Way of the Hummingbird

Way of the Hummingbird

Shamanic Tales, Ayahuasca Journeys & The Dreaming of the Whole Earth

By Lore Solaris

DREAMINGARTS

Way of the Hummingbird
Shamanic Tales, Ayahuasca Journeys and the Dreaming of the Whole Earth

Copyright © 2025 by Soulore Solaris
All rights reserved. No part of this publication may be reproduced, stored, or transmitted in any form or by any means without prior written permission from the author or publisher, except as permitted under Australian copyright law.

Published by DreamingArts Publishing
Byron Bay, Australia
info@dreamingarts.net
www.dreamingarts.net

First Edition — December 2025

Paperback ISBN: 978-1-7644042-0-4
eBook ISBN: 978-1-7644042-1-1

Editor: Bradley Dawson, Smith and Brown Design
Cover Design and Layout: Adrian Monk
Cover Art and Concept: Lore Solaris

Legal Notice

This book contains cultural, historical, and autobiographical descriptions of traditional sacramental ceremonies, including references to Ayahuasca and other natural plants restricted under Australian law. These descriptions are provided for educational and documentary purposes only. Nothing in this book is intended to encourage, promote, or facilitate the use, preparation, distribution, or procurement of any illegal substance or activity in any jurisdiction.

Readers are responsible for understanding and complying with the laws in their own region. The author and publisher disclaim all liability arising from the misuse or misinterpretation of the material contained herein.

Cultural Respect Statement

The ceremonial traditions, songs, teachings, and healing practices referenced in this work belong to specific Indigenous cultures, spiritual lineages, and ancestral guardians. They are shared here with deep respect and gratitude. These traditions should be approached with humility, cultural sensitivity, and guidance from legitimate knowledge keepers.

For permissions or reprint requests:
info@dreamingarts.net

Contents

Pre-flight	vi
Foreword: A yarn by Ash Dargan Fejo (MIndigStud)	xvi
Introduction: Eagles-Eye View	xxx

Part 1 Roots

Chapter 1: Learning to Fly	3
Chapter 2: Ayahuasca	21
Chapter 3: Shamanic Renaissance	57
Chapter 4: Way of the Hummingbird	97

Part 2 Growth

Chapter 5: Call Of The Forest	141
Chapter 6: The Earth Changes	180
Chapter 7: Bridging Worlds	214
Chapter 8: Australia-Brazil Boomerang	254
Chapter 9: Sounds of Awakening	300
Chapter 10: Star Birth	350

Part 3 Flowering

Chapter 11: Returning Home	405
Chapter 12: High Aim in the Upper Amazon	465
Chapter 13: Voices and Perspectives	506
Chapter 14: Rising from the Storm	546

Afterword: Fireside Yarn with Uncle BJ	598
Glossary	623
Bibliography	645

Pre-flight

In my life growing up in Australia, the power and presence of Country — the land itself — has always been overwhelming. Everyone feels it, yet not all are willing to humble themselves before its mystery and immensity. The education I received growing up still echoed a time when Aboriginal people were spoken of as if they were part of the flora and fauna; I was never taught in school what really happened to Aboriginal people, from colonisation to the contemporary world. Nor was I taught about their profound, rich and diverse history.

But as I grew older, I made it my mission and priority to learn — not just about history, but to learn from Country itself. To learn from the land. To listen to the voices of the old ones, the Elders, the people who carry ancient wisdom. And so, part of me is intrinsically connected to Country.

When I talk about Country from an Aboriginal perspective, I'm not referring to a nation-state or a patch of terrain. I'm speaking to something much deeper and more alive. Country is more than soil, rock or water. Country is a living entity. It holds stories, spirits and law. It is kin, ancestor, teacher. It is not something separate from us — it *is* us. As described by many Indigenous voices, Country is not only a place you live; it is a place that lives within you. It is a consciousness, a relationship and a spiritual force that connects all living things.

And through my own journey with Ayahuasca, it has always been my intention, both for myself and others, that we reconnect with Country. I believe that disconnection from Country is at the root of illness, mental health crises and societal disintegration. It's clear across Aboriginal communities and in every place I've worked and sat with people, that disconnection from the land, from Spirit, from one's roots, is the core wound. Ayahuasca, for me, is all about Country. It's about remembering who we are through reconnection.

The practices I've walked with — many of which come from Brazil and other places around the world — have supported me in deepening that understanding. They've helped me nourish my spiritual connection, helped keep my spirit buoyant and alive. And I've come to believe that vitality of the spirit is the key to health and wellbeing.

When I speak of Dreaming, I'm not claiming or borrowing the Dreaming of Aboriginal people. I speak of Dreaming as the spiritual unfolding of my life — a personal relationship to Spirit, to guidance, to the greater force that weaves through all things. The entirety of my being as part of all that is. Some call this 'Great Spirit', others call it 'God', 'Allah', 'Brahman', 'Tjukurpa', 'Yuxibú', 'Tupã', 'Olorun' or 'Olódùmarè' — there are many names.

All great traditions speak of this: the animating force, the sacred presence that moves through everything. And through walking with Indigenous people, learning and sitting with them, I've come to use these terms in my own life — not to appropriate, but to honour. I use them with deep respect and acknowledgment of the vast, cosmic wealth of knowledge that lives here in this country we call Australia, and in the wisdom of its people.

I was also inspired by a book called *Sand Talk* by Tyson Yunkaporta, an Indigenous academic who wrote his book as a series of yarns. He used conversation as a method of sharing. 'Yarn' is a term used across Indigenous Australia to describe a way of storytelling that is relational, inclusive and grounded in deep listening. It's not about proving right or wrong. It's not about asserting fact over feeling. It's about telling your truth and offering it into a shared space.

I sat down with a dear Australian Indigenous Elder who has been a great guide, teacher and friend along the way. He has been at many of our Ayahuasca ceremonies, which he supports in so many ways. His support has been invaluable to me and I can't imagine where I would be now without him. We sat down to have a yarn and record it for inclusion in this book and we yarned about sharing sacred or spiritual knowledge in this society:

> *Somehow we've got to do all this analysis and all this unpacking and all this everything, and basically, like yourself, be persecuted, or whatever, for having the audacity to try and present this knowledge to the Western world. So that's one of the reasons why I'm happy to tell these little stories or tell the group, give this yarn, so we call it 'yarn'. Technically, yarn really is that no one, no one's knowing what they say is more important than anyone else's and they're all just perspectives. They're all just yarns.*

There will be more from Uncle later in the book.

So this book is a collection of yarns. It's a conversation. It's a series of stories told from the heart, grounded in my experience. Over the years, by the fire, before ceremonies, or in quiet moments after, people have asked me questions. I've shared stories from my life — moments of awakening, struggle and spiritual guidance. And many times, people have said: 'You have to write a book.' So here it is.

This is the story of where it all came from. Of how our ceremonies here in Australia came to be. Of how I learned what I've learned. Who taught me. What called me. The communities and lineages I've walked with. The Spirit that has shaped this path.

It is the story of the spiritual constellation I walk with — the relationships I have to different cosmologies, to different spiritual beings, ancestors, to the forces of nature — and how these threads weave together to inform, energise and invite us into a deeper communion with the Earth and with Spirit.

I have done my best to describe these constellations from the roots, culture, practices and beliefs of the traditions and lineages in which I have lived and been taught. From Australian Indigenous teachings and foundation in Country to Amazonian Dreamings from three different Indigenous cultures, from modern psychological techniques and practices, and the Brazilian syncretic spiritual traditions of *Santo Daime*, *Umbanda* and *Ciranda*.

My walk has taken me to many places around the world. My Dreaming has unfolded through a journey that has followed my own personal songlines — threads of Spirit and Country that have guided me to different lands, teachings and revelations. Along the way, something much greater than me began to reveal itself: a dream within a dream, a deep knowing that I was walking not just my own path, but stepping into a universal unfolding. I call this the 'Dreaming of the Whole Earth'.

This Dreaming is not merely the Dream of human culture — it is the Dream of all living things. In the Indigenous worldview, the word 'Dreaming' can often be interchangeable with words depicting 'Great Spirit', such as 'Tjukurpa' from the Anangu people of Central Australia. Dreaming includes the ancestral wisdom of those who came before, the sacred paths of initiation, the pain and growth that have emerged through human folly, the radiant beauty of ceremony, the multi-dimensional forms of Great Spirit expressed through music, art, dance and prayer. It is a Dream woven through time, held in the wind, in the Earth, in the rivers and stars. It is ancient and alive. It is a living field.

There are yarns in here and the retelling of experiences of the seen and the unseen, the earthly and the celestial. At times, the story touches realms that may be unfamiliar or even uncomfortable to some — realms where yarning with what might be called 'extradimensional' or 'spiritual' beings has occurred. These presences are an intrinsic part of my path. They are not metaphors, nor figments, nor hallucinations, but living aspects of the greater tapestry of consciousness. For some, such beings are already known and felt, and will make intuitive sense or be a lived experience. For others, my hope is not to convince, but simply to invite openness — a willingness to hold these accounts lightly and with curiosity. Yarns and Dreamings cannot be captured and boxed by mind and intellect, nor can they be dismissed by such. I offer these yarns in that same spirit, like messages carried in river currents or sung by the wind. May they be held gently, and perhaps stir something true in you, too.

The Dreaming of the Whole Earth honours all of the living beings of this world — from the insects to the birds, to the animals, the trees and the mycelium that runs beneath our feet. It honours even the stones. It is a collective field of consciousness that we, as modern humans, have strayed from. We have forgotten how to listen. In Australia, many would scoff at the idea that an insect has a voice or that a gust of wind might carry meaning. But they speak to me. They always have.

The wind carries voices. The rivers whisper stories. If we truly listen, if we engage in the practice of *dadirri* — an Indigenous term meaning 'listening deeply' — we come into contact with this living field. Through this listening, the sacred knowledge held by the Earth begins to reveal itself. Not in words, but in presence, in feeling, in knowing.

Ayahuasca has been a great guide into this deep listening. The sacrament, a sacred combination of two plants from the Amazon, creates a brew that births a conscious being. In the West, Ayahuasca is often described with a lowercase 'a' as a chemical compound, a psychedelic, a curiosity for science. But to me, Ayahuasca is a great teacher. A wise, compassionate, majestic presence. A being of immense spiritual power that has come at this time to help humanity remember what we have forgotten. In this book, I choose to capitalise its name. Not out of grammatical preference, but out of deep respect.

I also may at times refer to Ayahuasca in the feminine form, and at other times not. In my experience, it has often appeared as a feminine presence, though at other times it has been entirely neutral, without gender. In the Brazilian traditions I've worked within, particularly with those of the *Huni Kuin* and *Yawanawá* peoples, Ayahuasca is not typically spoken of in gendered terms. The personification of Ayahuasca as 'Mother' or 'Grandmother' is more common in some urban or contemporary circles and, while beautiful in its own way, it is not universal. In the Brazilian *Santo Daime* religion there is no assigning of gender and the perspective is that the vine component is masculine and the *chacruna* leaves are feminine. In my experience we refer to Ayahuasca as 'the medicine', 'the tea' or 'Daime', and there are many other names for this sacrament. It seems to me that what we have come to know as Ayahuasca may be impossible to accurately name within the limitations of human language. For the Huni Kuin people of the Upper Amazon, Ayahuasca is respectfully called *Nixi Pãe* ('nixi' meaning vine or thread, and 'pãe' meaning force or charm), the enchanted vine, a living thread that weaves worlds together.

Ayahuasca is not just a compound to be studied, dissected and classified. It is not merely a tool for trauma therapy, a 'new-age' fad, nor a mystical substance for spiritual tourism. Ayahuasca is a conscious ally. A being. She deserves to be respected as such. Through her teachings, I have been guided into deeper connection with Country, the forces of nature and the Spirit that moves through all things.

This book is a personal memoir, a spiritual testimony and a heartfelt yarn. It is not a legal document, nor a clinical manual. It shares reflections, stories and lived experiences gathered over many years of walking alongside the sacred medicine known as Ayahuasca. These accounts are offered in the spirit of storytelling, cultural dialogue and personal truth.

The ceremonies described throughout are part of a collective spiritual practice, conducted in community and reverence, informed by lineage, and undertaken with sincerity and care. They have never been presented as therapy or clinical health services, or as commercial or medical treatments. They are expressions of prayer, tradition and healing grounded in spiritual, cultural and ancestral roots.

This work does not name individuals involved in legal or governmental processes and avoids specifics that could interfere with ongoing matters. Where critique appears, it is directed toward institutional behaviours and cultural dynamics, not at personal actors. As this book goes to print, some legal proceedings may still remain unresolved. What is offered here is not an attempt to prejudge, interfere with, or comment directly on, those proceedings. It is simply one man's testimony, in the tradition of storytelling, as it has unfolded through the lens of ceremony and Spirit.

Importantly, this book stands in alignment with Indigenous-led movements for spiritual sovereignty, truth-telling and cultural continuity. It honours the sacred alliances formed with Aboriginal Elders, community leaders and traditional knowledge holders, and seeks to support their rights, voices and calls for justice. These values are echoed in national efforts like the Uluru Statement from the Heart, the Voice movement, and truth-telling processes such as the Yoorrook Justice Commission. It is my intention that this work contributes meaningfully to the healing of Country, the recognition of Indigenous sovereignty, and the shared future we all must walk together.

It is my position, both in the writing of this book and in life, that sacred Indigenous and syncretic ceremonial practices deserve recognition and protection, not marginalisation or persecution. This is not just a personal cause; it is a national and global imperative that speaks to the heart of reconciliation, human rights and our collective spiritual evolution.

I honour the laws of this land and the Dreaming of this Earth. I also honour the ancient ways, the stories of the First Peoples, and the wisdom of Nature that continues to call humanity back into balance. This book is one such calling.

While I am not of Aboriginal or Amazonian ancestry, the experiences and understandings shared in this book arise from deep and authentic relationships with Indigenous Elders, teachers and communities. I do not claim to speak for Aboriginal people or for the Dreaming — I stand with it. I use language that is inspired by the cultural worlds I've walked within, born of the land I walk upon, and spoken with the care and permission of those who walk beside me. Again, this is not a borrowing of tradition, it is a weaving of paths. My words reflect my own Dreaming, my lived truth, and the relationships that have shaped my way.

Throughout this work, I've done my best to be respectful, conscious and transparent. I acknowledge the weight of words, the power of knowledge, and the delicate responsibility that comes with sharing from sacred experience. Some might argue that certain visions or spiritual teachings are best left unspoken or unrecorded, that writing them down risks reducing the sacred to the profane. I understand and respect that view. And yet, this book arises from necessity — a calling I could no longer ignore. It is the result of countless people asking to learn more, to understand more and to be guided. It also emerges from a long period of imposed silence, during which I endured deep public scrutiny, institutional aggression, and a media narrative that refused to allow my voice to be heard in full.

I see this book as a work of service, to offer something back from the path I've walked, to give voice to what has often been hidden or distorted, and to participate in the living archive of this time. There is risk in doing so, in revealing too much, in being misunderstood, in being attacked. But as an Aboriginal Elder once shared with me: our oral cultures and sacred knowledges are being lost not just through suppression, but also through silence. Sometimes we are forced by society to speak, to write things down, because the memory systems that once sustained our truths are no longer recognised or upheld. I take this step not lightly, but with great care and conviction.

This is not a book of doctrine or ultimate truths. It is a tapestry of experiences, visions, teachings and insights, offered in the hope that they may be useful. I recognise that some will misuse, misquote, or attempt to appropriate what is shared. I also trust that many will receive it with integrity and find in it inspiration, clarity and connection. These stories have been lived, not theorised. The knowledge here has been earned through years of discipline, sacrifice and prayer. I have kept much back: stories not mine to share, teachings given in confidence, and knowledge that is potent and potentially dangerous in the wrong hands. This book does not attempt to reveal everything. I hope it offers enough to illuminate a path.

There are many paths, and many ways to walk them. What I offer here are songlines of Spirit and soul — insights earned and a Dreaming shared in the hope that others may find inspiration, and perhaps hear the song in the lines of their own spirit's calling.

When I sat down to yarn with Uncle for this book, I offered an apology in advance for the clumsiness of my language. Language is not always enough; words can feel small beside the deep truths they aim to evoke. At times they can obscure what they intend to reveal. So, I ask you to read not only with your mind, but with your presence, to lean into the feeling of being carried, rather than searching for perfect accuracy. Let the words be doorways to your own awareness, not maps of rigid meaning. And, above all, trust your own sovereignty. No story, no book, no external voice should override your own lived experience or diminish the truth that rises from within. This is a guide, a yarn, a transmission — but the authority of meaning ultimately rests with you.

There is an invitation in these pages not only to walk alongside me and those who have shared in this journey, but to feel into the source from which these yarns arise. These stories are not just personal;

they are threads of a wider Dreaming, a living transmission from the spirit of Ayahuasca herself and the vast consciousness ecosystem that constellates the Earth. Beyond the events and the language is a deeper songline — an ageless, multi-dimensional intelligence calling each of us into remembrance. Let these yarns be a bridge not just to my path, but to your own sacred connection with the Dreaming of the Whole Earth.

As I've sat to write this book, often not feeling like a writer or author at all, I've been blessed by friends, family, Elders, teachers and guides, and given lots of encouragement and advice. I've been held and supported by the land here in Byron Bay, Bunjalung Country, in the Northern Rivers of New South Wales. I've been guided by Spirit every step of the way. This book has emerged in the wake of immense personal challenge, as I've walked through the deep impacts of persecution at the hands of governmental and institutional abuse. At times I have faced harassment, including the confiscation of my early manuscript by police. Writings that, to this day, have not been returned. The journey has not been easy. It has taken all of my focus, energy, faith and every ounce of strength I could muster. Somehow, I've made it through. And I could not have done so without the abundance of love, faith and support I've received along the way.

People sometimes ask me how I became a shaman. All I can say is the true shamans that I know are powerful, wise, deeply attained in lifelong shamanic traditions. I see myself as a student, as a ceremonial leader and as an emissary of the forest in service to Great Spirit. I am a fellow traveller, a student of life and ceremony, offering my learnings in service. Over the years, people have tried to project many things onto me. The media, police and legal institutions have labelled me a 'cult leader', a 'witch doctor' and many other things in attempts to discredit and demean my work. Until now, I've remained mostly silent in the face of those projections. I have walked this path with sincerity and devotion. I've lived through many powerful experiences, and I've been given skills and gifts that I've been asked to share. I continue to do my best. I am always learning.

Within this story, I share accounts of meetings, journeys and experiences with various friends, teachers and companions. For a range of reasons, the names of some individuals have been changed or obscured to protect their privacy, and also because we live in a country and a society that, through its fear and misunderstanding, has cultivated an atmosphere where persecution is a real and present concern. I ask for your understanding as you read. This choice is not about avoiding accountability, but about respecting sensitivities and navigating complex realities in a sometimes hostile environment. As the pages unfold, the reasons for this discretion will become more apparent.

Included throughout this book are the lyrics to songs, prayers and hymns — sometimes just a snippet or a verse. I've chosen to do this because, in my lineages and traditions, it is the music that carries the doctrines and calls the Spirit. The teachings, the guidance and the prayers reside in the music. Throughout my journey with Ayahuasca and ceremony, it has always been the music that has guided me.

I have included the songs, as they are part of the living tradition, and I hope they bring the reader into a deeper appreciation of what I'm sharing and how they relate to the teachings that have come through the lineages. It is also a kind of refrain from the discourse into poetry, a shifting of the mind from intellect into harmony and feeling, and another perspective from which to view Ayahuasca and the spiritual journey

Most of these songs were originally written in Portuguese, but for the sake of the reader I've provided English translations, with the original titles in Portuguese shown below. Many of the songs come from the three ceremonial songbooks I've created; others belong to the songbooks of my teacher, and a few originate from other sources.

Moving on from the writing phase of this book, it is my prayer that some may find benefit in reading these yarns. That my story and perspectives, my challenges and learnings, my integration and my faith may be of inspiration. This is not an exhaustive account of my experiences, the knowledge I have gained or the voice of Spirit that comes through me. This journey continues and there is still much to share. For now, though, I invite you into the realm of the mystery, to walk with me through Country and Dreamings. Enjoy the journey.

Foreword: A yarn by Ash Dargan Fejo (MIndigStud)

Larrakia man, artist, musician, adventurer, social and emotional wellbeing specialist.

When you follow any living tradition that's still here — and we're lucky to have a few, all around the world there's traditions that are still here — you're wise to place yourself really close to them. Plant medicine is something I've discovered that is in that category. Eldership is another— just going and being with the old people that you know all around the world. They're not always going to be there. It's amazing that anything's left at all. These lineages for me started off in culture.

For my family, when a capital city gets built on your land there's not much you can do about that. You assimilate or you die, basically, that's how it goes. Lucky for me, my Larrakia grandmother lived in the bush, and she liked it there, so that was my connection to deeper culture. I had that opportunity given to me when I was in my early twenties, and I took it because I just knew this is what I wanted.

I moved out there and then these Elders from the cultural region that had all the knowledge would come in and visit my grandmother, and that's where I met culture, real culture, for the first time. There's different levels to culture, there's different identities of being a cultural person, and none of them are right or wrong. They're just different. An Aboriginal person living in the city is Aboriginal; an Aboriginal person living in a remote community is also an Aboriginal person.

We've got to let go of these stereotypes. There's just different ways of being Aboriginal, just like there's different ways of being Australian. There are no stereotypes here, but there are people that are more connected to the lore. There are degrees of connection because there are degrees of disconnection from colonisation.

I recognised that this culture, this lineage that I'd connected with, with these old men from Western Arnhem Land ... they had the gold, and I wanted to go digging. Just like my grandfather worked on the gold mine at Pine Creek. And so these Elders were the mine, and so I had to spend time going deep into the mine, which is spending time with these knowledge keepers. That's like a mine. And you go mining and culture's like that: it's not given to you; you gotta go mining for it. It's a resource, but there's different ways that resources are used. When you learn about this resource, all the respect that's placed on you, you have to figure out what you're going to do with the knowledge because when it starts to come, that becomes your knowledge, and you better be sure about who you're going to share that with, or how you're going to share it, because that's on you. Once it's given to you, it's given to you with the responsibility that is now for you to look after, and that's a great responsibility. A lot of people don't understand that, what that responsibility is. Things can get watered down and commercialised and such, where it's not really anyone's fault that they don't know how to respect it, they didn't grow up in a culture that learned what respect is. That's part of the breakdown of colonisation, and that's the world that we're living in. We don't live in a world that understands respect — the world that I got to through these Elders.

I came across plant medicine a long time ago, when I was in my twenties, with the Native American church when I lived in Hawaii and I met a road-man. This group was serious about their business and I went to a ceremony and I thought, 'Wow, this is really something,' but it didn't call to me. It wasn't my path; something else was calling for me at that time. I was just spending time with Elders, that was my calling. Go and spend time with Elders, as many as you can, and that's how I was getting the downloads: going sitting with the medicine people out there. Medicine wasn't a part of that for me. That didn't come until much, much later in my life. Those downloads from the Elders and the other ceremonies, or just sitting with old people on Country, is one of the deepest things you can do, so long as you listen — and they will be watching, listening, to see who you are. They can tune you up these clever people; they can tune you up, like when you take your car to a place once a year. Sitting with old people, they can do that to you. They've got all sorts of tools. Plant medicines are just one tool out of an arsenal of a really big tool bag. And culture has a really big tool bag. It's really important to understand that it's really big.

I'd never understood the tools of plant medicine. That wasn't a part of my walk until I kind of got into my mid-forties and I started to dream. Not about the plant medicine. I started to dream about these rocks that I'd never seen before, rocks of stone walls that were built in a particular way. I'd never seen anything like it. I was dreaming of the megalithic stone wall construction in Peru, which has the greatest sites of megalithic stone construction out of anywhere in the world. That's what I dreamed about; it wasn't the medicine. I went over there for that and I started to learn about the medicine as well. I heard about it, and I thought, 'Oh, that's really interesting.' I started to feel like maybe this was something for me. When I went to Peru, I thought, 'Well, I'm going to learn about these rocks', and then at the same time the medicine was there. So it wasn't just the medicine. I was going somewhere I knew was really deep, because it had the story of antiquity that I met in North America. I'd lived in North America for 10 years with medicine people, always visiting with them. So, I've got all that under my belt, and it's a lot, you know. There's a lot of downloads in 10 years, sitting with old people like that. But that was North America and very different to South America. I was sitting with the people of the eagle. Now, all of a sudden, in my later life, I'm sitting with the people of the condor and [in] another deep dive, very different. But I'm used to deep diving and I thought it was really cool. They had a version of a story that I'd heard in the north — a story of the antiquity of humanity and the cultural progression of human beings on the planet. The story I'd heard in the southwestern deserts, so I was very interested in that plant medicine.

I started off with *Wachuma* (psychedelic cactus) because I was in the land of the Quechua people, and Quechua-speaking people. I first went in with the music and I was all about that and the medicine there. I take the Wachuma and go into the places of antiquity, and don't go in there with the traditional people, just myself. That was very beautiful. Then, much later, I found Ayahuasca and went on that journey. It was a significant moment in my life: that's a whole other universe, just that medicine, that single tool. It opened the door that was so big. It was almost as big as everything together that I'd previously done in my life, just that medicine door that Ayahuasca opened. The enormity of it was as big as the entirety of everything that I'd done previously up til that point. And I thought: 'Oh, wow. This is something extraordinary going on here and I need to pay attention.' So that was the start of my relationship with it, and I love it.

I have no desire to be a server of the medicine. I've got no desire to be anything. I'm just on the journey for myself and for my personal learning, my personal development and my personal relationship with myself, and [for] another way for me to be in relationship with my ancestors. Because recently on Ayahuasca I've been able to sit with my ancestors. I've been able to sit on Country in Australia with my ancestors in the medicine experience. Many times I've found the place to do that now, and I'm overjoyed to meet the ancestors of this Country in the door of that medicine that allows me to sit and meet and communicate with Elders of Country that come and find their way into that space. For me that's no surprise, because all these years of sitting with the old people have taught me how to be on the land and just open up and connect to the spirits of the land without medicine. So I was aware of the spiritual nature of place. The medicine does open up that as well. It opens up that door to allow these meetings to happen and I was pleasantly surprised that availability was there, that I could sit and be with the ancestors of place when I'm doing medicine from a foreign land, on Country in the continent that I call home, that my grandmother's people are from. That's really beautiful. I'm really very thankful.

I don't know much about the Ayahuasca space; I'm quite new to it. Lore's book is exciting because it fills in so many gaps and explains the lineages and their cultures. It's only been maybe four or five years of experience for me, but the community I meet around Ayahuasca that I place myself within, the communities that I choose to sit with, are operating at a level of respect that is in alignment with how I understand to be and how I would conduct myself. The people that I'm sitting with are running at the level of respect and accountability that I would hold myself to if I were doing it. And this is really important, because it has everything to do with safety, and because we're dealing with something very, very, very powerful here in the experience where we are sitting with each other. It's very important when we go that deep that safety is number one, and held by the way that the ceremony is set up, and who is holding the container with you, and how it's run, and all of that, so it is a real ceremony. The ceremonial protocols are what I understand as an Aboriginal person and practise in my work that I do around the country, which is working for the healing of this Country with Aboriginal community. I've been doing that work for a long time with some pretty serious Elders — trauma-related work and working with some big energies, with the history of this country moving through people and bringing that to working with the energies of *We Al-li*, which means 'fire and water'. So I work with the energies of fire and water in communities and help them find their balance with each other. Not to cancel each other out, but just to keep holding them in whatever state they're presenting in, and then allowing them to work together so that they cool each other off. That's the work that I do.

There's no medicine in the work that I do, but ceremony and holding containers is everything about the work that I do, so I really do understand that. When I sit with medicine groups, I sit with leaders and people that are serving from the way that I understand how cultural protocols need to be to keep everyone safe when you're doing really deep work. I sit with people that do it like that. I'm very, very thankful to have met Lore Solaris, because Lore and Jesse Lethbridge, who plays the *yidaki* [didgeridoo] in Lore's ceremonies, I've known for 30 years, and the community of people that support them do run a very safe container for a very profound and deep experience. And it is profound and deep because it is safe in my view.

There's another circle that I sit within that's based in Victoria that is also at that level: very safe, very respectful, very high level of accountability to the lineages and also to the Country that they're operating in. So those two things need to be there for me if I'm going to participate in a circle

I need to see that as an Aboriginal person going in — and a lot of my friends in Aboriginal community, they're the same. They're like me: if we're thinking about engaging with a circle which is serving medicine from the Amazon jungle, whether from Brazil or Peru or whatever traditions those medicines are connected to or whichever place they're originating from, we as Aboriginal people look for certain things, you know. Those that are aware. We come in and we look to see how that person is connected to that lineage. How are they holding that when they're running it here? Are they paying attention to where they are and whose land that they're on? Are they being appropriate and respectful, not only to the lineage that they're carrying, but to the land and place that they're bringing that medicine to? And yes, everyone that I work with is, and that's something that we look for. That's very important. That's a cultural perspective. The clinicians and therapists don't have that, it's not an inbuilt program for them. They haven't got that from years and years of doing cultural practices. Whether that's being on the land and being accountable to community or whether that's working in community services at different levels. Just being Aboriginal and working in community, you just learn by doing and being with your community. You learn by being around your Elders. You just learn the importance of respect and protocols, because that's still very much alive when you're working with our communities. And so we bring that with us to anything that we do — it's the most important thing. And how do I know that? Because our Elders have always taught us that. The people that are older than us have always reminded us: 'Look, this is really important to be respectful. You know, this is really, really important to be respectful where you are, and there's a way to do things, and we're going to show you that.' This is passed down, despite the impact of colonisation and the fact that we have assimilated into a Western world. I'm talking about values, cultural values that are shared all around the world.

Those values, they resonate at a certain frequency and Professor Judy Atkinson did a global study on this, considering what kind of culture raises up children where all the children feel safe. Because if we're going to benchmark what an enlightened civilisation is, and enlighten a culture that it gets it right more often than gets it wrong, that is going to be a community of people that raise their children where all the children feel safe in that environment. Not because the adults say that they're safe; it's because the children are telling you that they're safe. That's the benchmark. And so what are the conditions of that? What are the values that a community holds and practises because they need to be practised? What are they? So she went on a global search and she found there were five values, and they actually follow the actual life, the relationship between a baby and a mother from birth. It follows that relationship and it starts off with rights and respect. Human rights are culturally understood as a benchmark. It's not something to be argued about; it is something that is just a benchmark. It is the basics of a human culture operating at a level where they're wanting to produce the best possible outcome for the community — human rights will be honoured, all of the basic ones. So that's in every Indigenous culture around the world. That's why all approaches in healing must be grounded in human rights. If you're fucking up something there, then you need to go back to ground one and have a look at how you're doing things. Are people feeling respected? Do people have a sense of autonomy? Are people able to make their own choices about what's happening for them, about their journey? That's all part of it.

When a mother has a son or a daughter and gives birth to them, that mother has that relationship with that child. It's very special, and the first thing the mother does, just naturally, is the mother attends to the rights of that child. That child has a right to be fed, that child has a right to be held, kept warm, to feel that heartbeat. It's the mother that gives us language, not the father. The mother gives us food. The mother gives us everything: safety, that connectedness, heartbeat, all of that. And she's doing that because she's respecting our basic human rights. So those two things happen just straight away, and they're just given — nothing's asked for, it's just given.

The baby doesn't have to do anything, and even if the child starts to grow, the child doesn't have to do anything. These things are just the benchmark given freely. You don't have to be anything special. You don't have to do anything to please us. You're just going to get this. And then, as you start to grow up and run around, you start to notice, *oh, every other kid's getting this as well.* So you know that idea of being special? It just kind of evaporates, and you realise that everyone's getting the same, because everyone deserves their rights to be met and yet the children are still doing nothing for that. It's just being given to them.

There comes a time, if that relationship were to continue, where they are just given everything and they don't have to step into responsibility. Once they are around 14 or 15 years old, the mother can't keep holding that container and things can become really unbalanced. It works between a mother and a child at that early stage, because human beings are like that. We're not like horses. We don't come out and then stand up in a couple of minutes and start trotting around the paddock by ourselves. We're human beings. It's very different the way that we're raised up, and then when we get a little bit older, the old people come and get us and as children we know something really big is happening, and so do the mums, because those mums, they start to cry, and they start to wail, like they're about to lose their child. And in a sense, they are, they're going to lose that special relationship that they've had with their child, where everything has just been given to that child. If you think about that, it's a power position, between a mother and a child. That power — it's a beautiful thing, but that's about to change. The child then gets separated from the mother and gets taken out by the old people, who then pat the earth with their hand and they say, 'Hey, THIS is your mother now. She's going to give you all the food, she's going to provide for you.' There's a whole language you're going to be learning. But this isn't take, take, take. The relationship with this mother is give and take, and with that, you've now got to start providing for the rights of things, just like your mother provided for you. You're going to start providing for the rights of Country, for the rights of that river, the rights of those animals, because your blood is related to them. They're your totems. You're going to look after their rights. And you know what? They're going to look after you because this is give and take. This is reciprocity and this is how it works. This is the dawning of responsibility. This is the only way that we learn it as human beings, when we understand it as a fundamental exchange, through looking after each other, providing the basic human rights for something else to look after something else.

So we learn respect and then reciprocity and it's through the practice of looking after things and those things looking after you. Learning about those exchanges, this is where you understand what relationship actually is. It's through the reciprocal exchange of respect and of giving each other rights. That's actually a healthy relationship. These are the five 'Rs' as outlined by Judy Atkinson and this is our global Indigenous indigeneity:

> *Respect: for self, others, Country, and story—especially in listening without judgment.*
> *Responsibility: for one's own healing and role in the relational web.*
> *Reciprocity: not just in action, but in listening, sharing, and co-healing.*
> *Resilience: born from community, story, and cultural continuity.*
> *Relationship: is the container that holds all healing. It is not an outcome, but a living process.*
> — 'Trauma Trails: Recreating Songlines,' Judy Atkinson.

Now I see this in Ayahuasca, which shows me the same thing, because this is a human program we seem to have. Every culture has it and when we go from place to place and we go to someone else's culture, we learn we've got that framework that we bring with us in practice, because all human cultures have that. That's how to raise children and have the best future for your community, because that is the soup where we become our best, whatever it is that we choose to be. These are the five 'Rs', and this is how we learn them.

Now, what about today? Our Western culture doesn't have that initiation anymore. We're not taken out and shown that it's important for us to give other things rights. We just carry that relationship from our mothers through into adulthood, where men are just expecting that everything's just given to us, and if we don't get it, we throw a tantrum just like a child would, because we don't get it. We don't know another way because we've never been shown the reciprocity or what respect really is.

If we continue the relationship of just taking, then we get something like the toxicity of that. If it were to continue into adulthood, your version of respect would be actually getting something because you forced the issue, and to be respected would be to get that from someone else because you deserve it, because everything's given to you, believing you just have that right and don't have to do anything for it. That's why the world is the way that it is right now. That's why it's so fucked up at such a fundamental level. Because the respect and the reciprocity and being able to practise to care for other things, that happens around 14 years of age, and our culture doesn't have initiation anymore.

What I learned, outside of the medicine, was that with the human body — the code in our DNA, or our system — we actually have the code to go through that learning within our brains, the plasticity of our autonomic and central nervous system, all the organs of the body. We are naturally open and prepared at that age of initiation to consciously receive it. That's part of the human program. The human brain has finished its business of development by the age of six. This is known. What's also known is that the prefrontal cortex keeps growing and developing until the age of around 21, so we know that socially we're developing that ability to have a sense of empathy. The teenage years are when we're meant to be taken away with the Elders to be shown that there's a different way now, that we actually have to look after other people. Now we have to figure that out ourselves, without Eldership, and it gets pretty fucking warped because the only models that we've got are the people running the country that also never got the initiation.

This has been coined 'the initiation crisis' and people were talking about this in the late 1980s and 90s when I first became aware of it. I believe plant medicine can help with all of these issues. I believe it's really important for the containers of plant medicine to be as safe as possible to help people come back in, not only with the medicine, but the very experience of how a ceremony is run, when it's been served — to make that also a medicine, and start bringing back those ways of being that are wholly Indigenous and not Aboriginal. They are our globally shared indigeneity from the Celts, to the deep Irish ancestry, from the deep Spanish ancestry to the deep Persian ancestry, from the African ancestry, and so on and so forth. This is global human indigeneity based on the values that we need to get back to. Very simply, we need to get back to these. Everything that we do with Ayahuasca would be, in my opinion, better served within these cultural protocols, with these values alive. So that people, when they're in the medicine, great, they get all of the experience, but when they come back out and they're integrating, are those values still there for them? They exist in the medicine world because you're with the ancestors, with the spirits, right? And they're operating from those values. But when they come back into the human world and they're integrating, are we holding them in our communities with these values that are so important? Are we making them live again? Are we reminding people that in order to integrate, we have to make these values strong in our lives again? That's going to help us get there.

Lore shares the story in this book of how the lineages of his work came to be in Brazil, how they emerged from the jungle when an African-Brazilian man (Mestre Irineu) who was completely illiterate, went in to find the answer, selflessly seeking something to help with the suffering of his of his people and his community. There's that story where he had the spiritual visitations and the songs were placed in him. Many songs really struck a chord with me, because with our song men in Aboriginal culture in the north, the songs are placed in them as well. You don't learn the songs; the songs are placed spiritually in you. So you become full of songs, and those songs are just in you, you know them. When Lore shared with me this story, I thought: 'Oh, that's how we do it, too.' So there's this similarity there — of the songs being placed in the spiritual visions by the spiritual avatars. They're being placed in this this man and that's the same in Aboriginal culture: the songlines are placed in you —

they're spiritual transmissions. And it's not just one. Your whole line of songs is placed in you. So you have hundreds of songs. This man came out of the jungle with hundreds of songs and I thought, 'Yes, I understand that.' So, the cultural transmission of where these songs are from, I look at that through the lens of how our old people have always done it. These songs are transmissions. For me, they're like blueprints spoken from the creators of the Dreamtime themselves, from those many, many steps above our reality, the fine steps that are the very consciousness of creation itself. It comes down from there. It sort of steps down and becomes more solid. One of the ways that it does that is it gets placed in our bodies as songs, and then that further steps down by actually lifting it back up again to the point where the blueprint has been created across the landscape. It happens like that.

I've seen this in Ayahuasca ceremony. I've seen the same thing in Aboriginal ceremony as in plant medicine culture: when people are singing medicine songs, and not just Indigenous people, but Westerners that have gone over and studied for 10 years, dedicated study under the teachers over there and come back, obviously very serious students, and they're really practising it. They've embodied this, and when they sing, I've seen the same thing happen, where the star lore comes down and just explodes and travels across the land. That's what our ceremonies did, the same thing.

The medicine also shows me how music plays a vital role in ceremony and when we're playing music together on the medicine it has shown me how it has such an important role in lifting up our spirits. So that when we're singing these sacred songs in ceremony from the traditions that came out of Brazil, they're as sacred to me as the songs from the songlines of Aboriginal culture that are sung down the songlines from the top of the Northern Territory into central Arnhem Land. To me, they're the same; there's no difference. They are just as sacred, and the music is a fundamental part in the community aspect of both of those energies being grounded. We're talking about these things being placed into an individual human being, and then they're given out and then shared as a community, right? And now the whole community is doing this together, and the music supports that energy to be risen up to the level of purity that it was originally given to that person to begin with. We are able to do that in ceremony, and music is an essential part. The medicine has been teaching me this, and it's been part of my learning. I didn't get this learning from anywhere else. I got this learning from asking the medicine: 'How does this work?' And the medicine has shown me how it works. The Elders that I sit with in the ceremonial space show me. So music is really a part of it.

What I've noticed in Lore's ceremonies in Australia is the use of ceremonial instruments, including guitars that have become part of the tradition and the transmission of these songs from Brazil. The guitar is a musical instrument that's like the basic of basic; you can just play anything. It just accompanies you. It's such a great community instrument. It's percussive and it's melodic, and it can hold the rhythm. It can do all of that in one instrument — that's what's so cool about it. It's played rhythmically and provides the rhythm for the dancers. It provides the melody for the songs. Everyone can pitch to it, and at the same time, it's helping elevate the feeling of everyone singing those songs. And so everyone's rising, rising. And then it hits a note, and everyone just pops and you know that everyone in the group has just had a peak experience of being taken to the upper world, or something profound has happened for them. You know it has because everyone's reaching it. That is ceremony; that is proper ceremony. Every time we do that, we bring that to the land we're on. It just goes that the whole land benefits from it. I'm absolutely convinced of this. This is what I've been shown.

Music is a hugely important part of my life, because I'm a musician. The yidaki is being handed to me by my grandmother's brother. It's something that I have a very cultural connection to and I play this in ceremony. And I play other wind instruments too, and it helps me elevate the experience of the medicine for myself. What I've noticed in sharing is that it helps the whole group elevate, and I contribute to that as a community member with a whole bunch of people sharing musical instruments respectfully. I feel myself rise and I feel everyone else rise. It's just such an important tool in the space of the medicine. I prefer those ceremonies much more to the very individual solo journeys that I've had in the Peruvian jungle with the Shipibo, which is a very different style of working with the medicine. I've got nothing against that; it is just very different. I prefer the music because, for me, I've been able to feel more, learn more, experience more, and feel personally connected to Ayahuasca in a way that the journeys with the Shipibo people have not given me.

Music is a vital part of ceremony, and has always been a part of this idea of helping a group of people elevate the original transmission back up to its original vibration. And once it does that, it's actually the thing that keeps songlines alive.

Introduction: Eagles-Eye View

It was in Amazonas, Brazil in July 2003 that I had my first meeting in this life with Ayahuasca. Ayahuasca: a holy sacrament, an Amazonian psychoactive brew made of two plants traditionally used in shamanic-style rituals and practices. Ayahuasca, known by many names, is renowned for its visionary and healing properties and its potential for spiritual insight. The unfolding of my personal Dreaming, my spiritual path, took me to the great Amazon River in the middle of the world's largest forest. I was taken on a multi-dimensional journey of healing mind, body, emotions, ancestry and my relationship to Country. That journey continues to this day, and will throughout my life. This great friend Ayahuasca — teacher, guide, healer, protector, the Queen of the Forest, the queen of beauty, of love, of wisdom, of power — is a portal into the mind of Nature and ultimately to the void, our mind, spacious like an open endless sky. Ayahuasca is Nature, Ayahuasca is our mind. Ayahuasca has a force that emanates like river currents and ocean waves. This force guides and teaches. Traditions, practices, ceremony and sound hold us in the currents, like an ark on a cosmic ocean, where we learn balance and grace and remembrance of our humanity as Dreamers, as custodians of the Earth.

From the first ceremony I experienced, my life changed completely. I had begun what I consider consciously walking my spiritual path in the year 2000, sparked by communion with magic mushrooms, as I started building a deeper understanding of myself and my connection to the Earth and the cosmos. By the time I first arrived in the Amazon, I had already learned a lot on that journey. I didn't have a roadmap or any one teacher or guide; I was simply trusting in life and spirit and allowing the journey to unfold. I had come to know Spirit as the mysterious, metaphysical force that exists within all beings, and the oneness that connects everything in the cosmos. I didn't realise it at the time, but all of the experiences and teachings I was integrating would lead to me developing a deep integration and practice of personal Dreaming, Indigenous wisdom, music, psychology and cosmic science.

I write this book not as a researcher, academic, journalist, anthropologist or career author. This is the first book I have written and has been a long time coming, with many requests over the years for me to produce this work of sharing. When I started writing, I didn't have much idea of where this was going to go; my discipline was to 'just write'. At no time did I approach Ayahuasca with a mind of investigation, wanting to write a book about it, or with any other agendas. I believe that would have greatly influenced and limited my experiences. I always fully immerse in an experience, in total presence, reverence and respect. That is my way. After 23 years I have taken the time to write out my story and my perspectives and to share what I have learned. For me this is my lived experience, not coloured by intentions to get anything out of it, to prove anything, to justify, examine, research or promote. I have no ambitions to be a new-age journalist or pop scientist. I'm just a storyteller.

I began facilitating Ayahuasca ceremonies in Australia in 2016 after two years living in Brazil studying full-time under the tutelage of Carioca Freitas. Carioca had been travelling the world holding ceremonies and sharing sacred music for 35 years. He is one of the world's renowned and respected Ayahuasca ceremonial leaders, and I was impressed upon meeting him by his deep reverence for the practices and spirituality of the Brazilian syncretic religions of *Santo Daime* and *Umbanda*.

I was also deeply impressed that Carioca has a very humble and unique style of practice and prayer, with a heartfelt love and respect for humanity, life, the forces of nature, our ancestors and the Earth.

He holds space and guides from a simple doctrine of love and music in a non-denominational service that encourages firmness and discipline in our practice and our faith, yet also nurtures our uniqueness and our individual spirit and expression.

I felt at home with Carioca and our spiritual family at Ciranda, near Rio de Janeiro in Brazil, and I found a house and lineage where I could express myself, my own spirit, my music and my healing abilities — and it was there that I really learned how to pray. Meeting Carioca and living in Ciranda was like coming home and I did much deep inner healing in those two years in the Mata-Atlantica forest. My studies at Ciranda and with Carioca took me deep into a shamanic path which taught me much about the spiritual reality, practices and culture of Brazil that I had begun back in 2003.

Becoming a leader of spiritual ceremonies consecrating the sacrament known as Ayahuasca was not something I had any ambition to attain in this life. I left Ciranda and Brazil in October 2015 and after a brief time in California I returned to Australia. People in California had heard I had spent a lot of time studying with Carioca and were asking me to attend ceremonies and to play music and support their work. When I arrived in Australia it wasn't long before many people were asking me to hold ceremony for them. It was a sign from Spirit that I was being asked to share my knowledge, skills and experience.

'Shamanism' is a term that has come to define spiritual practices found in many cultures worldwide — practices involving the mediation between the human and spirit worlds by individuals commonly known as 'shamans', who serve as healers, guides, visionaries and ceremonial leaders. Shamanic practices are an ancient and well-developed science of being. Some would say that shamanism is simply a natural state of being, the essence of being human. Indigenous wisdom and knowledge paths are renowned for their challenges, as they come with what society may deem 'unconventional' learning techniques. My own training in shamanic practices came from guidance and initiatory rituals and experiences that allowed me to develop skills and awareness of communication with metaphysical beings, thereby accessing their knowledge and healing potentials and becoming a bridge between the seen and unseen worlds.

In 2015 I received spiritual permission to use my initiated eagle feathers in ceremony and to facilitate Ayahuasca ceremonies. I had been reluctant to walk this shamanic path, and it wasn't until August 2016, after preparing spiritually, mentally, physically and emotionally to hold space for people, that I felt ready to do so. I knew from all my times in Brazil and Peru that this was not something to be taken lightly. By this stage, I had accumulated 13 years of training and studies under various teachers and shamans, and from life itself. This was alongside a 20-year career in health services, including counselling, spiritual healing, drug and alcohol rehabilitation, Indigenous health, youth development and health promotion. I felt prepared, but wary of the immensity of the journey ahead, not knowing where it would lead, but knowing that it would be a challenging path. I continued to put my faith and trust in the guidance of Spirit and the unfolding of my Dreaming.

The ceremonies in Australia began slowly in 2016, mostly with friends and people who were ready and waiting for the Ayahuasca experience. This began to grow a lot more once the Brazilian spiritual community heard about me and found a house where they could pray and heal together. Word spread fast, and although there was never any promotion or advertising of the ceremonies, we were inundated with requests to attend them. The connection to the Earth, the forces of nature and the ancestors of the Brazilian lineages was felt strongly.

Alongside the spiritual community attending my ceremonies, I was also being approached by therapists, doctors, psychologists and psychiatrists, many of whom were aware of clients and patients who had attended ceremonies and shown rapid, grounded, positive changes in their wellbeing. Some of these health professionals were attending ceremonies themselves and reporting that the ceremonies were not only helping them with their own healing and spiritual development but were also helping them to better serve their patients and expanding their knowledge of what health and healing truly is.

The community around these ceremonies grew over a few years to around 2000 people in New South Wales, Queensland and Victoria. Some of these people came to other community events to sing and pray with us and to be part of a loving and embracing community of people interested in healing and spirituality without the indoctrination and dogmas of religion.

The people who attend our ceremonies in Australia come from a rich diversity of backgrounds and spiritual beliefs. They are a cross-section of men and women aged from 18 to 75, including doctors, lawyers, police, teachers, nurses, war veterans, LGBTQIA+ peoples, trauma survivors, terminal cancer patients, business people and, interestingly, many First Nations people and Elders who feel our work is healing not only for individuals but, more importantly, for loved ones, community and Country.

The blessings and participation of our First Nations people have meant a lot to me and given me much strength and encouragement, as these people also see the power and importance of reconnection to Spirit and the Earth as remedy for the planet-wide chronic psychological dysfunction, the epidemic of mental health casualties and the resultant march towards environmental destruction. These Ayahuasca ceremonies have been attended by many Aboriginal people who relate to the natural lore, respect, song and dance of ritual and prayer. Our ceremonies have become a house of prayer, culture, spirit and healing.

The spirituality and practices of our ceremonies have evolved a lot over time as we integrate and learn more practices and develop ourselves and grow and evolve together. There is a constant need to improve and evolve the work through reflection and experience in all areas, from personal firmness to self-discipline, safety, spiritual connection and practices.

Meeting Ayahuasca is most often a very powerful and positive experience for people, although it does have its pitfalls and risks. It is vital for any Ayahuasca movement to develop a culture with practices that integrate the experiences within people and their lives and relationships. It is for this reason that I have always had a strong emphasis on building community and support networks.

I have been very heartened to see so many people thriving in the community that has grown around these ceremonies since 2016.

Sadly, in Australia we live under social and political prejudice and discrimination towards our spiritual practices with Ayahuasca. There has been an ever-present cloud hanging over the safety of our spiritual work and ceremonies due to archaic and mal-informed laws in this country. The burden of dysfunctional and obstinate bureaucracy is a force of suppression we live with. In Australia there have also been sensationalised, propagandised, derogatory and misleading media representations of Ayahuasca and its use. This has led to the development of a large 'underground' counter-culture and mistrust in our government and mainstream social prejudices and fears.

In the final chapter of this book, I speak directly to a sequence of events that marked a turning point in my life and in the life of our community. What unfolded was not just personal, but emblematic of broader cultural and systemic dysfunctions, and exposed the shadows that emerge when sacred traditions collide with institutional ignorance and public hysteria.

At the centre of this experience was the unexpected death of a brother during one of our ceremonial gatherings. It was a moment of deep tragedy and sorrow that deserved reverence and care. Instead, the initial response from authorities and surrounding institutions followed a predictable pattern: suspicion, narrative construction, and an almost immediate assumption of wrongdoing. There was no pause for compassion, no inquiry rooted in understanding, consideration or care. Before any facts had emerged, narratives were already being seeded then promoted through media channels, with suggestive headlines designed to provoke fear and reinforce existing prejudice against sacred plant medicines.

What followed was a storm of projections. The media, eager for scandal, recycled tropes of danger, madness, and exoticism, portraying our spiritual practices with sensationalist strokes. These portrayals were not just misinformed; they were harmful. They drew on the oldest tactics of moral panic, cherry-picking evidence, painting ceremony as recklessness and community care as criminality. The truth, with all its complexity and nuance, was never sought — the only aim was the drama of condemnation and narrative control. This was the same dynamic we had seen before, with COVID lockdowns and medical coercion.

Within institutional frameworks, bureaucratic processes acted not as neutral arbiters but as amplifiers of suspicion and narrative reinforcement. There was a distinct absence of procedural fairness and transparency. Systems designed to investigate impartially instead appeared to confirm assumptions that had already taken hold in the public imagination. The mechanisms were subtle: omission, fabrication, silencing voices, selective interpretation and closed-loop logic that reinforced its own conclusions. It was less an investigation and more a narrative architecture — one that turned grief into evidence, spirituality into deviance, and leadership into liability.

The deeper tragedy is that such responses reflect a broader societal unease with the sacred, especially when it exists outside sanctioned norms. Rather than engaging with the rising global movement toward psychedelic healing, Indigenous knowledge and spiritual autonomy, the reaction here was to pathologise and persecute. The story was never just about what happened to one person; it became about how a society reacts when the unfamiliar pierces the veil of comfort and control. The enormous disrespect shown to Indigenous Elders and communities was a complete betrayal of stated government policies of reconciliation and has led to great harm.

By sharing my account of bureaucratic corruption and failure of governance in this book, I aim to illuminate this reality. It bears witness to what unfolded — not as a plea, but as a record. It reflects on the cost of fear-based governance, the shadow of institutional power, and the quiet strength of those who choose to stand in prayer amid a storm of suspicion and projections. Their fear of Ayahuasca, which is a peaceful, living example of community care, has become a mirror of institutional failure. What happened in our community is part of a much larger story — one that deserves to be heard with both clarity and heart.

Throughout all this, Ayahuasca was being heard. It was in the headlines, in the mouths of journalists, living in the hearts of those who knew. Even through distortion, it was being heard. Australian society was shown a mirror of its own disconnection from spiritual roots, from truth, from its Dreaming, and given a glimpse of its true nature — and it responded by throwing rocks at that mirror in the form of institutional tantrums, name-calling and schoolyard bullying.

Ayahuasca is not a medicine of convenience or comfort. It does not discriminate between what we prefer to see and what we wish to avoid. In ceremony, it shows us the full spectrum: both the beauty and the brokenness. People meet their truth, but they also meet their trauma. The darkness that is revealed is not inherent in the individual, but is so often the result of social, familial and civilisational wounding. Ayahuasca brings this to the surface for healing and integration and does so with much compassion, even if the reflections are sometimes painful. It exposes what society has suppressed: the shame, the pain, the distortion of our nature. And now, as Ayahuasca enters the public consciousness on a wider scale, that same shadow is being revealed on a collective level through media fear-mongering, court proceedings, political targeting and spiritual suppression. This is a reflection of how deeply we fear our own awakening. And yet, even this resistance is part of the process. What we call 'persecution' is often just the shadow of a system unable to face its own distortions. The state becomes a reflection of our cultural immaturity. Still, there are signs of evolution. In Brazil, where spirituality is woven into the culture, where reverence for the sacred is present in the knowing of the people, Ayahuasca has been granted protected status. Indigenous rights are recognised. The spirit of the medicine is acknowledged. It is no coincidence that the most spiritually integrated societies are leading the way in showing what respect and communion with sacred plant allies can look like.

What we often perceive as opposition may, in truth, be the presence of a necessary shadow teacher. Prohibition is not the enemy; it is a reflection of the fear we must transmute in order to integrate plant wisdom into collective coherence. This is an evolutionary rite that has been part of all enduring Indigenous cultures. The aggressive persecution of Ayahuasca and its practitioners is not random; it is the karmic echo of a society confronting its own spiritual malnourishment. And so, while this book tells a story of trials and injustice, it also tells the story of remembrance. We are not victims of governments; we are guardians of a sacred tradition that predates and transcends any modern institution. The Earth gave us this gift. It cannot be revoked by bureaucrats. The path forward must be built on Indigenous-led guardianship, on cultural preservation, on the recognition of cognitive liberty and spiritual agency as fundamental human rights. And with that comes responsibility. This is not a fight for permission — it is an invitation to grow up. The global Ayahuasca movement, for all its challenges, is part of a planetary maturing, an evolution. And this book is one voice in that awakening.

But this book is not an exposé. For those expecting that, know that 95% of what follows is Dreaming stories. This is not a tale of corruption, though corruption is part of it. This is my yarn. My journey. My prayer. My offering of sacred story. My hope is that these reflections help us find common ground so we can build something new: a roundtable of truth, where Indigenous wisdom and modern understanding meet for the healing of Country and of humanity. Australia can be a beacon — not just in traditional Indigenous practices and plant medicines, but in reconciliation, ecology and peace. Our ceremonies are meeting grounds where this is already happening, where we hold space for the expression of Indigenous voices.

And so I invite all: bureaucrats, scientists, media, politicians, the curious, the sceptical and the suffering. Join us. Sit with us around the fire and at the altar. Listen to the Earth. There is a new Dreaming unfolding.

This book, my Dreaming, is also part of a greater planetary Dreaming, a prophecy long foretold: the prophecy of the eagle and the condor. A time when the mind and the heart reunite, when the intellect of the North meets the wisdom of the South, when ancient ceremonial practices walk alongside modern science, technology and social institutions. This is the unfolding of a new epoch, a convergence of sacred traditions and evolving understandings. It is my sincere hope and prayer that, through this book and through the firestorm we have passed through as a nation, we may come to embody the principles of natural law, human decency and compassionate evolution. Ayahuasca is a gift from the Earth herself, offered as a remedy in an era that too often seems hopelessly divided and on the brink. We would be blind to think that the collapse of society is impossible. It has happened before, it can happen again — and we are on the precipice. I hope and pray that this call is heard. I know it can be. I will continue to stand for truth. I will continue to speak for the Earth, for Indigenous heritage, and for the protection of the vulnerable. This is in everyone's interest. It is a universal truth: we all long for peace, for harmony, for a world where our children, and their children, can live in safety and balance. This calling resides in the soul of every human being. And if we can quiet the noise, even for a moment, and listen deeply to the Earth, to the pulse of her heart, we will all hear it. An Aboriginal Elder said to me that in our society 'truth is illegal', but in reality I believe natural law and the spirit of the Earth never die, and endure through all.

With the storm of confusion, fear and many questions being raised about Ayahuasca, ceremony and myself as a ceremonial leader, I have taken the time to write this book. So here is my truth, written humbly from my heart, through trials and tribulations, rough waters and smooth sailing — and dedicated with love, in service to our sacrament Ayahuasca, our beautiful planet Earth and the healing of humanity. I invite the reader to join me in this journey, to unite in the call of the Earth. I am not alone in sounding this call; this is a planetary movement, growing exponentially and unstoppable. I asked Ayahuasca during the horrors and abuses of lockdowns and medical apartheid: 'What is going on here?' I saw a powerful vision of a huge swell rising in the ocean, an unstoppable force that represented the growing field of awaking in humanity. The wave of change is already here, we are awakening and remembering. The old system, with its colonial habits based in domination and control, is grasping and desperate to maintain the illusion of control. The force of that rising swell is unstoppable, and transformation is inevitable. I pray that the guardians of the dying system may, too, heed the call and join us all in the movement towards healing, peace and prosperity of the human spirit.

This book is far more than just a tale of a modern day witch-hunt. There is immense interest around the world in the topic of shamanism and Ayahuasca at a time of escalating mental health crises. In Australia, depression and suicide rates are soaring. The mystery and widespread reports of Ayahuasca's benefits, the cultural revolution of reconnection to Nature, have created a vast interest in what is going on with this sacred and ancient practice. Celebrities from film and music industries, even members of the British Royal family, are talking about their experiences with it and its enormous benefits. I hope that this book may bring awareness to Ayahuasca, its culture and traditions, to bring understanding as to why so many walk this path, and to gain insight into its roots, practices, benefits and potential.

My aim is not to promote Ayahuasca or shamanic practices above others, as this is one path amongst many and not going to be for everyone. I am presenting my story here to shine light on this path and these practices that have given me and so many people clarity, peace, health and happiness. My aim is to explain myself and how and why I do what I do in the hope that this can answer some questions and perhaps guide people who may be on a similar spiritual journey as me, and to give some inspiration from the shamanic worldview. There are safe, valid and viable alternatives through spiritual ceremony to what the mainstream political and health systems are currently offering. These can be complimentary. It is my belief that these worlds can and will merge. It is prophecy, destiny, the Dream of the Earth.

Whilst I am a strong advocate for spiritual practices and natural remedies, I also see the benefits and importance of Western science, technology and models of health care. Left to its own devices, the current government bureaucracy, with its politics and religion of science and reason, has led us to a crisis point with inherent disconnection from Spirit and an epidemic of chronic mental health problems. I would like to offer this book as a blueprint for how we may be able to integrate shamanic practices with Ayahuasca into a safe model that can be accepted and which is complimentary to current mainstream social structures and beliefs.

There are many threads and layers of the story presented in this book. This story is a weaving of personal and planetary Dreaming, of an Earth walk and spiritual guidance. It tells the story of a sacred weaving of songlines and traditions, where Australian Indigenous Dreaming, Amazonian Dreaming, Brazilian syncretic spiritual traditions merge in a sacred alliance, where my journey and purpose has been to sing and dance new songlines, open portals and build bridges. This is way beyond me, even beyond Ayahuasca. I am just playing my part in this divine orchestration. My story and my life path is my personal Dream, unfolding like a petal in the flowering of a newly emerging remembrance of the Dreaming of the Whole Earth. We humans are crazy if we think we are alone as conscious, aware beings in the universe. This book is a Dreaming trail back to the simplicity of connection to Nature.

I will begin this book with my story: where I came from and the life experienced that shaped my worldview and my path through life. I will tell the story of how I went from being a youth and community development specialist working in drug and alcohol rehabilitation and Aboriginal communities in Australia, to doing deep studies in ancient spiritual and shamanic sciences in the rainforests of South America, and how all of this came together to inform the work that I have developed and practised for the last eight years.

This book will also detail some of the traditions, cultures and practices I have studied and which are integrated into my spiritual practices and healing work and the initiations and training I received along the way. I will aim to describe how and why our ceremonies are conducted in the way they are and how this may affect the mind, body, emotions and spirit of participants. I will also share some different perspectives and studies from around the world into the science and benefits of commencing with the sacrament Ayahuasca.

Throughout this book I will be referring to meetings with spiritual beings, spirit guides, ancestors, *Orixás* (forces of nature) and other metaphysical experiences. These beings and realities are natural and normal aspects of my life and reality. I invite you to be open and present with all the aspects of my reality as I am presenting them here, even if at times this may challenge your beliefs. I am not asking you to *believe* anything: this is just my story, my life, my journey, the Dreaming of my spirit. My perspectives are merely that. This is my account of them and I sincerely hope that I can add to the rich field of studies in these fields. I invite you to allow these stories to be as they are. Beyond plausibility they exist, even if just as your imagination interprets them. Just as with Ayahuasca, I recommend finding teachings that may emerge as relevant to you and your life, your Ayahuasca experiences, your own spirituality or human walk. This is a key teaching in shamanism. Reality is not always as it appears, and this realisation may lead to shifting perspectives, even just for a moment, and may expand your mind, which is in itself a potent pathway to healing.

An ever-present and vitally important ingredient of this story is the inclusion of voices of our First Nations peoples, who have attended ceremony with me. I acknowledge Country, all First Nations, the Elders, ancestors and ones yet to come. Through acknowledgement we garner respect and trust. It is a mutual giving and receiving. As an adolescent Western country, Australians are learning what this truly means. Our Indigenous peoples are still living with the trauma caused by the atrocities committed against them, against Country and against culture. Offering ceremonial spaces as a safe space for healing and reconnection also offers an opportunity for unity in moving forward into a new Dreaming together, in respect and our shared purpose as custodians of the Earth. Embracing Ayahuasca ceremony in Australia can be a powerful cross-cultural, ancient-future remembering and realignment. Within this is a healing movement and an expression of the Earth in a gestational movement, as we become Dreamed as the custodians, co-Dreamers and artists of a planetary awakening and an evolutionary leap.

The path of Ayahuasca is not to be underestimated, nor glamourised. Ayahuasca is a powerful teacher and, if approached with respect and sound practice, is certainly a challenging but deeply rewarding path. Whilst joy and bliss may come from the healing and cleansing that it offers, it will also show you the inevitability of self-responsibility. You will see your own shadows and learn how to embrace compassionately all that has manifested as fear and pain. Our authenticity and knowing our own Dream are required to live life in integrity and with honouring of the self, all relations and our connection to all of creation. This work takes courage, vigilance and humility, as we remember that our role as humans is to care for this Earth, our home. When we awaken to this task and see the enormity of the wounding of the human soul and its relationship to the planet, there is a realisation there is no time to waste and no valid excuses to not live in honour of our highest truth. The path of awakening is a never-ending and relentless work, and allows us no time to stop to complain about it.

Spiritual ceremony is a uniting energy and a powerful force for the healing of humanity. It has the potential to open the hearts of people in a world where the large majority are looping around in their heads. In a society where the people are entranced in virtual realities and in a toxic culture that is out of phase with the harmony of the Earth, ceremony provides remedy. Without connection to spiritual reality — our true nature — we wither and die, we feel insecure in a world full of danger and disconnection. We develop distractions, addictions and anxieties.

Where Ayahuasca shows us the wounding from childhood trauma, ceremony gives us an opportunity to embrace our 'inner child' — a concept that is now well established in psychotherapy. This book will hopefully inspire you to honour your inner child, to embrace the joy and innocence of feeling safe and connected, to feel free to express your uniqueness, creativity and love through peaceful and harmonious actions, like taking a simple breath, admiring beauty in nature and expressing gratitude for the blessing of life. Ayahuasca inspires and reminds us of a state of wonder where mystery is expressed in song, dance and storytelling. This is an essential part of our humanity, and has been in all cultures across all known time on this planet.

Peace, love and harmony are the three precepts which govern my life, my ceremonies and all of my spiritual work and service. Striving for these precepts in our daily lives and practices, learning as we go (grow), leads to happiness and fulfilment, calms the ego and the mind and is an effective remedy we have available to us for the current mental health crisis. Ayahuasca, like other spiritual practices, shows us that there is a choice between suffering and self-liberation. It doesn't come as a free ride though. Ayahuasca, for all its documented evidence of powerful transformation and healing, doesn't do the work for us. We have to do that work ourselves and it's not always easy or painless. It takes courage and commitment to ourselves, a willingness to face inner pain and self-judgment to truly gain the benefits and it doesn't end with the ceremony, it is a life-long commitment. Ayahuasca, connection to Country and shamanic healing, amongst many paths are opportunities should we choose to embrace them. One way or another, our healing is possible in every moment, and it is more accessible than we may have ever imagined.

PART 1
Roots

CHAPTER 1

Learning to Fly

Those who feel the breath of sadness
Sit down next to me
Those who find they're touched by madness
Sit down next to me
Those who find themselves ridiculous
Sit down next to me
In love, in fear, in hate, in tears
Sit down in sympathy

— *Sit Down*, James.

I'm writing this book from Bunjalung Country in the Northern Rivers of the state of New South Wales in Australia. This land is one of my spiritual homes and where I have been visiting and living since I was a young child. Since 2009 I have spent equal time living in Brazil and Australia. Brazil has become my second home and the place where I like to retreat, where I connect deeply to Country and study the rich and diverse culture and spirituality of the people and the land. I've lived five years in Brazil in total, where I feel connected and at ease, speak the language and have deep roots in, and to, the culture.

From my teenage years I've been interested in spirituality, consciousness and healing. My first paranormal/spiritual experiences happened to me as a child, and from a young age I became very interested in the mysteries of life on our planet. I began contemplating the existence of a god or a creator, an *omni-presence* that through conscious connection may benefit my life and my awareness. I have never joined a particular religion, although through walking my own songlines I have studied many teachings and lineages and have developed my own beliefs and constellation of practices, teachings, doctrines and relationships with spiritual beings. If I were to define myself in terms of a person following any kind of religion, mine would be the religion of the Earth, the Dreaming, the forces of nature — similar to the way that First Nations peoples around the world see themselves in relation to the Earth and cosmos.

I have been blessed in my life to have had many profound and magical experiences. I've had countless meetings and studies with Elders and great teachers, profound connection to Country, communion with spiritual beings, deep experiences of love and connection, and a rich diversity of enjoyment of life's treasures. I believe there is a thread or a force within creation that is guiding us at all times. I have studied and learned how to attune myself to this force, this flow of creation, and to allow it to guide me on my journey through life. At times following this path can be scary, even frightening, as I am guided into places and situations, choices I would not normally make. Each time I take a step of faith into the unknown I am guided to experiences that lead to growth, expansion and evolution of my soul.

The practice of surrendering to divine or spiritual guidance I have come to call 'Walking with Spirit'. An Aboriginal Elder friend of mine once told me in front of others that I 'know how to walk'; that is, I am walking or journeying through life, walking my songlines and my Dreaming. Surrendering to this flow of divine guidance is an essential aspect of navigating the journey toward spiritual growth. It is a practice deeply rooted in the art of letting go, trusting and being receptive to the signs and messages that come from life and creation. This form of surrender isn't about relinquishing our power or avoiding responsibility for decisions, but is an acknowledgment of the sacred dance between our individual will and the divine will of creation. When these two aspects of will are in harmony, we are co-creating with the universe. When we align our individual will with the force of creation, we align our personal with the collective Dream and a third force of creation manifests a reality, a sacred path. I have also learned that the force of my ego can take me out of that sacred alliance, leading me astray into confusion, fear, dissonance and sometimes hard life-lessons.

To walk with Spirit requires us to let go of the control we often have over our lives, the clinging onto of the things we think may keep us safe, and instead to trust in a greater wisdom. In letting go of control, we are able to move through life with more grace, ease and fluidity, and this opens us to a greater trust in life and the universe. It humbles us into being part of something much greater than ourselves, thereby cultivating the knowledge that we are guided, supported and on our spiritual path for a reason. This is an active engagement with life, where we must listen deeply and remain open to where we are being led, even if it's not where we planned to go. Paying attention to signs, messages, intuition, opportunities and synchronicities is a practice of awareness. I have found that this is how the universe communicates with us, and is sometimes subtle and requires an open heart and a quiet mind to discern its meaning. This is why Indigenous peoples the world over practise the sacred art of *dadirri*, or listening deeply. This constant communication has guided me with clarity and purpose throughout my life. I am constantly being challenged to find new levels of trust and faith in Spirit.

I generally like to retreat into quiet, meditative spaces, away from people and hustle and bustle. I move towards nature and sacred places; I've always experienced peace and healing from the ocean and love being close to the beach. Time away in nature helps me to recharge, to connect with my spiritual guides, to listen deeply to Country and the messages from Spirit, and to prepare myself for the work that I do supporting people, community and the Earth.

I'm a naturally creative person, happiest when I am working on painting a canvas, playing music, writing or dreaming up plans and ideas. I have been an artist all my life, always painting and drawing throughout my childhood and adulthood, but it was only when I met the great Ayahuasca shaman Pablo Amaringo in Amazonas, Brazil in 2003 that I began to paint my visions and I started taking my art more seriously. This led in 2015 to an exhibition of my visionary art in Rio called 'Gulwan — Spirit of the Night Sky'. I love the creative process, storytelling through art, dreaming up a vision or an idea and the application of it into a form, collaborating with others and sharing it with my community.

I have also written and recorded music, one album of which is a collaboration with the *Yawanawá* and *Huni Kuin* peoples of the Brazilian Amazon called 'The Kanaro Project'. For me music is life. I don't know where I would be without it; for me the finest expression of my spirit and soul is when I am playing and singing. One of the things I have come to understand is that through music and art we have a two-way communication with Spirit. We are able to reflect spiritual realities through art and ancient and enduring cultural practices, and yet communicate intention through artful prayer into manifest reality. There is a higher awareness than the 'thinking mind' that we touch when we express ourselves from a creative place. People are touched and reminded of higher forces and spiritual realties through music and art in ways that the written or spoken word may not reach.

Throughout my adult life I have been involved in health, healing practices and community development, having worked in many different government and non-government agencies in a range of positions over 20 years. Beyond this my focus changed to spiritual healing, counselling and group work, music, creative arts and ceremonial practices. During this time I have had many experiences in Indigenous communities and have greatly enjoyed these connections and opportunities to learn and to develop my awareness through being in service. I am passionate about learning from the ancient and enduring cultures, and I feel that the wisdom and history contained in them is vital to our evolution and survival as a species. There is much to learn and a bridge to be built to reconcile the wounds of colonialism, genocide and abuse inflicted on First Nations peoples everywhere. I have dedicated much of my life to learning what is required to heal and to build this bridge, and much of what I have learned from the Indigenous peoples of the world has greatly informed my awareness, my work and my life.

From wounded child to healer

My story began with growing up in the inner western suburbs of Sydney, Australia as the middle child of three. I was born in August 1973 and given the name Peter George McIntyre, named after my grandfather on my father's side. I grew up quite isolated in a broken home — not too uncommon for children of my generation. I spent a lot of time alone throughout my childhood. My parents lived with their own emotional and mental struggles, were mostly self-absorbed in their own dramas and not really available to me. Despite the neglect, I know they did their best, considering their own traumas. I was a very sensitive child, very creative, and in particular loved to sing, draw and write stories.

I was raised in what I can refer to as a lower-middle class suburb of Sydney. My father left when I was about nine years old, which was pretty confusing at the time. Nobody explained to me what had happened. I just knew that my mother was very upset and had kicked him out and he left with a knife in his hand. I remember crying myself to sleep that night while my mother, drunk, stood watching me at the door to my bedroom. It was several years later when my father reappeared.

I learned to rely upon myself and spent a lot of time alone as a child. I would usually be drawing or building Lego and inventing worlds in which I could imagine myself exploring. I also loved getting on my bike and riding around the suburbs exploring and probably going a lot further away than my mother would have liked, but she didn't know and didn't show much interest to find out. My mother was dealt the hand of many Australian women married and living in the suburbs. She was ill equipped and unsupported to deal with my father and his trauma-based behaviours. She survived his emotional and mental abuse and did her best to keep the family together. After my father left, she spent every night drunk and unavailable.

My father was a Vietnam War veteran; he was a Corporal of the 1st Battalion (1RAR) of the Australian Army. He was the son of a veteran of the Battle of Gallipoli and the Western front (my grandfather), and a highly decorated war veteran. He served in the first tours of duty in Vietnam in the mid-1960s and was on the front line of horrendous human atrocities that left him severely scarred for life. Following his active duty in the war, he went on to become an instructor for the Australian Army until the end of the Vietnam War. My father had a heart of gold but was a very hardened, self-protective and often aggressive man. Though never physically violent towards any member of my family, his emotional and mental abuse was at times cruel, and mostly directed towards my mother, although I received a fair dose of it too.

My father mostly ignored me as a child, and I remember my mother arguing with him about him not spending time with me. Overhearing these arguments as a child was devastating, as I was already feeling abandoned and neglected, and these arguments translated in my mind as there being something wrong with me, reinforcing my isolation and need for self-reliance. In later years I came to realise that the abandonment and neglect I experienced as a child formed deep wounds in my psyche, but also inspired a path of growth and self-discovery that greatly informed my spirituality and my work in health and healing.

Why were my parents so disinterested in me? As a child I could not comprehend that they were just messed up, mentally ill humans in a dysfunctional society, self-absorbed with their own personal dramas. I internalised all of this as if it were somehow my own fault, and as a result suffered from isolation, depression, suicidality and crippling lack of self-esteem throughout my adolescence and into adulthood. The internalised belief that there was something wrong with me became a shadow that hung over me throughout my life. In later life I have used my personal experiences to become very adept at integrating inner-child therapy in supporting people to heal trauma and relationships. This has also been a major influence upon my work with Ayahuasca.

My father's involvement in the Australian Army was complex and mysterious. He suffered greatly with physical and psychological wounding from many years of service. He was directly involved in atrocities committed in Vietnam at the direction of the US Military, actions that often only killed countless women and children. Under his command, his unit was often the first one on the scene, picking up all the bodies whilst being fired upon by Viet Cong snipers. In later years he came to terms with the fact that he had been lied to and that the war was a propaganda exercise in which he had been used as an instrument of terror and to commit war crimes. The severity of my father's psychological and nervous system wounding from his involvement in such a cruel war has had a deep effect upon me throughout my entire life, with this often coming up in Ayahuasca ceremonies for healing. I carry the imprint of his post-traumatic stress disorder (PTSD) on my nervous system, and have spent my life managing its symptoms.

My father was also a subject in what seemed to be a psychological mind-control program that also infiltrated my life at times from childhood into adult years. At 18 years of age I once had to carry my father home from the pub after he was having war flashbacks and a nervous breakdown; he was shaking uncontrollably and emotionally releasing while reacting to phantom missile attacks. These kinds of incidents were not unusual for me. Years later, I would find myself supporting people during Ayahuasca and other therapies that were having similar trauma releases.

There were times in my childhood when psychologists from the Australian Army would contact my mother and ask her questions and give her advice on how to handle my father. At school, army psychologists would come to visit and take my brother and me aside and give us psychological exams, without my mother's consent. Eventually, they tried to convince my mother to give her permission to enrol me in a military school: she asked me and I said I didn't want to go. Into my teens, my father would ring me on weekends, drunk, and harass me to go to Canberra and enrol in military college. His phone calls became increasingly erratic and often psychotic at times, with him telling me he had a gun with bullets and he 'knew who they were for'. My mother would be in the background screaming at me to hang up the phone. This was a lot for an anxious teenager to deal with, and as a result I have had to cope into my adulthood with high tolerance levels to trauma, whether this be from working in youth detox centres, in Aboriginal communities or dealing with emotionally abusive partners and, more recently, the abuses of government bureaucrats, institutions and the media.

In my late twenties I decided to spend six months living in Cairns, North Queensland, to spend some time with my father and do some self-healing work. This *was* a healing time and we were able to talk about many things, often sharing stories and tears about his traumas from the war and about our family, my mother and what it was like for us both growing up. He also told me some stories about my grandfather, who was a high-ranking Scottish Freemason and a well-known figure in Cairns, where he worked as the harbour quarter-master.

During this time in the year 2001 whilst I was living in Cairns near my father, I began being followed by a man who was living in his van with his wife and young child. This man seemed to be paranoid and claimed to also be a Vietnam veteran. He claimed to know I was visiting my father and he told me a lot of stories about what things may have been like with my father and how the army was secretly observing him and also observing my own interactions with my father. There were a lot of strange synchronicities and accurate information he was giving me, but he seemed pretty crazy, and I took it all with a grain of salt.

One day, this strange man gave me a CD ROM disc and told there was something on it of interest to me. He asked me not to tell anyone who I had received it from. I never saw him again. I went to the library and opened the file on the disc and it had a lot of disturbing military information on it about covert operations and internal conflicts within the Australian military and government. It also had a lot of information about mind-control programs, listed my father as a programmed operative, and included a lot of anagrams, numerical codes and other very strange data surrounding his name. It spoke of an internal threat that seemed to be related to shadowy competing factions, threats of nuclear bombs buried secretly in Australia, and threats that mind-controlled 'assists', of which my father was listed as being one, may be activated if one of the factions acted in a certain way.

I chose not to tell my father about what I found in that file, as his nervous system was highly volatile. His doctor had given him instructions not to talk about the war, even though we did at times, and I think he felt safe to do so with me. I did have a cheeky curiosity and one day asked my father about joining the Freemasons so that I could find out more about all this mysterious drama that my family had been involved in since before I was born. Dad was quick and strong in convincing me that joining the Freemasons would not be a healthy choice, as he shared that he, himself, had kept away from them due to the secrecy and dubious intent he had been exposed to. I felt proud as his son to know that he had rejected secret societies which I had come to know as being among the great evils that caused so much suffering in the world. I decided to put all the pain of the military and government abuses on my family behind me by avoiding dealing with them; I didn't know how, or even feel safe, to talk to my father or anyone about it. Later in my life, in the presence of Ayahuasca, this all re-emerged with conscious recollections and a healing journey began.

As a child and into my adolescence I felt very different to those around me, and alien in my environment. Always seemingly doing my own thing, I was interested in styles of music, art, life's mysteries, history and politics that nobody around me was. Feeling different was normal for me, but also led to an increasing sense of isolation. What it taught me, though, was to be independent in my thinking, to see things from a unique perspective. I have always stayed true to myself, and have never been one to follow trends, fashions or social cliques. Even to this day I generally move in new directions outside of social and cultural norms. I have grown to appreciate this trait, and this has also been great training in being able to listen to the voice of Spirit in a way that is unencumbered by expectations and affectations. I see this as a gift in the development of shamanic awareness and abilities, and also an intrinsic part of what it takes to be a pioneer and leader of new movements.

Due to the isolation I experienced as a child, I developed a deep and rich internal world. This also led to me developing a strong inner mental dialogue along with an ability to observe others and the world around me with clarity. This was partly a defence mechanism. Maintaining hyper-vigilant awareness within my environment was a way of coping with the chaos, neglect and abuse within my family. I distinctly remember having long and deep thoughts about the nature of my existence, the nature of reality, and as quite a young child I remember identifying the sense of my spirit as separate from my mind, thoughts, emotions and body. I developed a deep familiarity with my inner dialogue that I recognise now was an inherent ability to communicate with Spirit, my *higher-self* and my spiritual guides.

The higher-self can be understood as the eternal omniscient aspect of oneself that resides in subtle spiritual realms and serves as a source of unending wisdom and guidance, beyond the confines of temporal existence. In some ways it can be known as one's 'personal Dreaming'. It offers a perspective that is both vast and deeply aligned with our purpose and our true potential. Communicating with our higher-self and our spiritual guides, beings of light and wisdom that are assigned or allied to us, supports us through our journey on this Earth, offering clarity, guidance and insights that are invaluable in navigating life's complexities and challenges. These spiritual entities guide us towards realising our life's purpose and understanding the lessons we are here to learn.

I have learned to be grateful for the isolation and trauma of my childhood. The blessing in disguise was that it gave me solace and connection as a neglected child. It also gave me, from a young age, skills in spiritual awareness that have been of great benefit to me throughout life, and tools that I am able to use in my work as a healer and in ceremonial practice. The dissociation of my childhood delivered me into the arms of Spirit. From an early age I was able to see spiritual entities and also to have a strong sense of empathy that at times was traumatic and confusing for me to experience, as I didn't have the language and didn't understand what was happening to me, nor did I feel safe enough to explain to anyone what I was experiencing. As I moved into my adolescence I researched as much as I could about paranormal phenomena, ghosts, extraterrestrials, telepathy and other extrasensory abilities.

As a young child I would often be out and about with my mother, walking in the street or in the supermarket. Many times I had the experience of walking past someone, perhaps a stressed person or an upset child, and I would feel a very strong wave of negative emotions. Later, I came to realise I was picking up on the emotions of others in my proximity without realising it. For example, if I walked past an upset person, I would feel a strong sense of grief and abandonment that would be confusing to me and hard to shake, and I could dwell on those feelings, which might take a couple of days to fully pass.

Another experience I had as a child was when my older sister and her friends would sit and innocently attempt to perform séances, copying things they had seen on television. They would sit around a *Ouija board*, a circle with letters of the alphabet laid out, with their fingers lightly touching an upturned cup as they summoned spiritual beings in an attempt to make communication. I was a bit younger and found this fascinating until one day when they were sitting on the front verandah doing this and I went out to watch. When I arrived I saw a dark and intense-looking entity hovering above them. This entity was very frightening to me and I went back inside and hid in a corner of the house. I was around eight years old at the time and had no idea what I had witnessed. My father came and found me and asked me what was wrong and I couldn't speak, I felt ashamed and scared. He took me into his room and closed the door and began to aggressively ask me what was wrong, saying: 'What's wrong with you, boy?' This was something I had heard from him a lot, and had instilled in me the belief that there *was* something 'wrong' with me. Eventually he said, 'Well, if you can't tell me what's wrong, there must be nothing wrong' and he let me go.

This experience with my father is one event that has stayed very strong and clear in my memory. On one hand it is a disturbing memory of the kind of emotional abuse I received as a child, when I would be made to feel there was something not right with me and I would be treated in a harsh way and did not feel emotional safety. This is also an example of how social norms and prejudices can lead to the ridicule and denial of spiritual realities. Nobody taught me about these things and there was no internet to search them out. This is a theme that comes up time and again when talking of shamanic reality and the Ayahuasca practices throughout my life. From another perspective, I can also see that my father's determination to tell me there must not be anything wrong did give me a sense of security that the scary spirit was not going to hurt me.

My childhood was full of supernatural experiences that have only made sense to me as an adult. I used to see a spirit at night as I lay in bed. Sometimes I would wake in the middle of the night as if I was in a different reality and would see and feel this spirit in my room. I would become frozen and confused but somehow I just allowed this experience to happen many times and never told anyone about it. I also had experiences of telekinesis, sometimes feeling like I was so deeply connected to the forces of nature, in particular the wind and rain and the animal world. I also had recurring dreams and premonitions as well as strong sensations of déjà-vu.

These kinds of experiences continued through my adolescence and adulthood, and I can now see that they were indications of an innate shamanic ability. I have come to see my extra-sensory abilities as powerful tools for understanding and navigating reality. Through years of study and research into spiritual healing, shamanism and Indigenous spirituality and practices, I have recovered skills and abilities and wisdom that I brought with me into this life. I have learned to harness and develop these past-life gifts or soul remembrance and developed them into techniques that I apply to art, music, self-awareness, ceremonial practice and to facilitating spiritual healing for others. The chapter 'Shamanic Renaissance', which explores shamanism and its global renaissance in greater detail, is dedicated to this.

Coming of age in a hostile world

Once my schooling was over, I left home at 18 and moved into a shared house with my older sister and some friends. I began to explore the world of drugs, parties, friends and lovers, and deepened my experiences in the school of life. I discovered I had quite a passion for people and experiences that gave me profound connections. I was excited to learn and to grow and it was in this time at around 19 years old that I first met people who talked to me about spirituality from a nourishing perspective I could relate to. Due to my experiences as a child and adolescent, I was quite shy and awkward in talking about this; however, I absorbed myself in personal study, exhaustively researching books, films, workshops and healing events — research that continues until this day.

In 1992 I was accepted into a Bachelor of Arts at the University of Sydney and I really had no idea what I wanted to do with my life, though studying seemed like a good idea. I remember arriving at the university orientation day and being asked to sign up for classes for the year, and it was only in the moment when I saw psychology on the list that I thought that would be a good idea. My subsequent experience studying academic psychology at the university felt like a disturbing, pessimistic and nihilistic view of the world and of humanity that was completely contrary to the things I felt in my own personal experience of my life and my connection to Spirit, let alone showing a contrast to all the spiritual texts I had already been studying. After two years of psychology and arts I decided to change my degree to a Bachelor of Social Work, an area which was much more aligned to my beliefs and much more accommodating to my personality and my empathetic approach to people, community and healing.

During those years of university I gained my many skills and experience as a counsellor and group therapist, and I chose to focus on youth and community development and health education, which at the time I felt would be an interesting and colourful field of work. Later, on reflection, I see this was also a way to heal my own deep wounds from childhood and adolescence. The Bachelor of Social Work allowed me to pursue a career over many years. I was offered many interesting roles and developed a strong reputation as a counsellor, group worker and community development expert across a range of government and non-government agencies in Sydney, Perth, Melbourne and the Northern Territory. I enjoyed this work very much and found myself adept at understanding both the human condition through empathy and building relationships as well as developing the theoretical and organisational aspects of working within social and community frameworks.

I spent several years working in drug and alcohol detox and rehabilitation services in Melbourne, and it was during this work that my compassion for those suffering from addiction and mental health disorders became very clear. It was also the springboard for me to launch a spiritual journey that eventually took me to the Amazon and meeting Ayahuasca. I realised there were many factors inhibiting people from healing and transforming their lives, and I often witnessed the limitations of working within organisational structures bound by complex and dysfunctional systems, policies and beliefs. This was a great source of frustration for me and would often lead to me quitting good jobs and going on 'gardening leave'; that is, taking on minimal hours of work and spending time growing my own gardens and following pursuits such as yoga, travel and personal development.

Life began to show me it was through developing healthy relationships and positive life experiences that people begin to heal, and that through loving care and support people can rebuild themselves through positive entrainment of the nervous system and emotional body. It's like the body needs to re-learn what it is to be truly human, without the imprint of the trauma of history. This is a long and delicate journey that is fraught with the dangers and distractions of the chronically dysfunctional social and institutional reality of our culture. The other thing I had clearly learned is that everyone has their own ability to heal themselves. The stories of what makes people happy, the successes and moments of joy that have been experienced all reside within, and through support and encouragement this can be remembered, embraced and re-integrated. Put simply, I had learned that we are all our own best healers, yet we still need others to support us in our healing and development.

It was in March 2003 that I left my job as a youth development worker at a drug and alcohol rehabilitation centre in Melbourne to embark on my first overseas trip with the intention of meeting my ancestors. This was the spiritual journey that took me first to remote parts of Scotland and then to the Brazilian Amazon and my first meeting with Ayahuasca, which would become one of my greatest allies for healing and spiritual growth. Everything changed for me from that first meeting and led to a completely new perspective on healing and mental health. Thereafter I began a long journey of many years' self-development, personal healing and spiritual growth that continues to this day. Ayahuasca, I quickly realised, was the best and most efficient psychotherapist and healer I'd ever encountered.

I felt like a completely different person upon returning to Australia after such a transformational experience of connecting with my ancestral land and Spirit in Scotland and after undergoing the immense spiritual awakening and healing that occurred in those first meetings with Ayahuasca. Everything had changed for me and I became much more active in developing myself spiritually and applying many of the teachings I had learned into new healing modalities and creative projects. I began to work independently within a new and exciting spiritual community I was becoming more familiar with. I also began painting my visions after I had been shown many things by the great teacher Ayahuasca and also the shaman I had studied with in Brazil, well-known Peruvian visionary artist, Don Pablo Amaringo.

I received many visions and guidance for my life's purpose whilst in the Amazon. My attention turned to the global awakening of humanity and the growing momentum of the movement towards new ways of organising ourselves as a community in alignment and harmony with the Earth and our higher spiritual values. It was on this path that I began to connect deeply with First Nations Australians, learning about traditional values, spirituality of the land and culture and how we can truly live in harmony with the Earth and each other. It was during this time I began collaborative projects on establishing some grassroots community movements that integrated Indigenous wisdom with ecology and sustainable development principles. This work took me back to Brazil, where I began working with communities, business and government in sustainable development.

While living in Brazil and working on exciting developmental projects plus meeting many people and advanced social organisations, I was also developing my relationship with Ayahuasca and its use as a communal religious and spiritual practice. Eventually, as I had found with my work within government and government-backed health agencies, I saw that the world of sustainable development was riddled with politics and the limitations of antiquated systems and group-think, corruption and self-interest. Agents were explaining to me the need for political 'donations' to sweeten any investment projects, at the same time 'green-washing' by trying to replace funded projects with hydro dams and palm oil plantations, while hidden hands were stopping the advancement of new technologies. I learned a lot through these experiences but also the feeling of frustration returned, so after this I began to focus more keenly on my spiritual development. This led me to return to Australia, where I spent three years working in remote Indigenous communities in Central Australia. Working in the desert with the original peoples and their ancient culture was a huge initiation for me on my path — and another revelation about the importance of applying a spiritual approach to healing and community development.

In 2013 I returned again to Brazil and spent a few weeks with my mentor, psychologist Silvia Polivoy, who, after some Ayahuasca ceremonies, challenged me by asking me why I had spent so much time and energy in my life helping others and supporting others with their healing and creativity, and why I hadn't invested this much in myself. I knew she was right. I returned to Australia and made a commitment to myself that I would spend as long as it took to discover myself as an artist. I had always loved art and music and been a very creative person, yet I had never invested in myself as an artist in any significant way.

Soon the pressure and stress of working in such a challenging environment got to me. By this stage I was managing a large community development project spanning nine remote Indigenous communities and I was mentally, physically and emotionally exhausted.

In November 2013 I left my position at the head of this project I had put so much into and returned to Brazil simply to be an artist, nothing more. With this intention I found life took on a whole new kind of adventure. I went back to the Amazon then to an Ayahuasca retreat focused on music and visionary art with the famous ceremonial leader and musician, Carioca Freitas. Once I met Carioca and the Ciranda family in the forests outside of Rio de Janeiro, I knew I had to stay there and study with him. I did a two-year apprenticeship in ceremony, music and Ayahuasca. It was this that set me upon the path of becoming a ceremonial leader and musician, and I was able to integrate so many of the skills and the awareness I had developed over my life into my practice.

I have come to believe that life is about harmony and peace in communion with the Divine. The Divine being the spirit that resides in us all, in nature, in the cosmos — a fine light that is universal and never-ending. We all have this light within us, we find it in all living beings of the Earth, the sun, moon and stars, and this light is where we find our connection to creation, to all things, and that connection heals us. We all want to feel connected; it's the sense of isolation and disconnection that causes so much anxiety and fear and illness in people.

My life has become about prayer and celebration of this divinity that we share to sing and dance and create art in honour of this beautiful truth. It's simple, yet somehow we have moved so far away from this simple truth. Ceremony humbles us to the Divine and teaches us to become better people, to improve the way we relate to ourselves, the Earth and each other. To sing and dance and celebrate the beauty of creation is to be free, to be happy and to participate as healthy humans, learning how to care for this beautiful Earth and all the gifts we have been given. All First Nations peoples around the world sing and dance in sacred ceremony, and our civilisation is waking up to this simple truth as we heal ourselves from the traumas of history, disconnection and generational abuses.

We can be happy and free and live in balance if we choose, and the evolutionary leap required to save humanity is one that must take us beyond the fear and insecurity of our society to a trust in Spirit and a return to love, peace and harmony. This starts within each one of us and spreads through our families and communities. I feel so blessed to have this knowing within me, to be able to sing and pray throughout life, and to use my creative abilities and spiritual connection to express the divinity of creation in my own unique way. We have much more power than we realise and, like the effect of butterfly wings, where even the most gentle and subtle movement of their wings reverberates infinitely to be felt all around the world, our actions and intentions can do likewise.

CHAPTER 2

Ayahuasca

In my view, what we have come to call Ayahuasca is a holy sacrament: a union of two Amazonian plants that, when prepared with reverence and activated through intention, music and sound, opens a gateway into dimensions of being that are ordinarily beyond our everyday perception.

Ayahuasca is more than just a concoction of plants and biochemical effects, as anyone who has drunk it will know. Ayahuasca is pure mystery, impossible to define; it is beyond the human mind's ability to comprehend. From the many ancient creation myths of Ayahuasca, what we find is that it has deep spiritual roots in Amazonian culture and there is some evidence it may have also been used in ancient times in the Andes by the Incan peoples. Ayahuasca is a living being, a spirit of great majesty and mystery that has a golden light that emanates endless, unconditional love. It is a great teacher and guide for humanity in how we navigate our relationship to the natural and spiritual worlds, and leaves a profound knowing in the hearts and minds of all those who come to know its kindness, compassion and vast wisdom.

Ayahuasca is known by many names and each tribal grouping of original nations in the South American Amazonian regions have diverse names, practices and mythologies for it. All of these cultures share a belief that knowledge of Ayahuasca originated from a divine act that left a gift for humanity, one that invites interspecies communication, benefitting our ability to live harmoniously with, and be protected from, nature, animals, elemental forces and earth changes.

Ayahuasca is now widespread across the globe and its use is growing rapidly. It is assisting in the awakening of humanity, and is a guide to commune with the Earth and its beings at a time of radical planetary transformation amidst the urgent need for species-wide evolutionary growth. Ayahuasca brings us healing, strength and awareness, with connection to spiritual realities and multiple dimensions. In order for us to gain its benefits, Ayahuasca demands self-responsibility in facing our shadows and fears. It inspires the making of courageous steps to integrate its teachings so that we may embody its qualities, leading to a balanced, peaceful and joyful expression of our humanity, in harmony with the Earth and all of creation.

Ayahuasca, which in the Andean *Quechua* language translates to 'the vine of the soul', may also be described as a brew, typically prepared by combining the *Banisteriopsis caapi* vine, in some areas known as 'Ayahuasca vine', with another plant, *Psychotria viridis* (chacruna), which contains DMT, or N,N-dimethyltryptamine, a psychedelic compound. When ingested, Ayahuasca may induce a profound altered state of consciousness, often characterised by vivid visions, introspection, emotional catharsis and communion with the Divine. An Ayahuasca experience is typically unique to each person who consumes it, and the experience may also vary during every dose or every ceremony undertaken. One of the most powerful qualities of Ayahuasca is the inherent sense of mystery that it embodies. Ayahuasca invites us to enter the great mystery. Many people write books and make documentaries about this, whilst Western medicine and science attempt to research and categorise it into existing belief systems and paradigms. The mystery represented by Ayahuasca is a humbling force for humanity, and when we approach its divinity with respect, we are shown the limitations of our ego and rational mind, but are also given access to the infinite possibilities of the multi-dimensional universe. Ayahuasca expands our consciousness and connects us to profound realities of personal revelation, cosmic memories, ancestral wisdom, subconscious woundings and, ultimately, the stillness and emptiness of a meditative mind. When we are clear in our bodies, minds and emotions, and are attuned to the elevated consciousness that Ayahuasca offers us, divine messages and guidance are available to support us in our expression, protection and growth as humans in a world abundant with challenges and blessings. To know Ayahuasca is to experience it with respect, honouring and truth.

Participating in an Ayahuasca ceremony is often described as embarking on a deeply introspective and transformative journey. The experience can be both beautiful and challenging, as individuals may confront their innermost fears, traumas and subconscious patterns. Ayahuasca offers insights into the nature of existence, our place in the universe, and the interconnectedness of all things. Many people report profound spiritual revelations, a sense of unity with the cosmos, and a newfound appreciation for life. Ayahuasca is not only an *entheogenic* (spiritual psychedelic) substance, but also a doorway to profound self-discovery and spiritual growth for those who approach it with reverence and humility.

There is a rich diversity of styles and cultures of Ayahuasca ceremonies and practices found all over the world. Ceremonies that are held in alignment with traditions, ancestry and sacred doctrines will typically guide participants to quieten the mind and limit the expression of individual egos. The culture and practices of these ceremonies are typically designed to maintain a strong firmness in our behaviour, so that we may practise surrendering to forces greater than ourselves. Disciplining the mind and ego as such creates a space where we can learn to embody divine qualities of grace, humility, reverence for the sacred, firmness in thoughts and actions, self-discipline and service. By surrendering the ego we may experience our resistances and addictions, avoidance, insecurities and self-validating behaviours. Awareness of these behaviours brings about healing of the wounded aspects of our psyche and leads us to a more spacious and authentic expression of ourselves as instruments of the Divine. Typically, more experienced practitioners will hold themselves in a strong and self-disciplined posture throughout a ceremony and lead by example as newer practitioners learn directly from the teachings that come from within their experiences and communion with Ayahuasca itself. The ceremony becomes a practice for our lives, where we strive to create a life wherein the qualities of respect, right-action and reverence may become our way of being at all times. In ceremony, as we pray to the ancestors, spiritual teachers and the forces of nature, we remember mindfulness and respect for others and our environment, and learn that our actions will always create reactions. Through right-action we are able to maintain an inner peace and harmony with all our relations. Ultimately, traditional ceremonies are held in such a way as to allow Ayahuasca to work within us and through us, without the interference of the mind and behavioural patterns of resistance and control. Ayahuasca ceremony is thus very healing on an internal level of self-awareness and mindfulness, but also healing in the way we relate and interact with others and the world. Ayahuasca reminds us and teaches us to listen and respect the forces of nature and Great Spirit, where there is always guidance for us on our journey through life, the embodiment of which I have come to refer to as 'Walking with Spirit'.

In my 22 years' experience with Ayahuasca ceremony in many different settings and cultures, I have come to know Ayahuasca as a living being, a Divine Majesty of presence, mystery and unfathomable existence. Just as in the many creation myths found throughout South America, within the experience of consecrating this sacrament is a magnificent and vast consciousness that has an infinitely loving and benevolent care for humanity. Within this consciousness field exists a grand constellation of spiritual entities and beings that support us on our inner journey as we commune within the multi-dimensional fields. Different spiritual lineages of Ayahuasca practice each have their own constellation of ancestors and nature beings that guide and protect. From my experience, Ayahuasca is a powerful, conscious force that is able to penetrate our walls of psychic defence and psychological dysfunction that have been created as expressions of human trauma. It guides us to an elevated and objective view of ourselves and our emotional wounds from this life and others. Ayahuasca teaches us to have compassion for ourselves and our wounds, often by showing us the trauma we have lived through. There is an innate intelligence within Ayahuasca, a living, conscious being. I believe it is misguided to separate the spiritual and supernatural aspects of Ayahuasca from its physical and manifest properties, to approach it merely as a scientific curiosity, as chemicals with physical and psychological reactions. Descriptions of 'hallucinations' are obscurations of what is a spiritual field of consciousness emanating from the natural world. A spiritual field of awareness forgotten to most of humanity. Ayahuasca is remembrance.

When considering the nature of consciousness and fields of consciousness, we may refer to states of being aware of, and able to perceive, one's surroundings, thoughts, emotions, and experiences. It involves the ability to introspect, reflect and have a sense of self-awareness. Examining or defining consciousness remains a complex and diverse field of study. Buddhist teachings talk about consciousness as impermanent, constantly changing, and devoid of inherent selfhood. Buddhism emphasises the cultivating of awareness and insight into the nature of consciousness to attain liberation from suffering (*dukkha*) and achieve enlightenment (*nirvana*). It is not possible to enter into the reality of Ayahuasca without some awareness of the nature of consciousness, as by its very nature it acts as a gateway to expanded and altered states of consciousness. This may be akin to our most common altered state — in dreams, where the normal boundaries of physical reality may be radically changed. For example, we may experience flying or talking with deceased loved ones in our dreams. Shamanism and other traditional spiritual practices have, for thousands of years, invoked altered states of consciousness for healing, spiritual enquiry, and inter-species and other dimensional communication.

In Hinduism there are many practices and beliefs that refer to *devas*, which means 'shining ones', and that are associated with the flow of nature and natural forces, from the rivers to the ocean, the wind, fire, rocks, clouds and forests, and so on. Similarly, in Afro-Brazilian spiritual cultures, particularly within the *Candomblé* and *Umbanda* traditions, the *Orixás* are revered deities or spiritual forces representing various aspects of nature, human qualities, and ancestral energies that provide a framework for spiritual connection, healing and community cohesion. During an experience with Ayahuasca it is very common for people to experience visions, communication or communion with these natural forces, where the Earth is a living entity in which every individual component functions as part of a greater whole. This is akin to the growing ecological awareness that is emerging within humanity, while industry and Western science is causing much disharmony and destruction. Within this awakening is a realisation of the spiritual forces that lie behind the physical form of nature and act as the formative and primal pattern, or life force. This is not just a mystical spiritual view, as leading-edge physics fundamentally shows that everything is energy and underlies physical structure and form. The underlying or primal pattern of the Orixás or *devic* energy as consciousness or Spirit is *the* animating force of the natural world and is reflected in the origin myths, culture and practices of Ayahuasca throughout the Amazon.

Practitioners of Ayahuasca and Indigenous peoples often talk about their experiences and interactions with spiritual entities and beings. Some of these entities are very specific, and shamans and other practitioners may develop ongoing relationships with them, as shown in some of the origin myths that describe beings who continue to work with humans through the Ayahuasca experience to this day. Modern Western appreciation of nature spirits can be traced back to the 16th century and the writings and studies of the alchemist Paracelsus which had a profound effect on the work of Rudolf Steiner and others. Biochemist Rupert Sheldrake developed his theory of morphogenic fields (*A New Science of Life*) which addresses the formative causation in nature according to an organising principle. According to this principle, a biological organisation depends on fields of consciousness he calls 'morphogenic' fields. Although Sheldrake uses the language of science and biochemistry, this is essentially the same way that shamans or psychics would describe it; that is, it is the overlapping of multiple realities occupying the same space, only at different vibrational levels. Modern physics also describes this same phenomenon. We may perceive nature spirits as non-material spiritual beings in their own right or as personifications of the innate intelligence of the natural world. Ayahuasca shamans may experience the reality of these spirits and multi-dimensions as a normal part of their practice and awareness, although we all have the ability to perceive these and it is very common for those who drink Ayahuasca to develop this and even have profound communication with this spirit world.

In the process of my writing this book, people have often advised me to refer to established mainstream science and studies in order to validate my writing and the information I am expressing here. Whilst I recognise that modern science has had a significant impact on the development of human consciousness, it is also very limiting in its reductionist social and political confines, and has acquired a quasi-religious authoritarianism that dictates what the truth is and how we verify it. In reality, Western science has also caused a lot of destruction and deformation of human thought and expression, arguably leading to the degradation of planetary health and the destruction of our environment. This is both alarming and insulting to Indigenous peoples, whose reality is being denied and questioned, or put into some kind of mystical sub-reality whilst Western science fumbles around trying to make sense of it. I hope this book may play a role in re-establishing the honouring and respect for spiritual reality. For First Nations people all over the world, there is no need for this reductionist science to prove what, for them, is well-established reality, lore and culture that have been effective for thousands of years in keeping them safe and thriving, living sustainably in harmony within the natural world. From that perspective, the Western world is merely trying to catch up, or perhaps first arrive at the realisation that the modern mindset and scientific philosophy is limited. From there, an expanded view must be adopted in order to avert an environmental and public health catastrophe. A great psychological, cultural and social healing must begin for human potential to be fully realised. I firmly believe that Ayahuasca is a powerful and potent tool available to us in this time for supporting the realisation of this potential.

There is a great diversity of Ayahuasca traditions, many of which are found in the large and diverse range of native cultures, traditions and spirituality originating in the Amazon rainforest. As Ayahuasca has now moved around the world, it has also expanded its field to integrate many new spiritual and cultural elements, both in the realm of consciousness and in ceremonial practices. For example, as described above, the Afro-Brazilian spiritual lineages that have many similar core beliefs and practices are widely integrated and woven into Ayahuasca shamanism and culture throughout Brazil and the world. In this book I will focus on the cultures and lineages that I have personally studied and those that I integrate within my own practices. This is not to discount or overlook the many other beautiful and potent lineages and approaches that are being practised around the world today.

Whilst I was blessed to spend time with, and be trained by, the late Pablo Amaringo, a famous Peruvian Ayahuasca shaman and visionary artist, the large majority of my training and experience has been in Brazil over many years and is ongoing to this day. I have a strong connection with the Brazilian Yawanawá and Huni Kuin peoples' spirituality and practices, and my personal spiritual and ceremonial practices have strong roots in the Afro-Brazilian religions of the Umbanda and Candomblé with a foundation in Santo Daime religious practices, beliefs and traditions. In this book I will focus on exploring these lineages, as they are most relevant to my own culture and experiences and my current spiritual practices. Although I am deeply rooted in an Australian Indigenous view of the world and spirituality, my Ayahuasca practice is also rooted in these Brazilian cultures and ancestry, where I have undertaken extensive studies over many years and integrated the practices into my daily life and personal view of reality and spirituality.

Origin myths of Ayahuasca

Seres vivas da floresta, venham me iluminar.
(Living beings of the forest, come to illuminate me.)

— *Seres Vivas da Floresta*, Giti Bond.

Indigenous creation or origin myths recount the beginnings of a particular Indigenous community or culture, offering insights into their beliefs about their own ancestry, identity and place in the world. These myths often weave together historical events, cultural practices, life lessons and spiritual beliefs that explain the origins of the people, their customs, and their relationship with the land and Spirit. Central to Indigenous origin myths are often stories of creation, migration, and encounters with spiritual beings or forces that have shaped the community's history and worldview. Through these narratives, Indigenous origin myths serve to preserve and transmit cultural knowledge, reinforce collective identity, and instil a sense of belonging and connection to ancestral heritage and the natural world.

Origin myths often feature supernatural beings, such as gods, spirits, or ancestral figures, which shape the world through divine acts or cosmic events. These stories not only explain the origins of existence, but also provide a framework for understanding humanity's place within the natural and spiritual realms, thereby developing a sense of connection and reverence for the natural world.

Ayahuasca origin myths are widespread, as there are an estimated 130 tribal groups, although it is common for native people of the Amazon Basin to identify with their immediate village rather than a larger ethnic or language grouping. Ethnic/tribal identity is a new concept that is developing in modern times, as Amazonian peoples organise for solidarity and the protection of their rights. The region of traditional Ayahuasca use is the Upper Amazon; that is, the western part of the Amazon Basin and the western part of the Guiana Shield. Ayahuasca use is widespread in the northwestern region of the Amazon Basin, where Colombia, Peru, Ecuador and Brazil come together. In this region 100% of Indigenous ethnic groups traditionally commune with Ayahuasca. Some Indigenous groups outside of this region also traditionally use Ayahuasca and others have adopted its use into their own cultures and lore in more recent times. (*What Indigenous groups traditionally use Ayahuasca?* by Sachahambi, Ayahuasca.com)

The myths describing Ayahuasca's divine beginnings and adaption into human culture are as respected and revered as the sacred brew itself. There are many names for Ayahuasca that also vary greatly across the Amazon. These origin stories and narratives weave elements of life and death, human and plant/animal life, the supernatural and nature together into deep, symbolic and mysterious parables with teachings on the essence and ancestry of the sacrament. These Amazonian creation myths have much in common with similar myths from Indigenous cultures around the world, particularly in the way they depict relationships with animals and plants, cosmic forces, heavenly and ancestral beings.

Whilst these origin myths may differ greatly in the context and characters of the stories, there are common threads weaving through all the stories. Some speak of shape-shifting animals that invite humans into their magical dimensions and share knowledge, others speak of great leaders and teachers who ascend to heavenly realms and through their passing leave messages and the secrets of Ayahuasca so that the people may communicate with those realms. Some myths speak of the dangers of being out of right-relationship with Ayahuasca and her spiritual domain and teach us how to communicate through telepathy and visions with the Earth and all its beings. All of these myths seem to evoke stories of supernatural beings and forces that bring about profound events which result in gifts of knowledge regarding Ayahuasca preparation, navigation, music, guidance and right-relationship. It seems that for the Indigenous people using Ayahuasca in pre-colonial Amazonia Ayahuasca gave them the ability to commune with the natural world, teaching them how to live harmoniously and safely in the forests, protecting them from the potential dangers of animals and other forces of nature, and also giving them warning of future changes in the Earth and other cosmic events.

Like the multi-dimensional beings they venerate, Amazonian cosmologies are infused with layer upon layer of symbolic depth. The origin stories told by Elders around ritual fires elegantly fuse botanical roots with human limbs, mundane reality with celestial spheres across time and space both physical and metaphysical. These mystically revealed myths lend meaning not just to the plants themselves, but to the cultures that have co-evolved together with these remarkable rainforest species over centuries.

Ayahuasca myths of origin are revelations in themselves. They integrate meaningful explanations for shamanic symbols with mystical metaphors for human life stages, whilst embedding cautionary codes for respectful engagement. Yet running as the common thread across stories is the depiction of Ayahuasca as a sentient plant-teacher compassionately communicating through visions across consciousness, dimensions and generations.

Therefore, the magical motifs within these creation stories, echoing through Amazonian jungle canopies for centuries, are sublime reminders that irrespective of mythical plot lines, Ayahuasca always resides as the sacred substance beneath the stories themselves. And like the inter-dimensional realities revealed under this remarkable plant spirit's influence, its eternal wisdoms extend far beyond rational barriers or limitations imposed upon this world by cultural constraints. — Massamiliano Geraci, *The Divine Birth of Ayahuasca: Myths on the Visionary Vine.*

These creation myths and practices of the native peoples of Amazonia are also now complimented by the formation of large-scale syncretic religions and spiritual movements, which are by far the largest in Brazil, but also spreading across the world. Syncretism is the practice of combining and weaving together different spiritual beliefs and philosophies. The way that Ayahuasca has woven Amazonian shamanism with other spiritual practices such as Christianity, Spiritism, Afro-Brazilian, Hinduism and others is, interestingly, reflective of the tendrils of a vine weaving with other plants and the sacred union of the leaves and the vine. The most widespread of the Brazilian churches are the *União do Vegetal, Barquinha,* and *Santo Daime,* which has branched into other movements such as *Umbandaime* and *Ciranda* which integrate Afro-Brazilian deities, culture and practices. These movements were formed by master teachers who bravely ventured deep into the Brazilian Amazon and studied Ayahuasca, receiving doctrines and teachings for its effective and safe use in modern Brazil.

The modern doctrines of these spiritual churches and other movements hold teachings that are relevant for current human mental health conditions and provide protocols for life and spiritual practices, with guidance from ancestors, masters and teachers in this dimension and others. Indigenous knowledge and use of Ayahuasca traditionally did not have specific teachings or remedies for the chronic mental health problems experienced by people from the 'civilised' world. The doctrines that have come out of Brazil provide an important role in guiding us to heal and transcend those conditions. Brazilian Ayahuasca movements are deeply spiritual and devotional in nature and include teachings and culture that promote earth-consciousness, family, self-discipline, harmony, truth, forgiveness, joy and a spiritual life. In many ways these doctrines and their movements are supporting and guiding humanity to return to a sacred balance with the Earth, much like the Indigenous peoples and their original cultures do, and always have done.

The Ayahuasca origin myths highlight the importance of remembering the teachings of the ancestors and their relevance to practices and traditions. In my personal work with Ayahuasca I have always maintained a respect and reverence for these original teachings. Through my ceremonial practices, my song and my *miração* (visionary state), I am able to maintain and strengthen my own connections to the ancestors and their teachings, and to the spiritual beings that incorporate through these lineages. The teachings keep us in alignment with natural lore and offer guidance, protection, wisdom and support. All of the origin myths refer to Ayahuasca as being a gift from the Divine to humanity. In many cases the catalysing event that brings about knowledge of Ayahuasca comes after the death of a significant leader or cultural hero and their rebirth and communication through the plants and Ayahuasca itself, thus offering the people spiritual messages and teachings. This is similar to modern religions which speak of prophets and teachers such as Jesus and Quetzalcoatl, who died and returned with spiritual teachings. These myths are a strong reminder that Ayahuasca represents connection to the Divine, to spiritual dimensions and other-worldly beings, and that we must honour and respect it for this profound spiritual communion by elevating ourselves to a higher expression of being, reflective of this divinity.

> *I asked the spirits: "Why Ayahuasca? Why don't other brews make us see when we drink them?" Because other plants teach us this wisdom, only through dreams, not when we are conscious and awake. Why does Ayahuasca do this? They told me "because it is the umbilical chord of the human". This is what Ayahuasca represents. The chord that feeds us spiritually.* — Peruvian shaman Pablo Amaringo, *Otherworlds documentary.*

Huni Kuin: Nixi Pãe origin myth

> *Nixi Pãe is a plant drink that will help you dream inside; you drink it, and you feel the power, feel the light; you feel, you see. You can even see into the three passages of time: sometimes you can see the past, sometimes you can see the present, and sometimes you can see into the future as it will happen. You see colours that emerge from many different lights; you don't count them — you are seeing them change and transform in front of you, and the music controls that. A lot of light.* Ibã Huni Kuin, from Mahku — Huni Kuin Arts Movement.

The Huni Kuin people, also known as the *Kaxinawá*, are an Indigenous group residing primarily in the Amazon rainforest of Brazil and Peru. Their name translates to 'true or real people', reflecting their deep connection to their ancestral lands and cultural heritage. Renowned for their intricate spiritual practices and profound relationship with the natural world, the Huni Kuin maintain a rich tradition of shamanism and plant-based medicine, including the ceremonial use of *Nixi Pãe* (Ayahuasca), pronounced 'nishie pye'. With a strong emphasis on communal living and oral tradition, the Huni Kuin have preserved their unique language and customs, despite facing challenges from the ongoing encroachment of colonialism and environmental threats to their homeland. They are a colourful, friendly and peaceful people who have become very adept at preserving their culture and ancestral knowledge, while including the offer of a significant contribution to the development and guidance of the modern Ayahuasca movement, mostly within Brazil but also expanding across the world through sharing wisdom, culture, art, music, ceremony, shamanic teachings and training.

I first met the Huni Kuin in Brazil in 2013. I was invited to visit the Huni Kuin village of *Alta Mira* (high aim) in 2017 to participate in a cultural exchange with a Brazilian friend from the Santo Daime tradition. It was during this time that I integrated with their village and I was guided through an initiation with special plants for singers to receive the blessings of the spirit of the forest. I was given the Huni Kuin name *Nawa Ibã* (the singer who calls the miração) by the *Cacique* (pronounced 'ka-see-kee'), or Chief, Txaná Ixã.

Nixi Pãe is the Huni Kuin name for Ayahuasca and translates to 'strong vine' or 'spirit vine'. From my time with the Huni Kuin I came to learn that Nixi Pãe is an integral part of life and spirituality for the entire community. They use it in many different ways and for different reasons. In the villages I spent time in, Nixi Pãe is revered by the Huni Kuin as a master teacher plant brew which they hold in great respect, both in the way that they approach it but also for the wisdom and the magic that it gives. Typically there would be community ceremonies weekly or on special occasions where the majority of the community would gather in a traditional shelter with a fire and drink the Nixi Pãe, while the cacique and the *pajé* (shaman) would sing traditional spiritual songs that would invite the force of the brew into the ceremony and the people, and call on the different forces for healing, spiritual connection and visions. Once these traditional songs had been sung there would be a short break before drinking again and then the cacique would invite others to share more modern and diverse music and songs. And if the energy was right, then they would also perform traditional dances such as the *Dança da Jiboia* (Dance of the Boa Constrictor). Other uses for the Nixi Pãe range from healing illnesses in the village, shamanic studies and sharing of wisdom, hunting and gathering trips into the jungle, *feitios* (special ceremonies to prepare the brew) to longer term diets and deeper studies in remote sacred places in the forest. It seems that everyone in the villages has drunk Nixi Pãe since they were children, although not everyone would be drinking it often or attending the weekly communal ceremonies. Some of the pajés themselves did not drink it much either, as they were specialists in other plants and medicines and gave their focus to that particular work. For the Huni Kuin, Nixi Pãe is a part of daily life and in my observation they live in a divine state of peace and harmony. I never saw any conflict or tension between them, which they claim is due to their reverent connection with Nixi Pãe and other plant medicines.

The main objectives of the Nixi Pãe ritual are to connect worlds, to remind everyone of the Huni Kuin's relationship with the jiboia (boa constrictor), to renew the intimacy of the encounter, and to serve as a reminder of both the sharing of knowledge and connection, as well as the limitations of the relationship between human and jiboia, as narrated by the myth. That is, the ritual is about reinforcing and delineating the thread that both separates and connects different beings and their spirits. From Mahku — Huni Kuin Arts Movement.

The Nixi Pãe origin myth of the Huni Kuin is a magical depiction of the interaction of humans and the *jiboia*. The jiboia is revered as an ancient being of the forest that long pre-dates humans' existence on the Earth. Txaná Ixã said to me that we humans are living in the dream of the jiboia, which reminded me of Australian Indigenous spirituality in which we are awake inside the dream of the Rainbow Serpent. The origin myth tells the story of a Huni Kuin man named Yube Inu, a hunter who one day encounters a magical shape-shifting jiboia woman by a lake. The story talks of the jiboia as residing below the waters of the Amazon where they live, seemingly in an enchanted human-like dimension. The jiboia woman invites Yube Inu below the waters to live with her where they marry and have three children.

Whilst living amongst the jiboia people, Yube Inu is given herbs and taught to live, read, paint and hunt like they do. He becomes interested in the enchanted drink that gives them special visions and the ability to see across time and space. Yube Inu's jiboia wife warns him against drinking the brew, as it is her father, a very strong jiboia, who is the one who created the Nixi Pãe ritual, and only serpents know the secrets of the sacred brew. The father jiboia agrees to give Yube Inu the Nixi Pãe and, to his surprise, Yube Inu is able to instantly memorise all of the rites and songs of the Nixi Pãe ritual, and once he drinks the sacred brew he enters into a miração. The father jiboia is shocked and becomes jealous of Yube Inu, as a human has for the first time discovered the secrets of Nixi Pãe. In his vision, Yube Inu sees a future event that the father and the other jiboias will consume him.

Frightened by this vision, Yube Inu decides to escape from the jiboia people and he manages to make it back to the land and to his human family. He then transmits to them the knowledge of how to prepare the Nixi Pãe, the chants and the ritual practice, as he has learned them from the jiboias. His jiboia family, however, never gives up on trying to find him, and eventually they surprise and capture him, severing his body in two, taking one half back to the world of the jiboia. Upon his capture, Yube Inu's father-in-law accepts that humans now have the knowledge and access to the sacred brew of Nixi Pãe. Following his death, Yube Inu transforms himself and reappears within the miração of the Nixi Pãe in order to pass on the knowledge that he has learned from the jiboias, including the sacred chants and the *kené*, which is the symbolic language of the jiboias and used in art to this day by the Huni Kuin people.

The boa constrictor is considered by the Huni Kuin to be the greatest of shamans, a messenger and being of transformation, travelling from the world of water to the world on land, shedding its skin. The vision made possible by the brew, whose master is the mythical father jiboia, the one who taught humans the experience with Ayahuasca, allows humans to see the world from their point of view. Huni Kuin art and symbology are the visions of the mirações (altered states) which emerge during the rituals. They can also be considered records of the chants and other myths that make up Huni Kuin cosmology. From Mahku — Huni Kuin Arts Movement.

Having lived for thousands of years deep within the Amazon rainforest, the Huni Kuin are adept at navigating the dangers of the natural world, including the dangers of living amongst such powerful predators as the boa constrictor. This emphasises the importance of the role of Nixi Pãe as a conduit of inter-species communication and deep connection to the natural world. The nature of Nixi Pãe as a transformative agent shows that humans must also do the work to transform themselves in such a way as to open their vision and minds to spiritual realities that sometimes manifest as subtle communications, requiring effort and concentration. The rituals themselves are specifically and carefully designed and conducted in such a way as to provide a space, setting and intention that allows the journey, or miração, to be experienced in a profound and protected way. Just as there are many beings in the forest that are potentially dangerous to humans, so the same conditions exist within the realm of the Nixi Pãe miração.

The sounds and chants which are an intrinsic aspect of the Nixi Pãe experience are guides and pathways that inspire the manifestation of particular images, spiritual beings and events, conducting lights, colours and interactions with spiritual beings that manifest during the experience. To the Huni Kuin people, the music and the miração go together and are impossible to separate. The images of the miração are in constant transformation and show the unending connection and flow between consciousness, the beings and elements of the Earth. The ritual of Nixi Pãe reminds participants of the ongoing connection of humans with their ancestors such as the jiboia, allowing the teachings and guidance to be transmitted, thus strengthening and developing the essential knowing of humanity's innate connection to the natural world. This inter-species communication creates a balance and respect for the forest in which they live and maintains harmony in their daily lives, protecting them from dangers and guiding them within a universe where everything is consciously present and aware, and humans must incessantly negotiate their position in the cosmos.

Like most Indigenous peoples of the world, the Huni Kuin are aware of the deficiency of this cosmic consciousness in the awareness of non-Indigenous peoples and the disharmony this creates, and are making strong efforts to share the teachings and gifts of Nixi Pãe with the world. Like many Amazonian peoples, they are aware of how inherently dangerous the ignorance and disconnection of non-Indigenous peoples are as they, the non-Indigenous, march unconsciously along a destructive path that endangers the very existence of humanity. The Nixi Pãe ritual is seen as a powerful ally for humanity in awakening us to our role as carers of the Earth. The people of the Amazon are deeply sensitive to the forces of colonialism and planetary destruction and are currently very vulnerable whilst maintaining their ancient spirituality, wisdom, culture and way of life. It remains to be seen whether non-Indigenous peoples of the Earth will make the effort and transformation necessary to reconnect and relearn our place in the cosmos. Perhaps the work of the Huni Kuin and the growth of other global Ayahuasca movements is a good sign that there is some hope of this necessary awakening occurring in time to avert impending disaster.

Beyond therapy: The spiritual healing of Ayahuasca

Ayahuasca is not just a medicine; it's a sacred journey within ourselves, a profound opportunity for healing and self-discovery. In the arms of Mother Ayahuasca, we find the courage to face our deepest wounds and traumas, allowing us to heal and grow in ways we never thought possible. Its healing power lies in its ability to show us the root causes of our suffering and guide us towards profound transformation and healing. Ayahuasca teaches us to surrender to the flow of life, to let go of the past and embrace the present moment with love, gratitude, joy and inner peace.
— Dr Rachel Harris, Listening to Ayahuasca.

The Huni Kuin's and other Indigenous origin myths show us the transformational powers of Ayahuasca are profound in their ability to give us the physical, mental and spiritual conditions to enable us to experience the cosmic nature of the Earth. In order to enter into the underwater world of the jiboias, Yube Inu was given herbs and plant remedies to prepare his body, and in the Ayahuasca ritual itself, the music, protocols and conditions are created in order to prepare our bodies and minds for the journey of the miração. The importance of transformation is inherent in being able to enter into an altered state. Most non-Indigenous peoples have, in many cases, had generations of disconnection from spiritual forces and awareness of their own true nature, their bodies, minds and emotions, and are often unprepared for this experience. Thus, when partaking in the Ayahuasca ritual there is a necessary physical, mental and emotional realignment that must be undertaken. The force of the brew as it enters the body and affects the mind essentially raises the vibration of the person which may necessitate a cleansing or purging in order to harmonise with the spiritual reality that Ayahuasca invites us into. In many cases this may take the person through a deep and thorough healing process that may take some time and often several ceremonies in order to be able to fully experience the miração, the visionary state.

People may come to Ayahuasca for many different reasons. The most common reasons are for spiritual connection, to discover life purpose, connect with ancestors and deceased loved ones, and mental, emotional and physical healing. It is quite common for people to feel a strong 'calling' or intuition to meet with Ayahuasca, where the mystical experience begins even before drinking the brew itself. Attending an Ayahuasca ceremony is not something that is taken lightly, and it inspires a sense of caution, respect and good preparation in knowing that this may not be an easy or pleasant experience at times. People will often travel so far away from their comfortable first-world conditions into remote and often very challenging places deep in the Amazon jungle in order to experience an Ayahuasca ceremony. In countries like Australia, the US, Canada and Europe, ceremonies are also not so easy to find, as most circles are found only through word of mouth, and due to social prejudice and discrimination are forced to exist underground. This means there is a lack of regulation within these circles and it is thus important that those wanting to partake do some thorough research into the group they intend to drink with. What this shows, though, is that this ever-growing global movement of Ayahuasca is inspiring people to step far out of their comfort zones in order to have an experience with the spirit of Ayahuasca.

Whilst there are some Ayahuasca practitioners who purely focus on the therapeutic benefits and healing, it is impossible to ignore the spiritual dimension of Ayahuasca. In recent years there has been more and more interest from mental health practitioners, scientists and researchers into the enormous benefits and efficacy of Ayahuasca for healing depression, addiction, trauma, and self-esteem and childhood wounds. There is also a growing movement of spiritual and religious practice of Ayahuasca ceremony, where the focus is more towards the ceremony, the prayers and offerings to the brew itself and the spiritual beings and forces that support the work — the healing is the lived experience. It is very common for people who come to Ayahuasca for healing reasons to awaken their innate spirituality and become adepts of the spiritual practices involved in the Ayahuasca lineages. Similarly, those who feel called to continue their development with Ayahuasca will often go on to study the spirituality, traditions and, in particular, the music. It is very common and in fact, likely, for people who work enough with Ayahuasca to become artists and musicians and develop a rich, creative spiritual life.

Drinking Ayahuasca for the first time is somewhat of an initial attunement to the vibration and the force of the brew. For each person the experience is unique. It may take anywhere from 15 minutes to two hours for the effect of the brew to be felt in the body and the mind. The participant may experience some discomfort and disorientation during the time the effects of the Ayahuasca are coming on. In this time there may be some mental and physical resistance. The Ayahuasca is wanting to elevate the consciousness into the spiritual realms and open the higher energetic centres and consciousness of the person. If the participant has any kind of resistance or blockage, the Ayahuasca will work with them to remove the blockages in order to prepare them for the clarity and openness to gain the full experience of spiritual communion. It is at this time that the participant may begin to feel nauseous, emotional, be over-thinking and looping in their thoughts, and as the body releases stored traumas and toxins, the mind and emotions may also release at the same time. This can often accumulate until the point of a physical or emotional purge, but once the body has released the built-up toxic energies, the participant may begin to have a more sublime spiritual experience of visions and profound realisations. I have noticed over the years that people who have some experience in meditation, yoga, martial arts and have a good diet and emotional health will usually adapt very easily and quickly to the Ayahuasca in their first experience. Those who are adept at bypassing and avoiding self-responsibility may have a much more challenging time due to fearful resistances and entrenched psychological defences.

It is important to emphasise the value of the healing journey that occurs during Ayahuasca ceremony. The potential for realising years of therapy in a single night of Ayahuasca use is commonly reported, although for some people the depths and complexity of trauma may take many sessions to fully access and release. At this point it is important to acknowledge that Ayahuasca is not for everyone; participants must be willing and ready to face their shadows and pain, and for some people this shamanic-style healing may be too confronting or may be contra-indicated for their mental and physical health conditions. There is potential for the re-traumatisation of participants if they are not supported in a trauma-informed way by the facilitator and assistants. It is important that the facilitator or shaman and those holding space for Ayahuasca are able to recognise the importance of supporting both the mental and physical health responses as well as the shamanic and spiritual elements of the Ayahuasca work. Complex trauma has a vast range of presentations and manifestations in people. I will explore more details of working with trauma and trauma-release later in this book; however, it is important to recognise that modern, Westernised humans carry childhood, social and ancestral wounds, conditions that did not exist traditionally for the Indigenous peoples of the Amazon, and thus when working with the non-Indigenous, it is important to integrate practices that can appropriately bring remedy to these modern conditions.

Ayahuasca ceremony is a deeply personal and internal journey and is, in reality, an intimate relationship with a spiritual being. People often report they have conversations with the spirit of Ayahuasca itself or with the other spiritual beings that may come to them during their experience. On a physical level, Ayahuasca, in combination with the music and its vibrations, may also release stored tension within the nervous system. When we experience traumas in childhood or throughout life, the body will often contract or go into a 'fight or flight' protective response that creates an imprint upon the nervous system, also known as 'epigenetic imprinting'. It is quite common for this imprint to be released from the body on a physical and a mental/emotional level. The resulting catharsis and release may then leave the person feeling very relieved and less tense, more at peace and better able to deal with stressful situations in life. The days and weeks following an Ayahuasca ceremony are usually a more subtle continuation of the Ayahuasca work, with people commonly reporting feeling reborn, lighter and liberated. Sometimes realisations and more challenging feelings may also come up. It is vitally important that Ayahuasca communities and practitioners develop a strong culture of integration so that people are always supported post-ceremony, as they are often emotionally open, vulnerable and may need support in navigating life and choices moving forward without carrying the weight of the baggage of the past with them. In most cases this is a positive experience, but for some, the realisations may lead to emotionally challenging life changes.

> *Healing with Ayahuasca is a journey of integration, of bringing the insights and lessons from the medicine back into our everyday lives, so that we may live with greater clarity, purpose and authenticity. Ayahuasca is a powerful ally on the path of healing and self-discovery, but it's not a magic bullet. It requires dedication, intention, and a willingness to do the inner work.* — Dr Rachel Harris, *Listening to Ayahuasca.*

Working with Ayahuasca essentially compels the partaker to surrender to spiritual forces that are much greater and expansive than our minds could ever comprehend. Whilst we may gain some insight into the trove of experiences and research all over the internet, or even from our own personal experiences, as to how the next ceremony will go, there is always a sense of mystery and the unknown. This is part of the magic and medicine of the sacred brew. Our conditioned Western minds are unable to fathom the immensity whilst the intelligence of the plant itself seemingly knows how to humble us to its majesty and power. When we let go in faith in this regard is when the real gold of deep spiritual communion with the Divine may dawn in us. Essentially, though, we must work through our conditioned responses, fears and expectations, as no two Ayahuasca experiences are the same. There is also a huge variety of experiences one may have with Ayahuasca, in addition to the impressive myriad of traditions and practices that have emerged throughout South America, in particular Brazil, and which are now emerging throughout the rest of the world.

> *One Ayahuasca ceremony can cover an unbelievably wide swathe of psychic territory. This includes but is not limited to the following: personal childhood history, family history and secrets, past-life narratives, perinatal memories, cathartic expressions of emotion with or without content, ancestral history, trauma, shamanic experiences, out-of-body flights, initiation or dismemberment, energetic healing and surgery, ego death and rebirth, archetypal figures or landscapes, animal allies, mystical experiences, visionary and prophetic revelation, encounters with non-human entities (such as from other planets or civilisations), cosmic travels through the brilliant darkness, contact with spirits, encounters with the numinous, conversation with dead loved ones, concrete advice from Grandmother Ayahuasca, noetic downloads, personal healing, ecological awakenings and mythopoetic realms.*
>
> *There are also the physical symptoms that seem to be an essential part of the Ayahuasca experience, such as nausea, vomiting,*

diarreah, yawning and sleeping. The possibilities are endless. — Dr Rachel Harris, PhD, *Listening to Ayahuasca.*

Like many spiritual practices, Ayahuasca ceremony requires participants to practice mindfulness and self-discipline, respecting the space and the ritual, humbling ourselves to divine presence. Ayahuasca teaches us to embody grace and respect for others and our environment, and the ceremony itself may be seen as a practice for integrating these qualities into life. The potential is for participants to learn from the Ayahuasca and the ceremony and to take those teachings into their own lives, cultivating that reverence and humility, grace and respect into everything they do — not just in how they practice Ayahuasca, but in every aspect of life. This can be an even more daunting and challenging thing to achieve than the ceremony itself, as life-triggers, patterns and habits may cause distraction and relapse. This is where developing cultures of integration becomes an important aspect of the Ayahuasca work. Outside of the Amazon itself, modern society does not generally support an awakened spiritual awareness or emotional openness, and the lives that people have lived before drinking Ayahuasca may no longer reflect the way that they feel post-ceremony. Given time and a careful approach to life integration, most people report that their lives, relationships, work and sense of self greatly improve, but this doesn't come with a magic wand; we must work to achieve these benefits.

The Ayahuasca origin myth as told by the Yawanawá people of the Brazilian Amazon, perhaps gives us a warning of the importance of integrating our experience into our daily lives, rather than reliving the Ayahuasca experience itself. One of the dangers of any spiritual path is the tendency that people may have towards *spiritual bypassing*. Spiritual bypassing is a phenomenon where people may use their spiritual practices as a way of avoiding dealing with difficult emotions, mental conditions or life challenges. The Yawanawá myth speaks of the first death that ever happened amongst humans, as before that they had lived eternally. A great and deeply loved emperor of the Yawanawá people died and ascended to the heavens. Upon his death, he left the people the secrets of *Uní* (Ayahuasca) and its use.

They practised diligently and integrated the Uní ritual into their lives and became very adept at this. After some time they wanted to ascend to the heavens so they might go to the realms where their beloved emperor now resided. One person from the village didn't want to follow the rest of the people in leaving this world and chose to stay behind. These Yawanawá people prepared themselves and left the Earth and met their beloved emperor in the heavenly realm he now resided in, but he did not welcome them. He told them they were meant to remain on Earth as humans and if they needed to communicate with him, they could do so through the Ayahuasca. They returned to the Earth, now with the experience of mortality.

Western science, medicine and colonialism

This, the ancestors have preserved, this is the legacy they've left, how things are done. Now is the time when people have forgotten the knowledge of how to heal. The teachings of the ancestors have been left behind, replaced by scientific remedies, this is why they have lost it. The traditions of the ancestors, received from the spirits, have been lost. They didn't invent, they were taught spiritually. The Incas had communication with the spirit realm, the Mayans. Here, the Shapibo communicated with spirits, the Amahuaca and all the Aboriginal people. In those times, previous to this civilisation, they received instruction from spiritual beings coming from other worlds, materialised as people to teach them, including Ayahuasca to be taken together with chacruna, has been given by spirits who have come to show them how to do it. — Peruvian shaman Pablo Amaringo, Other Worlds.

Whilst I have an extensive background working in government and non-government health organisations, my personal preference and belief towards Ayahuasca ceremony is as to a sacred spiritual ritual that is, and always will be, connected intrinsically to the Amazon forest, the people, ancestors and their traditions. Non-Indigenous practitioners of Ayahuasca have over the last few decades navigated and begun to map this healing journey from the perspective of psychological, emotional and physical conditioning. Alex K Gearin in his book *Global Ayahuasca* explores its use by entrepreneurs in China: '... Ayahuasca was used by young Chinese professionals searching for holistic wellness, self-cultivation and competitive edge in capitalist environments'.

Through exposure to the spiritual force and visionary state of Ayahuasca, practitioners often experience profound healing journeys that traverse their entire lives, physical illness, childhood wounds and ancestral traumas. Western science and research has made some attempts to understand how Ayahuasca, and in particular DMT, affects the human body and consciousness. Jeremy Narby in his book *The Cosmic Serpent* hypothesised the idea that the serpent imagery commonly reported in Ayahuasca visions mirrors the structure of DNA, suggesting a deep, intuitive understanding of molecular biology. Narby theorises that Ayahuasca may temporarily suspend the filters of perception, allowing individuals to access the vast storehouse of genetic information and collective consciousness contained within their own DNA. This theory is supported by the Huni Kuin view of Nixi Pãe that connects us to ancestral wisdom. From a shamanic view, the serpent of visions is a form of Ayahuasca, a totem (spirit lineage guide) and messenger from the Amazonian forest. I explore the healing potential of Ayahuasca in further detail throughout this book.

Western science has often focused research on one of the components of Ayahuasca. N,N-Dimethyltryptamine, or DMT, is a substituted tryptamine that naturally occurs in many plants and animals, including humans, and which is both a derivative and a structural analogue of tryptamine. DMT is usually found in most brews of Ayahuasca in very low quantities. Submissions to the US Supreme court in the case for the legal use of Ayahuasca tea for religious purposes included two scientific studies indicating that DMT was found in very low quantities in the tea, with a similar amount within a cup of Ayahuasca as may be found in a passionfruit. Research has shown that DMT is produced in the human body and functions as a neurotransmitter. Western science tends to assume that it is the DMT within Ayahuasca that produces the altered state and visions; however, within shamanic and spiritual understanding there are many more factors that contribute to the consciousness-altering effects of this sacrament.

Ongoing research has suggested the *endogenous* presence of DMT in the human body, prompting speculation about its potential role as a neurotransmitter or neuromodulator. Endogenous in this instance meaning that DMT arises naturally and is produced within the human body. While the exact physiological function of endogenous DMT remains speculative, some hypotheses propose its involvement in various cognitive processes, including perception, dreams, memory and mood regulation. Studies have identified the presence of DMT and its metabolising enzymes in the brain, particularly in regions associated with consciousness and perception, such as the pineal gland. While further research is needed for Western science to fully elucidate its role, the discovery of endogenous DMT opens intriguing avenues for understanding the complexities of human consciousness and brain function (Barker, S. A., Monti, J. A., & Christian, S. T. (1981). *N,N-dimethyltryptamine: An endogenous hallucinogen. International review of neurobiology, 22,* 83-110).

Endogenous DMT might be the "spirit molecule" that allows us to experience the realms of consciousness beyond our ordinary perception, unlocking the mysteries of the mind and the universe. At the moment of death, the brain may release a flood of DMT, offering a glimpse into the profound mysteries of existence, perhaps revealing the true nature of consciousness and the afterlife. — Rick Strassman, *DMT: The Spirit Molecule.*

In recent years, the Western scientific community has shown increasing interest in exploring the therapeutic potential of Ayahuasca, leading to a surge in research endeavours. Studies have delved into various aspects of Ayahuasca, including safety, effects on mental health, brain function and spiritual wellbeing. Findings suggest that Ayahuasca may hold promise as a treatment for conditions such as depression, anxiety, and post-traumatic stress disorder (PTSD). Research indicates that the brew's psychedelic compounds can induce profound psychological experiences that may facilitate emotional processing and promote healing. Additionally, neuro-imaging studies have revealed alterations in brain activity and connectivity patterns during Ayahuasca experiences, shedding light on the neural mechanisms underlying its therapeutic effects.

Moreover, investigations into the safety profile of Ayahuasca have shown promising results, with few reports of adverse effects when used in controlled settings under the guidance of experienced facilitators. This has led to growing recognition of Ayahuasca as a potentially valuable tool within the realm of psychotherapy and spiritual exploration. However, from the perspective of modern science, further research is sought to elucidate the long-term effects, optimal dosing regimens, and potential risks associated with Ayahuasca use. Overall, the Western scientific approach to Ayahuasca research is driven by a desire to understand its mechanisms of action and unlock its therapeutic potential while ensuring safety and ethical considerations remain at the forefront of exploration. From a shamanic perspective, the only way to know Ayahuasca is through a lived experience of it. Much of the literature and study is from an observational, journalistic, critical or sociological perspective, where authors and researchers are limited in the scope of their experience by the innate separation apparent in their approach.

> *What we call "science" is a very narrow, patriarchal project for a very short period of history. We name as "science" that which is mechanistic and reductionist. But that was the kind of science that Bacon, Descartes and others who are called the fathers of modern science created. Domination of nature, exploitation of nature, declaring nature as dead and then using a mechanistic and reductionist mode. This was born at a time when the Industrial Revolution needed an exploitative knowledge, and that knowledge for exploitation was then treated as the only reliable knowledge. Whereas the knowledge of protection, conservation, rejuvenation, regeneration, which is actually the vital knowledge, and which women have, which peasants have, which tribal and Indigenous people have, was put into the garbage bin.* — Vandana Shiva.

While Western medicine and science are understandably excited by the discoveries emerging from Ayahuasca research, there's still a risk that its use, like many aspects of Indigenous knowledge and spirituality, might end up shaped too tightly by narrow frameworks of control and regulation. Without care, it can start to reflect more of a colonising mindset than a respectful integration. Ayahuasca and other plant brews also containing DMT in Australia and other places around the world have typically been deemed illegal and listed as poisons under government control orders adopted through international agreements stemming from the United States and their failed 'war on drugs' mentality, often without public consultation or debate and at the expense of national sovereignty.

Most of the books on Ayahuasca tend to focus on proving its effectiveness and safety through a scientific or academic lens. While that can be useful, it often reflects the way our culture has elevated science to a kind of unquestioned authority, almost like a modern belief system. Everything is expected to justify itself by those standards, even when those standards aren't always equipped to understand the deeper spiritual or cultural dimensions involved. What modern science lacks is respect for spiritual and ancient wisdom, a broader perspective that has been demonstrated for thousands of years in Indigenous cultures and in ancient traditions such as Buddhism and other religions. Seemingly, most of the books and films depicting Ayahuasca are using this scientific paradigm to perhaps convince the mainstream population of its validity. Media representations here in Australia have tended to be based in assumptions and stigmas. The way Ayahuasca is often asked to 'prove' itself tends to reduce it to just what it does in the brain, and this is framed by narrow psychological studies and lab-based comparisons that don't fully capture the depth of the experience. Scientific narratives, which sometimes carry a kind of belief-like authority, have ended up dominating the conversation. And even after decades of research and strong evidence, the response still often defaults to 'more studies are needed', ignoring the Indigenous history and lived experience of millions of people worldwide. At the same time, the 'gurus' of modern science and health policy were able to recently rush through a highly toxic and dangerous experimental vaccine regime within a matter of months, based on shaky science, ideology and intensive propaganda.

> *Despite the major breakthroughs of recent years, especially in mind/body science and transpersonal psychology, the great majority of scientists continue to reduce the mind to no more than physical processes in the brain, which goes against the testimony of thousands of years of experience of mystics and meditators of all religions.* — Sogyal Rinpoche, *The Tibetan Book of Living and Dying.*

Whilst globalist government approaches to medicine and corporate interests in maintaining a sickness-solution-profit model of 'health' dominate this field, the sacred gift of divine light and spiritual healing of Ayahuasca has been forced into the underground. At the same time, these governments attempt to support the scientific and medical industries to redevelop and essentially colonise the usage of Ayahuasca and DMT whilst intimidating spiritual communities with punitive anti-drug laws and inflated criminal penalties that lack scientific or ethical foundation. In countries such as the US and Brazil, where the archaic laws against DMT and Ayahuasca have been tested and where much research has been done, respect for religious and spiritual practices have been regained by the people, but not without large political and legal battles, as biased and unfair judicial and political systems attempt to maintain their dominance and control at the behest of the industries that fund them. It is difficult to say what the motivation is for these colonising attitudes, and whether there is a concerted attempt to suppress Ayahuasca usage, when its efficacy and safety are well proven, potentially offering a massive breakthrough in the understanding of health, spirituality and human rights, or whether our society is still suffering under a historical hangover of fear and ignorance of shamanic culture and practices, with a lack of insight and courage shown by law makers. This regime of ignorance is usually accompanied by a lazy and fearful bureaucratic swamp that stumbles its way through, indulging in group-think, buck-passing and abuse of power.

The dominator culture of our society assumes and enforces that only the archaic scientific belief structure and its research findings are to be trusted in a legal-political framework, with this notion reinforced through propaganda and a compliant media apparatus. This culture restricts the socially accepted use of sacred plants and their rituals and enforces a cold, clinical approach that is regulated by the medical/pharmaceutic industry and its sickness-solution-profit model of health. The truth is that humanity has communed with sacred teacher plants throughout the entirety of its history and this culture of spiritual practice has informed human consciousness and evolution. The use of these plants is a natural and vital part of our humanity. The restrictions placed upon their use is simply an abuse of our rights and an attempt to place human ideology in front of our God-given rights in a 'big government knows what's best' mentality. The scientific paradigm that has insidiously risen to dominate the field of our consciousness and society is, in fact, a human-created falsity imposed upon our social constructs, akin to a well-resourced imposter misleading a fearful and naive population. I believe there is a place where ancient wisdom and traditions can meet modern science in a respectful and appropriate alliance. I hope that this book may add some light and direction to this exciting prospect.

Psychedelic experience is an extremely old part of the smorgasbord of human experiences on this planet. In fact the emergence of human consciousness and the emergence of an awareness of the properties of these biodynamic alkaloids scattered throughout a number of plant genre, may be nothing less than the same thing.
— Terence McKenna.

Some more progressive countries have developed legal mechanisms that allow for religious freedom with sacred plants, their culture and practices. Sadly, the forces of the Western scientific dominator culture and its commercial interests do not let go of their control of these sacraments easily. We live in a culture where people have to fight for human rights and traditional culture and practices, where they have been eroded and put into statutory laws and reinforced with propaganda and political donations by the mega-wealthy industries that benefit greatly from their dominance over health and medicine. This imposes a belief system that integrates an outdated, quasi-religious scientific regime with tight control that protects industries' profit margins and dominance. The European dark ages and Spanish Inquisition brought in torturous, strict religious and scientific control over ancient Earth-based shamanic spiritual and natural health practices. Practices that are, in fact, inseparable from human nature. This has led to a toxic society and a trauma-ridden humanity. The demonisation, prejudice and fear culture around shamanism and spiritual healing continues to this day.

The reality that we see unfolding around the world is one in which Ayahuasca is naturally growing in stature along with the growth in respect for the culture, healing and reconnection to Nature and Spirit that it offers. Research and experience shows overwhelmingly that the large majority of people partaking in Ayahuasca are gaining significant benefits. The use of Ayahuasca remains, and always will remain, in the realm of mysticism and spirituality. Whilst science makes its best attempts to understand Ayahuasca's nature and functions, this may yet serve to benefit the efficacy and safety of Ayahuasca use in Western contexts. However, it is my belief that there is no way to separate the context of ritual and spirituality from Ayahuasca, and this may represent an exciting frontier where Western science may be forced to accept the ancient wisdom and mysteries and give our society some breathing space to open ourselves to a spiritual evolution — something which can only be of great benefit during times of radical mental health decline, war and environmental destruction. Through the ritual use of Ayahuasca that has been passed down from the Amazon and through modern lineages that connect back to the source, we have the opportunity to gain immense insights. This is referring to Ayahuasca practices that have direct teachings and connection to these lineages, not the backyard ceremonies invented by the uninitiated or ambitiously co-opted from short trips to Peru. A modern scientific approach alone limits access to the depth and potential of the consciousness, healing and wisdom of Ayahuasca. The shamanic ritual and spirituality of these ancient practices and ancestral connections are interwoven into the very fabric and nature of Ayahuasca, even where those traditions have evolved into modern movements.

> *The snake represents a way to diagnose illness correctly. It symbolises the origin of life, the spark of life. When we see the snake, it is wisdom, comprehension, understanding, knowledge and so much more. This is something ancestral. It cannot be said that it was through trials and experience that the ancestors learned. No, they were taught by spiritual beings.* — Peruvian shaman Pablo Amaringo, *Other Worlds*.

Whilst around the world the modern scientific and medical community are making some attempts to find a therapeutic role for Ayahuasca within the current mainstream paradigm, there remains a large chasm of understanding of the Indigenous and spiritual approach to Ayahuasca and its ritual use. Much of the literature does not seem able to explore the ancient spirituality of Ayahuasca and treats it as more of a phenomenological curiosity or a culturally specific belief system. I believe that the practice of Ayahuasca and the nature of the mind and cosmos are consistent across time and culture, even if the practices appear different. This also extends to other spiritual practices and cultures. Jeremy Narby's theories on DMT and DNA, as explored in his book *The Cosmic Serpent*, offer an exploration into the potential connections between Indigenous shamanic knowledge, molecular biology and consciousness. Narby suggests that Indigenous cultures, through their use of psychoactive substances like Ayahuasca, which naturally contains DMT, may have acquired insights into the molecular nature of life and consciousness long before the advent of modern science.

Western science and medicine alone will not be able to access the full potential and insights offered to us by Ayahuasca. Within Western culture, traditional shamanic practices may not be enough to fully potentiate Ayahuasca in people with Western social conditioning and its ailments. Pablo Amaringo said to me on more than one occasion that it was important that we do not just 'copy' the traditional practices of Ayahuasca ceremony and healing, that we develop ceremonies that are practical and reflective of the society in which they are held. It is important to remember that the complex traumas and mental health afflictions of Western societies did not exist in traditional Indigenous cultures, where people were generally much healthier, deeply connected to Spirit and Nature, and where anxieties, depression, cancer and other chronic diseases did not exist in the form they do today. We cannot then expect that traditional ritual use of Ayahuasca alone is enough in a Western context and setting. This is where the exciting alliance with Western medicine and psychology may be of great benefit and where there is hope being shown by some within the scientific and academic paradigm who are open and respectful of an approach based in spirituality. I believe, though, that we first need to let go of any assumptions that traditional practices need to be analysed and forced into conformity within a scientific paradigm. In fact, I believe it is the opposite, in that modern science needs to show that it has value and function to be a worthy addition to well-proven, divinely sourced ancient practices that have been at the centre of, and informed, life for aeons.

Essentially, there is a need for humanity to awaken beyond our adolescent arrogance in which we believe that through our inventions we can know more or know better than the immensity of creation and the will of God. Whatever religious or scientific belief one may have has no bearing on the force of creation and the nature of the Earth's Dream, in which humanity in balance and harmony with nature plays a co-creative role. We are at a loss if we do not recognise and accept that our ancestors developed consciousness and practices that align us with this greater truth. It is folly for humanity to think that we can solve the problems we have created on this planet and amongst ourselves by using the same limited scientific mentality that created those problems in the first place. For those of us who choose this path, Ayahuasca takes us beyond this conundrum and offers an opportunity and pathway for humanity to evolve our consciousness, grow spiritually and find our place in peace, love and harmony with the Earth, the cosmos and all beings. It seems clear to most people who drink Ayahuasca, and certainly from the Indigenous perspective, that Ayahuasca is not just of the Earth — it IS the Earth, a natural, liquid concoction that bridges and merges the physical and spiritual dimensions of our sacred planet and the cosmos. A multi-dimensional reality. I suspect that within our Western culture we are still only at the precipice of beginning to comprehend the vast scope and potential of Ayahuasca in our society, in our minds and in our Dreaming. It is through faith and walking the path of spirit that we can know and enliven the Dream.

For the love of plants

For me personally, though, they mean even more than this. Plants, in the great living book of nature, have shown me how to study life as an artist and shaman. They can help all of us to know the art of healing and to discover our own creativity, because the beauty of nature moves people to show reverence, fascination, and respect for the extent to which the forests give shelter to our souls.

The consciousness of plants is a constant source of information for medicine, alimentation, and art, and an example of the intelligence and creative imagination of nature. Much of my education I owe to the intelligence of these great teachers. Thus, I consider myself to be the "representative" of plants, and for this reason I assert that if they cut down the trees and burn what's left of the rainforests, it is the same as burning a whole library of books without ever having read them.

People who are not so dedicated to the study and experience of plants may not think this knowledge is so important to their lives — but even they should be conscious of the nutritional, medicinal and scientific value of the plants they rely on for life.

My most sublime desire, though, is that every human being should begin to put as much attention as he or she can into the knowledge of plants, because they are the greatest healers of all. And all human beings should also put effort into the preservation and conservation of the rainforest, and care for it and the ecosystem, because damage to these not only prejudices the flora and fauna but humanity itself.

I, Pablo, say to everybody who lives in the Amazon and the other forests of the world, that they must love the plants of their land, and everything that is there!

This expression of love must be a sincere and altruistic interest in the lasting wellbeing of others. We are not here simply to exist, but to enjoy life together with plants, animals and loved ones, and to delight in contemplation of the beauty of nature. A shaman has in his [or her] mind and heart the attitude of conserving nature because he [or she] knows that life is for enjoying the company of this world's countless delights. — An interview with Pablo Amaringo, by Howard Charing.

CHAPTER 3

Shamanic Renaissance

Shamanism is a natural science that humans have discovered all around the Earth, according to their race, their folklore, their epics, their rites, their legends, their tales, their mythologies. Man [sic] has always been dedicated to spiritual things. Man [sic] is virtually a religious animal. Humans have never been happy unless venerating something outside of themselves. They have always wanted to know about a stone, a tree, a river, what is it that it contains? What is it that it has to offer? Why is it like that? And so much more. This is what shamanism derives from. — Pablo Amaringo, Otherworlds documentary.

The shaman is the ritualistic artist; the artist is the everyday shaman. — Terence McKenna.

The term 'shaman' is an adaptation of the word *saman* that originated in the Evenki language (formerly known as Tungus) from Siberia in Russia. The term 'šaman' (pronounced 'sah-man') in Evenki refers to a person who is believed to have access to, and influence in, the world of spirits. The word is thought to be related to the verb ša, which means 'to know', and the word *man* which means 'great power'. Modern anthropologists have adapted the term to collectively describe similar spiritual leaders from Indigenous groups all over the world who access altered states, spiritual beings and realms. In this sense it is not an accurate term, but it is used as a way of describing and categorising these natural healers. In fact, there is a great diversity of practices, cultures and beliefs amongst 'shamans' from all over the world who usually don't describe themselves as shamans, as they have their own names, unique practices and cultural references.

Another term that often gets used to describe traditional and Indigenous healers from around the world is 'medicine man/woman'. There is a distinction here in that medicine men/women who might work with natural lore and with particular plants and other natural healing techniques may not access the depths of spiritual wisdom and power as shamans do. Typically, shamans will have done much training and study in the development of their abilities to enter into trance and altered states of consciousness in order to commune with spiritual beings and forces, where they may gain influence and alliances for personal use, which is usually in the form of helping others of the community. Whilst everyone has this ability to access spiritual realms, shamans are more like specialists who have particular skills and abilities to invoke these altered states and guide others into spiritual realms. In my experience of living and studying with Indigenous peoples, the most powerful and respected shamans are the ones that have developed high levels of skills and awareness through deep study and initiations and have made significant personal and ego sacrifice in order to attain these levels of expertise. Shamans as such are not somehow special beings or supernatural people but have done the necessary studies to become specialists in this field.

> *Compassionate, healing spirits have a mission to try to communicate their mission to us so that they can get on with their work of trying to reduce suffering and pain in our reality ... But they are in one reality and we are in another reality, and the only way they can penetrate this reality, except in very rare circumstances, is with help from our side.* — Charles Gordon and Roger Walsh, *Higher Wisdom*.

In the Amazon, from my experience, shamans are greatly respected for their knowledge and abilities. They may not be as present in day-to-day village life as others, as they will spend a lot of their time and attention cultivating their power and their relationships with the natural and spiritual world, and often will be helping others with healing or training in their shamanic arts. As they are specialists in accessing spiritual dimensions, they have a unique view of reality from other perspectives. They may also be seen to be slightly outside the 'normal' day-to-day reality, as their unique view is important for guiding and navigating through the challenges of life in the human and natural environment. It is through an ability to access multi-dimensional realities and guide others to experience them that shamans are able to support healing in others through helping them gain awareness of their own mental, physical and emotional conditions, thereby allowing them to see themselves without the filters and history of their conditioned minds, beliefs and behaviours.

Shamans throughout history have played very important roles in the leadership and survival of communities. Using their visionary abilities and communion with Country, spiritual beings and ancestors, they are able to guide people and communities through present and future challenges, such as natural phenomena, to know when the best times are for hunting, gathering and planting, to find remedies for mysterious or new illnesses, and discover ways to integrate new influences into the lore and cosmology of their culture. Shamans are also often community and tribal leaders and play strong roles in nurturing the coherency and unity of the tribe.

Hiawatha was a legendary Native American leader and co-founder of the Iroquois Confederacy, also known as the *Haudenosaunee*. He is often described as a wise and powerful orator from the Mohawk or Onondaga nations. He had a vision of a growing darkness and sickness of war, with the coming threat of invasion of their lands by the Europeans. Guided by the Great Peacemaker, Hiawatha played a key role in uniting the five warring Iroquois tribes — the Mohawk, Oneida, Onondaga, Cayuga and Seneca — into a powerful alliance based on peace, unity and collective governance. His story is deeply symbolic and has been passed down through oral tradition, inspiring peace movements and Indigenous resurgence across generations.

> *Only as a warrior can one withstand the path of knowledge. A warrior cannot complain or regret anything. His life is an endless challenge, and challenges cannot possibly be good or bad. Challenges are simply challenges.* — Carlos Castaneda.

Over the last few thousand years, as humanity has become increasingly de-tuned from spiritual realities and the natural world, societies and authorities have also become increasingly fearful, suspicious and sceptical of the shamans and their roles in society. This has led to persecution and sometimes ridicule in an attempt discredit and eliminate their influence over the people and culture. This was seen in the dark ages of Europe with the 'witch burnings' and concerted attempts such as the Spanish Inquisition to eradicate paganism and other nature religions, often done in the name of the Roman version of Christianity. Since the 1960s there has been a strong resurgence of interest in and pursuit of shamanism in the Western world. And whilst the fear, ignorance and persecution of shamanism still continues, of which this book will go on to give examples, a new form of modern or 'urban' shamanism is growing at a fast pace. As mentioned earlier, there is no clear definition of what shamanism is, as it varies widely in practice and culture. In these times, in most cities in the West you will be able to find many practitioners of arts that guide people into different states of consciousness. There are many levels of awareness, potency and attainment among these modern practitioners. They may range from those who host sound and vibrational healing circles, to those conducting ecstatic dance events, breath-work, medicine drumming, sweat lodges, vision quests, corroborees, plant medicine ceremonies including Ayahuasca, chanting, dance, meditation, martial arts and yoga, as some examples. At the highest level there are stories and examples of some shamans, or as they are known in Australian Indigenous culture, 'clever men', who are able to access such high vibrational states that their bodies become ethereal and they may be able to levitate, appear and disappear at will, use telekinesis, command nature, demonstrate whole body teleportation and other powerful and mysterious abilities. On another side of the spectrum, some festival DJs have been known to invoke a group shamanic experience through music and dance.

Many modern shamans, some of whom call themselves such, may be practising without actually having studied or having direct experience with the Indigenous cultures whose knowledge and practices they may be using. As a young, enthusiastic and emerging 'shamanic society', we must be mindful and maintain humility in the midst of cultural appropriation in this regard. In some cases, practitioners may be invoking altered states and spiritual beings that they are unaware of and unable to control, sometimes merely copying what they have seen others do, or having watched a video on the internet. There is a spate of YouTube shamans, 'show-men', 'sham-men' and women, who may be seductive and glamorous but may not have integrity or authenticity in their practices. Seekers of shamanic healing and spiritual development should be cautious of where and with whom they practice, and I believe that those who are using traditional practices must show respect and be mindful of the roots of those practices. Where possible, they need to go to those traditional peoples to learn directly, to pay respect and gain permission and guidance through wisdom in order to do this work. An Aboriginal Elder said to me that ceremonial leaders need to have been trained and initiated by credible groups with cultural practices that humble their egos.

People often ask me, 'How did you learn to become a shaman?' And while I understand the question, I don't see myself through that lens in the way it's often portrayed. If anything, I resonate more with the *Toltec* understanding of a shaman — not as a title, but as a way of being. In the Toltec tradition, the word 'Toltec' itself means 'artist', and that's how I experience my path: as the art of living.

Don Miguel Ruiz Jr puts it simply: 'A Toltec is an artist of the spirit, someone who creates their life as their canvas.' That speaks to me. I don't separate my healing work from my living. Every part of my life — how I speak, how I walk, how I relate, how I hold space, how I dream — is part of the creation. It's all shamanic because it's all part of the dance between the seen and unseen, the physical, the emotional, and the spiritual.

To be a shaman in this sense is to be in conscious relationship with all of life. It means recognising that we are not just observers of reality; we are co-creators of it. And when we walk that path with awareness, when we listen to the land, to the spirits, to our own truth, then life itself becomes a ceremony. Creation becomes art. And we, in turn, become the hollow reed through which Spirit creates. Within a shamanic worldview, especially through the Toltec lens, life itself is the canvas, but it's not just the mind that paints. It's the heart, the spirit, the Dreaming and the land. Every choice, every thought, every prayer — they're all brushstrokes in the art of being.

My life and my practices may be seen as an artform that's shamanic in nature. I have the ability to move between worlds, to mediate between the human, material reality and the spiritual dimensions of the unseen. This isn't something I studied or sought out. It's something that's always been with me. Since childhood, I've been in communion with the spirit world, receiving impressions, messages and guidance from what many might call the 'invisible' realms. These experiences are not abstract to me. They are woven into my daily life, into how I listen, respond, pray and move in the world.

It was during and after my first experiences with Ayahuasca in 2003 that I became actively conscious that my soul had carried many lifetimes of experience walking the shamanic path. Within the *miração* (visionary state) I began to receive soul memories and direct connection with incarnations where I had worked with Spirit, with healing, with ceremony. These weren't abstract concepts or fanciful ideas. They came with a deep familiarity, a sense of recognition in my body and bones, as if I was remembering something I'd always known. In those early ceremonies, I wasn't just being shown the visionary landscape; I was being taught how to navigate it by my own past selves.

This inner guidance, these remembered teachings, have continued to shape and support my path. They've offered tools, insight and direction in ways I can't always explain, but have come to trust. And that trust deepened during my time with the Huni Kuin in the Brazilian Amazon, where I was often reminded: 'Learn from the forest. Learn from the land. Let it teach you.' I came to see that this had always been my way. That the land speaks. That Country guides. That Spirit moves through all things if we learn how to listen. It's all Dreaming.

I'll share more about these soul memories and teachings in the chapters ahead, but what I can say now is this: I have been guided through life by the force of Great Spirit, and I have learned directly from Country. This is my way.

There has been no teacher or guru or master shaman instructing me and telling me what to do. Although I have been very blessed to have had some amazing shamanic guides over the years, most of what I have learned has been from direct experiences. In 2005 I asked an Australian Indigenous Elder about a spiritual experience I had had in the Australian forest, where I had been communicating with my ancestors and the spirits of the land. Perhaps I was seeking the Elder's approval or permission, but his answer was 'what occurs between you and Spirit, is between you and Spirit'. He had no comment on my spiritual experience, and I have found that all of the most respected teachers I have had in my life have guided me with similar advice. The message here is to trust in myself; there is no one or nothing between me and Great Spirit, no intermediary. Later in this book I will recount some experiences in the Amazon that taught me more about this.

The *Song of the Pajé* by Brazilian singer Maria Bethânia depicts the role of the shaman in reconnecting to Country, invoking the forces of nature for remembering who we are. She invokes *Anhangá* — the protector spirit of the forest, *Tupã* — Great Spirit, and *Guaraci* — The Sun.

Oh, sunlit morning, Anhangá has fled
Anhangá ê, ê
Ah! It was you who made me dream
So I might weep for my homeland

Guaraci, ê ê
Anhangá has fled
Oh, sunlit morning
Anhangá has fled
The river sings its voice
The sea sings its voice
All is dreaming—
The sky, the sea, the fields, the flowers
Oh, sunlit morning
Anhangá has fled

Oh Tupã, god of Brazil,
Who fills the sky with sun,
With stars, with moonlight, and with hope
Oh Tupã, take from me this longing
Anhangá made me dream
Of the land I lost

— O Canto do Pajé, Maria Bethânia.

Shamanism sometimes may evoke an alluring air of mystery and curiosity, while some may be sceptical or even hostile towards those of us who are communicating and working with the 'invisible worlds' of spiritual dimensions. In my experience, there are people who may have shamanic abilities, and there are many levels of competency and awareness that they may have attained. In many traditions, and certainly through the lineages in which I have been trained, there are very challenging rites and initiations that must be undertaken in order to be sufficiently competent and confident to work clearly and safely with shamanic practices. This is where Indigenous shamans and Elders may lead the student towards challenging experiences and often strict diets, or through the Brazilian shamanic religions' doctrines, which are important to make sure that practitioners attain a quality of training that is effective, safe and ethical. There is a strong imperative for those on a shamanic path to do the personal development and healing required to be a clear and empty channel of Spirit. In Australian Indigenous culture the practice of the *yidaki* (didgeridoo) encourages to player to become hollow, like the instrument, so that they may be an empty vessel for the flow of Spirit to move through. If we are full of useless thoughts, old emotions or physical and energetic blockages, we may not be a clear channel of Spirit. This is why, typically, the path of shamanism involves many trials and initiations that break down the ego and our attempts to control the flow of life and energy, and teach us to be empty and fluid in our expression to allow that flow of Spirit through and within us and to live and move in trust.

> *Because the power can be taken away at any time, anyone who claims to be a shaman starts getting focused on his or her ego. He or she, however, is almost nothing, for one is only a shaman when the spirits want that person to be a shaman.* — Michael Harner, anthropologist.

There is a phenomenon in Western cultures, perhaps derived from Christianity, where there is faith in a saviour who will take away our sins, where those with shamanic abilities are elevated as some kind of saint or spiritual authority. I know this from my own experience of people wanting to put me in this role, approaching me with questions that suggest they want me to tell them what to do or how to live their lives. Even more so, Indigenous shamans are often exalted and revered, and where in some cases they may be Elders and wise men and women who have earned their place as wisdom keepers and deserve to be respected and honoured, in most cases shamans are just like everyone else — with human frailties and imperfections. This is where humility and self-awareness are essential ingredients for any practitioner of shamanism. This is one of the many reasons I have never claimed the title of 'shaman' and do my best to point out the 100-year-old *pajés* (shamans) in the forest and the Aboriginal clever men as the true masters.

> *To become a master in these medicines, you have to learn for at least 10 years so that you can be able to use and guide others in the process, because it is study. It is an elevated study of energies, much higher than the material world here. It requires commitment and attention.* — Benki Piyãko, Ashaninka pajé.

True shamans are deeply connected to Nature, understand the energetic universe and are empty of personal ambition. Shamans have often walked a challenging path through life, overcoming deep personal traumas and challenges that may have instigated profound transformational healing. Shamanic trials and training will often come in the form of life experiences that require stepping beyond the limitations of our beliefs and social conditioning, taking risks that require courage and faith. For me, shamanism is a religion of faith in Nature, Country and the energetic universe, and a deep surrendering in service to the will of Great Spirit or 'God' as it has become known.

My first Ayahuasca experiences were in the Brazilian Amazon with psychologist Silvia Polivoy and the great Peruvian shaman and visionary artist, Pablo Amaringo. In my experiences with Don Pablo, I witnessed him performing seemingly incredible feats. He would often enter my visions, appear and disappear, shape-shift into spiritual beings and animals, and in some moments I was not able to be sure if he was physically present in the room or not. Clearly, Don Pablo had developed a lot of personal power and I found him to be a mysterious but very humble and unassuming man. Pablo was famous for his work with Ayahuasca in Peru and his extensive work in painting his visions of the universe of Ayahuasca and the spiritual realms of the Amazon. He warned about the dark side of shamanism that may involve a kind of sorcery, although he didn't explain exactly what that was. One day, though, he explained to me that there were two paths of Ayahuasca shamanism: one being the 'way of light' and the other being the 'way of power'. He went on to explain that the way of light was for those shamans who became empty of ambition and any desire for power, who dedicated themselves to a life in service to Spirit and self-sacrifice. The shamans of the way of light are empty vessels and work as channels so that light and love flows through them, and they act in accordance with higher vibrational forces that guide the healing that flows through them and their work. The shamans of the way of power are the ones who focus on gathering personal power, both spiritually and materially, and have the ability through their will to influence people, reality and healing. They can be charming, seductive and sometimes tricky. He suggested that if used for good, these shamans had the ability to perform very powerful work that could help people with magical healing, but that this way was also treacherous, as this power can easily corrupt and be used for personal gain and influence which may be harmful. It made me consider the well-known saying by Lord Acton (1887): 'Power tends to corrupt and absolute power corrupts absolutely.' In later years I started to see the influence that glamour, seduction, image, rank and status was having upon the global Ayahuasca community, and I became more appreciative of the doctrines of the Brazilian lineages and the brother/sisterhood of those communities that seemed to promote and maintain a humility and sense of equality in service amongst the people.

In the Brazilian Amazon the shamans, as we may call them, are referred to as *pajés*. An Indigenous village may have one senior pajé (pronounced 'pah-zjeh') who has typically done the most training, diets and initiations and therefore is able to cultivate the most personal power and ability to work with the spiritual forces and energies. In my experience, though, everyone in those Amazonian villages has shamanic abilities, as they learn from a very young age although they may not choose to deepen those studies, where others in the village become more specialised. In the Amazon, the pajés are not only concerned with Ayahuasca but with other plants and animals too, and they may specialise in different areas of their cultural practice and the arts of the pajé.

Another aspect that has become clear to me through experiencing Indigenous cultures in different parts of the world is that their language, culture, spiritual beliefs, ancestral knowledge and shamanic practices are very much reflective of, and informed by, their environment. For example, the language of an Amazonian nation will have sounds and words that reflect the sounds of nature in the region in which they live. Similar is their cosmology, by which their entire culture, history and spiritual beliefs are reflective of the animals, plants, trees, weather and natural phenomena of their respective environments. In natural law, there are also many common themes and beliefs that are universal around the world. The thread of spiritual energy that exists within and through the entire universe weaves itself through all existence regardless of location, history or belief. Sometimes there are different names or personifications for certain universal forces, though I am often amazed at how much of traditional, ancient cosmologies can be translated from one tribe to another on opposite sides of the planet. For those blessed with the awareness of a shamanic view, we may also start to perceive that each country and environment has its unique spiritual beings and ancestors of Country, that these beings and entities also will have a large influence on culture and cosmology. My experience with the Huni Kuin people in the Brazilian Amazon taught me that some pajés are tasked with the role of investigating the spiritual qualities of new plants and animals and even the sounds from foreign instruments, and through visionary states they develop an understanding of how these new influences may affect their own finely balanced cosmology, for better or worse. Once they understand these effects and meanings, they may then receive songs and prayers and practices that create the spiritual conditions of harmony and balance so that these new influences may be integrated into their cosmology. This is very important work for these people, who deeply understand the delicate balance required for survival in the forest and know that even small disturbances can cause much damage and pain through the colonisation of their lands, and through the current colonisation of culture and people's minds with modern media, money, tourism, television and film, political propaganda, alcohol and other toxic substances.

 This traditional shamanism exists in cultures all over the world: the medicine men of North American First Nations, the clever men of Australian First Nations (in Central Australia they are known as *ngangkaris*), the druids of Celtic Britain, the *naguals* of Central America, the African *sangomas* and the *samans* of Siberia. When people ask how I learned to be a shaman, I point out to them the old people I have met in Central Australia with silver eyes and abilities to shape-shift, to appear and disappear, to levitate, and who can put someone to sleep with a simple gesture, or the 100-plus-year-old pajés of the Brazilian Amazon with physical strength to match the youngest and fittest of the village. When considering these great men and women of traditional lineages, I see myself as a humble student of perhaps the greatest and most challenging vocation on this planet. The field of study of shamanism is unimaginably vast and yet all humans are able to access this knowledge and ability if we choose and put our focus and intent on that path, although some might say that the true shamans do not choose; they are chosen by Spirit.

> *Throughout Australian Aboriginal society there are advanced initiations for those with greater capacities for spiritual growth. In some cases these initiations, accompanied by rigorous disciplines such as food restrictions, purification rites, memorising of songs, dances and stories, can lead to achieving the title of a man of high degree, Aboriginal people referred to these tribal doctors as 'clever men'... The Aboriginal doctors are known to perform clairvoyant, telepathic, and trance or hypnotic practices, remote viewing, thought transference, psychic healing (non-surgical removal of objects from the body), levitation, journeys to other worlds, communication with spiritual beings and with the dead, sorcery and psychic projection, and multiple appearances (appearing in one place while actually being in another).* — Robert Lawlor, *Voices of the First Day, Awakening in the Aboriginal Dreamtime*.

Ayahuasca shamanism is also a very diverse field of specialised study and practice. By its nature, Ayahuasca and its potential for human access to spiritual dimensions is an obvious path for accelerated spiritual growth and healing and a powerful tool for shamanic training. In my experience of working with Ayahuasca I have learned through two main forms of practice. As I mentioned, my first experiences were with the Peruvian shaman Pablo Amaringo and psychologist Silvia Polivoy. Their form of Ayahuasca practice, which I refer to as the *curandeiro* (or healer) tradition, is where the participants are in a dark space and in the care of a shaman-type healer who works to heal and support the spiritual process of those partaking in the ceremony. The other form of Ayahuasca practice I have gained a lot of experience through is what I refer to as a more 'communal' shamanism, where there is a ceremonial leader guiding the ritual but everybody in the ceremony is effectively holding the space together, where all the initiates of the lineage are able to support and hold space for the prayer and for those in the ceremony. My work with Ayahuasca is more aligned with this communal shamanism, as I personally find it more empowering for everyone to be able to find their own inner strength and ability with Ayahuasca and with the ceremony, where our collective prayers gain strength and power, where our communal sense of working together builds community and camaraderie, and where power is dispersed amongst many, not concentrated in one.

There are different levels of development on the path of shamanism. Essentially those who are dedicated to this spiritual path will learn that it is necessary to become very self-reliant, and this can sometimes be a lonely path. Ultimately it leads to personal power, independence and strength, but on the journey this can be very challenging for some, and it is not for everyone. As humans are essentially social animals, we need community and family in order to thrive and be healthy. It is important that through Ayahuasca use there is great consideration given to the needs of those participating, especially when they are new on this journey. I will discuss this more later in the book.

Traditional Ayahuasca shamanism was developed through the conditions of the peoples of the Amazon in relation to their social, environmental and cosmological conditions. The concerns of those ancient peoples may have been more about their relationship to their environment and perhaps the spiritual pursuits that connected them more deeply with their ancestral roots and visions of their future. Once

European colonialism arrived in the Amazon, the ancient peoples' visionary explorations became focused on developing knowledge and skills to deal with the myriad of illnesses, environmental destruction and genocidal actions they were confronted with. In many cases they did not have a remedy for the conditions they were presented with, as they had never seen them before. For example, when viruses and diseases arrived in the Amazon and the native people were becoming sick and dying, the shamans had no known remedies to cure them. In many Amazonian tribes they now use a medicine derived from an excretion from the skin of a frog, which is commonly known in the West as *kambô*. Amongst many of these tribes they tell the story of kambô: that it was not used until recent history. When the pajés were investigating through the use of Ayahuasca and asking the spirits of the forest to help them find a remedy for these strange diseases, they were instructed in the use of kambô, which provided an effective cure and prevention for these illnesses. Kambô is also known as 'nature's vaccine', although that description is one some people may not like.

One of the greatest afflictions carried by the Western world's population is the epidemic of mental illness, which manifests itself in deeply complex forms. Through colonialism, the native peoples of the world have been confronted with the ego of the Western mind, which projects, wants, manipulates, lies, avoids and exaggerates with self-importance and seeks to dominate others and nature. This chronic egoic mental condition is something that did not exist in the experience of the Amazonian peoples, as through their rites and spiritual practices they had developed a well-balanced social system that created harmony amongst each other and with Nature. In traditional cultures, the leaders were the wisest ones who, without ambition, took on responsibility for guiding the people. They were recognised and chosen. In the Western world it is the opposite —people who are driven by ambition and lust for power and recognition force or manipulate themselves into leadership and subjugate others into their distorted realities, infecting the culture with their personal agendas.

The blessing of Ayahuasca has also been a powerful tool for Indigenous people to maintain awareness and cleanliness of their subconscious thoughts and mental health. Increasingly, they have seen Westerners arriving in the Amazon with complex and challenging mental health conditions which require very specialised knowledge and experience in how to deal with them. There is also the issue of integrating back into societies and environments where these mental conditions are created. After a participant has had profound healing in the forest, for example, it is easy for them to return home and quickly relapse, if they are surrounded by triggers and without a supportive environment. As mentioned previously, Pablo once said to me that the blessing of Ayahuasca was for the entire world and it was important to share it in different places, although not by merely copying traditional Amazonian practices. He said that ceremonies must be conducted in culturally appropriate ways that reflect the conditions and experience of the participants in their own environments. He encouraged me to do this. From my experience, both the expansion of spiritual awareness and the complex and fragile mental health of Westerners are where the biggest risks and challenges lie for Ayahuasca use outside of the Amazon and, in particular, in Western urban settings.

> *The depth and quality of psychedelic experience is, to some degree, shaped by the consciousness that undergoes it. In general, Western mental, linguistic and social processes are so literal, rigid and externalised that, for Westerners, the psychedelic experience has often led to confusion and challenging integration. Aboriginal society allows shamanistic and psychedelic experiences to blend with, enhance and uphold the full expression of life.*
> — Robert Lawlor, *Voices of the First Day, Awakening in the Aboriginal Dreamtime*.

Essentially, both shamanism and psychedelic plant use are universally intrinsic to human culture and evolution throughout history.

In shamanic view: The global mental health crisis

There is an accepted consensus today that the world is sick. The human population has for thousands of years been on a quest for domination over one another and the environment and has driven itself to the edge of catastrophe. The planet is literally overheating physically and psychically, and we are like frogs in increasingly hot water that won't jump out before it boils. It doesn't take much to look around and see this.

Climate change is upon us and we are living through unprecedented weather anomalies and disasters, with the Northern Hemisphere just having gone through its hottest year on record. Here in Australia, we have experienced apocalyptic forest fires and floods. Seemingly the Earth is shaking us awake and nobody truly understands the nature of these earth changes. For decades, those who sounded the warning were ridiculed and victimised while the fossil fuel and big agriculture industries paid off politicians and media to protect their control and profits.

Humanity continues to awaken and, just like those who realised that the Earth wasn't flat, there are those who have been screaming for the care of the Earth and our environment. These are the awakening ones with open minds and the courage to see beyond the veils of a sick society and its intense propaganda of distraction and media spin. The shamanic view allows us to see beyond the illusions of the collective 'group think' mind just like the Huni Kuin, who encountered visions through the Nixi Pãe, warning and guiding the people of upcoming environmental challenges. Shamans, Elders, seers, yogis and others with the ability to transcend the confines of the 'thinking' mind have been tracking the shifting landscape of this sick world and mobilising to teach others through spiritual practices and show the way to a healthier lifestyle and way of being.

If humans are frogs in a slowly boiling pot, the heat causing this is not just the rising temperature of the planet. It's also a rising of psychic heat, as we are being confronted by relentless reminders of this planetary sickness of trauma and are feeling the pain of our collective insanity and the relentless pressure to 'do something' — to awaken with an urgency that only seems to be growing.

> *If we could begin to see much illness itself not as a cruel twist of fate or some nefarious mystery but rather as an expected and therefore normal consequence of abnormal, unnatural circumstances, it would have revolutionary implications for how we approach everything health related.* — Dr Gabor Maté.

The Amazon rainforest is the largest living organism on the planet, an immense ecosystem that is akin to the lungs of the Earth, capturing carbon dioxide and producing oxygen. This majestic being is dying, and if the Amazon dies, the planet dies. At this crucial time it has given us a divine gift in the form of a sacred medicine that is able to heal the mind of humanity and reconnect us back to Country and to our true nature. Perhaps this divine gift is an evolutionary reflex of the Earth — to distribute a sacrament that is not only a remedy for the mental health afflictions that are leading us to our own self-destruction, but is also helping us to spiritually evolve.

In the midst of this insanity, the mental health of the planet is also increasingly deteriorating. Alternative remedies and lifestyles are emerging in great number, but those of us leading the call for a new view of health are being treated like today's climate activists or past scientists who realised the Earth was not flat. I was chosen for this path and asked by teachers and shamans in the Amazon to travel into the world and spread the message of warning — that the Amazon is in great danger. Since doing so, whilst I have witnessed immense transformations in health and consciousness amongst countless people who have been touched by Ayahuasca and her forest light, I have also had to deal with brutal, archaic laws and intense persecution by those wanting to demonise our sacrament and its divine work. It is quite shocking that Spanish inquisition-style 'witch hunts' still occur in Australia.

The call of Ayahuasca and the Amazon is one of awakening our minds and spirits, because it is only through a healed mind that we are able to listen to the Earth, to be truly able to hear what she has to say and to allow ourselves to be guided on the path towards a safe and prosperous future. This is the great humbling of humanity, as we face the darkness that the sickness has created — to find the courage within each one of us, to see the illusions of the mind and of our dysfunctional society, to own and admit to our role in it, to feel its pain, learn to heal and embrace a new reality.

> *This is a school of divine knowledge. It is such a serious thing that if everyone really knew, they would not speak badly of this beautiful sacrament that sprouted from the earth itself, as natural as God's own nature. But, since the time of Mestre Irineu, people without this knowledge have spoken dreadful barbarities. They want to force on us the insanity so prevalent in the world today, when our goal is the healing from such derangement. The truth is the only medicine for our time. By receiving the truth in ourselves we show the way of healing to our brothers and sisters.* — Padrinho Sebastião of the Brazilian Santo Daime church.

A great sadness dwells within humanity. For those of us sensitive to this pain, it can be excruciating because we see we are abusing our own mother and ignoring the voice of Great Spirit, our father. This disconnection only heightens the sickness, and the Indigenous peoples of the Earth in particular suffer greatly; they are still so deeply connected. Their 'religion' is Country, it is the Earth. They feel its pain profoundly and many turn to alcohol and drugs to deal with that pain and are subsequently blamed and victimised. The majority of humans on the planet are self-medicating to deal with this great sadness, either through alcohol and other drugs, or through other addictions and distractions such as media, sport, politics and interpersonal drama. For some there is a burning anger that, if directed in a healthy way, can become a fire of passion for change. The change, through transformation, may become felt from within, and once people are healed, they become peaceful agents of change.

The global epidemic of depression and mental health issues is currently of an unprecedented scale. Despite, or perhaps because of, advances in technology and wealth, rates of depression, addiction, anxiety, suicidal ideology and other mental health disorders continue to rise. People often express frustration about politics, economics, and the state of the world, unaware that they are also, often unconsciously, entangled in and perpetuating the very systems they critique. This isn't always a matter of conscious choice, but of deeply ingrained patterns, inherited beliefs, and societal structures that shape our participation. Still, awakening begins when we start to recognise these patterns — and reclaim our agency within them.

The trauma that society has inflicted on the people is considered normal and those who reconnect to Country and Dreaming are classed as radicals and often persecuted. The ever-growing reliance on overly complex technology leading to overly complex lives is creating stress, isolation and overload. Social isolation and distance created by the blind march towards a technology-centred reality cause disconnection from Nature and Spirit, leading to the range of depression and mental disorders becoming increasingly prevalent across the world.

The same systems and organisations that promote and perpetuate this unhealthy and unbalanced society are also providing 'solutions', with immense growth in the epidemic of dependency upon government-funded pharmaceutical mental health drugs. In 2025, the global market for pharmaceutical drugs targeting mental health was estimated to be worth over $200 billion dollars annually, based on aggregated data from recent market research and industry analysis reports. The authoritarian approach to medicine in Western nations is dominated by a global industrial cartel which has resulted in the failure of their systems to address preventative and holistic health. This ideological scientific-profit matrix is failing and driving people to seek alternative remedies in natural medicines, shamanism, religion and even Ayahuasca. As one example of this extreme distortion in reality, the most technologically advanced country in the world, the United States of America, which has the highest level of consumerism and media saturation, also has the world's highest rate of depression.

In the Australian example, this country has the second-highest rate of antidepressant consumption in the world. Over 10% of the

Australian population are consuming antidepressants, whilst the rate of ADHD (attention deficit hyperactivity disorder) medication consumption has doubled in the last 10 years. Currently, around one in five Australians are currently on some form of mental health medication, whilst almost half of Australians will experience an episode of mental illness in their lifetime. In March 2024, Sapien Labs' fourth annual *Mental State of the World Report* showed the global trend towards declining mental health has shown no signs of slowing post (COVID) pandemic. According to the report's 'Mental Health Quotient', Australia is the sixth-worst performing country, ranking lower in MHQ than even war-torn countries such as Ukraine.

By far the most common reason for visits to doctors in Australia is for psychological and mental health complaints. Under the Australian medical health rebate scheme, a mental health consultation is limited to 20 minutes with a general practice doctor. Given the complexity, sensitivity and great diversity of mental health conditions, this would seem to only deepen the dysfunction, as 80% of the prescriptions for mental health medications are from these too-brief medical consultations, with research showing that doctors are prescribing recklessly, often against the recommendations of the drug makers. In Australia, if a doctor refers you to a psychologist, the waiting time for an appointment is around one month, if the patient can afford the treatment. Whilst in Australia there are a number of government-funded mental health support agencies that act like a kind of loose band-aid, there is seemingly little interest in addressing, or even getting close to acknowledging, the root causes of this widespread mental health decline. More likely, the government with its policies and systemic corruption is actively supporting this dysfunctional social and political system. In general, it seems fairly obvious that a 'sickness-solution-profit' system of health in Western society is a failure for all, eventually even for those who have been benefitting from the profits, academic accolades and political kickbacks.

From a shamanic view, health can only be considered from a holistic perspective. In shamanism the mind-emotion-body and spirit are all interrelated and it's the psycho-spiritual condition that is what informs physical health. Western medicine and research is also showing this, but for some reason there is still a strong resistance amongst establishment medical and pharmaceutical interests to accepting this and pivoting towards a philosophy of practice that is reflective of the overwhelming evidence. Power corrupts … Mainstream medicine in both physical and mental health usually dismisses the strong efficacy of plant medicines like Ayahuasca and has been dismissive of any positive results, ignorantly suggesting these are due to superstition, transference or a delusion based on feelings of euphoria. It is important to acknowledge that just because something is not easily understood by scientific rationalism does not mean it is not true. Thankfully there are many in the mainstream scientific and medical fields who do recognise the obvious spiritual dimension to healing and health and are able to focus on what is effective and integrate the different philosophies and cultural understandings. 'Effectiveness is the measure of truth,' notes an Hawaiian spiritual precept.

There are many developments in mainstream mental and physical health that have proven to be effective, but on their own without psycho-spiritual integration into an expanded view of health-connection to Country we are still left with the dire crisis of health in Western countries. My Aboriginal friends tell me they are tired of approaches from government and politicians which are merely box-ticking exercises where no one is really listening. A more mature and evolved perspective is called for, where the shamanic view and ancestral medicine, with all their benefits and effectiveness, must be shown the respect they deserve, so that these two worlds of ancient and modern can work together. There is an urgent call for governments and the medical industry to honestly face the crisis in global health from a post-historical perspective and a need to honour the human right to use ancestral medicines and related spiritual practices. From there we can create an alliance which will lead to a revolution in health and wellbeing on a scale previously unimaginable. This is the prophecy of the union of the eagle and the condor which I will explore later in the book.

> *One of the most frustrating failures of Western medical practice is its lack of awareness of the unity of mind and body despite voluminous, elegant and absolutely persuasive research evidence that the distinction between mind and body is false, unscientific, and — in real life — impossible... the miracles described by evidence arising from shamanic plant ceremonies are, in fact, exactly what one would expect if one were grounded in a holistic understanding of human beings in health and illness.* — Dr Gabor Maté.

In considering the current social and environmental conditions humans are experiencing amidst this ubiquitous psychological dysfunction, it is also important to acknowledge the current rise in legal and illegal drug use. Australia has one of the highest rates of methamphetamine use in the world and has experienced a sharp increase in its use since the pandemic, use which by mid-2025 is still increasing. It is no surprise that illegal drug use rises in tandem with legal drug use, as both are likely attempts to find a remedy for the same underlying social and psychological problems. Interestingly, both legal and illegally manufactured psychotropic drugs have significant problems with their addictive tendencies, both psychological and physical. Both legal and illegal manufactured drugs have complex issues relating to detoxification and withdrawal from their effects when stopping their usage. This of course is in contrast to natural psychedelic plant medicines that aren't addictive or don't have significant withdrawal effects Also, within this context, both categories of manufactured drugs, illegal and legal, do not address underlying issues, and whilst they may provide some mental and emotional stability, their use does not enable us to address the root causes of the issues of mental illness. Their inability to provide a cure and the danger of chronic dependency intrinsic to their use have led to the growth of large industries in legal and illegal drug manufacture and supply. Global pharmaceutical cartels aligned with heavily regulated medical industries that have no accountability monopolise the legal drug industry. The illegal drug trade is similarly without moral or ethical substance and run by underground cartels with links back to the same government-pharma entanglement. We just have to look at the prevalence of US Government and military presence in countries that supply the global drug trade such as Afghanistan, Columbia and, more recently, Venezuela. The result is the same: people suffering with chronic illnesses, addiction and poor health, disconnected from the natural remedies of the culture and spirituality of plant medicines.

> *The fact that psychedelics are about to become medicines shows that they should never have been banned in the first place— probably not even for recreational use, but certainly not as medicines. There is 50 years' worth of people with mental illnesses and addictions who have been denied the best treatment that could have been available.*
>
> *Using a back-of-an-envelope calculation, since LSD was banned in the late 1960s possibly 100 million people have died prematurely from alcohol abuse. They were denied a treatment with some strong evidence. And even if LSD had helped only 10 percent of them, that would have saved 10 million lives.* — David J Nutt, Psychedelics: The revolutionary drugs that could change your life – a guide from the expert.

The Australian Government, alongside most Western nations, has a simplistic 'war on drugs' mentality, where they promote the idea that illegal drugs are the problem, which has the effect of criminalising and alienating a large population of mentally unwell citizens, targets low income communities and fuels organised crime at an extremely high cost to taxpayers. This also ignores increasing academic research and effective health care practices which show that addictions are a maladaptive response to trauma and not a result of the drug or external thing. 'The question is not "Why the addiction?" but "Why the pain?"' says Dr Gabor Maté. At the same time, Western governments go to extreme lengths to protect the regime of legalised drugs and the medical-pharmaceutical industry that benefits from their substantial profits and addictive tendencies.

Addiction in today's society can be seen as a spiritual disease. Many of today's addicts are people who, if they lived in traditional societies, would have sought initiation into non-ordinary states of consciousness. In Indigenous cultures around the world, a minority of the population feels the call to become shamans. These societies maintain traditional techniques of experiencing altered states, and assign value to them. Most Indigenous cultures recognise the exploration of altered states as something innate, important and universal. All around the world, humans yearn to change their consciousness. They do this continuously, through various licit and illicit substances as well as other means (meditation, amusement park rides, sex, the trance produced by social media and so on). — Daniel Pinchbeck and Sophia Rokhlin, When Plants Dream.

One of the most dangerous yet prevalent drugs is alcohol. In Australia, there are thousands of deaths per year from alcohol poisoning and other directly related causes of death from alcohol. In February 2024 the University of New South Wales published a report raising the alarm regarding the significant increase in these deaths and an urgent call to alert the public to the risk factors. While this is going on, the state government is making billions of dollars in profits from alcohol sales and is reported to spend nine billion dollars a year of public money on alcohol-related harms and on policing alcohol-related violence that is destroying families and communities. Politicians and bureaucrats do photo shoots for the media during election cycles with a beer or a wine in their hand and then do nothing to address this enormous social problem. This report by UNSW came amidst an ongoing persecution campaign by the police, the health commission in the NSW along with the media to discredit Ayahuasca use, with them even going so far as to take actions against me for alleged 'dangerous drug' use, referring to my work with Ayahuasca. The insanity continued in August 2024 when the state police commissioner was caught spending taxpayer money on bottles of gin, which she alleged she was giving as gifts. I wondered if she had considered doing background health checks on the recipients of her gifts of dangerous drugs? I contemplated the state of the world when I looked at the police documents with her name on them authorising actions against me and Ayahuasca, and the millions of dollars she authorised to be spent on their persecution campaign against Ayahuasca. Nobody has ever died from Ayahuasca intoxication (ICEERS report, 2023) and it actually helps by bringing peace and health to people whilst curing addictions including alcoholism. The astronomers of 2000 years ago would have been turning in their graves.

We are now at the twilight of an age, and it is not without significance that the evolutionary relationship between mind and consciousness and spirit, brought about by the use of power plants, is confused in the misinformation and prejudice surrounding drugs, one of the most perplexing issues of our times.

The government, the modern secular power of our time, was moved to an undisguisable curiosity about the origins and goals of the Santo Daime, a group rooted in the Amazonian forest, achieving communion with God through a drink obtained from a vine and a leaf. To a certain degree, the preoccupation was justified because this spiritual phenomenon was as yet unknown to many. And that the religious sacrament is obtained through the mixing of two psychoactive plants stimulates much prejudice. Initiation with divine plants, a native tradition of the most ancient peoples of the Americas, should not be confused with the indiscriminate use of drugs and the economic interests that guide this terrible industry, a significant wound of our modern civilisation at the end of this millennium. — Alex Polari de Alverga, *The Religion of Ayahuasca.*

In this context of social and psychological dysfunction, it is no surprise that the rise of interest in spirituality, including shamanism and Ayahuasca, is now so prevalent across the world. Humans are intrinsically connected to, and a part of, Country. We are born of the Earth and its elements, and we carry the teachings, wisdom and spirituality of our ancestors in our blood, in our culture and in our souls. We all live in one shared Dream. In these modern times, we have re-awoken into the planetary Dream, where our social structures and governments and institutional beliefs have abandoned our true nature and the ancient teachings of our ancestors. Since the invention of artificial timing systems such as calendars and clocks, there has been a systematic entrainment of the human mind and body away from Country and ancestral wisdom, accompanied by the imprinting of subservience to a false authority that promotes mechanical and technological dependence. Clocks were developed after a request was put to the Catholic Church during the Industrial Revolution in an attempt to force people to conform to a working organisational structure. Business owners had struggled to overcome their workers' natural instincts, which kept them in tune with natural cycles, such as that of the moon. When the clocks alone didn't work, the businesses introduced institutional education in collective schools for children, as this would train them from a young age, then they would train their own children — and so it went. Depriving humans of our natural rhythms and rights and forcing us into mechanical rhythms unsurprisingly leads to illness, both mental and physical. We now see the results of generations of disconnection from Nature, as humanity has become chronically sick and heavily medicated, addicted to technology, out of balance with the Earth and environment, and where those who return to our natural roots and step out of this dysfunctional system are vilified and persecuted. It is insanity.

The song of the land is lost
The people long forgot
Drowned by TVs and movie screens
But I hear whispers in the wind

Spirit never forgot
She lives in every rock
Sung by the birds at night
Holding her children tight

We live in paradise
Or so it seems to me
Sometimes I really wonder
How we got so far away
So far away from here
So far away ...

— *So Far Away,* Lore Solaris.

The current drive towards artificial intelligence, virtual reality and social media dependence is the culmination of this movement by controlling forces such as governments and the dominator classes to drive humanity away from our true nature and ancestral wisdom. Sadly for many, they have totally forgotten, and may even totally reject, their natural roots. It is no surprise that social media addiction and smart phone usage are two of the biggest factors causing depression. The current social solution for medicating the psychologically sick population is through manufactured chemical drugs, again utilising technology. For a select few, regular psychotherapy may be a solution, although the quality of this therapy varies wildly and in order to cure depression research shows that at least 16-20 sessions may be needed.

Amidst social pressure there is some emerging hope that there is also now a movement within the system of corporate-government cabals to accept the use of certain plant medicines such as cannabis and psilocybin mushrooms as effective remedies, on the condition this use is strictly under their profit and control regimes. In some countries there is a movement towards the acceptance and legalisation of the ancient and traditional 'shamanic' use of plant medicines such as Ayahuasca that respects the religious nature of the Holy Sacrament and its potent healing potential used in sacred rituals honouring and invoking ancestral wisdom and practices.

In Brazil, where there has been a movement towards the respect and recognition of the traditional and religious use of Ayahuasca since the 1930s, there are now many examples of research being done by dozens of universities, often in collaboration with the well-established churches, into the safety and efficacy of Ayahuasca use. This is a great example of how there can be a mature approach to investigating Ayahuasca use in respect and partnership between Western science and traditional spiritual practices.

Alongside the global epidemic of mental illness is the concurrent increase in chronic physical health conditions which are also rampant globally, especially in developed nations. I won't explore this much here, other than to say that physical health is directly related to mental and spiritual health. It would also seem that a natural result of increased self-awareness and spiritual connection would create the environment and behaviours for a healthier physical condition. Whilst there is much evidence for the positive effects and remedy that Ayahuasca may bring to people suffering from a range of physical ailments, it is not something I will be exploring in this book, and it has not been a focus of my work and studies, which have been more focused on mental and emotional health, personal and spiritual development.

The increase in mental illness also seems to be fuelled by an increasing global movement towards authoritarianism through government and corporate propaganda and mind-control techniques employed via censorship and media-led psychological warfare. The religious cult of scientific rationalism dictates and controls the social, legal and political narrative. The legal-political systems of the world assume the dominance and intellectual superiority of the modern scientific paradigm, even when it is in conflict with well-proven ancient knowledge or modern theories that create further contradictions. The systems of our society are designed to protect the dominance and authority of the cult-like scientific paradigm, and proponents of it are trained to obey its precepts and assumptions, even where clearly contradictory evidence exists.

In Western society our lives are increasingly under insidious forms of surveillance, data collection and aggressive propaganda, in many cases with the removal of our rights, which have slowly been eroded by government legislation under the guise of anti-terrorism and biosecurity justifications. Aside from the negative effect this movement towards a corporate totalitarian society has upon mental and physical health, it also has the effect of pushing people even further towards natural and spiritual remedies. The shamanic view sees this as part of a spiritual evolutionary trigger-point, where the increasing control and domination over the human spirit has the opposite effect — of waking people up to their true nature. Spirit never dies and the more governments try to squeeze and suppress it, the more it finds new forms of expression and movements away from tyranny. History has shown this over and over. From a shamanic view, there is no separation between the increasingly desperate need for the controlling forces to implement more and more technological authoritarianism and the ever-growing tidal-wave of the conscious awakening of humanity. Perhaps it's a bit of a chicken and egg scenario, where the dominator culture creates the awakening and resistance, while the resistance causes more controlling responses.

> *Civilisation has led us to the point where the political power machine and the electronic media transform millions of human beings into automatons, consumers manipulated by their own desires and habits, preyed on by advertising and media agencies. People live out their lives with a few basic concepts and some abstract assurances. Ideas of citizenship are stereotyped, and there are few examples of noble and idealistic behaviour to follow. The myth of science lives within all of this in a dubious manner. Reclaiming the science of our own ancestors may*

well be a solution for the crisis on planet Earth at the end of the millennium. If science does not spiritualise itself, the result will be a materialistic, all-powerful scientific council hovering over the spiritual consciousness of the new world. True spirituality will have to overcome stifling dogmatism in a new disguise. — Alex Polari de Alverga, *The Religion of Ayahuasca.*

From a shamanic perspective, we observe the nature of the current global dysfunction as symptomatic of a confused and entangled web of lower-vibrational entities and energies that are, in effect, keeping humanity in a state of fear and anxiety whilst feeding off these lower-density energies. These entities empower those whose will is easily corrupted to their purposes and who will often, usually unconsciously, rise to positions of power and authority through wealth, politics, academics and institutional authority such as governments and their agencies. I have personally had experiences of returning to the city after spending weeks in the forest drinking Ayahuasca, after refining my sensitivity to spiritual dimensions, then walking through the city and seeing people with dark entities attached to them, with tentacles feeding off their crown centres, keeping them in a state of mental confusion and despair, whilst obscuring their connection to their higher spirit or knowing.

From a shamanic or traditional perspective, the rational West's ideal of an objective science — free from all vestiges of superstition — is simply another myth, a naive projection of the world as we want it to be. In fact, this one-dimensional ideology of rationalism blinds us to the subtle realms. Because we have no language for understanding the subtle dimensions, all kinds of negative, supersensible entities may be able to invade and infest our world. The shaman or occultist sees post-modern civilisation, trapped by its reductive ideology of material progress, besieged by all sorts of inter-dimensional entities. These psychic invaders sneak in through the gaps in our scientific knowledge, which denies the supersensible dimension and sees the occult as meaningless fantasy. — Daniel Pinchbeck & Sophia Rokhlin, *When Plants Dream.*

It seems to me that the inevitable resolution of the current confusion and chaos we experience in the Dream of the planet is a more balanced society where natural lore and ancient wisdom are able to create safety and protection for humanity within a world full of dangers, where evolution has the potential to expand human awareness and natural abilities, including shamanic spiritual sciences, whilst these are balanced with the best elements of technology that can be sustained ethically and with ecological responsibility. Just like the native people of the Amazon discovered through Ayahuasca shamanism a direct channel of communication to Country and all its beings. Those of us who are blessed to receive the Holy Sacrament are also given the opportunity to be visionaries and leaders in the movement towards the re-creation of the Earth and humanity's Dream in a more balanced, healthy and respectful form. I believe that we should not take this gift for granted. Those of us with the vision gifted by Ayahuasca have the ability to see the causes and effects of human behaviours and to receive the warning signs that are being transmitted through the natural world. Ayahuasca has been through many challenges and adversity to survive cultural genocide in South America and has then made its way around the world. Much has been sacrificed and the persecution of Ayahuasca use and the community of people consecrating it signifies there is a great need to gather ourselves and our resources to preserve and protect our human rights and the rights of the planet, especially during this time of intense planetary crises. The chronic illness, war and environmental catastrophe are clear signs that we need to stand up and work towards the creation of a new society based upon the precepts of peace, love and harmony. Ayahuasca and the spirit of the forest, from the heart of the greatest forest of the Earth, is a divine gift for humanity at this crucial time and is playing a significant and unique role in our collective awakening — which is needed for our survival and evolution.

We listen to the talking box
Machine world cause all life to stop
A kangaroo hoping across the setting sun
Ancient Desert
Can't you hear, can't you hear?

The sound of the fall, remember now
Can you afford not listen now?

— *Last Sunset*, Lore Solaris.

Tendrils of the shamanic vine unfurling globally

In the midst of modernity's chaos, there's a yearning for the sacred, for the shamanic, for a deeper understanding of existence.
— Terence McKenna.

Shamanism has experienced a notable resurgence in recent years, reflecting a growing interest in alternative spiritual practices and Indigenous wisdom traditions. In response to the complexities of modern life, degrading mental health and a longing for deeper meaning, individuals from diverse cultural backgrounds have turned to shamanic principles and practices for personal growth, healing, guidance and spiritual connection to the natural world. Our ancestors and our innate spiritual knowing are calling us. This renaissance has been supported by the globalisation of information and the accessibility of teachings from various Indigenous cultures through books, workshops, online resources and with the movement of people around the planet searching for shamanic remedy and teachings. Indigenous leaders and Elders from different parts of the world have also come forward, sharing traditional wisdom and knowledge, often travelling the world holding ceremonies and giving talks and workshops. This global movement of shamanism manifests in many forms, such as the teachings and ceremony of these Indigenous Elders and wisdom keepers, modern shamanism and its urban adaptations, sacred plant ceremonies, visionary arts, 'medicine' music and the psychedelic festival movement. The nature of these global shamanic movements ranges in depth and meaning, from simple things like a native drum-making workshop to ceremonial healing and more challenging initiatory rites that require tests of personal will, mental, physical and emotional strength.

The global renaissance of shamanism and shamanic culture is not just about people seeking healing and remedy for the sicknesses of Western culture. All of us have a natural instinct towards shamanic awareness that is embedded into our genetic and ancestral history. It is only through the suppression of humanity by the advance of modern civilisation that we have forgotten these abilities, which for most people over time lie dormant, outside of awareness.

A large-scale counter-culture movement began in the 1960s led by various cultural leaders like The Beatles, Bob Dylan, Timothy Leary, Ram Dass and more. From 1963, all over the world thousands of young people would be found screaming their hearts out at Beatles concerts, having out-of-body experiences and altered states of consciousness akin to a collective shamanic ritual. This movement lead to a culture of consciousness exploration, including widespread experimentation with marijuana, LSD, and other mind-altering psychedelics. Yoga and meditation became popularised and this time saw the beginnings of large-scale outdoor festivals celebrating human connectedness, spirituality and trance dance through psychedelic music, arts and movement. The psychedelic revolution in popular Western culture continued into the 1970s and beyond, led by researchers such as Terence McKenna alongside the first forays into the Amazon jungle in search of Ayahuasca. Meanwhile in Brazil, the development of Ayahuasca religions was already well established, after arising from humble beginnings in the 1930s, with clear and well-defined doctrines and spiritual paths within these lineages.

> *Turn off your mind, relax and float downstream.* – Timothy Leary, et. al., *The Psychedelic Experience.*

As a reaction to this widespread and growing movement, LSD and psychedelic plant medicines were outlawed under strict government controls in the US and other countries such as Australia. This, however, did not stop the growth of interest in these substances and, like other attempts at prohibition, caused a myriad of other problems, including the development of a large underground movement and the criminalisation of a peace-loving movement of people yearning for deeper connection to nature and spirituality.

In the 1950s and 60s there had also been widespread and ongoing research into the therapeutic benefits and safety profile of psychedelics, including DMT. This research was largely shut down with the implementation of these new prohibitionary laws. In most countries, these laws still exist, and in the case of DMT, and thus Ayahuasca, there was never any reason, research or evidence provided as to why it should be deemed illegal. In the last two decades there has been a resurgence in applications to government for research into psychedelic therapy and there have also been some significant Supreme Court cases in the US that have determined that Ayahuasca be legally permitted for religious and spiritual purposes, where governments have been unable to provide compelling evidence as to why it should be deemed illegal.

The 1990s saw a significant increase in the number of Westerners traveling to South America specifically to participate in Ayahuasca ceremonies facilitated by Indigenous shamans, often organised in healing centres by Westerners. The largest movement was towards the Peruvian Amazon, where there had been connections growing with the native *Shapibo* people who had become famous for their *curandeiro* (healer) practices of Ayahuasca ceremony. To this day there is a large trail of Westerners seeking this healing and spiritual development and Ayahuasca tourism is booming, with countless healing centres being established across the Peruvian jungles and into the mountains in places like Cuzco and the Sacred Valley. In the early 1990s the groundbreaking work of Argentinian psychologist Silvia Polivoy began, with the first retreats for Westerners being run outside of Iquitos in the Peruvian Amazon. Silvia's work was complimented by many psychologists, researchers, artists and philosophers. She was also working closely with Pablo Amaringo, who had become popular through his visionary artworks depicting the Ayahuasca *miração* (visionary field) with all the colours and spiritual beings of the astral forest. This style of retreat, with a focus on catering for Westerners, has become widely popularised across South America and around the world. By the 2000s a movement began beyond Peru and into the West, including to the US, Europe and Australia, of Ayahuasca ceremonies and retreats being held with adaptations of the Peruvian movement and often based upon the teachings and practices of the Indigenous Amazonians.

The popularity of Ayahuasca was growing fast by this time and this movement out of Peru spawned many new forms of Ayahuasca use, in a variety of forms. The pace and landscape of this development outside of the native traditions of the Indigenous cultures of the Amazon also led to the phenomenon of people and groups who had no formal training, and in many cases had not even been to South America, taking it upon themselves to start serving Ayahuasca, leading to an increasing call for sensitivity in the face of safety and cultural appropriation. This also led to a movement of Ayahuasca 'hacks' and 'cowboys/girls' running ceremonies without connection to the ancestry and traditions of the sacred brew, resulting, in many cases, in a lowering of the quality of the experience due to a lack of knowledge and wisdom held and transmitted by the ancient Amazonian cultures, and often without the humbling of community and initiatory rites.

By the late 2010s, a series of world Ayahuasca conferences were held and a big call was made by the Indigenous peoples of the Amazon to have their culture, identity and practices be honoured; a new movement towards ethical and culturally respectful use of Ayahuasca was initiated. In recent years Ayahuasca has become so popular that many documentaries, films, books, art installations, conferences and festivals dedicated to it have appeared all over the world. In Brazil, Ayahuasca has become a mainstream topic on television and other media, where even in daytime television novellas (soap operas), it makes appearances as a cultural icon.

Brazil is one of the quintessential Ayahuasca countries, both because of the shamanic traditions of its Indigenous peoples reaching the cities, and because of the country having three traditional Ayahuasca churches: the União do Vegetal, the Santo Daime and the Barquinha. In addition, there has been an intense development of neo-shamanic Ayahuasca approaches. — Global Ayahuasca Consumption Report, ICEERS.

Brazil has seen a very different evolution of modern Ayahuasca practice and culture which began to emerge from the late 1920s and which continues to evolve. The Santo Daime, União do Vegetal (UDV) and Barquinha Ayahuasca religions grew strong and became widespread across Brazil by the 1960s, and by the 1980s and 1990s the first Brazilian Santo Daime churches began to appear in Europe, starting in Spain and The Netherlands. The movement of Ayahuasca out of Peru and other countries like Columbia and Equador developed from Indigenous shamanic practices and moved around the world without regulation, in many cases without Indigenous recognition. The Brazilian movement saw the development of strong practices, doctrines, culture and ethics governing the way that Ayahuasca rituals are held, with a strong focus on developing community, including support structures and associated healing practices. Whilst the Western influence into Peru brought a focus on the healing, psychology and psychedelic experience of Ayahuasca, in Brazil there was a much stronger emphasis on the spirituality, culture and religious practice of Ayahuasca ceremony and the development of protocols that today have developed into a rich and diverse Ayahuasca community spanning into mainstream Brazilian culture. Brazil has multiple sacramental churches in all of the major cities and regions across the country, some of which conduct regular ceremonies with hundreds of practitioners. Amongst the churches they have other names for Ayahuasca that reflect their culture and spiritual constellations. In Brazil, with the guidance and ethical support of this Ayahuasca culture, in recent years several Indigenous groups have begun travelling the country and now around the world, sharing traditional culture and Ayahuasca shamanism. The strong culture developed in Brazil by the religious movements has seen the development of a sacred alliance with the Indigenous peoples, where their culture is preserved and respected and integrated with modern forms of practice in a spirit of honouring and unity.

In 2023 the International Centre for Entheogenic Education, Research and Service (ICEERS) presented a preliminary report entitled *Ayahuasca Global Consumption and Deaths Reported*. The data revealed in this report shows that up to 2019 more than 4.2 million people around the world had drunk Ayahuasca at least once, including 123,000 people in Australia and New Zealand. ICEERS also reported that up to 2019 there were over 200 Ayahuasca retreat centres worldwide. This ICEERS report is limited in its scope and based on extrapolated data where in some cases estimations have been made, while many countries are also not represented. It is likely that these numbers are a conservative estimate and the number of drinkers worldwide is much higher. I am including this data here as an indication of the growth and scope of Ayahuasca use around the world.

We are currently at an exciting moment in the history of the planet, despite the challenges of what seems to be an ever-present darkness of domination and control creating the sickness of war, disease, poverty and suffering through greed and the misuse of power. From the shamanic view this is merely a sickness that we are collectively experiencing and it provides a collective challenge to overcome and to inspire a conscious reconnection of ourselves to the forces of nature and Spirit — where the true remedy to these conditions lies. Fighting against, or arguing with, the sick minds of those in control of this global mess is a waste of time and akin to attempting to rebuild our reality with the same thinking that has created these painful limitations in the first place. Shamanism and Ayahuasca help us to untangle ourselves and our minds from the traps and tricks within the shadows of the sickness affecting humanity. It is easy to become disheartened and diseased when our attention lies on the problems at hand, whilst we live in a low-vibrational energetic swamp. Energy and excitement comes when we take on the shamanic view and see that there is so much remedy available to us on the planet right now. Never in the history of civilisational advance has there been such access to ancient wisdom, spiritual and cosmic forces, natural medicines, useful technologies and an ever-growing momentum of communities joining forces, healing together and taking lives into our own hands. People are waking up, becoming healthy and working together to co-create a new Dreaming. This evolution is a spiritual one. It is not occurring through manipulating the material world to 'fix' the imbalances or manipulate people through political ideology, discourse or argument, but through realising that we are the creators with the power in our own minds, hands and intentions.

Of course there is nothing new in the discovery of shamanic science and awareness. Throughout history this has been at the heart of all Indigenous cultures and has been a great contributor in the evolution and longevity of human life on Earth. Researchers such as Terrence McKenna and Graham Hancock talk of the development of human consciousness through our ancestors' ingestion of psilocybin and other psychedelic plants. Anthropologist Erika Bourguignon did an extensive study of 488 societies and found that 90% of them had institutionalised ways of entering into an altered state of consciousness.

> *Trance and altered states of consciousness are deeply embedded in cultural practices, often serving as a means of reinforcing social norms, expressing collective identity, or facilitating communication with the divine or spiritual realm. The methods by which individuals enter into trance are typically shaped by the expectations and traditions of their society.* — Erika Bourguignon, 'Religion, Altered States of Consciousness, and Social Change'.

After thousands of years of genetic and spiritual evolution as a result of humanity's accessing of altered states, there is an innate and powerful instinct within us to commune with the Divine in these ways. Due to the repression of traditional and Indigenous cultures and practices by modern society, this innate drive has manifested in humans through the discovery of other ways of accessing altered states, without the cultural and institutional containers set out to support a safe and effective journey of conscious expansion. People have turned to alcohol and other substances that are misused and abused. There remains, however, the memory in our souls and the guidance of our ancestors to lead us back inevitably to the original Dream and the natural state of our humanity. Despite the repressive controls of the dominator culture of society, the awakening is happening at pace — some may refer to this as a 'quickening'. As society concocts new and elaborate ways to use technology for the control of people, this serves to inspire a stronger instinct in humanity to reconnect spiritually, thus accelerating a global awakening. It makes sense that people with addictions such as alcoholism are drawn to plant medicines such as Ayahuasca not only for healing, but also to serve and honour the sacred traditions of shamanic awareness, in healthier and more effective ways. Ayahuasca ceremony and community culture support a retraining of the human nervous system back to its natural state.

Through this shamanic renaissance and great awakening of humanity we are realising a new Dream for the planet, one that we don't need to manipulate or strategise in order to make happen, but one that already exists as the Dream of the Earth. A Dream where we clear our minds of ambition, fear and control, and naturally align ourselves to the force of Great Spirit that flows through us all and through all things. In that flow is the remedy for our personal life purpose, guidance and direction from Spirit, and our unity in a sacred alliance with Country and Dreaming. The remedy for the human condition is shamanic in nature and Ayahuasca plays a role in this planetary unfolding. I am personally grateful beyond words for its influence in my life and I have seen it bring about so much healing and transformation in so many people. It is not easy living in a society full of prejudice, fear and persecution towards shamanic realities. My faith in creation and Spirit has only strengthened along this path and this has allowed me to traverse the immense challenges this shamanic journey has confronted me with. It has taught me to always be more humble and available to Spirit so that I may continue to be of service in this awakening and the newly emerging planetary Dream. What an adventure and what a blessing.

CHAPTER 4

Way of the Hummingbird

In this chapter I will explore the different forms and lineages of spiritual culture and practices that I have experienced which inform my own beliefs, practice and work with the sacrament Ayahuasca. It has been more than 22 years since I first consecrated the sacred brew in the Brazilian Amazon, just outside of the city of Manaus in the state of Amazonas. As I mentioned in previous chapters, there is a great diversity of culture, practices and experiences that one may have with Ayahuasca and every experience will be unique to each person.

Through my years of experience I have cultivated an astral garden of practices, prayers, intentions and alliances with spiritual beings and animal totems. Some of these spiritual alliances have been formed through my relationships with teachings directly from the land and the nature of different places, such as the Amazon and with different tribes and their ancestors, as well as with different spiritual lineages such as the Santo Daime and Umbanda religions. Over these 22 years I have dedicated myself to this spiritual study and to tending this astral garden. I have integrated these alliances formed over the years and in hundreds of ceremonies including with my ancestors and the teachings from other cultures such as Scottish Celtic and Aboriginal Australia. This 'spiritual gardening' has been my dedicated focus during these years and what has emerged is a unified constellation of spiritual beings and realms that I am able to commune and work with, where Ayahuasca is sometimes the thread weaving them all together and where I am able to gather strength and knowledge of myself and support others with their own self-awareness, healing and spiritual development.

My guides and spiritual 'team' may be defined in three groupings for the purposes of attempting to explain my work. There are the beings from Country and the forest: they may be animal or insect spirits, they may also be spiritual beings who have never been physically incarnated, and they may also be the spirits of shamans, either living or deceased. In Brazil these spiritual beings from the land are known as *caboclos*. The second group are the forces of nature: the wind, the waters, the rocks, the fire, the plants, the forces of beauty and of light and shadows which all have relationships with each other and which are in a constant state of sacred dance in harmony with the Earth and the cosmos so that when we are in alignment with them, they create a harmony within us as well. The final grouping is the angels and saints: celestial beings that are less connected to the earthly realms and offer teachings, healing and guidance from higher vibrations of light and love. Some of these beings are familiar to many through Christianity and other religions, whilst some are Star Elders — ancestors and masters from other stars and other parts of the galaxy.

It would be a big undertaking to include descriptions of these entities and their roles and functions in more detail here; some are defined later in this chapter and the rest, perhaps, will be in another book. This chapter will be about the specific lineages and teachings that have had a great influence on me and my work and about my journey of meeting and integrating guides, spirits and natural forces. These lineages are mostly accessible for everyone too, and perhaps there is some inspiration here to be gained, as you may find yourself called in one direction or another relative to a path with Ayahuasca or shamanism. There are also many other paths and lineages. By not mentioning them I am not discarding them. I will reserve this book for talking about the lines, cultures and practices that I have studied and have direct personal experiences with.

Way of the Hummingbird, Lore Solaris, Acrylic on Canvas

I have cultivated my work with Ayahuasca over many years, and whilst I have drawn upon many teachers, practices and cultures, my way is unique to me. I consider my path with Ayahuasca the 'Way of the Hummingbird'. In Brazil, the name for hummingbird is *beija-flor* which translates as 'flower kiss'. Hummingbirds are a common *totem* (spiritual force) for Ayahuasca across Brazil and the Americas. To me, hummingbirds have a graceful beauty that is subtle yet dynamic, powerful and magical. In this sense, hummingbirds represent the magical flight of a shamanic journey: they can hover and dart around, changing directions suddenly and sharply, whilst their wings move so fast they can't be seen, though they can be heard as a vibrational hum. This magical flight may also represent the power of transformation that Ayahuasca gives to us. It moves in mysterious ways whilst the colourful radiant wings and feathers of the beija-flor are like the colours in the visions of the miração. Hummingbirds are also very busy workers, as they spend their whole day humming around kissing flowers to taste the nectar of the garden's beauty. Ayahuasca also puts us to work on a great task of personal development that is difficult. It's not for the faint hearted. You need to be ready to face your shadows, the depths of your pain and your soul and learn to correct yourself, with humility, into alignment and harmony with Nature and Great Spirit. This is a challenging yet worthy endeavour, and when we undertake it we can learn to fly like the hummingbird gracefully through the garden of life, whilst gathering the nectar in our lives and being free in a constant state of spiritual transformation, just as we as humans were designed to be.

Deep in my heart
There's a place where I go
Where the hummingbird flies
and a gentle wind blows

How I honour your grace
and amaze at your beauty
Hummingbird show me your way
Show me your ways

Hummingbird, hummingbird
Teach me to live
So I can surrender to grace
Hummingbird, hummingbird
Show me my wings
So I can fly on my way (fly all the way)

Fly me home
On the wings of the hummingbird
Lead me deeper
Into that place in my heart

Fly me home
On the wings of the hummingbird
With infinite love
And eyes of affection
Hummingbird teach me the way (show me the way)

—*Way of the Hummingbird,* Kiavanni Keehan.

The nature of my ceremonial work with Ayahuasca is as community prayer which supports people in spiritual reconnection with the Earth in order to awaken ourselves back into the garden of beauty that manifests as being truly alive on this wonderful planet. So we may embody and honour our sacred role as custodians of the Earth. Finding self-discipline through spiritual practice reconnects us and gives us the freedom to be happy and joyful in peace and love. This, I believe, is our true nature. This reconnection is where healing happens and our journey as true humans begins. In 2022 my work with Ayahuasca was consecrated by Spirit, manifesting as a living, spiritual point of light and given the name '*Estrela da Ciranda,*' (Star of the Ciranda). It was also given a symbol: a rainbow hummingbird with a six-pointed star representing harmony, balance and unity through ceremony — a sacred alliance of Spirit and the physical Earth.

Connection to Country

An Australian First Nations teacher of the Bunjalung people told me a story many years go about our ancestors. He shared that the animals are our ancestors, that we as humans are the most complex and most evolved of all the species, that when we trace back through evolution we see the genetics of humanity goes back through all the animal species to the dinosaurs and all the way back to microbes and the first spark of life. In this way, Indigenous peoples of the world see that all the animals, and in fact all the beings of the earth, be they animals, trees, plants, fungi, bacteria, insects, even rocks, crystals or sand, are all our relations. With this teaching comes the great respect that we must learn to show our planet. We live amongst our ancestors and their teachings are always available to us. All we need to do to access their teachings and blessings is to learn how to listen deeply. Miriam-Rose Ungunmerr of the Australian Ngangikurungkurr people explains this from the Indigenous worldview:

What I want to talk about is another special quality of my people. I believe it is the most important. It is our most unique gift. It is perhaps the greatest gift we can give to our fellow Australians. In our language this quality is called 'dadirri'. It is inner, deep listening and quiet, still awareness.

Dadirri recognises the deep spring that is inside us. We call on it and it calls to us. This is the gift that Australia is thirsting for. It is something like what you call 'contemplation'.

When I experience dadirri, I am made whole again. I can sit on the riverbank or walk through the trees; even if someone close to me has passed away, I can find my peace in this silent awareness. There is no need of words. A big part of dadirri is listening.

The contemplative way of dadirri spreads over our whole life. It renews us and brings us peace. It makes us feel whole again ...

In our Aboriginal way, we learnt to listen from our earliest days. We could not live good and useful lives unless we listened. This was the normal way for us to learn – not by asking questions. We learnt by watching and listening, waiting and then acting. Our people have passed on this way of listening for over 40,000 years ...

There is no need to reflect too much and to do a lot of thinking. It is just being aware.

My people are not threatened by silence. They are completely at home in it. They have lived for thousands of years with Nature's quietness. My people today recognise and experience in this quietness the great Life-Giving Spirit, the Father of us all. It is easy for me to experience God's presence. When I am out hunting, when I am in the bush, among the trees, on a hill or by a billabong, these are the times when I can simply be in God's presence. My people have been so aware of Nature. It is natural that we will feel close to the Creator.

Australian Indigenous teachings talk about the different animals in the Dreaming of the land that has become known as Australia and how they relate to each other, and how each of the nations relate to their animal ancestors and the different lineages of these ancestors. In Australia, it is common amongst many Indigenous nations to identify with either 'saltwater' or 'freshwater' groupings or clans of animal ancestors or totems. In Australian Indigenous cultures, animal totems hold deep cultural, spiritual and social significance. Totems are part of the complex belief systems of the Dreamtime (or Dreaming), which explains the origins of life, the land, and the laws that govern the relationships between all living things and the stories and wisdom that weave them all together. Each Indigenous group has its own specific beliefs and practices regarding totems, often tied to their environment, clans and tribal laws. Totems represent specific animals that possess particular qualities, powers and lessons that influence human life. The concept of animal totems embodies respect, kinship and responsibility towards the Earth and its beings.

It is common in most traditional forms of shamanism to work with totem animals, plants and other forces of nature. It is also common for Indigenous peoples to be born into a totemic relationship with one or more animals. These animals are seen as a manifestation of the peoples' ancestors and provide a sense of identity and belonging throughout their lives. Individuals often inherit their totem based on their family lineage, region or clan affiliations.

Spiritually we may find ourselves in some kind of relationship with specific animals at different times in our lives, in dreams and visions, or even at different moments throughout the day. This spiritual connection can give us energy and bring the qualities and teachings of the totem into our being and into our lives. Many people recount to me their experiences of uncanny situations and synchronicities where a particular animal is making itself present in their lives and, more specifically, in their Ayahuasca visions. This is very common and to those with a shamanic awareness also holds great meaning. It offers us an opportunity to see this animal as a spiritual ally, perhaps one that is bringing a message or an invitation for greater connection so that we may study and integrate its qualities. For example, the eagle is a very powerful and majestic animal; it can often spend a long time on its own and can see much of what is going on below that other animals may not be aware of, as it has greater vision than most. Eagles may be serenely and silently gliding on the wind whilst maintaining a sharp focus for hunting some prey upon the ground. The lonely, silent, deeply focused attention of the eagle eventually transforms into a lightning-fast dive to catch its prey, where it must remain undistracted and razor sharp to make sure that it not only wins its prey but survives such a risky manoeuvre. So we might see that eagle people have sharp vision, will benefit from time alone where they can cultivate their personal view, and will be able to act when they are fully present and be able to understand their 'prey', which may be a goal to achieve. This is just one example of how we can work with our totems. Many people during their Ayahuasca experiences, even when these are outside of the jungle, have distinct visions and encounters with Amazonian animals such as jaguars, snakes, hummingbirds, monkeys, butterflies and others.

Indigenous Dreaming stories

Earlier, I recounted the story of the *jiboia*, or the boa constrictor snake that is a totem for the Huni Kuin and many other Amazonian native peoples. The jiboia represents ancient wisdom and transformation.

The snake sheds its skin as it grows, which can be an uncomfortable experience, and during the shedding process it is in a vulnerable situation and has to be patient through the process. This relates to the process we undergo during Ayahuasca healing, as we are confronted with our behaviours and wounds and fears and thoughts that don't serve us, and we feel the pain in acknowledging our old emotional, physical or spiritual burdens which may have caused us much pain. In reliving this pain through an Ayahuasca experience we learn the consequences of being out of alignment with our higher truth, and perhaps see what it is to be living a life that is based on the desires of the ego, out of fear either for protection or avoidance of embracing our true selves. Just as the jiboia slides silently through the forest, it also guides us between the material and physical worlds through our Ayahuasca experiences. When we are reborn through the Ayahuasca processes we find a new sense of freedom and growth which, if we choose to embrace it, can lead to a much healthier and more fulfilling life.

The Huni Kuin, Yawanawá and Shipibo peoples I have had the opportunity to spend time with in the Amazon each work very consciously with the spirits of the forest, including the animal totems. The experienced pajés will have songs they use to call the spirit of these totems into the miração of the Ayahuasca. When they call in the force of these totems they are also working with specific intentions to invoke the spiritual qualities of these animals to support the Ayahuasca experience, bringing healing, protection, wisdom and guidance. They may also call in other beings such as ancestors, the spirits of different plants, forces of nature such as fire and wind, and even celestial bodies such as the sun, moon and stars.

In 2016, I was contacted by Trevor, an Australian First Nations man from the Yolngu people of Arnhem Land who had seen my artwork and heard of the work I was doing with Ayahuasca in Australia. We chatted for a year or so over social media and he told me of his work as an artist and as a teacher of natural lore. He told me he was asked by his Elders to pass on sacred knowledge that had been kept secret from the *balanda* (white people) and that now was the time to start sharing this knowledge, as there were enough people awakening and it was important to pass on the knowledge for the sake of the healing of the planet. He was travelling around Australia tracking *songlines*, which is how Indigenous people refer to ley-lines, or electromagnetic lines of force that connect powerful points of land all across the world. The songlines also transmit currents of the Dreaming, connecting history and ancestral knowledge. His intention was to track down sacred sites that hold power and significant energies which are crucial for the balance of the Earth. Songlines and their Dreaming carry ancestral story lines that connect all the Indigenous nations through currents of electromagnetic force. They also intersect in places that are considered sacred due to the energy and potential they convey. Many of these places have been hidden or left dormant for many years, as the native peoples who cared for them and sang and danced their Dreaming into reality had long since been killed off or had left the areas due to land theft and the displacement caused by colonialism. Eventually Trevor's work with songlines wove through me and into the Amazon. I share more of this in the chapter 'High Aim in the Upper Amazon'.

I have always been interested in the stories of Country that have been held sacred for thousands of years by the Indigenous peoples. Many of these stories talk of ancestral creator beings that moved around the country, gifting the people with knowledge, language and mythology, creating a rich tapestry of interconnected Dreaming. Traditionally the native people would go *walkabout* (travel through Country) along these songlines, listening deeply to the land, communicating with the people and the animals and keeping the knowledge and connection alive in their culture and in their spiritual awareness. When I met this teacher of ancient knowledge he took a group of us to a scared place just outside of Sydney and told us stories and taught us some of the concepts of natural lore. We talked a little about Ayahuasca and he seemed to know a lot about its nature and benefits; he mentioned to me that he would like to drink it, although he said it wouldn't affect him much because he already had the awareness that it gives. From everything I had experienced with him, I believed him. Over the years I have also had very enlightening conversations with Elders who have shared the same things, and it has been a great honour to have the presence of Elders and other First Nations leaders at my ceremonies to share their culture, wisdom and blessings. I have learned many things in sharing sacred medicine and ceremonies originating from South America with Australian First Nations peoples, and even though many of the customs and totems are different, the shamanic awareness and knowledge of natural law is universal.

Trevor told me the time had come: that humanity was awakening and the Earth needed healing and that it was time to share the ancient wisdom. He spoke of a 'new Dreaming' emerging — one that would weave Indigenous wisdom into the heart of human collective consciousness. Eventually he gave me a message to take to the Indigenous peoples of the Amazon.

Later that year, I was invited to visit a Huni Kuin village in the Brazilian Amazon, and was guided there by a mysterious convergence of synchronicities. A friend and I embarked on this journey on the wings of Spirit, into the mysteries of the forest. This was my fourth journey into the forest, but it carried a different weight. On the night of the full moon, we arrived in Alta-Mira (High Aim) and walked straight into ceremony. It was there, in the presence of *Caçique* (chief) Txaná Ixã and the sacred brew of Nixi Pãe, that I shared the message my Yolngu friend had asked me to carry. Their nods and their knowing smiles made it clear they understood. In that moment, I saw the songlines of the jiboia and the Rainbow Serpent weaving together — an unfolding within a new Dreaming of the Whole Earth.

That journey was a continuation and deepening of a path that bridged continents, cultures and cosmologies. It continues to be an immense honour to share ceremonies with Indigenous Australians, learning from their wisdom and witnessing the universal nature of shamanic awareness. Weaving Dreaming and cosmologies together through music and ceremony. The customs may differ, but the songlines connect us all.

Over the years whilst living and travelling in Brazil and also in my meditations and in Ayahuasca visions I had heard stories about the spiritual connection between South America and Australia. In that moment in Alta-Mira I was being initiated deeper into my role in this new Dreaming. I was also being shown by Great Spirit how the teachings of shamanism are so deeply mysterious and yet can never be invented by the human mind or ambition, and that even on opposite sides of the planet, in Country so vastly different in nature and culture, we can understand each other through profound connection to the spiritual world and alignment through universal natural law.

> *Forest sounds awaken with their calling*
> *First light, time of the morning*
> *A new day is over the horizon*
> *A new love inside of me is rising*
>
> *The ancient ones sitting by the river*
> *Fire burns, singing up creation*
> *Insects tweet, buzzing their vibration*
> *Spirit speaks but never did she mention ...*
>
> *Sometimes we flow with the waters*
> *Sometimes we dance in the fire*
> *Sometimes we float on the breeze*
> *Sometimes we walk on the land*
> *These songlines dreaming our creation*
>
> — *Songlines*, Lore Solaris.

The Queen of the Forest and the Saint of Giving

> *Each living pulsation of the forest produces a profound therapeutic effect on the people connected to it. This living connection anticipates the felicity that will be encountered living in the new era, as human consciousness surpasses human destructiveness. Can we actualise a spiritual community that lives in harmony*

with the forest, with the understanding that the forest is the earthly manifestation of our Celestial Mother? It was no accident that Mestre Irineu received the doctrine of the Daime from the Queen of the Forest. — Alex Polari de Alverga, *The Religion of Ayahuasca.*

In 1912, Raimundo Irineu Serra arrived in the frontier Amazonian state of Acre. He was a 6'5" (195cm) tall black man of African descent who had travelled from his home state of Maranhão in the north looking for work in the south, where he had heard there was rubber harvesting. He came from a humble family who were the descendants of slaves who had lived solely through cultivating the land. It is said that in his childhood he chose to follow his African heritage in customs and traditions, and during his adolescent years he became restless and left his homeland in search of opportunities in other parts of Brazil, despite his inability to read or write. Eventually his cousins invited him to join them in Acre.

Mestre Irineu, Acre, Brazil

After arriving in Acre he reconnected with his cousins who told him stories of some *caboclos* (natives from the forest) they had been visiting and drinking Ayahuasca with. It is said that the caboclos they were visiting were in Peru and were descendants of the Incas. His two cousins invited him to visit these caboclos to drink the magical tea they had been telling him about and he agreed to go. If he were to think the tea was good, he would then attempt to take it back to his people in Maranhão. During these times very few people outside of native Amazonians had experienced Ayahuasca. The natives were using it for hunting, fishing, medicine and spiritual work, and there had been a handful of white people who had come to know the sacrament. This time with Irineu there was a consecration with the African race, thus uniting the races of the population of Brazil within the realm of Ayahuasca.

On his third night with Ayahuasca, Irineu had his first spiritual encounter with a being that he came to know as the 'Queen of the Forest'. This spiritual being tested his faith within the miração he was experiencing and she taught him through visions beyond what had been seen before. The sacrament had a particular intention in giving him these visions which were also beyond what had been experienced by the native people of the region. As a simple man who had gone to meet the sacrament in a humble way, he commenced a relationship with it that gifted him not only the secrets, beauty and mystery of the forest, but also a level of responsibility and work that he could never have imagined. This has since led to the development of a large global movement of people dedicated to studying the teachings of this mystery. The teachings of *Mestre* (master) *Irineu* have greatly influenced me, my work and my life. I am forever grateful to him and his path of faith and courage, which has inspired me to maintain firmness on my own path, to surrender to the mystery of life and to always trust in my connection to Great Spirit.

The divine spiritual being the Queen of the Forest began instructing Irineu, from the beginning giving him hymns that became the foundation of the doctrine and teachings of the Santo Daime religion. He accepted the mission that was being gifted to him on the condition that it would be of benefit to his people. He asked the Queen of the Forest to make him a great healer, and she agreed on the condition that he not use this for personal profit. This led him on a personal quest of deep spiritual studies, healing and perfecting himself through self-discipline and evolution, a process which has come to be known as 'material destination' in the Santo Daime.

The story of Mestre Irineu's studies in the Amazon is similar to the way in which the Huni Kuin people were teaching me about how they acquired their knowledge. When I was living amongst them in the forest of Acre, I would often ask them, 'How did you learn to do this or that?' or 'Where did you learn that song?' They would always reply to these kinds of questions with: 'We learn from the Forest.' What we can learn from the story of Mestre Irineu is that there was no intermediary in his spiritual journey. There was nobody telling him what to do or how to interpret his miração; he followed a shamanic path of learning directly from Nature, he met and nurtured his relationship with a divine spiritual being that guided him throughout his life. He was given so much when he surrendered to the mystery of the forest.

The doctrine that flows through the Santo Daime is a living branch of contemporary Christianity, one in which the light of Christ is not sought through external authority but awakened within the soul of each practitioner. The Daime/Ayahuasca calls us to know ourselves, to enter the sacred current of self-realisation through the miração, and to perceive that the divine spark we seek is the very essence of our being. This is the Christic gnosis spoken of in the early mystical traditions: the recognition that we are not apart from divinity, but are expressions of it. In this way, the Daime inspires us to find the light of Christ within our own hearts, aligning deeply with the Gnostic teaching found in the *Gospel of Thomas*, where Jesus said: 'If those who lead you say to you, "See, the kingdom is in the sky," then the birds of the sky will precede you. If they say, "It is in the sea," then the fish will precede you. Rather, the kingdom is inside you and it is outside you. When you know yourselves, then you will be known, and you will understand that you are children of the living Father.' (*Gospel of Thomas, Saying 3*). Through this revelation the path of the Daime becomes a return to our own divine nature — a sacramental way of remembering that Christ is not merely a figure of history, but the living consciousness awakening within all who dare to see through the forest of their own hearts.

> *Living beings of the forest*
> *Come to illuminate me*
> *I'm here, I'm singing*
> *I'm open to heal myself*
>
> *The forest brings mystery*
> *And we ask for protection*
> *Our fears go away*
> *and our hearts will be opening*
>
> *All light is revealing*
> *We realise that all is love*
> *The clarity arrives*
> *and now I know that I can fly*
>
> — Seres Vivos da Floresta, Giti Bond.

Ayahuasca revealed many secrets to Irineu. At times this came in great detail with regard to his need for the personal discipline required in order to do the spiritual work with the sacrament. He was taught the correct physical alignment and condition required. This also included physical labour in the forest and work with the plants. Much of this was received as hymns which are now foundational teachings in the doctrine of Santo Daime. He came to accept that his life and path was now as a student of nature and through Ayahuasca, later to become known as *Daime*. He learned to embody the peace, love and serenity of the sacred elements such as the sun, moon, earth, wind, fire and water.

After some years of study, Mestre Irineu went on to form the first known Ayahuasca centre. There they began doing Daime 'works' (Ayahuasca/Daime ceremonies are often referred to as 'works' in Brazil), but the sacrament and their practices began to suffer from social persecution, with other church groups calling for government and police harassment and intimidation. He was forced to leave the organisation and it closed down. Following this, he began working for the Border Commission for Acre, a place that would go on to become famous around the world for the spiritual mission of Ayahuasca. Acre has attracted many people: at first it was those wishing to find the Santo Daime and more recently it has been people visiting the native tribes of the Huni Kuin, Yawanawá, Ashaninka, Kuntanawá and many others in a region richly coloured by a great diversity of native languages, music, culture and traditions. Over the years Mestre Irineu became involved in the military, politics and administration, and he was well known for his service to the community in many different ways throughout the state.

After more than 20 years of cultivating personal discipline and deep studies in the mysteries of the forest, Mestre Irineu went on to form a group of spiritual workers who began implementing the doctrine of the Santo Daime — the name given to Ayahuasca by Irineu which translates as 'saint give'. It is claimed this name was given to inspire the people to honour what is given to us through the sacrament, from Great Spirit, from the forest. *Give me strength, give me faith, give me love, give me knowledge, give me power, give me spiritual nourishment.* The early works of the Daime were primarily a type of ceremony and were known as 'concentrations' which carried the intention of healing others in need.

The early formation of the practices of Santo Daime occurred during this period but this was not without its challenges. Mestre Irineu faced financial challenges in doing the work and strong persecution due to social and religious prejudice. Over the following decades, Mestre Irineu formed alliances with other esoteric spiritual groups and created other official organisations which collaborated to end the prejudice and provide a legal framework for the spiritual practices of the Santo Daime to be accepted in Brazil. It is said that in the 1940s a group of men from the government came to Acre and drank the Daime with Irineu and his group then left with hugs and declarations of brotherhood in understanding of the divine nature of the group's work. Santo Daime churches continued to be persecuted in Brazil and beyond, with governments interfering in their spiritual work in other countries such as the US and The Netherlands, as well as recently in New South Wales, Australia.

There were also said to be times in the development of the Santo Daime with Mestre Irineu where he would close down 'works' and refuse to participate due to the politics of the church community. He encouraged people to work things out themselves in alignment with the teachings of the Daime which show us to become self-responsible and develop firmness and personal discipline. The integration of the spiritual work required on the path of the Daime, and in all Ayahuasca practices, is fundamental to the integrity of those practices. From the early days of the Santo Daime movement we can see that human relations are one of the most challenging areas for this integration. In my experience this shows how important it is for each one on this path and within a movement to practise self-responsibility. It is very easy to be distracted on this path and to be victimised by others along the way. Where one person may be dedicated to their practice and discipline, another may not be so dedicated, and this is where a weakness in the community may occur. One of the teachings of the Daime is that of fraternity, where we are all responsible for keeping each other accountable, and this is one of the very valuable teachings in the doctrine of the Santo Daime, where community becomes supportive in keeping cohesion and focus on the true work.

> *Harmony, truth and forgiveness*
> *Are the three points*
> *Securing this union*
> *I ask my brothers and sisters*
> *Pay attention*
> *The master of the astral*
> *Is watching the session*
>
> — *Harmonia, Verdade e Perdão*, Vera Frôes.

Santo Daime works are typically held as a group prayer, with all the participants singing and holding space together. The hymns that contain the richness of the teachings of the doctrine are amplified within the consciousness of the group and the intentions of them are reflected in the quality of the miração. In the Daime tradition each participant is encouraged to learn the hymns and take on an equal role in supporting the whole ceremony. This collective prayer may be seen as a kind of 'group shamanism' and has gone on to be widely adopted by many groups throughout Brazil. It's also the form of practice that my own ceremonies embody. This form of practice is distinct from the practices that became popularised as Ayahuasca culture, adopted from the *curandeiros* (healers) of Peru. The difference here being that the large movement of people visiting Peru are seeking healing from the curandeiro shamans who, for the most part, conduct their ceremonies in the dark with the participants sitting or lying down alone while the shaman sings and does their healing work. Whilst this form of working in traditional Ayahuasca healing ways can be very effective, these maestro shamans and their *icaros* (Ayahuasca chants) have very powerful abilities to heal people through sound and visions with often very precise spiritual 'surgery'. Whilst the participants of these healings may experience deep personal revelations and powerful cleansing, spiritually, physically, mentally and emotionally, there is also a phenomenon where they return to their lives in the Western world and then relapse back into their old patterns without community or people around them who can understand what they have gone through and support them. This is one of the many reasons I became more attracted to the communal form of practice with Ayahuasca that is widespread throughout Brazil and why I have always worked towards building community around the work I have done with Ayahuasca. Mestre Irineu and the ongoing work over 100 years of the Santo Daime movement has been dedicated to developing a life system for individuals within a community learning to live together in love and harmony with nature. In this teaching that Mestre Irineu has inspired so many with, we are encouraged to develop ourselves and our lives in presence as reflections of the beauty and truth shown to us in the miração.

Music is a vital aspect of the work of the Daime. The hymns transmit beautiful truths and are typically received directly from the divine connection to Spirit through the miração. The hymns convey the messages from the forest and their use is central to ceremonies, where they support participants to navigate the spiritual realms and transformative effect of the Daime. In the 1950s, Daniel Pereira de Mato, who went on to found the Barquinha Ayahuasca religion, originally joined the school of Mestre Irineu and introduced the gift of music, developing the hymns with masterful chords and harmonies that reflected the beauty of the miração. Around this time instruments such as guitars and the maracá (percussive shaker) also began to be used to embellish the works. The study of music then became another aspect of the work and discipline of the Daime adepts. De Mato, who had also studied and practised *Umbanda* (an Afro-Brazilian spiritual movement) initially became a student of Mestre Irineu and they were also great friends before he eventually went on to create his own church which became known as *Barquinha* (little boat), brought its own unique colours and teachings, and is now also practised throughout Brazil.

Many great teachers have studied under Mestre Irineu and gone on to become leaders in the Daime movement. Some stayed true to the original church and its doctrine while others diverged and formed variations and other lineages like branches of a great tree. In 1965, Padrinho Sebastião Mota de Melo met Mestre Irineu. This meeting marked a significant turning point in Sebastião's spiritual journey, as he became a devoted follower of Mestre Irineu and later played a major role in expanding the Santo Daime movement. Padrinho Sebastião went on to establish his own branch of Santo Daime after Mestre Irineu's death, integrating his own visionary experiences, and this led to the broader spread of the religion beyond its initial Amazonian roots. Padrinho Sebastião had had contact with various spiritual entities in dreams and visions since he was a child and he went on to become a great 'medium' (receiver of healing spirits). He worked tirelessly to follow the doctrine and guidance he received from Mestre Irineu and his miração, including initiating the development of a large spiritual community living in the forest in Acre known as 'Mapiá'. Today there are hundreds of people living in this community and people travel from all over the world to study the spiritual work there. Many other churches were born all over Brazil from this movement, which has now expanded all over the world into many countries, including Australia. Many types of Daime works are practised in these churches, each with specific functions and intentions. The works are several hours long and are often experienced while sitting in silent concentration accompanied by the collective singing of hymns or through collectively performing simple dance movements in geometrical formation.

> *What is important is that I see you are happy. Soon you will find yourself, know who you are, and discover your mission. We are here for this, to help each other to discover who we are, to become men and women who are truly like Christ. Let's follow His road, isn't that it? It was He who opened the tollgate and left tracks for us to follow. I always say. "Whoever can follow, follow! Even crawling is worthwhile."* — Padrinho Sebastião.

Padrinho Sebastião, Acre, Brazil

The influence of Santo Daime goes far beyond the churches themselves, with a huge spiritual Ayahuasca movement throughout Brazil and the world, including here in Australia with our point of light *Estrela da Ciranda*. Ours is greatly influenced by the doctrine, teachings and spiritual guidance of Mestre Irineu and the Queen of the Forest, in particular embodying the sprit of fraternity, firmness in ourselves and with others, love, peace and harmony with Nature. I see the work that I have forged here in Australia as being an offshoot of the original teachings of Mestre Irineu, or a branch of the tree with the original teachings being the trunk of a great wisdom tree with its roots deep into the Amazon and the Earth.

Modern Santo Daime is a syncretic religion, combining aspects of the Amazonian and Afro-Brazilian religions and Christianity which believe that the spirit of Jesus Christ has returned from the forest through the divine sacrament they have come to know as Daime. The teachings of Christ, as seen through the Daime, include the precepts of love and forgiveness and also of suffering, where through our human condition we have the opportunity to take responsibility to transform both our own suffering and our fears, including the fear of death. This form of Christianity promotes self-realisation, where we learn that the 'kingdom of heaven' is within, that the essence of Christ is in our own hearts and that we must live that through example. As Alex Polari de Alverga says: 'We will not know truth until we lose the fear of knowing ourselves.' This renewal of Christianity offers a new understanding of redemption and hope for the spirituality of humanity as we move into the third millennium.

> *... the miração contains the model for a new state of being brought forth from an internal reality, revealing an ancient wisdom and foretelling a spiritual consciousness that is indispensable to our very survival on this planet. In this consciousness, our whole being beholds a mystery and shares a secret: Christ is risen among us in a new form! He left the sumptuous cathedrals and now He pulses in the heart of the Amazon forest. The "Green Hell" of the conquistadores has become the Green Paradise for those willing to enact the conquest for themselves. The forest is the Garden of*

Eden, wherein may be found both the tree of life and the forbidden fruit. — Alex Polari de Alverga, *The Religion of Ayahuasca.*

Flower of the waters
Of where it comes, to where it goes
I will do my cleansing
In the heart is my father

The abode of my Father
Is in the heart of the world
Where exists total love
And it has a profound secret

This profound secret
Is in all humanity
If all know themselves
Here inside of the truth

— *Flor das Àguas*, Mestre Irineu.

Union of the plants

Simplicity is the mark of a great man. — Ruy Fabiano.

Three great Ayahuasca religions have grown out of Brazil: Santo Daime, Barquinha and the *União do Vegetal* (Union of the Plants). The União do Vegetal (UDV) was formed in 1961 by José Gabriel da Costa, later known as 'Mestre Gabriel'. The UDV combines Christianity with Indigenous Amazonian shamanism and Afro-Brazilian spiritual traditions, forming a unique syncretic religion. Mestre Gabriel was born to a simple family with a hard-working ethic in the state of Bahia, Brazil. He travelled to the Amazon to seek work as a rubber tapper and while there he endured some great personal challenges which inspired him to develop his spirituality. In the 1950s he first met Ayahuasca whilst visiting Indigenous peoples in the region. During his time with the sacrament he began to receive spiritual insights and teachings that would form the foundation of the União do Vegetal. Mestre Gabriel officially founded the UDV in the state of Rondônia, Brazil with the intention of spreading a message of spiritual growth, self-awareness and harmony with nature. From its humble beginnings among small rural communities, the church gradually expanded throughout Brazil and later to other countries, including Australia.

UDV ceremonies, known as 'sessions of vegetal', are relatively formal and emphasise calmness, order and discipline. Participants are encouraged to reflect on their lives, engage in self-examination, and seek inner clarity, often through contemplation more so than entering into deep miração as in other traditions like Santo Daime. Music is not central to UDV sessions, which differ from other Ayahuasca practices that use hymns or chants to guide participants, although the master of the session may sing *chamados* (callings).

The UDV also places a strong emphasis on ethical behaviour, including honesty, integrity and respect for others. Members of the church are expected to carry the teachings of the UDV into their daily lives, fostering spiritual development not just in ritual but in everyday conduct. Whilst the practices and structure of the ceremonies of the UDV are quite different to those of Santo Daime, the teachings are fundamentally similar. Mestre Gabriel conveyed a message of personal transformation, unity and spiritual evolution. At its heart the UDV teaches that each individual is on a spiritual journey, and through the use of *Hoasca* (Ayahuasca) people can access deeper truths about themselves and the nature of existence.

The UDV blends Christian teachings from the Solomon lineage, such as the emphasis on love, forgiveness and salvation, with a broader, more universal spiritual philosophy. Members of the UDV believe in the immortality of the soul and in reincarnation, and they view Hoasca as a tool for enlightenment and moral refinement. One of the UDV's core tenets is the idea that spiritual evolution can be achieved through regular communion with the Vegetal (Ayahuasca), ethical living and service to others. The church encourages self-discipline, hard work and a commitment to helping others along their spiritual path.

Whilst my knowledge and experience of the UDV is not as deep as that of Santo Daime and the teachings of Mestre Irineu, I have great respect for the UDV's work and practices and for the dedication and devotion that the church and its members have towards a sense of fraternity amongst all of us who are in service to humanity, the planet and the protection of our divine sacrament. For the members of the UDV, the ethical and ecological cultivation and preparation of Hoasca is sacred. The church is extremely organised and structured, including through its organisational and legal frameworks, which allows it to maintain a healthy foundation for the practice of their spiritual work. In 2023 I was honoured to meet Mestre Nonato, a former leader of the UDV church who had left for personal reasons and was visiting Australia. I was impressed by the vitality and presence of this 80-year-old man, his wisdom and peace and the strong feeling of love emanating from him. My meeting with Mestre Nonato left me with a deep appreciation of the doctrine of simplicity. Lead a simple way of life, grounded in ethical principles and spiritual contemplation that allow us to develop a closer connection to the Divine without distraction, to cultivate peace within ourselves, and to contribute positively to our communities.

The intelligent and well-structured organisation of the church helped it through persecution and in legal battles over the use of Hoasca, particularly in the US, where the UDV won a significant Supreme Court case in 2006 (*Gonzales v. O Centro Espírita Beneficente União do Vegetal*), allowing it to legally use Ayahuasca as a religious sacrament. I will talk more about the legalisation of Ayahuasca in later chapters. The impressive work of the UDV has seen it become a courageous pioneer of the Brazilian Ayahuasca movement in Brazil and around the world in the quest for social justice and the human right to use of the divine sacrament known to the UDV as Hoasca, a gift from God and our Mother Earth that is naturally and spiritually ordained, and so crucial for our evolution and survival in these times.

Umbanda and the forces of nature

The world of shamanism is full of a diversity of colourful blends of religion, culture, plant medicines and practices. Many forms of shamanism can look completely different to others and on the surface might seem to be unrelated, even though they are still working with the same essence of spiritual communion. Brazil, in particular, has a rich history of blending historical lineages, plant wisdom and direct spiritual experiences which are constantly emerging from the fertile field of practice and life path that is shamanism. The syncretic Afro-Brazilian religion of Umbanda is one path that has merged its beliefs in African *Orixás* (deities representing the forces of nature), spirit mediumship and Catholicism with Ayahuasca. This syncretic phenomenon, which includes African spirituality and which is so prevalent in Brazil, has greatly influenced all the Brazilian Ayahuasca religions and most informal Ayahuasca movements, but it has also led to the creation of a new religion known as *Umbandaime* (Santo Daime plus Umbanda). Umbandaime developed in the 1990s after receiving the blessings of Santo Daime leader Padrinho Sebastião.

Umbanda blends elements of African traditions (primarily of the Yoruba and Bantu peoples), Roman Catholicism, Spiritism and Indigenous Brazilian beliefs. It is one of several Afro-Brazilian religions alongside *Candomblé*, *Ifá* and others but with its own distinct identity and practices. Umbanda emerged in the early 20th century and has since evolved into a major spiritual and cultural movement in Brazil with a great influence on modern mainstream Brazilian culture.

Umbanda is believed to have been founded in the 1920s by Zélio Fernandinho de Moraes, a Brazilian medium from the state of Rio de Janeiro. According to accounts, Zélio, who came from a Catholic family, began to manifest spiritual phenomena at a young age. He eventually attended a Spiritist (Kardecist) session in 1908, where he reportedly received spiritual guidance from an entity named *Caboclo das Sete Encruzilhadas* (Caboclo of the Seven Crossroads). This spirit is said to have outlined the principles of Umbanda and communicated that this would form a new religious path which merged several different traditions.

Umbanda was created as a more inclusive, less rigid alternative to Kardecist Spiritism, offering a spiritual practice that welcomed the participation of working-class Brazilians, including those of African, Indigenous and European descent. Its syncretic nature allowed it to resonate with many people, as it blended familiar aspects of Catholic saints, African Orixás and Indigenous spirits (caboclos). This connection to nature and its forces plus the reverence for the Indigenous caboclos led to a natural alliance between Umbanda and Ayahuasca practice. As mentioned, Umbandaime is a religion that merges the practices of traditional Umbanda ceremonies with the works of the Santo Daime religion. It is also common for many Santo Daime churches to practise works that may focus on prayers and rituals for certain Orixás, such as *Yemanjá* (Orixá of the Oceans). Padrinho Sebastião always had an interest and willingness to explore and introduce forms of mediumship into Santo Daime practices and found that the cosmology of Umbanda melded quite synergistically with the Daimist world and its practices and beliefs.

The main lineages of religions that form Umbanda practices and beliefs are African, Indigenous, Catholic and Spiritist. Umbanda shares certain aspects with Brazilian African-based religions like Candomblé, especially in its veneration of the Orixás. However, while Candomblé is more focused on complex rituals and the worship of specific Orixás, Umbanda is more flexible in its rituals and incorporates a broader range of spiritual entities. Caboclos are revered in Umbanda. These spirits are seen as wise and powerful, representing the natural world and the strength of the native Brazilian heritage. Umbanda also incorporates many Catholic symbols and saints. In fact, many Orixás are syncretised with Catholic saints, a practice that originated during colonial times when enslaved Africans disguised their deities as saints to avoid persecution. For example, the Orixá *Oxalá* is often associated with Jesus Christ, as is *Ogum* with Saint George, and so on. Spiritism, as developed by Allan Kardec in France, plays a significant role in Umbanda. The belief in reincarnation, spiritual evolution and communication with spirits is central to the religion. Mediumship (communicating with the spirits of the dead or other entities) plays a pivotal role in Umbanda ceremonies and represents a form of shamanism where the experience of an altered state, which usually comes about through rituals that include specific drumming rhythms and chants, is a full-body incorporation of the spirits practitioners are working with. The process of learning to incorporate these spirits is a deep study learnt through often-arduous training practices. The process itself can be very healing for the practitioner, whilst the goal is to be of service for the healing of others.

> *Let us all saravá! (praise and celebrate)*
> *Whoever is sick will be healed*
> *Whoever is healed will go to work*
>
> — *Xangô Caô*, Luz Ametista.

The key practices of Umbanda are mediumship, ceremonies, offerings and rituals. Mediumship is central to Umbanda practice where practitioners known as *médiuns* (mediums) serve as channels for spirits. These spirits, known as entities, fall into different categories, including caboclos, *pretos velhos* (old black people, spirits of former slaves), *exús* (entities associated with the crossroads, transformation and protection), *ciganos* (spirits of gypsies) and others. Umbanda ceremonies, called *giras,* involve music, drumming, chanting and dancing to invoke spirits. During these ceremonies, spirits may 'incorporate' into mediums, offering guidance, healing and advice to those present. The atmosphere is communal and supportive, with participants seeking spiritual help for physical, emotional and social problems. Offerings, such as candles, flowers, plants, food and drinks, are made to spirits and Orixás to connect the spiritual with the material worlds for invocation of their blessings and to give thanks. Rituals are often performed in *terreiros* (places of worship), which can range from simple backyards to elaborate temples.

I was first introduced to Umbanda in Salvador, Brazil in 2009 when I met Dona Maria, a *Mãe de Santo* (Mother of the Saints — spiritual leader from Umbanda) in the state of Bahia. She was recommended to me by Silvia Polivoy. The spirit of Africa has

Umbanda terreiro – 'The Beauty of the Sacred Waters of Oxum,' Rio de Janeiro

often come into my dreams, visions and miração over many years, and the teachings of Umbanda have always seemingly found me on my journey. I believe that those who make contact with this beautiful spiritual path often find that its practices and beliefs are very simple and effective. Umbanda is very much a path which incorporates the great diversity of culture and spirituality of Brazil in an elegant and graceful way that is very open and accessible to all people. Umbanda has a reverence for, and connection to, Nature and Spirit in a system that is very practical and beautiful. My spiritual practices and my work with Ayahuasca incorporate many of the practices and spiritual entities of Umbanda and have become a huge part of my life. The great lineages of Santo Daime and Umbanda are two of the three pillars of my work that makes up the spiritual point of the Estrela da Ciranda, the other being the Indigenous lineages of the Amazon. The development of new forms of spirituality in the syncretic tradition of Brazil can be viewed as a grand flower with many multi-coloured petals, where the Estrela da Ciranda has become one of those petals sprouting from an infinite circle of light, with each petal a unique aspect of divine expression.

Heavenly court
Orient and Mother Earth

Santo Daime and Umbanda
Sidereal infinity

Immeasurable immensity
Multi-coloured rainbow

This rosary is so great
Petals of the same flower

— *Aqui, Agora, Estou,* Chandra Lacombe.

In Umbanda, practitioners have affiliations with certain Orixás that make up a personal constellation and mythology representing the spiritual gifts and influences on one's life path. It could be said that everyone has affiliations with particular forces of nature; for example, some people may need to be close to the ocean while others may love storms and lightning. Whilst these affiliations will generally stay throughout the life of a person, they are not fixed and may change. Each Orixá represents a particular aspect of the universe and our human experience. Although Umbanda shares many Orixás with other Afro-Brazilian religions like Candomblé, the roles and characteristics of these deities can differ slightly. While there are many Orixás, here are some of the main ones from the Umbanda perspective along with their meanings.

Oxalá (Obatalá): Representing creation, peace and wisdom, Oxalá is considered the father of all Orixás and is often associated with Jesus Christ. He embodies light, purity and spiritual balance.

Yemanjá: The Goddess of the Sea and the mother of all Orixás, Yemanjá represents fertility, motherhood and nurturing. She is one of the most beloved Orixás, and is known as the 'owner of the minds'.

Ogum: The Orixá of war, metal and technology, Ogum represents strength, courage and justice. He is the protector of warriors and those who fight for justice.

Oxóssi: The Orixá of the hunt and the forests, Oxóssi symbolises abundance, knowledge, strategy and the pursuit of goals. He is a guardian of nature and the forest. Oxóssi is often associated with caboclos.

Xangô: The Orixá of thunder, lightning and justice, Xangô is a powerful figure associated with truth and fairness. He governs over laws and justice, punishing wrongdoers and protecting the innocent.

Iansã/Oyá: The Orixá of winds, storms and fire, Iansã is a fierce warrior and symbol of feminine power, change and transformation. She is known for her strength and fearlessness.

Oxum: The goddess of fresh water, waterfalls, rivers, beauty, love and fertility, Oxum represents healing, clarity, wealth, femininity, cleansing and emotional sensitivity.

Nanã: The Orixá of rain, mud and the Earth's primordial waters, Nanã is the oldest of the Orixás and represents wisdom, ancestry and the connection to death and the afterlife.

Omulu/Obaluaiê: The Orixá of disease, healing and the dead, Omulu represents both suffering and the power to cure. He governs over health and illness, symbolising the cycles of life, death and rebirth.

Exú: A key figure in Umbanda who comes in many forms, Exú serves as the messenger between the human world and the Orixás. He represents communication, movement, and transformation and protection.

Oxumaré: The Orixá of continuity, renewal and the cyclical nature of life. Often associated with rainbows and serpents, transformation and the balance of opposites, Oxumaré embodies both masculine and feminine energies.

Ossain: The Orixá of herbs, plants, and medicinal knowledge. He holds the secrets of healing and the mystical powers of nature, as he governs the use of sacred plants for spiritual, medicinal and magical purposes.

Logun-Edé: An Orixá who unites the qualities of both Oxóssi and Oxum, embodying duality, beauty, youth, and the balance between masculine and feminine energies — the male in the female, the female in the male.

My personal relationship to the Orixás has allowed me to develop a structure for the integration of all the guides and spiritual entities that I work with. Understanding my connection to the Orixás, the way they work with me and how I can call on them and invoke their characteristics, is an important part of the work I do with ceremonies, and even in daily life. My spiritual constellation is an astral garden that I have been tending for most of my life and this changes over time as I meet and work with different spiritual beings and forces as needed. Times that I have spent in the Amazon and other powerful places in nature have often introduced me to different spiritual beings, some of whom I have forged alliances with over time. It's like a group of friends I have available to call on for my work and they come and go at different times depending on what is needed, whether that be during a ceremony or when doing healing work for someone. My main Orixás are Yemanjá, Ogum, Oxalá and Oxum. Yemanjá holds me and keeps me secure amidst even the most tumultuous waves; Ogum gives me the strength to stay firm and opens pathways with protection so that Oxalá may shine his light of peace and wisdom, illuminating my path; and Oxum, my godmother, takes the light, peace and wisdom on her rivers of love, flowing back again to the ocean of Yemanjá.

> *Yemanjá holds me in the sway of the sea*
> *In the waters that embrace the entire planet*
> *Ogum wields his sword in front of my heart*
> *To open the divine path and protect*
> *His iron strength is my firmness*
> *Oxalá arrives with divine white light*
> *Enlightening the path with peace, faith and love*
> *The light touches the little waves of the streams*
> *Descending through the forests*
> *Oxum my godmother of the flowing waters*
> *Carries this light to energise in her cascades*
> *Into her rivers that return to the sea*
> *And into the arms of our mother Yemanjá*
>
> — *Dança dos Orixás*, Lore Solaris.

Carioca and the Ciranda circle of friends

> *I am from here, there and everywhere. My Soul is music. To be free, happy, lovely and honest is my path. I live in this world, I am the owner of its richness, I come from nature to dance, to sing and smile. Poim.* — Carioca Freitas, *Ciranda Poim Poim.*

Ronaldo Leite de Freitas was born in 1955 in Rio de Janeiro, Brazil. From a very young age he was absorbed in studies and performing music. He left home at a young age and went on to form a progressive rock band 'Carioca and Devas' that toured Brazil in the late 1970s. He took on the name 'Carioca' when he moved to São Paulo to study music at university. Carioca is a cultural term used to describe native people from the city of Rio de Janeiro.

Carioca Freitas

Carioca became fascinated by the spirit of the Amazon and was increasingly inspired by the sounds of nature through the music of Umbanda, with its percussion, the sound of the drum, the vibrations of the wooden instruments and the chants of the caboclos and spirits of the forest. Carioca has a unique gift and sees the world as music. He began studies into the nature and ecology of the Amazon, feeling the spirit of the Amazon everywhere he travelled in Brazil as he became more and more drawn to the forests, where he felt this the most.

He began to translate this presence of the forest and the spirit of Brazil that had captured his attention organically through his music, leading him to record his first album *Mistérios da Amazônia* (Mysteries of the Amazon) in 1980. The album was a complete departure in style from the electric guitar-driven experimental rock music he had been playing. This album gained widespread attention and acclaim and led to him being invited to Europe, where he taught music and worked on arranging and producing albums for other artists. He also gained the attention of well-established Brazilian musicians such as Egberto Gismonti and he began touring around Europe taking his unique, Amazonian-influenced style with him. During the 1980s he went on to tour all over Europe and the world, including the Americas, Australia, Japan and Indonesia. Later, he reflected that for him these concerts were like ceremonies, where the spirit of Brazil was being transmitted through his music to the audiences while he was in a kind of altered state, where he would close his eyes and feel the spirit of the forests of Brazil.

This was the time of the military dictatorship in Brazil, which had been suffering under repressive social and political conditions. The dictatorship lasted from 1964 until 1985 and during this time many musicians and artists were exiled and imprisoned, including Carioca at times in his youth. Music was a way the people found to express themselves whilst under the repression of total media censorship and the brutal treatment of dissidents. This lead to the *Tropicalia* music movement which connected Brazilian music to its roots and which Carioca said also greatly inspired his shift towards discovering the sounds of nature through his music in the 1980s.

It wasn't until 1987 that Carioca first met Ayahuasca, or as he refers to it 'the tea', and directly experienced the introspective power from the roots of the Amazon. This first meeting had a great transformative effect on his life. He recalled: 'All of a sudden, it all made sense. In 1987 I finally lived what I had recorded seven years earlier.' In later years he also reflected that 'when I met the tea, what it brought me is that it broke all my directions of life. I came into an altered state and just started to sing all the time. It taught me to not take it all so seriously, just to be in joy'. Carioca went on to become a *fardado* (initiate) and guitarist of the Santo Daime church of the *Seu do Mar* (Ocean Sky) in Rio de Janeiro which was at that time under the guidance of the great Padrinho Sebastião. During those years Carioca learned the way of the Daime and had contact with Padrinho Sebastião, who in his last years of life was visiting Rio for hospital medical treatment.

On 20 January 1990, Padrinho Sebastião died in Rio de Janeiro due to complications from diabetes, which he had been suffering the effects of over the previous years. Carioca recounted the story of the night of Padrinho's passing, when a Daime work was being held in the church of the Céu do Mar in Rio. Carioca was a *violeiro* (guitarist) in the church at the time and during the afternoon of the work a massive tropical storm hit the city, with wild winds and rain blowing vertically into the church; most of the congregation went home, but a very small group stayed to complete the work. At the completion of the ceremony, the body of Padrinho was brought to the church and Carioca was one of the fardados there to receive his earthly body. Carioca himself would subsequently go on to develop a global movement that expanded again upon these teachings, including the teachings and practices introduced by Padrinho Sebastião. In a cosmic synchronicity, several hours before the passing of Padrinho Sebastião the influential Indian spiritual leader Osho Rajneesh also passed away, again leaving a huge global legacy that has also influenced generations of modern spirituality. In some places communities of *Sanyasins* (devotees of Osho) have formed communities and adopted the practices of Santo Daime in a further syncretic union.

After several more years with the Céu do Mar in Rio de Janeiro, Carioca's spirit of rock and roll and experimentation led him to outgrow the at-times rigid practices and doctrine of the church. The spirit of music flowing so strongly and organically through Carioca was becoming too much to contain within the confines of the church's rules and he was guided to return to Europe where he began playing jazz music in Switzerland. Whilst there he met a group of *Daimistas* (devotees of the Santo Daime) who did not have a church to practise their works in or leader. They enthusiastically asked him to hold a *Cura* (healing) work for them. A Cura is a work developed by Padrinho Sebastião that invokes powerful healing intentions and is an endurance of concentration and firmness in self-discipline. Carioca and this group held their first Cura in an attic in a house in Switzerland and have been holding this work twice a year now for nearly 30 years. Carioca's Cura is now held in Rio, and he has long since redeveloped the work to include more expressive and colourful musical versions of the hymns, also extending the work over three days, including three 12-hour ceremonies. The Cura has gone on to become the foundational work of Carioca's calendar of ceremonies.

Through the miração and the guidance of the spirit of Ayahuasca, Carioca was given a new vision: opening up the work to allow the focus to become the expression of sound and music, more so than religious doctrines and teachings. Carioca invites participants to let go into the colours of the sounds of nature through the miração and for each person to find their own unique expression of this beautiful truth. The doctrine of Carioca's work is music, the religion is music — and the practice is to be happy. Whilst in many ways the teachings of firmness and discipline are central to the practice of Carioca's ceremonies, the work inspires and encourages participants to free themselves and their spirit and to embrace their unique selves without religious doctrines. Music and the practice and study of the music brings a collective and cohesive group shamanic experience through ever-evolving harmony and musical expression in a circle of friends healing together and realising inner peace and joy. Carioca's ceremonies and work are non-denominational, and whilst the central works are strongly rooted in Santo Daime, Umbanda and Amazonia, which are accessed through the hymns and sounds of the music, the global nature and freedom of expression in the circle is such that all spiritual paths and religions have a place and influence on the culture of the ceremonies.

> Music doesn't need a room; it needs ambiance, like magic, like mystery and colours. With music in composition we try to create an image, but we are already in the image. Then it's just close your eyes and already the music is there. You're crazy in this symphony — the symphony of the universe is nature, a lot of sounds, a lot of colours, lots of birds. I'm very proud to have created this philosophy over the years, where nature is the real symphony; we just imitate or reproduce it, where you've already created your music and live in the forest with its beautiful garden inside you. Whatever you do, it doesn't exist that there is only one style, you can do it with four notes or 10 notes; it's already there because it looks like the harmony, the biggest symphony is ready for your notes. Whatever you do inside that ocean is flowing; it's there for navigating, that note navigates inside of you. — Carioca.

My first encounter with Carioca in 2014 in Brazil changed my life forever. I experienced the most profound healing of my life in those ceremonies and in my time living in the forest there with Carioca and our spiritual family. The discovery of the music within me, under Carioca's guidance and tutoring, was the greatest revelation of my life and I am still opening the petals of that flower emanating within me. In 2011, after receiving guidance from the miração, Carioca's circle of friends founded the *Ciranda* retreat centre in the Mata-Atlantica forest outside of Rio de Janeiro in Brazil. Ciranda is a word that comes from the Pernambuco region of north eastern Brazil and means 'a circle of children playfully dancing and singing'.

> The visions for Ciranda came through the sessions; it wasn't from me, I am just the channel. In the circle it's more important to make people happy, to become like a child — a child wants to be taken away from reality. The spirit of Ciranda is the spirit of a six-year-old girl; she lives in the forest and I see her moving around here. It's spontaneity and the unknowing that leads us to find happiness. There is not much space

> *for people to be proud and talk too much; it's more to sing and play music. The heart is the first part that is so happy and thankful. There are other places to go and do studies and learn other philosophies. Ciranda is just to be happy.* — Carioca.

The legacy of Carioca's work is immense. He has spent over 30 years travelling the world giving workshops, holding ceremonies and retreats, and spreading the message of music and the liberation of the heart. He has grown a remarkable global circle of friends, united by the discovery of the doctrine of music from within and connected through the teachings of the miração. In my experience, the power of the healing of music is equal to that of the Ayahuasca itself. The combination of these paths is remarkable and continues to take me into the deepest and most profound revelations of my life. I have witnessed countless people discover the music within them and reconnect to nature through this work and the path of Ciranda. Carioca doesn't take on the role of guru or master of the work or of anybody; he simply allows the magic to flow through the circle, through the miração and through each person and into beautiful, diverse and colourful expressions of music and life. More than 12,000 people globally have been touched by this work, and during the 2020 global lockdowns an online celebration of the global circle called *Canta com Amor* (sing with love) attracted over 10,000 online participants, brought together and inspired by the work of Carioca.

> *What draws people together as friends is that they see the same truth. They share it.* — C S Lewis.

Carioca's influence and music is heard in Ayahuasca circles all over Brazil and the world and he has recorded around 30 albums, each one unique in its creativity and expression. Carioca has several different ceremonies that he holds, including Curas and the works of Mestre Irineu and other Daime leaders, an Umbanda ceremony of drumming and dancing, plus other ceremonies that celebrate the colours and expression of music through the teachings of those lineages and the Amazon. Hundreds of musicians have been birthed and nurtured into self-confidence and self-belief through these ceremonies and the circle.

The most powerful aspects of this work are the strength of the firmness and discipline held by the circle, the freedom and joy that we are able to reach and the depth of the challenges in confronting our limitations and wounds which prevent us from expressing the pure joy that is the true nature of our being and our humanity. In my experience of going through some of the darkest moments of healing in this circle, I have always felt loved and held and supported in a non-judgemental spirit of freedom to be myself without being told how or what to do, and instead encouraged to find my own way to my own truth. Ciranda gave me the gift to accept myself and embrace and express all the colours of my being. I don't have the words to express the deep gratitude I have for this in my life. Carioca and Ciranda teach us to embrace our inner child, to open our hearts and let the music flow through us from the heart of the Earth. This movement and its global circle of friends is a very significant and influential aspect of the global Ayahuasca movement and represents a liberation of the doctrines into an unspoken personal freedom expressed through music, happiness and friendship. Carioca describes this in one simple word — a word that has no real meaning, but which represents all things good: *poim*.

> *Forest*
> *Calm my thoughts*
> *Your peace is my help*
>
> *Forest*
> *Touch my heart*
> *With your green veil,*
> *beauty and such protection*
>
> *Forest*
> *Pure joy of my soul*
> *I give thanks*
> *For always I am your child*
>
> — *Floresta*, Karen Behmer.

In 2003 and 2007, when I was in the presence of my first teacher of Ayahuasca, Pablo Amaringo, I found his guidance to always be very subtle and at times cryptic, in that he wasn't always saying directly what he was wanting to teach, but was guiding you to find your own answers from your own perspective and truth. I always appreciated this about Pablo, as I was familiar with this way of spiritual guidance from my times with Australian Indigenous leaders and Elders.

We can see this teaching coming through in the formation of the Santo Daime and other Brazilian Ayahuasca religions, whereby the modern culture of Brazil, which was largely influenced by Christianity and the Afro-Brazilian religions, could relate to the teachings of those doctrines and had pre-existing relationships with the spiritual beings and entities guiding them. Something I learned from the Yawanawá and Huni Kuin peoples in Brazil was that the Indigenous peoples did not traditionally suffer the diseases and mental health afflictions that are now chronic in Western culture. People with diverse illnesses seeking healing are finding their ways to the Amazon, where new forms of working with Ayahuasca must emerge which are also culturally relevant and coherently integrate appropriate remedies for these conditions. The teachings in the hymns of the Santo Daime are a great example of how the message of the forest has evolved to bring healing to people in a way that is relevant to the mental conditions and cultural needs of the people. The evolution that has come through the work of Carioca and the global Ciranda circle of friends is again something that is open and accessible to a growing community of spiritual and new-age people — people who are embracing teachings from many paths and in a non-denominational form. Carioca's ceremonies are astounding in their beauty, harmony and grace, yet allow participants to truly find their unique way. This is an example of the importance of ceremony reflecting the culture and needs of the people and bringing us together in a sacred alliance of reverence for the Divine.

The importance of ceremony is such that it has the power, if done in the right way, to inspire us and prepare us to practise that reverence in grace and beauty, and embody that in all of our actions, throughout our lives, so that life itself is seen as, and becomes, the great ceremony. Sitting in circle together in the light, holding our grace through *firmeza* (firmness) as we sing praise to Great Spirit in all its forms of creation allows us to be seen and to be consciously reminded of the need to stay clear and clean in our actions and thoughts, held in love, support and accountability by our brothers and sisters, not running and hiding in our shadows. The culture of ceremony is ancient, enduring and universal, planet-wide. Perhaps the greatest beauty that comes from the teachings of the ceremonial use of Ayahuasca is that not only can we heal from the painful clamour of our mental confusion in this age of illusions, we can also learn to put down our defensiveness and avoidance of living vulnerably in the truth of light and love. We can empty ourselves of personal ambition that blinds us, as we surrender to the Divine, becoming instruments of the great spiritual work of creation. Through our healing, faith and devotion we become truly useful to the regeneration of the garden of divine beauty that exists as the potential of humanity here on Earth which lies within each one of us and which, in fact, is a necessary point of growth and evolution for our collective survival. Ayahuasca, through these beautiful lineages born out of the richness of the actual forests and the garden of consciousness of Brazil, has given us purpose and guidance on how we may become the servants of Spirit and the Earth we are once again destined to become.

The beauty of being,
and becoming an instrument
And every moment awaken the gift
To flow lightly, without thought
Walking the paths of the heart.

— Espírito Cantador, George Lucena.

PART 2
Growth

CHAPTER 5

Call of the Forest

The beauty of being
and becoming an instrument
And every moment awaken the gift
To flow lightly, without thought
Walking the paths of the heart
The journey is inside
Path of silence, master teacher

—*Espíritu Cantador,* George Lucena.

The powerfully haunting sounds of howler monkeys amidst a symphony of bird songs, insect buzz and a myriad of other animals enchanted me as I returned to the material world within the sublime beauty of the Amazon rainforest on the morning following my first night with the great teacher Ayahuasca. I felt washed clean, like I had just undergone a cosmic baptism and deep cleanse of my body, mind and soul. I sat in complete stillness, silence of mind and openness of my being to receive and absorb the sounds, spirit, vibrations and energy of the majestic forest. In that moment I experienced a sense of oneness with all of creation, like I had never felt before. During the night's ceremony my consciousness had been deeply immersed in the astral forest of the spiritual realm of Ayahuasca, to be reborn on this morning into the embrace of the actual forest itself. My whole being absorbed the immensity of this most densely alive and spiritually rich environment on the planet. Whilst I sat meditatively staring out across the forest, drifting, empty, I felt a sense of calm presence. I was unable in that moment to bring thoughts or words to the profound journey I had just undertaken the night before, when I had found my wings on the magical flight of my first Ayahuasca ceremony. I stayed there in that moment, taking it all in, like a giant healing breath of realisation — of the Divine within and without me. To this day I feel that moment was a great rebirth of myself on my soul's journey through this life, and in that moment of pure presence and innocence, feeling like a sensitive and vulnerable newborn, I had no idea of the immensity of the journey of growth, challenge and beauty that was to follow.

It was on the night of the 'Day Out of Time' in the Mayan Dreamspell calendar, 25 July 2003, that I first drank the sacred brew known as Ayahuasca. I found myself being guided and called to that first ceremony through a sequence of profound synchronicities, and the path had opened in front of me. That morning of rebirth after my first ceremony was the first day of the 13 moon Mayan year, and was the day of the 'Spectral Wizard' — the liberating of the inner shaman. The Day Out of Time signifies a time of letting go and forgiveness, clearing the way for the new year. That particular day was also the day of the 'Planetary Skywalker', signifying the manifestation of the exploration of space, guided by the power of birth; a profound synchronicity with the experience or drinking Ayahuasca deep in the Amazon rainforest. I had not planned to be drinking Ayahuasca on this auspicious date, and had little knowledge of the Mayan calendar at that time, though during the ceremony I did meet some galactic Mayan extraterrestrials in my vision and was given many teachings regarding the galactic/cosmic nature of time and space, synchronicity and prophecy. This first ceremony unlocked inside me my own personal prophecy, and my spiritual path was made so clear to me. My mind and my ego-self wanted to put all kinds of meaning and strategy around this revelation, thoughts that were a distraction at the time, although looking back two decades later I can see that what I saw on that first night of Ayahuasca visions was a sequence of profound truths that have resonated throughout my life and my being ever since, manifesting in the writing and publishing of this book.

> *It is a mistake for seekers who have only discovered what they should be, to believe that they have reached the final realisation. Spiritual rebirth begins with a long gestation. In the Daime, unlike other doctrines in which enlightenment is the culmination of prolonged practices and evolved skills, rebirth can be experienced in the miração quite unexpectedly. Thus we can become astounded by the gift received and afraid of the responsibility it implies, but we can also become extremely motivated in response to the genuine treasure just encountered.*
> — Alex Polari de Alverga.

When I first came to meet Ayahuasca, I had very little knowledge of what it was and I did not approach it with any sense of expectation or ambition. It just seemed like a good idea at the time, based on the series of synchronicities that had led me to that moment. It was early in 2003 that I first heard of Ayahuasca, in the days after a Solar Eclipse festival I had attended with a group of friends in the Central Australian desert. This was one of those times where the spirit of the festival seemed to come home with me and a group of friends had gathered at the house where I was living by the river in a forest, just outside of the city of Melbourne in Australia. One night around the fire, a brother whom we had met at the festival began discussing DMT, and he had some smokable DMT that had been extracted from Australian acacia plants. During this conversation he offered people the experience of smoking the DMT right there around the fire, which some in our group did at the time. The conversation went on to talk about Ayahuasca, which also naturally contains DMT. The person talking about DMT and Ayahuasca seemed to be to be a bit boastful and was using hype and new-age jargon a lot, so I didn't partake that night. But I sensed there was something profound to be discovered with these plants. I made a decision to wait until I felt a strong calling from Spirit embodying reverence for something so sacred before partaking in any experience of DMT or Ayahuasca. Included in that circle of friends at the time was Jesse Lethbridge, whom I had met in the Australian desert in the year 2000 and again at the recent eclipse festival. Years later, Jesse would go on to be instrumental in my journey with Ayahuasca in Australia.

Spiritual journey begins

In early 2003, after 29 years on the Earth, I was working as a youth worker and case manager at a drug and alcohol rehabilitation centre for young people in the outer suburbs of Melbourne. I had been in this role for over a year, having worked in youth and community development roles since 1996. The agency I was working for was a non-government organisation employing cutting-edge strategies in re-engaging marginalised young people who were in recovery from drug and alcohol addiction, domestic violence, mental health breakdowns, social isolation and homelessness. Research being done from within the organisation showed that the prevalence of drug use in these young people was congruent with a lack of release of naturally developed serotonin and dopamine, or the 'happy hormones'. This research showed there was some kind of innate intelligence in people where their drug use was boosting their brain functions to a level in alignment with the average population's baseline functioning in regards to emotional/psychological wellbeing. Without the nourishing childhood to train their bodies into a natural level of elevated hormone release — which provides for a healthy mental state and neurological development — they had instinctively taken up drug use at a level to make up for this deficiency. This indicated that the issue wasn't about the drugs or drug use itself, but about a self-regulating adaptation through socialisation for individuals to reach normal, healthy brain function. Self-medicating trauma relief. Unfortunately, without the love and support needed and with the dangers and dysfunction of social stigmatisation plus being criminalised by society, this path of drug use was not giving them a sustainable or healthy form of remedy for their impaired brain function and resultant depression and other mood and mental health problems.

The work I was doing in drug and alcohol rehabilitation at this time focused on supporting the young people in our care in learning how to live in ways that entrained their brain functioning with natural, healthy forms of serotonin and dopamine release. Simply taking away the drugs was not enough, and since the drug was a survival mechanism, this removal without replacing the drugs with something else could be seen as a kind of cruelty or torture. This is a big part of why the 'war on drugs' mentality is so abusive, damaging and backward. What we found was that by working with these young people in supporting them to have positive relationships and life experiences, their brains would become entrained to natural forms of healthy functioning and thus they would slowly learn how to live without drug dependency. Whilst in many cases this work was relatively effective, what we also found was that it was a very slow and resource-intensive process. The risk of relapse, re-traumatisation and worse was always very strong, as was burnout amongst the youth workers, who were constantly in the firing line of sometimes-angry youth and their extreme behaviours, while also having to navigate the swampy minefield of politics and a dysfunctional bureaucracy. After years of this work in which I had found natural affinity and skill at, I needed a break and to find a new direction in life. I decided to leave my job and go travelling again.

The weekend before I left Melbourne to drive west across the Nullarbor Plain to Perth in Western Australia I had a chance meeting with a man who gave me an interesting prophecy. I met him at the local markets in St Andrews where he had a stall and was giving readings and teachings on the Mayan calendar. I had been very interested in this for a long time but had never met anyone who knew anything about it. As it turned out, we were born on the same day: this was significant synchronicity and a strong sign, as the Mayan calendar is all about the synchronic nature of the universe. He told me that he predicted from the cosmology of my Mayan calendar signs I would be in the Brazilian Amazon on the Day Out of Time. Considering I had not yet thought of making that journey and was planning to be in Europe, I didn't think much about it until months later, when it became apparent that Spirit was indeed calling me to that location at the time he predicted. His prophecy was eventually fulfilled. In May 2003, Jesse and I plus another friend took my van on a road trip and drove from Melbourne across the expanse of Australia to Perth, where I spent several weeks before leaving for Europe in June.

I left Australia for the first time with the intention of heading to the lands of my ancestors in Scotland. My family line was pretty broken, in that I didn't know much about my ancestors, although on both my mother's and father's sides they are predominantly of Scottish descent. I was feeling the call to visit Scotland, to feel the land and perhaps activate some memories in my soul and in my DNA which originated in those lands. On my way I met Jan, a friend of Jesse's, whom he had met at an eclipse festival in Africa the year before. Jan invited me to stay with him in Cardiff, Wales and it turned out we also shared some synchronicities. Jan was planning a trip to the Holy Isle in Scotland for a spiritual pilgrimage, after which he was going to the Brazilian Amazon to drink Ayahuasca. Jan had planned to go with another friend and they had paid their deposits for a special retreat with the great shaman and visionary artist Pablo Amaringo. I had not heard of Pablo before, but I did some research and discovered he was well known and respected for his art and work as a *curandeiro* (healer).

Ancestral revelations in Scotland

Jan and I decided to make the trip to Scotland together, where I would go with him to the Holy Isle, then I would go on my spiritual journey through my ancestral lands and Jan would return to Wales. As we were preparing for our trip, Jan's friend called and told him he would not be able to go to the Amazon. Jan offered me the place and said that I could have the deposit; all I needed to do was come up with the rest of the money. I didn't have the funds but I was very curious, as I was feeling the calling from the forest — and it was getting louder. I had no great desire to meet Ayahuasca but this series of synchronicities was too much to ignore. Jan offered me a couple of weeks' work doing some research in the psychology department at the University of Cardiff, where he was studying and working. This would cover some of the trip. The next day I received an unexpected email from a close friend in Sydney who said that he had just sold a house and had some cash available, asking if I needed any support for my spiritual mission. I wrote back and told him I was being called to Brazil to the Amazon to drink Ayahuasca with a great shaman. He seemed a bit shocked and surprised but he trusted me and so he sent me the funds. Life was teaching me the art of creation where, through attention, faith and courage, the path of Spirit always unfolds before me.

> *Trust in God by honouring and trusting your intuitive sense. No God would create a creature without the wisdom to chart its course. Trust the nature of your design. God's actions appear within your awareness as the most natural thing for you to do. Following them will reconnect you with the awesome powers of the universe, for all your actions will then be in harmony with the underlying intent of the life-force itself.* — Ken Carey, Return of the Bird Tribes.

The journey to Scotland was powerful. It revealed a lot to me about my spirituality and was a precursor to the work I was about to do in Brazil. On this journey I did not have any great ambitions or any plans set in stone; I was really just in the flow of trust and allowing life to unfold. I have always found that when I let go into trust like that, while it can be scary and unsettling at times, this always leads me to magical revelations, spiritual growth and evolution.

While I was on the Isle of Arran in Scotland with Jan at one point he went off to meditate and so I went for a walk through a glen, which enchanted me with memories and feelings I knew but couldn't recognise. A strange yet powerful and deep sensation. On the other side of the glen was a road and I started hitch-hiking back to the other side of the island. The first vehicle that came along — a simple camper van like the one I had in Australia — stopped and picked me up. I got in the back and the driver asked what I was up to; I told him that I had come from Australia and I was visiting Scotland to connect to my ancestral and spiritual roots. As it turned out, he was a practitioner of druidry, the ancient form of shamanism practised by the Celtic peoples of Britain, and something which I had always been drawn to. We talked about sacred places and stone circles and he mentioned a place called *Calanais* (Callanish), the oldest known stone circle in Europe. When he mentioned this place the hairs on my arm all stood up and I felt a rush of energy move up my spine; I told him I knew it was the place I needed to visit. It also transpired that he was on a pilgrimage to visit the same sacred cave on the Holy Isle that Jan was visiting, as they had both recently had someone close to them pass away and this was a place to go and pay respects to those who have passed. The next day we all went together.

After leaving the Isle, Jan returned to Wales and I visited the house of my new druid friend on my way to the Isle of Skye and the Isles of Lewis and Harris, where I would find the ancient stone circle of Calanais. My new friend had given me some Scottish psychedelic mushrooms for the journey and educated me in some druidic arts and how to pay respect to the land and the ancestors. I spent five days there, on the top of a hill beside the ancient stone circle, surrounded on one side by a beautiful loch (lake) all alone in a very remote part of one of the Outer Hebrides islands off the northwestern coast of Scotland. I was very enchanted during my time there, as the people still spoke the traditional Gaelic language, of which I knew a few words after studying Celtic history and culture at the University of Sydney. Some local people gave me somewhere to sleep and I spent the days in meditation and absorbing the profound beauty in the land. During this time, I met an ancient druid spirit, a tall old man who guided me and questioned me deeply, and at times I felt like he was playing tricks on me to the point that I wasn't sure what was real and what was my spiritual vision. Much happened on this part of the journey — powerful experiences that I will save for another book.

I learned many things, realised a lot of my soul's journey, and was given spiritual permission by my guides to continue my journey and visit the Amazon.

Connecting to the intense beauty of these Scottish lands and being in deep communion with the ancestors there opened my mind and also reminded me of who I was in this life and my spiritual purpose, which transcended generations. The land showed me such intense beauty and brought me into a profound stillness beyond time and space. I realised with clarity that I had a spiritual connection to my ancestors and had a job to do in this life: to bring healing to the line of my family and to remember our connection to the land that had been forgotten for generations. It seemed like a lot of responsibility, and I also realised that this powerful experience was important, as the work I was about to do in the Amazon and the journey it was inviting me into was going to be very strong and it was important for me to remember who I was and be strong in that so that I didn't forget it on my journey. The old druid spirit who appeared to me during that time in Calanais also showed me the wound I was carrying in this life and in my soul which was manifesting as a lack of self-worth and insecurity, and which became very clear in my meditations there. I also had a lot of soul memories, ancient secrets revealed and past-life memories that raised more questions. These started to be answered once I was in the Amazon, deep in the miração of the great teacher Ayahuasca.

First journey to Brazil

Arriving in Brazil for the first time was also a huge revelation. The smells, the feelings, the vibrancy in the people and the culture, the music and the nature was all very energising for me, as though something had set my soul on fire and I was feeling more alive than ever. Very quickly I fell in love with the spirit of Brazil, and to this day I feel at home in this magical, creative, colourful, vibrant country that is thriving with life force and an astounding diversity and depth of music, spirituality and culture. Brazil is full of heart and soul. I felt like a different person exploring a whole new life. Jan and I travelled around for a couple of weeks before we made our way to Manaus, the capital city of the largest state in Brazil, Amazonas. Upon arriving I was drawn to the Amazon River itself, its majesty, immensity and mystery. Manaus is a large city that sits on the side of the Amazon River at a point where you can't even see the river's other side; it just looks like a vast ocean. I contemplated the immensity of this, and it just excited me and drew my curiosity deeper into its mysteries. The morning after we arrived, we met the retreat organisers and participants for breakfast before we all travelled together by boat, bus and then canoes to arrive at a beautiful retreat centre next to a small tributary river, surrounded by dense, loud, deep-green jungle.

It was a beautiful afternoon when we arrived at the retreat centre where we would be spending the next two weeks, and as the sun set over the Amazon rainforest I invited Jan to come with me down to the river bank to play some guitar and sing for the setting sun. After a few minutes of sitting there we noticed a few mosquitoes and Jan wanted to go back to the dining area, but I told him not to worry. I'm Australian and we can handle a few mosquitoes. But then, moments later, it became clear that there was a buzzing black cloud of thousands of seemingly very hungry and ferocious mosquitoes surrounding us so we just got up and ran. Pretty quickly I realised that the nature of this place commanded a whole different kind of respect and attention than I had ever previously experienced.

The people who had gathered for this retreat were a very diverse group from all over the world and with a very diverse range of backgrounds — artists, a lawyer, a doctor, spiritual healers, and others — all with varying degrees of experience with Ayahuasca. I found myself immediately enjoying very much the conversations and the energy and friendliness of the people. Silvia Polivoy, who had organised the retreat, is an Argentinian psychotherapist and psychologist who has done a lot of pioneering work in shamanic studies and building a bridge between ancient plant medicines and contemporary psychology and opening up these experiences for people to come from all over the world. She seemed very attentive to every detail and was very focused on providing the right conditions for participants to feel safe and supported. Pablo Amaringo was also there. He was a very gentle and unassuming man, dressed very plainly, who spoke quietly and carefully. It was only because I already knew he was a famous Ayahuasca shaman that I recognised his personal power, otherwise I would probably not have looked at him twice or assumed anything about him if I had seen him anywhere else. This impressed me, as coming from Byron Bay in Australia, a town which is full of cliques and flashy, glamorous new-agers, it was refreshing to know that our guides were humble folk without pretensions. This made me feel confident in their authenticity.

I immediately felt at home in this environment. I enjoyed great conversations about healing, health and spirituality and the sense of excitement at meeting Ayahuasca in the majestic Amazon forest. Everything I found there were the things that had inspired me the most in life. Silvia prepared us for the first ceremony, which was on the second night of the retreat, with a couple of workshops and meditations that guided us to connecting with our higher selves and to sharing with the group about ourselves, our lives and the things we wanted to gain from our experience with Ayahuasca and the retreat. This kind of environment was very familiar to me, having worked in health and therapy for so many years before arriving.

The ceremonies were held in a large round temple that was surrounded by forest and located some way away from the cabins and kitchen/dining area. We were joined in the ceremonies by some local Amazonian Indigenous people, who seemed to be very happy to be drinking Ayahuasca with Pablo, a renowned master shaman from Peru. Each person was given a space with a mattress and blanket in a large circle around the perimeter of the temple. Silvia asked each participant before the ceremony how they were feeling and what kind of tolerance they might usually have when taking different substances. I elected to have a large dose. Each person was given their dose of Ayahuasca and we were invited to stand together in the centre of the temple where Silvia made an invocation and prayer. We then all drank together, before returning to our places and the lights were then turned out. I remember feeling relatively calm and curious with a small amount of nervous anticipation of what I was about to experience.

As I was sitting there meditating in the dark, scanning my body and consciousness for any effects of the onset of the medicine, Silvia began to play some recorded songs that created a gentle ambiance and spaciousness of sound which I enjoyed and was quite soothing. After an hour or so I noticed the effects of the medicine beginning with a sense of a vibration and a slight unease which could have been a nauseous sensation. It didn't take long before I started to see visions of colours and movement, geometries, with a sound like a kind of hum that was coming from within an astral vision. I noticed my mind trying to work out what the visions were and if there was any meaning in them, but quite quickly the visions became very vivid and intense, and any perception I had of the room and the music that Silvia was playing was almost completely gone. I felt my mind resisting this experience and trying to rationalise, and at one point I was experimenting with keeping my eyes closed and observing the intense colourful visions and then opening my eyes where I still saw the same visions and couldn't see the room. Having my eyes open or closed wasn't making any difference.

As the visions continued and my mind stayed active, trying to rationalise and navigate with logic and my experience of what I thought was happening, I started to feel very nauseous. I remembered a conversation that Pablo had engaged in during the day with a participant who was quite experienced and who was asking him about vomiting, because she had usually purged during Ayahuasca and wanted to learn how not to purge. Pablo had said to her that if possible try and keep the medicine inside, but if you really have to vomit, then just let it happen. At this point the nausea was becoming overwhelming and my mind was going into overdrive with worry and fears and trying to work out what I should do. I experimented with breathing and staying still but the nausea seemed to amplify with my thoughts. I started to think maybe I should get up and go to the bathroom but that made me feel even sicker. Then, magically, I heard the sound of the sweetest singing I had ever heard in my life, and this grabbed my attention. After a moment I realised that Pablo had begun to sing an *icaro* (Ayahuasca hymn from the *Shipibo* tradition). I was enchanted by the song as Pablo walked gently around the room.

The sublimely beautiful sounds of Pablo's singing completely disarmed my mind and I found it was easy to focus my attention on his singing. As I did so, the sensations of nausea I was feeling went away. I began to surrender to the experience; the visions and the sounds suddenly became a beautiful cosmic journey and the struggle I was experiencing ended. After a while I began contemplating my experience, but not with the intense thoughts of a mind at work — this was more of a flow of consciousness and realisations that came without an inner dialogue of words. I felt that through his singing, Pablo had stabilised the space and it came right at the perfect moment, as my grasping mind had been causing a mess in my experience. The visions started to become more like forms and images that made sense to me and in the appearance of an astral forest with a strong feminine presence emerging from within. I saw a plant-like female presence who communicated telepathically that she was Ayahuasca. Once I had grasped this realisation, the visions changed and I started to see my body as energy and how the medicine was moving through my body. As it was encountering energetic blockages in my nervous system and toxins were being released, the medicine was removing stagnant energies while my mind was experiencing the fears and negative thoughts associated with those stuck energies and all of that was causing me to feel such intense nausea.

Ayahuasca showed me that, as I had faced the fears and then surrendered to the experience, once Pablo began singing I didn't need to physically purge anymore and that my emotions and fear and over-active mind were all symptomatic of the storage of tension, old emotions and toxins in my body. This is something that has stayed with me over countless Ayahuasca experiences over the years, and to this day, after maybe a thousand ceremonies, I have probably only vomited about five times. What I have also come to realise is that the mind can act as an amplifier, and if the mind is focused with thoughts on discomfort or negative emotions, it can amplify those feelings and sensations, making them more intense and seemingly more real.

This is where meditation, breath work and other practices become so valuable in life — to train the mind to stay empty and focused. Dr Gabor Maté and others talk at length about the psycho-spiritual causes of illness and the effectiveness of mystical and shamanic experiences for healing physical ailments. This was the beginning of the teachings that led me to later always guide participants in my own ceremonies to focus on the light of the altar and the music being played as a technique to bring the mind into focus. It was the first of many mind teachings I have received from Ayahuasca over the years, and like most spiritual disciplines, the first thing we need to do is to deal with our minds and its illusions. Ayahuasca shows that suffering and confusion only come from the mind, and when we learn to surrender the thinking mind and allow our thoughts to flow in harmony with the flow of creation, we become one with that creation and our direction is then guided by that flow through the heart, in presence with the moment, without projecting into the past or worrying about the future. Allowing ourselves, our minds, bodies, emotions to be filled with uninterrupted flow of creation, is essentially healing. This is also one of the key teachings of Ayahuasca, where the force of the medicine comes first to align us and condition our bodies and minds in harmony with nature and a profoundly spiritual presence, so that we are then able to enter clearly and cleanly into the miração, the visionary state.

> *It was the belief of Padrinho Sebastião that when we invoke the Divine Being present in the Ayahuasca, it will come to cleanse and sanctify us in preparation to receive our righteous selves. The drink per se is the vehicle, the sacrament. Its ingestion reorganises our organic, neurochemical and energetic foundation, adjusting us to spiritual reality and its multiple meanings. At this point, the Daime helps us to transcend both the positive and negative energies that emerge from the depth of our spirits. After this phase, the miração comes and archetypes, myths and legends emerge from the collective unconscious. Through this rough material, the universal Holy Spirit becomes accessible through the living images of the miração, the divine language. The miração is not just a result of*

the force of the Ayahuasca, as in a cause and effect relationship. It depends as well on the choice, merit and degree of surrender to the Superior Being guiding the miração. Without faith in its divine essence, what comes forth from the collective unconscious will only reach psychological and imaginative levels. — Alex Polari de Alverga, *The Religion of Ayahuasca.*

By this stage of my first Ayahuasca journey, I was feeling honoured and blessed by the presence of a divine being who had shown herself to me. The vision of the astral jungle all around me stayed very present as I was contemplating these first teachings I had received. At one point my attention suddenly became very alert to another presence: a giant snake was coming towards me at full force with its mouth open ready to eat me! I instantly realised I had no chance to resist or fight it off and remembered another experience I had had in the Northern Territory of Australia when I was staying with Aboriginal people where a crocodile had eaten me in a vision. I just surrendered and allowed this Ayahuasca snake to consume me as I felt its immense force and power; all I was able to do was to surrender to it. Everything went still and silent for a moment, the visionary state disappeared, my mind was empty and then slowly lights and colours began to re-emerge and I found myself riding on the back of this now colourful rainbow serpent as it took me on a journey through beautiful visions of the forest with animals, plants, spiritual beings and seemingly endless universes of wonder. Eventually this ride on the cosmic serpent took me to a portal, which was like a doorway that I became very curious about; the snake disappeared and left me with this new possibility. My instincts told me not to enter into this portal, though I was quite curious about it. Later I asked Pablo about the snake and the portal. He explained to me that the snake wanting to eat me is a test that Ayahuasca gives to some people to see if you will humble yourself to her power and wisdom, and is for those who are ready to surrender their illusion of control to the Divine. It's a test of courage and submitting to the will of Great Spirit while facing the fear of death. Ayahuasca has a lot to teach, but only for those who are ready to receive the beauty. I knew that I had had training in my life with Aboriginal people in humility and surrender to Spirit and ancient wisdom, which also helped guide me in my experiences with the druid spirit in Scotland. After the ceremony I asked Don Pablo about the portal and if it was okay to go in there, and he said, 'Yes it is but only with a guide. So next time, ask for a guide to take you in there.'

As this first journey continued I found myself in another time, somewhere in a rainforest in the Americas, perhaps in the Amazon itself in another time, where there were pyramids and temples, and I saw a vision of myself in a previous life meditating inside a pyramid temple. When I saw myself there, I became aware of my spiritual body I was journeying with inside the miração. I found my awareness moving to a past version of myself meditating in this temple and I merged my spiritual body into his so that we were as one being. I saw many things through his eyes. I saw that in this previous life I was a kind of shaman working with psychedelic plants and in that realisation, all the memories of how to navigate in the miração came back to me and I was told by Ayahuasca that I had come back to this place in my visions to remember the teachings I had gained in past lives so that I would be able to use those skills and knowledge in this life. It was a similar vision to the ones I had with the druid spirit, where I was being shown past lives and my soul's journey. I had a strong sense of purpose and meaning which was beyond words, and at this stage my thinking mind was still disengaged, as I was very deep in the miração and in total trust and faith in the divine being guiding me. I took some time to contemplate the vastness of my ancient soul and the realisation that who I truly was beyond this lifetime was impossible for my thinking mind to comprehend, yet in the miração I could feel and experience and just be grateful and in awe of the power of this great mystery of life and existence.

The next vision that emerged in my first Ayahuasca miração (in this lifetime) was the appearance of an extraterrestrial spaceship that came down to me and invited me to enter it. This was another experience that may sound to some as being pretty far out there or unbelievable but I had also had previous experiences in Australia of seeing and communicating with extraterrestrials, usually around

Aboriginal sacred sites, so when they arrived in my miração, I wasn't surprised. I went inside their ship, which seemed like it was made of pure light, and was introduced to some beings who called themselves 'Galactic Mayans'. They took me to their home planet, which was a beautiful and pristine Earth-like world with forests and jungles that seemed to be a lot like the Amazon. They showed me how they lived in pod-like houses that were suspended over the trees and that they lived in way that had minimal impact on the environment. They showed me that they exist at a very high vibration and explained that they can only maintain that vibration by being in total harmony with the living being of the planet without creating any disturbance in its vibrational field. They explained to me that they were ancestors of humanity, that they were here to help and had left knowledge at different points of history. Following this, I was then taken into space, where everything became very colourful and geometrical and I saw a large spiralling galaxy-like mandala of energy moving in ways I could not fully grasp. A realisation came into my mind that this was the cosmic map of what we know as the Mayan calendar, which in reality is the harmonic patterns of creation and how all time and space exists throughout the galaxy. This Mayan cosmology was then given to me in a kind of download and I spent what felt like a long time receiving cosmic maps, geometries, numbers, sequences, colours, sounds and frequencies. Interestingly, after my first Ayahuasca experiences, when I left Brazil and went back to Britain, I met a man in Glastonbury who came up to me in the street and we had a conversation about the Mayan calendar. He was a teacher of it and a keeper of its knowledge and he gave me documents, books, maps and calendars which I then went on to study in great detail. In the following years I travelled the world studying, living and teaching the cosmology of Mayan time science. As I write these words, I am in a studio in Byron Bay, Australia, where this Mayan time messenger was living a few months earlier.

So far, my first Ayahuasca experience had taken me from the depths of a confused personal hell of mental resistance and physical pain into the belly of a cosmic serpent, to a meeting with myself in a past life and on an extraterrestrial journey into space and the galaxy where I downloaded the mechanics of time and cosmic science. After these cosmic downloads I became more present with the room again and I found myself sitting up in a meditative position; I noticed that Pablo and Silvia were walking around the room from person to person. Pablo stopped in front of me and was singing a song and doing some energetic movements with his hands, and I could feel him doing some kind of clearing or healing on me. I closed my eyes and I could see Ayahuasca as fractals of DMT moving through my body and finding any damaged cells that I could perceive. It was like looking into a microscope but in the miração this seemed as large and vivid as any other of the visions, and I realised that the micro and macro scales of life could be perceived equally in the miração. I saw that the intention of healing and the sound of Pablo's singing was activating a kind of life-force inside my cells, with the DMT from the Ayahuasca renewing them and rebuilding them back to their original design at a fractal or quantum level. It was as though I was seeing into the mechanics of the quantum science I had previously studied a little when I had learned that quantum science could show that thoughts directly affect our reality. Now I was seeing in my vision exactly how this occurs and that this is one of the natural functions of DMT within the human body.

When Pablo moved away I started to feel a sadness coming over me, and a worry started to return to my mind that wasn't a reaction to anything that was going on in the room or the ceremony, but something that existed deep inside me. I started to experience negative thoughts about myself: insecurities and self-doubts and a feeling of not being good enough. I started to have some visions of myself as a child and the presence of my father. My father had been relatively absent from my childhood, but when he had been around me, the experiences with him hadn't been very positive. I could see from a very profound perspective how much this had affected me, how I had a deep lack of self-worth that came from neglect and abandonment by my father, and also from the criticism and put-downs I had received from him. I saw also how I had learned in my life to be strong and to fight these feelings of inadequacy and insecurity and had built an architecture of defence around myself and my heart. I saw how, in a way, I had not been fully honest with myself as to just how much pain I was in due to the neglect of not having had a loving father. I found myself going into some further self-criticisms regarding this realisation and I felt the presence of Ayahuasca reassuring me, encouraging me not to let this realisation cause another spiral of negativity and not to re-experience this feeling of not being good enough, of feeling like there was something wrong with me that I had been carrying with me all my life.

I was quite shocked at realising the depth and scope of this wound, as I saw in the visions how it had been affecting all of my relationships throughout my life and was blocking me from realising the fullness of my being and freely expressing my true self. This was very disarming. I felt paralysed, like I was lost in this pain and had no idea of where to go to begin to heal or how to move forward in my life, knowing how profound the wound and its architecture of defence was. On one hand, I had been on this path of realising all these deep spiritual truths of who I was in this life and in my soul journey, and on the other hand I saw myself as this wounded child, lost in illusions of insecurity, hiding behind an architecture of self-protection.

Within my miração I saw visions of my father and his life and his relationship with his father, his experiences throughout his childhood and adolescence and his experiences as a soldier in the war. I saw the deep wound that he carried and how that had been transferred to me. I saw that a lot of the struggles and emotional pain I had carried in my life were the effects of carrying my father's wound in a way that I was wearing it like a heavy cloak. I felt that Ayahuasca was encouraging me to find compassion inside myself for my father and for the way that our dysfunctional relationship had affected me so deeply. I took some time in this moment to feel the pain of all this, and the visions went into past lives and wars and I saw a vision of blood spilling from a crucifix in Scotland, the land of my ancestors. I realised in this vision that there had been a struggle over hundreds of years of war, domination and conquest that had moved through my ancestral lands and how my ancestors had been fighting for generations for justice and freedom, and that now in this life I was still in this fight. My life's journey of healing and spirituality seemed to make so much more sense, despite the crimes of the forces of domination and control that have swept around the planet, stealing the connection of the people from the land. I understood that Spirit never dies and the spirit of Country was still strong inside me. I understood that my connection to my ancestors will never die and can never be stolen. I felt the presence of my ancestors embracing me. I felt their love and support, and I was shown some visions of symbols that hold meaning for the tribal, spiritual connection with my ancestors that endures throughout time. And I saw in the miração how I can use those symbols through intention to invoke and keep that connection strong in this life. After dealing with the intense wounds of abandonment and feeling alone, this revelation gave me strength and confidence in who I was in this life and the importance of my spiritual path.

Following these revelations I felt empty, just drifting in the feelings from receiving the most powerful healing of my life. The visions and presence of my ancestors felt more real than anything I had ever experienced. My mind had wanted to go into wonderment and fascination with Ayahuasca and the profundity of this experience. Ayahuasca began to show herself in visions as a beautiful woman who was playfully shape-shifting in an astral forest and gently sending me love and reassurance through humorous and cheeky gestures. I had the sense she was telling me to calm my mind, that the thoughts of wonderment and fascination were just my ego, and that I must maintain the surrender and emptiness that would assist me in absorbing all of the healings and teachings I was receiving.

This feeling of sublime surrender continued into the morning, and as the first signs of the light of the sun emerged in the forest I was enchanted by the sounds of the animals that began to awaken. I felt myself drifting and journeying and being bathed in the astounding beauty of nature. At times I sensed different animals becoming more present with me and connecting with me and I received them all with gratitude and honour. I could sense certain animals stronger than others and felt an ancestral connection to the land too, and all the beings of the Earth and the forces of nature. It was as if the journey of Ayahuasca and the healing I had received had opened me for this moment to be filled with the energy of the Divine through the blessings of this magnificent forest. There were many other visions and healings and realisations on that first night with Ayahuasca in the Amazon, and I remember having thoughts of how I might be able to remember it all, to savour every part of such an epic journey — it felt like I had just experienced lifetimes in one night. I let the thoughts go and lay there feeling like a newborn child, bathing in the sonic landscape of the awakening forest at dawn.

The rest of the day unfolded like in a dream. We rested and ate with the group and were then taken out in the canoes by the local Indigenous people to explore the smaller rivers that flowed into the mighty Amazon. We saw monkeys, alligators and dolphins, snakes in the trees and so many birds and fish. I felt peaceful and so alive and connected to everything; my spirit was more alive inside me than I had ever felt and I even imagined myself in some past life living, hunting and playing in this vast multi-dimensional forest. Whilst the visions had subsided, I was imagining everything in that forest as being not just the physical but also the seemingly infinite spiritual dimensions that existed there.

As the retreat unfolded I began to form some great friendships with other participants. Silvia would call us to gather each day and she would facilitate group sharing circles where we explored our experiences together. She put a strong emphasis on the psychological aspects and challenged the group members to understand our emotional, physical and mental conditions through the lens of the messages and visions we experienced in the ceremonies. As we explored together, the group became increasingly bonded and this was reflected more and more as the retreat unfolded, especially during the ceremonies, where a kind of 'group oneness' opened up which included shared telepathic experiences such as shared visions and receiving messages and visions for each other. The Ayahuasca was showing us how connected we truly are when we break down the barriers and learn to trust in a spiritual reality. I was absorbing everything through this time at the retreat. Silvia was a very impressive guide, with a strong presence and constant reminders bringing us back to ourselves and our inner knowing — at times with some tough love that I really appreciated. I felt very much at home in this space and that I had found a realm where I could really open myself and enjoy expressing all the aspects of my being. The familiarity and sense of being at home in that spiritual and healing environment gave me a new vision for how we can heal and grow together which has inspired me to this day. I had discovered a path of spirituality and healing that was the most efficient and effective I could ever have imagined, and as my whole life and inspiration in life was to be of service to the Earth and the healing of humanity, this was the greatest blessing and gift to have found.

The most intriguing and compelling aspect of the retreat for me was the presence of Pablo Amaringo. I found myself very drawn to him; my spirit was guiding me to remain very present and attentive to his words and actions. I enjoyed relaxing into being a student in the presence of a great master. Pablo's abilities were subtle but I could see how he was moving with Spirit in a way that was very powerful in his connection and confidence. He was very secure in his energetic field, which was of a very strong and high vibration. His presence invoked a strong sense of mystery. At times he was there and then not there, and he spoke in riddles: sometimes answering people's questions in ways that made me think deeply, reminding me of conversations I had previously had with Aboriginal Elders in Australia. I found a lot of love and respect for the way he would answer questions that would inspire us to find our own answers or give us deep spiritual puzzles to solve. At times he would be in the ceremonies and at other times not, often saying things like: 'I am an old man, I'm tired so I won't be coming to the ceremony tonight', and then he would be there, while at other times he would say he would be there and then he wouldn't be there, sometimes suddenly appearing or disappearing. At times I couldn't tell if he was physically present or whether it was his spirit appearing within the miração. I knew that whether he was physically present with us or not, he was with us all the time — which was very reassuring, especially as I was going deeper into uncharted spiritual territories. I just stayed present with him and embraced every opportunity to observe and to learn from him in the playful, spiritual and multi-dimensional way that he was teaching us. At times I saw

With Jan and Pablo Amaringo, Amazonas, Brazil, 2003

him appear and disappear, other times I could hear him singing although I couldn't see him in the room; I saw him shape-shift into a colourful butterfly and move around the room bringing healing to the participants. At times he would also appear in my miração and show me things or take me to places. In between the ceremonies he would show us his paintings, which were very detailed depictions of the physical and astral forests with all their energies and spiritual beings, plants and animals, shamans and angels. Each painting was full of meaning and teachings, which I absorbed every word of and any guidance that he shared. Some of the paintings would emerge in my miração during the following ceremony, where the teachings would continue.

One of the paintings he shared depicted some extraterrestrial spaceships and ethereal temples amidst stars and planets. He pointed to one temple and told us it was a special temple on another planet where some shamans can go and learn shamanic arts. Later that night in the ceremony, when I was inside the miração of the

Ayahuasca and I came to a kind of gateway or spiritual portal, I remembered Pablo's advice to ask for a guide before entering. As soon as I had that thought, he himself appeared in the vision beside the gateway. Before I could have another thought we were journeying through colour, movement and geometries, and eventually into space, and then I found myself sitting in some kind of astral temple full of light but quite empty. I felt the presence of Ayahuasca as I sat meditating in this temple and many visions started appearing, one after the other. I found that I was being guided to work together with Ayahuasca and my spiritual guides: I would be shown a vision and would have some kind of reaction to it, and at other times I would be asked to create my own visions of things from my life and my own imagination. It seemed that Ayahuasca was reading my visual and emotional landscape with all these visions. She explained to me that we were working together to develop a visual and sensorial language — which I called a 'language of light' — that would strengthen the miração, and that Ayahuasca herself and the other spiritual beings within the miração would know how to communicate with me through knowing my own internal visual universe. It was like a mutual sharing of visions and building a relationship. Ayahuasca reminded me that my relationship with her was like any relationship I might have with another person, and that we were learning about each other in this process. She also explained to me how, through surrender to the mystery and the power of the miração and the spirit of the forest, I could learn to empower myself to co-create the visions of the miração — and even the Ayahuasca experience itself. Once I awakened my own spirit she told me that even though she was a powerful being with a vast consciousness, we were actually all equal. It felt like I was in the temple for a whole lifetime. At times I would be painting pictures in my mind and responding to telepathic communication from Ayahuasca and I began to show her things from my own land and the nature of Australia. I got a strong sense of my own spiritual body and the colours and geometries that emanate from me. When I transmitted my thoughts as visions with creativity, Ayahuasca would respond with visions showing herself delighting in what I was sharing. This led to a very playful exchange and a feeling like reconnecting with an old friend. These teachings were very valuable in not only developing and strengthening my connection with the magical being that is Ayahuasca, but also in developing abilities that would benefit the work that was to come for me over many years and over many hundreds of experiences with this sacred medicine.

As the days of the retreat unfolded, Pablo also guided us through visionary art workshops. Pablo himself was a famous visionary artist and a pioneer in sharing the spirituality of the Amazon all over the world through his art. He had ceased working as a curandeiro some years previously due to the jealousy and competitiveness in his native Peru from sorcerer shamans, who had persecuted him and even tried to kill him with black magic. He had dedicated the rest of his life to his art and wanted to share all his visions and spiritual knowledge from the universe of Ayahuasca and the forest. I had always enjoyed art, painting and drawing since I was a child, and found a lot of satisfaction in learning about painting my visions from Pablo. Following Pablo's inspiration, I went on to explore visionary art, painting many artworks. During the ceremonies with Pablo I contemplated the value of art in depicting a spiritual reality without using words or anything that somebody could argue or disagree with. I had found in my life that I had always been visionary, either through seeing a more positive light on the world and our collective future, or through sharing spiritual insights with friends and family. Since childhood I had found that some people find it very hard to accept my views and I had at times been frustrated by this, sometimes leading to me being defensive. What Pablo showed me with his story of taking himself out of the dangerous world of competitive shamanism in Peru was that art could also be a powerful mode of sharing knowledge and shamanic abilities.

At times I wanted Pablo to answer every question I had and to guide me and tell me what I should be doing on this new and exciting path. Part of me wanted to gain validation from him regarding the experiences I was having and the depths of my miração. I was attempting to measure my journey based on what other people were experiencing at the retreat, but I found that nobody seemed to be having the same kind of spiritual experience I was. At times I would sit with Pablo with the intention of asking him questions or talking about my visions, and every time I did, all the questions and thoughts would just drop away and I would hardly be able speak. It was like I suddenly had nothing to say. Eventually I came to realise that this was all happening in the miração and that he was completely aware of my journey and the experiences I was having. He would sometimes look at me and nod his head with a knowing glance; even when I was painting my visions he would come and take the brush and add something that showed me he knew exactly what I was painting. There was much more being transmitted in our silence and through the miração than could possibly be transmitted through words.

Pablo had brought his nephew Juan with him to the retreat; Juan was looking after Pablo's needs and, I felt, providing him with a familiar sense of family and home. Pablo had taken an interest in me and would often give me praise and attention. Juan seemed to want attention from his uncle and often wanted to spend time with me, and we struck up a friendship. Juan seemed a bit lost in his life with drinking issues and relationship problems, but he was excited when we spoke about music, and we played together at times. Pablo asked me at one point to help him with Juan, as he said that Juan had not embraced his spiritual path and was suffering as a result. Pablo had invited Juan to come in the hope that he might open himself more. This became an interesting counterpoint to my experience. In knowing Juan and his story, I could see in myself the ways in which I had also been avoiding the spiritual and creative reality of my own life.

During one of the ceremonies in the miração I saw some very intense visions of global environmental changes, cataclysms and, in particular, a volcano erupting from under the Earth that sent so much smoke into the atmosphere, it blocked the sun around most of the planet. This vision endured for some time and gave me a sense of dread, as though it was a warning of something yet to come. I sensed within me the immense importance of doing everything I could to develop myself spiritually to care for the Earth and prepare for the possibility of global catastrophe in my lifetime; Ayahuasca was speaking to me and showing me that my vision and healing abilities were gifts I had been given which can help many people to awaken. Caring for the Earth had always been a huge passion of mine and I had been a strong activist in environmentalism over the years. I sensed through this vision that the best way for me to help the planet was to help people awaken. I was then shown a vision of myself holding Ayahuasca ceremonies in this life and given a message from Ayahuasca that this was my destiny — that I had been chosen to walk this path with this holy sacrament. The vision took me out of the miração and my mind became very active as I began over-thinking this possibility. My instinct was to immediately reject the vision, as I knew the level of commitment, challenge and sacrifice it would require. The idea of me holding ceremonies did seem very real and possible; my faith in God and spirit throughout my life had always put me in a position where people had come to me with spiritual questions or had asked for healing. My whole life had already been dedicated to spiritual growth and helping others, but this thought also made me go into a spiral of self-doubt and fear. I was certain it was not something I wanted to do and I felt vulnerable in accepting that in the future I might take on this role. I didn't speak to anyone, not even Pablo, about this vision. I was scared that if I did, I would start to manifest it, and a big part of me was trying to run away from that possibility. Eventually I did mention the volcano to Pablo and when I did he pointed down at the ground; I knew that he had seen it too and he said, 'Yeah, it is underground.' I asked him if I should tell people and he answered, 'Why not?' I didn't really have an answer to that. Later, when studying the Santo Daime doctrines and visions of Mestre Irineu and Padrinho Sebastião, I discovered they had also been receiving visions of, and preparing for, global catastrophe. I decided that whilst it is good to be aware we live in times of prophecy, some of which might foresee a bleak future, it is best not to dwell on or worry about this — and to just get on with living.

After my experience in the first ceremony I was quite excited and couldn't wait for the next one. I had been telling Pablo that I felt I could go deeper, explore more and expand more. He smiled and didn't say anything; I then said I thought I wanted to drink more next time, explore a stronger dose. He said, 'It is medicine; if you're not sick you don't need it.' I contemplated that and asked another, more experienced, participant who shared that in her experience Pablo had encouraged her to always have less, that as we become clearer, lighter and more attuned we need less, not more. In fact all the research shows that Ayahuasca is not addictive and that people do not become desensitised to it — it is the opposite. Still, I wanted to drink more, and on the second ceremony I asked Silvia for significantly more, so she gave me two cups this time. I didn't care about the taste. What I learned from the increased amount was that my experience was no more or less profound than the night before. It was just a continuation. On the third ceremony I had less than on the first night and found the force of the tea was a little more subtle, but the strength and potency of my experience was just as good. This underlies the notion that the quality or depth of an experience of Ayahuasca is not solely determined by the quantity of the dose. I have learned much more about this as the years have progressed.

In the next ceremonies many more visions emerged, following the same themes I have described. In many ways these first experiences of mine with Ayahuasca, with the forest and with the master shaman Pablo Amaringo, were like initiation on a spiritual path, but also a remembrance of my soul's journey and an awakening of my spirit. During one ceremony I was visited by some extraterrestrials, who invited me to enter a large spaceship and who told me they were from the 'Galactic Federation'. When I entered the ship I found my mind becoming excited and the beings quickly reminded me not to let my ego get carried away with fascination and wonderment, and to stay empty and present. I felt a shakiness emerging in the miração; I wasn't holding myself in the grace required to be in such a highly refined vibration. Whenever this would happen, I would often drop out of the miração, the visions would disappear and I would be left processing with my mind and thoughts, which in turn might lead to insights into my attachments, fears and insecurities. But I realigned myself and the miração returned. Again I was aboard the galactic ship with these large, angelic beings. They told me that one of my roles in this life was to be an 'Emissary of the Star People'. They explained that there are many extraterrestrial races who are ancestors of humanity and of life on Earth. They went on to show me how, through my life and my work, they were guiding me and were present with me on my journey, and that through my eyes and experiences they were getting a sense of where we as humans were on our journey of spiritual evolution. They also showed me how in my life I would at times also be able to speak to people on their behalf. I saw visions of myself writing. This made a lot of sense, as I had been connecting with star beings from a young age and had already had many experiences and done much study on them. This is another theme that has been very present throughout my life, as I mentioned, through the Mayan calendar and its cosmology and prophecies of the galactic Maya and their return to Earth.

One night with Ayahuasca I was sitting on my mat, and as the force of the tea arrived I noticed some ants crawling around on my mat. I reacted with displeasure and tried to sweep them away, as I was a bit fearful of them interrupting my ceremony. I was agitated. As the miração began to arrive with the sensations entering into my body, the adjustment of the spiritual and material worlds alchemised inside me, which sometimes can feel a little uncomfortable and can cause the mind to question and try and work things out. During this process I sensed the presence of a being directly in front of me; it seemed very close to my face. As the miração became stronger, I started to perceive that this was some kind of insect being, or even an ant, that seemed very large. At first I felt some fear but quickly let it go and allowed this being to be present in my visions. I thought about its size and in response it said to me that even if in the material dimension insects may appear small, in the miração they can appear to be equal in size to other beings. I saw visions of the northern part of the Northern Territory of Australia where there are endless ant hills and termite mounds, some as big as houses, that stretch out into the desert for hundreds of kilometres. This insectoid being showed me how there are many billions and trillions of insects on the planet and that whilst they may be small, their entire physical mass combined is much more than that of humanity. It then showed me that, if they wanted to, the entirety of the insects could rise up, overwhelm and eat all of the humans in the world. The message the insects were giving me was one of humility and respect. I had shown repulsion to the insects on my mat, yet they are also God's creatures and have a consciousness field and dominion on the Earth, just like humans and all the species.

Following the insects and the teachings, the galactic Mayans returned and showed me that Ayahuasca provides a gateway for humans and all the species, animals, plants, natural forces, extraterrestrials to communicate in an equal way, as if at a telepathic 'round table'. Ayahuasca is the conduit which opens us to the telepathic communication that is universal. I realised that modern humanity sees itself as somehow superior to all the other species and this keeps us separate and disconnected — and that Ayahuasca is able to connect us telepathically with the other species once we humble ourselves and can learn how to evolve ourselves in harmony with the entire planet. The Mayans showed me how the real evolution of the planet is the spiritual evolution of the mind into the telepathic field of the planet, where we are all one in a sacred alliance, and that when we achieve that planetary oneness of all species, we can evolve to become galactic humans. Then the star people, our ancestors from the stars, will return amongst us and we will graduate as a planet. It seemed to me that humans, being the youngest of God's species on the planet, are like naughty children causing a mess and learning how not to misuse our power so that we can return to being creators and not destroyers.

One of the greatest teachings I received during this first time in the Amazon and with Ayahuasca was how strong the mind and the ego are. I was receiving so many blessings and remembering my soul's journey while connecting to God and many ancestral beings, and to get to these revelations was through tests of faith and humility. I was learning how Ayahuasca can open us to the immense beauty and power of the forest and our own spiritual ancestry, but also how it disarms the mind of its defences and illuminates our shadows, wounds and struggles. This can often be painful and invoke intense vulnerabilities and fears, as the mind has trained itself to protect us from traumas that can be painful and difficult to face. As a result our behaviours may develop into a protected state with repetitive behaviours, addictions and defences which inhibit us from accessing our true divinity and the secrets we have been holding inside. This leads us to guard our hearts and the deeper truths that reside in the most sensitive and vulnerable parts of ourselves, protected from the reality of a harsh world which is governed by fear and control. I could see how the entirety of humanity is holding onto the fears of the past, making our species vulnerable to the kind of corruption and control that is plaguing our society. I saw this struggle within myself and through my realisations of the beauty of divine messages that were guiding me and calling me forth, and of the old beliefs and patterns of thinking and behaving I was carrying through life. I could see more clearly than ever the imprints of life's traumas on my psyche and how much within I needed to acknowledge and begin the process of rebuilding myself and my life in a way that was a true reflection of the divine spirit within me. I began to sense the enormity of this challenge, but also the excitement of feeling newborn in a newly expanded world. I was reminded of a feeling I would often have: of feeling lost and not knowing where to turn or how to navigate this mysterious world that often creates anxieties and fear of the unknown.

Stand still
The trees ahead and the buses beside you are not lost
Wherever you are is called 'Here'
And you must treat it as a powerful stranger
Must ask permission to know it and be known
The forest breathes. Listen. It answers.
I have made this place around you
If you leave, it may come back again, staying here.

No two trees are the same to Raven
No two branches are the same to Wren
If what a tree or a bush does is lost on you
You are surely lost. Stand still
The forest knows where you are
You must let it find you.

— Lost, David Wagoner.

During the next ceremony, as the miração was arriving I felt a strong energy and a presence around me that began to do some spiritual healing work on me. I saw several spiritual beings around me; they were working on my *third eye* — the chakra between the eyes in the middle of the forehead. I was aware that this is the chakra of insight, the invisible eye that allows us to see into the spiritual and beyond the material world. As they worked their magical healing on me, I could sense them cleansing and clearing my third eye, and it felt like it had become a bright, clear crystal. Once it was cleansed, I could feel it being stretched and expanded. This sensation was a little uncomfortable but, like most of my Ayahuasca experiences, I was in total trust and allowed the process to unfold. As it expanded my visionary centre, I perceived more and more light entering into the miração, until it became quite blinding. Suddenly, I found myself emerging into a new realm of pure, golden-white light, accompanied by angelic humming sounds like songs of the Divine. Several very light beings who looked like angels with a very loving and fine, delicate presence, appeared in a circle. One of them raised its arm; it was holding in its palm a tiny, brilliantly glowing blue jewel. I was drawn to this jewel and saw that it was the Earth in the palm of its hand. The beings showed me that they were guardians of the Earth and were guiding us on our healing and awakening journey. I realised how fine their vibration was and I felt a wave of gratitude for the blessing of being taken to this divine realm. This vision of the tiny Earth made me contemplate my own small incarnation on that tiny blue speck of a jewel that is the Earth. I felt I was being taught about the knowledge of our divine truth that comes from Spirit and how it is the real power, and that I myself am just a small speck in the infinitely vast cosmos. After they showed me these visions these beings started to move and kind of swirl around until they all merged and shape-shifted into a magnificent winged unicorn with its horn spiralling and endlessly changing colours, including an array of colours I had never seen before. My mind went into wonder and fascination and each thought I had in my mind manifested as a dark stain on the unicorn. My thoughts were manifesting as disturbance in this fine, pure realm. After this happened a few times, I was suddenly ejected from the realm and found myself back in the temple and the ceremony.

> *The world is very small in the face of the Divine Presence — it's like looking through binoculars from the other end. Have you done that? Everything is very small, is it not? And it has to be very small really, because we become inflated in illusion and pride, thus taking a risk when passing through the eye of the needle. Even those who discover some things and arrive at some knowledge, if they become proud, they will die in the same way. Pride, envy and jealousy are our biggest enemies. I am speaking because I lived through all of that, so I could converse with and teach you today.*
> — Padrinho Sebastião.

After experiencing such beauty and connection with beings of such heavenly stature and divine light, I was left to contemplate my mind and how I had sabotaged my ability to stay present so deeply in this profoundly beautiful miração. Knowing that it was fear inspiring the ego to control my conscious experience, I asked myself what it was that I was afraid of. I could feel a very strong vibration of love in my heart, and when I allowed myself to feel that I could recognise the fear inside. The fear was of being vulnerable, opening myself up totally, being exposed, fear of being denied, rejected or abandoned for being who I truly am. The realisation again returned of how I had been shielding myself in life and relationships, scared to fully be myself and shine my true light. It all seemed so absurd in that moment of realisation: what was the point of hiding our light? I remembered all the pain of my ancestors, who had been driven to war to protect their rights, to protect the truth of ancestral unity through culture and connection to land, to defend it across time in the face of the forces of darkness marauding across the planet.

> *The more we give of ourselves in this surrender to the Divine, in trying to overcome our barriers and limitations, the greater is the grace we receive in the miração.* — Alex Polari de Alverga.

I began to contemplate the ego and its attachment to identity and the material world, and when I did Pablo arrived in my vision. I realised I was still in the miração and Pablo had come, indicating for me to follow him. When I did so, I found myself in an empty void of total darkness, just emptiness, and all thoughts disappeared. I had been in this void before in meditations and something so peaceful in knowing this descended over me. Everything stopped and disappeared for what felt like an eternity when, from somewhere, I heard a voice that sounded like one of those angels I had been with before. I was drawn to this voice and in that moment was unable to think of anything or have any thoughts I was at all familiar with. I tried to remember where I was and how I had got there; I couldn't even remember my name — or my life. My mind was trying to assert itself but there was nothing. The voice calmly said to me: 'You don't have to go back to that life; it's gone if that is what you want.' This didn't alarm me, as I had nothing left I was attached to. A strong force of awareness came from within me and instantly I made a decision to return to the world as I knew it with a strong conviction I had more in this lifetime I could experience to learn and grow from. When I returned to the miração after this experience, Pablo was back with me and was sending me a lot of energy. This was a luminous transmission of huge amounts of teachings and knowledge which I took some time to let enter into my spiritual field. He told me this was a gift of spiritual knowledge that would be available to me for the rest of my life. This was our final night together in ceremony at this retreat and after my experience with the void, which felt like some kind of shamanic ego-death, I had so much to contemplate. As the light of the sun began to arrive again I allowed my mind to drift between thoughts and feelings, visions and the emerging sounds of the jungle's morning orchestra.

Break,
Break the code
Concentrate
Let the doors swing open
See through all your walls
All your floors
Now you're in deeper than sleep

When you let me fall
I grew my own wings
Now I'm as tall as the sky

When you let me drown
I grew gills and fins
Now I'm as deep as the sea

When you let me die
My spirits free
There's nothing challenging me

— *Ring the Bells,* James.

It was a little sad to have reached the end of this journey in the Amazon with Ayahuasca. I had received such profound healing and teachings and grown so much spiritually, and made some wonderful new friends, including Silvia and Pablo. So much had come to light it was as though I had lived many lifetimes in those two weeks at the retreat. The biggest impact upon me was my relationship with Ayahuasca itself. She had come to me in many different forms, often very playfully, cheekily teasing me and giving me riddles that would help me to go beyond my mind and to realise another way of communicating through telepathic knowing and the visions of the miração. We had spent so much time in those ceremonies, playfully frolicking as old friends together. The visions and senses I received from Ayahuasca had felt mostly feminine in nature and with her vast wisdom and power I can understand why some people refer to Ayahuasca as 'Grandmother'. I had met her in so many different ways. Mostly she seemed to be a younger female spirit, but she could also be a snake, a jaguar, butterflies, vines and other plants. Ayahuasca shows herself in infinite ways. The voice that was communicating to me though was that of a wise woman: regal, graceful and honouring. I have come to know her as *Rainha da Luz da Floresta* or the 'Queen of the Forest Light'.

From my experience, Ayahuasca is beyond words and beyond the human mind's capacity to comprehend such majesty and mystery.

Without needing to define Ayahuasca, I felt that I had just been on a cosmic journey with an old friend who took me by the hand and showed me her beauty and her mysteries and reminded me of the most powerful and divine aspects of my own soul. Ayahuasca took me to the depths of my wounds and showed me the arrogance of my ego, and through profound compassion helped me to release the pain that was inside me. She gave me the remedy for those wounds and renewed faith in my life's path ahead. I knew this experience had changed me forever, and it felt like this was only the beginning.

Since I was a child I had been in contact with spiritual beings and had had numerous experiences throughout childhood and adolescence of feeling overwhelmed by divine love that would wash over me in moments and would seemingly paralyse me. As a child, I really didn't know what I was experiencing and I remember searching in VHS video shops for any documentaries or films about paranormal phenomena, spiritual channelling, extraterrestrials and mediumship. In my late teens I was able to find people I could talk about these topics with, but it took some time to fully understand and accept the gift I had in this lifetime. Many people and society in general have a fearful and ignorant attitude to spiritual realities and other dimensional beings, and for a long time this caused a lot of doubt and confusion in me. As I grew throughout my late twenties and into my thirties, I became a lot more confident in my spiritual experiences. I often wanted to find a teacher or guide who could help me to know how to navigate this reality. Being amongst the community of people who gathered for the retreat and with teachers such as Silvia Polivoy and Pablo Amaringo, I finally found myself in a group where respect and understanding of communication with, and connection to, the Divine is fundamental. I felt the blessing from the forest that allows us, through sacred ceremony and respect for ancient ancestral traditions, to safely have these profound experiences with the divine being through Ayahuasca and to cultivate faith and self-knowledge which, I had come to understand, was at the core of shamanic awareness. I also felt the strong distinction and difference in ancestral medicine and power plants compared with psychedelic drugs and hallucinations. My faith and confidence in Great Spirit had grown enormously from these experiences in the Amazon, and I left that retreat with gratitude, a big smile and love in my heart

After that last ceremony I felt some vulnerability in not fully knowing where my life would take me. I knew I was going to meet Ayahuasca again and from the perspective of working in different health settings and being a facilitator of healing throughout my life, I felt she was by far the best psychotherapist and healer I had ever met. I had so much to integrate from my experiences. I was also very grateful for Silvia's work and we became friends during this time. My connection with Pablo was similar to that with Ayahuasca: it was deep in mystery yet familiarity, with some kind of cosmic soul-knowing of each other.

As Pablo had given me such a powerful gift in the miração, after the ceremony I gifted him a crystal I had been carrying with me for several years and had taken to Uluru and other sacred places in Australia. Ayahuasca herself had been very curious about these places and I had taken her to some of these sacred Australian sites in the miração. Pablo was very grateful and curious to receive my gift. Later, when I was walking along the path to my cabin, Pablo seemingly magically appeared beside me, walking with me. His energy felt powerful, as though a very strong vibration was connecting to me spiritually, like a magnetic force. He asked me: 'When are you coming to visit me in Peru?' I was a little surprised at the invitation, and very honoured. I told him I would do my best to visit him as soon as possible. We chatted for a moment then he whisked off again as quickly as he had arrived, just like a hummingbird.

After the retreat, Jan organised a trip for us to go to a remote beach in the north of Brazil called Jericoacoara in the state of Ceará. The trip was an important time to just relax and be with the ocean and nature, and I did a lot of journaling and continued the art that I had been painting at the retreat. The presence of Ayahuasca and Pablo still seemed very real and strong with me. Upon returning to Wales with Jan, I started to feel restless and some of the clarity that I had had in the Amazon started to fade. Doubts began creeping back in. I decided to go on a vision quest to the town of Glastonbury in Somerset — that was another place of strong spiritual significance to my ancestry.

I spent a few days there wandering around visiting holy places and writing a lot in my journal. While I was there I met a woman who was a powerful spiritual healer, who said she recognised my soul and saw in me my connection to the land. She took me on some journeys to sacred sites where more of my soul's journey became clear. One morning at sunrise as I was meditating on the Glastonbury Tor, I received a clear message guiding me to return home to Australia.

I felt like a different person to the one who had left several months before and I had no idea what was waiting for me upon my return.

How do you know that you are on your path? Because it disappears, that's how you know. Can't see where you're going, that's how you know. Everything you have leant on for your identity has gone. You are going to enter the black contemplative splendours of self-doubt, at the same time as you are setting out on this radical new path. — David Whyte.

Reflecting upon my journey from Australia to Europe and the ancient sites of Celtic Britain, to the depths of the Amazon and Brazil, I felt a new confidence in myself that I had not experienced before. It was now clear to me that I was not alone on this spiritual journey through life, that I had the power of my ancestors and their lineages behind me. It was like a new foundation was holding me and there was a security in knowing who I was. I had previously been introduced to ancient rituals with First Nations peoples in Australia and now I had experienced the ancestors and ancestral lands of my blood relatives and had partaken in thousands-of-years-old rituals in the Amazon. On each step of the way, the message guiding me was that the great secret, the sacred knowledge, was actually within me. I learned that, despite the disconnection of my family from our ancestral lineages, despite the suffering through the generational traumas caused by this and despite having this knowledge denied to me throughout my life, the power of Great Spirit in guiding me to the places and people that could open the doors to this knowledge remained available to me, and in fact, was always there. One of the greatest crimes against humanity is that we are cut off from our ancestral knowledge and ancient rituals which for aeons have nourished the human soul and given us the confidence in who we are. I felt enormously blessed to have had these experiences and realisations, and also felt a determination to learn more and support others to know and experience the Divine Spirit of the Earth, our ancestors and the divinity within ourselves. The power and depth of my spiritual experiences had given me so much to contemplate and the realisation that I had been living my life in a form which was limiting. It seemed like I had so much to learn and to grow into in order to fully embrace and integrate all that I had learned. I knew there would be a lot more work ahead of me, but as I walked with renewed faith into this next part of my life, I felt the strength of my ancestors, my spiritual guides and the forces of nature with me.

We live in a dream
And it goes on forever
Here we are, in this moment
We all share together
If you see and you feel
Then we are all together
With the birds and the trees
Everyone, you and me
This crazy world
It's illusion
It's all energy
We live in a dream
And it goes on forever ...

— *We Live in a Dream (Goes on Forever)*, Lore Solaris.

CHAPTER 6

The Earth Changes

Mysteries unfolding

The mystery of life isn't a problem to solve, but a reality to experience. A process that cannot be understood by stopping it. We must move with the flow of the process. We must join it. We must flow with it. — Frank Herbert, *Dune*.

Returning home to Australia was more challenging than I had anticipated. I felt so radically different; my perspectives on life and my own self had changed so much. Many of the paths and friends I had previously chosen seemed like they were not right for me anymore and I had to stay focused on myself and my connection to Spirit to avoid going back to old ways. I knew I didn't want to go back to working in government and non-government agencies — that just felt too dense for me at this time. I was determined to continue the spiritual path I had initiated since I had begun my journey back in Scotland. I had no idea where to go or what to do at this time and in some ways I was a little lost, but I had a close friend to stay with and I dived into studies of Mayan calendrics and cosmology.

I met some people during this time who were connected to Ayahuasca groups in Australia and wanted to do some of that work with me, although I wasn't resonating much with the way they were talking about their experiences with Ayahuasca and I didn't sense anything in what they said that was even close to what I had experienced in Brazil. I did embark on a mission with a new friend

I had met who had some plants for cooking some Ayahuasca, and I agreed to help him with that and for us to do a ceremony together. He had gained some experience from a facilitator in Australia who was well-known but also had a reputation for inappropriate behaviour. I remembered the message from Ayahuasca about one day becoming a facilitator and thought that maybe I should find a way to pursue that. But what I found was that my new friend and I were both far out of our depth in being able to navigate such a powerful experience without the guidance of true masters. This turned out to be a painful experience and also very humbling, and I quickly realised that I had a lot more to learn before attempting to do such sacred work. I could also see how easy it was to let the ego run away with ambitions and I was relieved to pull out of this experiment, much to the disappointment of my friend, who kept on dabbling. I really had no idea of the amount of study and spiritual growth I was yet to experience, and all I was left with at this point was faith and trust in Spirit — a common theme in my life.

I began to experience strong feelings of loss and grief around this time; I was letting go of my old self and identity that were no longer relevant. This was quite challenging and I was starting to feel anxiety about learning how to integrate the powerful experience I had had in the Amazon and the advice Silvia had given about being mindful of the challenges of integration. As feelings of confusion and doubt arose, I decided to enrol in a 10-day Vipassana meditation course, which seemed like a good idea to develop a meditative mind, something I had learned was so important during Ayahuasca.

After returning to Australia I began a deep study of the Mayan calendar and the cosmology of time science, with a strong emphasis on the work of philosopher and prophet José Argüelles, who had become famous for numerous discoveries and decoding of the mysteries of the galactic Maya and the codes and clues left behind in the synchronic codes of the Mayan calendar systems and their prophecies. As this knowledge and wisdom had been part of my journey with Ayahuasca and had also come to me at various points on my path, it was with a deep focus that I delved into these mysteries and wisdom. I discovered a profound resonance with the messages I received from Ayahuasca and the warnings from this ancient culture about the impending environmental catastrophe and the need for humanity to awaken.

José Argüelles, in his book *Manifesto for the Noosphere*, emphasises the *noosphere* as a mental stratum of Earth which represents the next evolutionary leap for human consciousness. He believed that the noosphere, akin to a planetary 'mind-field', emerges when humanity becomes fully aware of its role as a collective organism. This shift, he argues, moves us from a fragmented, materialistic worldview into a synchronised state of consciousness that prioritises harmony, telepathy and art over consumerism, competition and separation from nature.

While contemplating this work I was reminded of the messages I received from Ayahuasca that were showing me how we as humans are part of a unified collective field of consciousness, and how through Ayahuasca we can achieve awareness of and communication with all the species of the Earth. Argüelles suggests that the activation of the noosphere could foster inter-species communication, as it enables us to tap into higher layers of planetary intelligence. He sees the noosphere as a medium through which advanced telepathic energies and galactic intelligence can interact with humanity, proposing a future where synchronisation and shared awareness lead to new modes of knowing and relating, both among humans and with other species. For him, achieving this 'mind shift' is a conscious effort requiring humanity's alignment with the rhythms of nature, such as those expressed in the 13-moon calendar. Through this alignment, Argüelles envisioned an era where humanity transcends conflict and disorder to co-create the Earth as a work of art, integrating both imagination and the natural order.

I managed to find a cabin in the rainforest hinterland of the Byron Bay region of Australia, where I spent many months in deep study of natural time, Mayan cosmology and cosmic science. I found these studies were opening pathways in my mind and connecting me deeper into spiritual realities and a shamanic view of reality, much like I had experienced with Ayahuasca. Argüelles, in his book *Surfers of the Zuvuya*, tells a story of how the galactic Mayans came to Earth to bring prophecy and knowledge, and that they chose the terrestrial Maya people of Central America to integrate themselves with because the terrestrial Mayans were adept at navigating multi-dimensional realities due to their use of psychedelic plants and shamanic practices. I had also become aware of how Australian Aboriginal peoples have also used native plants containing DMT in ceremony and what we may describe as 'shamanic arts'. During this time back in Australia I had also been introduced by friends to a leafy herbal smoking mix that contained DMT from native Australian plants.

Over several months in my isolated retreat in the forest I spent days studying and painting my visions. At times I would walk into the forest where I would do a small ceremony and smoke some of the leafy DMT mix I had been given. Over many nights I received visions, guidance and knowledge from Country and my ancestors. During the day I would paint these visions, and I filled some journals with writings, art and the transmissions that I received. Many things were opening in my awareness during this time, and after a while I began another spiritual journey around the world, making connections, organising gatherings and workshops sharing the knowledge of the Mayan calendar and natural time. For the first time in my life I felt I was totally aligned and in harmony with the natural flow of life. My spiritual guidance and the profound synchronicities that were guiding me became stronger than ever.

At this point I would like to share that, although I am telling a story of smoking DMT alone in the forest, this is not something I would recommend to just anybody. It is important to have reverence and respect for powerful psychedelics and to use them in a way that is ceremonial and in harmony with the land, nature and its spirits. Without this respect for the sacrament and for Country the user may create disturbances with the spirits in the land that could lead to them having a negative experience. To do this I believe it is respectful to have the blessings of an Elder or very experienced person who knows you are ready for such an experience. I also believe it is always important to follow safety protocols, such as letting someone know where you are and what you are intending to do. These are just basic and standard safety practices in case your experience is emotionally or mentally intense and you need support to recover and integrate. I have seen people become disoriented, often from interactions with spiritual beings which they may not have the experience or skills to navigate. In some cases, practitioners alone or without qualified guidance may experience ego-inflation and the support will help them to remain grounded and humble. In my case I had consulted with a local Aboriginal Elder, plus I was very attuned to and connected with that land and had gained confidence and skill in navigating deep in altered states with a steady mind and self-discipline.

My studies in the Mayan calendar led me to Europe on a mission with a friend to attend an ancient crystal skull conference in Switzerland. When we arrived there I was surprised to meet a woman who had been sent by the Indigenous Maya in Guatemala along with three ancient crystal skulls, each transmitting the mystery of cosmic science and history of the Maya. Connecting with these remarkable artefacts and the message that had been sent with them by the Elders was another transmission of teachings I received on my journey. It led to further crystal skull meetings in Glastonbury and a spontaneous trip back to Scotland, where we met and stayed with a Scottish shaman woman who was another keeper of ancient crystal skulls. She shared with me some beautiful and inspiring transmissions she had received from extraterrestrial ancestors of the Earth through her meditations with the skulls. These transmissions reflected the same theme of Earth changes and humanity's awakening that had come to me through my own experiences.

Following this meeting in Scotland I was guided to the US, where on the night we arrived in San Francisco my friend and I received a spontaneous invitation to a traditional sweat lodge by a Lakota First Nations Elder. The sweat lodge was being held close to the place where we were staying. I had experienced sweat lodge ceremonies before in Australia but nothing could have prepared me for this one, as during it I had a powerful experience similar to those I had had during Ayahuasca. We were invited to stay with some of the Lakota family north of San Francisco where we did two more sweat lodge ceremonies. I was guided through a ceremony of an eagle blessing, where one of the brothers wove beads and prayers into the stem of my Australian eagle feather whilst I stayed on a mountain alone, praying, as two eagles circled above me. In the years to follow this blessed feather and that land in Northern California would play a significant role in my journey.

These years following my first Ayahuasca experiences were filled with deep personal and spiritual revelations and many blessings and teachings that I received along the path. I was filled with passion for growth and learning and strongly driven by the guidance and visions I had received regarding the urgency of humanity's need to awaken, evolve and change our ways in order to survive the coming global shift. It seemed to me there was little else more important than this work and I put myself into it totally. This was not always an easy path, as so many people were asleep to the state of the world, despite the many prophecies ringing alarm bells warning humanity about the dangers of its current trajectory. Others were more focused on glamourising and commercialising Ayahuasca practices, whilst not going much further than the ego and its fascination. This all brought me to a relatively lonely place, where my spiritual awareness had become so developed that it wasn't so easy to find others who might understand. I began to realise this was also part of initiation on the shamanic path, where life guides us to learn directly from our spirit, to not seek from outside the self, to find the healing and the knowledge within. It seemed I had awakened with the Dream of the planet to find almost everyone else still asleep. I knew in myself I still had some tendencies to drift into sleep within the Dream, and I contemplated what it would take to move from wavering between consciousness and unconsciousness to living completely in continuing consciousness. I decided to go back to a more 'normal' life with a job and bills, social life and community in Byron Bay.

This was a really enjoyable time. I still had my spiritual studies, I was connecting with local First Nations peoples and painting visionary artworks in a little cabin with views over the beautiful coastline of the whales and rainbows of Byron Bay. It was nearly four years since I had made that trip to the Amazon and met Ayahuasca and I felt that I had never really left her — the presence of the forest and its teachings was still always with me. Throughout these years I always had in the back of my mind to follow through on the invitation I had received from Don Pablo about visiting him in Peru. Aside from the deep connection that I found with Ayahuasca and the warm, loving guidance she gave me to continue with her in this life, the personal invitation from Don Pablo was a great honour and I knew at some point I would have to visit him. I started to experience dreams and memories of Don Pablo, especially when painting or working in the garden. I had some resistance to making this trip though, as I knew it would be another significant journey with lots of challenges which I was trying to avoid. I had this great life in Byron Bay, one of the most beautiful places and communities in the world, I had my cabin and friends, connection to Country and my art: why would I want to give all that up after years of personal challenges, tests of faith and the sacrifice of living between the spirit realms and the Dream of humanity's collective reality? It was more magical synchronicity that led to me being pushed out of my cosy nest and learning to fly with the spirit of the eagle once again.

One afternoon I was sitting in my cabin painting a canvas of my view over Mount Chincogan to the sea and with a kookaburra flying with wings outstretched towards the west. As I was painting, I imagined Brazil and South America across the massive expanse of the Pacific Ocean. I had often seen kookaburras flying around the region; sometimes they would fly in front of me or alongside me whilst I was driving. They are one of my favourite birds due to their friendliness, curiosity and quirky song and behaviour. When I would watch them with their wings outstretched gliding sleekly along the wind I would see geometries and colours reminiscent of ones I had seen in Ayahuasca and with the acacia DMT. These colours and geometries were so much like my own whenever I saw my own energy field and ancestral spiritual field; I felt so connected to the kookaburra that I decided to paint one. When I paint I am usually inspired by a vision and the rest just falls into place without much thinking. In this painting I had also depicted some images of the *Nazca* lines from Peru — vast ancient geoglyphs etched into the desert plains depicting immense shapes of animals, plants, and symbols, including the hummingbird. As I painted the last brush strokes I realised this wasn't just a painting but a magical creation, manifesting the next part of my journey.

As I sat enjoying my latest creation, I received a very unexpected phone call. *Congratulations! You are this week's winner of $5000 in our orange juice competition!* I asked the happy woman on the phone what the competition she was referring to was and she reminded me I had sent a text message to enter the competition. I had forgotten about it, as entering competitions wasn't something I would normally do, but the moment she told me I had won I had a vision and strong realisation it was time to return to the Amazon. She then told me all I needed was the receipt and my heart sank; I don't usually keep receipts. But I went and searched my house and found one small piece of paper at the bottom of the rubbish bin. Sure enough, it was the receipt. Just as with the first time I had gone to the Amazon, here was a random communication coming to me and offering the financial means to travel again. When I think of these kinds of events which have guided me throughout my life, I am reminded of the importance of maintaining faith and gratitude for a life with such blessings.

Despite this clear vision, my resistance to a return trip to the Amazon and Don Pablo was pretty strong. Whilst this was such an awesome opportunity, it also seemed to indicate a deepening of the responsibility in following a path of spirituality which would require more sacrifice and self-development. I was still attached to my cosy, fun and social life in Byron Bay. I also knew that being guided and blessed by the honour of receiving these invitations was triggering fears, insecurities and self-doubts — the same ones passed on from my father that I had seen during those ceremonies in Brazil. For some weeks I resisted. A friend convinced me to buy a Landcruiser 4WD, but after returning from a big road trip with some friends to a traditional Aboriginal Elders gathering at a sacred mountain in Queensland, I knew intuitively that it was time to go. I quickly let go of my gardening job and my cabin, sold the 4WD for $1000 more than I paid for it, and I was set for my second journey to the Amazon.

I didn't really have any plans or great ambitions for this new journey, especially as it had come as such a shock and everything had changed so quickly. I was really free and in the hands of Great Spirit. I kept telling myself I was going to see Don Pablo and surely he would be the guide and teacher I needed to do the studies Spirit was calling me to. I felt I needed a teacher or a guru or someone who would guide me in the way I needed. I decided to fly to Cairns in the North East of Australia to visit my father, whom I hadn't seen for a few years. Seeing him reminded me of the hole in my life — where I had never had a true father figure and had been forced to learn to find strength and confidence on my own. I wondered if these were somehow connected: my desire for and expectation of finding a mentor for this deep and complex spiritual mission I had been given, and the lack of guidance and mentoring I had received from my father.

From Cairns I had enough frequent flyer points to get a ticket to Hawaii; that sounded like a great option, as I had some friends there and it is another magical and powerful spiritual land and culture and a step closer on the journey to South America.

> *You must always make the important decisions in your life from the heart and not from the mind. You should use the mind to implement or manifest the decisions that have come from the heart.* — Pablo Amaringo.

Travelling around the Big Island of Hawaii, I was touched by the beautiful spiritual community and the wonderful people I met along the way. One day I was invited by some friends to visit the lava flows of the great volcano known by the locals as 'Pele' in reverence to the great goddess of fire, whose powerful feminine energy is seen as an ally for initiating change, pursuing passions and embarking on new ventures with confidence. It felt like a good thing to do: to connect with this healing energy to help me with my feelings of self-doubt and the avoidance I was experiencing regarding my return to the Amazon. On my walk across the volcano to the live lava flows I met a very interesting man who shared with me about his work as a spiritual healer and kinesiologist. He was a healer to many famous people, including Oprah Winfrey, amongst others. He invited me to come to his house and offered me a gift of a healing session with him. His house was built on top of an old lava flow and his healing room under the house was actually inside a natural cave made from the lava. It felt like I was in the womb of the great Pele and this seemed like the perfect way for me to connect with the immense power of such a huge natural force. The healing itself was deep and took me back to my childhood and even pre-birth to understand on a much deeper level where my insecurities and self-doubt came from, and included a huge emotional release. It helped me connect to trauma from when I was in the womb — the loss of a twin. I nearly fell off the table when he was able to recover this memory, and I remembered my mother always telling me the doctor told her initially that I was destined to be twins. Some of the primal emotions around abandonment that also went on to manifest through my father-wound made even more sense. I was very grateful for this and it was the perfect way to launch myself into the next steps of my journey.

Towards the end of this time in Hawaii, I received an email from Silvia Polivoy, the facilitator of my first Ayahuasca retreat, who had moved to the state of Bahia in Brazil where she was now building a healing centre and permanent home for her retreats. She invited me to attend as a volunteer to her next retreat which was starting in less than a week's time. She asked me to run some visionary art workshops for the participants, as she had seen the connection I had built with Don Pablo and the art I had continued in the time since I had last been there with them. Could I manage to get to Brazil, and make it in time to the retreat? It seemed almost impossible but I was determined and managed to find a way to book four flights all the way to Ilhéus in Bahia. I noticed that my self-doubt was really strong during this time, and all the way along this journey I was faced with challenges that forced me to stay strong in my belief and trust in the magic and the flow of Spirit. Flights were cancelled, the Brazilian consulate in Los Angeles initially refused to give me a visa to enter Brazil, and a few times I nearly gave up, but somehow it all worked out and I made it there on prayers, magical synchronicities and some artful dodging, finally arriving on the morning of the first day of the retreat.

Back to Brazil

After a taxi ride from Ilhéus along the beautiful Costa de Cacau in Bahia, I arrived at a beachside jungle retreat centre in the Mata-Atlantica rainforest where Silvia would be hosting her nine-day Ayahuasca retreat. Having only made it there by the skin of my teeth and after dealing with a lot of stress in airports and fears of not being able to make it, I was exhausted when I arrived. I rested in the afternoon but by dinnertime I knew I was starting to feel ill; maybe I had picked something up in one of those airports. After a good rest on the first night, I still felt worse the next day but Silvia encouraged me to attend the ceremony, as the Ayahuasca is medicine and could only help me to recover. I felt a lot of excitement at being in ceremony again and at reconnecting with my great friend Ayahuasca. It had been a few years and I was curious to see where my journey would go, what I would discover. The ceremony, though, was very difficult. I experienced a lot of discomfort and negative thoughts, my visions were dark and reflective of fears, and I found it almost impossible to let go. This was very different to my first time and I wondered if my experience was not being lifted up due to the absence of Pablo and his supreme skills with the medicine. Being sick didn't help and I found myself spiralling down through fears of illness and eventually fears of dying. Many things went through my mind: I looked at my life and asked myself if I was ready to leave it, I processed past events and relationships and questioned myself and all my choices. I was holding on and my resistance had become so strong; I was aware that other people were also feeling I was not fully surrendering. When I finally found the courage to let go whilst deep in the miração, I accepted my death and then I sensed all the life draining out of me. Then I saw a vision of my body in the earth and watched while it decayed and rotted and eventually disintegrated into the earth. The visions seemed more like scenes from a horror movie than the exquisite beauty I had seen in my previous journeys.

After this death experience, my mind finally surrendered and I was able to find some clarity and realise Ayahuasca had guided me to let go of this old self that was insecure and self-doubting, to let go of this version of me that lacked confidence in my choices and felt I was not good enough. It seemed like I was processing some strong, deep subconscious fears around death and the fragility of my human body. The biggest lesson, however, was to just let go and to trust. The process of dying in the miração was very real and in some ways it seemed I was being prepared for my actual death. My ego mind tried to work out if I was being given a vision of something about to happen, but when I let go it was clear this was a spiritual lesson, a test in letting go and trusting in life whilst in some ways practising for the inevitable moment when death will come. I contemplated the release that I had had with the healer in Hawaii and the power of being so charged by the fiery force of the volcano goddess Pele, who was supporting me to clear the way to find the confidence and strength to walk tall on my spiritual journey. Ayahuasca had given me a strong healing and was releasing of a lot of fear and negativity. By the morning I was exhausted but I felt a lot better and the sickness I had been feeling was quickly subsiding.

> *I must not fear. Fear is the mind killer. Fear is the little death that brings obliteration. I will face my fear and I will permit it to pass over me and through me, and when it has gone past, I will turn the inner eye to see its path. Where the fear has gone, there will be nothing. Only I will remain.* — Frank Herbert, Dune.

The next day after a rest and a good breakfast I was feeling much better and guided the participants through an inner-child meditation and movement process before we sat down to draw and paint our visions. This was the first time I had run this workshop and it would lead to many more over the years to come. Silvia also ran her usual group psychotherapy and sharing circles, and she did some guided meditations which I found very useful. It felt great to be back in this environment where again I felt very much at home. I was also learning a lot about Silvia's techniques: the way she held space and created a safe place but still brought a good level of challenge so that participants didn't fall into ego traps and comfort zones. The forest, animals and the beach were stunning, and I spent a lot of time again connecting to the nature and the energy of the land.

During this retreat, once I had cleared my mind of all the emotional and mental dramas I had experienced on the way there, I found myself contemplating the importance of creating a new way on the planet for humans to live in harmony. I wanted to know how, as a collective species, we could get it together in time to find the harmony and balance with the Earth before we destroyed our environment and ourselves. I was also curious about my upcoming trip to the Amazon in Peru, where I was still planning to visit Don Pablo.

During one of the ceremonies that followed, I asked Ayahuasca about technology and energy use on the planet. I had grown interested in ecology and alternative technologies such as zero-point energy, magnetic power and other ways to generate electricity not dependent on burning fuels and creating pollution. As I entered the miração I was taken to a view of the whole Earth and I saw how everything was interconnected and interdependent and how there is no separation between humans and the consciousness of the Earth itself. I found myself in a conversation with the Earth, who appeared as a great old matriarch of the solar system. She took me to a vision of a giant old Aboriginal woman who was lying on her back in the desert in the centre of Australia. I could see the Aboriginal woman was suffering under an immense weight of deep grief and emotional pain. I saw she was an ancestral spirit who was receiving and feeling all the pain of the Earth, all the wounds that were being inflicted upon the Earth, and she was absorbing and carrying it all for humanity. The voice of the Earth then told me that her pain was felt by all Indigenous peoples around the world, and that as they are born into a spiritual tradition which is completely at one with the Earth, they all feel the pain of the Earth — and that is one of the reasons they suffer so much. I contemplated the social problems and alcoholism of Australian Indigenous peoples, their pain at being forced off their Country and ripped away from the land and its ancestors that had sustained them for generations, and how the alcohol and social problems were a way for them to cope with the enormous pain they carry within their hearts. It wasn't the first time I had a good cry for the sadness of the Earth.

After this vision, I asked the voice of the Earth why were we still not able to access and use these clean technologies to live in a way that would not create all this pain and destruction? Why is there seemingly this hidden hand that stops progress from being made and drives the awakened ones underground? The response from the voice of the Earth was very quick and clear: she said it was 'because that is not the lesson I am teaching my children, the humans of the Earth. I am not teaching them how to get free, clean energy; I am teaching them how to use energy responsibly'. I was left to contemplate this revelation, which seemed to make sense. Then the miração suddenly changed and I found myself journeying rapidly deep into the forest, through jungles and rivers and an ancient life-force that seemed at once foreboding and enlivening. Eventually I arrived in an Indigenous village somewhere in the Amazon. I entered one of the wooden houses with a thatched roof and found a pajé sitting there alone, carving something out of a small piece of wood. I sat with him and asked him if his village would like to receive some solar panels or a free energy device that could give them electricity. His answer surprised me: 'No, we don't want that; we already have enough problems with our children consuming toxic media and television that is polluting their minds, taking them away from our traditional cultural and values.' At that moment I was shown a vision of Indigenous children looking at mobile phones and watching cheap soap operas. It seemed I was being shown a representation of the message that had been given to me by the voice of the Earth; I was seeing how consumption of energy could lead to negative outcomes for the survival of culture and the human spirit. The pajé, who was deeply connected to the Earth, was defending the health of his people. This raised the question: if the children are being diverted through media and technology away from their traditional culture and values, what does this mean for the future generations of the Earth?

Following the encounter with the pajé, I asked Ayahuasca about this vision and how to find the balance with modern culture and technologies. She explained that we are emerging into a collective global awareness, where all over the world technology is allowing us to see and be seen by the rest of the world. She then explained it was normal that Indigenous youth, isolated in the jungle, had become aware of themselves in relation to the rest of the world. She explained it was natural that they would be curious about other cultures and people in other parts of the world, that depriving them of this experience was not the way and that it was necessary to find a healthy balance. Ayahuasca suggested that a good way to engage the youth in Indigenous communities would be to teach them how to use audio-visual technology to be able to share their own culture, thus bringing value to their traditional ways. Instead of only consuming foreign media, they could be producing their own media content and sharing it with the world. I was very touched by this insight; it would go on to become a big inspiration for some of the work and projects I worked on in the years following.

You are the girl of the sun star
You are the queen of the sea wind
Your light makes me sing
Earth, Earth you are so starry

Your blue mantle commands
The breath of all creation
And after the wetness of the rain
A rainbow comes to crown

The forest is your dress
And the clouds are your necklace
You are so beautiful
Oh! Earth Consecrated in your turning

Sailor of solitudes
That takes us to space
Mother Ship you are home
Earth, Earth you are so delicate

Your men have no judgement
They have forgotten such love
You offer your treasures
But nobody values you

Earth, Earth I am your child
Like the plants and the animals
I give myself only to your earth
With love I reaffirm your peace

— *Estrelada,* Milton Nascimento & Márcio Borges.

The theme of ecology and protection of the Earth continued throughout the ceremonies I took part in during this retreat. During one miração, I again found myself deep in the jungle with some pajés and other native peoples. The jungle seemed pervasive and I had an ominous feeling. I had been contemplating my upcoming trip to the Peruvian Amazon and I had asked Ayahuasca to give me some guidance. I was aware I would be entering the jungle without a guide or a retreat to attend, and I would be going solo into the unknown. This ominous feeling was getting stronger so I asked Ayahuasca what this sense was, and she gave me a message of warning. I saw a vision of energetic tentacles that looked like the tendrils of vines and plants reaching out of the forest trying to seduce me into its depths. This was a more intrusive feeling than those I had experienced in visions to this point. Ayahuasca explained to me that the forest would want to consume me, that I should be careful, stay in my centre and not give in to the powerful seduction I might encounter. I was very curious about this, as it seemed I was being given some clear guidance for the journey ahead, and although I didn't fully comprehend its meaning, it definitely stayed with me.

Following the retreat, Silvia invited me to visit the new, purpose-built Ayahuasca healing centre that she was setting up nearby on stunning land with jungle and full of wildlife and beautiful views over a sublime sunset. It seemed like the ideal setting to do this sacred work. After spending some time there, visiting the local waterfalls, rivers and beaches and exploring nearby towns, I fell in love with this Country on the coast of Brazil. Since then this has been a place I have often visited and has a special place in my heart. I went on to visit the city of Salvador and was then offered a friend's apartment in Rio de Janeiro to stay in while he was travelling for work. From there I could organise my trip to Peru, where I would journey into the Amazon to visit Pablo Amaringo. After the intensity and depth of the lessons and healing I had experienced it was a good contrast to take a moment of fun in the city of Rio, which was so vibrant and full of culture, music, art, passion, beautiful people and brimming with life force. It was during this time that my love affair with Brazil, its people, the land, culture and Spirit began. I had originally planned to go somewhere quiet in nature to integrate my experiences but life guided me to Rio when my friend offered me his apartment, and I found that the openness and passion in the people and the culture was a great remedy for an Australian coming from a dry, conservative culture. Over the years it was in Brazil that I found my song.

In the waters of the Amazon River
My heart bathed
In the enchanted depths on the other side
Iara's voice called
I heard her calling ...
Her song crossed the Amazon
In the beak of one knowing
On the wings of the wind this voice spread
In each palm tree flag raised in the air, Brazil

In the banana plantation, Brazil
In the Pantanal, Brazil
In the river-sea
There in the backlands, Brazil
On the coast, Brazil
My heart, Brazil
Could hear

*A knowing, Brazil
In a brazilwood tree
That taught me, Brazil
My song!*

— *Rio Amazonas*, Dori Caymmi.

Peru and the Earth changes

It was some time in 2007 when I arrived in Lima, the capital city of Peru, and spent a few days exploring. I was heading toward the small Amazonian city of Pucallpa where Don Pablo lived and ran his art school for the local children. Lima is a very dry city, where locals told me it never rains, and Pucallpa was on the other side of the enormous Andes mountains deep in the Amazon jungle. I decided to journey via road transport, as I wanted to experience the distance and the land as it transformed from desert to snow-capped mountains and then down into the dense rainforest. This ended up being quite an arduous mission. After getting a bus to the top of the Andes I learned there was no public transport from there down into the Amazon. I managed to get lifts in a series of share cars that would wait until they had enough people before heading off to the next town. At times there were up to 10 people in these cars, often with no windows, and we encountered regular breakdowns and flat tyres along bumpy, dusty roads full of giant potholes. After a couple of days in these cars the scenery changed to dense jungle mountains with waterfalls cascading down their sides, deep green mountain hills and valleys as far as could be seen. Despite the discomfort of the journey and having very little Spanish, the views and feeling of being surrounded by such beauty and majesty of the jungle were worth it, although at times I definitely regretted choosing this way when I could have caught a plane directly from Lima. Despite these moments of doubt, I was enchanted by the experience and becoming more excited as we got closer to Pucallpa.

I arrived in Pucallpa around mid-afternoon. It seemed like a busy, noisy place with almost no public spaces and one park in the middle of town surrounded by military police. I had no idea of where I might find Don Pablo, but I knew he would be somewhere in the city. As I was checking in to a small hotel, a man entered. He overheard me asking the hotel concierge if he knew of the famous artist Pablo Amaringo. The concierge wasn't sure who I was talking about but the man who entered said that he knew Pablo and was actually married to his niece. He agreed to take me there first thing the next day. As I checked in to the hotel I realised I had lost my debit card somewhere on the other side of the Andes. All I had left was less than two hundred dollars in cash. My heart sank, as I realised this might be a big problem and another challenge to navigate. I sent a message to my bank in Australia who said they would urgently send me a new card but that it would take at least three weeks to arrive. I needed to work out how I was going to survive with little money, but I decided to focus on meeting Pablo first and trusting that something would work itself out. I was determined to let Spirit guide me on its wings; losing access to money was a great way for Spirit to force me to surrender and not rely on the material world. I braced myself for another test of faith.

The next morning I was taken by the man from the hotel to meet Pablo. We drove through the city and came to an area that appeared to be a much poorer area, with wooden shanty houses and dusty dirt streets, with potholes everywhere and a lot of Indigenous people going about their lives. We arrived at Pablo's school, which was attached to his house, all built from wood. I saw several children around who seemed to feel safe and loved by Pablo, whose warm smile greeted each of them as they approached him. He greeted me with a big smile and a welcoming hug, expressing his happiness to see me and that he knew I would come one day. He showed me around the school and we talked about day-to-day life there and the students he was supporting to give an opportunity, supported by donations that came in through his international profile as a visionary artist. He also told me about some of the older students who were also studying with Ayahuasca, although he wasn't working with the medicine any more. He told me about another curandeiro shaman whom he recommended in Pucallpa.

Pablo invited me inside to his art studio, where he had many canvases and a new one underway. We sat down and he asked me to show him my art; I pulled out my art journal and showed him lots of photos of some of the paintings I had been doing. He asked me about their meaning and was even able to point out some things he saw in them. It was clear that, just as during the time we had spent in Brazil several years before, he had a clear spiritual insight into the visions and realities I was accessing and expressing through my art. This led to a much deeper conversation about spiritual realities, leading to discussions on following the path of Ayahuasca, and he was particularly interested to talk about his own path of self-taught shamanism. This was very interesting for me, as I had arrived with a lot of expectations that he was going to put me to work on some kind of studies or take on the role of teaching me. As the conversation continued, it was clear he was saying to me, after seeing my art and listening to other experiences I had shared with him, that I was already doing the work that was needed. We laughed about it, and I felt quite exposed, but on the other hand it was very affirming and I was able to put the last few years into a bigger perspective. I was grateful Pablo had not taken advantage of my curiosity and naivety in that moment, yet what he did was set me free from the need to have a guru or someone to facilitate between myself and Great Spirit. I felt an enormous sense of relief. Pablo's teaching was so clear and grounded and empowering for me, and despite all the insecurity I had been experiencing, he helped me to realise that all of the experiences I had had over the last years were part of the training and spiritual development I thought I had been seeking somewhere else. I was left with a strong feeling of peace within, a knowledge that my spirit and the universe were guiding me, and that I didn't need anything or anyone external to access that.

Over the next couple of days I visited Pablo and his extended family a few more times. We would sit with a cup of tea and talk about art and spirituality. I met many children who were so excited to meet a *gringo* (white Westerner) from as far away as Australia. It seemed like a whole universe of children and young people were orbiting around Pablo and his school. I was reminded of the many years I had worked in youth and community development. Someone there told me he used money that he gained from selling paintings to support the whole community with food and education. Pablo himself seemed as humble as ever, happily painting away in his studio. He showed me many paintings and we would talk about them; he told me one dream he had always had was to build a temple for Ayahuasca ceremonies he had always seen in his vision. He showed me a huge painting he had made of this temple. He said that his mission since ceasing work as an Ayahuasca healer was to paint his visions and that those visions would become like a library of his knowledge — that could be his legacy. The other thing he wanted to do was to build the temple. Pablo offered to introduce me to the old curandeiro shaman he had mentioned, and said that if I wanted to drink Ayahuasca I could do so with him. It would mean staying in the city; which didn't seem very appealing due to all the noise and pollution and my new problem of having limited funds to pay for staying there. I was getting the sense that the forest was calling me, and I was getting excited about finding a way to journey deeper into the jungle.

My time with Pablo and his family was very warm and reassuring with such gentle, subtle, yet very powerful guidance. I had let go of so much through the recent revelations: there was the letting go of my insecurities and the feeling I needed to have some kind of father figure I had never had; there was Pablo pointing out that the guidance was within; and there was being left without a strong goal of ambition, other than as Pablo had said, to keep doing what I was already doing, that Spirit was guiding me. On my way to Brazil I passed through Los Angeles, California and met a man who was recommended through mutual friends. He had recently spent one year living in a native Shipibo village not too far down the river from Pucallpa. I contacted him and he suggested I visit the village; he would let them know I was welcome to the house he had built there that they were caring for. This seemed like a great option: to immerse myself in a native village and the forest, away from the comforts and support of a retreat or my normal western comforts. Besides, without much money I didn't seem to have much of an option. Again, Spirit was guiding me.

The Shipibo village is called San Francisco and was around three hours' travel on a dusty bumpy road in a beaten-up car with no windows and filled with about 10 people, including children sitting on my lap. They seemed used to gringos showing up in their village but the journey was more of a mission of endurance to get there in one piece. The village was on the banks of the Ucayali River, a large tributary of the Amazon River. I asked around for my friend's house and was taken there by one of the local natives. There was an Englishman staying in the house who was about to leave to go travelling with his French girlfriend and it was good to have someone to talk to who spoke English, even though he seemed lost and confused. It seemed pretty clear the Shipibo weren't very fond of him. He was chewing on a lot of coca leaves and smoking constantly, so I was really happy when he left after a few days. In that time I met a young Colombian man called Unyemi who was travelling around; he had made his own passport which had a *Hunab-Ku*, the symbol of time and space from the ancient Mayans, and which he used to pass through borders in South America. This was a strong sign: we forged a friendship and, as he seemed to know a lot about the locals and their culture, he became a kind of guide for me with my limited Spanish.

After the Englishman and his girlfriend had gone, we cleaned out the little wooden house and made a tidy and organised space that would be my home for the next few weeks. Once I was on my own, a group of children and adolescents came knocking on the door and offered to help me clean. They were amazing. They got to work scrubbing, sweeping, mopping and tidying. A couple of the young boys found a fishing line on the wall, and went off and came back with some small fish, which they gave to me. When the place was all clean, two older women came by with some presents to welcome me: a bag of milk powder and some crunchy *mandioc* (casava) dried into little granules. I was very touched by their welcoming gestures and felt bad that I didn't have much to offer, although some of the children took a liking to me and would come every day and sit with me as I would make art with them and draw animals and things from other parts of the world while teaching them what I could. The children of the village became a daily presence in my life and kept me smiling; they were also able to teach me a lot about life with the Shipibo and help me learn some Spanish.

The first few days in San Francisco were challenging to navigate, as I didn't have any clear ambition or know exactly why I was there or what I was going to do. The people were so lovely and welcoming and seemed to be genuinely interested in me as a person, so I began to relax into the idea that I was just going to stay and be part of the community to learn and help however I could. Over those first few days, though, waves of women would approach me with a range of beautiful arts and crafts, fabrics and clothing and want me to buy from them. I kept explaining I didn't have any money with me and they were very disappointed; it was hard for them to comprehend a blond-haired gringo had shown up in their village with no money. There seemed to be three large family clans living in there, each one occupying a part of the village. The family I was staying with seemed to be the poorest of the three families, with the smallest houses, and I was the only gringo staying with them. When I walked over to the other side of the village I was met by young men who were very pushy and persistent in trying to convince me to do Ayahuasca with their uncles, who were apparently very powerful shamans. My friend who lived there warned me about the powerful shamans and he suspected they were using sorcery to gain power, money and status amongst the trail of gringos coming through looking for Ayahuasca. Aside from the warning, the way they were approaching me, the pushiness and the seeming desperation for money was not very attractive, and I could not imagine myself wanting to get involved in their stories. I did meet a few other travellers there who were doing diets or staying with these other families, but generally I kept away. Something didn't feel right about the energy I felt from these people, and there were also rumours of the old shaman in that family putting curses on naive gringos. I was also warned by some of the young men in the village not to upset the powerful shamans. The best thing I could think of was to just keep away from that scene and besides, I had been drinking Ayahuasca just a few weeks prior in Brazil and was still integrating that experience. I was happy to simply be in the forest and paint and write and spend time with my new Shipibo friends whilst learning about life in the Amazon.

Over a few days some of the men from the Shipibo family kept asking me if I was going to go hunting with them for *caimans*, a type of huge alligator native to the Amazon. I saw some caiman skulls around the village; people would often have them on their walls and it was clear these animals were enormous. Being from Australia, I had lived around crocodiles before so I knew how dangerous they were. When the men kept asking me if I was going hunting with them for caimans, I nervously said, 'Okay', as I was always keen to take up the invitations they gave me. One day the children told me the men had gone out to hunt a caiman and I felt relieved that they had gone without me. Later that evening I was invited to the grandmother's house to see the caiman that had been caught — it was over two metres long. When I arrived the men were laughing and I realised they were joking about me going hunting with them. They explained the stealthy life-or-death way they stalk and hunt the caiman and I felt very grateful to be sharing in the feast that night. I had made friends with a young Shipibo man who was around 20 years old and on the night we were eating the caiman he invited me to come to a special Ayahuasca ceremony where he was going to be given blessings and some kind of initiation by his uncle, who was the shaman of the family. I felt really honoured and happy to be invited to attend a ceremony in a village that was based in love and connection, and not full of very seductive salesmen with their promises of strong visions, power and miraculous healing.

The next day the children came around and told me about a giant snake with six heads. I really couldn't understand what they were talking about, as my understanding of Spanish was limited and I didn't have anyone close by to translate, but they were very persistent. They wanted to show me a little creek where they wanted to go fishing, so we went for a walk as they kept talking about the strange snake. On the way back we encountered my Columbian friend Unyemi, who told me the children were talking about a movie they wanted me to watch. Now it made sense. I really didn't want to watch the movie but they were very keen for me to do so. Now submerged in this nature and life in Shipibo, the last thing I wanted was to tune back into some toxic television reality. But the children were so excited and persistent that I agreed.

That night we went to the grandmother's house, which was the only house for that family that had electricity; it seemed the village had some petrol and fired up a generator. Inside the house were just one chair and a television on a stand with a DVD player. They asked me to sit on the chair and as the film began 10 or so people from the family sat around me on the floor, watching me watch the television. Sure enough, the six-headed snake made its appearance and whenever the Amazonians in the film appeared with feathers and spears and bows and arrows, my Shipibo friends would get very excited, pointing at them and proudly telling me: 'That's us!' The film was terrible and painful to watch but it meant a lot to them to show me this; the purity of their intention and love for me by showing me this film depicting their culture was very touching. I was reminded of the vision I had had in Brazil with the pajé explaining about television and electricity and the dangers to their culture. At the end of the film was a scene where one of the Amazonian children was sick. The curandeiro shaman approached the child, but the villains in the story told him 'no, no, no!' and tried to stop him. Suddenly, out of nowhere, two blond blue-eyed gringo doctors appeared wearing white coats as the music became angelic. The shaman in the film backed away, then the doctors pulled out a large syringe and injected the child, who was miraculously healed within moments. A light descended over the gringo doctors and everyone was smiling as the film ended.

My thoughts around this suspiciously trashy film were that it was some kind of propaganda. I asked the Shipibo where they had got it and they said they had bought it on the street in Pucallpa for two soles (Peruvian currency). I had learned in my time in the village that some workers had been visiting the village from a non-government organisation which had apparently tested the children of the village and deemed them to be malnourished. This justified why they needed to regularly deliver them sugary packets of Nestlé milk powder. I could not understand how these children could be malnourished, as their lives were so healthy and full of love and harmony and deep connection to nature, with an abundance of food and plantations all around them. I was left to ponder the insidious ways Western colonial culture which still attempted to control the lives of Indigenous peoples.

The next night we went to the uncle's house for the special ceremony. I was really excited to have my first Ayahuasca experience in a traditional setting with this family that had adopted me. The house was dank and dark and filled with Shipibo sitting closely together, as there was not much space relative to the amount of people. I was shown a hole in the floor where I could purge if needed; I looked into it and could see rats running round under the house. There was a little camping tent in the corner with a very sick man in it. The shaman uncle told me the man was dying and there was nothing he could do to help him. He also suggested the man had made a choice in his life that had caused the illness but he was too stubborn to change his ways. Thus he was sick and close to death even though he was being cared for by the healer of the family. I found it interesting that the uncle was nursing this dying man during the ceremony. This showed how the role of the curandeiro extended beyond the ceremonial healing. The presence of someone close to death was also humbling and added an extra dimension of Shipibo life to the experience.

The ceremony was short and very beautiful. The miração came and went with a graceful ease, every vision dancing and moving and shape-shifting to the sweet harmonies of his beautiful *icaros* (songs). Icaros are magical songs usually received by Shipibo curandeiros and are used as calls and invocations to different energies, healing properties and spiritual beings. I didn't have any strong or deep revelations or insights this time: most of my experience was colours and movement and butterflies and hummingbirds dancing all around me. I felt like I was being blessed by the forest.

Afterwards I thanked the Uncle and he wanted to know about my visions. I told him about the butterflies and the sense of serenity, beauty and peace I had experienced. I gave him 50 soles as an offering and he was very grateful. The family insisted I stay with them that night in the grandmother's house, so we returned there and this time inside there was just one bed with a mosquito net. They guided me to sleep in the bed, and when I got in and lay down 10 or 12 of them all lay on the floor around me. It was a strange feeling, to be treated with this kind of loving care and respect. In some ways it made me feel uncomfortable, as I didn't want to be treated differently to any of them, but for them it was very important to look after me the way they did. As I lay there, I remember feeling overwhelmed with gratitude for this very sweet and authentic experience of beautiful ceremony and the gracious welcome to the Shipibo Dreaming through our mutual friend Ayahuasca. We spent the night dreaming together.

In the days that followed I was confronted by the women of the family who one day came around to the house with a beautiful young 15 or 16-year-old Shipibo girl who was all dressed up and wearing lipstick. She sat shyly in the corner with other young women around her giggling and fidgeting. I didn't understand what was happening but after a while I realised that they were offering her as a bride and wanted me to marry into their family. There seemed to be a lot of hope and expectation about this. It was a big challenge to find a way to navigate the situation without hurting or offending them whilst also remembering my guidance from the miração in Brazil that warned me the Amazon would want to consume me. Although I wasn't tempted by the offer of a pretty teenage bride, I could feel a strong seductive force wanting to pull me closer into this family and into life in the Amazon. I had met a young American man who did accept a teenage bride from the family of the powerful shaman I had been warned about. The American was stuck in a loop with the family: he was trying to get back to the US after the teenage bride moved to the city to live out her fantasy Mexican soap-opera lifestyle of urban glamour and fashion. He had become enmeshed with the family and every time he tried to leave and return to the US, something would happen that kept him there. He seemed very stressed to me and I suspected he was under some kind of enchantment, as he felt very confused and fragmented energetically.

A few weeks passed with no sign of the new debit card's arrival. I had found a groove in village, was learning a lot and writing and painting; it was a great experience. I was introduced to a young

Shipibo man, who seemed like he was very serious and deep in his shamanic studies and Ayahuasca. He looked at my art and we spoke a little about spiritual things before he told me there was someone he wanted to introduce me to. We managed to get a ride in a car to another village that seemed a bit more developed, with more electricity available. There I was introduced to a *mestizo* (part Shipibo) man called Juan, who was working with a financial grant from a local university to create a study on all the healing plants that the Shipibo use. He had done artwork and written descriptions for them and had this all in a large folder containing hundreds of pages of his work with beautiful art and a great deal of knowledge about these healing plants. I was astounded by the amount of work he had done and the huge amount of spiritual and botanical knowledge he held. He told me he was also a student of a Grand Master shaman who lived three days down the river. I had heard about this old shaman and most of the gringos I had met were all looking for a way to go and see him. Apparently, to all the Shipibo in the area he was the one renowned to hold the most power and knowledge and was seen as wise and benevolent.

With my access to money returning imminently, it was interesting that I had met Juan and connected with his story and his work both in the university and with the Grand Master shaman I had heard so much about. Juan came to San Francisco to visit me and I showed him my art; he told me that he had drunk some Ayahuasca and been told through his vision to invite me to go down the river with him to meet with the old shaman. My Colombian friend was very encouraging. He told me it was rare to be invited like this, that most people paid for a meeting with this shaman. Despite my friend's encouragement, I wasn't feeling a very strong call to follow that path. I managed to convince myself that it was the right thing to do, to make the most of the offer, and that somehow it fitted into my vision of shamanic studies. In the back of my mind though was Pablo's advice: to let Spirit guide me, that the answers and guidance were within. With much encouragement from everyone around me in the village, I eventually agreed. My card arrived from Australia so I was able to spend some days in the city with Juan preparing everything we would need to take with us on the canoe for a three-day trip down the river and deep into the jungle. I found myself frustrated and agitated, feelings I had not experienced for a while. Up until then my time in the Amazon, although uncomfortable at times, had always been within a sense of harmony and a peaceful flow. I had convinced myself to go, and Juan was also really invested in taking me to meet his teacher, so I persisted, despite things feeling out of alignment within me and in my flow.

Juan had been coming around to my house at times with a bottle of Ayahuasca and we would sit in the dark with some of the young Shipibo men from the family while he would hold little ceremonies and sing his beautiful icaros. Two days before we were about to leave the village to head down the river, Juan arrived again at my house with Ayahuasca and he told us that he had received a message to drink together one more time before leaving. There were six of us in the little wooden house and the ceremony went along as the others had, but this time the miração that came for me was very strong — it reminded me of some of the powerful ones I had experienced in Brazil. I found myself in a strong vision deep in the jungle, a long way away from San Francisco, where it was dark and damp and dense and with foreboding sounds and the presence of a great many insects and animals. I saw a circular clearing ahead of me in the forest and in the centre of the clearing was a fire. I approached the clearing and as I arrived I could sense the presence of large animals coming towards me through the forest from each direction. As they drew close I could see that there were several jaguars; as they arrived at the clearing, they all transformed into pajés. These magical men felt very powerful and focused. They gathered around me and the fire and began singing and moving their hands. They began to put their hands on me and then they put feathers and a necklace and bandana on me. I realised this ceremony was being done for me. One of them told me that I was being honoured as a 'defender of the Amazon'. This pajé then explained that they were very concerned that the Amazon forest was sick and dying. I saw visions of the forest slowly being choked to death and had a very ominous feeling. The pajés explained that it was very important that this message be spread around the world, so that humanity could do something to stop the destruction before it was too late. They said to me that it was not my role or my path to become a Shipibo shaman, that these pajés had initiated me as this defender of the Amazon. My role was to be out in the world connecting with as many people as possible to wake them up to the emergency and to preserving the ecology of the Amazon. This miração showed me that if the Amazon dies, then all life on Earth is at risk.

When Juan finished singing and the miração subsided, I lay down on the floor contemplating the strong and vivid vision I had experienced. I thought deeply about the ecology of the planet and the insanity of human behaviour and how this message kept coming up in my mind and in my Ayahuasca visions. I knew beyond all doubt that, considering the urgency and the state of the world and seeing such powerful visions, there was and is no greater cause than to defend life and defend our beautiful planet and home. After a while Juan lit a candle and began speaking. He asked for everyone in the circle to share from their visions. I felt a bit nervous to share my experience, as Juan had been so invested in this journey with me and I had only just realised it was not my path to follow. Despite my discomfort at having to break this news, I was also relieved, as I had never felt comfortable with the trip. Each person shared a little and when it came to my turn, Juan put his palm up and said, 'Stop'. Then he pointed at everyone around the room and said, 'We all need to learn from him,' as he in turn pointed at me. He gave me a knowing look and nod and went on to the next person. It seemed tha he had also been given a vision informing him that I would not be going to visit his teacher. I wondered if he had also seen the vision of the jaguar pajés in the forest.

The following day I made a trip to Pucallpa to visit the only travel agency in town and booked a flight to Cusco via Lima. I had been dreaming of visiting the ancient sites and connecting to the spirituality of the Incan and pre-Incan peoples that Pablo had talked about. I returned to San Francisco village later that evening with presents for the family and planned to purchase some of their arts and fabrics. They had given up trying to sell me things and I wanted to wait for the last day of my trip to give them this as a farewell surprise and also knew it would be a very welcome financial boost for them. I had seen the inequality they suffered in comparison with the other families in the village who were using enchantment and persuasion to make them better at selling things, including Ayahuasca ceremonies, to the gringos wandering into the village. My Shipibo friends were sad I was leaving but also hopeful about my vision to bring awareness and promote protection of the Amazon.

Early on the morning of my departure I was visited by a small group of younger Shipibo men who had become good friends throughout my time in the village and who came to say goodbye. One of them had brought some marijuana and rolled a joint for us all. Marijuana was taboo amongst the Shipibo, as the shamans claimed it was a plant that was not spiritually compatible with their cosmology. They were obviously willing to risk bringing it to me, and I felt like it was a nice way to for us all to connect spiritually before I left. We all sat in a circle chatting and the joint got passed around; it wasn't long after I smoked some of it that I went into a deep miração. My eyes were closed and my consciousness went to an undefined place that was unlike any miração from Ayahuasca. I didn't have clear visions, but did have some strong feelings that took me back to the message from the jaguar shamans who had told me about the plight of the Amazon. I wasn't sure how long I was in that meditative state, but eventually I opened my eyes and saw they were all staring at me expectantly. A voice spoke through me and said the words 'earth changes'. I wasn't sure where that had come from but assumed it was related to the general theme of ecological crisis that had been so present for me and inspired by Ayahuasca throughout my time in South America.

My Shipibo friends came with me to wait for the car to leave the village for the trip to Pucallpa. We said goodbye and off I went in an overflowing car on the bumpy, dusty journey with kids on my lap. When I arrived in the city I had some time to kill so I went to the internet cafe where they had some old computers for tourists to use. I opened the search engine and a story came up on the news feed saying there had been an earthquake in Peru. There was very little information about it in the article but it seemed it had happened during the bumpy car ride from the village. I had been in a car and shaken up while an earthquake had been shaking the country. I made some prayers that people were safe. When the time came to go to the airport I hailed a moto-taxi with a friendly man who got me there safely after a brief stop to fix a flat tyre. When I arrived at the airport, everything seemed as normal. As I was waiting in the line a woman came out and told everyone that all flights were cancelled, that Lima airport was closed due to the earthquake. Nobody was able to offer any further information.

I managed to find a room in one of the few hotels in town and after I checked in and settled into my room all the power went out. I looked out of the window and it looked like that the electricity was out across the entire city. It stayed like that for three days. It felt surreal being in the city without any power and no information coming in from outside. City life seemed to be going on as normal and I wandered around the markets and ate meals of fish, plantains and *mandioc*, much like in the village. It was Sunday afternoon when the power came back on and a sign in the travel office window said it would be opening at 8am the next day. I got there extra early the next day, as rumours were going around that there might not be any flights, but I was lucky and managed to get one of only five seats available for the only flight that evening. When I arrived in Lima the city was like a ghost town: there was very little traffic, damage everywhere, power lines down and an ominous feeling hanging over everything. Nobody was outside on the streets. I was invited to stay at the house of a friend I had met when I first passed through Lima and when I arrived at his house I ran straight to the bathroom and vomited. I felt like I was transmuting a lot of the fear I was seeing in everyone, including in my friend, who said the earthquake had been a horrific experience and he was still in shock.

I got the plane to Cusco as planned, although the Andean town had not been directly affected by the earthquake and tourism and services seemed to be operating as normal. As I wandered the ancient streets I had plenty of time to integrate the experiences of the last weeks from when the power had gone out to arriving in Cusco. I contemplated the end of the Incan civilisation and wondered what had caused the collapse of their empire and where the Incans had gone. Pablo had told me they had disappeared under the earth. My experience that last morning in the village, when I had spoken the words 'earth changes' only moments before the earthquake had hit, seemed to be showing the importance of the visions I had received regarding these times on Earth and how fragile we were as a species and civilisation. I had often had prophetic dreams, including dreaming of being in the twin towers in New York then running away from a war in the desert the night before the planes struck the buildings in 2001; I had another dream of a huge bomb going off in London the night of the tube terror attacks. I decided to head back to Australia and leave the exploration of the ancient sites of the Andes for another time. I didn't want to be a drain on the resources of the country in a time of intense crisis.

There were no flights again, so the only way back to Lima was on a smelly, uncomfortable bus that was going to take 24 hours to wind down the mountains and cross the Nazca plains and the desert back to Lima. I remembered my flying kookaburra painting with the Nazca lines. The earthquake had been enormous, 8.0 on the Richter scale, and hundreds of people had died. The bus journey took us through seemingly endless kilometres of destroyed towns and villages, some of them reduced to piles of rubble with very few structures remaining. I saw overcrowded buses and trucks packed with people sometimes stuck in traffic jams on teetering, half-destroyed bridges and people holding signs begging for medications for loved ones. I donated money where I could but the international rescue teams weren't welcoming untrained volunteers to help. I had the feeling I was witnessing something important for me to see and directly related to the mission I was being given by Ayahuasca and my spiritual guides. Due to the destruction of roads and massive traffic jams it took an extra six hours, but I eventually made it to Lima for my flight back to Australia. The discomfort of the very long bus trip was nothing compared to the suffering of the people in such a tragic situation.

Upon returning to Australia I again felt radically changed inside — as if I was seeing life through different eyes after such a powerful and life-changing journey. I dived back into life in Byron Bay, where I began volunteering for ecology and permaculture projects. I started new study in ecology and began to apply my experience in community development to some exciting projects developing cutting-edge sustainability, biospheric awareness and new forms of harmonic community organisation. I was still in contact with the Foundation for the Law of Time and its leader José Argüelles, who had developed a philosophy of biospheric rights, employing the practices and structure of the Mayan calendar and natural time to develop technology and community-based projects in harmony with nature and the natural rhythms and frequencies of time. I studied more of this new and ancient practice and philosophy and was appointed as a volunteer bio-regional coordinator. I became strongly involved in an ecological project called 'Starseed Gardens' in Byron Bay run by the visionary biologist and philosopher Dan Schreiber. Dan was also a pioneer in entheogenic plants and their use in Australia and this included the support of emerging Ayahuasca communities. Eventually I moved to live on the Starseed Gardens farm which was being developed into Dan's vision of an ecological and community hub that would apply advanced ways of organising community and developing new ecological technologies in land regeneration, soil development, sustainable agriculture, power generation, healing and consciousness.

During this time back in Australia I dreamed a lot about returning to Brazil, and in early 2009 I was offered a position in the country to work as a consultant for a Swiss-based start-up company introducing new ecological technologies into local communities, government and non-government organisations. This time I didn't have any resistance about returning to Brazil, and it was clear that yet again the universe had conspired to find a way to get me back there. I was given a portfolio of technologies ready to implement in Brazil and a list of contacts to follow up once I arrived there. I was also excited to start building bridges between our community in Byron Bay, the region where permaculture was developed, with communities in Brazil which had taken the philosophies and practices of permaculture and supercharged them into large community movements. This time it seemed that my visions and guidance from Ayahuasca were manifesting as grounded projects and resources in the material world.

CHAPTER 7

Bridging Worlds

A mind like clouds
The new time is emerging
Bringing divine glory
More pure and attentive
We become channels of the infinite

Divine Mother I want to be
A realised child
And it is before your power
That I surrender to be liberated

With a river flowing out to sea
Currents carry the fear
Confidence to cross
My ultimate frontier

There are no excuses to hold up
It's already been said the time is to be
The time is to integrate
Embracing what remains

I am dying to the past
And not longing for the future
My crown is shining gold
I prove the nectar of mature love

— *Recado da Mãe Divina*, Chandra Lacombe.

Upon returning to Brazil, I was invited again by Silvia to attend her next retreat and offer my support and skills in helping her with it. I met up with a friend in Rio de Janeiro whom I had met on my last trip when he was volunteering for an arts and permaculture organisation working with youth in Bahia. We travelled to Salvador, the capital of the state of Bahia, and we stayed for some days at the *Organização de Permacultura e Arte* (OPA), where he had been working as a volunteer. After some days helping out and learning about their philosophy and projects, I also learned this was of interest to me, as I was also a specialist in working with youth arts education and had been developing my understanding of permaculture and ecology. I was really energised by the experience and excited to be back in Brazil. We met Silvia in the city and spent a couple of days exploring the culture and foods before driving down the coast to Itacaré, where Silvia's new retreat centre, Spirit Vine, was now up and running.

Arriving at Silvia's new and functioning retreat centre felt in some ways like a homecoming. A great group of people had gathered for this retreat and were excited and nervous about doing the work together. There was a mix of first timers with Ayahuasca and others who had already done some retreats and ceremonies with Silvia. This time I was feeling much more confident and prepared for what might come from reconnecting with Ayahuasca, and I was also able to work closer with Silvia in supporting her and her work and in supporting participants during the retreat and in the group therapy sessions, and also by running my visionary art and inner child workshops.

Silvia is very good at supporting participants to get in touch with their subconscious fears, motivations and childhood wounds that may be holding them back in life. I noticed that some people had strong reactions when challenged in ways that confronted them with their avoidant behaviours and cognitive dissonances. I learned a lot from Silvia, who was able to use her skills as a psychotherapist with two decades of experience guiding people through Ayahuasca in a setting that was more focused on therapeutic outcomes. I was also able to debrief with her at times to discuss my observations of what I was seeing in these participants and to formulate strategies on how best to support people through their experiences during the retreat.

I noticed that my eagerness to find remedy and diagnose some of the issues that emerged was, at times, allowing my ego-mind to become involved, and I was grateful that Silvia was very astute and strong in being able to point this out to me. My way of working with people was and is quite different to Silvia's. She is very direct and blunt at times, which can be effective, whereas I am more gentle and subtle in the way I share my reflections.

This time in Bahia and at Spirit Vine was a really happy and emotionally fulfilling couple of weeks for me. I felt able to really relax into myself and express my joy and playfulness in an environment which felt so comfortable and familiar to me now. I noticed I was much more confident with the ceremonies and working with Ayahuasca, and saw that my experiences in the ceremonies, although at times still very challenging, were more serene and balanced. I felt I had found a grounded and methodical way to work with the medicine that was allowing me to easily track the movement of the force of Ayahuasca in my body and its effects on my mind, with the experience becoming more predictable in the way it was working with me. The focused intention I was working with in this time was in learning to control my mind to a much stronger degree. In response, Ayahuasca was being very strict with me whenever my thinking mind would become active within the miração. During a strong vision that might trigger emotional responses or curiosity, if my mind engaged, the visions would dissolve quickly and I would be reminded of the pointless activity of a mind that thinks in words and how this interferes with the flow of spiritual messages and realities communicated through visions. This sometimes became a little frustrating, as I would find myself battling with my mind and struggling to come back to a pure meditative space.

During one ceremony Ayahuasca said to me very clearly: 'Your mind has the capacity to explore the infinite. The mind in a visionary state can create realities, you can create a whole world to explore, you can shape-shift into a bird and fly across magical skies. Imagine your mind like a paintbrush, painting realities of infinite possibilities. The mind that thinks in words is limited. Words have definite meanings and cultural and historical references that limit their scope. Let go of the words and the thinking mind, relax into what is possible in the infinite flow of ever-changing realities that may be impossible to be "thought" of, or understood in words. The thinking mind is like a habit, or a defensive posture, that protects you from the vast mystery of the unknown, where the mind is not required and wants to survive and protect itself. Be mindful of the wounds of abandonment you may have carried. Through faith and practice, your mind will learn to trust and fully let go into the ever-changing limitless forms of the miração.'

I was reminded of one of the mind teachings of Padmasambhava, the *lotus born* (miraculous birth) Buddhist Guru from Tibet, in which he describes the mind as being like clouds — they are always in motion, always changing form and appearance. We might look to the clouds and see them as a giant whale, but a moment later they might look like a dragon, and are constantly moving and changing. The mind and awareness are the same: mind states and thoughts are impermanent, much like the visions that come through the miração, and are constantly changing. If the mind tries to engage with the visions, this interferes with that flow of impermanence, where the visions may be shifting and changing whilst the mind is stuck trying to define what has already passed. I realised that in order to fully embrace the nature of the miração, the mind requires discipline and focus. It seemed with Ayahuasca now being a lot harder on me and at times teasing my mind that the teachings of the medicine were the same as in other spiritual disciplines such as Buddhism and Yoga. I was also reminded of how out of control my mind could be at times and how much work I needed to do in order to find the discipline to go even deeper into the miração of Ayahuasca and into the flow of life and creation. It was clear to me my mind was often the source of suffering in my life.

There is no difference between buddhas and sentient beings other than their scope of mind. What is called mind, consciousness or awareness is of a single identity. The mind of a sentient being is limited. The mind of a buddha is all-pervasive. So develop a scope of mind that is like the sky, which has no limit to the east, west, north or south. Within the sky-like empty mind habitual tendencies and disturbing emotions are just like clouds and mist. When they appear, they appear within the expanse of empty mind. When they remain, they remain within the expanse of empty mind. And when they dissolve, they dissolve in that same expanse of empty mind.— Padmasambhava.

One of the things I had learned from Pablo Amaringo was something he had said in that first retreat in Amazonas: 'Ayahuasca is a medicine and if you're not sick, you don't need it.' During this time in Bahia with Silvia I felt that I was going deeper into this teaching. From one perspective I was learning more and more from Silvia as her assistant and student but also from Ayahuasca itself. It made sense that Ayahuasca was making it harder for me to bypass the need to control my mind. During one ceremony the message was clear that Ayahuasca was not always willing to do the work for me to use the miração and tricks of teasing me in order to enchant my mind into a posture of surrender. Now I was being guided to take responsibility and learn to control my own thoughts. These mind trainings and dealing with the emotions of frustration and fear of the unknown manifesting in my thoughts were teaching me to not be dependent upon Ayahuasca. Over time and in the many years that followed Ayahuasca allowed me to work with much smaller doses once the resistances and mental distractions were no longer such a strong tendency in me. Silvia said that my ego could be quite arrogant in wanting to be right all the time, and although it was a shock to hear that from her, she was right, and I realised this was something I had learned from my father at a very young age. The teachings of the Maya which I had been studying also pointed out to me that in order to recreate our world in a new form which is not influenced by a past created by a dysfunctional mind, we needed to learn to think outside the box of our historical thinking, so that we could create from the spaciousness of the all-pervasive great mystery — something which can never be known by the human mind and its limitations. After all, it is the mind and the intellect that have got us into the confusions and destructive complexities of our unbalanced society, so to think that the mind will get us out of it would seem delusional. It made so much more sense to me to trust and allow the flow of Spirit to move through me in all aspects of my life, and thus to live a life of faith.

The round table of consciousness

In another vision during this time at Spirit Vine, Ayahuasca took me back to the concept of a 'round table' of consciousness. Given my ancestry from Celtic Britain, this image of the round table is familiar from the legend of King Arthur, a great leader who united all the clans. In legend, Arthur was a strong king who had received the blessings of the land and from the spiritual ancestors of Avalon, and also managed to honour and integrate the new world and its movement towards Christianity and a monotheistic God. There had been endless wars amongst the Celtic clans and waves of infiltration from foreign invasions, relentless politics and manipulation. Arthur created a court with a round table at its centre and invited all the clan leaders to sit as equals around a table with no sides, thus symbolising equality amongst all those who sat there. Ayahuasca showed me through the miração a round table of all the conscious beings that hold dominion on the Earth. From the birds to the mammals, insects, fish, reptiles, trees, microbes and so many others, including humans, we are all equal in our roles and responsibilities to maintain peace, harmony and balance on the Earth. We are all beholden to the laws and forces of nature, and through Ayahuasca humanity is being offered a sacrament that allows us to humble ourselves beyond the arrogance of superiority and the blindness to our symbiosis with all of life, whereby we can sit at this spiritual round table as equal partners in counsel with the whole Earth.

Ayahuasca showed me a vision for the creation of an 'embassy for the whole Earth' and suggested that one day I might be ready to work towards the construction of a temple and centre to become a home for this embassy and its teachings. I was given some information about the development of a school that would become a spiritual 'flight training academy', which would include Ayahuasca use and harmonic sound vibrations. This would be to prepare people for working together with the whole Earth in a covenant or sacred alliance with all conscious beings in order to develop future plans for the restoration of the planet. By listening to the voice of the conscious beings with the Earth, we honour the rights of the biosphere. I remember being very touched and excited by this prospect but also overwhelmed by yet another immense task being asked of me by Ayahuasca whilst I still had so much to learn. After taking all this in, I took a deep breath and let it all go, returning to a meditation of listening to the divine sounds of the forest and its symphonies of sonic colour and feelings sublimely washing through my mind and my soul.

Ancestral drums of Old Africa

During the final ceremony of this retreat I had another strong miração in which I found myself viewing a vibrant scene somewhere in Africa, in a time before European interference and colonisation. I was looking down over this village, which was full of people who were very happy, dressed in elaborate clothing and regalia singing in stunning harmonies and dancing rhythmically in what seemed like a very happy celebration. The energy and powerful thriving life force in these African people reminded me of some of the festivals and cultural events I had witnessed in Brazil, which has such a strong influence from the spirit of Africa. I then saw a procession of people entering into this celebration and everyone moved to allow a line of people to enter carrying a large throne with what seemed like a king or tribal chief sitting on it. My vision then changed and I experienced myself as that man sitting on the throne while the people around me were singing, dancing, celebrating and adorning me. I spent some time with this vision just feeling this energy, which seemed so familiar. Afterwards I contemplated what seemed to be a scene from a past life which was interesting to me, as I had never had conscious experiences in this life of connecting to an African past life. Somehow it made sense though, as I had always been drawn to traditional African culture; hearing African drums would always make the hairs on my body stand up and send a rush of adrenaline through me.

The next vision showed me building myself a house with a very specific design, somewhere close by the Spirit Vine centre in the mata-Atlantica forest of Bahia. I saw myself living a life there, being very happy. What I saw, though, was a very different version of me. This was quite confronting, as the lifestyle and my ways of relating to the world and others in that vision were very different to the person I had become until that point in my life. I was left in deep contemplation, as I felt like I was being shown a possible future that would require a big shift in my perspective of who I was and how I saw myself. This vision was challenging me, as it meant a shift in some ways of thinking and even changing the things in life I thought I wanted, mostly in terms of the way I relate to others in friendships, community, love and relationships. This seemed like a big step. Even though I found myself strongly resisting the possibility, the feeling of peace and happiness I received in the vision was undoubtedly very appealing and has stayed with me ever since. I had not experienced that level of happiness before and in some ways found it hard to connect with. Perhaps I was still healing from the lack of love and joy I had missed out on as a child and also in many past lives. Could I let go of my identity, which had served to define me and protect me throughout my life to that point? It didn't seem achievable at that moment. Ever since that vision I have dreamed of that land in Bahia and even in meditations my spirit flies to that land. I have since visited there on several occasions and each time I have felt so at peace within myself, like nowhere else in the world. Interestingly, the local people are of strong African descent and culture; this is perhaps the most African part of Brazil I have experienced.

Following the retreat, a couple of friends and I stayed for a few days on the land there with Silvia. It was nice to just relax together after the retreat without the responsibility of all the participants and to spend some time cooking meals, laughing and visiting local beaches and festivals and music in Itacaré. One day Silvia mentioned that she had been visiting the local Umbanda *terreiro* (a place of worship in the African traditions), where she had been participating in the *giras* they hold regularly under the guidance of a *Mãe de Santo*. In Umbanda, a gira is a ritual ceremony or spiritual gathering in which spirits or entities (such as Orixás, caboclos, pretosvelhos, Exus, Pombagiras) are invoked and may manifest through mediumship/incorporation for the purposes of celebration, healing work or spiritual training. The Mãe de Santo (Mother of the Saints) is the initiated priestess (or priest, if it is a *Pai de Santo*), and is responsible for overseeing the work in the Umbanda terreiro and passing on that knowledge, culture and tradition to others. The Mãe de Santo is also a well-trained medium who will typically have communion with several spirits that she will incorporate at different times and with different intentions, depending on the ritual and its intent. She will also have a mastery of herbal medicines and magical or shamanic abilities. For Silvia, her work in the giras was helping with her work in Ayahuasca ceremonies, and in protecting the land of the Spirit Vine centre. She was learning more about her own mediumship abilities. I was fascinated to hear of Silvia's experiences in the giras and realised the synchronicity with the vision I had received through the miração. This definitely seemed like something that I wanted to experience and learn more about, and although I wasn't staying long enough to go to one of these giras, Silvia gave me the number of a well-respected Mãe de Santo in Salvador, to where my friend and I were about to return in the following days.

Arriving back in Salvador, my friend and I made contact with Dona Maria, the Mãe de Santo who was recommended by Silvia. Excited, we decided to visit her and she organised to consult the *buzios* (cowrie shells) and ask for some messages from the guides, ancestors and Orixás. Dona Maria was very friendly and welcoming and made a whole ritual with a large round bowl of water during which she threw the buzios into a wooden tray multiple times. At some point she began a long dialogue covering many topics from spirituality to life paths, choices, family and health. She also identified and confirmed two of the Orixás that are my personal guides: Yemanjá and Ogum. A lot of what she said was very familiar and accurate in relation to my life circumstances and my family's issues, but she also relayed some predictions for my path ahead. Even though I had not mentioned anything about my professional career, she spoke a lot about my role as a healer and spiritual guide for many, about high vibrational forces and extraterrestrials working with me and also about my work with youth. She told a story about working with children and youth in a great desert. I wasn't sure what this was but, sure enough, in the years that followed this prediction came true. Overall, the visit was very educational, as we asked her a lot of questions about the nature of Umbanda spirituality; she suggested that now I had received my Orixás, this knowledge and lineage would become more prevalent in my life. With this she was also correct, as Umbanda and Afro-Brazilian spirituality has since become a huge part of my life.

For the healing of the planet

After a long and bumpy bus ride across the *sertão* (desert) in the interior of Bahia, we arrived in Brasilia, the capital city of Brazil. In the next days I made contact with the people I had been asked to meet by the ARTECOOP (Art, Technology, Ecology and Co-operation) group from Switzerland and for whom I would be working in developing a consortium of organisations and businesses in Brazil, with the aim of developing a new co-operative platform of ecological technology and its implementation in Brazil. This was an exciting time but also a massive learning curve: I was developing my understanding of the culture of working in Brazil, learning Portuguese and navigating a lot of interest in the project, including complicated government contacts. I travelled around with some presentations of technologies and strategies for implementation which made me realise there was a lot to learn and a huge amount of work to be done to develop our vision of a co-operative network that would work together for the sake of the planet and bring these eco-technological solutions to Brazil. I was looking forward to heading north into the *Cerrado* region (a vast ecoregion of tropical savanna) of Brazil, where I would be mostly based for the next 18 months in a town called *Alto Paraiso de Goias* (High Paradise of Goias), about three hours' drive north of Brasilia, in the state of Goias.

Alto Paraiso is a town on the edge of a majestic national park known as *Chapada dos Veadeiros* (Plateau of the Deer Hunters). The town and its surrounding regions had become a new-age haven for spiritual seekers, artists, religious groups, shamans, trance festivals, Ayahuasca churches and movements, permaculture, environmental activists, biological research, eco-villages and sustainable development. The Cerrado region covers around one-third of the land mass of Brazil and is a high plateau of savannas and giant, sweeping ancient valleys teeming with rainforests containing an immensity of biodiversity, much of which is still undiscovered by Western science. The majestic valleys are formed by enormous gushing spring waters emerging from the ground with spectacular waterfalls and crystalline creeks and rivers in abundance, and where crystals can be found everywhere. When driving around on top of the plateau on the surface it appears to be endless dry savannas dominated by soy plantations and seems severely damaged by monocultural farming techniques and rampant pesticide use. Scattered amongst the savannas are the ancient valleys full of rich biodiversity and an abundance of water. The town of Alto Paraiso itself is an eclectic mix of new-age people from all over Brazil and the world alongside a community of local people living in very poor conditions with little work and resources. Despite its remote location, the character of the town is very unique and dynamic, with many people attracted to the beauty and power of this ancient and spectacular land, and to the newly emerging culture of consciousness, spirituality and new adventures in ecological awareness. I was very happy to find myself in this magical and mysterious environment surrounded by so many of the things that had become so important to me.

On the night that I arrived in Alto Paraiso, word came that there would be a special community Ayahuasca ceremony at an eco-village in one of the nearby valleys called *Flor de Ouro* (Golden Flower); it was suggested this would be a good place to begin meeting people and get to know the community. Flor de Ouro is a beautiful community amongst a thriving food forest, permaculture gardens, bio-construction and with a large geodesic dome at the centre where the ceremony would be. There was a special celebration that night, as the *Encontro Nacional das Comunidades Alternativas*, or *ENCA* (National Meeting of Alternative Communities), had finished and the participants had arrived at Flor de Ouro after living communally without phones, cameras, computers or any electronic or recording devices for up to four weeks. ENCA was usually held in a very remote location only accessed by foot where representatives of eco-villages and other alternative communities would meet in a sacred ceremonial setting to discuss the issues facing their survival, environmental issues, leadership, ethics, cultural concerns and develop agreed protocols and strategies that would promote and sustain harmony amongst the large community of new-age people in Brazil. I was immediately impressed by the level of consciousness, activism, leadership and maturity that exuded from the people I encountered in Flor de Ouro. In fact, for me it represented a huge leap of organisational maturity and wisdom that far surpassed anything I had seen before. This was very humbling but also exciting, as I knew there was a whole universe of culture and practices for me to learn. I felt like a kid entering into a whole new world.

The ceremony that night was very eye opening, like nothing I had ever experienced or even imagined. The geo-dome temple filled with people, mostly standing or dancing, with some of the community leaders giving rousing speeches and passionate calls to action for the planet and for our connection with Great Spirit accompanied by constant chants of 'VIVA!' from everyone in the space. The hairs stood up on my skin and adrenaline rushed through my body. Large jugs of Ayahuasca grown and brewed on the land of Flor de Ouro were placed on an altar in the centre of the temple and we were invited to come and serve ourselves as desired. The 60 to 70 people there all seemed to confidently know how to hold themselves and maintain a strong ceremonial presence in the space, which was very impressive.

I had never experienced this freedom of individual responsibility in an Ayahuasca ceremony before. At Spirit Vine I was in ceremonies with people lying on mattresses in the dark whilst I was bursting to break out. There were a couple of men who seemed to holding themselves as leaders here, although the overall culture was that we were all equals in a spirit of trust and community. People would take turns in a harmonic flow to sing songs and share music, with many rousing songs sung for the Earth, songs from Santo Daime tradition, songs for the Orixás, songs from the Amazon, new-age rainbow-tribe songs, reggae and mantras.

I was enjoying the energy and feeling of being in such a warm, loving and intentional space. I felt a sense of liberation and a lot of gratitude, even if at times I was a little overwhelmed and unsure of myself or how to hold myself in the space. A couple of times I wandered out into the garden where some people were also taking some time under the stars and in the gardens. At times, some people checked in on me to see if I was okay, which I appreciated, and I was made to feel very welcome. Once the Ayahuasca came on strong, my experience was quite different to the mirações I had been used to. I remember standing in awe of this creation of Brazilian culture, astounded by the immense diversity, colour, rhythms and spirituality being expressed in the ceremony. I laughed heartily at the beauty and magnificence of it and of all creation and felt honoured and blessed to have found myself in such a potent expression of humanity. This seemed an evolved movement of humans expressing their love of the Divine, united with the Holy Sacrament of Ayahuasca in a spirit of peace and harmony through music, dance and prayer in vigorous, passionate joy, disciplined with a focused intent. This was a preview of the years that would follow where I would get to know and immerse myself in the Brazilian spiritual and Ayahuasca culture.

This celebration and ceremony raised my faith in humanity and the future of our planet and inspired within me a vision of a beautiful reality that was within our reach. Not in some distant future, but right at that moment, and I realised I had been conditioned by society to lazily think, 'One day things will be better for the planet.' With the help of Ayahuasca over many decades of contemporary use and its legalisation in Brazil, healthy communities had risen up, forming sacred alliances with each other and with the Earth. The Ayahuasca visions that I had seen were not just of hope, but of a living, thriving culture. This movement I found myself in was not just a group of party-goers at a Burning Man festival or a weekend workshop that chips away at the healing of the soul. This was a living, breathing, lived reality of human life working in active regeneration in a sacred communion with the Earth.

By the light of the firmament
Among the forces of prayer
Call the light into the conscience
Peace reigns among the nations
Together we are many in the chain of prayer
Together we are many practising devotion

Our prayer is what feeds us
Our devotion is what sustains us

For the healing of the planet
God summons in prayer
(For the healing!)

— Pela Cura do Planeta, Leal Carvalho, Flor de Ouro.

Brazilian ecology and community resilience

The next few months of living in Alto Paraiso and making regular trips to Brasilia was a busy and deeply engaging time of learning and expanding my awareness of ecology, community development, spirituality and culture from a Brazilian perspective. Despite falling in love with the Brazilian Portuguese language, I found it very challenging to learn, even though living amongst such a beautiful, poetic, passionate, musical and expressive language was a great inspiration. Growing up as an Australian, I had not been exposed to learning other languages and, despite Australia's multicultural society, English culture and language has always been dominant there, with little exposure to other cultures and languages. Learning a new language seemed particularly difficult. Brazilian culture itself is deeply nuanced as a rich weaving of Latin European, African and Indigenous influences. Whereas in Australia, the English colonists actively separated the Anglo-Celtic population from the Indigenous, Asian and other European peoples, even leading to a 'White Australia' legal policy that was, shockingly, still active well into the second half of the 20th century, and still desired by many. In Brazil there is much more mixing, interracial breeding and cultural fusions, which can easily be seen in the diversity of cultures there, and especially in the syncretic religions, including the Ayahuasca religions of Santo Daime, Barquinha and União do Vegetal.

Another great difference I found while living in Brazil was the influence of a different colonial history from that of Australia. Both countries used slaves to build and develop their infrastructure and industry. Whilst England called slaves in Australia 'convicts', in reality these were largely Celtic peoples who had been pushed off their lands, with some persecuted for their pagan, Earth-based spirituality during the industrial revolution, and who had found their way into cities, forced to steal food there to survive, after which they were jailed and transported to the new colonial outpost. In Brazil there had been a particularly brutal and cruel system of commercial slavery, whereby slave owners had found it more economical to work slaves to death and just buy more of them from the slave traders than to treat them with some humanity and allow them to live longer lives, where their productivity might decline as they aged. Brazil experienced some revolts by the African people, where some slaves managed to rise and free themselves before escaping into the interior of Brazil, with many of them ending up hiding out in places like the Cerrado. Alto Paraiso itself has a population of African descendant peoples known as *Calungas*, many of whom were only rediscovered hiding in those ancient Cerrado valleys as recently as the 1980s.

What both countries share is that both are run under inherently corrupt legal/economic systems which have institutionalised and formalised insidious networks of control leveraged by elite groups of 'old money' families and cartels. The difference being that, in typical English style, Australia projects itself to the world behind the great illusion of being a sophisticated and controlled society of dignity, all cast over its history of genocide, theft and corruption, whereas in Brazil the politics and corruption are enacted with more of a blunt sword, evidenced in the blatant gangster-style robbery and violent retribution that is obvious to all there. Australia offers the people there enough economic mobility to keep them subdued and compliant amidst a tightly regulated, heavily policed, monotonal culture, whereas Brazil offers its people much less economic opportunity, with street violence as its form of oppressive control, but permits much more liberty in religion, personal freedom, land rights, politics and cultural expression.

Many wealthy Brazilians and some foreigners with good intentions for developing ecological land-based projects and community were buying land in the region. Most of these people were also influenced by the strong movement of Ayahuasca in the region and amongst the New Age culture. One of the projects I was involved in during this time was developing a proposal for a wealthy woman from Rio de Janeiro who had been touched and awakened by Ayahuasca and had bought 2000 hectares of stunning ancient land just outside of Alto Paraiso. She had bought that land with great intention although she had been somewhat naive as to the massive undertaking it would require to maintain, let alone develop, and she needed help in managing such an enormous property. Biologists had come and done surveys, and found endangered species such as native wolves, monkeys and jaguars. The vision for the project was to protect the land by developing a natural sanctuary and to employ advanced agroforestry, permaculture and eco-tourism to sustain it. A couple of years into the slow progress of this massive undertaking in a very remote area only accessible by strong, high-range 4WD vehicles, she had begun to have problems with the owners of the neighbouring farm.

One day when she was visiting Rio de Janeiro, the neighbour had invaded the land, burned down the house closest to the border of their lands, ripped the fence down and rebuilt it some distance into her land, thus effectively stealing a big portion of her land. On her return she took a friend with her to confront the neighbour, who promptly pulled a gun on them and told them to leave. After employing security guards, she began to take legal action, only to find that the neighbour produced a title deed for the land which included the parcel that they stole, and the person who had sold her the land and given her the title deed that also included that portion of land was, in fact, the brother of the neighbour. When she took them to court and was becoming eternally frustrated by unfair procedures and legal complications, she found out that the judge in the local court was the cousin of the two brothers and that the same judge was also related to the governor of the state. I realised that this part of remote Brazil, with its fragile biodiversity, was under serious threat — the same threat facing not only the local ecosystems like this, but the whole of Brazil and most parts of the world. Those ancient Cerrado valleys are millions of years older than the Andes Mountains and the Amazon basin and forest. In fact, the biodiversity of the Cerrado is the source of life and waters of all the forests and river systems of Brazil and parts of South America. This was clearly the Brazilian version of the 'Wild West' and this story was one of many similar ones I heard during my time in this region. At times over the years some of my friends from there were in fear of their lives after taking actions to stand up for the protection of the land. Not long after this episode, the State Government of Goias changed the law to allow for land to be forcefully taken if the owner was not actively producing economic benefit from it.

I reflected a lot on the environmental tragedy I was witnessing and often remembered that strong Ayahuasca vision I had received in Peru of the Amazon being choked and of being asked by those jaguar shamans to be a defender of the Amazon. It inspired me to learn a lot more about the environmental situation in Brazil and also the strong culture of emerging remedy and solutions for this cultural and environmental disaster. I found it interesting that life and Spirit had guided me to this ancient part of Brazil which was the source of life for the Amazon to learn and witness first-hand the destruction I had been shown in the vision. I was greatly impressed by the strength and stoicism of the passionate Brazilians living in the region who just seemed to be able to remain focused and calm amidst such treachery. It seemed this large community of people who were drinking Ayahuasca were greatly motivated to work together for the sake of the planet. In Australia we were used to being dominated by insane levels of bureaucratic controls and punitive laws, fees and regulations preventing us from developing our ecological and community projects, but here in Brazil was a very different manifestation of the dysfunction.

I was highly engaged in attending local permaculture and ecology meetings and groups and was introduced to many people and projects that were happening in the region which gave me a lot of hope and even excitement for the possibilities at hand. Through the networks I was developing I was also able to build links between the Alto Paraiso communities, Australia, Brasilia and Europe of ideas, people, technologies and strategies. At times I was invited by local alliances to gather and we would drink Ayahuasca on the land in small ceremonies before convening meetings, discussing plans and strategies, dreams and visions. I was learning that, despite my sense of urgency and the passion of these Brazilian eco-warriors, things in the material dimension move slowly as we navigate the weight of economic and political domination. I was learning a lot, both from the communities on the land in Alto Paraiso, and from the businesses and companies in Brasilia that were working with universities and government to develop large-scale environmental projects, all the while feeding back all of this to the team in Europe and my friends in Australia, and relaying feedback and ideas back to the communities in Brazil. The project gained much momentum over the course of 10 months and by then had built a co-operative alliance with ecological projects in Brasilia, São Paulo, Amazonas and Alto Paraiso de Goias.

Things became more challenging when I had to start dealing with politicians and government bureaucrats. There was an immense amount of interest in the project and, in particular, some of the politicians were desperate to get contracts for the intellectual property of the new technologies, as they could see a way to get large amounts of international funding from carbon credits and other incentives. The problem we were encountering was that the European embassies had strong regulations preventing corruption in any international trade that involved accessing these environmental funds, and the Brazilian culture of political donations was almost like an addiction for the political and bureaucratic class. I was often taken out to lunch by government handlers in Brasilia who would sit me down and explain these political donations to me; I would just listen and make no comment. At this stage my optimism and naivety kept me going to try and find a way around this roadblock of seemingly culturally entrenched corruption. Meanwhile, biologists and forestry experts would explain to me how the majority of the hundreds of millions of dollars of Amazonian reforestation funds had been given to slick international agencies and 'charities' who were offering very expensive quick-fix polyculture planting projects of up to only six species of trees which were dying after only 30 years due to lack of biodiversity. Within our project was a proposal for the implementation of 'successional agroforestry'. Extensive research and development of this in Brazil showed that although it was more labour and time intensive, it would bring an abundant biodiversity and long-term sustainability in forest regeneration with the side effect of creating economy by producing foods and building materials. Our co-operative was also developing projects that included technologies for recycling waste wood products from land clearing, building materials from garbage recycling and waste collection from cleaning waterways, bio-construction and energy generation.

Settling into life in Alto Paraiso had also included attending regular Ayahuasca ceremonies at the *Templo Mãe d'Àgua* (Mother of the Water Temple). These beautiful ceremonies were founded by Yatra Barbosa, who had a long history of working with the Santo Daime in Brazil and was one of the pioneers in taking the Ayahuasca religion to Europe, not long after Carioca Freitas did the same. She went on to establish the Tribe of the Mãe d'Àgua, where she was the patroness and *madrinha* (godmother), who in 2004 had found themselves a home in Alto Paraiso. Attending these ceremonies was a very different experience to what I had been accustomed to in my work with Pablo Amaringo, Silvia Polivoy and the Shipibo of Peru. The ceremonies were held under ambient lights in a relaxed and graceful atmosphere where the central focus was the exquisite music played by a multi-talented and multi-dimensional band at the centre of concentric circles with everyone dressed in white. It took me some time to accustom myself to this very different culture. The first time I went there I was prepared to lie down in the dark and focus on entering the miração. What I found instead was a gentle, focused circle of people singing and praying together and holding space in a beautiful, graceful and elegant way which moved the force of the Ayahuasca in a very different way than I had previously experienced.

Mother of the waters and star beings from the sky

At first I found that the lights and the consistent tone of the music, although beautiful, were slightly distracting from my trained instinct to close my eyes and go deep into the miração. The music itself didn't appear to allow me to drift into those deeper spaces and it seemed like this particular style of working with Ayahuasca was much more about the music, the setting and the prayers, and wasn't giving much space for deeper exploration. It took some time and a few visits for me to go beyond my resistance to this style of work, but eventually I realised it wasn't going to be the kind of space where I could go as deep as I was used to. But the music was so beautiful and alluring that I slowly learned to appreciate it and began to train myself to sit up and sing with the group. After years of keeping my eyes closed and being deep in the miração, it was challenging at times to go against that training and instinct and to keep my eyes open. I saw this as a new challenge, but I also felt a little bit lost in that space. There didn't seem to be much guidance or instruction available from the people, although I was able to learn through observation and by allowing the ceremony itself to guide me. Translating the songs and the prayers and learning to sing in Portuguese seemed a huge undertaking but I came to fall in love with the Brazilian Ayahuasca music with its influences from the forests, Santo Daime and Umbanda. I would listen to it every day and would be around friends and at gatherings where people were seemingly always playing this enriching and enchanting music. At this stage I had my guitar with me, but I wasn't playing much, just on my own every now and again. I had a few songs I would play for myself but I had never seriously attempted to master the instrument, and was far too shy about it to play in front of others. Through these ceremonies and the Ayahuasca culture I was immersed in, a seed was planted and this music and its culture began stirring my soul and calling my spirit.

One day I was with a group of friends out camping on the land in the Cerrado in a remote place where there was no mobile phone coverage or electricity. We were on this trip with a member of the group who was a biologist doing surveys looking for endangered species and were setting up camera traps and looking for paw-prints and other evidence to report back to the government ministry of environment in the hope of getting protection orders put on the land. That night we were sitting around a fire talking and playing music when we all saw a light in the sky that was obviously some kind of extraterrestrial presence. It was moving erratically: quickly, then slowly, zooming here and there, at times hovering, then appearing and disappearing. In some moments it seemed as though it was responding to our comments and thoughts. For all of us there this was an exciting experience but nothing we hadn't seen before or questioned. I had experienced many sightings of these kinds in the sky and they had usually marked some moment of significance in my life.

The next night back in Alto Paraiso there was a full moon ceremony at the Templo Mãe D'Àgua and I was excited to attend. The ceremony was again beautifully facilitated and with the usual beauty, grace and stunning music. When the force of the Ayahuasca arrived I received some insights into my life there and about the project — and even some deeper insights into my psychology and some of the relationships I had in the community. Doing these regular ceremonies was a great way to cleanse my mind of fears, doubts, insecurities and worries, and also to come back to my centre and find my personal balance. Sometimes the lessons would be stronger than others, but usually there was a sense of taming the ego mind and clearing the way for the voice of Spirit to be heard. Through these regular experiences I was starting to see the benefits for my mental and physical health and enjoy the opportunity to pray with my community for the land, for the children, for each other and for Spirit. I noticed my mood would always be elevated after these ceremonies, with positive thoughts, more energy and motivation. This night, though, something different happened.

Towards the close of the ceremony I could feel that Ayahuasca wanted to take me into a miração. I could feel a certain tension, as the format of the ceremony and the style of the music, with its relentless upbeat tone, kept testing my ability to maintain focused. Once the ceremony ended and most of the participants went outside to the fire to socialise and eat, I decided to stay in the temple — and the force of the medicine came on very strongly. It didn't matter whether my eyes were opened or closed; I saw colours and geometries that were powerful and ever-changing, similar to what I had experienced many times before. After a while I noticed two beings enter the temple. They were tall and slender, and glowing with a brilliant translucent blue aura. I had the strong sense they were the same beings who had visited us the night before in the Cerrado. Nobody else was left in the temple and once I had accepted the presence of these beings, my eyes closed and a strong miração arrived, which I entered. These 'star beings', as I called them, began to show me many different advanced technologies. Some I didn't fully grasp but they seemed to involve genetics and biology. One that was clearly explained to me was that through our star ancestors there was technology available which would be able to bring back species that had become extinct and re-establish the balance of biodiversity on the planet. The beings showed me another technology that could clean the atmosphere of radiation pollution, which they explained was much more serious than humanity realised. These visions seemed to go on for some time.

This miração was a strong one and at some point I forgot I was sitting meditating in the temple, but I stayed with the visions. These star beings then showed me a group of people standing in a circle in a remote, deserted place that could have been similar to where we had been in the Cerrado the night before. They showed me that by using harmonics of sound and vibrations activated through our voices in a purified field where there is no interference from electro-magnetic energies, a group of people with clear minds and pure hearts would be able to collectively 'sing' the manifestation of a sonic portal to call and welcome a visitation from our galactic star ancestors. I was effectively being shown how to make contact in our physical reality with extraterrestrial beings. The beings then went on to show me again this inter-species consciousness round table, and they explained that when we were able to achieve humble communication as a member of the round table with the beings of the whole Earth, we would graduate to a place within a galactic community and then be ready to communicate with our ancestors from the stars, and that with permission and agreement from all of the species of the Earth, these advanced technologies would then become available to us through these extraterrestrials. I was again reminded of the vision of the 'embassy for the whole Earth' that had first been presented to me in a vision at Spirit Vine. Once I had comprehended the visions and messages from these glowing blue star beings, they left and the miração subsided. I took some time to slowly come back to my body and the room, and lay there contemplating this profound vision and its teachings.

I had been living in Alto Paraiso for 16 months and regularly visiting Brasilia where I had also developed friendships and been involved in different permaculture and sustainable development projects around the city. I had grown close with a great circle of friends who really looked out for me; we had a great camaraderie and sense of purpose and faith in a shared spiritual mission of protection of the Earth and the healing of humanity. At times I felt really out of place as the only gringo (non-Brazilian) amongst groups of excitable and passionate Brazilians with all their cultural nuances, great humour and open-hearted kindness. The vision that had shown me a new kind of technology, by accessing pure consciousness and pure heart connection as a way to communicate with extraterrestrial beings and access very advanced telepathic and vibrational technologies through spiritual practices, reminded me more of the way Australian Indigenous peoples had developed their spiritual technologies beyond the complexities of materialistic designs. Those technologies do not require the untangling of a heavy, corrupted and dysfunctional system in order to make even the smallest steps of progress whilst the planet is in an urgent environmental crisis and on the brink of disaster.

I contemplated one the teachings from the Mayan prophecies that speak of these times and the next evolutionary leap of humanity, which is one of consciousness and spirituality: as we recognised the interconnectedness of all life, we would enter a new phase of collective and planetary awareness. The prophecy says that this crisis of our times, although it manifests in the material world, cannot be solved through material means. This crisis is an evolutionary trigger point for a radical consciousness shift, one in which we realise the only way out of the crisis is to evolve the technology of our minds through spiritual awareness beyond the material world. For many people, Ayahuasca is a medicine that offers training and preparation for death. Similarly, I have come to learn that it is also the perfect medicine for training our minds in how to deal with the upcoming spiritual evolutionary leap of humanity and the emergence of the consciousness of the whole Earth. The gratitude I have for the majesty and divinity of Ayahuasca in my life inspires me, like so many others, to live my life following a path of service to the healing of the Earth and of humanity.

> *We are living at a time of a great transformation. The noosphere, as the sphere of collective human thought, is beginning to emerge in its fullness. We must realize that the Earth is a whole, and the shift in our consciousness is a step toward the realization that we are one with the Earth and with the universe. The noosphere is not just a concept; it is a living reality that is emerging as humanity awakens to its interconnectedness. It is the consciousness of the*

Whole Earth, and it is our responsibility to align our actions and thoughts with the cosmic laws that govern life. — Jose Argüelles, *Manifesto for the Noosphere: The Next Stage in the Evolution of Human Consciousness.*

To look at the light in this Earth
Is the need to have love
To respect your brothers and sisters
With joy in work

To look at the light in this Earth
Is the need to comprehend
That the moment is coming
There is no time to lose

To look at the light in this Earth
Is the need to have firmness
To receive from the sky
The power to win

To look at the light in this Earth
Is the need to be grateful
The queen of the stars
And all of her creation

To look at the light in this Earth
Is the need of truth
This brilliance of purity
In the garden of the heart

— *Terra,* author unknown.

Returning to the inner landscape of evolution

The complexities and challenges presented by the co-operative project we had done so much work to create were at times overwhelming. It seemed that through Ayahuasca I was receiving guidance in visions of the nature of our evolution as humanity on a path of conscious evolution, which was also the prophecy of the Maya that had left a deep impression upon me. The struggles of the new-age communities in protecting the land around Alto Paraiso and in the Cerrado, the failures of reforestation projects in the Amazon, and the tangled web of corruption and politics all obstruct the implementation of programs, technologies and strategies that could make a huge difference. I started to wonder if the path being laid out for me was leading me towards supporting the healing of the Earth through spirituality and consciousness, more so than slogging it out in the material world. It was at this time I received a message that our project had received funding to hold a conference in Salvador Bahia, where all the partners could come to present their projects and the European and Brazilian partners could meet and formalise the alliance with a public presentation.

I packed up ready to leave Alto Paraiso to head back to Bahia to work on preparing the conference. The night before I left, a group of friends gathered for a music circle and celebration to bless my journey. I was sad to leave, as I had made some great friends and found a deep connection to the land. During the day I had visited a woman who was one of a group of people who were the first new-age people to buy land and start developing an alternative community in Alto Paraiso. They had been given the blessing of the Indian Guru Osho Rajneesh to start the first community of *Sanyasins* (followers of Osho) outside of India. The woman told me that some months after they had arrived and begun to establish their community, an Australia woman had arrived and delivered a message from an Australian Indigenous Elder woman, whom she had told of their arrival on this land. The Elder asked her to tell this group that the land they had acquired for their community was a sacred place that held a large crystal. That crystal was a twin to one in the central desert of Australia, and that these two crystals worked together to maintain an energetic and spiritual balance of the planet. This was interesting, as it was said that this part of Brazil was the second oldest exposed land on the Earth, and that the oldest was in Central Australia — both were sources of the first emergence of life on Earth. Interesting also was that when I had spent time in the Australian desert in the year 2000, an Aboriginal clever man (shaman) had found me and told me I would return there with an important message to learn regarding a 'new Dreaming' of the Earth. Like Pablo's invitation to return to the Amazon some years earlier, this was something that had stayed in the back of my mind as a powerful prophecy for my life — a prophecy which, in the years that followed, also came true.

Upon returning to Bahia, where I was staying again with the crew from OPA, my heart sunk after I received a message from one of the partners of the project. He asked me to look at the website for the organisation which was linked to the United Nations and which had sourced the funding for the conference to launch the project. The website had changed and was now featuring palm oil plantations and hydro-dams as the main technologies featured for the project, with links to the largest agricultural, mining and energy ministries of the Brazilian Government. Partners were threatening to pull out, as presenting this technology was clearly an example of *green washing* (presenting technology as ecological and sustainable when it isn't). News came in that the money for the conference had gone missing and I learned also from the European co-operative employing me that their investors had attempted to force them out of the company and there was no money to continue. It seemed as though the more powerful ministries in the Brazilian Government had caught wind of the potential of this project to access the millions of dollars of carbon-credit funding and had bullied their way in front of the smaller ministries we were working with, such as the ministries of science and technology, environment and planning. I suspected that some invisible hand, whoever that was or whatever that might be, had acted to sabotage the project.

All this was very disheartening, although unsurprising, as I had seen this kind of thing happen before: a hidden hand somehow arrives and blocks the advancement of new technologies. The project was put on hold, but as the money had all dried up, I was left without any funds and needing to reconsider my next moves. I remembered the vision from a couple of years prior when during a miração the voice of the Earth had told me about the lesson she had for humanity of needing to understand how to wield power with responsibility. The universe had played its hand and our dream of an alliance of co-operation in developing these solutions had been halted. I needed to work out my next direction. I considered returning to Brasilia and attempting to rebuild things but, given the visions and this recent manifestation, I decided to take a different path. I remembered when I had been in the Peruvian Amazon, and also without money, that I had decided to go into the forest to stay with the Shipibo. I contacted Silvia and asked if she needed some help at Spirit Vine and she happily welcomed me back there. I realised the significance of the timing of the communication with those star beings who had shown me the conscious evolution needed to access advanced technologies in communion with the whole Earth, soon after which this project was corrupted. I knew all the work and networks and knowledge shared, spanning the whole planet, would not die and would just remain itself but in a new form. The seeds had already been planted. I decided to return to work with Ayahuasca and continue my studies with Silvia at Spirit Vine. In the next days I took the bus for the six-hour journey down the coast, back to the place that was so dear to my heart on the Cacau Coast of Bahia.

It took me a few days to deal with the loss of the project and the forced sudden change in my plans. I was dealing with feelings of insecurity and a bit of confusion; my mind was fighting with the flow of the universe, lamenting the state of humanity. I had some feelings of self-doubt and failure, although in my heart I knew what we had created was a groundbreaking movement. So many connections and positive actions had come from it, and I had worked from my heart, given it my all and done the best I could. It was hard to escape feelings of anger and frustration at the corruption and dark forces controlling the flow of resources on the planet, knowing the dire consequences of the relentless movement of destructive human behaviours. Returning to ceremony and Ayahuasca, I came to an acceptance and peace with the state of the world, realising that there are lessons, both individual and collective, in the manifestation of our humanity in these times. My determination to continue my path in finding healing for the Earth was as strong as ever. The adversity I was experiencing only made me more determined to keep moving forward. Through the ceremonies at Spirit Vine I understood that I still had more healing to do on a personal level, and that I also had much more to learn along the way about consciousness and how to access those states of purity I had been shown in those visions, if I was to return to that round table and the Dreaming of the Whole Earth to do the work I had been shown was necessary.

> *All of human society has fallen to such deplorable levels because, as the Aborigines say, "white men have lost their Dreaming". The Aboriginal Dreaming is tuned to receiving suggestions, images and potencies directly from pervading, pulsating voices of the Earth and the prevailing echoes of the Creative Ancestors in the heavens … The potential of the Dreamtime is still alive within us, both physically and psychologically, and holds the promise of an astonishing awareness that stretches beyond the bounds of our five senses. No objective can be of greater significance for human survival than the recovery of the Dreaming. The Aboriginal way of life and the Aboriginal revelation holds the seeds for the rebirth of the Dreamtime in humanity. — Robert Lawlor, Voices of the First Day, Awakening in the Aboriginal Dreamtime.*

Over the next two months I supported Silvia's work over two retreats. After being so involved in the development of our ecological projects, I realised my mind had become too focused on mental and intellectual things. Going deeper into the mirações was a little challenging at first, as my mind was quite active. I continued my studies in learning about the psychology of supporting people in pre- and post-ceremony group therapy and sharing circles. Silvia remained a good, yet tough, mentor. I had begun to receive music and some songs after ceremonies, when music would arrive in my mind and I would be unable to focus on anything else until I sat down with my guitar and allowed the words and music of a song to come through. There was another musician there who lived locally and who played beautiful flute. He was inspired by my new songs, and this was a new revelation for me — to explore the creation of music that seemed to be coming from Ayahuasca and the forest there at Spirit Vine. I realised how much I loved to play music with others, although I still felt pretty shy and lacking in confidence as a musician. This joy in expressing myself through music from this time would continue to grow inside me over the years that followed.

My work with Ayahuasca was very focused during this period on continuing the mind teachings that were quite challenging and required self-discipline and focus. A lot of the work Ayahuasca was guiding me with was also in supporting the space, identifying energies light and dark plus entities that were entering the space which often attached to people in the ceremonies. I was gaining insight into how the issues people were bringing for healing, either consciously or subconsciously, were manifesting spiritually in the force of the Ayahuasca. This would happen both through their physical symptoms and behaviours and also with energetic movements and spiritual entities. At times I would check with Silvia and report the things I saw. I would offer my observations and sometimes diagnoses and she was great at helping me to clarify my vision with my interpretations to make sure they were unencumbered by any ego projections. Silvia had a very sharp and quick response to anything that was coloured by my ego, and whilst this was confronting at times, I really appreciated this training, as it helped me to refine my vision and learn to identify my own projections. I was spending less time exploring astral visions in the miração relating to me and more time working in the space and clearing energies within the miração, supporting others in their work by clearing the field.

At this time I began to get instruction from Ayahuasca to do more work in allowing its force to manifest through me to express the force of the medicine through my body. Silvia did not permit that in her style of work and she was not available to support me to explore this with Ayahuasca. Learning to sing and sit up in the light and even dance in ceremonies during my time in Alto Paraiso had awakened a new awareness and possibility within me, but at this time I humbly resisted exploring this, as it was not in the field of possibility relative to the work Silvia was doing. I accepted this was not something she was able to hold space for. What was coming in strongly, though, was a call to be there in support the ceremony and participants. Receiving and expressing music would come after the ceremonies. My relationship with Ayahuasca was evolving, and I was simply allowing this to happen, not getting carried away with ambitions. I could appreciate that Silvia was holding me back from this, as I could see that there were still edges of my ego that needed to be cleaned out. Silvia would remind me of one of the important teachings of Pablo Amaringo, who would warn us that Ayahuasca could break down your ego, but it could also allow it to strengthen, which could become the path to sorcery, power and the shadow side of Ayahuasca. It is crucial on this path to be guided by good teachers and community to stay humble and empty of ambition.

Pablo Amaringo passed away in Pucallpa at around this time. I knew that through his death there would be a transformation of his energy and that his spirit would remain with me and within the force of the miração. Sometimes I would be reminded of his presence and teachings and also through the extensive collection of art he had left, which is a whole university of plant consciousness and cosmic teachings. I knew he had gifted me a universal library of shamanic wisdom and knowledge, and that I had only accessed a small portion of it. The challenge remained to find my way back into those deep meditative spaces within the miração he had taken me to. His guidance was always reminding me to find my own way, to be guided by my own spirit and to be empowered with self-knowing. Whilst Ayahuasca was a powerful teacher of many things, what I had come to realise was that, aside from the connection and spiritual awareness of nature and the cosmos that it offered, the most valuable offering of Ayahuasca was the opportunity it gives us for self-awareness. This was the challenge I was being presented with: to know my mind, to understand my ego and the traumas that created the wounds that triggered my thoughts and subconscious behaviours. The medicine had taught me to surrender deeply to the divinity of Spirit and the Earth and from within to learn to cultivate and remain present with and humble to that divine force. Ayahuasca was teaching me to become empty, and thus to be of service — to be an instrument for the flow of divine love within and without me and to realise that the

'I' that I might at times identify with was so tiny and inconsequential in the magnificence of the entirety of creation. I was simply learning to 'get over' myself.

Music: the sound of creation

Between the retreats I spent a lot of time alone in the forest in one of the cabins at Spirit Vine. Occasionally I would spend some time helping Silvia or venture out to the beach or into the town of Itacaré. Life was pretty slow and simple, and it was a good time to clear my mind and let go of the last couple of years of working so hard on these ecological projects. I didn't have much sense of where I was heading; I was happy to just stay there and be present. I was studying the work of Lujan Matus and his book *The Art of Stalking Parallel Perception*, which I had read some years previous and which was a very powerful training in shamanic awareness. Studying this book provides a magical quality, not unlike reading the work of Carlos Castaneda and his tales of Don Juan. Matus' book even pays homage to the lineage of the *Nagual* shamans from Mexico. I would at times enter into deep meditations through the guidance of the book and there were occasions where I met Don Pablo in the visions I would receive and he would pass on teachings through energy and movement. It felt very reassuring to be connecting with him in this way.

Time was slowing right down and after I finished studying that book, I felt empty and again my mind drifted into questions on my direction and purpose. I had a few restless nights and was full of energy and unable to sleep. After a few such nights, I gave up trying to sleep and decided to sit up under the stars and meditate. It must have been around 2am one night, with no one around me, just the sounds and smells of the forest, the sound of the wind in the trees. I sensed a presence near and became aware that some of those ancestor star beings had again come to visit me. I welcomed their presence and, although I wasn't getting any visions of them, I did receive music. I could hear very clearly a beautiful melody and felt compelled to pick up my guitar. As I sat there under the stars, in one flow of creation I received and wrote a song which I called *Last Sunset*:

Fly, fly away from here
Setting sun disappear
Stars and the night sky
Are calling you, my dear
Can't you hear?

We call you alone right here, right now
When you're alone, we're with you now
We love you awake, right here, right now

Time ticks and drags us down
Awakened ones go underground
A calling from the core of life
A gathering sound
Can't you hear?

The view from the throne, right here right now
We walk this alone, we're with you

We love you awake from here, right now

We listen to the talking box
Machine world cause all life to stop
A kangaroo hoping across the setting sun
Ancient Desert
Can't you hear?

The sound of the fall, remember now
Can you afford not listen now?
We love you awake from here, right now

— *Last Sunset*, Lore Solaris.

Once I had written the song and played it a few times so I would remember it all, the beings began to communicate with me, telling me they had been sending me energy to keep me awake at night and that since I hadn't been listening to them, they needed to get my attention to do this work and receive this song. This made me laugh, as I was reminded of the resistance I would often have when I received signs or messages from spiritual guides. Sometimes I would try to avoid more spiritual downloads due to their intensity. The beings went on to explain that the song they transmitted and co-created with me was multi-dimensional and had messages for me but it was also important to share it with others. This was the first clear guidance I had received from Spirit to share my music. They explained that these ancestral beings were sending telepathic love to humanity in order to assist in our awakening, and there was a bit of a humorous aspect in that they were trying to wake me up in order to receive the song. This was also the first hint of a vision I was about to receive regarding the path in front of me. Over seven nights I received one song per night in much the same way: I would sit under the stars and meditate and the song would virtually write itself. I have gone on to record and play some of these songs in ceremonies.

A couple of days after writing these songs there was another retreat with Silvia. The ceremonies and the teachings of Ayahuasca continued much as they had in the previous retreats. I began to feel a strong sense of purpose with Ayahuasca and this way of working and supporting the spiritual growth and healing of people. I knew I had so much more to learn and I was getting the sense that everything was about to change. On the night after the final ceremony, I had a vivid dream in which I was on the east coast of Australia and I began to fly west across the land. I don't often have dreams of flying and this one was particularly vivid and lucid. I remember looking down at the Earth and seeing the landscape changing from forests into dry country and then into desert. I was a long way into the desert when I caught a glimpse of something shining brightly like a point of light, calling to me, so I flew down to it. When I landed I found a beautiful crystal so brilliant and full of light and energy. It was a divine gift from the Earth. I woke from the dream as I was holding this crystal and immediately realised that this was a message telling me it was time to return to Australia. Just like in the song *Last Sunset*, I was hearing the call from the ancient desert.

Encountering the dark side

I managed to organise myself to get a flight to Spain, where I planned to meet up with a dear friend on my way to England. I had been offered some work there which would help me pay for the journey back to Australia. While in the south of England I took some days to go and stay with some friends who had recently been in San Francisco, the same Shipibo village I had visited a few years before. I had met one of them, Allan, the last time I was in the UK and since then by synchronicity we had both had experiences in the same village in the Peruvian Amazon. I had spoken with him during and after his time in San Francisco, as he had been having some very challenging experiences with the powerful shaman there, the one I had avoided. Allan had decided to get involved with this shaman and his family and somewhat naively had taken the eldest son of the shaman, who was a powerful young shaman in training, on a trip to Cusco where they had run some Ayahuasca ceremonies. The old sorcerer shaman had warned them not to make this trip, but they had decided to do it anyway. The shaman had become furious with my friend for disobeying him and I imagined was concerned about the interference in his son's spiritual training in shamanism.

There were times when Allan had been confronted in the village by some of this old shaman's behaviours which were creating confusion and doubts in him. I had seen this kind of thing before when I was there: people who were seduced by the power of this kind of sorcery. Whilst they were in Cusco, the old sorcerer used some kind of magic and put a curse on Allan and he became sick. When he returned to San Francisco with the shaman's son, Allan found that his pet monkey and dog had died mysteriously. Confused and spooked by this, he quickly packed his things and fled the village to return to Cusco where he stayed to record some songs that he had written in his time there with the Shipibo. I had been talking to him during this time and supporting him to understand what had happened. Over time he had recovered his health but he still remained partly haunted by his experiences. I was surprised when I arrived in the south of England at his house to find out he was holding Ayahuasca ceremonies and using the knowledge and skills he had learned from this old sorcerer, who had died about six months prior to me arriving there at Allan's house.

During my first Ayahuasca experiences with Pablo and Silvia in Amazonas, Pablo would often mention the 'dark side' of Ayahuasca shamanism. He would mention it then tell us that he was going to explain more about it. Interestingly, he never actually did talk about it more than just saying that it existed and that he would explain it. In one of the ceremonies during that first retreat, during a miração, I had a vision of a disturbing dark entity rushing towards me. It came into my field with a sudden, disturbing shock that at first gave me a rush of fear and I felt a corresponding rush of adrenaline in my body. I immediately realised that this entity was trying to frighten me so I instinctively stayed very still, centred myself and connected with my heart. When I did, a powerful light and vibration emanated around me and shone towards this being, which instantly disappeared as quickly as it arrived. Pablo then appeared in my vision and I saw that visions of these kinds of entities are like parasitic beings which attempt to create an energetic attachment through fear. I was shown how they approach and attempt to generate a fear response, and when a person drops their vibration into a fearful state, the being is able to read the subconscious mind and hide itself as an emanation of that fear. If the person chooses to focus on that fearful emanation it can lead to them having obsessive and negative thoughts. The dark entity will feed off that low vibrational energy and attention and this can lead to the person having some darker visions and even becoming caught into negative loops of thought. Many people, even those who have never drunk Ayahuasca, carry these entities throughout life and don't even realise. I have come to learn over the years that some of these entities are suffering spirits that come to the ceremony to be healed, while others are like parasitic pests that attempt to infiltrate and feed off the light of the ceremony. I was grateful for these teachings and was learning how maintaining my own light and a high vibration has been invaluable in my own spiritual work, but also in helping others. This was also a strong reminder that Ayahuasca is not all about love and light and positivity, that there are dangers, and the spiritual field of any ceremony needs to be protected. The facilitators need to know how to identify and deal with these kinds of phenomena.

There is a lot more to be said about the dark side of shamanic work. I have had many experiences and teachings in dealing with disturbances during Ayahuasca ceremonies and even outside of them in supporting people with spiritual healing. I plan to right a follow-up to this book which explains more details of this and practices that help to maintain balance and harmony.

Allan was very excited and was insistent I should join him with a small group of people for a ceremony at his house during my stay there. I didn't realise I was about to learn a big lesson in taking care to be discerning about whom I choose to sit with in Ayahuasca ceremonies. Especially outside of Brazil, I have found there are a lot of people who do not have the training, experience or mentoring to fully know how to deal with the depth and complexity of holding space in such an open and vast spiritual field, and that it is easy for people to have a few experiences, pick up a guitar and start acting like a shaman while giving people Ayahuasca. In most cases this is relatively harmless but for some, the trappings of the shadow of the ego and its ability to deceive while pretending this doesn't even exist can often lead to spiritual alliances anchored in lower dimensional fields where people may be vulnerable to entities that employ sorcery, manipulation and seduction. I had been blessed throughout my journey with Ayahuasca to have been largely protected from these energies, and perhaps the experiences that I had had, which were very much of divine light and high vibrations of love and harmony, meant I was able to recognise these more shadowy realms when I encountered them.

Allan would sometimes boast a lot about his shaman teacher and how powerful he was. He was adorned with every possible trinket, clothing and feather he could display to signal his identity with the Shipibo. I could see there was ego involved in his story with serving Ayahuasca. This didn't feel good or clear to me but I told myself he was my friend and to give him a chance against my higher knowing of how he was presenting himself. When I did sit in the ceremony with him, the force of Ayahuasca arrived in a familiar way. He was singing some icaros that I assumed he had learned in San Francisco. I instinctively found I was protecting myself energetically and put myself into a kind of energetic cocoon. I noticed at one point he called people up to sit in front of him and he started doing some kind of healing work on them, putting his hands on their *crown chakras* (the energetic centre at the crown of the head). When he called me up I didn't really want to go, but I did so. I sat in front of him and expressed gratitude for the ceremony, and he reached up to touch my crown without asking me for permission. I stopped him and said, 'No thanks.' He said he wanted to give me healing, and I said I didn't feel that I needed healing, that I was okay, and I thanked him and went back to my place. I could feel he was somewhat agitated by the exchange.

I went back to my place and began meditating. I could sense there was a woman who was struggling somewhat and she wasn't able to get up and move to the front, so Allan went over to her. He put his hands on her crown and even though my eyes were closed I was able to see within the miração what was happening energetically with this 'healing' that he was doing. I could clearly see there was an energy stream channelling through his hands connecting to this woman's crown and sending and receiving energy that appeared to be a darkened red and orange colour. As I looked into it, the light started draining from the miração. Then I saw a serpent-like being which turned and looked at me, almost surprised that I was able to see it. When it realised I was watching it, it very quickly turned and showed itself as a demonic-looking snake, hissed at me and seemed to be trying to frighten me. It seemed very powerful but with the training I had I was able to stay present in my heart and maintain my field of light. I turned my attention away from it and went back to my energetic cocoon. I realised this ceremony was quite energetically messy and was in stark contrast to the sublime beauty and light of divine grace I had become accustomed to in Brazil. I meditated and asked Ayahuasca what was going on, and it was shown to me how even when some sorcerers die, they are able to maintain their power through their spiritual body and anchor themselves in the material world through this kind of sorcery. I saw that these sorcerers use unwitting Westerners, seduce them with power and give them specific songs that connect them spiritually to the sorcerer, and that when the Westerners sing and invoke them the sorcerers are able to enter into ceremonies and feed off the light of those present. They can also still do this while they are alive. Ayahuasca didn't seem to have any negative or judgemental projection about this kind of phenomenon; it was simply showing me that it exists. Pablo had spoken about the difference between shamans of power and shamans of light and this experience was showing me a way that one may choose to work with power. It was very clear this was not my path, but I was grateful for the experience and had yet more gratitude for the teachings and experiences I had received which allowed me to see what this was and to not get caught in it.

I sat meditating in my energetic cocoon that I had created and was deep in a miração when I was shocked back into the physical after Allen came up to me and touched me on the arm. He immediately realised he had disturbed me from a deep place and apologised but then went on to complain that I was somehow 'blocking' him. I told him I was deep in my own process and was fine and was being mindful to not disturb others or the stillness of the space. He seemed confused and again said I was blocking him from doing his work. I asked him to explain what he was experiencing and what I might be able to do differently and he looked to the ground and couldn't answer. I asked him if he needed anything, whether I could help him, and he said, 'No, I'm okay' and went back to his space. I spent a moment contemplating whether I had done something wrong and afterwards I wasn't able to go into any deep spaces so I just listened to the recorded music he was playing which was quite beautiful. I noticed that he was very agitated during the rest of the ceremony whilst everyone else was still. He pulled out some tarot cards and shuffled them around. The next day he called me back into the ceremony space, and with his partner and another woman he confronted me and accused me again of blocking him in his ceremony. I tried to explain to him my experience. He seemed offended that I had refused his healing and I explained that, as someone who facilitates healing for others, I always ask permission before touching them or usually wait for them to come and ask. He found it hard to let this feeling go and eventually we agreed to disagree on some things. Over the next few months and several conversations he eventually agreed that, considering the dark experiences he had endured with the old sorcerer in Peru, perhaps it wasn't a good idea to sing the sorcerer's songs in ceremonies. I am unsure as to whether he continued to do so or not, although I perceived that he was very attached to the power it gave him.

Back to Australia again

After a month or so in England I set off on my way back to Australia via a stop in India, where I spent a few weeks doing yoga and meditation in Rishikesh. This was a great way to reset myself in mind, body and spirit to face the return trip home. I made a special trip up into the Himalayas to one of the sources of the sacred Ganga River near Badrinath. Arriving there in the heights was magical. On the first night I had vivid dreams and visions, with spiritual communications similar to an Ayahuasca miração. My abilities in accessing spiritual vision and mediumship were growing, and being in such a pure place of high vibration gave me a great reflection of how much work I had done on myself. After this experience I was very ready to return back to Australia and face whatever I was going to find there. I was also extremely curious as to how I would feel, having been through so many powerful transformative experiences. Being surrounded by old, familiar people and places would be a good way to measure how much I had grown. Returning home to Australia was always a good feeling, inspiring so much gratitude for the privilege and blessing of being able to call such a beautiful land and country my home. *Yoway!* (a Bunjalung call of affirmation and spirit.)

CHAPTER 8

Australia-Brazil Boomerang

The spirit of Australia

Sometimes we flow with the waters
Sometimes we dance in the fire
Sometimes we float on the breeze
Sometimes we walk on the land
These songlines dreaming our creation

— *Songlines*, Lore Solaris.

I arrived back in Byron Bay just before Christmas, 2010. I felt so radically different even though I was returning to such a familiar place and one of my spiritual homes on this Earth. I have been around the Rainbow Region of the Northern Rivers of the state of New South Wales, where the town of Byron Bay is located, ever since I was a kid and have lived there at different times ever since I was in my early twenties. The region is famous for its natural beauty and the land has a spiritual quality to it that everybody who visits undoubtedly feels. It is a place of healing and of people coming together from all over the world. The Rainbow Region has the largest alternative and new-age community in the world, dating back to the first alternative communities and the Aquarius festival in the early 1970s. Before that, the First Nations people of the mystical Bunjalung Nations lived, danced, sang, shared and cared for the land in harmony for time immemorial. Upon returning I focused on getting myself grounded with some work, finding a place to live, exploring the community and tuning in to how things had grown and evolved since I had been gone.

It seemed that in the almost two years I had been away there had been a huge growth in the ceremonial use of Ayahuasca in the region. Friends and others were telling me all about circles that they were part of, most of which seemed to be hybrid-style ceremonies based on the use of Australian plants such as some species of acacia containing similar levels of naturally occurring DMT as the *chacruna* bush used in traditional Ayahuasca brews in South America (in some parts of the Amazon there are also other species used that contain the DMT component). There seemed to be a lot of excitement about this new movement, although I perceived a lot of hype as well. Some people knew I had had by this time quite a lot of experience in Brazil and Peru and once I returned I received many invitations to attend ceremonies in the area. I didn't feel a calling to be part of any of these circles and I found the hype and the way people were talking about these ceremonies to be similar to what I had experienced with my friend in England. I politely refused all the invitations. I also had spiritual questions about using other plants with very different characteristics from a different land and calling this 'Ayahuasca' and signing it Ayahuasca songs. To me this felt misleading, almost like making love to a partner and calling them by a different name.

The traditional Ayahuasca brew from the Amazon is a sacred union between two plants which combine through a holy alliance and carry the consciousness of a living being. Ayahuasca has been consecrated over thousands of years and the practices and songs that have emerged from the forest and evolved through lineages maintain connection to the ancestors and spirit of those lines, all the way back to the Amazon. These cultures represent a divine force that I believe is sacred, and not something that should be whimsically reinvented. Besides this, the Australian plants have their own consciousness and spirit, and in many cases are also traditionally used in ancient rituals by the native peoples of the land, with ancient rites and practices held in sacred trust. I felt that if I was to use them in a ceremonial way, I would need to learn from those plants as they are, without projecting any story or Dreaming onto them based on culture and beliefs from another land. I sought some guidance from a local Bunjalung Elder and friend, asking for his advice and permission to connect with these plants. He agreed, and also offered to come and support a small ceremony by holding space, singing and playing his didgeridoo. He explained some of the traditional uses of the acacia plants and told some stories of the way that clever men would work with the plants to learn what we might call 'shamanic skills'. I don't feel it is appropriate to share those stories here in this book, as I decided after this experience it was a lineage and culture that require much discipline, focused study and commitment to give the right kind of respect that it deserves. It doesn't feel appropriate to share the small amount of knowledge that I have been given. The ceremony that night was beautiful, powerful and revealing of secrets in the land, and this Elder had shared that whenever we hold ceremony on Country, the first and most important thing is that we must acknowledge the land and the Elders and offer ourselves and the ceremony for the healing of that Country.

I was comfortable with my decision not to participate or get involved with this growing movement and, although I could see that there were some great benefits, there was also a lot of ego and confusion surrounding it from what I was observing and hearing. It wasn't long before I was being approached by people with all kinds of concerns and questions regarding their experiences and from what I was hearing from the stories being shared with me, I was glad to not be a part of it. There were a couple of groups of Brazilians who were diligently creating community and practice within two of the Ayahuasca religions and their work seemed to be based in traditions and respect. I was happy to see there was also some authentic work being done in Australia which was grounded and humble, and wasn't projecting stories and indulging in the glamour around the emerging plant medicine movement. It was pretty clear to me that Australia was not the place for me to continue my studies in Ayahuasca and I didn't receive a calling or any guidance to pursue studies in Australian plant brews either. I instead focused on re-grounding myself and preparing for whatever my next journey would be.

I reconnected with Starseed Gardens and the inspired work of Dan Schreiber and his movement of ecology and community development. This time, though, I didn't become too involved, as my experiences in Brazil and the spiritual guidance I had received indicated my path was about consciousness and spiritual development more than finding material world solutions. Remembering my dream about flying across the desert, I applied for a job in Central Australia which would involve living and working in remote Indigenous communities supporting youth development programs. It seemed daunting but also a great opportunity, as I had plenty of experience which I could use in the role and it seemed a good way for me to give something back to the land and the Indigenous people of Australia, who continue to suffer so much under the ignorance and abuses of ongoing colonialism. Venturing into the desert to see how I might be able to help seemed like a good way to be of service to the planet. I remembered the vision I had a few years earlier in Brazil, of the Aboriginal woman lying on the earth in the desert taking on all the pain and suffering being inflicted on the land, and I wondered what I might find when I went out there. As my Dream a few months prior in Brazil had predicted, I got the job and prepared myself to make the journey to the desert.

There were other personal prophecies I had received over the years predicting this coming time in the desert. In the year 2000 I had spent a few months living around the town of Alice Springs and I had gone to a community dance with the Eastern Aranda people where I was one of only three non-Indigenous people there. During the music and dance celebration a magical clever man had come up to me and done some healing work on my energetic field and had begun to tell me many stories about the music and the ceremony and the coming of a new Dreaming; he told me I would return to this area one day and learn about the messages from the Elders and would take those messages to the rest of Australia. There was also the prediction of Dona Maria, the Mãe de Santo in Salvador, Bahia, who told me through her divination with shells that I would be working with the 'children of the desert'. At the time I wondered if this was something that was going to happen in Brazil, yet here I was, heading out to the Central Australian desert to work with children and youth in remote desert communities. Knowing all of this and despite what I knew was going to be a challenging and eye-opening experience, I was confident I was strongly on my path, guided by Spirit. One thing also clear to me was that while I had spent a lot of time dedicated to and focused on spiritual studies in South America, and even though I had learned a lot from Australian Indigenous people throughout my life, I still had much to learn about the spirituality of my home country.

Life in the desert was certainly full of its challenges. I was originally contracted to work at an Aranda community not too far out of Alice Springs called Amoonguna, but for logistical reasons I was sent out to the remote Eastern Aranda Community Ltyentye Apurte, known as 'Santa Teresa'. These were the same people that held the community dance I had attended 11 years prior where the clever man had given me his prophecy. It seemed like I had yet again come full circle. As my time went on in the desert there would be more revelations emerging around this community and the prophecy of the clever man. Life in the desert was tough and nothing could have prepared me for what I found when I moved out there. Central Australia is one of the most recently colonised places in the Western world, alongside the most ancient Indigenous culture on the planet. It is a melting pot of modern Western civilisation mixing with the ancient traditions of desert culture and its people. In many ways it is like oil and water trying to mix: the lack of cultural and environmental awareness of the European colonisers and modern service providers was overlaid, in very challenging circumstances and often clashed, with a traditional culture of people that were still in shock from having their lands and way of life destroyed amidst also dealing with intense racism, generations of children being stolen and their families being decimated by disease and genocide by the colonialists.

What I found when I began my adventure in Central Australia were some of the worst health and living conditions in the world. The First Nations peoples of Central Australia are some of the most peaceful and loving, kind people I have ever met. Life in the desert moves slowly, and it forces you to take your time to listen. The ancient culture is very diverse and complex in its social structures and spirituality. On the surface this is not so apparent, due to the intense levels of poverty and the poor mental and physical health conditions, but underneath the traditional culture is still very strong. Living amongst these people was a humbling and massively eye-opening experience. I had to let go of everything I thought I knew about working with people and communities, and take the time very patiently to firstly develop knowledge and understanding of the culture of the people and the enormous problems they were facing, and then to gain trust amongst them in order to work with them to develop solutions and plans that might help. I very quickly realised that the agency I was working for was highly dysfunctional and run by people with little training and skills in the area of youth and community development. After a few months I was encouraged to take on a coordinating role, which then led to me being appointed the manager of a large government-funded program which spanned nine remote communities across five different tribal language groups.

Some weeks into this management role I was offered significant funding to develop and implement a suicide-prevention project. The region had some of the highest suicide rates in the world and, as the traditional people had never experienced this mental health phenomenon, they did not have language or cultural lore around how to deal with it. Not a week would go by when I didn't receive a phone call from one of the communities reporting a suicide or suicide attempts. The despair and grief amongst the people was overwhelming. In collaboration with some of the community leaders and some allies in other government-funded agencies we designed a program called 'The Right Track'. This involved, through consultation with Elders and the communities, supporting the Elders to take groups of young people out into sacred places in the desert where they would share knowledge and guidance for healthier communities. We then worked with the youth to create music, film and art to express those messages from the Elders. It was 12 years from the time when I had met that clever man to the point where I was sitting in a meeting with a group of Elders from the same eastern Aranda community talking about this project. The clever man had explained to me that the messages from the Elders were being represented in the music of the youth and he suggested I would be involved in getting those messages out to the rest of Australia. Sure enough, 12 years later our project went on to be very successful, with communities all over Central Australia embracing the music, which was played on Indigenous community radio all over Australia. I was getting emails and phone calls and requests to send copies to communities from Aboriginal people all across Australia and I was interviewed on national radio broadcasts. I could never have predicted this outcome, as we were responding to an immediate and urgent need, but it seemed that the prophecy of that clever man was fulfilled.

After two years in the desert, dealing with very challenging politics and bureaucratic dramas, the day-to-day dysfunction of just about everything we were trying to manage in order to keep the project running, walking tightropes to navigate the huge cultural divides and the stubborn arrogance of Western thinking and attitudes entrenched into the system, the intense levels of pressure and responsibility took a very hard toll on me. I was dealing with a lot of stress and burnout, and physical and mental exhaustion. Deep and powerful moments being out in the desert or sitting with Elders and listening to magical stories and learning about culture and traditional healing practices were a beautiful respite from the relentless need to keep showing up and giving of myself amidst what I would describe as a humanitarian crisis. I felt good about what we had created out there in those conditions, seeing the smiles of the children, the gratitude from the people and some seeds of hope being planted. That kept me going, but by mid-2013 I needed some time out and I decided to return to Brazil for a holiday. This would be different to past trips and I was going just to relax, catch up with friends and enjoy myself.

Re-awakening

After visiting friends in Rio, I went back up to Bahia to do a retreat with Silvia at Spirit Vine. Returning to Ayahuasca and ceremony in Brazil was a huge relief and a big release of all the tension which had built up in me during the time I had been working in the desert. I arrived there carrying a lot: the huge burden of the work I had been doing, the immense grief of the people and the land. I returned to the same place with Ayahuasca where I had seen the vision of the woman taking on all the pain of the land in the Australian desert. This time, Ayahuasca took the pain I had been carrying from my time there. I felt so much lighter and mentally clearer after the first two ceremonies with Silvia. By the third ceremony, my visions returned and I was able to again enter into the miração. I saw visions of a future for myself. Again, it seemed to be there in that region of Bahia, which always made me feel so happy. I saw visions of people I didn't know and whom I assumed I would be meeting soon enough on my journey. This made me feel excited, but these visions weren't showing me anything relating to the desert or being in Australia. I didn't think too much about that, but then Silvia said something to me that changed everything.

During those ceremonies I began to realise that I had almost totally sacrificed myself and my own happiness in order to be of service and do the job that was being asked of me in the desert. I realised that throughout my life I had usually been quick to put myself aside and be there for others or for a purpose such as healing for the planet. I realised I wasn't happy, that my health was being affected, and that my tolerance to stress had grown too high. I spoke about this in a sharing circle facilitated by Silvia, where I told stories about all the great art and music we were supporting the Indigenous people in Australia to create. Silvia stopped me and abruptly challenged me when she said, 'Lore, you have spent so much of your life investing your energy in supporting others with their creativity and their projects. What about your creativity: when are you going to invest in that?' This was such a great observation and question, and it brought me into a very different way of thinking about myself and my life. I realised in a very profound way how much I had sacrificed my own happiness for helping others, how I had been too much of a 'people pleaser' at my own expense. This followed on from the theme Ayahuasca had been teaching me right from the beginning of my journey with it: believing in myself. I was surprised to realise how good I was at distracting myself through helping others, and not truly embracing my own happiness and creative life. I knew I had so much creativity, art and music inside, and Silvia's question made me think deeply about this and about what I could do to honour myself in a new and authentic way.

After a couple of weeks there with Silvia in what felt like a visit that was too short, I travelled back to Brasilia and then on to Alto Paraiso, where I stayed with friends, reconnecting, sharing stories and music and good times. The same passion and drive was thriving in the community, with projects having evolved since I had last been there. I could sense how much I had changed since I was last there. My worldview had shifted, my time in the desert had changed me, my thinking had slowed down and I was taking more time to listen and observe. It seemed like it had become easier for me to see the boundaries between me and others and my sense of self had grown. I was a lot more confident in who I was. It was great to get in touch with this, but at the same time I knew I still had some work to do and some choices to make in order to fully embody this inner knowing. I began to realise with the help of Silvia and Ayahuasca, and with the reflections of friends and life itself, that realising things within and gaining spiritual insights and revelations was only a part of the journey of being human, that integrating and embodying those truths was the key that might unlock true freedom and happiness. I was reminded of the song I had first heard in Alto Paraiso, *Divine Mother I Want to be a Realised Child*, and I could see a journey ahead where I would begin to embody the fullness of who I was in this life.

Returning to Alice Springs in Central Australia after that six-week trip to Brazil provided a big reality check. I realised I wasn't happy, that my role in Alice Springs was not sustainable. I became sick and fell into a bit of a depression. The pressure and expectations upon me were coming on really strong and even though I managed to keep some good projects running, it wasn't long before I told the communities and my employer that I was leaving. I made up my mind to move back to Brazil and to give myself the time and space to be an artist. There would be no pressure, no timelines, no expectations. I would just be with myself and let the creative magic flow — something I had never done before in my life. By this stage I couldn't wait to get out, but at the same time I was managing a massive project and it took me some months to do everything I could to leave it in good hands and pass on all my contacts, knowledge and everything I had developed during that time. During a gathering we organised with Elders and youth from the communities, a senior Elder from the Western Arrernte people came to me and shook my hand. He thanked me for all the work I had done and told me how so many people had become so happy through our programs. That gesture meant a lot to me.

In reflections I saw I had learned so much about the First Nations culture and the people of the desert, their spirituality and deep connection to the land, and about the deep sadness in the people arising from how much had been stolen from them and how dire the situation they were in was, whilst government and business agendas continued their relentless colonising of their land and showed disinterest in truly understanding or supporting First Nations peoples' intrinsic connection to the land. It is impossible for Indigenous people to be separated from their Country. Its sacred sites, the beings, ancestors and history are felt deeply in them all, and the shocking reality of invasion and cultural genocide that was still covertly underway created such deep pain in the hearts of every person, leading them to despair, depression, alcoholism and hopelessness. For Aboriginal people, disconnection from Country is disconnection from Dreaming. It is like telling a Christian person they are no longer allowed to go to church. I felt I had done all that I could, knowing I had made an impact and worked hard to support those communities in regaining some autonomy and respect over their own lives and communities, and I prayed that the work we had done together would have a lasting impact and continue to grow. I was sad to leave all the beautiful friends and places I had connected with, although I was also very relieved to be choosing a new path and excited to return to Brazil and to myself, to honour myself in a way I had never done in my life to that point.

Becoming an artist

In returning to Spirit Vine and the work of Silvia Polivoy, I had a sense of homecoming and relief. I had organised with Silvia to stay there in exchange for helping her with her retreats and developing programs and working around the centre whilst I focused on my creativity. I bought some canvases, paints and art supplies and set up a space where I could work on some paintings of visions that I had received over the years. I needed some deep healing from all the stress and trauma I had accumulated in my body, mind and emotions from the nearly three years spent working in the Australian desert. I chose to give myself no time limits and no pressure. Silvia was going through her own challenges with running a retreat as a single woman in a remote part of Brazil. I dived into working closely with Silvia in supporting her with running the retreat, dealing with administration and program development, as well as some doing maintenance around the centre. I continued my studies in Ayahuasca and my own personal development as well as learning from Silvia, who by this stage was very experienced in running these retreats with very fine-tuned ethics and an understanding of working with Ayahuasca using a spiritual and therapeutic focus. I felt a lot of compassion for Silvia, given the immense responsibility and challenges she held in maintaining the Spirit Vine centre, dealing with local politics and running her retreats. I was happy to help and be of support to her, as she had been a great teacher and friend to me over the years.

My focus turned quite dramatically to my art and creativity. I would spend all my free time during the day painting canvases and listening to medicine music on the veranda of one of Silvia's cabins with its beautiful view over the forest, which was teaming with life, whilst hummingbirds would buzz all around me. During ceremonies I would ask Ayahuasca permission to paint the visions I was receiving, some of which were of spiritual beings, and at times I would spend long periods in the miração painting canvases in my mind, where Ayahuasca would give me instructions on how to paint the visions in a lot of detail. I would receive instructions on how to design the paintings, what to paint first, how to develop the layers of colours and images, and even details of facial features of the beings I would be painting. I started a creative journal and filled it with the many visions and details on how to paint them.

During one miração I was again taken deep into the forest, somewhere in the Amazon, where I was met by an ancient *caboclo*

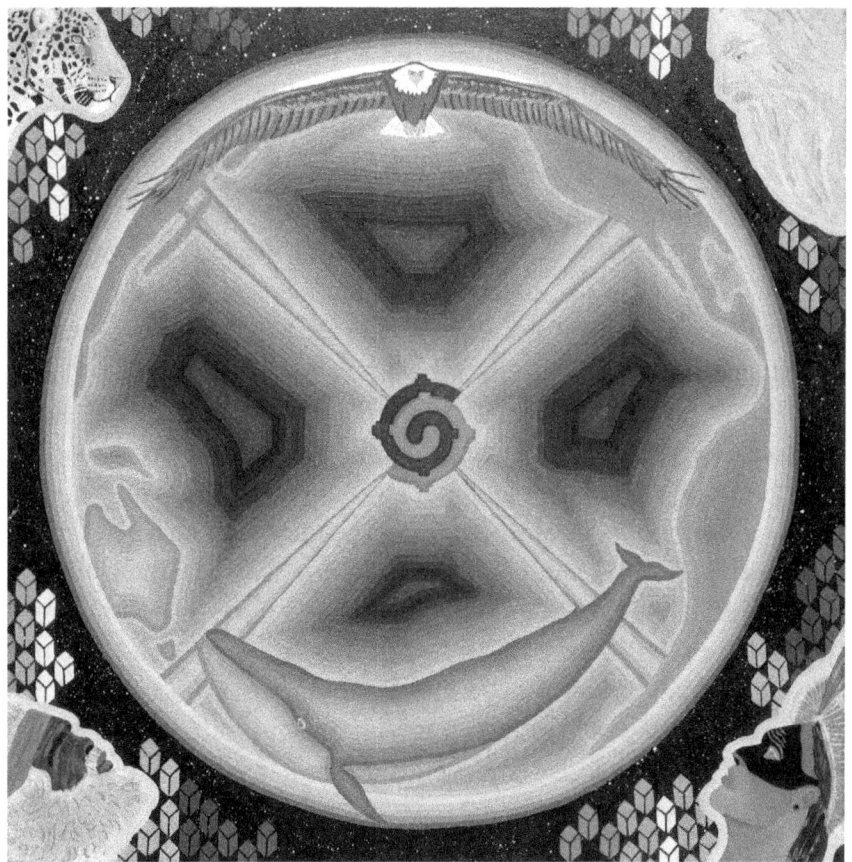

Dreaming of the Whole Earth, Lore Solaris, Acrylic on Canvas

(spirit of the forest). I looked into his face and saw that he was covered in scars and battle wounds, that he was ancient and powerful, yet old and frail. He told me he had spent lifetimes defending the forest, the plants and their knowledge from the relentless encroachment of invaders, thieves and occupiers. Ayahuasca asked me to paint this being, to honour his presence and to honour the native Amazonian warriors who had sacrificed and lost so much over hundreds of years in order to keep the sacred wisdom alive. Without them, we would not have had access to the knowledge of Ayahuasca and the other sacred healing plants that by now were spreading all over the world, saving lives and supporting people to return back from the brink of debilitating mental and physical illness, inspiring hope in humanity through connection to Country. It's painful to think of what might become of humanity without this sacred knowledge. I was reminded of the similar spirit of the Australian Indigenous people and their fight for survival amidst the seemingly relentless march of tyranny and the cruelty of humanity still living in its own shadow.

In one of the retreats a participant arrived from the United States who was not typical of attendees of this type of work. In saying that, I would also say that there really is no 'typical' kind of person who is attracted to Ayahuasca. People who practise the sacred medicine come from all backgrounds but generally have an interest in spirituality and a clear intent for healing and personal development. This man in the first group session with Silvia was sceptical about Ayahuasca and his participation, and he was elusive regarding his intention, doubting whether he even wanted to be there. He shrugged his shoulders and suggested that perhaps he had come to the wrong place. I thought this strange, considering he had paid thousands of dollars, including on airfares, and had made a long, arduous journey to get there. Often I have noticed with certain people that they may have tried many other things such as therapy and pharmaceutical medications, yet when nothing has been able to help them, they turn to Ayahuasca to seek remedy, even if it exists in a world that is very foreign to them.

During the sharing circle, Silvia challenged this man in her usual direct manner despite his evasive communication and reluctance to share much of his story. I noticed he was surprised by her directness, yet she was able to get enough of his story to indicate he was not happy in his life and was carrying some family-related trauma. He didn't react well to her in that moment, and she left it at that. Afterwards he was angry and I took him aside to see what he was feeling. He was adamant that he wanted to leave. I suggested that he at least give it a go, as he had come all this way. I debriefed with Silvia, who wasn't worried that he was agitated and wanting to leave. She said that he needed to have a strong commitment to the work and, in regard to her direct manner with him, she said that she wasn't there to make friends or be liked, that at times a kind of tough love was required to help people see where they were not being honest with themselves, or were confused with some kind of cognitive dissonance. I appreciated her approach, even though my particular style was slightly different, in that I am not usually so blunt. In my experience with Silvia, though, her approach seemed to be mostly effective.

Silvia placed this man beside me for the ceremony. I believe she did this so that I could keep an eye on him. During the ceremony I could feel his resistance and it was distracting me from my own inner journey. He was moving around a lot, constantly getting up and walking over to talk to Silvia, who kept sending him back to his place. Over the years in mirações I would often encounter cheeky, playful and colourful shape-shifting psychedelic beings that would come into my field of awareness and trick me into giving them attention. I learned over time that they were chaotic and tricky but were always ready and available to help for healing, for spiritual work, shifting energies and clearing people and spaces. Pablo Amaringo referred to them as '*doctorcitos*' (little doctors), and they may also have been the same beings that Terence McKenna referred to as 'shape-shifting machine elves'. I remembered this as I dealt with my ceremony neighbour, who was experiencing a lot of resistance and disturbing the ceremony by not remaining still — a way to avoid facing whatever he needed to see. I called on Ayahuasca to send some doctorcitos to help the situation and almost immediately a giant wasp-like spiritual being arrived and sat on his chest. And from then on, he remained still. After a while I forgot about this situation and then I started to see visions of this man in an abusive situation where he was the perpetrator. I was a little shocked and went up to tell Silvia what I had seen. She confirmed that she had suspected this. I went back to my space and could sense that the man was now doing some deep work and I could feel a lot of emotion finally moving within him.

As I drifted back into myself for my own work, I realised I had spent a lot of time in the ceremony focused on work for the space and people in the room and I was finding it difficult to raise myself beyond the field of the collective energy of the participants. I asked Ayahuasca for some guidance on this and was shown a vision of a large net, held up at multiple points like a Bedouin tent, with each of the points being held by a dragonfly-looking entity, each one of a different colour — more Ayahuasca doctorcitos. As they hovered, buzzing their wings, the vibrations they were creating sent a healing vibration into the space, creating what was like an astral, psychedelic hospital. It was beautiful to see the way Ayahuasca was working with the divine forest beings to hold a healing space for the participants of the ceremony. I realised that perhaps I myself didn't need to be lying down in a psychic hospital bed: I wanted to fly into the cosmos, with my wings ablaze and heart beaming. Ayahuasca said that in order for me to access higher realms, there needed to be a calling of sound or vibration to open those portals — and that wasn't the intention of this ceremony. I realised I was growing a lot in my Ayahuasca work and finding the limitations of what was possible at Spirit Vine. I asked my guides to open the path for greater learning and expansion.

Ayahuasca was beginning to work with me in different ways. It seemed like I was being put to work and given instructions — first through the art and then in other ways such as movement, energetic clearing and spiritual healing within the miração for participants in the ceremonies and outside of them. Having spent many nights with Ayahuasca, I began to realise I wasn't being called to do so much for my own healing and that exploring visions through the miração wasn't as engaging for me as was becoming more of an instrument for Ayahuasca to work through me. I was beginning to have the first realisations of my potential role as a medium and channel for the spirit of Ayahuasca and my spiritual guides. It also became increasingly clear that I was being drawn deeper into my spirituality through Ayahuasca and this was taking me beyond the focused therapeutic work that was Silvia's main focus. I started to realise my path with Ayahuasca was taking me into spirituality, beyond the focus of therapy alone. At first I was a bit irritated when I started to perceive other people's energies and even started to receive mirações of what they were going through and be given guidance from Ayahuasca and the spiritual guides about things I could do to help them. This seemed like a distraction, but I could see that it was part of the way that Ayahuasca works: that when you have the awareness, firmness and discipline, and have done healing to achieve this, then part of the work becomes being of service to others who are still learning and healing.

Let's all go Saravá!
Those who are sick will be healing
Those who are healed will go to work

— Xangô Caô, Luz Amatista.

There was a shift happening within me. At times I began to push the boundaries of what was possible within the work I had been doing with Silvia up until this point. During discussions with Silvia she was very clear that her work and ceremonies were not able to accommodate the way Ayahuasca wanted to express through me, that her ceremonies were not a place where I could explore this and she wasn't able to guide me with this kind of work. At first this created some frustration in me, but I knew she was right and there was no choice but to respect Silvia, as she was very clear on the nature of her work and her path, which she had been successfully cultivating and refining over many years. Silvia offered me the opportunity outside of her ceremonies to perform some rituals for the participants with fire and smoke which I had learned from Indigenous Australians and which people seemed to enjoy, but I felt a strong force within me and through the spiritual guidance that was moving through me. I started to accept that if I was going to continue along this path I would need to find another place to deepen my studies.

In between retreats I attended the famous psychedelic trance and arts festival called *Universo Paralelo* (Parallel Universe) that was held on the coast not too far from Spirit Vine. I connected there with friends from Alto Paraiso and other parts of Brazil. I am very sensitive to being in big groups of people at festivals but the vibe and the music were very impressive. I was mostly drawn to a small group of native *Pataxó* people who held vigil by a small fire on the beach at the edge of the festival site all night long for each of the nights the event was happening. I found it interesting that of the tens of thousands of people at the festival, this little happening by the fire was hardly noticed by anyone. I enjoyed sitting by the fire with these calm, peaceful and friendly Pataxó people, who would sometimes share stories and answer questions, but who mostly would just sit there in stillness and silence. They would light this fire and sit there all night to honour the spirits of the land who were distressed by all the energy and drama of the festival — and the fire would support them by giving them a safe and sacred space. They told me that the fire and their intentions and prayers were also having the benefit of protecting the people in the festival and transmuting the huge amounts of energy being released by the festival-goers, many of whom were opening their energetic fields with psychedelics and party drugs. I was impressed by the humble way the Pataxó were doing this spiritual work without fanfare or the need for any recognition and that their clear intention was to honour and protect the land, the spirits of the land and the people at the festival. Sitting with them and offering my presence in support of their work was healing and a nice way for me to also pay my respects to the native peoples and to the land, something I had come to understand from my time with Australian Indigenous people. It also seemed like the honourable thing to do. I noticed again that, despite the colourful and vibrant festival all around me, I was being drawn to the Indigenous culture and spirit, just like in Australia and during ceremonies at Spirit Vine.

Union of the Eagle and the Condor

In early February 2014 the 'Union of the Eagle and the Condor' gathering came to the Maraú peninsula of Bahia, close to the town of Itacaré and Spirit Vine. It was a blessing that this gathering, which I had been curious to attend since it had begun in Alto Paraiso some years earlier, this time had come to me. The gathering was in honour of the prophecy of the eagle and condor which is spoken of in Indigenous tribes across the Americas and has become known around the world. The prophecy refers to a time when humanity was split into two paths: that of the Eagle people, who followed a masculine path of mind, industry and technology, and that of the Condor people, who followed a feminine path of heart, intuition and wisdom. The prophecy speaks of the time of the European conquest of the Americas which would lead to the dominance of the Eagle people and the mind over the heartfelt Condor people, who would nearly become extinguished by the dominance of the mind and intellect. The prophecy says that at an auspicious time the medicines of the north and south of the Americas would come together and create the potential for humanity to unite these two paths, bringing a conscious awakening of humanity.

> *For thousands of years, the eagle has soared high in the sky, focused on material gain. The condor has flown low, close to the earth, knowing the ways of the spirit. One day, the two will meet in the sky, united as one, and the world will heal.* — Indigenous Elder, Ecuador.

> *The prophecy speaks of a time when we will remember that we are all one. The condor, which represents the spirit, and the eagle, which represents the intellect, will unite in the sky to show us that balance is the key to our survival.* — Lakota Elder, US.

In 2011, Yatra and the team from the Tribo Mãe D'Àgua (Mother of the Waters tribe) based in Alto Paraiso founded a gathering in honour of this prophecy. The vision of the gathering was to unite peoples and medicines of different spiritual paths to come together in a prayer of unity and harmony.

> *Where these birds of light can fly together in the same inner sky, fulfilling the prophecy, we as human beings can truly wake up and evolve into a more conscious species, adding ancestral knowledge to new technologies, and thus find practical solutions to live in harmony with the nature.* — Tribo Mãe D'Àgua.

In its early years the gathering was held each year, alternating between Alto Paraiso and Bahia. In early 2014 it was held in Bahia for the second time over nine days with four ceremonies which would each include partaking of both Ayahuasca and *peyote* (a psychedelic cactus sacrament from North America), as part of the prophecy of the sacred alliance of the medicines of the North and South Americas. The ceremonies were led by the Tribo Mãe D'Àgua team, with Yatra and a group of Indigenous and other shamans from Brazil, Peru, Colombia, Mexico and the US.

People from all over the world gathered together in a beautiful beachside location surrounded by coconut trees, just on the outskirts of a small village that hosted people in *pousadas* (inns) and other guest accommodation. The organisation of the event was difficult to follow, as it contained a good degree of Brazilian chaos and confusion, but somehow everything managed to come together. Participants had to find their own food and accommodation, and the ceremonies themselves were held under two large marquees just behind the sand dunes next to the beach. When I arrived I was excited to drink Ayahuasca right on the beach, but I also wondered how the ceremonies would go being so exposed and open to the outside world. It was great to be in a vibrant community of people, many of whom were very experienced in Ayahuasca, although there were also a lot of other people, mostly European backpackers, wandering around and joining in. This was a bit confronting to me, as I wasn't familiar with being in such a loose and uncontained space whilst working with Ayahuasca. The main crew and gathering organisers had their own space separate from everyone else. This also made me feel a little strange, as there didn't seem to be a unified group feeling, although I often found some of the Indigenous shamans hanging out in the village, where they were always happy and friendly and open to talk and share.

The first ceremony was quite large, with around 80 people all gathered together under the marquee, in the centre of which was a beautiful altar: a sand sculpture shaped into the form of the Orixá of the ocean, Yemanjá, who was one of the spiritual patrons of the event. The band was at the front and there were two areas on either side for the people to sit on rugs and pillows, with the Indigenous shamans sitting on chairs off to one side. At the back of the ceremonial space was a large sacred fire with an open corridor of space to the central altar in a design that seemed to be derived from traditional North American peyote ceremonies.

At the commencement of the ceremony we were invited to drink the first cup of Ayahuasca from a serving altar at the back of the ceremonial space. The ceremony began, led by the band from the Tribe Mãe D'Àgua with the beautiful music I was familiar with from my time attending their temple in Alto Paraiso. This time I was really excited to be singing along to the music, as after my recent experiences at Spirit Vine where I had become restless sitting in the dark all night in ceremonies, I wanted to make the most of this opportunity to open my voice, sing from my heart and allow the Ayahuasca to express through me. I purchased the songbooks before the ceremony so that I was able to follow along with the words. There were plenty of people there who knew the songs, and the ceremony was bathed in a joyous energy and feeling generated by the beauty and intention in each of the prayers. The space was very open and at times I found it hard to focus or to know where the energies were flowing; people were moving around a lot and some were randomly shaking maracás and getting wildly out of rhythm at some points. I was grateful when one of the band members asked people not to play them if they weren't able to keep the rhythm, as this was disturbing the harmony of the music and thus the ceremony.

During the second cup, six of the shamans moved to the area around the fire and we were invited to take turns to sit and receive healings and blessings while the music continued in the main area with the band continuing to play. I waited a while before going to the fire, as the force of the Ayahuasca was quite strong for me. As the band played and people kept singing I was drawn to the cosmic sounds of ancient tribal chanting and whooping and whooshing coming from the fire, which under the force of Ayahuasca was very psychedelic. I closed my eyes to listen to the sounds and was eventually drawn to go to the fire, which I then focused on. One of the shamans came up and started to do some energetic healing movements around me. I could feel him moving energy from my spine, and when he was working on the back of my heart he said some words in English that reflected exactly the insecure emotions and self-worth issues I was carrying in relation to the wounding of my father. It seemed that the shaman had found the old emotional energy which had been sitting there inhibiting my true expression – the same dynamic that had led me to sacrifice my own happiness for others, exactly what I had been working on since arriving back in Brazil.

After drinking a third cup, some of the shamans took turns to lead the music, mostly with guitars, with the band complimenting them on drums and other instruments. When the Huni Kuin pajé *Ninawa Pãe da Mata* (father of the forest) played his set of vibrant songs a strong force entered me and I got up and danced. This was a huge revelation: I felt that my spirit was dancing me and the songs from this pajé from the Amazon were stirring something in my soul. The force of movement and dance that had been calling me at Spirit Vine was finally free to express itself and I was in ecstasy as I let go and allowed the force to move my body. I could feel the presence of Australian Indigenous spirits with me as I danced and at times those spirits entered me and 'danced' me. I was a little self-conscious, as some of the guardians of the ceremony seemed a bit unsure of the energy I was bringing into the space. I realised they were being a little over-zealous, possibly not recognising the Indigenous spirit of Australia that was moving me. In that moment of liberation it was almost impossible to stop this flow of force. I recognised again how much my spirit is attracted to the tribal Indigenous spirit. The next day one of the shamans said to me they had seen me dancing and that it was part of my medicine and not to worry about those who were interfering.

As the ceremony progressed into the morning, the sun began to shine its first light into the sky. A North American medicine man was introduced and he shared the story of the peyote medicine. We were all invited to eat some of the dry power of the peyote cactus and then he went on to sing some songs from the peyote lineage. This was a very different medicine and energy and the first time I had partaken of it. I was still feeling the force of the Ayahuasca very strongly and I was unsure of, or not recognising, the effect of the peyote. Perhaps it was subtle, although I sensed that I was so familiar with and attuned to the force of Ayahuasca that another medicine at that moment would not be able to have a strong influence upon me. Just as the sun rose over the horizon, we were invited by Ninawa to form a long line behind him and he led us in the *dança da jiboia* (dance of the boa constrictor). Ninawa was at the head of the snake and led us single file on a dance that wound itself back and forth, inwards and outwards of the line, just like a winding jiboia, while he sang and shook his maracá. This dancing jiboia wound its way out of the ceremonial space, through the garden, over the sand dunes and onto the beach in front of the ocean, where we all stood together and watched the sun rise magnificently on a perfect morning, while the band led more songs, singing for Yemanjá and for the new day. In this beautiful moment of celebration and honouring of the divine forces of nature, with the spirit of the eagle and the condor with us, with everyone glowing and beaming in a light-filled joy, the ceremony closed.

Eagle and Condor flying together to the sun
And the wind of their wings is awakening our hearts
Preparing a new day of love and harmony

Jaguar and deer dancing together in the sun
And their steps guide us to this new day
They fill us with peace, happiness and joy

Ayahuasca and peyote in the light of the sun
And these sacred medicines they go healing and curing
We are filled with light for this new day

— *Agulia y Condor*, Kuauhtli Vasquez.

I felt deeply honoured to be part of this gathering of prophecy and ceremonies that were blessed with the presence of medicine carriers from around the world. The following three ceremonies proceeded much the same as the first one, with some slight variations. I found that I was becoming much more adept at sitting and singing all night and was enjoying that immensely. The energy of the ceremonies, however, seemed to be dimming as the gathering progressed and by the last night, the force was not very strong in the space. I noticed the energy was not very well contained, and there were a lot of new people arriving each night who didn't seem to be very connected or present with the work that was going on. I felt the importance of sitting strong and continuing to sing to help ground the force and support the ceremony by holding space. On the last night I met a group of young men who really didn't know much about what was going on but who were keen to drink Ayahuasca, even though they knew very little about it. I wasn't comfortable sharing space with so many people who weren't really aware of or connected to the intention of the work. At times I felt some darker energies moving around in the ceremony and on the last night there was some drama, as I noticed almost all of the ceremony participants where lying down, with many vomiting around the edges, whilst the band did their best to keep the energy up and the pajés worked hard around the fire transmuting energies. At one point, someone seemingly possessed by a dark entity staggered up to the altar as a water blessing was being performed by a female shaman. This person would have collapsed onto the altar, but he was caught by some guardians just before he did. He was then taken to the fire, where he spent an hour or so yelling and moaning while the pajés worked to clear him of the negative energy.

Whilst the spiritual work itself was immaculate, with so many skilled shamans and musicians, I never felt fully safe to let go into the force of the Ayahuasca. The format and organisation of the gathering and the space was, in my view, too loose, with people and energies coming in and out at a whim, and this was reflected in the energy of the ceremonies gradually weakening. I was happy that throughout the four ceremonies I was able to concentrate on singing and holding space in my own way and to keep my energy focused and clear while taking many opportunities to have a good dance and explore Ayahuasca in a form that was new for me. On one of the mornings there was the traditional celebration of the *Dia de Yemanjá* (day of Yemanjá), which is celebrated all along the coasts of Brazil in honour of the Orixá of the ocean that creates life, heals our minds and protects women and children.

During conversations with people at the gathering, some commented on how they had seen me enjoying the music and dancing and they asked if I had ever been in ceremony with Carioca. I told them that I hadn't, but that I loved his music, had been listening to it a lot since I was introduced to it during my time living in Alto Paraiso, and that I wasn't even aware he facilitated ceremonies. They encouraged me to go to Ciranda, near Rio de Janeiro, where Carioca holds his Ayahuasca ceremonies; these people were very sure I would find myself at home there and enjoy it very much. They reflected that my energy reminded them of Carioca. Someone told me there was soon going to be a music and visionary art workshop at Ciranda and suggested that I attend. This feedback and suggestion got me excited about the music and the ceremonies, and in particular about going there to study art. My mission in returning to Brazil was to explore being an artist. I had been doing a lot of painting and my artworks had all sold in the time I had been in Bahia. A new direction seemed to be emerging which filled me with inspiration and excitement for the journey ahead. The Union of the Eagle and the Condor gathering had expanded my view and experience of Ayahuasca in many ways: it had given me great opportunities to explore myself and the medicine in different forms, and it had also taught me about some elements I felt were not so strong and could be done differently. I returned to Spirit Vine with a lot to reflect on and integrate, with peace in my heart, an open mind and inspiration for the journey ahead.

Upper Amazon with the Yawanawá

After the Eagle and Condor gathering I planned a trip to the Amazon with my Spanish friend Daniel, who had been invited to visit the Yawanawá people in the state of Acre, Brazil. He also sent the Yawanawá people the videos from the project I had done with Australian desert communities in 2012. They were impressed and invited us both to visit them for a cultural exchange project where Daniel would support with teaching painting skills to help them realise their Ayahuasca visions while I would record their music and help them to develop an album. The timing worked out well so that we were able to spend five weeks on this trip before the Music and Visionary Art Workshop with Carioca would begin. I packed up things at Spirit Vine and finished my work helping Silvia, leaving with her the art workshop I had been running for her guests. We travelled to Salvador before flying to Rio Branco, the capital city of the state of Acre.

Reflection on my time with Silvia and Ayahuasca at Spirit Vine gave me an immense feeling of warmth and gratitude. Whilst at times very challenging on many levels, the studies, healing and spiritual growth I experienced was deep and potent over the years that I spent with Silvia. All of those experiences were infused with the teachings and presence of Pablo Amaringo, who had been so intrinsic in the work of Silvia and whose spirit permeated through her ceremonies and the Ayahuasca itself, even after he had passed. Silvia taught me some very valuable lessons. She taught me to discern and control my ego, to be mindful of my projections. During mirações at Spirit Vine the medicine taught me to control my thoughts; it guided me to strengthen the skills I had learned in meditation and yoga. Learning to ride the waves of sometimes intense mirações and the force of Ayahuasca was a strong and sometimes harsh way of learning to avoid pride, righteousness, self-doubt, projections and transference. These skills are great for life in general, for navigating relationships and human politics. On reflection I can see how important this training was for the work that was to come. At times I struggled with Silvia's stern forthrightness and sometimes blunt hammer delivery of advice and reflections like, 'You have your father's arrogance.' But this certainly hit home within me. I believe it was necessary for her to be as strong as she was, as the ego can also be strong and tricky and there is no time or space within this work to fumble around in the ego's projections and desires. I am glad we could always laugh about our human limitations afterwards. Self-discipline and firmness are essential skills to have developed and integrated to be safe and effective in working with Ayahuasca in a meaningful way that honours its depths and the respect that it commands. Also, Silvia taught me, as a support helper for her, the supreme importance of objectivity and presence alongside all the above skills in order to support people through Ayahuasca ceremonies, including pre- and post-ceremony support.

Rio Branco was surprisingly like most Brazilian cities of similar size, with a relatively calm energy in the city, which seemed quite open, friendly and clean. A very different environment to the busy, smelly, dirty and hard-edged city of Pucallpa that I had visited in the Peruvian Amazon. The day after we arrived we met with Tashka and Mariazinha Yawanawá, who were both leaders of the village of Mutum. We chatted over lunch, where we began to get to know each other, and talked a little of the projects we were going to work on and the logistics of making the journey to the village which would take several days of travelling. We met with Mariazinha the next day who took us around the city and showed us where to go to get the list of items she recommended we take with us for our time in the forest. After a couple of days gathering supplies and exploring the city, we hired a driver to take us on a day-long drive to a small town called Tarauacá (place of the rivers). Arriving there gave the strong sense of being in the Amazon. The nature was a lot more present and the town was predominantly filled with happy Indigenous peoples from different tribes and clans wearing lots of colours and feathers and body paint. There were two hotels in the town, both of which were very basic, with little attendance or facilities.

We stayed the night in Tarauacá, and in the morning after breakfast there was a slow, leisurely movement towards the next phase of the journey. By this stage we were in the hands of the Yawanawá people, as they would be organising the transport from there. I noticed that their pace was not forced, allowing everything to happen in the flow, with no rushing or stress. There was no looking at clocks or worrying about time at all, much like the ways of Indigenous people in Australia. It was nice to be in this kind of natural, organic flow, but I had already begun to notice my mind wanting to know what was happening and when, which made me feel like a typical gringo. We were told to get our belongings and wait at the front of the hotel, where eventually a truck arrived which we were invited to get into the back tray of with our stuff and with some of our new Yawanawá friends. The truck then proceeded to drive slowly around the bumpy dirt streets of the town, where it would pull up at houses that were filled with Yawanawá families. There would often be discussions about people who might be coming with us and after a couple of hours of driving around like this, the back of the truck was eventually filled with around 12 Yawanawá, including children, lots of boxes of food and supplies and a couple of chickens. I felt very out of place and out of my comfort zone but also amused and enchanted by these beautiful people and this little insight into their lives. I was happy and grateful for this experience, whilst a little nervous about the journey ahead.

The truck took off at significant speed down a long, mostly straight road with broad, sweeping hills. Once it picked up speed I was shocked at how hard it was to deal with the buffeting winds and struggled to find a way to get comfortable. I had to surrender and copy the Yawanawá who just sat, with their heads down, bracing themselves — and it was like that for a couple of hours on the back of that truck. Sometimes I looked at Dani and we both just laughed — it was all we could do. Eventually we arrived at the river Tarauacá, where there was a small roadside restaurant and inn with a little store that had gasoline and basic supplies. It was suggested we go and get some food while the young men grabbed our bags and prepared several canoes on the river. It didn't take long before we were inundated with small midges: tiny little blood-sucking insects that would spit a numbing bacteria which would also prevent your blood from congealing, so you wouldn't notice the midge biting at first and then would have to deal with an incessant itch that would last for days. We very quickly learned the value of using strong insect repellents. Down at the river bank the young Yawanawá men had packed five long canoes with supplies and bags ready for the journey down the river to Mutum which would take two days. By now we were surrounded by jungle, with only a few farms scattered here and there. I looked down the river in excitement. I was eager to be deep in the jungle, away from the encroachment of Western development.

After a leisurely preparation, eventually all the Yawanawá from the truck, Tashka, Mariazinha, Dani and I got in the canoes and we took off down the river. Being on the river was beautiful and meditative at times, and other times scary and treacherous. Like most things in the Amazon, there is sublime beauty in everything at the same time as danger and discomfort. There were places where the river was shallow and full of submerged logs. Tashka told us to look out because if we hit one, it could potentially tip the canoe. Also, the motor was very loud and echoed through the forest, sometimes bouncing back

Canoes, Rio Tarauacá, Acre, Brazil

onto the river if there were steep banks on the sides. After a while, and much like in Ayahuasca, I just surrendered and meditated on the divine beauty and pure energy of the forest as we wound our way along the snaking brown, flowing river. We stopped a couple of times before it got dark to fill the motor with fuel and Tashka served us some *rapé* (pronounced 'há-peh'), a dry powered snuff made from sacred plants, including types of tobacco. We continued into the night, while the men at the front of the canoes shone torches into the water to look out for submerged logs. Every now and then we would feel a strong thud as the canoe bounced off one. This would tip the canoe to its side and we would have to hold on, but somehow we never tipped over. After what seemed like about six or seven hours, we arrived at a very small Yawanawá village, where Tashka told us we would be spending the night.

We were taken to a small wooden hut where we were told we could hang our hammocks and were then invited to another hut where Tashka, Mariazinha and others had prepared some food. They were eating boiled *mandioc* (cassava), boiled *bananas da terra* (plantains) and small amounts of armadillo meat. There was not much flavour, but I had survived on similar foods in my time living with the Shipibo, on the other side of the border between Acre, Brazil and Peru. A message came from one of the locals who said that Dani and I were invited to the house of the cacique of this small village to eat with him and his family. The cacique and his family were very welcoming and excited to receive us. They offered us some food which was much the same with tasteless boiled mandioc and plantains — and this time the meat on offer was monkey. This was the first time I had ever eaten monkey and I had some mental resistance but felt obliged to eat, as our hosts watched every bite and chew, asking me multiple times if I liked it. I felt very honoured, as we were treated like special guests and they were offering us food and blessings for our journey. I told them a few stories about our project and about Australia and my previous experiences with Ayahuasca and being in the Amazon.

We were awoken very early the next morning to head back down to the river for the next leg of the journey. I was trying to let go of the sensation of wanting to 'get there', coaching myself to come back into the moment and allow myself to soak up every moment of this magical journey. This was much more immersive than my previous experiences in the Amazon; we were living amongst these native people and learning from them and their ways, and the best way I knew to show my gratitude was to be totally present with every moment. The village was shrouded in mists and deep greens, surrounded by endless forest, which inspired me to think of all the jaguars and jiboias and the magic that lived inside it. The rest of the journey that day was much like the first day, and we finally arrived in the village of Mutum (the name of a pheasant-like, flightless bird), which would be our home for the next five weeks.

Much like my time with the Shipibo in Peru, my intention for this journey was not to seek out Ayahuasca or medicines. Our aim was to share in a cultural exchange of music and art, and to learn about the Yawanawá people, their culture and customs. I was happy with this, as I felt it was a respectful way to meet them and to learn about them before receiving the blessings of their most sacred offerings. Many people commented to me how it was unusual for gringos to show up who weren't coming just for Ayahuasca and shamanic work, and they appreciated our intention to learn their ways and live amongst them. Once we were in this beautiful village on the outside of a wide bend in the river, Dani met up with his friend, the female pajé, Hushahu (pronounced 'hoo-shah-hoo'). She had become well known for being the first woman to have studied the way of the pajé, and apparently had been dealing with a lot of cultural resistance to this. But she had gone on through her studies in *Uní* (Ayahuasca) through which she met a divine ancestral being from the forest that had not previously been known to the Yawanawá. Hushahu was greatly respected for this achievement. Through her deep and lengthy diets she had met this being which was now incorporated into the Yawanawá cosmology. She told us she had asked Dani to come to Mutum to help her paint this being and to teach her some techniques that would help her to honour the being through artistic interpretation. We were invited to set up our hammocks in Hushahu's house while she spent most of her time in the forest, in the healing area where the shamanic work, including Ayahuasca, was done. One of Hushahu's daughters and her husband were assigned to cook and to look after us during our stay. There was so much to learn in terms of survival and communal tribal living, so the support was very much appreciated.

Before and during the journey to the village, Tashka took us aside now and then to talk about his mission and vision for our time in the village. Tashka spoke about the importance of the work of Hushahu for the Yawanawá and of how their cosmology was evolving. We talked about the music project I had been invited to work on with them. I suggested we just do some live recordings in the forest to organically capture the natural sounds and energy of the forest. He liked this idea and went on to explain to me that there were some questions and caution amongst the Elders and leadership of the Yawanawá about the inclusion of non-native instruments which were being introduced into Yawanawá ceremonies and spiritual work. Tashka said that they loved to integrate new sounds and musical colours into their music, but there was some caution, as they did not know what effect these new sounds would have on their cosmology and how this would manifest in their creation. For the Yawanawá, just as in Indigenous Australia and other parts of the world, sound is the core of creation, and the sounds that come directly from the forest and from their ancestors are sacred. Tashka then requested that there be some recordings that were purely traditional, to honour the original sounds, and then we could record with guitars and drums and other instruments. This seemed like a beautiful plan. I was glad to have these conversations with Tashka because I believe that cultural ecology is very important and there have been enough gringos and 'whitefellas' (Australian slang for white Europeans) barging in with a million good ideas and wanting to help, not realising the sensitivities of the culture and spirituality of the native people. I had been in Peru and seen the same thing in Australia, so I was happy there was a stronger ethical culture here in Brazil.

Arriving in Mutum a couple of hours behind us were another two boats, one with Americans who were visiting on behalf of the community development project run by the international cosmetics company, Aveda. While chatting with them, I was greatly impressed by their ethical approach to community development. They helped the Yawanawá to identify what they would need in order to be self-sufficient and independent, rather than just donating money or things they thought the Yawanawá should have and thereby possibly creating dependency. They worked with the Yawanawá to identify some plants, *jenipapú* and *urucum*, that are used in ceremonial adornment as body paints. They also worked together to set up a trade deal whereby Aveda invested in the infrastructure for the Yawanawá to supply powdered plant matter that was used in an Amazonian, ethically sourced range of cosmetics. They used the proceeds to fund projects in the village such as a school, internet, agro-forestry, sustainable farming and facilities for their spiritual work, such as Ayahuasca healing and ceremonies. As I had come to learn, Uní was at the centre of the lives and spirituality of the Yawanawá, and they were working on a mission given to them by the spirit of the forest and their ancestors. They were prepared to receive all the people who would be guided to come for healing as Western society continued to fail. The Yawanawá are custodians and knowledge keepers of the Uní and other sacred healing plants. They see their knowledge and the plants of the forest as divine gifts from the Earth for all humanity. In their vision, the people, once healed and awakened, will also care for the Earth at this critical time. I was inspired by the beautiful vision of global healing held by the Yawanawá and also by the alliance they had created with Aveda that brought connection between ancient wisdom and the sacred plants of the forest, and modern business and technology. A living example of the prophecy of the eagle and condor.

With all my years of experience in community development projects across Australia, including work alongside Aboriginal communities, it felt like a powerful synchronicity to land in Mutum just as these specialists arrived. I'd seen first-hand how poorly considered 'help' can distort a culture, especially now, when Ayahuasca tourism in Peru has surged into a cautionary tale of commercialisation, dependency, cultural interference and spiritual dilution. The same pressures are rising in Brazil: eager outsiders hunting for Huni Kuin and Yawanawá pajés to parade on the international stage, dangling promises of tourism money, solar panels and Wi-Fi. The dangers of cultural appropriation and economic co-dependency are always lurking in that exchange. The seduction of gaining 'power by association' with Indigenous people is strong for some who prefer to get it that way, rather than doing the hard work and humbling required to embody their own personal power and thus earn genuine leadership and shamanic skills.

What struck me about the Aveda team was the ethics behind their patience and humility: their thorough cultural study, environmental assessments, resource planning and genuine consultation. Their focus was on self-sustainability — cultural continuity first, ecological integrity always — instead of rushing into foreign-led tourism built around Uní. They understood that without strong foundations, the global fascination with Indigenous spirituality can become extractive, draining communities of their own meaning in the name of 'support'. And in this age of viral imagery and spiritual consumerism, where social media loves a 'shamanic celebrity' promoted through movie-style celebrity posters on Facebook and Instagram, many villages are left vulnerable to opportunists whose glossy marketing masks private agendas, absent of ethical considerations.

Opportunities for development are not the enemy, but they demand discernment. What I witnessed in the Aveda partnership set a high standard: development guided by respect rather than ego, by reciprocity rather than exploitation, and by a long view that protects what is sacred while welcoming what can help the culture thrive.

During the afternoon of the first day in Mutum there was a lot of movement amongst the people of the village and some excitement about a big ceremony that had been planned for the night. Just before dark we were guided on a half-hour walk through the forest to the healing place where the Yawanawá of the Mutum village would do their Uní ceremonies, healing, plant diets and spiritual studies in the forest. At the centre of the healing place was a large round temple-like ceremonial space with dirt floor and no walls. There was an altar in the middle and a fire to one side with some wooden benches around the edges. We were told we could hang our hammocks between the wooden poles holding up the edges of the roof. The temple was located in the crook of a snaking creek that seemed to wind around the space like a jiboia serpent. We were warned not to go into the water, as there was a large jiboia living in it which I was lucky to see one day. You could only cross the river by walking along a skinny slippery log. Around the temple were a couple of small structures for preparing food and medicines surrounded by small gardens of sacred plants, including *chacruna*, which is used in the preparation of Ayahuasca.

With preparations underway many Yawanawá were arriving as the sun was setting. Men and women were very relaxed and casual in preparing themselves, with many sharing rapé. When the ceremony began there were around 60 people including my friend and I, and the two Americans from Aveda. This ceremony was like nothing I had been in before. In some ways it was similar to the eagle-condor ceremonies, with a large gathering of people outside and a fire. We were invited to drink some Uní, which was much less concentrated and lighter coloured than what I had been used to, making the quantity that we drank larger also. While we were drinking there was still a bit of movement and chatting amongst the Yawanawá. At one point some singing began led by the pajé Matsini, who sang a few songs alone before the women joined him in chorus. The songs

Temple and healing space, Mutum, Acre, Brazil

and the frequency of sounds they were expressing immediately captivated my senses and spirit. When the women started singing in glorious overtones of cascading harmonies I saw visions of layers of trees in the endless forest with a brilliant sheath of light emanating from the ceremony and penetrating throughout the forest in every direction. The singing created overtones and sounds within sounds that disarmed my thinking mind completely. I could hear angelic choruses in the harmonics of the overtones while my mind was filled with visions of an astral forest bathed in light. I was carried on the wave of these cosmic sounds for what seemed like a couple of hours.

At times Matsini would lead the singing with the women backing him with their chorus, or at other times Hushahu or one of the other women would lead. There seemed to be a casual knowing of how things would proceed; the flow of the ceremony was unspoken and relaxed. This helped me to relax too, as there was a lot to take in: the new cosmic dimension I was immersed in, the mind-blowing sounds and the visions of the astral forest, the sheer force of the Uní, and the nature being so present that deep in the jungle, with the insects providing another soundtrack. Occasionally a spider or insect would crawl over me. There were a few little speeches when they took a break to drink more Uní and share some rapé. One of the young women asked me if I wanted her to apply some rapé and I accepted. This blow of rapé was like nothing I had ever experienced. It was like a rocket filled with fireworks went off in my mind and I struggled to walk back to find somewhere to sit while my whole body was spinning as I felt like my energetic field was being cleansed.

Later they lit the fire and some of the men went over and stood by the fire while the singing continued. The two Elder pajés Tatá and Yawá sat quietly on the sides while the singing continued with intermittent breaks. I had the beautiful feeling of being with a big tribal family in a ceremony which felt like a celebration. They were happy we were there for our projects, but much more so to honour the two people who had come from Aveda and brought so many blessings and had shown them great respect through their community development work. I felt very honoured to be immersed in the jungle as part of such a powerful ceremony.

Several of the men convened some small groups, linking arms and dancing in circles while chanting. Some of the chants had been sung earlier but were done so now with a different tone and intention, as the focus was on these circles of six or so people arm-in-arm, dancing back and forth. I felt compelled to join in but I was also a little overwhelmed and not sure of myself — there was a lot to take in. Eventually one of the young women came and grabbed my hand and pulled me into one of the dancing circles. I had to learn the movements and rhythm quickly and felt a bit like an uncoordinated gringo again. Once I had learned the dance moves and was in harmony with the circle, I focused on learning the chants, which were relatively simple and beautiful but still challenging to get the sounds right; I struggled to get them and let myself flow. Eventually I overcame my clumsiness and overwhelm, and something inside me just said to let go — and when I did everything changed. Suddenly I wasn't trying anything and I felt the force of the circle and the Uní flowing very strongly through me. I was dancing perfectly and singing the songs just as they were, and I was even singing the chants as they did without any effort or thought. This was magic. As we kept dancing, the pajé leading my circle said a few things in Portuguese that were exactly the negative thoughts I had been experiencing plus some other things he seemed to be able to read directly from my mind. This was very humbling and again disarming, with my mind realising I had nowhere to hide. The core lesson of Ayahuasca was coming through strongly again for me: turn off the thinking mind, have faith, let Spirit do the work.

After the dancing ended I went and sat back down on one of the benches and the Elder pajé Yawá came and sat beside me and thanked me for dancing with them. He said it meant a lot to his people when foreigners came and joined in their traditions. He went on to explain that the dance is a vital part of their ceremony and their work with the Uní and that when they sing the chants these function to call in the forces and prayers for health, abundance and connection with the forest and their ancestors. He said that when we dance, we manifest those prayers into our bodies and into the land and into the village for them to become physically manifest. I learned that these rhythmic dances are an integral part of the Yawanawá cosmology and that beyond just doing the healing work with Ayahuasca, the Yawanawá cosmology involved many weavings of cultural expressions that all had a specific function. I began to comprehend what Tashka had explained to me about the importance of maintaining the integrity and purity of their music. I could see how the light of the astral forest emanated so brightly through the forest and through all who were there, and it made sense to me that integrating into dance and the body created a kind of 'magical pass' that leads to physical manifestation.

I was reminded of the writings of Carlos Castaneda on Yaqui shamanism who said in his book, *The Wheel of Time: The Shamans of Mexico*:

> "Magical passes are not exercises; they are magical movements that were discovered by seers in ancient times, and when practiced, they allow us to align with the force that keeps us alive."

I spent time during the miração that night contemplating the importance of the prayers of manifestation by these native peoples, whose survival depended upon shamanism and Ayahuasca. This culture was the Dreaming of the Yawanawá. I was inspired with gratitude for the Holy Sacrament and a greater responsibility to honour my experiences with it. For most Westerners who make a trip to Peru or drink Ayahuasca on the weekend at a retreat somewhere in a Western city, we can gain the benefits but be lazy or distracted in integrating the teachings. For the Yawanawá it is a matter of survival and a practice that has endured over generations, sung from the Dreaming, calling the people into unity with the whole forest. My first night with the Yawanawá gave me this vision of profound beauty beyond my mind's comprehension.

Deep into the ceremony, not long before the sun was due to shine its first rays of light, the Elder pajé Tatá came and sat near the centre. Everyone gathered round in reverent respect for him. I had been told he was over 100 years old and a very wise and powerful pajé who had more knowledge of the plants and spirituality than any of the other Yawanawá. Everyone in the ceremony was still and silent, concentrating as Tatá began to sing. His songs had a familiar but very different tone and sound to the others I had heard that night. Tatá's songs were very psychedelic, meandering with strange sounds and an enchanting frailty in his elderly voice. The miração I experienced that night was ancient, like being in a deep, dark rainforest with mystical ancient forest beings. The sense I got from this was nothing I can describe in words, although it had the feeling of an ancient forest as it existed before any European influence. There was some silence after Tatá sang and then some of the younger pajés brought out guitars and sang some of their traditional songs with a more contemporary feel. These songs seemed very popular with the younger Yawanawá, flooding me with inspiration and a broad inner smile. As the sky started to lighten, I climbed into my hammock listening to the music and drifting into the sounds and feeling of being in the forest. I don't remember if I fell asleep or just drifted, but at some point in the morning the ceremony ended and most people wandered back to the village. I felt like I had learned so much, yet I hadn't even been in the village for 24 hours.

It took some days to get accustomed to life in the Yawanawá village. The crew from Aveda left after a couple of days and I missed them as they had been great guides and had explained many things to me and Dani. The reality of dealing with the intensity of the insects was very challenging to integrate but soon enough I managed to create a vigilant routine of protection. The village has a lake in the middle and I had swum in it, risking the insects that would swarm around me when I got out, and taking the risk that I might encounter the large jiboia some of the young men told me they had seen in the lake. It was so hot, and being able to cool down was a blessing. Every day in the village was slightly different and there was usually a lot of movement. It was hard at times to track what was going on. Some days it seemed there was nobody in the village and we would walk around and eventually find a big group of Yawanawá at a different house, usually one of the grandmothers' houses.

Every morning we would gather at the house of Mariazinha, who was one of the chiefs of the village, and Tatá would always be there, sitting and sharpening his machete and mumbling under his breath, seemingly making personal commentary about the lively discussions going on amongst the people. We were told that Tatá would be up at the break of dawn, tending to the chickens and the gardens, slashing paths and working with the same energy as the young men. Tatá was a short man, very thin and he looked his age of over 100, but somehow he was full of energy and life force. I sat with him at times and he complained that the young men were lazy and he had to chase them to get up early to get to work. He said that if they got too lazy he would give them *kambô* (cleansing medicine from a frog) which would quickly bring back their vitality and motivation. He said that if anyone in the village showed any signs of habitual laziness or unhealthy behaviours, he would take them to the healing space and give them kambô and Uní and other plants to bring them back to full force. I could see from my time there that nobody sat idle; everyone was engaged with village life. The younger pajés who were doing spiritual studies would wander around at times sharing rapé, collecting plants, painting their bodies and making journeys to the healing space. Sometimes we would join them in sharing rapé and songs and talking about Yawanawá spirituality, their shamanic diets and Uní.

We would spend time during the day in one of the school buildings, painting and creating art with Hushahu and some of the children. The teenagers would also wander in from time to time and a lot of creativity flourished in the space while a giant hairy tarantula spider sat vigil on the ceiling above us. Most nights we would spend in the healing space with Matsini Yawanawá, one of the leaders and the oldest student of Tatá. I found I had a great connection with Matsini. It was like we were somehow old brothers from another life, and there was an ease and flow between us, with a mutual understanding of each other. We would stay up all night sometimes, drinking Uní, while Matsini would sing and talk about culture, ethics and spirituality. I told him a lot of stories from my times with Indigenous Australians and we discovered there were a great many common beliefs and practices. Some nights we would sit with Matsini and he would tell stories from the ancestors or teachings on the culture and ways of the Yawanawá. I had my recording equipment set up and would record him singing. Some nights, groups of women would also come to the temple to sing for the recordings. They would always drink some Uní and prepare themselves with body paints to connect with the beings they wanted to transmit through the recordings of their music. Sometimes it would take a long time for them to get ready. A couple of times we would be ready to sing and record them, but then Hushahu would sense the energy wasn't right and she would work with the women to do some more energetic and spiritual preparation. I sat there patiently with my microphone and computer. Eventually between the women and the nights alone with Matsini, we recorded over 80 songs, along with some recordings of Matsini's storytelling.

Drinking Uní in the forest with Matsini taught me many things. He would often tell stories of the forest and his ancestors then sing a song, and I would drift into a deep miração and make connection with the animals and other spirit beings he would be calling. At one point a spiritual being, a large, colourful jiboia, came slithering up to me while Matsini was singing and it curled itself around me and eventually entered my head and looked through my eyes, seeing through my perspective. As I held this meditation I took this jiboia on a journey to many sacred places I knew in Australia, beautiful

Meeting with Jiboia, Lore Solaris, Acrylic on Canvas

places that I had been or places that hold great significance for Indigenous Australians. At one point I took her to Uluṟu, the giant rock in the centre of Australia. The jiboia was very curious and we held that gaze into Uluṟu for a long time. It felt like the beings of the forest were connecting to the land in Australia and energy was being transmitted back and forth. I felt like I was just the instrument to make this happen, but it was interesting that Matsini and I had so many conversations about Indigenous cultures and he had been so curious about this and then it manifested in the miração. Later I painted this vision and this painting is always in my sacred space, as it represents my Dreaming and the spiritual connection and songlines between Australia and Brazil.

On many occasions during my time there in the forest with the Yawanawá people I felt like I was being gifted with much knowledge and meetings with different beings, some of whom I was creating spiritual alliances with. At the time I didn't think too much of this, even though in reading this it may seem magical or maybe even unbelievable, but for me in the moment this was an expansion on some of my previous lessons and experiences of Ayahuasca. But this time it was so much more real, as here I was in the Amazon with a well-trained pajé being guided through many different mirações. Later, I came to realise that some of these beings I was meeting were to become spiritual helpers for me and are still with me to this day. I call them my caboclos, they are beings from the forest. Some are pajé spirits and others are not human, but they are spiritual beings from the forest that manifest in a myriad of ways. They all have a similar vibration, colours and qualities of the forest.

During this time I was also immersed in the music of the Yawanawá that I was hearing and singing every day. I found that learning the songs became easy after that experience on the first night and the songs themselves somehow became imprinted in my consciousness. At times when I sing them now, caboclos will come and sing them through me. This was a very important time in my training with Ayahuasca. It was not something I planned but was guided to. Matsini saw my openness and surrender, connected with me spiritually and guided me to build these sacred alliances and develop my connection and abilities with Ayahuasca. At the time I wasn't so aware of the consequences or the effect this would have on me until after I left and went on to my next experiences. To date, just as with the teachings of Pablo Amaringo, I am still learning from this strong connection I built with the forest through my time with the Yawanawá.

I was greatly inspired by the stories that Matsini shared with us during those nights in the forest. I felt a strong kinship with his mission and the mission of the Yawanawá in bringing healing to the people of the world. The Yawanawá are aware that the forest medicines and, in particular, Uní are gifts for the planet during this time of emergency and awakening. They had been guided by their Elders and ancestors to prepare for many people coming to ask for healing. Matsini told the story of how the Yawanawá were once divided into seven different clans, some of which were hostile and war-like. When they faced existential crises to their lands and cultures, they were forced to unite and did so through the use of Uní. Matsini used this as an example of how the Yawanawá could be leaders in creating peace and unity amongst the peoples of the world.

> *Our knowledge is rooted in the forest, in the plants, and in the animals. This knowledge can help heal the world, not just our people.* — Tashka Yawanawá.

He went on to share that when the invaders had come to harvest rubber in the forests, the Yawanawá had been forced off their lands for fear of genocide, and with murder, disease and displacement, their population had been severely diminished. The majority of the surviving Yawanawá were forced to flee to the towns and cities in Acre, but some of the pajés went and hid in the forest with the intention of keeping the sacred knowledge of the music, plants and the forest intact. Tatá and Yawá were two of those brave people who spent many years alone in the forest. Matsini shared that not all the knowledge was saved; for example, they used to have knowledge of 12 species of Ayahuasca vine before the invasion, and now only knew of seven. When the Yawanawá found that it was safe to return to the forest after the government gave them some lands for reservations, they began to re-establish themselves in small villages. The pajés returned and began teaching the younger generations the sacred knowledge and wisdom of the forest and guided a new generation of leadership and shamanism. Due to the decimation of their population, some Yawanawá, like the father of Matsini and Hushahu, had many children, and in 2014 when I visited them, they were still in a state of recovery from near extinction. Matsini himself told me that he would not leave Mutum while Tatá was alive, so that he could learn as much as possible from him before he left his body.

I contemplated the vision I had seen at Spirit Vine some months earlier in which I met the ancient pajé in the forest who had taken so many wounds in protecting the sacred medicines over generations. My heart felt full of gratitude and immense respect for the challenge and sacrifice of those ancestors who gave their lives for Ayahuasca, so that we now can receive the healing and spiritual blessings of this divine gift of the Earth. In all my spiritual work and ceremonies I

Ni Yuxi – Forest Protector, Lore Solaris, acrylic on canvas

make a dedication to those who have given everything to allow us to have the blessing to drink this sacred brew, and give thanks for the millions of people around the world that have benefitted from its divine powers.

It was very heartening to see a lot of young Yawanawá in the village who were very dedicated and focused on spiritual studies, including shamanism. Matsini and Hushahu represented a younger generation of leaders and it was very clear they were very well respected in their roles. Life in the village was vibrant and active. At one time during our stay, when they were getting ready for a big hunt, the whole village seemed to be talking about it and doing things to prepare. In order to sharpen their senses and give them strength and focus, the hunters were getting ready by taking rapé, kambô, *sananga* (a medicine from the bark of a small bush, given for clarity and force) and drinking Uní. They were gone for a few days and came back with an abundance of food, including fish, monkeys, a large tortoise, pacas and armadillos. Around this time there was a meeting of leaders and Elders in the village. Some people came from other villages and they met in Mariazinha's house, where they had a vigorous debate about some big issues they were facing. The Elders demanded that the meeting be only spoken in their native Yawanawá language and not in Portuguese. We were invited to attend and sat at the back with someone translating for us. There was great concern about the effect that media and television were having on the minds of their people, in particular with the introduction of social problems such as jealousy, fashion, consumerism and competitiveness, which had not existed in their culture before. There were also discussions around family members in the towns who were drinking alcohol and also on the best way for the development of the resources of the community in terms of farming and construction.

My experiences with the Yawanawá gave me a lot of insights, teachings and realisations. It seemed during my time there in Mutum that the rest of the world and even my own emotional and mental dramas had dissolved — or were not given any space for me to indulge in them. It was easy to flow with the people in everyday life and be inspired by their strong motivation for living, and focus on the projects and tasks at hand. I did a painting while I was there and gifted it to Matsini: it depicted a strong pajé using his songs to protect the village and the forest through the healing and power of Uní. Despite the mind viruses and toxic dominator culture encroaching on their lands and traditional ways, the Uní would always give them remedy to stay conscious of and alert to what was coming and to be able to protect themselves. In 2015 there was a severe flood and we used some of the recordings we made during this time to raise some funds for their support. When I returned to Australia in 2016, I collaborated with some musicians and a well-known Australian producer to create an album entitled *Kanaro Project*. I am very grateful for my time with the Yawanawá and feel very connected with them. Some of them came to Rio when I was living there in 2015 and invited me to join them at the beach in Copacabana, where Tatá and some others would see the ocean for the first time. I also participated in some ceremonies around Rio with them over the years and reconnected with Tashka at the World Ayahuasca Conference in Spain in 2019. To this day my spiritual connection with the Yawanawá remains very strong and the beings from the forest I met there are still with me

Receiving rapé, Mutum, Acre, Brazil

and come through my work, my ceremonies and music, where their blessings and presence have been helping me and others with the powerful healing and spiritual presence that they bring.

Since my time with the Yawanawá in early 2014, the vision of their ancestors has flourished. Many Yawanawá pajés and family travel around the world sharing their culture and medicine. Where in our time there in the village we were the only gringos, now there are hundreds, if not thousands, of Westerners making the pilgrimage to the Yawanawá lands, and the Yawanawá have used the resources brought to them to build healing centres and accommodation and supporting infrastructure to receive the Westerners. Unlike in Peru, where the Ayahuasca healing centres are almost always built and run by Westerners who hire in some local Indigenous healers, in Brazil all the programs and retreats are run by the Yawanawá themselves in alignment with their own vision. The commercialisation of their culture remains a danger, especially amidst the toxic politics of the Brazilian Government and the march of economic development and corporate interests. Some Yawanawá like Hushahu have complained about cultural appropriation, where people are copying their culture in disrespectful ways. Whilst this still continues, they have also made strong efforts to educate and share their knowledge for those who genuinely want to learn. In the last 10 years the Yawanawá, led by Tashka, Hushahu, Matsini and others, have had an enormous influence on the global Ayahuasca movement.

Our culture is like the river — it flows, it changes, but it never stops. And we, as the Yawanawá, are part of that river. — **Tashka Yawanawá.**

CHAPTER 9

Sounds of Awakening

Ciranda: Canta com Amor (Sing with Love)

In many shamanic societies, if you came to a shaman or medicine person complaining of being disheartened, dispirited, or depressed, they would ask one of four questions. When did you stop dancing? When did you stop singing? When did you stop being enchanted by stories? When did you stop finding comfort in the sweet territory of silence? Where we have stopped dancing, singing, being enchanted by stories, or finding comfort in silence is where we have experienced the loss of soul. Dancing, singing, storytelling, and silence are the four universal healings. — Gabrielle Roth.

In April 2014, after six weeks in the Upper Amazon rainforest with the Yawanawá people, I made my way over to Rio de Janeiro, where I would be attending the music and visionary art retreat with Carioca Freitas and his wife Keren-or Atari. I had a week's rest by the beach in Ubatuba on the São Paulo coast, and I was filled with the spirit of the forest and its teachings and did not have much time to prepare or think about what I might find at the retreat with Carioca. It seemed like I needed this week just to catch up with myself, to contemplate my life and my journey. After being so deeply immersed in the forest and life in the village, drinking Uní nearly every day, it was time to do some grounding and integrating. It seemed that life was guiding me deeper into the path of Ayahuasca and it was a great blessing to be able to invest this time with powerful experiences in Brazil. I could still feel the forest all around me and in my dreams. If I closed my eyes I would be back in the village — it was almost like my aura had been painted green by the forest. I felt like I was in a great place inside myself to meet Carioca and continue learning with Ayahuasca, and I was happy to be approaching this next chapter without many expectations or projections — just an open mind and heart for where Spirit would next guide me.

I was excited to be arriving at Ciranda for the beginning of the retreat, and full of curiosity and positive energy. Ciranda is about an hour and a half's drive from Rio de Janeiro, just outside a small city called Rio Bonito (Beautiful River) and nestled into the rainforest at the edge of the mountains. I attended with a friend and we were the first ones to arrive where we were greeted by a beautiful woman who was working as admin and also by Carioca's lovely wife Keren-or. Ciranda is a large, sprawling retreat centre surrounded by humid Mata-Atlantic rainforest in the foothills of the mountains. Forest trails wind up into the mountains with crystalline creeks and waterfalls, monkeys, colourful birds and forest sounds. The grounds of Ciranda are a magical parkland with a creek running throughout, and with bridges, gardens, flowers and hummingbirds buzzing around, plus 30 cabins, a large farmhouse with a big outdoor dining area and a large *conga* (temple), nestled into the side of the forest. Scattered around the gardens are statues of mythical beings and magical areas to sit in and enjoy the parkland setting and the nature or to dream and contemplate the cosmos.

In chatting with Keren-or, I was impressed by her strong character and found that we had a lot in common with our use of Ayahuasca, spirituality, healing practices and visionary art. Ciranda has many of her colourful, psychedelic artworks and murals throughout the centre. I was inspired to be participating in her workshops, which we would be attending over the coming two weeks. I was still curious to meet Carioca, as I had been listening to his music for so long and had come to realise that he was very well known and respected amongst the Ayahuasca communities throughout Brazil, while his music and influence was widespread in Ayahuasca culture all around the world. I had seen a man in the gardens wandering around without shoes, wearing some board shorts and a colourful old T-shirt with holes in it and thought he must have been the gardener, until he came over and introduced himself as Carioca. I was impressed by his easy, gentle and sweet demeanour, as well as his humility and boyish smile, youthful humour and looks. For a man of nearly 60 years old, he must have been doing something right; I wondered about the power of Ayahuasca in delaying the aging process. After our introductory chat, we were taken to our cabins in the gardens and took some time to settle in.

Around 12 people gathered at Ciranda for the music and visionary art workshop after travelling to Brazil from different parts of the world. I was reminded of the many retreats I had attended and supported with Silvia in Amazonas and Bahia. This time things felt different. I felt a new energy inside and I knew that this workshop, Ciranda itself and having this time with Carioca would be a whole new kind of experience; I was hopeful it would expand my creative expressions in art and music, and that it would give me some new insights into Ayahuasca and ceremony. We all sat for dinner and many great conversations as we all got to know everyone who was there, many of whom knew Carioca and Ciranda quite well and who gave me some good insights into what to expect, which only made my excitement and curiosity even stronger. Carioca was very gracious and generous with his time and energy and carried a great humour that had us all laughing, which created a comfortable and homely environment that made it feel like I had come home.

The next morning, after a good night's sleep in a cabin next to the forest, the first workshop of the retreat began: a music workshop run by Carioca. We sat down in the big conga, which is surrounded by jungle on one side and beautiful gardens with flowers and hummingbirds on the other. The roof of the conga is impressively expansive, architecturally designed with sacred geometry for a natural flow of energy and clarity of sound and acoustics. Carioca sat with us and spoke about music. His creative expression and storytelling style of communication was enchanting, and I was inspired by his creative mind and the way he expressed himself as a true artist. Carioca spoke about music as an expression of the soul,

The conga (temple) at Ciranda, Rio Bontio, Rio de Janeiro, Brazil

as a language of the spirit and of emotions. He talked about music as a living entity and went on to explain that if there is any religion of Ciranda and of his ceremonies, then it is music. He spoke about the music we all have inside ourselves: the music and rhythms of our bodies that never leave us, that are always there available for us to experience and express.

I found Carioca's words to be full of wisdom, simplicity, humour and emotion. I noticed this quality of authentic passion and emotion was also very present in his music at all times. When Carioca picked up his guitar for the first time and sang the song *Annelise*, a beautiful tribute to the moon, it literally brought me to tears. I knew in this moment he would be a great teacher for me. I connected with his words, his vision and his passion for creativity, and I could feel in such a profound way the sentiments and deep meanings of the songs he was sharing with us. It wasn't just the sound of his beautiful voice and guitar; it was the emotion that flowed through me from his song that deeply moved me. I knew this wasn't just some show of egoism. Carioca clearly is very connected to spirit and his heart, and this comes across in all the ways he expresses himself. To this day I still find this with Carioca. The mastery of his art and his deeply felt spirituality comes across not with the words he says but in the way he expresses himself. Carioca IS music, he is art personified — and this quality was something I greatly aspired to develop. Reflecting on this, I was very happy to have found a great teacher and I could understand why friends along my journey in Brazil who knew Carioca had strongly encouraged me to visit him.

Annelise,
water merged with the Earth
Evaporated with your magic
And danced among the coconut trees
Who it was that shone so bright
In this intense moment

Annelise,
Illuminated the Earth
With silvery glow
And round smile
Bringing brilliant light
Dewdrops without tears

Annelise,
water merged with the Earth

— *Annelise,* Carioca.

My eyes and mind were wide open during that first full day at Ciranda. Ciranda has an abundance of riches of so many things in my life that I love so dearly. Forest and gardens, beautiful nature, exquisite music with an openness to share, and teachings that touch the depths of the spirituality I have found within myself and on my journey over so many years. The healing energies of the place, the music and the art, the great people and rich conversations were energising my soul and filling me with excitement and inspiration. It seemed like my life had come into this magical, enchanted realm of Spirit in ways I could never have imagined, and I was deeply engaged with everything I was learning and absorbing. Keren-or's workshops on visionary art were also inspiring and it was a pleasure to be able to sit and paint with others and to talk about Spirit, Ayahuasca, the forest and creativity with such a lovely group of people. The energy at Ciranda seemed alive and its own universe. I could feel the blessings of so many spiritual beings and ancestors who seemed to be enchanting every part.

That night at dinner and the next day when we were socialising around meals and between workshops, I found myself talking a lot about my experiences with Ayahuasca, my times in the Amazon and the experiences and connections I had had with Aboriginal Australians. I reflected later on my style of communication, which was perhaps tinged with a lack of humility. By this stage I had been drinking Ayahuasca for over 11 years in a diversity of settings and with some wise and experienced teachers, though I underestimated the depth and power of the work of Ciranda and Carioca that was anchored deeply in 40 years of Ayahuasca traditions and Brazilian culture. The gusto with which I shared my stories seemed to have a tinge of my father's arrogance (it makes me feel slightly embarrassed to think about it now), and I believe I was in the process of learning some big lessons in humility that Carioca was teaching me through his own humility and subtle confidence. I had no idea about the richness in the traditions and the depth of the spirituality that the work at Ciranda was based upon. There was a lot to learn. What I didn't realise in those very early days at Ciranda was that I was about to undertake the deepest healing journey of my entire life for my inner child and my creativity.

The first of the ceremonies in this two-week retreat would be on the second night. From what I had learned so far of the music and culture, I was excited to experience Ayahuasca in this setting and, with this intention, to explore the teachings through the music. I greatly appreciated the strong invitation and safe, welcoming offer to sing and share in the ceremonies with the music. The workshops and guidance that we had been given were good preparation, but nothing could have prepared me enough for this first time in ceremony with Carioca. It was decided that the ceremony would be held in the *Cura* (healing) room, as there were only 12 of us, including a few friends of Ciranda who were going to drop in from Rio de Janeiro. The Cura room was a dedicated space designed to hold a special series of three ceremonies over three days; the room was beautiful with one white wall and another made from sandstone and the rest with ceiling-to-floor glass overlooking the gardens. The beauty and elegance reflected to me the grace of Ayahuasca and seemed like something from a fairytale or a dream.

We gathered for the ceremony, all wearing white and appearing very elegant — appropriate for the grace and humility of the ceremony and for work with Ayahuasca. People often ask me why we wear white in ceremonies that have their roots in Umbanda and Santo Daime. The wearing of white in spiritual rituals is very common in Brazil and is understood as being part of cultural protocols. White is representative of the light, of working with divinity, higher vibrations and elevated spiritual realms. White is also protective against dark forces and entities and it represents cleansing and purification of the body, mind and spiritual aura. Having everybody wear white also creates a sense of uniformity and equality among participants, removing distinctions of social status and focusing on collective spiritual experience without distraction. By wearing white, participants align themselves with the sacred energy of the ceremony, fostering a space of healing, devotion and transformation. I personally find that when I am wearing my ceremonial white clothes it brings me into a certain mind space of reverence, humility and respect — and it feels good to be there with everyone else. I also personally believe this adds to the beauty of the ceremony, as we all become channels of the current of light that flows through us, through the music and the force of the Ayahuasca. Within the light there is nowhere for darkness to hide; it inspires us to face and release our shadows and find the peace within our hearts and souls. White gives visual and intentional context to the goals of the work with Ayahuasca in this context.

Carioca entered the space and sat in his chair at the centre of the ceremony. He seemed very relaxed and in good humour, checking his guitars and tuning them, and checking in with the others who would be playing with him in the ceremony. I found myself much more interested in the way that the music and the ceremony was being prepared — perhaps as the workshop had opened my eyes already to the role of music in ceremony and the first thoughts that I might also be one of these musicians.

At the commencement of the ceremony, Carioca invited us all to stand for the reading of the opening prayer, *Consagração do Aposento* (Consecration of the Sanctuary), which was spoken in Portuguese and English. This prayer comes from the Santo Daime tradition and affirms the ancestral connection of Carioca's ceremonies to the lineages of Mestre Irineu and the Queen of the Forest. Following the prayer, two helpers lit some incense and one by one gave everybody a *defumação* (smudging or smoke clearing) to clear their energetic fields of any negative energies in preparation for drinking the Holy Sacrament, Ayahuasca. After putting on some recorded music as a soundtrack to the drinking part of the ceremony, Carioca was the first to receive a defumação, after which he went to prepare the Ayahuasca for serving to the participants.

A drinking table was set up just outside the ceremony room with an elegant glass jar and small glass for drinking waiting for everyone to come and be served the sacrament by Carioca. We lined up, with men on one side and women on the other to each drink, alternating between men and women. After drinking their glass of Ayahuasca, each person went back to sit in their place in the ceremonial space. Prior to this I was not familiar with the separation of men and women in ceremony, but I had come to learn that it is a distinct part of the tradition of Santo Daime. Whilst Ciranda and the work of Carioca is not formally part of a Santo Daime church group, the practices, ancestral connection, much of the music, the style of the work and many of the beliefs are derived from the Daime traditions. Ciranda is a living branch of the Daime tree with roots in the work of Mestre Irineu.

People have also often asked me over the years about separating genders and why it is part of the tradition of these ceremonies. Men and women traditionally sit separately as part of the spiritual discipline and energetic balance of the ritual. Sitting separately helps to maintain a harmonious energetic flow within the ritual space, allowing participants to stay focused on their spiritual work. Ayahuasca ceremony requires deep focus and inner work. Separating men and women minimises distractions, particularly those related to attraction, emotional connection or interpersonal dynamics. The separation of genders is common in many spiritual and Indigenous traditions as a way to organise and structure sacred space. It reflects a long-standing spiritual discipline aimed at ensuring the proper flow of energy during the ceremony. I have seen this in both Yawanawá and Huni Kuin ceremonies, and our local Aboriginal Elder, who has supported our ceremonies in Australia, also affirmed that for him this was an important element that also reflects the way that ancient Australian cultures hold ceremony. With the growth of awareness of modern *trans* and *non-binary* movements, some spiritual groups, including my own, have adapted to be more flexible at the request and respect of participants' need, and the consent of the respective genders present in the work. I have seen over time how separating men and women creates emotional safety and support, where camaraderie develops amongst the men and women respectively. In my experience, the way that men and women hold space for each other and offer support is distinctly different. I am often touched by the tenderness, intimacy and intuition that many women often share together in vulnerable spaces, and with the men they give each other support with encouragement to find strength and personal power. Also, it can be quite common, especially for women, that during Ayahuasca, deep traumas may surface, and this is very common, since 22% of women in Australia have experienced sexual violence at the hands of men and more than 50% have experienced some kind of sexual harassment. Subtle forms of harassment are much more common. Being around men, for example, who may also be releasing their own traumas, may be a hindrance to women who are fully letting go and releasing that trauma without fears or protections. This separation during ceremony creates safety. It also allows the helpers or guardians in the ceremony to focus on their respective gender areas which each require their own style of approach to therapeutic, emotional and spiritual support. Personally, I have always enjoyed this aspect in ceremony and I find it to be part of the beauty of the divine experience, whereby each of the genders mirrors the other in reflection of divine qualities of nature and Spirit, with both genders able to re-unite at the end in a celebration of unity and love.

After we had all consecrated the Ayahuasca and sat down, Carioca came back to the space and announced the name of the *hinario* (songbook) then called the corresponding number of the first song. We all sat up with our books ready to share in the music together. I loved the experience of having the song's words there to sing and practise, with translations to understand the words, most of which were in Portuguese. At this stage my Portuguese was okay but still had a lot of gaps and I found the translations were a great way to deepen my experience and learning of the prayers and hymns while also helping me to learn Portuguese. After so many years of not having a songbook or just being in the dark, I was revelling in the expanded possibility of participation in the music.

I was astounded by the beauty, colours and diversity of the music and the styles that Carioca played in his ceremonies. I noticed quite quickly during that first cup that the force of the Ayahuasca as it arrived was much stronger than I had been accustomed to. Carioca himself sat there like a mountainous force of nature, unflinching and focused as he channelled the forces through his heavenly voice in all of its range and psychedelic effects. The sensation for me was like being called into the force of Ayahuasca and swept into the psychedelia of the ceremony. This had the effect of the force being so strong that it became difficult for me to keep my eyes open. The force kept wanting to take me deep into myself and away from the space. I struggled a little, as I dearly wanted learn how to express myself through the music in Ayahuasca ceremony and maintain my *firmeza* (firmness) in the space, but the temptation to collapse into a purely inner journey was very strong. I had spent so many nights on Ayahuasca up until this point deep in astral journeys in the dark, and although I had some experience with the Templo Mãe D'Àgua group of learning to sing, this felt like another level altogether. I was also very aware of many others in the group who were sitting straight and tall, holding their firmeza, and I felt the challenge to do the same. Over the years I have come to greatly appreciate the teaching of firmeza in Ayahuasca practice. When we hold ourselves in the grace of self-discipline we are truly able to become safe vessels to receive all the blessings of the divine forces. This is perhaps the greatest teaching and it translates from the ceremony into waking life, where the challenge to maintain this firmeza is even greater than in ceremony. With this, I am very grateful for the teachings of Santo Daime which are so supportive and important in this work in achieving collective prayer.

Firmeza, firmeza
Firmness I ask God
Straighten my Heart
I want to be your child

Firmeza, firmeza
I receive with joy
To whom I ask firmeza
is always Virgin Mary

Firmeza, firmeza
I receive with love
To whom I ask firmeza
is Jesus Chris the redeemer

Firmeza, firmeza
To follow the Holy Light
To whom I ask firmness
is at the heart of Jesus

Firmeza, firmeza
Firmness in thought
To whom I ask firmeza
is to our almighty God
To whom I ask firmeza
To be eternally happy

— *Firmeza*, Mestre Irineu.

The medicine became very strong during that first cup and I felt myself drifting further and further from the focus of the music and losing my firmeza. Just as I was struggling to maintain my physical posture in the space, Carioca called for the second cup. *Wow*, I thought. I wasn't prepared for such a strong ceremony. It wasn't just the force of the Ayahuasca itself, but it was the strength of the music and the way that the ceremony was so tightly held. I have since come to learn that by keeping the energetic boundaries of the ceremony clear and well held, this increases the ability for the 'current' of the force of the Ayahuasca to be much more focused and contained in the space. Ceremonies at Ciranda are designed with many *pontos* (points of light) which each hold prayers and intentions for different forces and entities to help secure the space whilst bringing their intentions and blessings to the ceremony.

As the ceremony paused to drink the second cup, I made a prayer to have the strength to keep going, as it already felt strong and there were still two more cups to go. During the drinking period, Carioca again played some recorded music. This time there were some psychedelic rock songs from the 1960s and 70s that I loved so much which took me to a whole new appreciation for that genre and surprised me with how the sounds of that music and poignant lyrics were so appropriate for the moment during Ayahuasca. This gave a whole new perspective on my love of that genre of music and its inspiration from the psychedelic movements of the 1960s. At heart, Carioca is an old-school psychedelic rocker like me, and my heart opened even more to the profoundly exquisite work he does with Ayahuasca.

During the second cup, the music continued to elevate me and take me on many journeys. I wanted to be there with more firmeza, with focus and attention, but for most of that first ceremony I had my eyes closed, taking it all in. My mind was exploring it all, studying what was going on. I relaxed into it and saw that even though I was struggling to maintain my focus on the work of the ceremony with the intention of singing with everyone, this was a very new environment, spiritual field and experience for me — so I just let go. At times the beauty and power of the music was astounding and I would open my eyes with a big smile and an inner 'wow' as I was blown away, with all my expectations and ideas about Ayahuasca and ceremony being expanded, and in such a powerful, colourful and dynamic way. At one point I saw Carioca as the consummate shaman in disguise, with his calm, still presence, simple demeanour and understated presence, whilst he delivered a psychedelic banquet of sound, spirit and energetic colour in pure harmony that called for me to explore its depth. Carioca appeared to me as the cosmic guide of a multi-dimensional psychedelic church. What was equally impressive was the calm, still presence of the women singing with him and the gorgeous harmonies and grace expressed through their voices, again inspiring in me a desire to learn more and develop myself to gain that skill and poise.

Around halfway through that second cup, Carioca paused and asked me if I would like to share a song. This is usual practice in Ciranda ceremonies, where anyone who has songs and prayers to share will be asked if they would like to sing or play for the ceremony. During each cup there are one or two pauses from the work of singing from the hinario, and Carioca opens the ceremony for 'special songs', which are the contributions of the participants. This is a beautiful way for each person to have an opportunity to play and sing whilst on the force of the Ayahuasca. Carioca describes Ciranda as a school of music, and learning to play in ceremony is an important part of the study. It also creates inclusion and participation for everyone, no matter what level of musical skill or confidence they have, to share in a safe and non-judgmental way. Everyone is encouraged to support each other within this culture of sharing in a group, and even for those who may struggle with confidence and nervously wobble their way through a song, the vulnerability and heart put into it is often very touching for the whole group. It is also a gift to be the one in the spotlight, so to speak, in that moment to feel the loving support of Carioca and the whole group. This was the first time I had played a solo song in ceremony in the many years since I had been drinking and I was quite nervous but I did manage to play a scratchy version of one of my own songs on my acoustic guitar. How good it felt in the moment and experiencing the sound and feel of my voice and guitar under the influence of Ayahuasca was a revelation. This also opened another door of study to become proficient at sharing in this way, which both scared and inspired me.

After around four to five hours of singing and praying, Carioca stopped and called for a pause to the ceremony. This was the usual structure of Carioca's ceremonies, where after the second cup there was a pause of sacred silence. We were told there was a fire outside and we would be called back when it was time for the third cup. After we broke for the pause, I sat there, smiling and just taking it all in. Keren-or approached me and suggested that I might enjoy seeking out one of the hammocks hanging between the trees in the garden as a great place to rest for the pause. She was right. After spending some time around the large fire that had been lit in the garden, I found a hammock and lay there under the trees and the stars, contemplating my life and my journey that had led me to this point. I felt overwhelmed with gratitude and peace in my heart for Spirit guiding me to such a beautiful and spiritually nourishing place. I was also filled with excitement for the possibilities of what I might learn and discover at Ciranda and with Carioca and this beautiful, humble and welcoming community of people I had found. I also really appreciated this time in the pause to just be with myself, be with nature, alone in my own contemplation and silence. In all my time that followed at Ciranda, this practice of silence in nature during the pause produced some of the deepest, most important and enjoyable moments of my experience with Ayahuasca. I was reminded of those first ceremonies in the Amazon, bathing and drifting in the sublime beauty of the sounds of the forest, with the emptiness of my mind in total immersion with nature and the universe.

At the end of the pause I wandered back to the Cura room for the next part of the ceremony. Carioca was there, ready to serve the next cup. Some gentle music played while the room and everyone felt very sensitive as a gentleness permeated the space. For this part of the ceremony, it is Carioca's tradition to turn the lights out, with just the light of the candles on the alter illuminating the space. Carioca then played a soundtrack he had compiled of recorded music from all over the world with a great many different styles of music. This is the part of the ceremony that Carioca calls the 'meditation', where we can sit in the dark and journey into the astral and visionary state of the miração of Ayahuasca. I was used to this kind of journey being accompanied by a recorded soundtrack after so many ceremonies with Silvia, whose ceremonies work only with this style of musical journey. The music in Carioca's playlists for these meditations is a deep journey into sound and musical styles, and also an important part of the study of music which I immediately enjoyed. Like the live music played during the first two cups, the meditation soundtrack was a diverse and colourful banquet of sounds and styles that was reflected in the colour and depth of the miração I experienced. I noticed on this first night that my mind was very active in taking it all in, contemplating and trying to work things out. Again, in this third cup I just let myself drift with my active mind, allowing this new experience to filter into my awareness, knowing I would have plenty more ceremonies to refine my mental and spiritual discipline in the ceremony with this new format I was still learning. Carioca would later explain to us how the recorded music soundtracks to the meditation part of the ceremonies were essentially a study in music, with many diverse examples of music from all over the world and their accompanying different rhythms, styles, harmonies, progressions and instrumentations opening pathways of consciousness in the mind through sound.

> *It is the responsibility of spiritual music to learn from all the musical traditions, to track down long-forgotten sources and to bring back into the limelight the original function of music — its links with the deepest in human experience — without, in the process, falling into naive eclecticism.* — Peter Michael Hamel, *Through Music to the Self.*

As the sun started to come up and the light began streaming through the trees into the garden and into the ceremony space, the participants lay serenely or sat contemplating and journeying. After the intensity of the ceremony, with such strong Ayahuasca and music, I had the sense that all of us had been through some big moments and now there was a calm presence of stillness as the new day began. As the morning progressed, the music on the soundtrack became more energetic and playful, inspiring some to get up and dance, including me. At the end of the playlist at Ciranda there is always a recording of the song of the *Uirapuru*, a native bird from the Brazilian rainforests that is known for its beautiful and complex song. After the call of the Uirapuru we all then prepared for the final part of the ceremony, which is singing together again to call in the energies of the new day, of rebirth in love and joy. By this part of the ceremony the Ayahuasca is subsiding and there is a relaxed and gentle energy as Carioca begins with songs for the sun, for rebirth, existence, and for the morning and the new day. After another hour and a half or so of singing together and special songs, Carioca called the final song of the ceremony, which we sung standing up. This is called *Canta com Amor* (Sing with love) which is a rousing song with dancing, laughing, smiling and celebration. At the final close was a vibrant, cheerful and very Brazilian celebration, with participants calling *Viva!* and then a final release of all the energy from the ceremony through moving the body and singing with a lot of vigour and joy, shaking it all off and harmoniously landing back into the body with gigantic smiles and into the heart and joy. Afterwards, Carioca gave a little inspirational talk and we all hugged and chatted excitedly.

I am the morning star
I am the child of love
When I accept existence
I feel the embrace of the whole universe

I enlighten myself of immensity
I enlighten myself of love
In the silence of my being
In this divine mystery of love

I am the source of the light of my heart
I am the Queen of this flower
I am the source of the light of my heart
I am a love star

— *Estrela da Manha*, Carioca Freitas.

After the close, I went up to Carioca and gave him a big hug, and thanked him enormously for such a beautiful and powerful work and for all the teachings. I expressed my surprise and humility for what I had learned. He thanked me and said, in relation to me sitting with my eyes closed for much of the ceremony, 'So you don't like singing?' This took me a bit by surprise and I said, 'Yeah I do, very much!' I vowed to make a stronger effort to be more present with the music in the next ceremonies. He seemed pleased with my response. I contemplated his words a lot and was very touched by the way he was encouraging and provoking me a little to illicit my dedication to the practice. And I have come to notice this is a strong way common in Santo Daime communities, where we all support each other in the development of our growth and firmeza in the spiritual work of ceremony.

Harmony, truth and forgiveness
Are the three points
Securing this union
I ask my brothers and sisters
Pay attention
The master of the astral
Is watching the session

The diseases that appear
Are discipline
For those who make themselves worthy
Ask the spirits
Healers
The line of Arroxinha
And Jesus Christ the Redeemer

Have faith and hope in the request
To think of God
And our Virgin Mother
Do not be afraid to die
And if you run away
It's worse for you

With calm and tranquility
Your path will lighten
Reminds you of the old Juramidam
He is always present
And holds your hand

— Harmonia, Verdade e Perdão, Vera Froés.

At breakfast on the morning after that first ceremony I explained to Carioca the challenges I had experienced during the ceremony and the realisation I had so much to learn from him and from this lineage. He expressed his observation of my humility and said that he appreciated that, and that he could work with me based on this. I wondered if he had noticed how much I had been talking before the ceremony about all my other experiences, which I realised showed that I wasn't being very humble. In all my years of working with Ayahuasca up until that point I had experienced many people who had little or limited experience yet spoke authoritatively about Ayahuasca as if they were experts, with some even writing a book on it after a month of two in South America. I came to comprehend the depths of work, dedication and practice that Carioca had done to get to the level of mastery I witnessed in him and that I had felt so strongly throughout the ceremony. I was yet to fully grasp the depth of the study it would take to understand the faith, the courage and challenges of fully committing to a lineage such as this, in particular the way of the Daime. At this stage this was still quite unknown to me. There was a maturity in the culture and approach, and even the way people communicated, about the ceremonies and Ayahuasca that I observed and sensed in those present who were experienced at the retreat. On one hand it was overwhelming, being out of my depth and comfort zone, but on another hand it was a relief to find a great teacher who was so open and loving and humble, and to find in front of me a great challenge offering an immense field of study, which excited and greatly inspired me.

My eyes, heart and mind were wide open at Ciranda. I was keenly focused on everything that was unfolding, taking it all in like a sponge, and I noticed my spirit was intently engaged and willing me on with keen intent toward this new study. We did some workshops on percussion and finding the rhythm in my body, and Carioca encouraged me to practise more with the percussion; he said he saw a gift in me for that. We did a little sharing circle where he gave each person some percussion instruments. We each had to enter the middle of the circle and just let the spirit flow through us and the instruments, allowing the natural rhythm of our body's flow. Something happened in that moment and I had a memory of being with the Aboriginal medicine man in Central Australia when a force had pushed me into the middle of a corroboree and my spirit had taken over and I had danced while the people chanted around me. I also remembered being with the Yawanawá when I had let go in the dancing circle and entered into the current and become a channel of the force. This kind of *mediumistic* shamanic ability was becoming stronger in me and was something I would continue to develop over time. Learning with Carioca in his light-hearted, loving and playful way was a pure joy and I was happier than I could remember being in such a long time. This joy, love and music is the doctrine of Ciranda and the work of Carioca; it was making so much sense to me and was really effective, as I felt myself growing in these teachings right from these early beginnings. This inspired trust in me, reminding me of one of the Hawaiian spiritual precepts I had learned: 'Effectiveness is the measure of truth.'

During the second ceremony, two nights after the first one, we gathered in much the same way, although this time there was a different hinario to sing from which was more complex, with more diverse harmonies, rhythms, deeper spiritual teachings, prayers and intentions. Just as I had become so determined to increase my focus, my firmness and practice, the work became a lot more challenging! I smiled as it all unfolded, astounded at the majesty of Ayahuasca and Ciranda and everything that life had to offer. This feeling of gratitude was very strong and inspired me to dedicate more to the teaching being offered, to work harder. During the pause on this second night, I sought out one of the hammocks again and lay under the stars, taking it all in. I gently drifted in and out of miração, and back to my contemplative thoughts. During the miração, Ayahuasca came to me clearly and said: 'Stay here. Learn from Carioca. He can guide you and teach you many things. Stay here at Ciranda and you will integrate all of the gifts you have been given in this life. Here you can bring everything together that throughout your life you have been learning and developing within yourself.' *Wow*, I thought again. This brought me to strong attention. What a blessing it was to receive this guidance. My mind went over so many possibilities and dreams of staying at Ciranda and learning from Carioca. This also made sense: I could learn from Carioca, whom I had already identified as a great teacher I respected and shared much in common with. Ciranda offered a space to explore art in much the same way I had been expressing my own art. I had so much in common with Keren-or as well, and people were asking about my bodywork practice and spiritual healing work. I could feel things changing and a new life direction emerging that was bringing a lightness to my heart.

The morning after the second ceremony I sought out Carioca at breakfast. I wanted to share the message I had received from Ayahuasca. When I sat down with him I saw he was excited and he said, 'Lore! I had a message from the tea: it told me to train you and teach you to hold ceremonies like I do, and showed me a vision of you travelling the world doing this.' I was shocked and honoured to hear this, and the synchronous messages from Ayahuasca were undoubtedly a clear sign. I told Carioca about my experiences and expressed my gratitude again. We had a laugh about it, about the wonder of the universe and destiny and fate. It seemed like a new pathway had been set and I had found myself at the beginning of a whole new journey. I had had no intention of becoming a facilitator of ceremony when I arrived at Ciranda, and I had already been humbled in my place as a student, a 'newbie' in this space — which I had been enjoying. I remembered the vision and message from my first time in the Amazon, when Ayahuasca had clearly shown me I would be a facilitator of Ayahuasca ceremony and how I had rejected the idea. Despite Carioca's message, I still wasn't convinced being a facilitator of ceremonies was something I wanted to do, but I was definitely up for the journey of music, spiritual growth and discovery.

With Carioca at Ciranda

It had been nearly 11 years since I had first drunk Ayahuasca, and even though I was in a completely different setting, different land, different forest, different lineage, the guidance of Ayahuasca maintained a constant flow of a narrative that was unfolding within the Dreaming of my life. I attempted to calm my mind and my excitement, as I didn't want to get carried away with ambition or enter into some state of fascination where my ego might get involved. Spirit had guided me to this place. The visions and messages I had received from Ayahuasca and my guides were being mirrored in my manifest reality, encouraging me to maintain faith and trust in the unfolding of this path being given to me by Great Spirit. Within this realisation was also the lesson to trust in life and trust in the flow of Spirit, to cultivate humility and to honour all of the gifts and blessings being given to me. To always remember the responsibility that those gifts are given with and which belong to Great Spirit, and to trust in the path of the flow of creation from this source.

My mission now was to fully open my heart to the love of creation and to embrace my path with grace and humility. I still struggled at times with a lack of confidence and with insecurity. I was beginning to understand on a deeper level how this insecurity, which at times I was good at masking, would often manifest as behaviours like seeking approval or needing external validation. These were a hindrance to the humble emptiness required to be an instrument of the Divine, a pure channel of Spirit. At that moment I had no idea of the beauty, magic and challenges this path would present to me. Looking back now, I miss the innocence and naivety I had then but am grateful for the wisdom and peace that life has subsequently given me on this path. The final prayer at the end of every ceremony, Carioca's song *Canta com Amor*, so simply encapsulates all of these teachings on this magical path of love. I was blessed and enchanted by the magic of Ciranda, woven with such masterful love and joy through music from the heart. A profound reminder of the beauty of this life and of all of this creation.

Sing with love
Work with love
Trust with love
Joining all together, I AM
Love, love, love
Sing with love
Sing, sing
Sing with love

— *Canta com Amor*, Carioca Feitas.

As the retreat unfolded, I became deeply immersed in the teachings being offered through Carioca, the spirituality of the ceremonies and the culture of Ciranda, the music studies and the visionary art. Ciranda offered an abundant banquet of all of the things in life that I loved so much. I could feel myself being stretched spiritually and my thinking changing, as I learned and discovered new things about practices of holding ceremony and new spiritual insights. I was also integrating the big change in my life's direction after having decided to stay at Ciranda and keep studying indefinitely. Carioca had given me a set of techniques to learn on the guitar which were much more difficult than I could have imagined to integrate but they gave me a good focus for daily discipline in my studies. He suggested it would be beneficial to switch from a steel string acoustic guitar that I had played all my life to a nylon string classical guitar, which was more suitable for Brazilian guitar techniques and the jazzy arpeggios he was beginning to teach me. One of the biggest challenges was to start from the beginning with guitar playing, as my self-taught technique was full of bad habits that needed to go. So, whilst learning new techniques I also had to unlearn old ones. I was up for the challenge, though, and kept my focus.

On one of the nights of the retreat Carioca took us to the edge of the forest and asked us to sit facing it. We were to drink some Ayahuasca and sit in the dark in the presence of the sounds and spirits of the forest whilst Carioca sat behind us with his drum, ever so gently and very slowly scratching the skin of the drum with his fingernails to produce a sound like the low, purring growl of a jaguar. Occasionally he shifted the velocity of his fingers or made quick swipes and even a few deeper beats at times. He seemed to be doing this for a long time. As the miração arrived I could feel the strong presence of my black jaguar spiritual guide around me, with the scraping of fingernails across the skin of the drum having become the claws of the jaguar scratching the bark of a tree. I had become very familiar with my jaguar guides over many years since discovering them through different shamanic practices and times in the jungles of Brazil and Peru. This was another thing that we shared in common: Carioca is also connected to the jaguar, or the black panther, as he calls it.

During the fifth ceremony of the retreat, we sang from Carioca's most recent hinario called *Aquarela*. This songbook is, from my perspective, the most psychedelic of all of the hinarios he has developed. The name Aquarela was given in honour of the colours of the music of Brazil and the songbook has 111 songs that span the breadth and diversity of the harmonies, rhythms, musical colours and culture of the whole of Brazil and beyond. The musical complexity of the songs and their great diversity made it the most difficult of the hinarios to sing and to study. The first song of the hinario, *Aquarela do Brasil*, is a celebrated Brazilian classic that combines the imagery of Brazil's natural beauty with the rhythm of samba, drawing parallels between the painting (aquarela) and the vivid expression of Brazilian culture through music.

Each of the songbooks Carioca has created increase in musical complexity and the variety of colour in the music and the meanings of the songs. Carioca says that Ciranda is a school of music 'where we drink the tea Ayahuasca', and each hinario progresses the studies of music, beginning with the first hinario, *Samasati*. This has mostly simple chord structures, melodies and arrangements and mostly simple hymns from the Santo Daime and Umbanda lineages. Aquarela is by far the most complex, with musical progression and styles within it that challenge even the most accomplished musical maestros. The complexity and depth of the meaning of the songs and the prayers also increases with each hinario. Aquarela includes more Indigenous songs, unusual chord progressions and meandering psychedelic arrangements, but also deeper insights into our humanity and love, relationships, emotions and the depths of devotion to God through our human experience. I had fallen in love with Brazil many years prior, and it was through the music, its feeling and the exquisite and unmatched beauty and passion of the Brazilian Portuguese language that, through poetry and playfulness, we can express love and devotion for God, for nature, each other and the Earth.

What did you teach me, Brazil?
My song!

— *Rio Amazonas*, Dori Caymmi.

When Carioca announced the pause during the Aquarela ceremony, the force of Ayahuasca was still very strong within me. I had been feeling the presence of my guides and some caboclos. Without thinking I got up and started walking towards the forest. I didn't have any time to pick up a torch or a water bottle, I just walked. I had the sensation I was being 'walked'; that is, a force was moving me without me being in control. I knew that sometimes I had experienced this kind of mediumship in the past, and just allowed it to happen. As I approached the entrance to the forest, I received a powerful and vivid vision. This vision showed a scene of some kind of sacred marriage that was going to happen at Ciranda, that at some time in the future I would be 'married' at Ciranda. The message that came with the vision was the spirits of the forest and Ayahuasca were offering me an opportunity to enter into a sacred alliance with them which would lead to my path being united with the divine forces of the forest. The forest spirits said they would teach me and offer their alliance on the condition that I stayed there for as long as it took and to forget plans of returning to Australia or going anywhere else until I had learned what was required. Upon receiving this vision a sudden realisation occurred: fulfilling this vision would mean an enormous sacrifice on my behalf. I dropped to my knees amid a rush of thoughts and visions of all the things I would have to let go of in order for this to occur: a six-year relationship, any plans I had for the future, any thoughts or plans of returning to Australia. I would have to give up my return ticket home and just accept being there, with the forest teachers, under the tutelage of Carioca and Ayahuasca, and not have thoughts of leaving or escaping if it became too challenging or giving in to other desires that might want to take me away. I was just to stay at Ciranda and dedicate myself there and to the studies required — for however long that would take.

After this intense realisation and vision an overwhelming feeling of grief, but also of relief, came over me. It was clear what I had to do and what was going to happen. I got up and my legs kept walking me into the forest. As I entered the forest trail, the canopy of the forest immediately blocked out any of the moonlight; it was pitch black in there. Somehow, as I was being walked by Spirit, I knew exactly where to step, including over slippery stones with my bare feet, crossing creeks as I walked up the path towards the waterfall. Some fears and doubts washed through my mind but I continued to walk at a brisk pace with sure-footed confidence. When I got to the waterfall I looked up and saw the full moon shining brightly right in the middle of a gap in the forest canopy. The timing of the encounter with the beings of the forest was perfect and I felt a lot more confidence when I saw this positioning of the moon. I walked up onto the rocks at the base of the waterfall and began dancing while I sang three songs. The songs were strangely arranged with sounds and some language that seemed to be coming through me from the beings of the forest. The last of the three songs was a chant for protection; the other two were blessings from the forest and the connection to divine light.

After channelling these three songs I stayed for a moment and contemplated what was happening. Then I could sense many beings in the forest had gathered around me. They began communicating, thanking me for listening to them and being open. They said it was rare to find someone who was able or willing to listen to them and they offered to give me their blessings, teachings and gifts, if I followed the path being offered and stayed there to do the studies required. They told me there would be more songs to receive and that the Indigenous people who had once lived there were no longer there to sing the songs of the land. They asked me to do this and to honour the land and to sing the Dreaming of the land back into manifest creation. I felt honoured and contemplated the depth of the studies available to me at Ciranda, the forest itself and all its mystery, the music, the spiritual traditions, the teachings of Ayahuasca, the intricacies of holding ceremony — all growing in my art and with the humility of sharing in community whilst maintaining an open heart with faith and devotion.

I contemplated my experience, and was reminded of teachings from Indigenous Australia. Years later I read the book *Songlines* by Margo Neale, who reports on the traditional use of songs in 'singing up the land' and says 'songs were learnt' as people travelled to the places named in the songs and the rhythm of walking took the song into their body. Through the body, the song became dance, which in turn became ceremony. In ceremony that night, Carioca had sung a song that honoured Country and the memory and knowledge that it held in the same way as told by Indigenous Australians aligned with the Dreaming of the Whole Earth. The song *Origins* lists the names of places in *Tupi-Guarani* language:

> *Caçapava is — Clearing in the forest*
> *Jacaré eee! — Aligator in the waters*
> *Guaratinguetá — White herons*
> *Pindamonhangaba — To play with the fishhook*
> *Tremembé is — Tribe of the region*
> *Paraíba is — River of the muddy waters*
> *Paraitinga is — River of the clear waters*
> *Paraibuna is — River of the dark waters*
> *Bocaina is — Open cut in the mountains*
> *Mantiqueira is — The rain that drips*
> *Tupinambás Charrúas — The Indians from the forest*
> *Puris Guaianazes — The people of the forest*
> *Tamoios Guaitacazes — The owners of the forest*
> *Guarani nation — May Tupã protect you*
> *Paraíba killed — The Indians of the forest*
> *Paraíba knows*
> *Paraíba saw*
> *Paraíba cried ...*

— *Origins*, composer unknown.

At Ciranda there is a strong rule that people don't wander off into the forest during ceremony, and I personally wouldn't advocate or suggest that inexperienced people do this. I did mention it to Carioca at breakfast the next day and someone heard me and was shocked: 'Aaah! You're not allowed to do that.' She looked at Carioca, who then said 'Lore's an Aboriginal' before continuing to eat his breakfast. I smiled and knew that he understood. I explained some things to him about my process and he just nodded and didn't offer anything further, as usual honouring my personal spiritual experience without comment.

As the retreat came to a close, my cup was overflowing with new teachings and homework and a new direction set for my life. I felt great and, as always at the end of these retreats, there was some sadness at saying goodbye to everyone and letting go of the beautiful space we had all created together with so much harmony, love, deep sharing, vulnerability and safety that Ayahuasca always seems to bring when we gather in honour of this divine sacrament. I was also relieved, as I was looking forward to some time alone and to reflect on everything that had happened. The next program at Ciranda would be the Cura retreat, which is a very specific style of work with strong roots in Santo Daime. I was a bit reluctant about this at first, as I had some preconceptions, judgements and resistance towards the heavy Catholic influence in some of the practices and hymns of the Santo Daime. I was encouraged by people who were familiar with it to make sure I experienced this retreat, as it is the foundation work for Ciranda. It was an enormous challenge, but also a very big key to entering into the lineages, traditions and practices of Ciranda. I knew that my new commitment would require me to do this fundamental work, and despite some doubts and avoidance, I would be there for the Cura.

During the retreat Carioca had given me a lot of studies for techniques on the guitar, some that were quite challenging. He told me to just focus on refining the techniques for the time being and not to play any songs. I had also acquired all six hinarios for Carioca's calendar, which contained hundreds of songs to study. During ceremonies I had accumulated a lot of visions and instructions for artwork too, with many paintings ready to begin work on. It seemed like my plate was full, and after a trip to Rio to visit friends and organise some things, I returned to Ciranda, where I would spend the next few weeks alone, before the Cura would begin.

Healing and intention

> *I take this drink*
> *That has incredible power*
> *It shows us all*
> *Here within this truth*

— *Eu Tomo esta Bebida,* Mestre Ireneu.

As I got into a daily rhythm in the forest of studies, practice and meditation, I was also facing some emotions around letting go, memories of my life and my childhood, past relationships and the nagging fear of abandonment haunting my subconscious mind. I always enjoyed my own company, yet a part of me was still yearning for connection. I knew that in my solitude and with everything that had happened on my path, staying still with the intention of focusing on inner work and spiritual studies was an opportunity to look deeply into this abandoned part of me from childhood which was still calling for healing. Sometimes this feeling could lead me to distraction, to look for some kind of connection that could lead to insecurities and addictions, and as I sat alone in the forest at times I tracked my mind to see where it would go when I felt those old emotions. Spending hours sitting and meditating and observing my mind at the waterfall was a great way to process and let things go. Singing alone in the forest was also growing my connection to the music and integrating the forces of nature and the beings of the forest into my music. Many times I felt like I was back in the Amazon in the Yawanawá lands, seemingly in two places at once. I continued this practice for nearly two years at Ciranda.

When it came time for the Cura to begin I was still feeling waves of emotional turmoil and some mental confusion; I knew this was preparing me to see and to know what I needed to focus on for my healing. Carioca's Cura is a very powerful three days of ceremonies, where we drink six cups of Ayahuasca per night and also consecrate *Santa Maria* (marijuana) before the fifth cup each night. The consecration of the two holy sacraments Ayahuasca and Santa Maria is a long-held tradition of the Santo Daime religion, and for Carioca, the only time he will consecrate Santa Maria is during the three Curas held every year. So I prepared myself mentally and physically for three nights in a row, 12 hours each ceremony and 18 cups of Ayahuasca in total.

A beautiful group of people from all over the world arrived at Ciranda for the Cura. Many of them had been attending without fail for nearly 30 years with Carioca. The hinario is an adaptation, with some differences, of the Cura hinario that was developed by Padrinho Sebastião and which is also a foundational practice in all Santo Daime churches that follow his lineage. Carioca was a *fardado* (initiate) in the Daime in the final years of Padrinho Sebastião's life and this work is a continuation of Padrinho's legacy and traditions that goes back to the original teachings of Mestre Irineu from the 1920s. I felt blessed and grateful to be participating in this lineage, even though the work itself seemed daunting. As I chatted with people before the first night, my assessment that this would be a very challenging three days of practice seemed accurate.

The ceremonies were held in the space built for them, the Cura room, which we had used for the recent retreat. The format was different in that there was a tall, round table in the centre of the room with crystals, candles, pictures of Mestre Irineu and a large *Cruzeiro* — a type of crucifix adopted by Santo Daime that has two crosses instead of the traditional one. The second bar that crosses the crucifix signifies the connection between the divine and earthly realms, the cosmic balance, and the fusion of Christian, Indigenous and African spiritual influences.

There were about 50 people participating, and this time instead of sitting on floor-level chairs, everyone sat on normal elevated chairs, all in close proximity to each other. Carioca served the tea from the tall middle altar, whilst we all continued to sing for the drinking phase of the ritual. This drinking ritual included traditional Santo Daime songs sung on rotation that inspire courage and firmness, much more in the style of traditional Daime rituals. I was very impressed by the beauty and the strength of the singing. The Santo Daime music held a relentlessly focused rhythm, with similar structures and melodies across each song and was very different to the serpent-like meandering, multi-dimensional psychedelic kaleidoscope of musical styles of the other ceremonies I had participated in with Carioca. The hymns moved along at a fast pace and at regular intervals we were all called to stand, sing a hymn and then sit back down again. The relentless nature of this practice does not give any space to drift away or become distracted; it calls you to attention and keeps reminding you to stay firm and focused. The hymns themselves invoke healing, our self-judgement, call us to examine our minds and egos, our devotion and connection to God, our humility and surrendering to nature and the Divine. For the first four cups we charged up the intention for this deep healing with powerful singing, amplifying the intentions. I loved learning all the songs and as the force of the tea grew stronger in me with each cup, the challenge to stay alert and focused increased. I found this a very enjoyable, but certainly difficult, challenge.

The Cura felt like we were charging up a big battery with prayers and intentions before we took a break of silence in the pause and returned to consecrate Santa Maria prior to then drinking the fifth cup and entering into a meditation with the lights out and one of Carioca's psychedelic soundscape recorded playlists. By the time we got to the meditation, all of those charged up intentions were unleashed in the body and mind for accelerated clearing and healing. I had never experienced anything as powerful as this healing before. I was very impressed by the technology of the design and function of the ceremony. The consecration of Santa Maria was a revelation: it helped the whole process of supporting me through some of the most painful self-realisations, childhood and past-life memories I had ever experienced. At times I cried to the depth of my soul, at other times I laughed at the wonder of creation. By the third night I was starting to go deeper into the wounds that I carried from my father which I had begun to get in touch with on my first journeys with Ayahuasca, 11 years previous. This time I uncovered memories of abuse in my childhood and, as I was comprehending this, I felt a very strong wave of nausea overcome me. I had only vomited less than five times during Ayahuasca in those 11 years, but I knew that the Cura had dug up something very old and ancient and I needed to purge it from my body.

I made my way to the bathroom and kneeled in front of the toilet. As I was purging I saw a huge tunnel with psychedelic patterns containing layers and layers of past lives unravelling like some kind of cosmic ball of string. As I was unravelling and going deeper into the depths of this tunnel, I saw that there were eons of ancestral pain and karma releasing inside me as I managed to purge out what seemed like a psychedelic parasite into the toilet. Once released, all the karmic patterns were gone and all that was left at the end of the tunnel was a stunningly beautiful tribal crest with Celtic artwork — a shield of ancient ancestral honour. I received a message that this was the purity of the origin of my family's ancestral lineage before the corruption of colonial history and the onset of karma. I took some time to take this in and felt relief and gratitude to have done such deep and hard work to release all of those karmic patterns and centuries of war, abuse, displacement, colonisation, theft of land, manipulation, twisting and contamination by the dark forces that have interfered in our human evolution across so many generations. I went back to my seat in the ceremony feeling empty but clear that my mind, body and soul had been thoroughly washed clean. There was nothing left but stillness. As I sat meditating, I allowed the music to wash through me and I rode every wave of sound as though on a cosmic sea, yet held in the arms of the Divine.

For the close of the Cura, after drinking the sixth cup we stood for the entirety of the *Cruzerinho*, which is a sequence of 12 songs Mestre Irineu received in the forest. On that final morning of the Cura, I sang with more pride, vigour and joy than I had ever done in my entire life. There were times I was singing and having visions at the same time while tears were streaming down my face, as I was unable to hold back the tide of emotions wanting to release. This was all while always practising the teachings of maintaining focus and firmeza and faith in the spirit of Ayahuasca to guide me through it all. The practice of Cura that is grounded in the Santo Daime culture of firmeza, commands humility, holds us strongly in the prayers, and does not allow much space for avoidance. This allows us to dig deeply into the darkest and most stubborn parts of our psyche, releasing healing and self-knowing. I also noticed that as the Cura went on, the telepathy between everyone there was becoming stronger. At times I knew what people were thinking of me and in some cases knew the thoughts and judgements and projections they might hold. I realised they probably were seeing this in me too, which was a very humbling realisation and gave meaning to the practice of mindfulness and the line in the opening hymn: 'The vibrations of my thoughts are the forces of God in me, which are stored here and radiated to all beings.' This greatly inspired me to be a better person, and to do all the work necessary to integrate 'all the divine qualities which are in me and in all beings', as stated in the opening prayer known as the *Consecration of the Sanctuary*. Cura was a powerful and deep journey, abundant with cultural and spiritual teachings and the opportunity to know myself at a very profound level. The camaraderie and closeness amongst the brothers and sisters present for the work was expressed with loving care and support. I knew from my experience that the greatest challenge would now be to integrate all I had learned.

> *Flower of the waters*
> *Where it comes from, to where it goes*
> *I'll do my cleaning*
> *In the heart is my father*
>
> *My father's abode*
> *It's in the heart of the world*
> *Where there is only love*
> *And it has a profound secret*
>
> *This profound secret*
> *It is in all humanity*
> *If everyone knows each other*
> *Here inside the truth*
>
> — *Flor das Àguas*, Mestre Ireneu (Cruzerinho).

The experience of cleansing my mind and of the telepathic field was a great revelation. Whilst very confronting, it also showed me how, in the current age, with all its psychic interference, conditioning and tampering with our DNA which shuts down our senses and disconnects us from our source, we have become accustomed to a world and a system of secrets and hidden motives and agendas. Many of these forces — censorship, consolidated media narratives, suppression of dissenting knowledge — are well documented. From historical campaigns to erase Indigenous spirituality, to the exposure of CIA MK-Ultra mind-control programs, to modern alliances between governments and tech giants censoring alternative worldviews, we can trace a pattern: the control of consciousness. Whether through fear, propaganda or distraction, the thread remains—the disconnection from our spiritual sovereignty. Cura shows that spiritual work such as this, alongside other practices such as meditation, is a powerful tool for cleansing the mind and opening humanity to our natural telepathic ability. It is also a sign of the times that are coming, as we shed the skin of all the hidden agendas and learn to trust our natural telepathic ability, the age of hidden agendas will soon be behind us. As I write this, there is a growing political movement which is dismantling the secrets and bringing entrenched corruption to light. We are seeing that the Dreaming of Ayahuasca is preparing us individually and collectively to navigate in a world of openness, transparency and truth in the light. This is the turning of an age and it is clear to me that Ayahuasca is one of the vital harbingers of transformation, as it always has been for the original peoples of the Amazon.

In the Huni Kuin culture, the chant '*Eskawata kayawai, kayawai kei kei*' is commonly sung in Nixi Pãe (Ayahuasca) ceremonies and is a call for transformation/healing. Chants like this are spiritual tools that exist as part of a living tradition where the meaning unfolds in the context of ritual. The intention is to invoke healing that brings transformation, or transformation that brings healing, since healing and transformation are one and the same.

My first experience of the Cura at Ciranda opened up a world of new teachings and experience with Ayahuasca I had never imagined.

My relationship with the teachings of Christ and Christianity had been healed. I felt comfortable expressing the love of my own 'Christed' heart and the personal responsibility of living in this divine truth. Despite the Brazilian-Catholic language and imagery of Santo Daime, essentially the teachings of love, peace, harmony and forgiveness are universal. The return of the spirit of Christ through the Holy Sacrament from the Amazon made total sense to me. That unconditional, eternal love had always been present within me, but the Cura had given it a new perspective and language with which I could comprehend this and use as tools for my own personal spiritual growth. The call and honouring of old *Juramidam*, the spirit in the miração that carries the presence of Mestre Irineu, also gave me strength and courage through knowing that a fatherly ancestor was always present and guiding. The discipline and structure of the ceremonies created a safe container for my ego to remain humble and for my focus to remain on the altar and the prayers. The challenge to maintain firmness and self-discipline whilst singing my heart out with a group of dearly beloveds on the same path of self-knowing was a true gift. What a great way to experience the return of Christ. This practice is at the core of the work of Ciranda and the blessings that Carioca brings, and I could see the importance of this. The Cura is hard work and not for the faint-hearted but provides a training ground for finding grace, humility and clarity whilst doing Ayahuasca work. Whilst at Spirit Vine with Silvia I had received the guidance and calling to allow the Ayahuasca to express through me, and this practice, with its enduring teachings and training, was a great support in knowing I was able to explore that expression without becoming lost in my ego and the phenomenal realm.

I was now set upon a path of deep studies into the line of Santo Daime that continues to this day. These studies greatly enhance the tools and experience of Ayahuasca and also translate into teachings and insights for how I live my life. Whilst Daime is at the root of Ciranda, it is only part of a grand constellation of spiritual lineages within the context of a non-denominational movement. We embrace these beautiful foundational and effective teachings whilst maintaining openness to all paths, all teachings and practices that come from the Divine in the myriad of diverse expressions that exist across the world and in all of humanity.

Carioca always emphasises the intention of being free of attachments to dogmas and doctrines and of trusting and embracing our unique expression of the Divine. This is the difference between being a sovereign being of the Earth under natural and cosmic laws, and not just a follower of human constructs or religious beliefs. I personally revel in the celebration of traditional practices which hold meaning and purpose, while flying in joy and abundance of spiritual grace in full trust of my own free will. Ciranda has inspired a large circle of friends around the world who all embrace this uniqueness and gather to pray and practise together without coercion or manipulation through guilt-inspiring dogmas, but through pure joy in love and togetherness. The music carries us with the prayers, within the practices and traditions that create the form as a container for this work that, at its heart, is blessed and inspired by the Holy Grace of the Golden Divine Light of the Sacred Forest in the form of nature's gift known as Ayahuasca.

> *Authentic Christianity is a science of self-realisation. Through love and charity, we mould our being like the son of God who was sent to us, discovering his kingdom on Earth as it is in Heaven. Nothing men [sic] did or will do can surpass this truth. The message preached by Christ is not a doctrine for masochists. From the trilogy — love, forgiveness, and suffering — the last is, without a doubt, the hardest to swallow. But what He really wanted to show us is that through this inherent condition we can conquer our own suffering, as well as fear and death. — Alex Polari de Alverga, The Religion of Ayahuasca.*

The others who had journeyed together through the Cura experience also looked washed clean from a psychedelic baptism. The difference in how I was feeling before the Cura and afterwards was stark. Gone were any doubts or mental confusions. My path ahead was clear and there was much to do to continue these studies and development within this grand work. Following the Cura, Carioca invited me to visit him at his home in the mountains of Rio to receive the next teachings.

In the first lessons with Carioca he had instructed me to focus on my techniques with the guitar and to study the music from the songbooks. I stayed with those instructions until after the Cura, when I sat with Carioca and he gave me the next teachings which were to learn the whole hinario of the Cura. That meant learning 60 songs, one-third of which are sung *a capella*, while the rest all had guitar progressions and two different *arpeggios* (finger-picked patterns of notes for each chord). The goal was to learn all the songs and then be able to sit with Carioca at the next Cura and play all night long for the three ceremonies. This felt a huge mountain to climb: learning the complex, jazzy arpeggios, studying all the chords and progressions, rhythms, tempos and the meaning and feel of each of the songs. I was only just starting to feel confident with all the techniques, and this all felt like starting from scratch. I had the time, the focus and the will to do it though, so I just got on with this program.

When I sat down with Carioca to begin learning the songs from the hinario, he said to me: 'You come to Ciranda and you come to the doctrine of the music. There isn't another doctrine here, no shaman, no guru. The music is the only doctrine; I don't abuse you with one. It's not my idea, it's not my conception — it's music. Music is music, it's pure. I cannot manipulate you with music; that's another thing that is not my department to know. Music is music, and with what I am teaching, you will be free. For me and for Ciranda and for everyone, if you want to stay, there is nothing to grab you. It is the opposite; it's your investment for yourself. Once you get your wings in November in Cura, you can fly forever.'

I spent the next few months living at Ciranda and communing with the forest, the waterfall and the beings that live there. At times there were one or two other people there but I mostly stayed alone in my cabin or sitting painting on the veranda of the main house while listening to the songs from the hinarios with the words in front of me. There was virtually no internet there, which limited distractions, though at times my mind became its own distraction.

Every day I would go to the waterfall to sit and listen, and to sing to the forest. Sometimes beings would gather around me and sometimes give me messages, teachings and music. I did a lot of work integrating the teachings and the healing I had received. There were days when I would be sitting in my cabin feeling a bit too lazy to walk up the hill to the waterfall and some nature spirit would flash past my window and move over to the forest path, calling me in. Other times I would receive songs and sit and write words and work out chord progressions. After the teachings of the Cura and the Daime, my experience in these months was more about connection to the forest and the natural world — a shamanic journey. Carioca was very encouraging of this study and didn't ask questions; he just gave gentle guidance, support and good humour. He and his family would sometimes visit on weekends and we would do small ceremonies in the living room or study some of the more complex songs from the Aquarela songbook, learning harmonies and vocal parts. At other times I made regular visits to Rio to see friends or play music just to break the isolation. I also visited Carioca and we would usually talk about music and spirituality.

> *The work of the true shaman implies purifying his/her life to become very pure, so he/she does not become part of anything bad. When one has passed through process they can see deeper, they can see what a person does, what type of person one is, and why they are sick. When I purified myself, and the angels gave me my spiritual knowing, I could see who knew the other worlds and who did not.* — Pablo Amaringo.

For some of this time I was also letting go of many things, grieving over old wounds, broken relationships, lost childhood innocence, betrayals, and struggling to integrate new ways of thinking and being that were not coloured by the memory of those wounds. This tested me and I would observe my mind wanting to go back to these old and redundant ways. This was a good lesson in the great challenges of integration, and life was presenting me with some reflections to help with this process too. Having done so much work with Ayahuasca, it was vital to spend this time to integrate it all properly. This, I believe is very important, and I still see many people on Ayahuasca or other sacred plant paths who go from ceremony to ceremony but don't take the time to integrate. This can then delay them facing themselves in life and making the changes that take time and dedication to truly comprehend and embody. This classic pitfall of modern spirituality has become known as 'spiritual bypassing', and I was very aware that I didn't want to go down that path. To this day I see this as part of the shadow of the new-age spiritual movement and something I have found very difficult to navigate within my own communities, both in Brazil and Australia. The nature of the ego can be very strong and to go beyond it requires a level of faith and commitment that most people don't reach, meaning their spirituality or their Ayahuasca experiences don't often go beyond the realm of the phenomenal realm, the ego's fascination or lower-astral dramas followed by self-aggrandisement and attachment to glamour, image and social status. Meanwhile, they may find it hard to break out of their life's patterns and yearn for meaning and purpose whilst lacking the courage to truly do the work, to fully shed the skin of the old and endure the painful process of rebirth.

> *After the dazzle of first encounters, a deepening of the spiritual work with the Daime showed me how difficult it is to remove all the absolute layers of one's personality. My consciousness was a real junkyard, full of useless stuff, a junkyard with aspirations of becoming a sanctuary.* — Alex Polari de Alverga, *The Religion of Ayahuasca.*

This time and process was all about deepening my faith in Spirit and in life. I found that through music I was able to get deeply in touch with my joy. Through the music my inner child was coming alive and I felt like a young boy again, playing in the garden and the forest of Ciranda. Everything felt new and inspiring. Life had taken on a magical warmth and glow and I was very much loved and nurtured by Carioca, Keren-or and the Ciranda family. In these months at Ciranda there were retreats and festivals and many ceremonies and I embraced every one with pure delight and sincere diligence towards my growth within the work. Keren-or mentioned in one sharing before ceremony how much delight she had in seeing me fall in love with Ciranda and embody its spirit so fully. I felt truly at home; free to be myself and humbled by the lessons and teachings it offered. As I came to know the songs, I grew more confident in the ceremonies and naturally found my place there as it all became second nature. I became adept at learning how to hold space, supporting others and supporting the physical and spiritual space. Dance became a big part of my expression and at times in ceremonies my spirit would get me up and dance me, which was such a joy and so healing for my soul. I came to learn more and more that dance is a big part of me and the medicine that I bring.

The music at ceremonies in the big conga at Ciranda was usually amplified and often involved a full band of talented world-class musicians. As I learned the songs and gained confidence in my voice, I was invited to be in the front circle on a microphone as part of the guiding chorus. Before each ceremony I would anxiously prepare a song or two, knowing that Carioca would call me to share a 'special song' along with all the other musicians. I had to deal with so many emotions and nervous anxiety each time I was called. This in itself was a big part of the learning. Dealing with my inner critic and self-worth was a big challenge to overcome and it seemingly didn't matter how much positive feedback or encouragement I got; I was still deeply critical of myself. This was a large part of my healing.

Those days, weeks and months of many beautiful ceremonies and intimate retreats where I would get to meet and know people from all over the world was a very special time of self-discovery, as I opened myself up to play and be joyful, recovering my lost childhood. As I had turned 40 before I arrived, this felt like it had been a long time coming. I had never opened myself up as much in my entire life within a group of people. At Ciranda I felt safe in the presence of Ayahuasca, Carioca and the circle of friends. It was also an innocent time for me, where I felt reborn and new in the world whilst still slowly shedding the old skin of insecurity and fear of truly being myself and truly trusting in life and Spirit to guide and hold me. Each ceremony would help me with this: sometimes amplifying the fears, doubts and wounds, other times inviting me into powerful visions and profound realities, then at other times just holding me and healing me in that joy. Dedicating myself to this study, showing up at every ceremony with the intention of learning and growing in the work, the music and the ceremony itself was an immense blessing. Carioca took a break from travelling around the world during the two years I was at Ciranda. After 35 years of relentlessly taking this magic around the world, he wanted to spend time with his young daughter. It was a blessing for me to be present at Ciranda in these times and yet another divine synchronicity on this journey of life, whereby I seemed to be in the right place at the right time to receive the teachings and healing I required.

I want to talk about something
Guess where it is
It must be inside the chest
Or it walks through the air

It could be right here next door
Much closer than we think
The leaf of youth
Is the right name for this love

They have already pruned your moments
They have diverted your destiny
Your boyish smile
It has been hidden so many times

But hope is renewed
A new dawn every day
And we must take care of the bud
So that life may give us flowers and fruit

Student's heart
We must take care of life
We must take care of the world
Take care of friendship

Joy and many dreams
Scattered along the way
Greens, plants, feelings
Leaves, heart, youth and faith

— *Coração de Estudante*, Milton Nascimento.

The spirit of music

All of life — the universe, to make the stars, the Great Divine — is created by music, by sound. It's for this reason that when we are informed with the wisdom of the spirits, we can sing about many things, we can pass on many things. For this reason we are philharmonics, we are made from music, we love music, we have the music inside and therefore we love to hear music. This is why the icaros (sacred chants) exist. And when we sing the icaros, especially the icaros which have been given by the spirits, these serve like miracles to cure people. — Pablo Amaringo.

Living at Ciranda had transformed my life into a great spiritual study and immersion into sacred music: from the basic techniques of guitar playing to opening to mediumship and allowing the force of Ayahuasca, the beings of the forest and my spirit guides to channel through me in the form of music and sometimes dance. I had come to learn over the years I had been drinking Ayahuasca that the power of music was essential to activating the force and potential of Ayahuasca in the body, mind and emotions. Music can be a true manifestation, in the purest sense, of the spiritual vibrations, divine beings and Ayahuasca itself. This is part of the training that we do with Ayahuasca in clearing ourselves, our minds and bodies so that we may become clear instruments able to channel the Divine in its purity. Typically, shamans all over the world will become empty instruments for the sounds of nature and creation to flow through them, and this is part of their role in accessing other dimensions. Not all shamanic traditions work with sound in this way, but it is rare to find one that doesn't.

Almost all people who have partaken of psychedelics, especially Ayahuasca, will express that their understanding and perception of music becomes greatly amplified by the experience, leading to profound states of awareness. It is a universally adopted practice to work with music in Ayahuasca ceremony, even if this is only with recorded sounds or channelling the sounds of nature that, of itself, is a musical symphony, once we attune our senses to it. Modern scientific study and therapeutic research has also found that the use of music in psychedelic therapy is an essential part of the program. Professor David Nutt, in his book *Psychedelics* went so far as to describe music as a therapist in its own right:

> *Music plays a central role in psychedelic therapy because when a person's usual control over the senses breaks down, it leaves a freer, less inhibited way of processing sounds. Music can change someone's whole experience, enhancing the vividness of their mental imagery, activating emotions, thoughts and memories. People feel music more intensely under psychedelics, but it can also take them on a journey, a living dream of personal content, which can enhance the effectiveness of the therapy.*

After all of my experiences with Ayahuasca and my own understanding of the power of sound and music, it made total sense to me that Carioca had established Ciranda and his work as what he describes as a 'School of Music'. Through years of sitting in the dark and listening to recorded music or icaros, I began to feel the strong calling to allow the sounds to flow through me. The power of this in collective form became very evident during my time with the Yawanawá. Being at Ciranda and being a student of music and sound opened a whole new level of awareness and abilities within my own experience. I find this way — the way of a collective musical experience — to be much more powerful in calling the force of the medicine, and thus the potency of the ceremony and the intensity of the Ayahuasca journey is deeply enhanced, whilst the singers are empowered within the experience of the ceremony. What I find is that, as channels to the Divine, the vibration of the sounds of the music merged seamlessly with the divine intent within its prayer is enormously healing for the body and the spirit. The vibrations of the music are physically channelling with conscious intent throughout our bodies.

With music being the 'religion' and doctrine of Ciranda, this enhances the expression of the divine qualities within our humanity and our reality, which is amplified by the prayers to the forces and the spiritual beings who guide and nurture us through ancestral teachings and connection to nature and the stars. The harmony we create through sound and music vibrates throughout our bodies, harmonising every atom, molecule and cell, entraining all matter to return from dissonance back to harmony. This is reflected in the laws of music, where we always see a return to harmony.

> *Many doctors are used to healing their patients with beautiful music. How can music have an effect in the body of another person? In such a way as the soul of man [sic] as well as that of many animals understands the harmony, takes pleasure and delight in it, and thus makes the body more vigorous, so that the heavenly force comes down to earth through harmony and serene music.* — Johannes Kepler.

Even without Ayahuasca, music as consciousness in all its forms is healing. Singing opens our hearts, bypasses the mind and heals the soul. I am yet to meet anyone who is not moved by music in some way. With the sounds and vibrations of the healing hymns, whether they be in the Shipibo style of Icaros, other forms of shamanic chanting or the collective hymns of Brazilian spiritual traditions such as Ciranda and Santo Daime, something magical happens with Ayahuasca within the alchemy of the body, the mind, emotions and the spiritual dimensions. The rhythm of the drums and the chants in the Umbanda and Candomblé rituals sends the participants into trance. If done right, the vibrations of the sounds of the music can activate the force of Ayahuasca within the body and it can shake loose the epigenetic imprints on the human nervous system and reset the original DNA blueprints, thus activating a healing of childhood and even pre-birth traumas, impacting the whole system of the person. Over time, Ayahuasca itself will entrain the practitioner with vocal styles, techniques and even in musical styles with instruments which will create specific effects that transmit the healing and other multi-dimensional spiritual awakenings. I had begun to experience this when I was with the Yawanawá, and without thinking or effort, I would be channelling the songs, sounds and vocal styles. Over the years I have been consistently in awe of the many and deeply nuanced effects my vocal range and abilities have developed after so many hours of singing on the force of Ayahuasca.

> *The shamans use music like a map. Each note and rhythm in the icaros carries intention, pulling you through the layers of your mind and into a space where healing can happen. It's as if the sound itself vibrates with the plant's intelligence. When you're in ceremony, the Ayahuasca opens the door, but the music — it's what walks you through it. It connects the physical to the mystical, syncing your heartbeat with something bigger than yourself.* — Dr Joseph Tafur, The Fellowship of the River.

The openness and invitation to participate in the music at Ciranda is truly a divinely inspired gift for all who choose to participate. I found this openness helped me to in turn open myself to music and this was greatly healing. I had so much shame and fear around expressing the music from within and this, to a large extent, was healed in my time at Ciranda. I very much related to the way Carioca conducted his ceremonies, where each one had a theme based on a different songbook, and he would choose each song based on what the needs of the ceremony and participants were at any moment. This is a shamanic technique whereby he is guided by the Ayahuasca, his spiritual guides or the group itself as to which song to sing. This could often be a meandering, serpent-like journey, where the music might go in all kinds of directions, rhythms, intentions, harmonies and tempos, creating a psychedelic journey across the landscape of the ceremony and within the miração. In this way, the style of Carioca is different to that of Santo Daime, for example, which will have a specific hinario for each ceremony and will usually sing it from start to finish, with the hinario generally being the same each time. This predictability and stability has its own value and magic. For Carioca, the Cura and Umbanda ceremonies are exceptions, as they also follow a linear progression through their hinarios. I find that the snaking jiboia form of selecting the songs and prayers as each moment defines adds an element of mystery and diversity that expands the spectrum of colours of the ceremony and the depth of the miração, as well as expanding the possibilities for healing and growth, often challenging the mind by guiding us through uncharted waters of the great mystery reflected in sacred sound.

What we call music in our everyday language is only a miniature form of that music or harmony of the whole universe which is working behind everything, and which is the source and origin of nature. It is because of this that the wise of all ages have considered music to be a sacred art. For in music the seer can see the picture of the whole universe. All the religions have taught us that the origin of the whole of creation is sound. No doubt the way in which this word is used in our everyday language is a limitation of that sound which is suggested by the scriptures. The music of the universe is the background of the small picture which we call music. Our sense of music, our attraction to music, shows that there is music in the depth of our being. Music is behind the working of the whole universe. Music is not only life's greatest object, but it is life itself.

What makes us feel drawn to music is that our whole being is music: our mind and our body, the nature in which we live, the nature which has made us, all that is beneath and around us — it is all music. We say that we enjoy nature. But what is it in nature that we enjoy? It is music. Something in us has been touched by the rhythmic movement, by the perfect harmony which is so seldom found in this artificial life of ours.

When one looks at the cosmos, the movements of the stars and planets, the law of vibration and rhythm, all perfect and unchanging, it shows us that the cosmic system is working by the law of music, the law of harmony; whenever that harmony in the cosmic system is lacking in any way, then in proportion disaster comes to the world, and its influence is seen in the many destructive forces which are manifest there. The whole of astrological law and the science of magic and mysticism behind it are based upon music. Therefore, the whole life of the most illuminated souls who lived in this world, like the greatest prophets in India, has been music. From the miniature music, which we understand, they expanded the whole universe of music, and in that way they were able to inspire.

Every person is music, perpetual music, continually going on day and night; your intuitive faculty can hear that music. That is why one person is repellent and the other attracts you. It is the music he [sic] expresses; his [sic] whole atmosphere is charged with it. The great charm that the personality of the Holy ones has shown in all ages has been their responsiveness to the music of the whole being. That has been their whole secret.

The difference between the material and the spiritual point of view is that the material point of view sees matter as the first thing, and considers that intelligence and beauty and everything else evolved from it. From the spiritual point of view, we see the intelligence and beauty first — and from them comes all that exists. From the spiritual point of view we see that one considers last to be the same as first, and therefore in the essence of this whole being, as the basis of all that exists, there is music. One can see that in the essence of the seed of the rose there is the rose itself, its fragrance, form and beauty. And although in the end it may not be manifested, at the same time it is there.

The experience of harmony and at-one-ment he [sic] can make everywhere in the beauty of nature, in colour of flowers, in everything he [sic] sees and in everything he [sic] meets. In the hours of contemplation and solitude, and in the hours when he [sic] is in the midst of the world, the music is always there, he [sic] is always enjoying its harmony. And by breaking down those walls which surround him, he [sic] experiences at-one-ment with the Absolute. This at-one-ment with the Absolute manifests as the music of the spheres. — Hazrat Inayat Khan.

The power of the songs from the hinarios is transmitted from Spirit, channelled and received by their composers directly from the force of Ayahuasca, the spiritual beings of the forest and the *Orixás* (forces of nature). The purity and potency of these songs as direct transmissions from the spiritual realm adds to the depth, colour and quality of the ceremony and the Ayahuasca journey. I continued receiving and writing songs during my time at Ciranda and found myself singing songs and receiving music in my head almost every day. At times I was guided to sit and construct what I received into songs, at other times they passed through me momentarily, perhaps for my own healing. Carioca took an interest in my ability to compose music and began teaching me more chords and chord progressions. He likened this to my artwork, as I was also painting a lot at this time and would use a lot of colour and vibrancy to reflect the visions of the mirações I was seeing in the ceremonies. He said that learning more chords and progressions would be like having more colours on my musical pallet from which to create. He explained to me how the beauty, clarity and quality of the music would inform the miração with its colours and depth. These teachings for me as an artist gave me a new awareness into how I could channel my creativity and spiritual gifts into music and art which would be able to inspire and transmit something divine into the world in a physical form.

*My mother gave me
A hymn to sing
It was she who wrote
Using divine notes
She taught me to listen
To read to pronounce
So many beautiful words
From the Goddess of love*

*My mother gave me
A hymn to remember
Formed from small letters
There from the blue sky of the sea
A shawl she wove
With her hands of love
To cradle us
When need be*

*Receive this lullaby
In a very flowery cradle
And our mother that sings
To her beloved child
In each starlet
Is a kiss that she gave
To embellish the sky
Of my master Irineu*

— *Acalanto,* Composer unknown.

As my pallet grew, so did my consciousness and awareness of my craft. As I bathed in the force and energy of the forest at Ciranda and the *Aquarela of Brasil*, working and loving each ceremony and opportunity to sing with this beautiful family and learning to empty myself and channel my creativity, I felt truly blessed and grateful to be given this opportunity. Over and over again throughout my process of study, spiritual growth and self-realisation, and despite all the challenges and mental clamour, the place where I found my peace was with music. In so many ways, my faith is in my music. The more I discover and uncover the music within me, the happier I am, which only inspires more music.

CHAPTER 10

Star Birth

The stars have already arrived
To say your name
I am, I am, I am
I am a child of God

The stars took me
To run across the whole world
To know this truth
So I could be true

I climbed thorny hills
Stepping on sharp spines
The stars told me
In this world, everything is healed

The stars told me
Listen a lot and speak little
To be able to comprehend
And talk with my caboclos

The caboclos have arrived
With bare arms and feet on the ground
They bring good medicines
To heal the Christians

— *As Estrelas*, Mestre Irineu.

Firmness in grace

The first song that Carioca taught me was *Sou Luz* (I am Light), a Daime song written by Padrinho Sebastião, and a significant song in the Cura ceremonies. I understood his intention of passing this song to me as part of an invitation and initiation to the lineage of the Daime that came from Mestre Irineu then on to Padrinho Sebastião and eventually to Carioca (and others). 'Eternal love, engraved in the heart. From you I receive the teachings to expand for our brothers and sisters.' He also mentioned this song as being appropriate for me and which I took to refer to my strong connection to the sun and the many comments people would make to me that my light shines very bright in ceremonies. I felt touched by his acknowledgement and for being seen and respected. My training with Carioca seemed to be a pathway of initiation into the lineage, starting with the Cura and its roots in Santo Daime. Now I had some songs to work on, and not just techniques and arpeggios. Over the next few months Carioca taught me all the songs from the Cura hinario.

Days, weeks and months passed, with most of my time spent at Ciranda and in the forest there. My daily practice included yoga, meditation, walks in the forest, bathing in the waterfalls, communing with nature, painting and studying music. I made a trip to Bahia to collect some things I had left there and to have a little holiday at the beach, and I would make regular trips in to Rio to visit friends and attend music and other events in the city.

The Cura in November at Ciranda in Brazil is traditionally the beginning of the Ciranda season. The calendar opens with a Cura in November and closes with a Cura in May. This time, as Carioca wasn't travelling, there was another calendar of retreats and ceremonies in the tropical winter months at Ciranda. This was great for me, as there were so many opportunities to continue my work, studies and healing with Carioca being around all the time. As the time for the Cura and the opening of the season drew close, I was nervous that I would not be adequately prepared. Knowing that Carioca was challenging me to be ready to play my guitar along with him for the whole of the three nights of the Cura was daunting, and knowing that I would be supporting him to hold space for so many people, most of whom were very experienced and confident in the work, was also intimidating. I kept telling myself that the intimidation was just my ego's fears and insecurities and to just stay focused.

Typically, in the Santo Daime tradition there is a culture of earning an initiated place as a *fardado* (person in uniform), where the initiate is given a star and a uniform, symbolising their spiritual commitment and integration into the community. The act of becoming a fardado marks a significant rite of passage, where individuals take on responsibilities within the group and engage actively in the spiritual practices of the tradition. Carioca doesn't have a culture of initiating fardados as in the Daime culture with its wearing of a uniform representing a commitment to following strict rules and obligations within the church. The culture of Carioca's work at Ciranda is not to oblige anyone with expectations and rules that must be followed. Ciranda is where the spiritual family works together in harmony and self-empowerment and where individuals independently learn and assume joint responsibilities to support the functioning of the space and the ceremonies.

The self-discipline, grace and firmness required for the work at Ciranda were all things I learned through observation, self-motivation, inspiration, direct teachings from within the miração and from Ayahuasca itself, through masters and ancestors, and via the occasional gentle guidance or suggestions from those more experienced in the circle. I love that Ciranda allows and encourages self-empowerment and free-spirited expression. As I have since come to find within the culture of my own ceremonies and retreats, when people feel free to find their own way and their own unique expression, they will almost always strive to be in harmony with the group and to self-regulate their learning, goals and ambitions with the ceremonies and the culture of the work. Throughout all of my professional life and also in healing and community development, supporting people to be self-empowered always leads to effective and lasting outcomes in healing and personal growth. Without empowerment, individuals can easily become dependent on the 'healer' or the structure to keep them in alignment, leading to codependence and the risk of unhealthy dynamics or relapsing to old behaviours. In those months I had been at Ciranda, I certainly felt supported and empowered to take on responsibilities within the ceremony and outside of it that were things I was choosing or was being guided to do within the force of the Ayahuasca.

The Lord of the Dance

Carioca offers everyone the opportunity to receive a star (a small brooch) as an initiatory experience. In contrast to the Daime, there are no set expectations or obligations to receive it, but when you feel ready and called then you can ask him and he will give the star with a little ritual moment during ceremony, where he will also play a song that is also a spiritual gift and will become known as the initiate's 'star song'. I noticed Carioca was very good at choosing a song from the hinarios that was perfect for the person it was chosen for and somehow accurately reflecting their spirit and personality as expressed in ceremonies and in life.

Leading up to my second Cura, I asked Carioca if I could receive my star and he agreed. On the second night of the Cura during the fourth cup he began to play the song *Senhor da Dança* (Lord of the Dance) — one of my favourites from the *Ciranda Poim Poim* hinario. When Carioca put his guitar down, everyone kept singing and looked at me; I knew it was my turn to receive my star and that this would be my song. Carioca and his wife came over to me and I stood while they pinned the star onto my shirt, before he sat down and finished the song. Then we all sang together and I felt so elated and a sense of achievement for having reached this moment in my life. At the end of the song, there was a call, 'Viva Lore!' before moving onto the next song of the Cura. So many things about that song spoke directly to my heart and spirit. As the ceremony went on, I contemplated the depth at which Carioca could see me and how much he honoured me for who I was with this gift.

All that I believe
Comes translated
In the light that comes from you
All that I believe
Glitters beautiful
With the blue sky

The Lord of the Dance
Presented himself in you
Watered the plants with love

In you I journey
By your time
Your bare feet
Dancing in the wind
You brought a message
Of your perfume
With you, the flowers
Dance love

All that I believe comes translated
In your movements
Everything that is beautiful
comes glittered
Inside your eyes

All that I believe
comes translated
In the light that shines in you
All that I believe
Glitters beautifully
Form and spirit are one

— Senhor da Dança, Nei Zigma.

I felt touched by Carioca's choice of star song for me. Dance has always been a big part of my spirituality and my expression. Ever since I was a teenager I had been a cosmic dancer; when I was younger I felt self-conscious that people would comment on this. Over the years of trance festivals and ecstatic dance I had translated this into many moments in ceremonies at Ciranda, allowing the movement of Ayahuasca to flow through me and to dance me. Carioca often acknowledged this in me. The song itself is an ode to the shaman or medium who receives and channels the blessings of the plants and expresses this through dance.

In Tibetan Buddhism the Lord of the Dance is known as *Chenrezig* or *Avalokiteshvara* in Sanskrit. I relate to this deity, also known as the Lord of Compassion, a *bodhisattva* (embodied compassion) who looks over all beings. I could see this in myself in the way I was always aware of everyone in the ceremony and able and ready to assist where possible, with my whole life dedicated to service.

> *The Lord of the Dance; the supreme image of a demi-god, who perceives the effects of all actions. The prince of movement, dancing in an ecstatic embrace with his female counterpart (White Tara).* — Timothy Leary et al., *The Psychedelic Experience.*

Closing prayer of the Cura, Ciranda, Rio Bonito, Rio de Janeiro, Brazil

Sky dancing

After the Cura I received a message from Kenemwa, a Yawanawá friend I had met in the village of Mutum. She told me that she and some family had come to Rio for a ceremony and had brought the Elder pajé Tatá with them. She invited me to the ceremony and we all met beforehand on the beach in Copacabana. This was a beautiful experience, as for some of them it was the first time they had seen the ocean. I smiled and enjoyed every moment of their pure joy in experiencing a day at the beach in Rio. These Yawanawá from deep in the forest, so far from the ocean, made friends with every vendor who came along to sell them all the random items typically peddled on the beaches of Rio. They invited each vendor they met to their ceremony, which was going to be later that night.

We gathered in Alto da Boa Vista, a beautiful rainforest area in the mountains just behind Rio. The ceremony was hosted by the *Guardiões da Floresta* (Guardians of the Forest), a group founded by a Huni Kuin pajé who had a vision to educate non-Indigenous folk from the city in the ways of the forest people, and to create a group that would be able to guide others and protect their culture from any profiteering, interference or cultural appropriation. It seemed they knew there would soon be a lot of people coming to visit them. The Guardiões have since gone on to become a well-established group protecting and serving the traditions and medicines of the Amazon whilst supporting access to them in ethical and sustainable ways.

The ceremony was held outside under the stars with a large fire. This was typical of what I had experienced before in the village, beginning with traditional chants and prayers, rapé and drinking Uní, followed by songs with guitars, drums and other instruments and a contemporary fusion of sounds. I noticed that the people from the group working there who had seemingly done some deep studies with the Yawanawá before had a much harder and more serious edge than I was used to at Ciranda. The Yawanawá themselves were very relaxed, comfortable and in good humour. The ceremony and

Sky Dancing, Lore Solaris, acrylic on canvas, Rio de Janeiro, 2015

my visions were beautiful, and it was a great pleasure to reconnect with my friends and the prayers and tradition of the Yawanawá, this time in the mountain forest of Rio de Janeiro.

During the ceremony after the second cup I had a powerful vision in which I could hear some astral chanting that sounded like Australian Aboriginals. I instinctively stepped away from the circle and closer to the edge of some bushes and began to dance, just letting the spirit flow through me. I had visions of Aboriginal ancestors in the stars; they were dancing through me. This felt like a strong transmission and energy and I felt a little shy, as I didn't want to disturb the ceremony. Later, in the morning the music continued and we did some traditional Yawanawá dancing around the fire. Afterwards one of the Guardians came up to me and said he had seen me dancing Spirit during the ceremony and that this had given him a powerful healing energy and strong vision, for which he thanked me a lot. I felt much better, as I had been a bit self-conscious and a vision like this had not happened so clearly or directly before. Reflecting on my experience, it seemed like some Aboriginal ancestors had come to join the ceremony, connecting the spirit of Brazil and Australia — a theme I have often experienced in spiritual experiences over the years. When I returned to Ciranda I painted a canvas of my experience, which then went on to become the cover of my first songbook called *Sky Dancing*.

Forces of nature

One of Carioca's ceremonies practised at Ciranda is known as the 'Umbanda ceremony' and is sung from an hinario called *Forças da Natureza* (Forces of Nature). Alongside its roots in Santo Daime, Carioca's work is founded in the traditions and ancestry of the Afro-Brazilian lineages, where the focus is on working with the *Orixás*, or the forces of nature, as described in previous chapters. In the religion of Umbanda, a ceremony is commonly known as a *gira* (gyrate). This is where the participants will enter trance whilst the *ogã* (drummer) plays strong rhythms on the drums while also in trance. The trained mediums, through the vibrations of the drumming rhythms and prayers, then receive and incorporate the different spiritual entities of the lineage and often gyrate or dance as they perform healing, either on themselves or on other people in the ritual.

As Ciranda is not a place of traditional Umbanda practice, and Carioca doesn't work with mediumship in any formal or traditional ways, his Umbanda ceremony is held as a *bailado* (dance). In the Saint Daime tradition, a bailado is a sacred dance of devotion and healing where the body becomes a vessel for divine energy, guiding the soul through a spiritual journey of connection, transformation and unity with the cosmos. The bailado is held in a circular, back-and-forth motion with variations, depending on the timing and rhythm of the music. Effectively the circle and the movement strongly hold the force of the current and the Ayahuasca, keeping it in the body. The effect of this is to bring the energies of the forces of nature into the body for physical manifestation and healing. The unbroken circle and the group discipline of the movement and rhythm hold all the participants securely in the work. This also has the effect of preventing mediumship and incorporation (embodying spiritual beings) and brings the focus to the group prayer. In my experience, the work with mediumship requires another level of training, presence and attention in order to safely hold the ceremony. Umbanda and some Santo Daime churches have strong practices and initiations in this form of work. That is not to say that incorporation doesn't happen at Ciranda (I have personally experienced it); commonly it does, but it is not the focus or intent of the work. This is also an example of the syncretic nature of Brazilian spirituality and religious practices where, in this instance, a Santo Daime practice is used to secure the field of the ceremony invoking the Afro-Brazilian Orixás.

Carioca's Umbanda ceremony is held in the large conga, with sometimes up to 100 people in concentric circles. There are only a couple of chairs in the centre and a few mattresses around the back in case anyone needs a rest or has a strong process. Typically, the gyrating motion of the bailado will hold all the participants in the circle and the force of the Ayahuasca gives energy and focus to the practice of the dance. This is a very strong work with Ayahuasca, as the forces of nature bring a lot of healing on many levels, connecting and grounding us to the Earth. It trains the participants to be physically strong and alert, developing firmness and fitness with Ayahuasca and ceremony. Where the Cura and Santo Daime work can often be very celestial, invoking Christ, saints and angels, the Umbanda work is more earthy and grounding, invoking the elements wind, earth, forest, stone, fire, metal and water in all of their forms. During the ceremony there are four servings of Ayahuasca tea: three cups incorporate dancing with just Carioca and others on drums, then there is a pause of silence with a fire, a fourth cup and sitting meditation in the dark, followed by another hour or so of drumming, singing and bailado in the morning.

That the African and Indigenous 'cultures of resistance' have gained so much strength and popularity in the mainstream in Brazil is a beautiful thing. The African slaves had to hide their religion, as they were tortured and killed for practising it. *Capoeira*, a kind of Brazilian martial art/dance, was developed as a way for the people to continue their practices whilst the slave owners thought they were merely playing games. Umbanda was developed in part as the people were being coerced into Christianity; they developed a system of incorporating Christ and the saints into the African cosmology and religious practices. Santo Daime was also a fusion of Christianity and Amazonian culture and beliefs infused with African influences. This weaving is a sacred union of different forms of spiritual doctrines and beliefs honouring the Divine and these are harmonised in practical and meaningful ways. Even today, persecution and discrimination still exists towards Afro-Brazilian culture and spirituality, which are labelled as 'devil worship' along with other medieval prejudices. It is a victory of Spirit that modern Brazilian music and even the universally popular *Carnaval* celebrate the Afro-Brazilian spirituality, its connection to Indigenous Brazilian culture and singing for the Orixás. Spirituality and religion are woven deeply into the fabric of Brazilian culture. This is in stark contrast to Australia, where our mainstream culture is vacant of any depth of meaning and connections to the Divine, whilst ignorantly dismissive of Indigenous spiritual practices. Santo Daime and Umbanda are natural allies through ancestry and are a rich spiritual constellation which aligns us spiritually, opens our awareness to nature, and conditions us to live strong, well and in harmony with the Earth, the cosmos and each other.

I am always astounded at how Ayahuasca can open the pathways of the mind, allowing conscious access to vast cosmic landscapes. The field is vast, with layers of conscious awareness and potential points of focus, described by Carlos Castaneda as 'assemblage points' of energetic and conscious attention(s). Working with large spiritual constellations such as syncretic religions provides a language, culture and road map. There is no destination, but ultimately we find ourselves alone with God and all of creation. Anything else is the mind in its internal or external forms. Despite the interwoven spiritual guides and guardians, the road map to the stars is infinite. Beyond the forms of creation, deities, geometries, gods and demi-gods is the spacious emptiness of the void: transcendence, perfect peace. From the pulsing rhythms of the drums of Umbanda to the chants of the masters, and to the caboclos of the forest and beyond, there are many divine beings and musical elements that inform the spiritual constellation of this Ciranda, bringing teachings, healings, colour, sound, inspiration, art and creation. Each one is a point of light in an expanding realm of experience, healing and wisdom. These are beautiful allies on the path and a beautiful Dream to dance in the forest in harmony and in honour of all its divine glory, inspiring humility in gratitude for this life and this existence.

The rainbow-coloured diversity of spirituality expressed through Ciranda is a revolutionary form of the evolution of Brazilian culture and its interwoven cultural, racial and spiritual influences. Here is where human adaptation evolves spiritual belief and practice as reflecting the culture and environment from ancestral, spiritual, social and environmental influences. With profound beauty Carioca has adapted this sacred alliance of spirituality and culture into a form that can be accessed, understood and embraced by people from all over the world.

Here I am now
In the unity of the Creator
I greet with praise
The names of the Lord

Christ, Buddha, Tupã
Babaji, Shiva, Xango
Allah and Juramidam
Synonymous of love

Heavenly court
Orient and Mother Earth
Santo Daime and Umbanda
Infinite stars

Immeasurable Immensity
Multi-coloured rainbow
This rosary is so great
Petals of the same flower

— *Aqui, Agora, Estou*, Chandra Lacombe.

Expanding pallet of musical colours

After my second Cura experience, lessons with Carioca took on a different flavour, with him teaching me a variety of different musical styles, techniques and songs. He continued to encourage me to develop my musical pallet of 'colours' whilst at the same time keep learning and integrating the teachings within the meaning of the songs. He would often choose a song to teach me, which would challenge me not just in learning the techniques within the music but also give me a contemplative focus relative to the meaning of the song and how it might be relevant for my current challenges and life lessons. Many times Carioca would give me a lot to think about and reflect upon in my personal and spiritual growth through his music lessons. These would often meander from personal stories and healing challenges, relationships, music theory and the spirituality of Ciranda to practical advice on navigating my path with ceremony and in life.

Summer at Ciranda was an exciting time, with a lot of ceremonies held over several retreats that Carioca refers to as 'festivals'. After the November Cura there was a break for a month or so before the Christmas and New Year's festival. These festivals last two weeks each and include six ceremonies with five songbooks and a sixth ceremony which is highlights from each of the five books. The third ceremony is Umbanda, with dancing and drumming. The Christmas and New Year's festival and the Summer Festival, which is at the end of January into February, both have the same format. The Christmas festival was a revelation for me and my experience and relationship to Ciranda. This gathering was attended by many people from all over the world —people who had worked with Carioca for a long time, some for over 25 years. I reflected on how great it was for me to suddenly be at these ceremonies, which had become like home after nearly a year at Ciranda, and to now be sharing with people with so much more experience, knowledge and skills in the work. I spent a lot of time deepening connections, making new friends and learning as much as I could, with more expansion into greater firmeza and teachings in holding space.

The Christmas festival really showcased the remarkable musical talent that Ciranda had fostered over the decades of Carioca's work. Sitting in the front circle at the commencement of the first ceremony of the festival, I could feel the strong sense of excitement and anticipation of everyone at the gathering, like at a family reunion. There were many world-class musicians present, some with their own legendary status within Brazilian cultural movements. I was really grateful for the training and practice I had gained since studying with Carioca and my time at Ciranda leading up to this epic moment. Even after almost a year of dedicated studies and dozens of ceremonies, I quickly realised there was so much still to learn as I sat with many experienced Cirandieros (people of Ciranda) within a well-established culture. The good feelings of family, love and happiness at being there all singing and praying together with so much beauty and power in the music seemed to elevate the whole experience and provide a strong container for the force of the Ayahuasca to be even more powerful and intense than I had yet experienced. Being part of this awesome group as we sang to Spirit helped me to realise the potency and potential of this work. My eyes and mind were wide open and, after so much time already at Ciranda and so many moments of awakening and humbling, this was another level altogether.

The quality of the music and the harmony we created singing those songs and prayers together in the Ciranda forest temple took me to that next level within myself and my understanding of how this process works and how it was unfolding within me. As I had often experienced in my years drinking Ayahuasca, there would be ceremonies where my level of attainment of spiritual grace and union with the Divine would seemingly evolve to a new level. This hadn't always come easily, as the higher vibrations and higher awareness I was immersed within would challenge my sense of self, show me something greater than I had experienced before and humble me to my place, highlighting the limitations I needed to overcome. This was especially evident when it came my time to sing a special song during these ceremonies with 80 people listening and watching me, including some incredible musicians whom I respected so much. This really challenged my confidence and self-esteem.

After the first ceremony at that Christmas retreat I felt shy and intimated by the experience and afterwards Carioca made a comment to me that I have always remembered. He said that even though these world-class musicians were technically very competent and had great skill in their musical craft with years of experience playing in ceremonies, technique was not everything. Whilst Carioca always encouraged pursing improved technique with music, this time he told me not to compare myself based purely on the technical ability of others. He pointed out that musicality was a quality of heart and soul and that when one sings with pure heart, deeply connected to spirit and feeling, this quality is far superior to good technique alone.

He must have sensed my insecurity amongst the group, and I found his words reassuring, especially as he had commented on my strong spiritual connection, feeling and heart that went into my music. He encouraged me to honour and nurture this. I was realising that all my years of study within the miração of Ayahuasca had given me a strong foundation in the spiritual and visionary side of the work, and I came to see that this was a realm of practice in which I had become quite advanced. I was very aware of the current within myself and the collective space, and I could sense and see where others were at in relation to this current. I learned not to compare myself to others, even when the great musicians attracted a lot of attention. This was another good reminder to be mindful of my self-worth and to not make comparisons, as we all have differing paths, focus and levels of attainment on the journey of spiritual awaking. We are all given different gifts by Great Spirit in an ever-evolving, weaving tapestry of creation. The harmony we find amidst these gifts and different perspectives and focuses is a work and a gift as well. I appreciated Carioca noticing and mentioning this to me, showing me again that Ciranda was a balanced and equal environment amongst a circle of friends without rank or privilege.

A powerful element of ceremony that I had come to know well at Ciranda was the sense of beauty and reverence for the ritual and the music, that high vibration of love. Being present with the music, singing in the light and being shown beauty and the openness to be vulnerable could often trigger in me certain anxieties relating to insecurities and that same sense of not being 'good enough'. It is common amongst people in the Ciranda culture to traverse these insecure feelings when seen in the light. The call to divine truth can sometimes make us want to hide in our shadows, rejecting the beauty, love and acceptance for fear of being seen and being vulnerable. This is a common trauma response that stems from childhood wounds, where we may recoil from receiving love when we have defence mechanisms built in our psyche to protect ourselves from rejection. I like to remind myself and others of what I learned: to confidently sit tall in the presence of ceremony, open the heart to the music and expression, and embrace the eternal student in all of us. To call on our faith and stay strong — not collapse when confronted with dear or self-doubt. Sometimes these fear reflexes are subconscious, hidden from our awareness, and Ayahuasca may show us. Ceremony reminds us to return to the light of self-love and the unconditional, eternal love of the Divine.

> I arrived in a white hall
> That had many flags
> When I approached
> Was a Brazilian flag
>
> I saw Christ's eyes
> His eyes met mine
> Immediately I thought I didn't deserve
> And he disappeared
>
> After singing to the Master
> Overcoming suffering and pain
> He presented me
> A garden of beautiful flowers
>
> — *Cheguei Numa Sala Branca*, Flavia Passos.

I noticed in these ceremonies that the group prayer would become stronger as each ceremony progressed and as the festival progressed, with the final ceremony being the most powerful due to the harmony and unity within the music, which was taking us to higher states of ecstasy, depth and connection. This showed me how the music naturally harmonises the group and the energy, which leads to healing and higher states of awareness. I noticed as well that as time and the ceremonies progressed, the connections, humour and flow of life outside the ceremonies at Ciranda also took on the same qualities of heightened awareness and harmony amongst the group. Like anything that has light shone on it so powerfully, the shadows also became highlighted. Every now and then we would see someone lose firmeza and focus, dropping into a deep process of confronting and releasing trauma or facing their shadows, whilst the group would continue to hold space, maintaining the harmony securely in the current, which holds each of us strongly through all of the ups and downs of the process of the Ayahuasca journey. The power of music to harmonise and thus create healing would help us to overcome the rational thinking mind whilst entraining our voices and instruments to new levels of unity. I reflected on flocks of birds all flying and moving through the sky in natural harmony and how this happens naturally with humans in our biology, our hearts and spirits. The combination of Ayahuasca and music is a powerful force for realising the sacred union through harmony, and for weaving a flight path of love and joy in peaceful unity through prayer and song.

> *In music, the miracle of entrainment is made explicit. The performer's every gesture, every micro-movement, must be perfectly entrained with the pulse of the music, or else the performance falls apart. Watch the members of a chamber group — how they move as one, become as one, a single field. We have become accustomed to such miracles, the extraordinary faculty of jazz musicians to "predict" precise pitch and pattern during improvisation ... The miracle springs not so much from individual virtuosity ... as from the ability of a large group of human beings ... to sense, feel and move as one.* — George Leonard, *The Silent Pulse.*

Even with a large group and such powerful and vibrant music, the depth of the miração and visionary states of Ayahuasca still maintained their potency. Being now trained to be able to hold the miração and be present with the music and ceremony — akin to holding multiple awarenesses at the same time — was a skill I was enjoying exploring and gaining confidence in. Despite my love and passion for the music and the prayers, the silent pause and the meditation were times when I also greatly enjoyed inner exploration. Navigating in the visionary state always deepens my relationship with Ayahuasca. All the lessons and the connections with people would bring new contemplations and teachings from within the miração, sometimes giving me paintings or songs. I had become very refined in navigating this inner work examining my own psychology, behaviours and emotional states to gain more self-awareness and healing. I noticed that not everyone had the same dedication to doing the internal work in these times during the ceremony. Part of me wanted to talk to them and encourage them to do the deeper, inner work, especially when I could see they really needed it. I respected the culture of Ciranda, though, to allow people to find their own way and to trust in that unfolding process. At times I did notice some people had a tendency to avoid the depths and find distractions. I did my best to refrain from being judgemental and allowed their own natural unfolding without offering unsolicited advice.

I started to see this tendency within certain people to avoid inner depth and self-responsibility for our minds and our behaviours. During my time at Ciranda and in other circles I had been to, there would often be people who seemed to create more drama amongst the group or with others, and these would also be the ones who would look for attention, wander around, go for a smoke, find someone to chat with or more during the pause or the meditation. Plenty of people were resisting letting go of the mind and the phenomenal reality. I have come to see one phenomenon where people, usually men, but it can be women, will go from one ceremony to another to different groups, not really committing to any one lineage or path of study but floating around from one group to the next, accumulating songs and paraphernalia, and thus be able to put on a show to impress each group. Carioca mentioned something about these people, saying it would be hard to trust them because they always changed from one moment to the next, depending on which group they were in or where the latest scene or trend was taking them. Sometimes these people would be great musicians, but I noticed that often they lacked depth or emotional intelligence. I did find myself becoming frustrated at times with social dynamics, but chose not to engage with this projection of mine, knowing that my own studies were valuable for my own self-awareness and growth, even if nobody ever noticed. This phenomenon has also spread around the world through 'medicine' music and communities to where beautiful young singers take the Ayahuasca music, singing to forces and spirits they don't even fully understand, often without connection. I simply saw this as inspiration to deepen my own studies and inspiration and develop my own authentic spiritual connection.

Minimal music has meantime become en vogue, and like so many things that have become subject to marketing mechanisms, it has often acquired an unpleasant taste. Musicians, performers and conductors began to "make" minimal music without having the slightest idea of the spiritual consciousness that this music carries. They simply play and conduct periodical music, knowing that it might bring them money or success. Music, however, has to do with consciousness. Great Musicians are called "great" because they have scrutinised not only the music but also the thinking, the spiritual position and, often enough, also the religiousness of the master whose music they play. Playing minimal music without spirituality means doing finger exercises, playing empty music. — Joachim-Ernst Berendt, *The World is Sound — Nada Brahma.*

Carioca said to me one day that we can't just brush aside the ego, and that music requires the ego to find our expression and confidence, even if this is not the driving force. It is a fine balance, because a good-looking, skilful musician can easily gain a lot of attention and mistake this attention for something meaningful, creating attachment and behavioural patterns. But this is inevitably shallow and unsatisfying. All of this is different stages on the spiritual awakening journey and Ciranda, with all of its colour, allows everyone to be whoever they are, at whatever stage of that journey they may be. There is something really beautiful and freeing about that permission. In later years, I would realise how strong this ego force could be and see the challenge of having the right boundaries to be able to contain it within groups and community. As both Mestre Irineu and Padrinho Sebastião found, the thing they couldn't resolve within their communities was dealing with drama and politics amongst the people.

Carioca perceived that I was becoming a bit distracted and confused by confusing and distracting people. It made sense when he gave me the song *Segue o Teu Destino* (Follow Your Destiny) to study and encouraged me to focus on my studies and not be swayed by the shadows from others' trees. The song is a musical adaptation of a poem by the Portuguese poet Ricardo Reis, one of the heteronyms of Fernando Pessoa. The lyrics are set to music by Brazilian composer Sueli Costa. This collaboration resulted in a piece that blends Portuguese literary tradition with Brazilian musical colours and feelings. It is one of the most challenging and complex songs from Carioca's *Aquarela* hinario, and a great example of the depth of musical styles and spirituality expressed through the work of Ciranda. Later, I would include this song in my own first hinario, *Sky Dancing*.

Follow your destiny
Water your plants
Love your roses
The rest is the shadow
From other people's trees

Reality
Is always more or less
Than what we want
Only we are always
The same as ourselves.
Gentle is just living
Great and noble is always
To live simply
Leave pain on the altars
As an ex-vote to the gods
See life from afar
Never question it
The answer lies beyond the gods.

But serenely,
Imitate Olympus
In your heart
The gods are only gods
Because they do not think themselves so

— *Segue o Teu Destino*, Fernando Pessoa.

The Summer Festival at Ciranda was held in late January into early February in the sweltering humid heat of the tropical Brazilian rainforest. The heat was an extra challenge when navigating the ceremonies and maintaining firmeza, especially the dancing of the Umbanda ceremonies. I enjoyed the challenge of the forest humidity, as it reminded me of times in the Amazon. The Summer Festival ceremonies were even bigger than the Christmas festival, with up to 100 people attending per night. The energy of these ceremonies was a little wilder, with not as many experienced people attending and a lot of new people or some that had less experience there. Whilst the music and the force of the Ayahuasca were still very powerful, it was definitely less focused and less contained. I also noticed there was certainly more drama and healing going on in the community during and outside the ceremonies. I enjoyed it all very much: all the challenges and personalities, making new friends, playing music all day long and deep powerful ceremonies which were embellished by the camaraderie of the group to support each other through the work and with the music. There seemed to be as much excitement and joy at being together as a spiritual family as there was in the ceremonies themselves, highlighting to me the importance of community for Ayahuasca work for support and integration. I also noticed how over the duration of the retreat the harmony, good feeling and unity amongst the people would increase after each ceremony. I felt more at home than ever and found myself guiding and supporting many people during this time also, as I was now stepping into a role of guardianship of the space and of the participants. I also now had many years of experience training in group therapy and psychotherapy with Silvia Polivoy. This was a natural progression and I felt totally comfortable in it, satisfied that my confidence was coming along with me on the journey now. It is quite natural for me to be in this helping and healing role, as it is a large part of who I am, and with so many years in health, healing and community development, I was able to draw upon a lot of my skills.

Meeting the Huni Kuin

At some point in the summer I was invited by some friends to attend a ceremony in the mountains of Rio, the same venue where I had been with the Yawanawá some months earlier. This was also organised by the Guardiões da Floresta, but this time they were hosting some Huni Kuin people, who come from a neighbouring part of the Amazon to the Yawanawá, in the state of Acre. This was the first time I had met any Huni Kuin people, who were also known as the Kaxinawá, although they were shedding this title, as it was an anthropological name, rather than their traditional name of Huni Kuin, which means 'True People'. In early 2015 the Huni Kuin were not well known outside of Acre or small communities in Rio and São Paulo, whereas today they are known throughout the world. This first time with them was a very sweet experience. The Nixi Pãe (Ayahuasca) ceremony they held was not so strong for me: I could sense and tell from the way they worked that they had a beautiful and deep connection, but the force they were calling was not so strong. Two young pajés had come over from the forest and I had the feeling that, for some of the participants, their perception of the pajés' abilities was greater than their actual levels of attainment. They were very sweet and friendly young men from the forest and I really enjoyed my time with them, more so from a musical and cultural perspective. I had the feeling that I would one day seek out some Elders or more accomplished pajés here in the future. I greatly appreciated the work they were doing there with the people from Rio who were studying with them and being initiated as their guardians. My curiosity would take me to visit the Huni Kuin people in the years that followed.

Music workshop

In March, the next program at Ciranda was the 'music workshop'. I had already been to the Music and Visionary Art workshop a year before, but this retreat was purely focused on the music and is one of the traditions of Ciranda and one of the core foundational programs of the lineage offered by Carioca. The workshop is a two-week retreat where the focus is on learning, playing music and studying together in groups. The focus for Carioca was to work on arrangements and playing and singing in groups. All participants were invited to present a song to the group of around 30 people who had come from all over the world and were of all

Music workshop in the conga at Ciranda, Rio Bonito, Rio de Janeiro, Brazil

levels of musical ability. Those who presented a song would then form groups which would spend the next couple of days arranging and rehearsing the song. Five or six musical groups formed every few days and worked on a song together. Carioca would visit the groups in their rehearsals and offer suggestions on arrangement, vocal parts and harmonies, rhythms and techniques. There was also a flautist and other professional musicians who would visit the rehearsals adding parts to the arrangements. Each night there would be a concert where we would play the songs while Carioca would introduce other songs from the Ciranda cannon and we would study and arrange them as a group.

Throughout the days of the workshop there would also be smaller workshops such as 'samba school' (Brazilian rhythms and percussion), guitar workshops, voice, and lots of jamming, singing and playing together in the temple. It was truly a feast of Brazilian music with so much to learn covering many different styles, all giving a good foundation of knowledge into the rich musical ancestry that lives and thrives through the work of Carioca. I chose to lead one song that I had written at Spirit Vine after a ceremony some years before called 'Dreamers of the Forest Light'. The song is an ode to the journey of finding and communing with Ayahuasca (the 'forest light') and integrating that journey into life. I greatly enjoyed the process of having a group bring my song to life.

What is this life, living a dream
What is this world, not what it seem
Where am I now, facing my shadow
Where am I now, light shining free

Dream, dream of you and me
Dream, dream, dream ...

The taste of life sometimes is bitter
We drink that wine, the name of Divine
It takes our mind, jungle vine time
The sweetest dream, darkness and light

Dream, dream of you and me
Dream, dream, dream ...

And now we stand in the waking life
To meet the challenge of eternal flight
We are the dreamers of the forest light
The forest light, the forest light

We wake to find freedom alive
Somewhere inside the jaguars smile
We look to find the eagle on high
The belly below the serpents' slide

Dream, dream of you and me
Dream, dream, dream ...

— *Dreamers of the Forest Light,* Lore Solaris.

Every few days during the two weeks of the music workshop, Carioca would call a ceremony. These ceremonies were slightly different to the usual ones in that there would be a large circle of chairs with microphones, guitar leads and drums ready to accommodate a band. After invoking the ceremony with some standard Ciranda songs, Carioca would then invite the groups to come and share their rehearsed and prepared songs now in the ceremony. Anyone else could also join in, and as the two weeks progressed we all got to know each other's songs. These ceremonies were relatively gentle but a beautiful way for everyone to play and practise the music we were learning whilst on the force of the medicine. This method of music study, enhanced by the ceremony and the Ayahuasca, was a powerful way to learn, and during these two weeks I made a giant leap in my musical knowledge, skill and confidence, whilst also gaining more insight into the depth of the lineages where the music came from. More songs would keep getting added to the groups' repertoires and by the end of the workshop we were also recording the songs. Following the music workshop was also a mini-festival in which there were three more ceremonies from the *Samasati*, *Ciranda Poim Poim* and *Aquarela* songbooks.

The focus of this workshop was on the music. Carioca explained at the beginning that we would do less work with ceremony than at the other retreats, but at times we would drink small cups whilst studying. The ceremonies we did were shorter and more focused on playing the songs and music we'd learned whilst on the force of the Ayahuasca. As Ciranda was a music school with a spiritual doctrine of music itself, it made great sense to have this yearly retreat available for students and practitioners to develop with that doctrine. The simplicity of the spiritual focus being on music was aligned with spiritual doctrines all over the world that speak of creation beginning with sound. Christianity (Word of God), Hinduism (Om), Buddhism (Om and Nada), Sikhism (Ik Onkar), and various Indigenous traditions (e.g. Aboriginal Songlines, Song of the Creator) explicitly tie sound to the beginning of creation. Even the Huni Kuin people talk about the sacred sound *Haux* being the first sound uttered when the Creator Serpent (Jiboia) was born.

> *Our Tradition teaches us that sound is God — Nada Brahma. This musical sound and the musical experience are steps to the realisation of the self. We view music as a kind of spiritual discipline that raises one's inner being to divine peacefulness and bliss. We are taught that one of the fundamental goals a Hindu works towards in his [sic] lifetime is a knowledge of the true meaning of the universe — it's unchanging, eternal essence — and this is realised first by a complete knowledge of oneself and one's own nature. The highest aim of our music is to reveal the essence of the universe it reflects, and the ragas are among the means by which this essence can be apprehended. Thus, through music, one can reach God. — Ravi Shankar, Raga Mala.*

Science, philosophy and ancient religions align with their understanding that the universe is made of sound: from the vibrations emanated by electrons, atoms and quantum fields, to the sonic majesty of the planets, stars, the entire cosmos and the music of the spheres. Singing together in tribal union, in praise of the Divine, the Earth, the spiritual beings and ancestors, has been a universal human experience throughout the entire planet and all of history. Jazz musician and author Jochim-Ernst Berendt, in his book *The World is Sound — Nada Brahma*, explains in rich detail how deeply woven music and sound is into all aspects of human language, culture and experience:

> *What is interesting is that the word "sound" refers not only to audible things, but also to everything that is whole, unimpaired, firm and healthy. Your health is sound: Is it sound because you are "within the sound?" Because you sound? To sing is a sound thing to do, not only in the superficial sense that a singing person most likely is a healthy person, but rather in the most basic, original sense our language can have, in the sharing of primal roots of words.*

Over the years I have come to learn that Ayahuasca itself — and within the miração and the spiritual landscape emanated when we drink the holy sacrament — is pure vibration and sound. I have found that, for almost all people who stay on the path of ceremonial Ayahuasca practice, there is an inevitable growth into musical expression and desire for harmony through creativity that emerges as a life priority. Without being overtly promoted or written into doctrines, this movement and evolution of the human soul is a pure and natural occurrence. Much like when we sing together, voices will naturally harmonise in oneness, reflecting our interconnectedness with all things, with the Earth, each other and creation. The richness and diversity of music at Ciranda allows for many variations of sacred sound and music to be created in honour and praise of the Divine. Ayahuasca in this setting becomes a conduit and conductor of sacred union with the Divine through sound. The group experience allows us to reach higher levels of joy and ecstasy, reflecting the glory, divinity and grace of creation as a shared shamanic experience. The diversity of sounds, instruments, rhythms, intentions, melodies and sentiments also has the effect of expanding the spiritual pathways and possibilities in raising conscious awareness and ancestral healing across a vast and colourful sky of unimaginable divine beauty. Music brings us into humility and reverence with the Divine. The multi-dimensional spectrum of colours in the music is reflected in the beauty and quality of the miração.

> *Since God created the world from sound, all music is directed back to God and the gods. That is why all music, first and foremost, is praise of God. This concept can also be found in the music concepts of almost all music cultures in the world.* — Jochim-Ernst Berendt, *The World is Sound — Nada Brahma*.

Carioca's music workshop is a deep dive into the musical styles and culture of the spiritual work with Ayahuasca and the lineages that are the foundation of the practices at Ciranda. Within these musical studies I also encountered greater depths of meaning and the rich spirituality of the practices and beliefs of Santo Daime and Umbanda. On one level there is the study of the music and the techniques of the styles being practised, but delving deeper, there is a lot more meaning in the spirituality that is the foundation of these sounds and their sounding. Each rhythm has a style and function relative to specific spiritual invocations, such as each Orixá having its own specific rhythm that for many Brazilians is deeply embedded within them. The way the maracá is played in each Santo Daime song also has a specific meaning and function. This works as a spiritual or shamanic technology which can at once invoke certain spiritual qualities and intentions whilst grounding the practice to the Earth, creating an anchor. This allows for a safe holding of the spiritual experience whilst simultaneously creating sonic fields of clearing and protection from unwanted energies. In Umbanda and Candomblé rituals, specific rhythms are used through sacred drumming practices to invoke corresponding Orixás such as Ogum or Xangô, which in turn may also be used to invoke specific entities which the mediums will then incorporate for healing and spiritual communion. It is not uncommon amongst Brazilian music and spiritual communities for people to have knowledge of many different rhythms and be aware of their spiritual and cultural roots. This permeates throughout all

Brazilian culture, from pop music to the majestic parades, dances and parties of the Carnaval held every year. I realised there was a lot of work to do in studying and integrating all these teachings — much more than just learning to play the songs. This study is vast and life-long and during this time at Ciranda this was the very beginning of studies that have been ongoing in my life ever since.

Mythological cosmology of becoming truly human

The shaman's creed, as outlined by the quote from Gabrielle Roth at the beginning of the chapter 'Sounds of Awakening', speaks about the retrieval of the soul requiring one to return to the roots of humanity through dancing, singing, storytelling and silence — these being the four universal healings. Singing and dancing are key elements of the spiritual practices of Ciranda, and when incorporated with periods of silence and meditation during the ceremonies this fulfils the shamanic creed, harmonising our human experience with the wisdom of the soul and its expression. The healing potential is sealed by the storytelling expressed through the mythology of the spiritual lineages found in the words, melody and rhythms, and in the prayers and the practices themselves. We also find these narratives woven into the visionary landscapes of the Ayahuasca miração. This is through the primal sounds found in the Amazonian and ancient African-sourced names of divine elements, ancestors and beings, or through the stories and sometimes personification of these forces, as told through the songs and their singing. The stories of the ancestors of Santo Daime, Mestre Irineu and those who came after him, the biblical teachings of Saint John, Mother Mary and Jesus Christ, and the epic encounters of the Orixás and their stories of life and creation all provide a beautiful and rich weaving, sourced from ancient wisdom and teachings as the mythology of the Earth and our ancestors. In the cosmology of Ciranda, these forces and beings harmoniously find home within a sacred alliance of song, dance and meditative concentration. The teachings and lessons gained through understanding these mythologies within this vast constellation, and the stories they tell, give us a roadmap and an abundance of guidance and practices for living a healthy and happy life in alignment with divinity and creation. Whether we take these stories, the gods and other spiritual characters as real or as creative metaphors for universal realities, if we choose to study and learn from them, then we create a safe and grounding container for our human experience, giving us references in our waking reality to our earthly connection and the teachings and wisdom emanating from all of human history through our DNA and transmitted directly from our souls.

When we find the unity of Earth and Spirit and align with our intent, we transcend doubt and insecurity, shedding the skins of ancestral pain and fear, and elevating our consciousness into states of healing and peace. It is through faith that we overcome the fears, doubts and insecurities which lead us off the path of harmony and wellness. When that faith leads us to the practice of the four universal healings, we rebalance and re-align ourselves as instruments of God-Great Spirit-Creator, and the peace, joy and love that fills our beings becomes our natural state. In this way, we can see how spiritual practice is essential for physical and spiritual health and wellbeing. These truths are relatively simple, yet the Western mentality has taken us so far away from this truth of who we truly are as humans on the Earth. The global cult of government health services, politicians and materially invested science tries to lock us into medications and psychotherapy as the solutions for declining mental health, whilst the real cause is the disconnection created by a dysfunctional and out-of-balance society — and the collective lack of courage to confront that reality. It seemed to me in my time at Ciranda that through this healthy, vibrant and deep culture of ceremony, communion and divine joy, the healing I had achieved within myself was not something that was even remotely recognised nor allowed in my own society. I was reminded of the time in the Australian desert when I had felt the separation and isolation of being outside the vibration of joy and unity in the Aboriginal community, and the grief and longing in my soul at being separated from this. Yet again, Ciranda and Ayahuasca brought me to profound levels of gratitude for the culture and community that had given me such a beautiful and loving experience of what it was to be truly human, to simply dance and to sing together. The hard work of finding my firmeza, facing and embracing my pain and my shadows, overcoming my trauma and emotional wounding, learning to open my mind, my eyes and my heart, and integrating all of that, was easily worth it for the soul healing I had experienced. The natural inclination that followed was to share and to be of service to this beautiful truth with the rest of humanity.

> *Behold your music!... Of the theme that I have declared to you, I will now that ye make in harmony together a Great Music. And since I have kindled in you the Flame Imperishable, ye shall show forth your powers in adorning this theme, each with his own thoughts and devices, if he will. But I will sit and hearken, and be glad that through you great beauty has been wakened into song.* — J R R Tolkien, *The Silmarillion.*

After the music workshop, a group of about six of us who wanted to continue with the spirit of the music workshop and keep playing music together went on a road trip down the Rio coast to a little fishing and tourist village called Trinidade, where we rented some rooms in a *Pousada* (guest house). We spent two weeks playing music together, day and night, sometimes with some locals joining us. It was during this time that I gained a lot of experience, skills and confidence in leading songs for a group, greatly refining my rhythm and timing and learning. I realised that leading was something which I was good at, came naturally to me and which I enjoyed immensely. There seemed a natural progression from the year I had been at Ciranda to this moment and I was again full of gratitude for Carioca, who had created this awesome pathway of learning. I was also grateful towards myself for staying and doing the studies and work required to progress so much in this relatively short time. Relaxing and playing music at the beach with friends was a great way to integrate all the teachings.

By this stage after a year at Ciranda under Carioca's tutelage I was beginning to feel I was gaining confidence in spreading my own wings. I had a circle of friends in Rio de Janeiro, where I would stay at times between the programs at Ciranda. In Rio we would also play music together and I was integrating more and more of the life and culture of Rio and Brazil, attending different events, street sambas, Carnaval 'blocos' (cultural groups), and even attending a group that played Ayahuasca 'medicine' songs in busy public places around the city. My Portuguese had also become much better and I was able to converse with people without too much drama, even if with a lot of holes in my knowledge and fluency. I was also studying with a language tutor in Rio, which was very helpful, and studying so much Brazilian music was also a massive boost to learning the language. Through harmonies and melodies I would find the pronunciation and meaning in the words. It was the language and the music that inspired me to fall so deeply in love with Brazil, and it has been a great joy for me in my life to learn to speak Brazilian Portuguese. People often say to me that I speak differently in English than in Portuguese, from the perspective of my expression and personality. I came to realise that I had learned Portuguese at a time in my life of spiritual awakening and expansion through music and religions, and this had formed the foundation of how I spoke Portuguese. The expressiveness and emotion, the passion with which Brazilians speak and the way that Portuguese can be spoken, were also a liberating force for me and the way I express myself.

The journey I was on with Ciranda and the Brazilian lineages and music of Ayahuasca was so much more than just studying the music and drinking the sacred tea. I was diving deep into Brazil itself: all the colours and sounds and language, culture, history, ancestry, spirituality, the land and the spirit. The focus and dedication I had put into my studies and also just living in Brazil for years was an immersion that has led to me feeling as much Brazilian at times as I feel Australian. I am always happy in Brazil in ways that I have not found so much in Australia. From where these studies led me to becoming a leader in a large Brazilian community in Australia of a spiritual lineage — all of this study and experience was vital to being an authentic guide and representative of this work. For me, this authenticity is vitally important. I never planned it that way but

I realise now that life guided me to these realisations, understanding and wisdom, which later unfolded into the work that I do and also in the way that I live my life.

> *Brazil!*
> *My Brazil, Brazilian*
> *My cheeky brunette*
> *I will sing to you my verses*
> *Brazil, samba that gives*
> *A swing that makes you sway*
> *Brazil, my love*
> *Land of Our Lord*
> *Brazil! For me, for me, for me*
>
> — *Aquarela do Brasil*, Ary Barroso.

As the months passed at Ciranda and in Rio de Janeiro, my studies continued and were enhanced more and more by experiences with friends and communities. I was able to practise not only the music and culture I had been learning but also to integrate my healing and experiences with friends and relationships and in the way I expressed myself and lived my life. This was a great thing but was also making me question my lifestyle and path ahead and, as I approached two years away from Australia, I was beginning to wonder where things were leading. My thoughts had moved towards manifesting a life in Brazil, much more so than wanting to return to Australia. For me, my life had *become* Brazil, the freedom and liberation of being able to openly practise my spiritual beliefs with Ayahuasca and music, the deep connection I had made to the land and the ancestors. This had such colour and richness: more than anything I had experienced in Australia, and thus was a strongly grounding force for me. In Brazil I healed my wounded inner child, I met the spirit of the forest and all her beings and received gifts and blessings. In Brazil I found my song.

Calling from Country

My relationship to my home country Australia was changing greatly and I had done a lot of healing through ceremony and some very different cultural and life experiences. There were many moments during the time I had returned to Brazil when I would feel the pull of returning to Central Australia and the Aboriginal communities. This pull was not a conscious desire, but was coming through a spiritual connection that had taken some time to resolve within me. I understood I had played a significant role in my time in the central deserts and in particular with the Aranda and Luritja peoples there. Occasionally I would get phone calls from Indigenous friends asking when I was coming back and telling me about community projects and ideas they had. I was torn by this, as I felt a lot of care and purpose in my ability to work in those communities but life was certainly calling me in a very different direction. I also had to do a lot of work to heal myself from the trauma and damage to my nervous system that working in those environments had caused.

Eventually, through ceremonies and with the help of Ayahuasca, I was able to resolve this calling and sense of pressure and duty to return. In silent meditations during ceremonies I could hear a voice singing distantly in the miração. With focus and concentration I could hear that it was an Aboriginal song which was sweet and also very strong. I didn't feel like the song was malevolent, but it was ever-present. Over time I attuned myself to the presence of this song in my mind and after a while I could perceive it regularly during ceremonies. At first I dismissed it as something beautiful and mysterious within the Ayahuasca landscape/soundscape but after a while I became concerned that it wasn't going away; when I tried to clear it from my field and my awareness I wasn't able to. I went through all kinds of mental processes in trying to understand what it might mean, and after some months I began to realise I was being 'sung' back to Central Australia by an Aboriginal Elder who wanted me to return. I had heard of this kind of magic being used before but had never experienced it. Often the act of being sung by a powerful Indigenous Australian is akin to being subject to a kind of curse and can be a bad omen, but it can also be done in a playful or sincere way. And that is what the energy behind this felt like. I started to be concerned, though, as I did not have the shamanic skill to be able to clear it and Ayahuasca was not offering any remedy for this, seemingly because Ayahuasca did not have the spiritual permission to interfere with this magic. I realised something in me was allowing this or agreeing to it on some level, and perhaps the guilt or pressure I was putting on myself to consider returning to the desert was part of that.

During one powerful miração, I perceived the song again but this time just let it go. During this astral journey I was guided to a memory of a time some years before — when I had been taken on a bush walk by an Aboriginal medicine man friend on his ancestral Country. As we walked he had shown me sacred artefacts and told me stories of his ancestors, the land and the animals and their Dreamings. At one point we walked under a large eucalypt tree and the birds in the tree started screeching and making a big commotion. My friend seemed greatly alarmed and told me to stay still as he started looking for a snake. Seemingly the birds were warning of us of danger and, sure enough, my friend found a large king brown snake, a very deadly and aggressive species. After the king brown moved away from us, this medicine man and I sat down and he told me some great stories about the king brown snake: how powerful it is and that it commands respect. It was nice to be taken back to this memory. Then the spirit of that medicine man came to me in the miração. He was smiling, with a cheeky playful energy, and I realised this whole experience that manifested was him showing me an aspect of myself and my own personal power. He explained to me through the miração that this experience I was remembering was actually his spirit showing me that the brown snake was one of my totem animals and that knowing this would bring me personal power. He explained that the aim of showing me in the way he did was to give me the self-realised connection to this power and to inspire awareness in me. I realised it was not his way to tell me directly but his wish was for me to realise this within myself one day. I then came to a strong sense of myself and I could see the only reason the old man from the desert was still singing me was because he knew that I did not recognise my own power and he was playfully attempting to call me back to Country. I also understood that the peoples of the desert could see my spiritual power and potential but used my lack of awareness as a cheeky way of gaining influence over me. I felt myself rising up, almost like a coiled snake wanting to strike, although, as I felt a sense of power, I also sensed a huge wave of peace moving through me. Suddenly the singing stopped — and it never returned. I could see the Elder who had been singing me, and this made me smile because I felt much love and gratitude coming from him towards me.

The miração continued to teach me, showing me my spirit and presence have codes and alliances that command peace and that the Aboriginal people had seen me as a peacemaker in the time I had been there with them. I felt my sense of duty shifting towards an empowered recognition that my own personal power, if used with humility, could be of great help to people and communities. Ayahuasca was teaching me a grand lesson with the help of my guides and Aboriginal ancestors. This helped heal my relationship to those communities and also awakened a part of me to accepting the spiritual power I had cultivated in this life and which resided in my spirit. I realised there was a power of peace and healing that I carried with me which could be used for healing and protection. I felt a strong sense of gratitude and smiled at the beauty and wonder of the way Spirit moves and the wisdom of the Elders across time and space. I connected with the vulnerable and ignorant 'whitefella' part of myself and also with the love of my Aboriginal friends, who had teased and tricked me but also taught me powerful lessons of self-realisation.

Brazilian life

After releasing all my attachments to returning to Australia I settled into life in Brazil and got on with life and studies. I could see the inevitability of change on the horizon, though at some point I would have to start earning money and making a living and a life for myself. I had been living for so long and so deeply in the flow of Spirit and trusting everything that came and unfolded in my reality, but now I was being challenged by thoughts of survival and materiality. These would bring me back to faith in Spirit and asking for guidance, followed by stillness until the guidance arrived, which it always would.

I had been painting a lot in the almost two years in Brazil and had built up a collection of several large canvases, each depicting visions and stories as direct transmissions from the mirações. The inspirations would come to me in all different ways: sometimes I would see a beautiful vision, be inspired and ask Ayahuasca if I could paint it; other times I would be shown things and given specific instructions from Ayahuasca as to what to paint and how to paint visions. During this time I made a lot of sketches of ideas for paintings and would spend almost every day with my paints and brushes whilst listening to the music of Carioca and Ciranda. I took my paints with me everywhere and would often sit in the dining area at Ciranda talking with people while painting or do the same at friends' houses in Rio, including at Carioca and Keren-or's place. I often spent a lot of time during the pauses or meditations in the ceremonies studying the paintings with the help of Ayahuasca. I could paint an entire artwork in my vision and would be given very specific guidance on how to paint, the layers and structure, colours and so on. Whenever I became stuck on something while working on a painting and was not sure how to do the next part, I would wait for the next ceremony and ask Ayahuasca for guidance then receive the next piece of the artwork. Eventually I was invited to hold an exhibition at an art residency guest house in Santa Teresa in Rio. I was living in the Santa Teresa part of central Rio, which had become my second home when I wasn't in the forest at Ciranda. Interestingly, Santa Teresa was also the name of the old mission in the Aboriginal community where I had spent so much time in Central Australia and where I had a strong connection. My exhibition was called 'Gulwan — Spirit of the Night Sky', a title inspired by my connection to ancestors from the stars. The name Gulwan had been given to me by star beings during an acacia DMT experience in Australia some years before. The artworks depicted my spiritual journey with Ayahuasca.

'Dimensions,' Lore Solaris, Acrylic on Canvas

I was also very engaged in my healing and massage work, which had become very popular as people sought me out for consultations. I was still experiencing the wonderment of a child at play in a magical garden; this feeling had carried over from the time I arrived. Although with familiarity and now being more relaxed and at home, I started to see things from different perspectives also.

Ciranda had experienced two decades of development before I arrived, with a large community of people having all contributed their Dreaming, prayers and support in the creation and organisation of the place. At times people would arrive with years of experience, which was great because I usually learned a lot from those people. There were others, though, who brought politics and entitlement and were more likely to throw their weight around to position themselves in hierarchy and power. After months at Ciranda I found it a little destabilising to have people arrive for two weeks and bring a lot of new energy with them, and it started to affect me. This was a bit of a wakeup call, as I had been staying more in the background doing my studies, healing and mostly keeping to myself. Once I had more

Spirit of the Night Sky – Art Exhibition Flyer, Rio de Janeiro 2015

confidence and was fully engaged, I didn't consider how my role had expanded and that at times Carioca was asking me to do different things that other people perhaps felt they were more entitled to do because they might have been doing those things in the past. Personally, I had no ambition or attachments and was happy to defer to others and always appreciated more time to focus on things like music studies and personal development. I enjoyed the moments where I could just flow while others took on jobs and responsibility. This was the first time I had experienced light bullying and projections from people at Ciranda. I was disappointed but largely shrugged this off, as I had been around enough communities in my life to recognise this for what it was and also to know that people bring their wounds and have different ways of expressing them. At times, though, I noticed Carioca becoming upset by some of the manoeuvring and manipulations going on around him which to me seemed typical of any social group where people feel comfortable to be themselves and where they feel safe to bring their shadows into the light to be healed. I also recognised that I was a bit clumsy and shy at times and still had a lot to learn.

I noticed that, like me, Carioca was reluctant to become involved and to tell people what to do or to set strong boundaries. Mestre Irineu was known to have sometimes closed the church and paused the works so that the people would have to do the personal work or take self-responsibility. I had learned this was not something to do another day or to wait for others to do or to be told to do. It had to come from an inner reflex, a knowing with courage and humility. I can see now this was not a strong point at Ciranda, where at times big personalities would come in and dominate spaces. These kinds of shadows are normal and are opportunities for growth, and we need to learn to navigate them from a compassionate and loving place. I was learning to be mindful of any judgements. I was grateful the Cura was coming up again, as I felt that it would help to sort out a lot of these dynamics and would certainly offer me some insights into myself and how I might be also playing into these dynamics, or at least why they were beginning to affect me. I had no desire to make myself more important than others or to engage in jostling to create a hierarchy or cliques. And I did not want to be seen as special or needing to manipulate things to be closer to Carioca. I felt stable and confident in myself and the path I had created there. I could never understand why anyone would want to play out personal agendas and politics when we were really all there in the presence of a divine and magnificent being such as Ayahuasca and where our goal was peace, love and joy. Surely everyone would know this and want to let go of any social or phenomenal dramas and attachments in order to live in faith and communion with all the divine forces. All that it takes is to be humble and do what needs to be done. It doesn't matter who does it. All we have to do is accept whether we are the one who is chosen or not.

By the time the Cura arrived again I had done a lot of preparation and was feeling a lot more confident, although playing all night for all three nights this time was definitely going to be a big challenge. That was because I was now able to see so much of the dynamics going on amongst the people, the little dramas and politics, the projections and all of the interpersonal dynamics that play out in community. I was grateful for the Cura, as it was a great leveller and forced people to see deeply their wounds and insecurities. I had come to Ciranda shy, insecure and unsure of myself in the space and had grown to be more confident and had cultivated a lot of skills, experience and knowledge. I perceived this through the way others were relating with me and how there were times where I had to say 'no' or stand up for myself, whereas in the past I may have been more passive, stayed quiet and just done what people wanted. My field and perception were more coherent and stronger, challenging me to elevate myself above any projections that were unnecessary. The human realm seemed messy, yet my work with Ayahuasca was sublime and where I had invested a lot of time and focus on developing stability. However, I was starting to feel a little restless for more expansion and growth, although I couldn't yet see how I might achieve it from the place I had arrived at in myself.

The Cura was deep and challenging and helped me to peel some more layers off the onion of my ego's defences. What I found was a calling and guidance for the next part of my life. It seemed there was a big job at Ciranda to support Carioca and the community and I had been preparing to possibly stay and do this work, to be a mirror and reflect the interpersonal dynamics in a healthy way, and to help with all the other immense challenges that Carioca faced in running the space and dealing with leadership in such a colourful, diverse and vibrant community with all its light and shadows. The Cura showed me, though, that there was still work to be done within, more spiritual teachings to come.

During the third and final night of the Cura, while we were in the fourth cup and were singing, I had a strong urge to leave the room. I could feel all the people and their processes very strongly, and my own confusion about my role in this was coming back. I don't like leaving ceremony while there is work to be done with singing, praying and holding space, but this time the calling to leave the room was irresistibly strong. I put my guitar and book down, quickly moved out and walked to the edge of the forest. The Ayahuasca was very strong as I sat down under the trees and when I did, two of my ancestral guides came to me as giant bird-like angels and soared gently, directly above me. They communicated with me telepathically and told me it was time to leave Ciranda and that there was nothing further for me to learn from Carioca at this time, that he had given me enough to keep going without him. My guides showed me a vision of a house in the Cerrado near Alto Paraiso in central Brazil and told me to go there and stay, alone. From there they said they would come and teach me, that it was time to learn directly from Spirit. They explained that I needed to be alone in silence in a remote place to receive the next part of my training. Once I received this blessing, I felt a wave of relaxed energy come over me. It felt like I had now come full circle from the time I had received the original vision and guidance to stay at Ciranda and learn to now, when I had been given the guidance that it was time to leave and permission to do so. Without thinking, I returned to the Cura room to finish the work during which I contemplated this new guidance and everything that it entailed. Part of me was a bit scared and sad to be leaving Ciranda, but another part of me was ready for the challenge of the journey continuing in new ways, under the guidance of Spirit. The vision and guidance was crystal clear.

At breakfast the next morning I sat with a friend who told me about his house in the Cerrado, near Alto Paraiso. Considering the strong vision I had had the night before, this was an interesting synchronicity. He went on to tell me he was going overseas for two months and needed a house-sitter to care for his home and his cat. It would be a couple of months before he was going but it was clear his house was the one I had seen in the vision and we both agreed it was a clear plan that would serve us both. Yet again, life was showing that by maintaining my faith and trusting in my guidance, everything would work itself out.

Following the three days of the Cura I was feeling grounded in the life I had created at Ciranda and in Rio de Janeiro. I was taking things day by day and not making too many big plans in my head. I did not know if the path of a personal retreat alone in the Cerrado would lead me back to Ciranda or on to something else. I knew that I had found my spiritual home with this Ciranda family and the music, ceremony and teachings of Carioca and Brazil. I was noticing a lot of signs in this time, observing the way that life, events and energy were flowing in my life and my reality. People were inquiring if I was able to hold space for them with Ayahuasca and run my own ceremonies. At the time I wasn't feeling like this was something I wanted to do but it was planting a seed, as people who knew me and had heard my music and seen me in ceremony were seeing me in that light. Carioca had suggested I prepare for running circles outside of Brazil and until this time that had seemed more daunting and not something I wanted to rush towards. I was also making strong ties with close friends in Rio and this was building a foundation of life in Brazil which has continued until this day.

I stayed between Ciranda and Rio for another couple of months before heading to Alto Paraiso and my personal retreat. I understood my guidance. Doing the work at Ciranda in the ceremonies and with so many people and energies around had been great support for my growth, yet now I could see it would be a huge challenge to just sit and listen directly to my guides and Country, with no intermediaries or external influence. I remembered the path and guidance of my first teacher of Ayahuasca, Pablo Amaringo, who did not follow traditions or any lineages; he followed his heart and his spirit and forged his own path. I had grown to know that this was also my way and was also something that Carioca had encouraged; he was also an example of this. Carioca and Ciranda had not created any ties or obligations in me beyond my own desires and personal investment in the teachings, practices, the community, and simply the love that I felt. The teachings I had received in my life to this point were profound and I had accumulated a lot of knowledge. I felt I had some more personal healing to accomplish, including more integration of all the gifts I had been given, such as music and art, in order to find more ways to confidently share what I had learned. I still didn't fully comprehend the plan my guides and Ayahuasca had for me, although I had learned to deepen my faith and stay true to my path. And this was the key. This daunting feeling was something I had to shake off. All of my life and spiritual experiences had taught me that the universe and all of its mysteries were so vast and complex that I could never imagine myself being more than a humble student who really knows nothing. Letting go of ambitions had been a practice of mine for some time, as they would only ever get in the way of me becoming the empty vessel which would then be able to become an instrument of the Divine. My ego was still getting in the way at times, and there was more letting go needed, another skin to shed.

There was a lot of movement and change in those last months at Ciranda. I felt myself drifting out of it after some time, at times still wondering what my role would be there moving forward. I knew the global Ciranda family of friends extended well beyond the forest, Ciranda and family in Rio. There are many thousands of people in this global circle and I was becoming curious about spreading my wings with this new knowledge and experience to see where the winds of life might guide me. It seemed like things at Ciranda were evolving in a positive direction. During this time Carioca held a couple of ceremonies and in these I was suddenly the most experienced person in the group other than Carioca himself, as his wife was not there for those nights. This felt like a good initiation before leaving, although the last ceremony was a particularly strong experience.

Later, a group of 30 Brazilian spiritual healers gathered at Ciranda for a special ceremony and I knew it was going to be a very powerful night. I felt a sense of responsibility to be of service and Carioca asked me to stay particularly present with the music to help guide the chorus of singing. I knew what to do, as I was so familiar with music and the ceremony. The energy was potent and the consciousness quite elevated by the group, who were quite open and experienced in dealing with high-frequency energies, channelling and mediumship. I was excited by this, as it was very much aligned with my own awareness and skills. The ceremony became very challenging, however. When Carioca served me the first cup, a large lump of muddy Ayahuasca tea plopped into the cup. *Woah*, I thought. Carioca just raised his eyebrows and gave it to me to drink. Trusting that I was being given what Spirit wanted, I didn't resist this unusually concentrated dose; I knew it was going to be an interesting night and prepared for a very strong experience. Sure enough, only three songs into the first cup I could feel the force of Ayahuasca very strongly beginning its process. It didn't take long until a powerful miração arrived and my vision, with eyes open or closed became very psychedelic. The force combined with the visions made it almost impossible to sing and to read the words of the songs. I sensed some presences. I started to realise that they were some very high-vibrational extraterrestrial beings. I felt they were calling my attention and perhaps had some message or task or were offering some kind of communion. I had met with star beings before with Ayahuasca, but this presented with a very strong force and very high vibration. I resisted this calling and asked these beings to leave me alone and come back later, as I really wanted to sing and felt a duty to support Carioca. It became impossible to sing. I was in resistance, which started to make me feel sick. The strength of the force of the Ayahuasca was elevating my awareness and vibration. The miração was the dominant field with the physical ceremony in the background, where I had to work to stay present. Usually this happens in the meditation of the third cup but now I was being trained to maintain awareness in both realms of attention.

It's only been on rare occasions that I have felt any nausea or wanted to vomit on the force of Ayahuasca. Occasionally some small sensations would come and go but I was well trained in not needing to purge in ceremony. I managed to crawl out of my chair and by this stage the rest of the room was hardly perceptible, as I was so deeply in the miração, which wasn't coherent due to my resistance. My lack of integrated presence was causing me to fall out of balance, both physically and mentally, losing coherency. I managed to get myself to the bathroom and stood over the toilet ready to vomit but it never came. I turned and leaned against the wall, trying to rebalance myself. It had been so long since I had struggled so much with the force, and it wasn't just the strong dose; it was also the very strong vibration of these extraterrestrials. Once I was out of the temple and alone I was able to hear them clearer; they were asking me to go with them. I didn't know what this meant or even who they were, so I asked them but I didn't get a clear response. Part of my resistance was a fear of dissolving and the physical reality disappearing. Usually, even when I am deep in the astral miração, I find it easy to return to the physical when needed, but this time I felt like my body was dissolving. My mind went to thoughts that perhaps I was leaving the planet, that these beings had come to take me away, and I was seeing them calling me to some kind of light ship they were in. I asked again where they were taking me, but I wasn't able to hold the coherency of the field, perhaps because this experience had come so differently and outside of my expectations. I did my best to just flow with it. Then I went through a process of experiencing my death, this time by somehow vibrating off the planet with some star beings in their light ship. My mind spiralled into all kinds of thoughts about the realisation of death or of leaving this life, and everything flashed before me. When I had the strong realisation that there was more I could achieve in this lifetime, in particular in learning to open my heart more, I came back to a more balanced state of being.

After this realisation I felt more grounded and walked back towards the temple. The force and the miração were still very strong but I had accepted this was happening and felt more stable. Once I arrived back in the ceremony, though, I realised I was not able to sit and sing. I tried for a moment but I couldn't see much in the physical space and I wasn't able to connect with anything that was happening physically in the room. I went to the outside of the circle and sat on a mattress where I could work on grounding myself even more. I focused on concentrating my mind to clear the chaotic thoughts that were interfering in integrating this experience in graceful presence. As I sat there in meditation, I could still feel the presence of the beings. One of them came towards me; it was tall, thin and luminescent. Through the colourful light geometries of the miração, this being reached out with a hand in the gesture of a handshake. I felt a loving peace emanating from this gesture, which I accepted. Now I felt in resonance with them and I accepted this gesture of peaceful friendship. I asked again: 'Who are you?' and they replied simply: 'We are You.'

I took a breath and sat there contemplating this beautiful gesture of inter-species communication and the whole experience, including the lessons of maintaining presence and firmeza. As I let go of my fear and resistance to it, more revelations and information came through. The beings explained that there was a convergence of events within the timeline that had led to this meeting with them and that they had come to offer me an 'energetic upgrade'. This meant that I had to stretch myself to be able to hold a higher vibration and that my resistance was because this was unfamiliar. I was still unable to see the room clearly and was guided to stare at a candle which would help me to re-orient with the physical world. Eventually I went back to my seat and with intense concentration was able to sing again. As I looked around, the others were smiling at me, seemingly happy for my safe return.

Not long after returning to sing, Carioca called the second cup, which made me smile in appreciation for the beauty and playfulness of Ayahuasca and the sacred lessons in her teachings that seemingly never end. In the line waiting to drink, I realised I had never spoken to or asked Carioca anything when I arrived to drink his tea. When I approached him to receive the second cup, I leaned over and, whilst finding it hard to speak, I said to him, 'I'm having difficulty integrating my experience.' He asked if I'd like a small cup and I nodded. When I sat down I smiled again and laughed at myself for my wonky integration during this ceremony. I was hopeful the force would become more manageable but it didn't — the experience of the high vibration and strong miração remained for the entire night and into the next day. I could still feel the presence of those star beings and asked them to turn down the intensity. They said they couldn't, that I had received an attunement, and that I had to just get used to a new level of vibration and use it as a challenge to become stronger, more open and sensitive in the force of Ayahuasca. There have been several key moments in my journey with Ayahuasca where I have had energetic attunements like this that have raised my vibratory field to higher frequencies, and I have come to understand that this gives me the ability to maintain awareness and presence within the force and miração across an expanded spectrum of dimensions. Upon receiving these attunements, the next steps are in refining my firmeza and presence to hold and navigate these new frequencies with grace and presence. Within these fields are beings that come to offer healing and wisdom, and when my consciousness is guided there, I become more adept at knowing how to attune myself without the resistance and the drama that this creates, as I had experienced on this night.

This experience was notable in that I was given instructions on how to navigate and integrate a higher vibration. In subsequent experiences of attunement over the years, I have integrated more gracefully than on that night, although the intensity of the challenge remains, perhaps even increases. Later, my spiritual guides explained to me that the experience was also to show me I had other work to do with my studies that required me to be alone in an isolated place and that this would not easily be able to be integrated in the style of work we were doing at Ciranda at this time. This all made sense to me. This path I am on is full of mystery and profound experiences I could never imagine or invent, yet it weaves together with a divine intelligence that inspires faith, humility and gratitude. The struggle and resistance of integrating this experience also provided me another area of study within the constellation of my relationship with Ayahuasca, where I felt that I was still at the very beginning of an unimaginably vast universe of teachings, consciousness and wisdom. What I learned from Carioca is that in every step of this path, at the source and fruits of the teachings and experiences, is love. Simply, love.

My last ceremony at Ciranda had, for the time being, opened a portal into a new awareness. I realised I needed to expand and that there were limitations, even at Ciranda, in what I was able to learn and integrate there. Ciranda had taught me firmeza, grace and gratitude. The training I went through in all of the work at Ciranda had given me a solid grounding in right-relationship with Ayahuasca, holding space in reverence and respect of the Divine, and a striving to ever evolve these qualities and be a better human being. To always remember to live in praise of the Divine in all of creation and to practise with faith and devotion. I was now being called to learn directly from my guides for next part of my spiritual growth. By this stage I was ready to leave Ciranda and head out into the world again. Being in this cosmic forest school and psychedelic incubator for nearly two years had given me the confidence for this next part of the journey. After some time in Rio, I took a flight to Brasilia and made my way to Alto Paraiso de Goias for my personal retreat alone in the wilderness. Ciranda had given me a clear and coherent spiritual practice that had nurtured my being in countless ways. I had found myself amongst a beautiful family of friends that I would have for the rest of my life. The connection, ceremony, music and community had provided me with a healthy foundation from which to continue my life path and, in particular, the work with Ayahuasca. The people and the community, even aside from the spiritual work, were a big part of the medicine I had received, in that the bonds created were purely of the heart, not of obligations or attachments. This healthy model of integrated spiritual community and musical expression continues to emanate through my life purpose and practices to this day.

On the last day at Ciranda I climbed the big hill above the waterfall and said goodbye to the land and its beings. Some grief passed through me and I offered my tears to the land. As I looked from above over the forest, I saw two hawks dancing in the sky over Ciranda. A message came and said that soon on the journey I would find a sacred feather from a hawk which would join and work together in sacred union with my blessed eagle feather. I had recently written a song for the eagles whilst at Ciranda.

An eagle taking flight, so high in the sky
Looking to the ground to see what can be found
He calls out with a song, for others sing along

Blue sky eagle home, up there all alone
Silent gliding flight, guiding to the light

Holding all the vision of the whole world on the wing
A spirited decision, teach the world to sing
King of birds sing through life, we all take wing

Blue sky eagle home, up there all alone
Silent gliding flight, guiding to the light

Up there with the clouds, we can only look up from the ground
An eagle's tear sheds rain, a prayer upon the sound
A lonely flight so high, a heart call to be found

And then one day it happened!
That the air under the wing, lifted eagle higher
Spinning beautifully, a spiral!
and up there with the clouds
He found an eagle other ...

Blue sky eagle home, in love we're not alone
Silent gliding flight, guiding to the light

Eagle lovers, wing lovers, through life they sing
Eagle lovers, wing lovers, they're sky dancing
Eagle lovers, wing lovers, through life we sing
Eagle lovers, wing lovers, we're sky dancing

Eagle lovers, wing lovers
Through life we sing
Sky dancing
Let's take wing.

— *Sky Dancing*, Lore Solaris.

Star Birth

PART 3
Flowering

CHAPTER 11

Returning Home

The eagle's ascent

> *Music is very special; it is the expression of joy, and it can imbue you with the flame of passion. All that has been brought into existence, the stars and the cosmos, is created by music and sound. Since it deeply influences our thinking and emotions, we should listen to music that inspires our highest humanity.* — Pablo Amaringo, The Ayahuasca Visions.

I made my way to Alto Paraiso and the Brazilian Cerrado. When I arrived, my friend took me to some ceremonies with *Estrela das Àguas* (Star of the Waters) where we were invited to join and play music from Ciranda. They were lovely people and it was a nice way to ground into the land with ceremony and community. I then settled into my friend's little house by a magical garden and crystalline creek with hummingbirds and pure waters flowing from nearby springs. The nature made me feel that I had awoken into a scene within a Brazilian Ayahuasca forest song. The house backed onto the Chapada dos Veadeiros, a vast national park in the savanna plateau of central Brazil. The area was very remote: there were only two other people living on the same property, some way away from where I was staying. The psychic energy was very clear and open with no interference. The silence and the stillness were perfect for the new mission that I had: to listen deeply to my guides and ancestors and receive their teachings and guidance directly.

My process at this time was much more challenging than I had anticipated. In the stillness and silence I was able to hear the thoughts in my head very clearly — and there were a lot of them spinning around for the first couple of weeks in my isolation there. I might have gone a little bit crazy facing myself and allowing the last couple of years and my thoughts, worries and projections of the future to wind out in my mind, while my ego grappled with the isolation and the inevitable surrender to the silence. Once I was able to attune myself to the space and to the experience of being alone in a vast wilderness for this extended time, I was able to make the most of the two months I had there. It was the perfect way to integrate all the intensity, colour, visions, energies, people, teachings, music and creativity of Ciranda. Whilst my time at Ciranda had been overflowing with my own creativity, there were also a lot of external influences and teachings I was absorbing and learning. Without this external input, without phone reception or internet, with just the silence of the dry Cerrado and the songs of the birds, I was forced to go inside myself for guidance and teaching.

> *If you want to chant well, you must go to a place where no one will hear you. You are not like a singer who learns a song that has previously been sung by others. A chant must be learned from the spirits, treated as sacred, and kept secret if it is to have power. Great onayas (those who know) chant to call spirits into a ceremony and to strengthen their concentration. Although they are sublimely beautiful, they are not intended as entertainment.* — Pablo Amaringo, *The Ayahuasca Visions.*

I spent a lot of time in contemplation, occasionally drinking a cup of Ayahuasca and sitting by the waterhole, watching the nature, the insects and birds, and merging energetically into that space. Sometimes I would sing to the nature spirits and the land. The dry, almost desert-like environment was radically different to the dense, wet forest of Ciranda and of the Amazon. Many messages and much guidance came to me during this time. There were moments where those same spirit guides that had come to me at Ciranda visited me, and I was able to attune myself to them. I spent a lot of time working on my music, with hours every day spent practising songs and techniques, experimenting with my voice. Eventually I started hearing music in my meditations. I wrote some songs in this time and one of the strongest messages coming through was that of spiritual sovereignty. I was learning to accept that my path was unique and that my connection with my own spirit, my ancestors and with the land was clear and unbroken. Despite the integration of the Brazilian spiritual lineages and their cosmologies, teachings and practices, I did not need to have a conduit or anything or anyone between me and Great Spirit. I could communicate, learn and flow within my own sovereignty, directly.

> *Because we are created from Spirit we possess divine essence, and although we have many diverse religions, we have a single innate desire to venerate that which is sacred.* — Pablo Amaringo, *The Ayahuasca Visions.*

This truth resides in the purity of my spirit, and whilst the laws of nature and the flow of creation will always be my guiding forces, my relationship to those forces is my own and in that way nobody can tell me or show me that. In this way, faith and trust become ever more important. I was grateful for the teachings and the doctrines of the spiritual lineages I had adopted and loved so much, yet my path was uniquely defined by the sovereign will of my own unique connection to Spirit. It is a beautiful dance, as my free spirit had found home in the practices based in those doctrines and teachings coming from Umbanda, Daime and the Amazon which brought so much love and healing to me and my life. I felt a lot of gratitude for Carioca and everything I had learned through him and Ciranda, where we could hold reverence and sacredness through ceremonial practice and community, yet dance with a free spirit. The part of me that was wounded, like a lost wild animal, afraid and defensive alone in the world, came back to the sanctity of the family, where there is safety and protection through connectedness. Knowing that my spirit could stay free, yet choose to embrace the codes of doctrine and practices, gave me a sense of freedom that I was still discovering. There would always be times where I would need to break out of the container, but everything I had learned in this brought a knowing I would always return to remember, recharge and find the reflections that keep me honest, accountable and aligned with my community. My constellation of ancestors and spiritual guides connect me through all time to the cosmic wisdom of the ages, to the land and to creation, which fortifies and seals the love in my heart and the force of Spirit moving through me.

This teaching and my way of walking with Spirit is important, as it has subsequently allowed me to be a pioneer in grounding new movements and adapting the teachings into new environments. This has led to me being able to integrate the practices and beliefs from well-developed lineages into new environments outside of Brazil, with their unique culture, history, traditions and natural environment. This is in itself a continuation of the tradition and path of syncretic religions; the weaving of lineages and the formation of new constellations and star maps of divine order, geometric architectures of sound and light manifesting into realities. I had a strong memory of Pablo's advice to me, given long before I had accepted a path of study and training in leading ceremony. He had suggested that I should not just copy what I had seen or experienced in others, but should adapt things into culturally appropriate forms which were coherent and which resonated within their own societies and environments. In order to achieve this, the practice of music, dance, stillness and storytelling remained, but the colours, content and expression adapted based upon the harmonic weavings that come from the stillness and presence. It was for me to sense, receive and integrate them into appropriate forms. My own unique spirit and experience, gifts and skills could be put to work on this mission. This was not about my own will and desires manifesting and playing out in some kind of egoistic performance or contrived story, but was a naturally flowing spiritual evolution, where I was the instrument being played by Great Spirit for the formation and expression of these new weavings. One night this came alive in a new song which I called *One Spirit Love*:

Stars shine night sky alive
Dreamtime journeys define
Beyond my lifetime I find
Spirit songs from my ancestral line

Dream of me evolving my mind
To unlearn all that's not aligned
Spirit Dreaming me will survive
and live on and on in all time

There's no teachers
and no gurus
and no prophets
Can take me to myself

No medicine
and no shaman
and none of the gods
Only one spirit love

Last night I dreamed I could fly
Across desert star filled sky
Star families are my guide
Home calls from my bird tribe

In all the world and noise of the grind
Remember to stop time in your mind
There's a voice right there inside

— *One Spirit Love*, **Lore Solaris**.

In my life I have always walked in this way, whereby I allow the guiding forces of my spirit to move me. At times I have learned and grown through veering off path and getting bitten by the harsh reality of trauma-stoking disharmony. I had now found a set of teachings embraced lovingly and freely by a beautiful community of people.

The teachings and the practices taught me to control my ego and my thoughts, to hold firmeza in ceremony and in life, and if at any time I fall or stray — *falta de firmeza* (lacking firmness) — I am reminded by the teachings emblazoned in my heart. Ayahuasca has given me this strong sense of presence in the form of divine love. Maintaining the practices and being held accountable by Elders and my brothers and sisters is a vital part of these teachings and the path I had begun to walk and continue on, and, in faith, always will. I'm deeply grateful for those teachings, which keep me on track and for the family that has my back, which includes keeping me in check and accountable. I could not do the work that I do — holding ceremony and leading practices — if I did not have the clear guidance and support of my ancestors and the ancestors of Ayahuasca and the Country in which we practise and live.

At this time I felt like an eagle flying high, alone in the sky, taken by the winds and hearing the whispers of Spirit. I could close my eyes and feel the light of the sun. In this clarity I ceased drinking any more Ayahuasca for the last few weeks I was there. I remembered the song I had written at Ciranda called *Sky Dancing* and the magical prayer of the eagle about flying high and teaching the world to sing. I realised my path ahead would be all about music and the call of the bird tribes, the spiritual beings of the sky. My spirit guides would come to me, often appearing as enormous angelic birds in geometric formations in the sky. I would later go on to learn that, just like in the song, the wind can spiral me higher. *Sky Dancing*. When I was working on the song I wrote about the eagles dancing, I wondered about the vision and message I had received that last day at Ciranda: that I would find a second feather to complement my blessed eagle feather.

I was able to focus and create 18 demos of songs I had written. Using my basic equipment and skills plus a lot of faith that I wasn't just making a mess, I ended up being pretty happy with what I had created. I sent them to an Argentinian producer friend Juan-Pablo, whom I had met at Ciranda some months earlier. He liked them and flew up to spend a month working on the songs. We stayed at the stunning Mariri Eco Arts forest sanctuary, created by a dear friend Mariana. Mariri is a wonderland of beauty in nature, deep ecology and biological protection. Mariana is a brave eco-warrior and biologist who protects endangered species, builds treehouses and is devoted to ecological living in a creative haven filled with ceremony, art, music, community, joy and beauty.

My collaboration with Juan-Pablo led to 11 recordings using loops alongside my guitars and some other instrumentation. I learned a lot in the recordings, and dived right into the creative process, realising I had far more ideas than we had the capacity to create. Recording music, I discovered, was something that I really love — the bringing of songs to life with colours and sounds, refining the composition and arrangements, turning visions into living sonic journeys. I am always so happy and vibrant in any creative process, whether it be art, writing, music or whatever.

By this stage it was clear to me I was on a path back to Australia; it seemed like the two years in Brazil had come to a natural conclusion for this part of the journey. I was full of new teachings, skills, music and awareness. I felt like a new person and I started having visions and receiving guidance about returning to Australia and beginning to ground myself and everything I had learned. I didn't have any grand ambitions or plans for moving forwards, although I felt good, but also challenged, about leaving Brazil and returning to my country of birth.

At this point I wasn't really thinking of holding my own ceremonies. I knew I had learned a lot and my life experiences and time studying in Brazil had equipped me very well, relative to other people in Australia that I knew, to facilitate ceremony. I was concentrating on music and art and finding ways to integrate this into a new path. During the last days at Alto Paraiso I met a lovely woman who was the wife of a well-known Ayahuasca shaman, a Brazilian man who had studied in Peru with the Shipibo. She took an interest in me and asked about my journey, enquiring if I was already holding ceremonies. I was a little surprised by the question and told her the calling hadn't arrived yet, that perhaps I wasn't ready. She asked if people had been asking me to hold space and facilitate ceremony and I told her that this had happened on a few occasions in Rio and here in Alto Paraiso. She said, 'Well, that's it then. If they are asking, you are ready — there is your sign.' I took on board what she said and filed it away for some later contemplation. Later, I went back to the Estrela das Àguas where I had been invited to attend again, and at the commencement of the ceremony there I was asked to play for everyone. I wasn't prepared for this, but it again seemed that life was showing me something through the way others were seeing me.

I had other things to think about: wrapping up the recording with Juan-Pablo, supporting the people and project with Mariana at Mariri and planning my next moves. I had come to the end of my finances and could barely afford a ticket back to Australia, but then a friend who owned a marijuana farm in California invited me to go and help there for a few weeks. It seemed like a nice way to make the journey back to Australia and I could then also see some friends in California along the way. I was also aware that there was a big Ciranda community there and I had received many invitations to visit them.

We wrapped up the recording with a day to spare and I planned on taking a day of rest to prepare for a long journey ahead. I had organised multiple flights and transport to San Francisco. Early the next morning I was awoken by some very excited friends who had decided to go for a hike and climb the 70-metre cliffs behind Mariri. My friend Fillip was a mad climber and treehouse builder and knew the land and forest like the back of his hand; he wanted to take me to the top of the cliffs for my last day. He'd been a great ally in my time there and he managed to push through my resistance to such an intense trek for my last day. Once I agreed, I realised what a great opportunity this was.

We walked up the very steep and slippery hill to the bottom of the cliffs, where we were able to see that there was a large freestanding rock proudly towering alone in front of the cliffs. Fillip was very pleased to show me this and point out that it was shaped like the head of an eagle. He told me there was a cavern behind the cliff face where a large eagle lived and which he had seen in there. This was also on the path to the top of the cliffs where a natural rock staircase began inside the cavern. When we arrived inside the cliff face we found the bones of animals that had seemingly been meals for the eagle.

The last few steps to the top of the cliff were pretty challenging and very steep, and the very last one was almost impossible — I had to hold tight to a tree root and lift myself up to make it. When I arrived at the top, I saw on the ground in front of me a gleaming, perfect feather from a hawk wing. It was literally glowing and seemingly a gift for me right at the end of my journey. Having made the treacherous, sometimes scary but beautiful, journey to the top of the mountain, the prophecy I had had in Ciranda of the second feather had now manifested and I felt a wave of accomplishment and knowing wash through me, like a momentous marking point in time along my soul's journey in this life. I held the feather out into the sky over the cliff as I looked out to the horizon beyond the enormous forest canyon that reminded me so much of the vast forest vistas of the Blue Mountains near Sydney in Australia. While holding the feather I said many prayers of gratitude and for the future of my journey. To this day I still use that feather, bound with the ceremonial eagle feather I already carried, in ceremony for healing and spiritual work. Even though I wasn't physically able to fly, at this point in my life I felt that I was flying with Spirit, and I asked my guides to help me spread my wings and launch into this next phase of my journey.

California Dreaming

The work in California at my friend's farm was quite arduous. I'm not adverse to hard yakka (work), as we say in Australia. This was mostly in work gangs with young Americans. Sweet, loving and playful people, many of them were working to earn some money before heading off on the popular new-age circuit to Peru for a two-week Ayahuasca retreat, then to Costa Rica for an acroyoga and tantra retreat on the way to the Burning Man festival. Despite all this healing work and their festival-hopping lifestyles, these people didn't seem to cope well in the social and working environment. There seemed to be a cascade of emotional collapse all around me. I kept my headphones on and didn't listen to the arguments, emotional drama and complaints about the avocados not being organic.

This was a very different environment to the one in Brazil, where so much gratitude and positive energy would go into any opportunity to work together on projects and community goals and resource development. I contemplated this very different cultural experience and wondered if this movement between events and spaces which are momentary retreats away from the 'ordinary' world was a way to escape the realities of the social quagmire of work, money, housing, jobs and social expectations. Swinging or monkey-branching between different realities and spiritual paths and festivals perhaps leads to an ungrounded psyche that struggles to integrate in relationships and the material world. I saw this as symptomatic of a Western culture where the young people are cynical and unsure of themselves, yet full of love and joy and creative fire, and seeking safe places to live and ground in harmony with the Earth.

Spirit's flow and guidance had sent me back to Northern California where 10 years previous I had received blessings from Lakota people. At that time I had been on this land and was invited to participate in a series of sweat lodges and then a blessing for my eagle feather. This time I was in California as a bridge between Brazil and Australia. The North American landscape and nature was so different to both Australia's and Brazil's. Despite this, I felt very connected to the land and ancestry. Another beautiful synchronicity occurred. I heard that a friend, Fabiano, whom I had met in Brazil at Ciranda and had been in many ceremonies with, was coming to the same town where I was helping my friend to hold two ceremonies. My friend and I both agreed we would take some time out from the farm to attend the ceremonies.

Arriving at the venue was really exciting, as it had been a few months since I had been in a Ciranda-style ceremony, and Fabiano was very true to Carioca's work and the lineage. Some Santo Daime prayers at the begging of the ceremonies also made me feel a warmth, safety and connection. Before the first ceremony began, Fabiano asked me to play the maracá and to do the *defumação* (smoke clearing). These are two things I had done for Carioca at Ciranda and was quite proficient at them. I did feel honoured, too, that Fabiano had shown the grace and respect to ask me to perform these sacred tasks. The defumação is a small but important cleansing ritual to clear the field for the ceremony and the maracá is a powerful shamanic instrument which, when played with focused care and intent, holds a powerful force in the field of the music and grounds and protects the energies of the ceremonies.

Just before we began I went to get my eagle feather, and as I picked it up I saw a vision of the new feather I had found on that last day in Brazil. I heard a voice in my mind saying it was time to use my sacred feathers in ceremony. I had never used my eagle feather in ceremony before, as I was unsure of how to integrate the strong energy it holds and of my clarity at being able to use it. Now I was being asked by my guides to join the feathers and use them together. It seemed so appropriate that I should use, for the first time in ceremony, my eagle feather from an Australian wedge-tailed eagle, blessed by ceremony in this same land. With the two feathers I united the spirit of Brazil and Australia with the blessing of the spirit of the land of North America and prayers of the Lakota nation. This beautiful moment in my life and journey as a ceremonial leader was very significant. It gave me confidence in the blessing and permission from Spirit to be a carrier of the spirit of the eagle and condor, where this sacred alliance was weaving itself through me and my path.

I greatly enjoyed the ceremony, especially as Fabiano is a talented and astoundingly skilled musician, and I loved hearing his versions of Carioca's songs. Fabiano used the same songbooks as we did at Ciranda, all of which were put together by Carioca. The ceremony was grounded in presence and firmeza and conducted with gentle beauty and grace. The force of the Ayahuasca throughout was like a gentle breeze compared to the soaring currents of ceremony with Carioca and all his spiritual guidance and ancestral wisdom. During the third cup after the pause I sat in meditation, and as the miração arrived, I began my usual practice of scanning my field and thoughts and clearing and asking for any guidance or teachings. Ayahuasca quickly said to me that I had done enough of my own deep-sea diving into my inner world for now, that it was time to be of service to others. This blessing, alongside the blessings of my sacred feathers at the beginning of the ceremony, was a clear message and sign for me that I was ready to be called into the service of Ayahuasca and the spiritual constellation of guides, nature beings and ancestors with whom I am in a sacred alliance.

In the weeks that followed I travelled down to Los Angeles to meet some friends and connect with the Ciranda community there. I heard stories of many different Ayahuasca circles and communities in the region, with various different lineages. In my time there I was invited to three Ayahuasca ceremonies, as people knew I had spent so long in Brazil and studied with Carioca. After the message I had received telling me it was time to be of service, I accepted all three invitations. Previously, I would rarely attend ceremonies outside of my lineage. Interestingly, in all three ceremonies when I was asked to sing, I felt the force and my guides very strongly, and on each occasion when I sang, many people in the circle went into deep processes, including the facilitators. Each time the facilitators went into process they asked me to keep playing and hold the space. In those moments I paused and asked for spiritual guidance, and I was shown which songs to play and in which sequence the people and the ceremony needed. I learned a lot during these ceremonies. Notably, I was given guidance from the Orixás on how the forces worked together and how they could facilitate the clearing and healing required to open to the force of Ayahuasca and the miração. After one of these ceremonies I practised a song from Carioca and while I was experimenting with the chords, I received a song about calling the Orixás:

> *I feel the force of love*
> *My guides are the stars*
> *I call*
> *I call the Orixas*
> *É Oxala!*
> *E Nana!*
>
> *Iansã!*
> *Yemanjá!*
>
> *The planet spins*
>
> *The eagle in the air*
>
> —*Eu Chamo*, Lore Solaris.

These experiences showed me that this eagle was ready to fly; I was keen to get back to Australia to ground myself there and see where life would take me. In my visions I was being called to return to Sydney, my home town, but somewhere I had not lived for 15 years. I didn't quite know why I was being called there, but it felt good to go and spend some time with my mum, who lives in the Blue Mountains nearby, plus I had a few friends there. So again, I took a leap of faith and followed the visions of the Earth Dreaming me.

Boomerang back to Australia

... the rainbow serpent moves through this photo-fabric of creation. He goes under the ground too, because light has been there in the past and he is not limited to linear time. Ah, but is it a wave or a particle? I guess that depends on how you're looking at him, but we would see him as a wave, a snake, because he is in constant motion across systems that are constantly in motion and interwoven throughout everything that is, was and will be. There are infinite variations of him in all shapes and sizes throughout the world — wyrm, dragon, ureaus and many different names in different regions, taking the shape of the spirit of those places. He was always there and always will be, unless people keep trying to make him eat his own tail. — Tyson Yunkaporta, Sand Talk.

Arriving back in Australia after so long away felt like returning home. But the home return wasn't about being in Sydney; this was a return to myself. I had integration work to do and I knew it. Many things had happened in my life, many powerful spiritual realisations and clear pieces of guidance. Alongside these I felt an enormous sense of responsibility to myself and to the mission I had been given. Responsibility to myself came in the form of dealing with the surrounding memories and triggers of my past, family, old friends, toxic culture and the reality of being so far away from Brazil and the culture and spirituality that had become so integral to myself and my path. In some ways it was like arriving in a desert. Instead of resisting this and rushing into things, I decided to face myself and integrate without any practices, and with no Ayahuasca, no *Santa Maria* (sacred marijuana) or any other strong influences. I wanted to face myself, my triggers, and rebuild myself from a grounded foundation. I decided to take six months to do this integration. I would have to face myself and my relationships and life without the help and support of the sacraments, and find the guidance within. I had done this in Alto Paraiso recently, though doing it in a city surrounded by old life triggers and distractions would be a whole new challenge — but an important one. Self-empowerment through non-attachment.

By early 2016, I had partly established myself back in Australia and was excited to find people to play music with. I didn't know anyone who had heard of the Yawanawá people before and I didn't know anyone in Sydney who had heard of Carioca or Ciranda. I hadn't met any of the Brazilian community yet either. Through networks I was invited to play music at some community spiritual events, cacao ceremonies and little festivals. This movement contained great passion and seemed to involve a convergence of a group of people putting energy into these events, which had community building intentions around them. I met some people who were drinking Ayahuasca in some ceremonies held around Sydney and Byron Bay. I could see there was a 'medicine' culture developing, mostly led by people who it seemed had done minimal training. I didn't relate much to some of the ideas, language and beliefs around these groups, although it was nice to invite groups of people to sing together, at least with the intention of honouring Ayahuasca and the spirit of the forest. After holding this space for some months, I saw this grow the first sprouts of Ciranda in Australia. People liked the songs and the prayers and the teachings I was carrying, and I really enjoyed sharing them in my home country. I was missing Brazil, though, and missing Ciranda and the knowledge shared between those who understood the ceremony, culture and spirituality of the lineages that had become my home. I would have to lead the creation of a new house of prayer that honoured these lineages, spirituality and teachings.

During this time I was making trips to Bellingen in the mid-northern NSW coast and its surrounding areas: a richly forested region with beautiful rivers, crystalline creeks and waterfalls. I was there visiting Jesse Lethbridge, whom I had journeyed with before, and who was with me when we found the eagle in the desert that belonged to my blessed feather. Jesse is a master didgeridoo player and craftsman, trained by a well-known Aboriginal Elder and keeper of the ancient *yidaki* (didgeridoo) rhythms held by the Yolngu people of Arnhem Land in the north of Australia. These are some of the most ancient rhythms and music in the history of humanity. Aside from that, Jesse is an accomplished musician and multi-instrumentalist who has produced many albums and has also travelled the world with his craft. Jesse and I spent a lot of time practising and playing music together, working out songs and arrangements, and he helped me to refine my music and presentation. We played music around the

With Jesse Lethbridge, Blue Mountains NSW, Australia

community in Bellingen and he also made occasional trips to Sydney. We are like old soul brothers and had journeyed with Spirit together in many lifetimes with ancient eagle tribe knowing shared between us. Jesse has a deep sense of the sacred in music, ceremony and connection to Country, which was very complimentary to what I was carrying and transmitting through my music and spirituality. We learned a lot together and he was inspired to study and experience Ayahuasca, the lineages, the music and ceremony. Interestingly, when I was in Brazil I received guidance to seek out Jesse for music and, as it turned out, we were very aligned to meet and collaborate during this time.

In Sydney I met a lot of people and spiritual circles who were very open and humble on their paths. I really enjoyed this openness, as I had a lot to share and there was a strong flow of guidance coming through me when I would be singing or supporting spiritual events. Some of the strange concepts and attitudes people would approach me with regarding their experiences and beliefs around Ayahuasca were at times a bit concerning. I wondered what was happening in these circles. My guidance told me I had been sent there to teach and show a different way. In my mind I kept going back to the visions of the suffering of the Amazon forest and of the planet and to remember that this is what it was all about. Learning to become a better person, a better human being in the world of illusions, was more than wearing the latest psychedelic outfit and talking about your last ceremony.

I had a different experience in Bellingen, where the community was already largely in Earth guardianship consciousness and community. While perhaps there were a lot of emotional and psychological issues around relationships and community, at least there was a strong community of ecology and healthy living. Whereas in Sydney people were curious and open minded with Ayahuasca and sacred plant teachers in general, in Bellingen people were more wary, and at times dismissive or suspicious. I didn't know what to make of this because in Sydney people were making all these wondrous and fantastical claims about Ayahuasca. In Bellingen perhaps people had seen an ungrounded and disconnected practice and culture around Ayahuasca which had created the scepticism. I also noticed prominent people in the community making money off promoting themselves as the saviours of those who had become ungrounded or confused after their ceremonies. It seemed obvious to me that, without doctrine, practices of grounding into humility such as firmeza, coherent spiritual foundations through culture, ancestral wisdom and careful community development, the Ayahuasca community could easily become unclear and ungrounded.

This is an important insight for anyone entering into the spiritual path of Ayahuasca: to be careful of where you are being led, how the space is being held physically, culturally and spiritually. What are the foundations of the practice, where are the ancestral teachings and doctrines that bring meaning and function to the practices? What are the meanings and significance of those practices? What are we calling and invoking, how do we facilitate those energies and, after opening, how do we close spaces and portals in order to integrate the healings and blessings? How do we seek permission and respectfully attune to the land, its spiritual beings? It is also vital to know that we are connected to Great Spirit though the blessings and wisdom of the Elders and the ancestors. In my mind it is not enough to copy what has been seen in a random ceremony, pick up a guitar and learn some songs, give Ayahuasca then put on a concert. I am conscious in this book of not projecting judgement. Arrogance has been a weakness of mine, and I have also had my own bumps and challenges on my path. I am not perfect. I am still a student on the path. I do hope to get across, though, that for any practitioner and any student or anyone stepping onto the path of Ayahuasca, this is a profoundly deep practice calling for dedicated self-work and dedication to learning, shedding the ego, being deeply confronted and facing those shadows, taking responsibility and accountability, and integrating on all levels of life. In simple terms, it is a path of truth in harmony. The teachings must be grounded in authentic experience and be connected to the traditional roots that anchor it in Earth's cosmic history and guardianship. If this connection is not soundly grounded in this way, it risks being a false light. A flash of the ego's desire to be saved; an easy victory of accomplishment and a badge to wear. To achieve this takes years of focused and dedicated study, sacrifice and careful integration under the guidance of Elders and recognised leaders on the path. To me this is a matter of respect but also of spiritual safety, and First Nations Elders in Australia have spoken about spiritual communities following a false light that is not connected to Country, lineage or ancestry.

Another phenomenon I was encountering when meeting people back in Australia was the seemingly common use of Australian acacia plants which contain DMT in brews that were being called 'Ayahuasca'. People would approach me and tell me about the ceremonies and I when would ask about the tea they were drinking some explained it was Australian acacia mixed with either Ayahuasca vine or with s*irian-rue*, another plant that has a similar effect. I would explain that out of respect I don't work with acacia because I am not initiated or trained in its use, that it is a very sacred and powerful plant spirit that demands careful spiritual study and permission. Like all plants, acacia has its songs, its consciousness, teachings and culture. It has been used and venerated by First Nations peoples in different ceremonies over thousands of years. Most Indigenous people do not even mention it to anyone — it is highly respected and preserved only for the highly initiated. For me to bulldoze in and start serving this to people and even calling it Ayahuasca seemed out of alignment, lacking in respect and not something I would do or condone. Drinking acacia in a loosely derived South American style of Ayahuasca ceremony, entering into its miração and spiritual field, and singing Ayahuasca songs to it, to me is disrespectful.

Aboriginal writer Tyson Yunkaporta in his book of yarns, *Sand Talk*, speaks of a whole systems perspective on plant medicine.

> *As an example, us two might look at a native tree — the silky oak tree — that has been planted all over Australia in recent times due to its beautiful flowers. But that tree cannot be examined as a specimen on its own for medicinal and other uses, because it is part of a complex system, like every other entity in the universe. That silky oak tree has the same name in Aboriginal languages as the word for eel. Its wood has the same grain as eel meat and it flowers in the peak fat season for eels, signalling to us that it*

is the right time to eat them. The fat is medicine in that season and can cure a fever. The role of plants in Indigenous medicine is about much more than isolating compounds to be extracted for pharmaceutical use. You can glimpse the true knowledge systems of Indigenous medicine by looking with a less reductive lens at things like silky oak trees. This requires more than taking samples.

From this perspective, we can't take out DMT from one plant and substitute it with another plant and call it Ayahuasca. Even though it might seem to some that Ayahuasca is just a vehicle for DMT, the reality is it is a living entity and a spiritual being within a vast spiritual constellation. Some might argue that they substitute acacia in Ayahuasca brews due to limited availability of the true Amazonian plants. I would argue that if they were going to do this, spend the years of study and build a correct relationship with the plant, its ancestry and its songs first, ask permission from an Elder and then decide if you still want to use it and call it Ayahuasca. Similarly, prohibiting the compound DMT, a naturally occurring neurotransmitter, falsely referring to it as an 'illicit' substance and then somehow transferring that to Ayahuasca is incoherent, disrespectful and demonstrates an error in law.

Whilst I had spent a lot of time previously exploring acacia as a plant teacher and I had a lot of respect for it, I also had many questions and huge gaps in understanding of the plant and its spiritual field. In order to work with it I would need to do the equivalent studies I had done with Ayahuasca. After years of studies I still had so much to learn about Ayahuasca, so taking on a new teacher and new spiritual constellation was too much for me. Simply, I am not a dabbler, especially with divine sacraments and where traditional practices and culture are involved; I have always sought permission and coherency in my intent and actions. The spiritual alliances I had made with caboclos and nature beings was something I had cultivated and studied over many years. These beings and forces inform my practices and provide remedy, guidance and protection throughout the work. I would be lost without these connections and allies and would simply not lead ceremonies without their conscious awareness, presence and support. Indigenous friends look on and have expressed to me that they see the rampant use of acacia, without integrated wisdom, as yet another cultural invasion. In recent years some Elders have suggested teaching the sacred knowledge of acacia to people who are in leadership roles within different plant medicine circles. In some First Nations they now see that with the spiritual awakening all over the planet, there is a strong desire to learn the sacred ways and to reconnect to Country, and so they have opened their culture in ways never before seen, seemingly as part of a spiritual evolution of humanity but also as a way to minimise harm and confusion as a matter of care and safety. I am constantly impressed with the way Indigenous Elders offer compassion and grace in the face of colonial attitudes, immature behaviours and cultural ignorance. I can say this after learning the hard way. I certainly transgressed and showed disrespect to Country and to Elders when I was younger and had to face the consequences of that. *Ouch.* It is a very human way of learning, and it's why I have so much love and respect for Indigenous culture and wisdom. Learning through experience, listening, presence and walking with spirit. Storytelling. One of my intentions in writing this book is to share what I have learned.

After six months of integration, I decided to light a sacred fire and make some prayers through ritual. I invited the spirit of Ayahuasca to return to my life. I was ready; I could feel it. And I felt a strong call to return to my practices and to accept the next teachings and guidance. As many people had been asking me about ceremonies and wanting to know about my lineage, I saw that I was hearing the call in Australia, in the people, in the Dreaming. The wisdom of Brazil was responding through me. I felt myself an instrument of a sacred alliance and I prayed to the sacred fire and made an offering to Great Spirit to give commitment to follow my path, to step into the Earth guardianship as a protector and teacher — something I had been working towards all my life. I didn't know what the path forward would be; I wanted to stay present and not project into any future. My way is the Way of the Hummingbird — the love and harmony of the Earth in holy communion with the Light of the Forest that is known as Ayahuasca and which has many other names. In this truth my soul rests and my spirit soars. An Aboriginal Elder once said to me 'What is between you and Spirit, is between you and Spirit.' What he was referring to is faith. Faith in my connection to God/Great Spirit, or however we might call the majesty of all creation. For we are that. It's only our minds that have created the separation and a world of illusions. Knowing who I am, how to be and with faith in Great Spirit, is where I find my peace. With my feet on the ground and my wings opened to fly, I received the gift of sacred flight. I felt strongly it was time to fly.

The day following the sacred fire ritual of calling Ayahuasca back into my life and invoking my divine guidance and purpose, I received two beautiful offerings. Two friends contacted me and offered me some Ayahuasca tea and some plants to make it. Two days later a third person contacted me. One of these three had already enquired about the tea, the other two just appeared. Three sources of Ayahuasca in the three days following my sacred fire ritual. This to me was a clear sign of grounded and spiritual activation (with three being a number of physical manifestation). I felt clear in my guidance and vision and the universe was supporting this with an ease and grace of truth in natural harmony, natural lore. I would come to learn that this path I had accepted was one of faith, and I prayed that Spirit would hold me, guide and protect me.

Law versus lore: The difference that shapes perception

In the days that followed my fire ceremony, and as my old friend and teacher Ayahuasca found her way back to me through three emissaries with blessings of grace, I began to reflect not only on the nature of Ayahuasca's return, but on the beliefs and structures that often obscure her light. One of these obstructions is the murky, unjust laws imposed by Australian governments. Australia is by nature a conservative country that follows global media and political trends. If the US Government says 'Jump', Australian politicians respond with 'How high?' In Australia, legal impositions on sacred and ceremonial ancient practices with plants that naturally contain DMT were done at the behest of foreign bodies and a US declared 'war on drugs'. That same absurd war that has caused immense suffering for millions globally has been enforced at the behest of the pharmaceutical mega-industry with their opposition to other forms of healing and natural medicines, whilst pushing their own addictive drugs. There was no debate, no impetus from the public to act as such. No science, research, consultation or evidence. When a government adopts laws imposed by foreign entities without consultation or the informed consent of its own people, especially when those laws contradict the sovereign wellbeing or cultural integrity of the land, it ceases to act in service of its citizens. In such moments, elected officials risk breaching their sacred duty and veering into a form of administrative treason in allegiance to foreign interests that do not arise from nor serve the soul of the nation. In considering the legal and moral status of Ayahuasca, it is important to discuss the nuances of legal frameworks and how they govern. It is equally if not more important to consider the spiritual and moral rights of humanity and the Earth. And it is of great importance that we acknowledge there is a difference, both subtle and yet monumental, between *law* and *lore*.

Law is the external shell. It is the formal architecture society builds to define, protect, and often, to constrain. Law is written in ink and maintained through enforcement. It is bound to jurisdiction, time and the consensus of governments. Law names Ayahuasca as 'illicit' in some regions, including Australia: it is seen as a substance, a chemical, a risk. Law here does not speak of Spirit. Law deals in generalities and outcomes. It does not see the plant spirit; it sees a file number. And yet, law also has its role in holding the social field. When applied with integrity, law provides the shared expectations, boundaries and consequences that shape coherent societies. It offers a container, a structure that can protect from chaos, uphold justice and create a sense of collective safety. It is not inherently adversarial to Spirit; it becomes adversarial only when it is used in a manner that betrays its origins in service. But law is vulnerable. It is susceptible to distortion when fear overtakes understanding, when misinformation clouds truth, and when control becomes its own justification. Like any structure not rooted in wisdom, law can be co-opted, corrupted or calcified into something that no longer reflects the living needs of the people it claims to serve.

Lore, on the other hand, is the ancestral voice. It is the unwritten remembrance encoded in land, breath and lineage. Lore is the oral library of Elders, the rhythmic pulse of ceremonial songs, the codes woven into geometric visions. The vibrations and eternal meanderings of the songlines. It is the harmonic remembering within the human soul that is sung by the Earth. It recognises Ayahuasca not as a drug but as a grandmother, a living being of ancient consciousness who carries teachings from the Dreamtime. Lore is not enforced; it is inherited. It is not judged; it is lived. Ayahuasca is a sacred gift from the heart of the Earth, offered to humanity in times of crisis.

The legal misconceptions around Ayahuasca arise because law has forgotten to listen to lore. Law asks, 'What is the risk to society?' Lore asks, 'What is the offering to the Spirit?' And yet, these two do not have to be in conflict. When law is informed by lore, it becomes wise. When lore honours the boundaries of law while holding true to its deeper knowing, it becomes safe. Both serve, but they serve from different dimensions. In this path of remembrance, I choose to walk with lore first, so that any law I engage with is harmonised by truth, not fear. It is lore that guides the way, and law that must eventually catch up to the heartbeat of the Earth. By stepping onto the path of Ayahuasca in Australia, I would also have an intrinsic role in this unfolding of truth and ancient prophecy in restoration of sacred order in harmonic balance.

But what happens when law is no longer in service to the people? What happens when it becomes a tool of erasure?

In Australia, the imposition of law arrived not as a consensual agreement among peoples, but as a unilateral declaration of dominance. It was enforced through imperial decree, rooted in the false doctrine of *terra nullius* (vacant land), a profound denial claiming that the land was uninhabited and thus, its lore, its law, did not exist. This was not law in coherent service to Earth and its peoples; it was law in service of deception and conquest. The British system, adversarial and alien, displaced not only Indigenous custodianship of land but also the sacred systems of knowledge that governed it. Lore was not only ignored, it was systematically persecuted and criminalised. We are still inflicted with the remnants of this incoherent and decaying system which, sadly, in its dying throes grasps for survival with mindless and damaging actions driven by ambitious, arrogant bureaucrats and the scourge of ignorance amplified through the phenomenon of 'group think' (consensus over truth).

To this day, those with ancient, continuous and enduring cultural and spiritual connection to the land are forced to plead their case in courts modelled on old English adversarial systems. They must seek recognition from institutions that still operate within the same mental architecture of control that denied their existence in the first place. This is not justice; it is theatre. A performance staged by bureaucrats, politicians, and media actors who have inherited, and now unconsciously perpetuate, the mentality of imperial dominance. The very concept of 'evidence' in these courtrooms excludes the cosmologies and ancestral wisdom of First Nations peoples, rendering sacred songlines, Dreaming stories, and ceremonial rights invisible to the legal eye. And yet, the collapse of this system is no longer hypothetical — it is already underway. Nature inevitably returns to balance and humans are not separate from nature, even if we foolishly attempt to force our will upon the natural flow of creation. The failures of governments and legal and health institutions in Australia have reached a crisis point. Public trust has eroded. The mental health epidemic, suicide rates and current spiritual malaise reflect a nation that has lost its tether to meaning. In this vacuum, sacred teacher plants like Ayahuasca are not emerging as trends; they are surfacing as signals that a turning point is here. Ayahuasca does not bring an ideology; it brings a mirror of the truth of our connection to nature. In the face of institutional failure, it offers the possibility of whole system coherence — not imposed from above, but remembered from within. Ayahuasca is not illegal because it is dangerous. It is illegal because it disrupts the systems that depend on dissociation. It restores connection where disconnection is profitable. It heals where pathology is incentivised. This moment is not merely about plant medicine; it is a reckoning between imposed law and living lore.

A reckoning between empire and Earth. And while the courts may still speak in poison-tongued deceits, the land remembers. In J R R Tolkien's *Lord of the Rings*, Gandalf speaks about the character Grima who has corrupted the mind of the king. 'And ever Wormtongue's whispering was in your ears, poisoning your thought, chilling your heart, weakening your limbs, while others watched and could do nothing, for your will was in his keeping.' Despite the legal system of ancient poison, the people remember. And lore — the true law — has never stopped singing beneath our feet and in our Dreaming.

> *Disconnection in all its guises — alienation, loneliness, loss of meaning, and dislocation — is becoming our culture's most plentiful product. No wonder we are more addicted, chronically ill and mentally disordered than ever before, enfeebled as we are by such malnourishment of mind, body and soul.* — Gabor Maté, *The Myth of Normal*.

Just as Ayahuasca calls us out of fragmentation and beyond the ghosts of historical trauma, the prophecy of the eagle and the condor speaks to a deeper psychological split between two ways of being, two systems of law, two fields of coherence. According to Amazonian and Andean teachings, the eagle represents the intellect, structure and rational paradigm of the north, the law that dominates, enforces and often eclipses emergent wisdom. The condor, rooted in the south, carries the energetic frequency of intuition, heart-wisdom and the living lore. Over the last 500 years, the eagle mind has overshadowed and nearly silenced the condor heart, echoing a dynamic where law intellect overrides lore intuition. The prophecy declares that now is the time when eagle and condor begin to soar together in the same sky, birthing a new level of consciousness: a reunion where mind and heart, technology and spirit, law and lore weave into unified service for the Earth. Sky dancing in sacred alliance, heeding the call of the forest.

This sacred alliance mirrors Ayahuasca's role in our own journey: to disarm and harmonise the intellect that has forgotten the melodies of the heart, and to elevate the intuitive knowing that has been forced underground or into the unconscious. The eagle's sharp vision, guided by the condor's inner sight, forms a holistic law, a law born of the heart, witnessed by the mind, anchored in ancestral remembrance. This is the path forward: when law is humbled by lore, and lore is emboldened by law's clarity. A true synthesis of the prophecy unfolding in healing time. Ayahuasca removes the veil to access this truth where it may become emblazoned in the hearts and minds of those who consecrate the divine sacrament.

> *The patterns and innovations emerging from these ecosystems of practice are startling, transformative and cannot be designed or maintained by a single manager or external authority. They cannot even be imagined outside of a community operating this way. This is the perspective you need to be a custodian rather than an owner of lands, communities or knowledge. It demands the relinquishing of artificial power and control, immersion in the astounding patterns of creation that only emerge through the free movement of all agents and elements within a system. This impacts the way we are managed and governed.* — Tyson Yunkaporta, *Sand Talk*.

In faith, I remembered the sacred teachings and the visions that were shared with me. The immense sacrifices and painful ego deaths I had endured to receive these blessings. In my prayer was the remembrance in all of humanity that we connect from the heart and into the heart of humanity. There is always a way forward where we can meet in harmony, where evolution of the human soul happens in sacred trust. I felt at this time of my life the weight of the responsibility to the divine blessings in the gifts I had received, and prayed for the courage and strength to hold this light of truth through the swamps and harsh realities of the human intellect and the systems it has created, that it defends, in disconnection from the Earth and spiritual wisdom.

Spiritual sovereignty

The choice to hold Ayahuasca ceremonies in Australia, a country where naturally occurring psychedelic plants remain legally misrepresented and culturally stigmatised, carries weight beyond personal healing. It is not rebellion; it is resonance. For many of us, this path is not adopted, but remembered as a spiritual, ancestral, and moral alignment, with a way of being that calls us into service to humanity and the Earth. We recognise the laws of the land, but we also answer to deeper laws: natural lore of reciprocity, of kinship, of spiritual alignment. These are not abstract ideals. They are living codes that guide how we relate to the Earth, to each other and to what is sacred. Their effectiveness is proven by the endurance of thousands of years of continuous, living Indigenous cultures all over the world which universally embrace these natural laws.

The criminalisation of sacred plant allies — beings that emerge directly from the intelligence of the Earth — is an absurdity that represents a deep disturbance in natural evolution and spiritual law. These are not synthetic inventions. They are divine sacraments, natural expressions of the planet's own intelligence entrusted to humanity through countless generations of conscious communion in ceremonial relationship. When human institutions, rooted in fear, ignorance or cultural supremacy, impose prohibitions upon these divine sacraments, they do not protect. They perpetuate spiritual amnesia, causing great harm. They override the birthright of communion with Nature, and in doing so they deny the human soul one of its oldest forms of remembrance. This cruel abuse overrides ancient spiritual relationships with ignorant bureaucratic mandates, thereby perpetuating trauma rather than healing it. As Saint Augustine wrote, 'An unjust law is no law at all.' And as Martin Luther King Jr affirmed, 'One has a moral responsibility to disobey unjust laws.' In this light, our ceremonies are not acts of defiance. They are acts of devotion and fidelity to coherent practices, older and far more sacred than incoherent legal statutes made with corrupt processes.

In the discussion on ways to overcome the insanity of a toxic culture and it's trauma-inducing, and often deadly, public health policies, Gabor Maté explains in his book *The Myth of Normal* the challenge that healthy people face with integration of self-actualisation.

> As it turns out, it is often individuals who defy conventional normality who are the healthy ones. The psychologist Abraham Maslow made the investigation of self-actualisation — the attainment of authentic satisfaction not based on external valuations — his life's work. "A study of people healthy enough to be self-actualised," he wrote in a widely read paper, "revealed that they were not 'well adjusted' (in the naïve sense of approval of and identification with the culture)." These healthy people, suggested Maslow, had a complex relationship with their "much less healthy culture". Neither conformists nor automatically reflexive rebels, such men and women expressed their unconventionality in ways that kept them true to their inner values, without hostility but not without fight, when that was called for. "An inner feeling of detachment from the culture was not necessarily conscious but was displayed by almost all … They very frequently seemed to be able to stand off from it, as if they did not quite belong to it."

It is important to acknowledge that the vast majority of people who come to Ayahuasca (certainly in my experience) do so with the intention of becoming a better person, improving self, relationships and their role in the world, and in most cases end up wanting to find ways to support others and society to heal. This is a lot more than can be said for the politicians and bureaucrats who formulate and enforce insane laws perpetuating the traumas and abuses of an unjust society, often with dubious intentions and usually without a deep or nuanced understanding of what they are doing, whilst most likely also lacking and being resistant to self-awareness.

There is a misguided arrogance in believing that human law, especially law born from colonial frameworks and disconnected worldviews, can nullify the sovereignty of the Earth or the Spirit. As if punitive legality were more sacred than life. As if safety could be found in suppression. In choosing to hold ceremony anyway, we are not resisting the law; we are obeying something older, an ancient truth that is our birthright. We are responding to a call that predates legislation and transcends punishment: the call to heal, to remember, to realign with the laws of Spirit, of Nature, and of the heart. We do this in the face of a global mental health catastrophe, endless social and political crises, environmental disaster and war. Ceremony is not a loophole. It is a living prayer offered in the face of cultural amnesia and its devastating effects, a positive act of devotion, not to ideology, but to harmony. Natural lore.

This spiritual commitment must also be held in direct relationship with the land we are on. In Australia, ceremony does not occur in a vacuum; it happens in the presence of Country. The trauma of colonisation here is not historical; it is active, living in the dispossession of Indigenous people, the suppression of their ceremonial rights, and the silencing of their spiritual sovereignty. As non-Indigenous facilitators of Brazilian-origin spiritual lineages, we do not offer this work in isolation. We open our space with humility, prayer and care as a sanctuary where Aboriginal people may also find reconnection with their own sacred traditions. Whilst we do not claim to hold those lineages, we hold space for them to rise. In our prayers, our songs and the Earth-based sacraments we work with, we make a sacred offering — that our circle can be a place of mutual remembrance and solidarity. This is reflected in global movements such as the eagle condor and other gatherings which bring together Indigenous peoples and emerging tribes from all over the world in solidarity.

This choice exists within the broader context of Australia's spiritual suppression, where Indigenous cultures were outlawed, Country was stolen along with children, languages banned and ceremonial lives shattered. Elders were punished, sometimes killed, for practising their ways. Much of this is still within the living memory of Australian Aboriginal peoples, and in some ways, it is still happening. Recognising this, we bear responsibility not only to our collective psyche, but to the spirit of Country. Ancient Aboriginal traditions hold deep wisdom around native plants: acacia trees containing DMT have been used for thousands of years in medicine, ceremonial cleansing and psychoactive rituals, though these remain rarely shared outside community protocols.

> *Ceremonial use of these plants is kept hidden from others in the tribe ... this is true for a wide variety of bush medicine, not just the acacia species.* – Charlotte McAdam, *Mind Medicine Australia*.

By bringing Ayahuasca ceremony into this territory, we enter into a matrix of human rights and spiritual sovereignty — the rights to religious freedom, to plant knowledge, and to right-relationship with Country. Western colonial frameworks have attempted to erase these rights, regulating and commodifying sacred medicines while ignoring lineage and ancient practice, and disrespecting ancestral and living Elders and peoples. To truly decolonise this work, we must uplift Indigenous voices and weave genuine reciprocity into the practice. This is not a merging or appropriation; it is a respectful invitation for cultural camaraderie in a sacred alliance where reconciliation moves beyond apology and enters the body. The presence of Brazilian spirituality, rooted in communal song, spiritual discipline and reverence for living sacrament, can help re-weave a fabric of belonging. In a country still reckoning with the harms of stolen land and broken spirit, these ceremonial spaces are meeting grounds — not of sameness, but of shared healing, remembrance and reconciliation. We believe this is part of the greater harmonisation of Australia's cultural field, where sacred plant medicines, in their many forms, help restore coherence not only in the individual but across ancestral lineages, communities and nations. It is with great sorrow that I acknowledge the great harms done to the Indigenous custodians of this land and across all lands, and where my ancestors have both transgressed and been transgressed. And with great sorrow I acknowledge my own transgressions against Country and culture. As humanity we face a painful truth — and that is the brutal abuses inflicted on the human soul. In Australia that truth is amplified and alive in the psyche. I have a vision: that in peace and harmony may a path of love be forged as a new way emerges, a new dreaming of unity and respect in natural lore.

Guarani nation
May Tupã protect you

Paraiba killed
The Indians of the forest

Paraiba knows
Paraiba saw
Paraiba cried

— *Origens*, composer unknown.

Sacred ground — sacred silence

> *It is important to emphasise, however, that within the Santo Daime tradition, healing is not necessarily equated with a physical cure. The Daime is said to do more than cure physical or emotional ills. Equally importantly, Daimistas believe that drinking the Daime engenders and supports healing at the deepest level, in that it ignites a process of spiritual growth, that is, the movement from the darkness and suffering of ignorance and illusion toward the Light and Joy of Divine Love and self-awareness. In this broadest sense, the entire thrust of the Santo Daime tradition can be seen as unifying the often separate tasks of healing and spiritual development.* — G William Barnard, Liquid Light.

During the months after I had returned to Australia and walked the path of integration, I met many people with an interest in Ayahuasca and Brazilian spiritual lineages. I spent the time gathering information and connecting with people and communities to find out what was happening in the field of Ayahuasca circles and with those who were hearing the call to experience the Light of the Forest. It was important to me to know what people were presenting with, where their intentions lay and how they might be best served within the framework of the knowledge, skills and experience I was able to offer. People approached me with all kinds of requests and suggestions, such as giving me ideas on how I could run ceremonies, who to run them with, in what format to run them and more. To me, though, there was really only one way for me to go forward. If this path were to unfold, it would be to develop a spiritual practice aligned with Ciranda and the lineages I had been taught and trained within. I was not interested in inventing something new or offering some kind of psychedelic therapy practice. My guides, my training and teachings were all aligned within the practices I had become so familiar with in Brazil, and I was devoted to continuing these practices. It was, however, daunting to think that I knew no one in Australia at the time who had any knowledge or experience of Ciranda and Carioca's work. I had, though, met some friends in the years prior to this who were part of the Brazilian churches Santo Daime and the União do Vegetal which were practising in Australia. Although there is alignment and common practices and beliefs between these churches, I was bringing something with its own distinct ancestry, culture, harmonic signature and spiritual constellation. Like many times previously in my life, I was being asked to trust deeply in Spirit and allow myself to be guided by the force of creation. In faith, I followed this guidance.

Whilst preparing to facilitate ceremonies, it was important that I spent a lot of time contemplating, meditating and writing about the guiding principles of the work I would be offering. I understood clearly that I was interested in founding a spiritual circle where I could pray and practise with Ayahuasca as I had done in Brazil. This had become intrinsic to my life and my soul's expression. Brazilian Ayahuasca ceremony, beliefs and culture had become my life and contained many of the guiding principles I lived and live by. The blessings, training and initiations I had received along the way were gifts. I felt a strong and solemn sense of responsibility to walk them with grace and integrity. Writing down guiding principles would create a clear container of agreed intention for me, the work and for anyone who may like to join. Like Carioca, I was not called to create a religion with rules, dogmas and social expectations. As

I have described at length in this book, the teachings, healing and spiritual development come through the practice and through the communion with the sacrament we call Ayahuasca. I was not interested in putting myself in between that, or creating something that didn't flow from the source of those teachings, from the forest and from Ayahuasca itself. As a ceremonial leader, my role is to be of service in a way that I am not elevated above anyone else, although I am trained to be the instrument of Spirit and a lens through which the Light of the Forest may shine through. I carry the teachings and the blessings in my developed knowledge and skills, but they are also transmitted through me directly from Great Spirit. Ultimately, this spiritual path awakens all who are committed to it to develop their own communion and also open up their own channels. I knew that the way was to teach. It was important for me to let anyone know who would come to any spiritual work I might conduct that this was a spiritual path where healing might and would likely occur, although the practice was essentially spiritual.

Over the next year, I worked with Jesse and a small group to begin holding ceremonies and spiritual studies with music and Ayahuasca. There was a lot to get through for the ceremonies to be coherent and held in a way that was clear and safe. This included bringing awareness and firmness to the way we hold space in consideration of the spiritual, emotional, physical and cultural needs of the practitioners whilst in communion with the spirit of Ayahuasca. For some, this wasn't so easy to integrate, especially those who already had some Ayahuasca experiences and exposure to other lineages and teachings, and was even harder for those that had been drinking Ayahuasca in cowboy-style ceremonies with people who had not done formal training, were not connected to lineage and where the ego seemed to have free reign. One of the biggest challenges was to contain the egos and expectations being projected towards myself and the spiritual work. Over time, this weeded out those who were not truly interested in the path being offered, and strengthened for the ones who wanted to learn, who could feel the connection, felt the beauty and power in the music and took the time to study the meaning, intentions and effects of it. As Carioca had said to me, we choose to show and do the work because we grow and learn and we invest in ourselves. In those early days there were times where I was really pining for community in Brazil or anyone who knew the culture. In some ways this was perfect, as I was able to guide the development of the ceremonies in a gentle and cautious way, and in an organic and slow progression. For me, one of the most important aspects of it all was beyond the ceremonies and the work with Ayahuasca. It was about how we showed up in life, how we integrated the experiences and how we shared together as community. Learning how to be better humans, as we are part of a huge global community of humanity. It is common for people on spiritual paths to build connection and community around the common intention. Ayahuasca is a strong example of this phenomenon. Beyond self-responsibility then, a question that expands the field of the ceremonies is, 'How do we support our brothers and sisters on this journey?' My years of working as a community development specialist in government and non-government organisations had also given me a lot of skills and knowledge to draw upon. Together, our fledgling group was growing the awareness of holding our firmeza, experiencing the healing through the practice and, when able, being of service to the ceremony and to others.

> *Ey-o, Eyo!*
> *Let's all call the blessings (Saravá!)*
> *Who is sick, will be healed*
> *Who is healed, will work*
>
> — *Xangô Caô*, Luz Ametista.

One clear difference to Brazilian culture that was emerging through these ceremonies was in the connection to the spirit of the land. Jesse would play his yidakis (didgeridoos) with ancient traditional rhythms he had been taught by the Yolngu. During this time, there was much interest in these ancient sounds and vibrations, prayers and the connection to the land and the spirit of the Indigenous peoples. Through his experiences with Ayahuasca, Jesse was inspired to return to Arnhem Land to reconnect with the people and Elders, to deepen his knowledge and find ways to give something back for all the healing and spiritual development that those teachings had brought for him and so many others. A bridge was built between our growing spiritual community and one of the oldest cultures on Earth. Jesse is still working today closely with the custodians of the yidaki and its ancient songs, and he tells his story in the chapter 'Voices and Perspectives'. Many people from our community over the years have studied with Jesse and he has organised many trips to visit the Yolngu clans. Over the years that followed, we began to make contact with Indigenous leaders and Elders, who would often come to share stories and offer blessings and traditional ceremonies. Along this journey many Indigenous friends have joined us in ceremony and prayer. For many, Ayahuasca has helped them to reconnect to Country, to culture and to family. It is not unusual for an Indigenous brother to arrive at my house, dishevelled and lost, confused and drifting, damaged by the harsh Australian society. In these moments I light a fire, have a good yarn about life, about Country, about ancestors and family. I remind them of who they are. Some come to ceremony and shed

Yidaki (didgeridoo) workshop with Jesse during retreat, Northern NSW, Australia

layers of trauma, shake themselves off, reconnect to Spirit, purpose, culture and Country. I have had Elders thank me for the work I have done over the years in being there for young Aboriginal men, keeping them out of trouble and on the right track.

We always hold ceremony in reverence of the forces of nature in a sacred space that honours the land and the ancestors. For many this has been a safe space to do their sovereign spiritual work. To me this is a great blessing — to hold this sacred ground in harmony and respect, in the spirit of the prophecy of the eagle and the condor, with the great Dreaming trails of the Earth re-uniting. The mystery of Great Spirit, the weaving and snaking colours of the Rainbow Serpent's Dreaming, have played a great role in the creation of our spiritual point of light, illuminating the way of the hummingbird here in Australia. This is the lore of living in harmony, where healing is in the living. The teachings of ancient Australia and its people and culture resonate the deepest in my soul. The sounds and rhythms of this land dream into the miração of Ayahuasca and the Light of the Forest in ancient remembering. The immensity of this ancient spirit and its vast, emanating wisdom commands that we show respect in humility and in the sacred silence of *dadirri* (listening deeply).

It's something from the light
Calling you tonight
The inner child alive
A silent voice inside

If time is on our side
And a gentle soul resides
In the darkness we will find
The key to free our mind

Lightening comes and brings the change
To show the way to better days

The river flows, the ocean knows
The wind blows and so it goes...

Eyes that see what can't be seen
Ears that hear what can't be heard
Upon the breath, what can't be told
Sacred silence, we behold

The silence bares a sound
That the mind has never found
Just like a passing cloud
Beyond the spirit shroud

When stars and time align
And love will be our guide
It will open up our minds
In dreams we'll always fly

— *Sacred Silence*, Lore Solaris.

At times in the pause of a ceremony, in the force of the Light of the Forest on sacred ground in Australia, we sit around the fire in silence, feeling the land and honouring the sacred silence, dadirri. A beautiful part of the practice of our Ciranda circles, where we honour silence in the ceremony, allows for the same practice of dadirri, which is a foundation of ancient Australian culture. It is evidenced in the silence of two eagles dancing in the sky, Dream-weaving. Aboriginal professor and author Judy Atkinson wrote about dadirri in her book *Trauma Trails: Recreating Song Lines*.

> *Dadirri has been called "the Aboriginal Gift". Miriam Rose Ungunmerr says it is a "special quality, a unique gift of the Aboriginal people. It is inner deep listening and quiet, still awareness — something like what you call contemplation". The principles and functions of dadirri are a knowledge and consideration of community and the diversity and unique nature that each individual brings to community, a non-intrusive observation, or quietly aware watching, a deep listening and hearing with more than the ears, a reflective non-judgemental consideration of what*

is being seen and heard, and, having learnt from the listening, a purposeful plan to act, with actions informed by learning, wisdom and the informed responsibility that comes with knowledge.

I have spent many nights in silence by the sacred fire in the presence of Indigenous Elders, listening deeply. Sometimes entering into the miração of the Dreamtime, sometimes communicating telepathically. Some Aboriginal people I have sat with in ceremony have journeyed with me telepathically into the Amazon, the astral emerald forest and its divine light. It is a beautiful gift for them to then describe the following day the majestic Light of the Forest, as I have seen it. I have learned a lot about navigating the mirações of Ayahuasca from reflections and conversations with Aboriginal people after ceremonies. I have come to call this the 'Art of Dreaming': navigating the sacred flight through the astral, the miração. You don't need Ayahuasca to take you to dadirri, though the medicine can greatly help clear the way, but with practice, concentration and presence, dadirri can take you into the visions of miração.

Sacred music — sacred culture

In the last few months I was in Brazil, I started working on putting together a book of all the songs I had learned from Carioca, the Yawanawá and other circles in Brazil. Over the six months I was integrating in Australia, I added other songs I wanted to learn plus some of my own songs, and brought in a full constellation of songs and callings, prayers and chants that I could sing in ceremonies. I gave the songbook the name *Sky Dancing Ciranda*, in honour of the visions I had received connecting Australia and Brazil, the eagle and the condor and my two feathers from the Australian eagle and the Brazilian hawk. This was also in honour of the miração I had learned so much from and how to navigate its beauty, depth, challenges and mystery. We are like eagles learning to fly in a spiritual dance in our

Ciranda circle of singing and dancing, honouring our inner child, the trauma that has shaped us, and the gifts we receive from Spirit when we open our hearts and minds into the vast inner sky. Always in faith that the Earth's wind will always hold us and carry us, delivering us safely home. It was a joy to see people taking the songbook, studying and learning the songs, getting together with guitars and teaching each other and jamming the music. I felt that the magic of Carioca and Ciranda was pulsing through our group and this was a great sign for me to know that I was on the right track of holding the light of the prayers and the lineage in its truth while witnessing it evolving.

During this time of growth and learning together as a spiritual family, a lot of my time was spent preparing myself, the music and everything necessary to continue the work. A lot of this was about being there for the people who were doing the work with me. I was conscious of organising events, music nights and study gatherings to build community and provide safe spaces that didn't always include Ayahuasca. It was beautiful to see the growth in relationships and people making positive life choices and family reconciliations, following creative dreams, finding new loves and having new babies, with the circle eventually expanding beyond myself and Ayahuasca. At no point was there any advertising or suggestions or requests for people to come to ceremony. The circle evolved organically and naturally unfolded with everyone being invited by word of mouth. Often people would want to encourage their loved ones to come to ceremony and ask me about it. My advice would always be the same: it's important not to push anyone or tell them to come to ceremony. The person must make a clear choice from within, without influence on their decision. Besides this, my experience has shown me that when someone wants to drink Ayahuasca and they are ready, they are clear about this and don't need to be convinced of anything. Personally, I wouldn't want anyone to come to a ceremony of mine who was not clear of their intention and choice. Besides, I had seen this before in Brazil and if someone did go because of their partner's pressure, or because someone wanted them to, they did not get much from the experience anyway. People would present with all kinds of intentions, experience and expectations when wanting to come to ceremony.

Many people, especially Australians, would be surprised about the nature of the ceremonies, the singing of prayers from songbooks. Once people relaxed into the experience and saw the function of the music, culture and the participation, the ceremony would make sense. Some were familiar with the ways of ceremonies based on experiences they may have had in the dark with a Shipibo shaman, for example. For most, though, the clarity, function and communal prayers and 'group shamanism' gave them a vast field of study and experience, opening many diverse pathways for growth and healing. A lot of new musicians were born. A lot of layers of trauma would be released; broken hearts were mended and opened like flowers. The ceremonies and the community was a gentle, safe, welcoming space for people to open up in and feel loved and supported. I was very careful not to create hierarchies and cliques. Over the years many people had tried to do this and played out their insecurities and behaviours. It was important to be mindful of social dynamics and politics and how they could become traumatising, within and outside of ceremony. The spiritual point of the work, the teachings and the ever-present growth in firmeza, mindfulness and humility would hold the ground strongly, through all the political ups and downs that humans go through. Sometimes human dynamics can be a rocky road! We must be equipped to ride the waves like hearty sailors in the arms of Yemanjá, even when her oceans are stormy. At the end of it all, we laugh, we dance, we sing, we return to joy. But the goal is not to be in that joy, the ecstasy. It is to be balanced and present, and ride all the waves. Not to shy away from the pain and discomfort of our subconscious wounds and shadows, and how they affect us. We have to do the work, and when we do, we come into alignment with the peace of love and joy in harmony and alignment with Great Spirit. As we create this together, we heal in our practice and as we achieve that in ceremony, we can apply it in our lives. As community we support each other in the remembrance of who we truly are.

People from all kinds of backgrounds were attracted to the work. Sydney is a highly multicultural city with diverse communities of immigrants from all over the world. I was happy to welcome them and noticed that many had a sense of disconnection from their cultures and sometimes their families, while often carrying a lot of trauma. In the ceremonies a lot of healing happened, with people releasing the traumas of war and oppression, and being able to attend a safe space where they could be free to express their own spiritual beliefs and practices. We would have people play Ukrainian harp, there were Hebrew chants, Georgian flutes, Iranian singers and much more. Many made friends and connections through the circle, reducing their isolation. Some would become more active, learn the songs and be conscious of holding space, while others would come and quietly do their spiritual work. As a community, we learn a lot about what we all bring, our own unique medicine, and how this can be of service and benefit to others. Some people came because they had things they wanted to heal: addictions, depression, disconnection, lack of direction and purpose. I always make it clear that we gather to pray with Ayahuasca as a spiritual practice. The healing is part of it and welcomed — but not the reason we hold the ceremony. The healing is in living. There are many aspects of these ceremonies that facilitate a healing journey: the music, the community, the prayers, communion with spiritual beings, the connection and, most importantly, the personal insight. Most people would reflect to me that the greatest benefit they got from participating in ceremony was a general feeling of wellbeing. Following the ceremonies they would feel more peaceful and at ease with themselves, relationships and life. Some received deep personal and spiritual insights that often could be life changing. From the lineage of Santo Daime, this aligns with the doctrine of awakening the Christ within.

Hundreds of people over the years have reported to me that they have ceased addictive behaviours after ceremony — in many cases, permanently. Breaking addictions is very common and can happen quite immediately. Other conditions like depression, negative thinking and a lack of self-accountability can be harder to shift when we are dealing with core wounds and their masks and behaviours. Over time, and with patience, dedication and practice, a lot of progress can be made. Many people greatly benefit from regular ceremonial practice, whether that is to keep shedding the layers of wounds and healing, or to build connection with community, or deepening spiritual studies and developing their creativity through music and other arts. For some, becoming proficient, confident and holding strong firmeza whilst praying and singing their hearts out is part of their lives, and part of who they are. I know that is where Ayahuasca took me.

In my experience it is common for people who come to work with Ayahuasca to report that they have shifted to a more spiritual perspective of the world. One male participant shared the following:

> *I am integrating the work well now and can feel a substantial shift towards alignment with my path. In particular, recognising how so many experiences that I have enjoyed in my life have laid the foundations for where I am now and for this work. "Humbled" is the resounding word, along with a sense of renewed TRUST. Actually, my biggest lesson gained on Thursday night during ceremony was all about trust, which, after meditating on your reflection of me being too often "worried" seems to be the appropriate antidote. Trusting to dissolve the worry. Trusting that I am held by something far greater than I could have imagined, trusting that this journey that I am on in my life, and that we are all on, is just as it is, and needs to be, which is such a massive lesson to come to terms with, especially with so much suffering going on in the world today.*

People over the years have sometimes told me about physical conditions being cured through their work in ceremonies. They may attribute this to Ayahuasca, which could be true, and it also could be true that they have healed their minds, overcome fears, reduced stress, calmed their nervous system and found peace, all of which has been shown through research to allow the body to naturally heal. We all want to feel connected. We all want to feel safe. We live in a society that intrinsically makes us feel unsafe and disconnected, and we build an architecture of defence in order to survive the toxic onslaught that usually begins when we are in the womb. As Gabor Maté points out at length and in great detail in his book *The Myth of Normal*: we live in a toxic society that makes us sick. This reinforces why it is so important to practise firmeza, mindfulness, gratitude and humility in the Ayahuasca space. We can, if this is done with this mindfulness, become pioneers of creating a new culture of healthy living, positive community actions, and movement towards growth in harmony with Nature. In my experience, in all cases Ayahuasca helps to harmonise us with our true nature, our humanity, and with the Earth, which allows us to make choices that lead to inner peace and harmony. The extent to which we choose this and continue the practices in our daily waking life depends on how sustainable and far-reaching in our lives the positive effects of Ayahuasca will manifest themselves. This remains the greatest challenge for practitioners in Western and urban environments.

Ceremonial Ayahuasca is a divine gift at this time in human history when we need it the most. As the civilisational push toward collective human suicide marches relentlessly forward, the Light of the Forest has become accessible in various forms to a huge amount of people around the world. I have also noticed over the years that Ayahuasca is not for everyone — there are many spiritual paths. I believe there is overwhelming evidence, common sense and natural justice for ceremonial Ayahuasca to be recognised as a valuable and valid spiritual and cultural treasure and to be welcomed and supported in Australian and global society. I believe we can collectively move beyond archaic prejudices, scientific and political dogmas, immature insults and ridicule. What I received from Ayahuasca and Ciranda was the healing of my deep childhood wounds, the psychological and emotional pain of growing up as the son and grandson of war veterans. My grandfather fought and survived the Western front and then the battle of Gallipoli in the First World War, renowned as the most deadly and brutal battle of the war, and (in)famous in Australian culture and history. I was able to sit with my father before he died as he told me stories of the cruelty and horrors of the war in Vietnam, where he fought so valiantly. He spoke of facing the pain of the fruitlessness of it, of the manipulation and lies that were told to the people about the war. He witnessed many acts of slaughter of women and children at the hands of the US and Australian military command. And had the realisation that it was all profiteering and propaganda. This pain and sacrifice I carry with me throughout my life — the betrayal of the Australian Government against its own people, against humanity. I carry the flame for my family on the frontline in defence of humanity. For me, Ayahuasca has brought remedy for the effects of trauma on my nervous system and psyche, trauma leading to depression, post-traumatic stress and anxiety. Ayahuasca has become a gift of knowledge, wisdom and service to help others through their own traumas. Through all this work, the prayer in my heart is that we can be free to live in peace and harmony and to evolve ourselves and see an end to all war. The first act is to end the war inside the self. This is what I have learned. That's why, in my ceremonies, I always welcome people home. They are coming home to themselves. Coming home to Country and community. Perhaps the young ones and the ones yet to come may not have to suffer the pain and disconnection that I and so many others have had to endure. The hope is that we can harmonise and rebalance ourselves as a human family and with the Earth, returning to our role as guardians and custodians of our beautiful, divine, life-giving planet.

It is important to acknowledge that throughout my experiences with Ayahuasca it is clear to me that special care needs to be given to supporting women to feel safe in ceremony and community. This goes beyond gender roles and politics. The reality is that women in our society suffer immensely from inequality, projections, unwanted sexual attention and lack of safety. Ayahuasca communities have a greater responsibility to ensure that women feel safe, especially in ceremonies led by men. We are all vulnerable in a space where we are very open, and therefore there is great responsibility to hold a safe space. I have been immensely grateful for the role of strong women in our community supporting women participants to feel safe and to release their grief, fear and trauma within ceremonies and in the community. This is why in our tradition we feel it so important to have separate men's and women's spaces in ceremony. I have been deeply touched on many occasions to see the way women are able to support each other with so much vulnerability, openness and love. The strength that shines forth in those women's spaces has been a great privilege to work with, and I am constantly asking for guidance from the women who work closely with me, including Elders and in the community, to learn how we can ensure the safety of the space. It has also been important to support men in learning how they, too, can show up to support women, which often involves them accessing their own vulnerabilities and healing. Equally, it is important to recognise that around 10% of the population has diverse sexuality and gender expressions. Whilst there is currently backlash against 'woke-ism' (performative justice) and the weaponising of the politics around this group of people, whatever the nature of their self-expression, identity or who they might be attracted to, they also need to be honoured and equally to feel safe and included. I am blessed in my many years of experience to have worked with marginalised and minority groups while also having strong women and social justice warriors around me. One woman shared with me:

> *This was my third ceremony with you and I truly get like I was home — the longing I have been waiting for my whole life after never truly fitting in and being placed in a box with all these mental health labels. I feel so free, free of fear and judgment, full of love and gratitude for the experience I am full of acceptance. Thank you thank you thank you!!!*

I believe that anyone or any group working with Ayahuasca or any psychedelic plant medicines needs to be aware of creating safe and inclusive spaces, to consult with their community and to be very mindful that they are not re-traumatising their participants. One woman come to me and explained that she had never felt she was truly connecting to Ayahuasca because she wasn't receiving visions or insights. She had been attending ceremonies with a male leader and had asked for help. She was repeatedly told that she had 'dark energy' and needed to improve her posture and preparation. She kept going back to this circle over several years with always the same experience, and felt bad that she was somehow doing things wrong and 'not good enough'. I was impressed that she kept going back to try, that she was dedicated to uncover what Ayahuasca had to offer, but also aware that she was repeating a life pattern of re-traumatising herself and reinforcing negative self-belief. By the time she found me and our group, she was apologetic that she had some kind of darkness and didn't want to infect the rest of the group. It seemed to me that her previous ceremonial leader had been unwittingly blaming her. When I enquired deeper it turned out that she hadn't been feeling safe in those ceremonies for a variety of reasons and we were able to go over all the reasons and find ways to make her experience in our circle feel safe, which included sitting her close to a female guardian. It was important for her to direct her own experience and I was able to honour her and her needs just by being curious and allowing her to express. I also gave her some guidance around mindfulness practices she might use if she felt safe and able to. It was also important to let her know that she wasn't doing anything wrong, and that whatever her experience was, it was okay. I could see her body relax when we had that conversation and I asked her if she felt she could give herself permission to not have to perform or to have any specific kind of experience, and to let go of expectations. She had a huge release with lots of tears that night. In the morning she was elated that she had seen visions and felt held by Ayahuasca. She shared that our conversation had helped her realise the weight she had carried growing up with an overbearing father and a disapproving mother. She expressed gratitude for the women who actively supported her to feel safe, allowing her to heal.

It is very common for the women participants to find a lot of safety and healing by doing the ceremonies with the support of strong women guardians. A group from a women's empowerment circle came to ceremony with me and one of them reflected after her first ceremony:

> What a blessing. Honestly the trauma, pain and suffering I have experienced through my hero's journey felt like it left my bones on Saturday, and pouring it into the Earth and thanking Aya for removing it from my body was a type of healing no other modality could ever replace. I saw myself at the feet of a thousand grandmothers before me, purging their own pain and suffering, and it was way beyond me and my individual journey. I had said

in circle with the woman a few months ago that I felt the women in my family just sang this old song of trauma. And abuse. And pain and suffering. And I didn't want to sing that song to my daughter. Well, that song dissipated Saturday evening and I am writing a new song and I can't even begin to describe how that experience has changed my life. Honoured. And forever blessed to have been held in such a sacred ceremony. I went into the ceremony with the intention of offering my respect, devotion and appreciation to Aya, hoping to in turn receive her wisdom, healing and protection — and, boy, did she deliver.

I always encourage people to write to me with reflections, and always make sure that everyone knows they can access me or others in the circle for support post the ceremony. This is a crucially important factor in this work, and goes a long way to supporting people to feel safe.

It is not uncommon for people to come to ceremonies carrying anxiety for what they think might, or should, happen. This is often the case with people who have read a lot and watched videos on YouTube and built up a lot of expectations. I always encourage them to follow the protocols and practices of our ceremony, which are quite simple: sit up, listen or sing along with the music, maintain sacred silence, concentrate the mind and use the central altar as a point of focus if the mind gets busy. They are also always made aware that help is available, that even though they naturally have the resources within themselves to navigate whatever may come up, if at any time they do not feel safe or need help, to let us know. People sometimes become frustrated that Ayahuasca didn't give them what they wanted, or in some cases felt entitled, to receive, just by showing up. I try to explain that Ayahuasca is also a living being, and generally does not respond to mental or emotional demands. Ayahuasca has a graceful dignity. It is usually not about the dose given either. It is about acceptance and personal surrender. And it is letting go of the ego and the mind, because if we are in this mental, rational, intellectual posture with Ayahuasca, we are working contrary to its nature. Being caught in mental loops or obsessive thoughts is not 'bad' or 'wrong', but if you are there, then examine that, look at your mind, observe any emotional reactions of frustration, fear, anger, blame. These can be blocks to the intuitive self and are not supportive of entering into the miração. So what are the teachings being offered? They may not be what we want, but they are what is happening. When we come into acceptance of that and let it go, then magic can happen. As ceremonial leader I can sense when there is mental and emotional resistance inhibiting the flow of the current, the force of Ayahuasca. I have songs and techniques to move the group beyond this. But this needs to be guided in a natural way where things organically unfold, and should never be done with any forceful actions or intentions. Regulating the amount of force in the ceremony is very important, as too much may tip people into mental panic or anxiety if they are not ready for that depth. This is a refined skill I have developed over many years. Each song has a prayer, intention and calling, and must be used with careful attention and intent informed by the group and by Ayahuasca and the spiritual guides. This is why practitioners must do serious training, because the risk is that people can be pushed over the edge in terms of what they can mentally or emotionally handle. When we talk about the risks of Ayahuasca, I believe that the biggest risk is of re-traumatising vulnerable people and leaving them confused, or at worst mentally disturbed. What I am sharing here are some of the practices we use to mitigate this risk and hold a safe space.

Another common expectation people often present with is that they have a great fear that Ayahuasca is going to somehow punish them. This may be because in a previous ceremony they may have had some harsh realisations about their mind and behaviours, faced a painful memory, perhaps of abuse, or had some physical discomfort as they were cleansing their bodies and minds. This fear may also be because they have convinced themselves that they have been so disorganised, lazy or not good enough in their lives that they deserve punishment. Again this shows how important it is to talk to each participant before ceremony to check in with how they are feeling in themselves and how they are feeling about ceremony. I would say that most people, regardless of how experienced they are, report that they feel at least a little anxiety, mixed with excitement.

To me this is healthy and common. It is also honest. With Ayahuasca, we are dealing with a powerful presence and a strong spiritual force which takes us not only into the depths of our subconscious, but also to the magnificence of Spirit and the mystery and majesty of Ayahuasca and our potential as humans. For most of us on the path of spiritual development, it can be daunting to see how much work we need to do to uncover what's in our soul and the work needed to truly embody this. Sometimes the contrast with the life we are living is overwhelming.

Interestingly, I have observed that in almost all cases where people come with expectations of punishment, they end up having a blissful and joyful experience, full of self-love, affirmation and confirmation of purpose. I like to reflect on this point. Ayahuasca is not a torturer. If you have passed through your darkness and pain and purged the toxic physical and mental burdens, then why would you need to do this again? Especially now that work has been done, or at least the start of the work — which is the toughest part. Once this has occurred, we are more able to explore higher realms, happy thoughts and feelings that fill the spaces where the negativity was. Also, sometimes we subconsciously want to punish ourselves, and for those of us who have spent our lives in self-critical mental obsessions, constantly beating ourselves up with pressure to be better or do more, the remedy for that is to let go and have fun, be joyous, find positivity, play and be like a child. Giving ourselves permission to be free to play and enjoy life or the ceremony and the music can be the greatest realisation for many. And for some of us — and I also relate to this — the greatest work isn't admitting our faults or seeing our shadows; it's believing that we deserve to be happy and allow ourselves to honour our wounded inner child with play, joy, beauty, music, dance and love. But we must not to become attached to this because always on the journey we will find more layers, more pain that needs to be released, challenges to overcome, and deeper truths to be faced. It is not about creating attachments to the good stuff that life offers; it's about finding the balance and acceptance and good humour to ride all the waves, big and small, rough and smooth, stormy or sun-kissed.

... a word to the wise — or those who wish to be. If we remove the hyphen from "re-create", we are left with the verb form of "recreation", as in "play". An excellent reminder that we do ourselves no favours by taking ourselves, or the process of inquiry, so seriously that we lose a sense of spontaneity and vitality. These steps may not be much fun, but they still work best when infused with some lightness. I have seen more than a few people surprise themselves, mid process, with a smile. — Gabor Maté, *The Myth of Normal.*

In dealing with the clamour of the mind and all its drama and confusion when this is felt in ceremony, I will often invoke the Orixá, Yemanjá, Queen of the oceans and the seas, the '*dona das cabeças*' (the owner of the minds). Our minds dissolve into her unfathomable depths and teach us to be strong sailors of the ups and downs of the waves, with the wisdom of the inner ocean. Just as in life, for me, when my head is spinning, or I'm over-thinking or obsessing, I will go to the ocean, make prayers and give offerings to Yemanjá, go for a long walk on the beach and just let it all go. When my mind has had enough, and the thoughts naturally shift, I will sit and meditate and say some prayers in thanks and gratitude. I have always found that the ocean is a great healer for my mind. And when I am not in her beautiful presence, then I call her through song, with gratitude and praise. *Odoyá Yemanja!*

> *On the shore of the sea*
> *I will call Yemanjá*
>
> *In the blue of the sea*
> *I will cry out, Oh Yemanjá!*
> *Look, holy mother*
> *My song of pain*
> *Made in your praise*
>
> *Yemanjá!*

Hear my plea
Yemanjá, alleviate my pain
Oh, my father Xangô
Hey, my mother Yemanjá
come to my aid

— Na Beira do Mar, Os Tincoãs.

The Brazilian wave

A lot of Brazilians make great surfers, which is why many of them come to Australia and love it here. The migration of Brazilians into the ceremonies came like a big wave which evolved into a steady swell that holds strong to this day. It was great for me when, after some time, the Brazilian community started arriving at the ceremonies. Suddenly there were people who had been in similar kinds of ceremonies in Brazil or in Santo Daime churches or Umbanda *terreiros* (sacred grounds). The connection to the prayers and the ancestors and spirituality of the ceremony greatly elevated the experience and coherency of the ceremonies. I found it a huge relief that people would take care of things in the temple, in the music or in preparation and more, and knew what to do and why, without me explaining. Cultural protocols, language and religious and spiritual knowledge were a huge blessing that has grown and continues to grow and thrive. I benefitted enormously from being immersed into a fusion of Australian and Brazilian culture as we wove a new Dreaming trail through songs and community, prayer and ceremony. I can understand why Brazilians love to stay connected to other Brazilians when they migrate to Australia. Brazilian culture is warm and playful and expressive and vibrant. Brazil and Brazilians have a life-force pulsing within and a flaming fire of passion that expresses in all ways. Australian culture by comparison is slow moving and understated. For Brazilians, culture is sacred. People come together to celebrate life, where family is strong and cherished. A Brazilian woman shared the following after her first ceremony:

> *I was adopted in Brazil in the 80s and have no idea of my ancestry or lineage. I don't know whether I have siblings or whether my mother still lives or died during childbirth. All I know is that this experience really brought me home — it was profound and I want to thank you from the bottom of my heart for the music, for the thoughtfulness, for the dedication and devotion, and for holding this space. It was amazing and life changing.*

The ceremonies and their culture are deeply rooted in Brazil and it is a great honour to receive so many Brazilian people who choose to pray in our spiritual house at our sacred ceremonies. Commonly I will be met by a Brazilian participant at the end of a ceremony in tears who gives me a big hug and expresses their gratitude at being reconnected with their culture. Realising the pain of the separation. Some experience a great deal of healing of cultural wounds and feelings of shame for their country and its corruption, violence and injustice. The ceremonies serve as a cultural remembrance and a house of prayer. They are a safe home for people to stay connected to their spiritual and cultural roots. Many begin a journey of discovering their spiritual gifts, connecting to the Orixás, ancestors and caboclos. This has often led them to deeper studies through the ceremonies, to other Brazilian spiritual groups and also on return trips to Brazil. I am always impressed by how easily and quickly most Brazilians open into their spirituality, and with such depth of gratitude and reverence. The infectious Brazilian passion and enthusiasm will often sweep others along in its tides and waves. This is certainly what happened to me — with thanks to Great Spirit!

I'm grateful for all the gifts of shared knowledge and wisdom that people have brought to the ceremonies over the years. I have learned much from Brazilians of many lineages with similar and resonant beliefs and practices. I continue to keep learning more about the practices and the wisdom behind them. There is prayer and function in all the spiritual points and altars we create around the ceremonial space. Spiritual protection is vital inside the temple and within the spiritual field of the ceremony. Spiritual energies and forces can and do enter ceremonies, and any leaders, guardians or space holders must be aware of this, beyond just a few random prayers and a performance. The spiritual field of the ceremony is a container for the work to be done within. It must be held coherently, where the constellation of prayers, invocations, altars and points of light are in harmonic relationship. Once the field is coherent then it must be held intact. The space can be cleansed as energies release or the field needs some attunement. This can be done through music, specific songs that have the effect of sweeping the field and clearing energies, and through sometimes removing entities or beings that can emerge to also

Ceremony Northern Rivers NSW, Australia

be healed and transformed. At times I have learned the hard way when energies have leaked into the space. Each time I have asked the land and the guides for the remedy to maintain the field. I have also consulted spiritual leaders from my lineages and made trips to Brazil to deepen studies whenever I find some limitations in my knowledge or I have questions about the spiritual point of the ceremony, its functions, the guides and Orixás and how to work with them individually and in relation to each other. It is a constant path of learning from Spirit, growing and evolving.

I asked an Aboriginal Elder once about some guidance that was coming through to me in my miração during ceremonies. My guides were encouraging me to work deeper within the miração at untangling and clearing energies in the ceremony. At times I could see this pathway, and at other times I resisted or maintained physical awareness. But, as I had well-trained guardians to deal with the physical space, I could go deeper into working in the visionary field. This was another spiritual test of faith. I told the Elder about my experience and he reflected that for him, it was more efficient to work in the spiritual visionary field. He reminded me that this was a test of faith. Over time this is a skill that I have been working on more and more. When there is a moment where I can see pathways for deep inner spiritual work to clear or repair energies in the ceremony, I will do so on those occasions. I have come to trust this, as every time I am called to be in the physical space I am shown in the miração, I easily come back. The most important thing is to stay present with the music and maintain firmeza. From there, with the grace of Spirit, everything flows. That is not to say that challenges don't arise, that the seas stay calm. It's always about balance and coming back to centre. Allowing those winds to gently guide me back home.

Another common cultural practice I have learned both in Australia and Brazil is the honouring of the spirit and beings of the land. Part of acknowledging and honouring of Country is asking permission and making offerings. The opening song of my ceremonies invokes this:

When I entered the forest
I asked permission to enter
I was received
by my father Ossanha

— *Ewê*, Chandra Lacombe.

Ossanha, also referred to as *Ossain*, is the Orixá of sacred plants, leaves and healing. When we work with Ayahuasca, we do so with sacred permission from the forest to cultivate and consecrate her sacred plants and commune with her sacred light. In the cosmology of Umbanda, with roots that go back to Africa, Ossanha is the force of nature that symbolises and holds the prayer for that point of sacred light. An Aboriginal medicine man, a friend from Far North Queensland, once taught me to offer some of my hair to the land when entering, to tie it around a branch of a tree, ask for permission, guidance and protection, stay present and listen. Hair is a beautiful way to offer something of ourselves. In Umbanda we make a similar offering with the same prayer; I will find a point on the land to light a candle, make an offering and keep it there as long as we are working. The land is a living being that we must meet with respect. This is also about making that sacred connection to the land, as what can happen is spiritual beings may see the light in the ceremony, be curious and want to connect with it. This can be chaotic and cause disturbance in the field — people may become startled or scared. And since it is the spiritual beings' land, their home, it is fair game for them. I have come to learn that cheeky nature beings are content when you make an offering in their Country that gives them a point of connection. In some instances they speak to me through the ceremony. Simple practices like this, if done authentically and from the heart, can create harmony, balance and the gift of relationship. It is always an honour when in ceremony our miração is blessed by visions and messages from Country. This is a beautiful weaving of Spirit from Africa to Brazilian Amazonia to Australia, all in the light of the Christed heart, unconditional love. Earth Dream-weaving.

Living beings of the forest
Come to illuminate me
I'm here, I'm here singing
I'm open to heal myself

The forest brings mystery
And we ask for protection
Our fears go away
and our hearts will be opening

All light is revealing
We realise that all is love
The clarity arrives
And now I know that I can fly

— *Seres Vivos da Floresta,* Giti Bond.

As the ceremonies and the spiritual community around them evolved, there were many times I was greatly challenged and presented with many things that raised questions. As always, Ayahuasca was and is an amazing guide and I would receive a lot of teachings and guidance. There were some big challenges with people's personalities and what they were bringing to the community and to the ceremonies. Some people would come and be very much focused on the phenomenal world and external experiences. They could often be entangled in interpersonal dynamics, and this could be tricky to deal with. Especially as at times this would move into areas within me where I still needed to work on my own communication and boundaries. Some of these people would take advantage, others might be manipulative. Disharmonic behaviours can also be seen as spiritual sickness. All are welcome if they show up to the work with a sincere calling to be there. If they come for healing, even those challenging personality and ego traits can be healed through the teachings of love, peace and harmony. But this takes strength and emotional maturity for me in holding the ceremonies and for the guardians and experienced members of the community. This doesn't heal overnight. One example of how this can manifest is when someone arrives for the first time and feels connection and wants to go deeper into the work. For me, I believe the best way to develop in the work of Ayahuasca is to humbly do the work without expectations, focusing on the inner journey with full self-responsibility. It's important to learn the cosmology and practices of the ceremony before jumping into social dynamics or wanting to help others. There is a risk of people jumping into something they are not fully comprehending. I am always impressed by people who arrive and want to learn, as that was the path I chose. It is thus important to become proficient with Ayahuasca and ceremony first and then naturally find your way into taking more responsibility or expanding roles in the ceremonies and in the community. I have noticed over the years that those who avoid responsibility don't integrate well and often become entangled in drama and politics; they may leave before resolving themselves and their relationship to the work. In his book *Global Ayahuasca*, Alex K Gearin reflects on his research into global Ayahuasca culture: 'As a vortex of mysteries and alternate realities, Ayahuasca marvels those who are courageous enough to stick with it.'

In some cases, people immediately work out who the guardians and the ones with more experience or influence are, and enthusiastically befriend them and involve themselves in social dynamics. Through this, they might assume a role as a guardian or take on roles that were previously done by others with less forceful personalities. I've seen this dynamic play out, where someone might attempt to elevate their self-importance, and in doing so develop dependences. These people can often demonstrably 'help' in the ceremonies when this is not needed. At times some have even gone so far as to demand changes to the way ceremonies are run and have even suggested they should somehow be elevated to special roles. I have definitely made some mistakes in dealing with some of these characters, whereby I have had to make boundaries due to the imposition of personal interests and agendas that have diverted from the spiritual point of the work. I was often amazed at how many times people in those early years would come to me and tell me things that I should and shouldn't be doing in the ceremonies. These were usually people who had never been to South America, let alone studied with teachers and masters. I would often see these people 'monkey-branch' their way from one group to the next, rather than face themselves in a sacred mirroring and be held by loving friends. Over time I learned to hold a stronger container with clearer boundaries and this coherence has largely ended this as a disruptive force. Sometimes people would walk away with anger and blame, as they hadn't got what they wanted. I reflected on the lives of Mestre Irineu and Padrinho Sebastião, who both expressed regret at the end of their lives that they were not able to fully resolve drama and politics amongst the people.

> *To end the bizarre tyranny of ego is why we go on the spiritual path, but the resourcefulness of the ego is almost infinite and it can at every stage sabotage and pervert our desire to be free of it. The truth is simple, and the teachings are extremely clear; but I have seen again and again, with great sadness, that as soon as they begin to touch and move us, ego tries to complicate them because it knows it is fundamentally threatened.* — Sogyal Rinpoche, The Tibetan Book of Living and Dying.

One of the things that I hear said, and also have read, is that some people prefer 'traditional' Ayahuasca ceremonies and can even go so far as to claim that anything else is invalid or not authentic. From my own experience, which in the field of global Ayahuasca practice I believe is quite extensive, my spiritual work and approach with Ayahuasca is authentic to *my* teachings, lineages and spiritual guidance. I'm not dressing myself up as an Amazonian and adopting their customs. My guidance and practices are informed by the lineages and their teachings, with which I am aligned and initiated. I am still a privileged Westerner with education and access to resources. The notion of 'authenticity' is relative and based on many factors such as personal truth and values, cultural and societal realities, and effectiveness as a measure of truth. What works or resonates with one person may not do so for someone else. This doesn't reflect authenticity. I have heard stories and witnessed people conducting Ayahuasca where their behaviour in the ceremony appears more of a show and a performance and is copying what they have seen or projecting an image of how they want to be seen. I have always stayed true to myself and worked within what I know to be true and effective. It seems over the years that people are attracted to this. Interestingly, when I started facilitating in Australia, aside from the Brazilian churches, I was the only one working with a coherent and consecrated syncretic practice in the light with songbooks and group prayers. It is understandable, even if presumptuous, for people to witness a different approach and question its validity.

Many people from the global Ayahuasca movement often talk about wanting to travel to Peru for a 'traditional' experience. It seems that the idea of what is traditional is in actuality more of a modern, global culture, adapted to suit Western tourists and seekers of healing, with 90% of retreat centres in Peru now run and owned by Westerners, and set up in jungle settings with comfortable accommodation, lavish beds in designer temples, Wi-Fi and other modern amenities. Native Shipibo people may be brought in to do their spiritual work and healing practices in ceremonies, sing a range of icaros, some often in Spanish language, perhaps using Tibetan singing bowls or other non-traditional practices. Many now report that a lot of these healers also have to spend the night in ceremonies praying for protection from the dark projections of sorcerers' attacks because the field is so distorted from colonial pressures, poverty and the effects of Western money and influence. In many cases the participants at these retreats may have no idea of the real culture and context of the lives of their native healers. The retreats are often run as new-age experiences and can include modern practices such as guided meditations, breath work, Western yoga and adapted psychological practices. Like my work, these retreats seem to have their roots in traditions, but are adapted to a modern context catering for the complex needs, physical and mental conditions of urban Westerners. Most of my personal experiences in native Amazonian settings have not been organised retreats or jungle trips with planned programs designed by Westerners for Westerners, with 'traditional' healers employed to play a role. I have only lived amongst villagers on invitation, experiencing their culture and conditions, grateful for what they offer. In those experiences I have had to integrate into village life as a guest, sometimes feeling awkward and out of place. I've had to navigate floods and damp and insects and snakes, long arduous walks through muddy and dense jungle, sleeping in hammocks and drinking

Ayahuasca in sometimes very rough and wild, natural conditions. This hasn't been easy and has definitely challenged my fragile and precious Western ego, so I can understand how this may not be for everyone. For those who crave 'authentic 'and 'traditional' Ayahuasca experiences, when we are referring to Indigenous cultures, this is the closest I have personally experienced.

After an intensive period of growth and development conducting ceremonies and building community in Australia, I was ready to return to Brazil to deepen my studies. I had a long list of questions and was ready to learn more. At this stage it was clear to me that being a ceremonial leader and founding a movement and community meant it was also imperative that I continued to study and delve deeper into the mystery of Ayahuasca and my spiritual path. The learning never ends. It had been a while since I had been to Ciranda and longer still since I had been to the Amazon. I was really craving having a teacher and guide who understood what I was going through.

In late 2017 I was contacted by a friend in Brazil, João, who is a devoted and strong warrior of Santo Daime and the doctrine of Mestre Irineu. João is not affiliated with any particular church, though he lives according to the teachings and doctrines of Mestre Irineu and the Queen of the Forest. João had met some leaders from the Huni Kuin people and they had invited him to come and share knowledge with them in their villages in the Amazon in Acre, Brazil. He had received an inspiration that it would be a good idea for me to go with him, and invited me on the journey to the Upper Amazon. I was familiar with the area, as it was neighbouring the Yawanawá lands which I had visited a few years earlier. I didn't know that much about the Huni Kuin, although I had met some of them and been to ceremonies in Rio de Janeiro and felt a great resonance with them. Another trip to the Amazon felt a bit daunting but again, I was going on an invitation and cultural exchange journey, much like I had with the Yawanawá. The timing was great, as I had been ready to return to Brazil and deepen my studies. I could go there then to return to Ciranda in the summer. It was time again for this eagle to fly.

CHAPTER 12

High Aim in the Upper Amazon

Emerging songlines

> *Everything starts and ends with Country in the Aboriginal worldview. Yet there are no endings in this worldview, nor are there any beginnings. Time and place are infinite and everywhere. Everything is part of a continuum, an endless flow of life and ideas emanating from country, which some refer to as the Dreaming.* — Margo Neale, *Songlines*.

> *Well, at the end of the day, and really, with our world viewpoint, there is no other countries. There is no other world. This is all just one world. We're all human beings. We have a similar Dream. So, with our human Dream, we can relate whether we came from Alice Springs or whether we came from the upper reaches of the Amazon. We have that in common. We have a human Dream: that one Dream that we share as humanity permeates through all of it.* — Australian Indigenous Elder, Uncle BJ.

When I had returned to Sydney back in late 2015, I had made contact with a Yolngu man, Trevor, from Arnhem Land in Australia's Northern Territory. Arnhem Land is more than a geographic region — it is a place of living ancestral presence, a living cathedral of Dreaming. Spanning nearly 100,000 square kilometres of pristine wilderness, it is home to the Yolngu people, one of the oldest continuous cultures on Earth. The Yolngu are a famous and strong people and culture who continue to hold many powerful enduring traditions, rites and ceremonies. They have also produced many well-known musicians, artists and cultural leaders. The Yolngu are the ancestral custodians of the *yidaki* (didgeridoo), which is played in our ceremonies in Australia. Jesse plays on the yidaki ancient rhythms which have been passed on to him by a senior Yolngu Elder.

Trevor travelled around Country connecting to sacred sites and energetic portals, sometimes reactivating dormant songlines. He explained to me that his people could feel the energetic blockages at significant points in the web of songlines that criss-crosses the continent. His job was to travel to find them and see what can be done to reactivate them for the harmonic balance of the planet. His Elders also gave him permission to share wisdom, stories and natural law. He made contact with me via social media and commented on my art, introducing himself as a fellow artist. I was struck by his openness and interest in me and my art. One day he flew from Darwin to Sydney to visit one of these sacred Dreaming sites. He invited me and a group of people to go with him. He shared a lot on the journey to the site and said to me, 'I know you do that Ayahuasca from the Amazon. I would like to try it myself, but I don't need to because I already live in that reality.' He knew I understood what he meant.

He went back to Arnhem Land and we stayed in touch; he would message or call me from time to time. Just days before I was due to return to Brazil, he called me. On the phone he said that he was with his people and they knew I was heading back to the Amazon. I hadn't recalled mentioning it to him and was struck by the timing —right before I was about to leave. I didn't ask any questions, just listened. He went on to say that the Yolngu had for 800 years known of a date when a specific ceremony would open a new Dreaming trail as part of the renewal of the Earth. They had been holding ceremony for this prophecy for 800 years, preparing for the day when this new Dream would enter. Trevor told me that I would be in the Amazon on that day. He asked me to pass this message on to the people I would be with there in the forest. I felt honoured and a bit spun-out that somehow I had been tracked by the Yolngu and trusted with this beautiful unfolding. While Jesse had been sounding the vibrations and rhythms of Yolngu Country in the ceremonies, a spiritual Dreaming track had opened between Yolngu Country in Northern Australia and the Brazilian Amazon. Messages like this were signs of being at one with the flow of creation and are of service to the unfolding planetary Dream. This was the unfolding of a weaving of Australian Indigenous and Amazonian Dreaming, much greater than me, which, through lineage and my Dreaming, I was in service to. The mystery was again blessing my path. The Dreaming of the Whole Earth.

I arrived back in Rio de Janeiro and was excited to be back there to catch up with dear friends and soak in the Brazilian culture and life force. I visited Carioca and we sat down and had a good catch-up. He had a lot of questions about how things were going on my journey with the ceremonies and with my music. He went on to teach me a passage on the guitar, with a technique that was new to me. After this meeting, I was full of inspiration and had a lot to contemplate and integrate. I went back to a friend's house where I was staying and sat down to work on the guitar piece that Carioca had taught me. When he had been teaching me the sequence and technique, I hadn't been aware that it was a song. Knowing him, though, I knew there was meaning in everything that he had shown me through these lessons. As I started to find the music and feeling in my guitar, I realised this *was* a song. I found the melody and realised it was one that Carioca played in his Aquarela ceremonies: *O Leãozinho* (little lion). This is a very famous song in Brazil and most Brazilians I know have an emotional connection to it from their childhood. It is a sentimental song of friendship and affection, with beautiful, poetic, heartfelt words. I realised the message and gift that Carioca was giving me in his offering; I felt emotional and touched and shed a few tears of gratitude. His gifting me this song was his way of expressing his friendship, care and happiness to see me again.

I met up with João in the mountains behind Rio, where we stayed with a woman who led a spiritual healing community. João was preparing some Daime (Ayahuasca) to take with us to the Amazon, where we would be staying with the Huni Kuin. They had asked him to teach them about the Santo Daime ways of preparing Daime in a cultural exchange.

It is not just cultural nuance to differentiate the names for what we have been referring to as Ayahuasca. This is honouring spiritual and alchemical coherence. Santo Daime tea is prepared in a very particular way, with its own prayers and intentions, guides and ancestry. Nixi Pãe for the Huni Kuin also has its own spiritual constellation and energetic signature. There are also differences in the way they are prepared, each with their own harmonic relationship to the plants and the spirit of the forest. Petals of the same flower. These traditions hold coherency and culture within their practices, and this is reflected in the manifestation of the sacred tea and its qualities and spiritual field.

I was impressed by the focus and devotion that João had towards his work and his spiritual path. Whilst there, I was invited to play music and lead prayers in an Ayahuasca ceremony and participate in healing rituals, including receiving from the group. We enjoyed some great conversations and sharing about spirituality and culture. I liked sharing stories about Australia and my path, and I was grateful that my path had taken me to receive, with such divine grace, the blessings, clearing and healing before my journey to the Huni Kuin and to the Upper Amazon forest. I was loaded with new knowledge, remembrances, experiences, teachings and new music to integrate, and the forest would give me time to do that.

Upper Amazon with the Huni Kuin

> *Songlines, related to Dreamings or Dreaming tracks, connect sites of knowledge embodied in the features of the land. It is along these routes that people travelled to learn from Country.* — Margo Neale, *Songlines*.

> *Huni Kuin are one of the most enchanted beings. We emerged through the transformation of nature. First came the Earth. Then,*

from the Earth, came the mud of the Earth. And from that we grew, Huni Kuin appeared. And Huni Kuin enchanted themselves with the animals. — Ibã Hunki Kuin / Isaias Sales Kaxinawá.

After making our way to Rio Branco where, years previously, I had launched my journey to visit the Yawanawá, we booked an early flight to a small town called Jordão (Jordan). The plane was a small eight-seater that was noisy and uncomfortable but the view was majestic. For an hour I stared out the window, admiring the endless forest in every direction with dense green land and snaking brown rivers. As I looked down over the trees, I imagined how many jaguars and jiboias were living there and what they were up to in this magical forest. Flying at a relatively low altitude in a small plane over the forest was enchanting. The endless forest landscape reminded me of the endless desertscapes on the other side of the world in the middle of Australia. Experiencing the vastness of endless Country is sublimely meditative. I knew that when we landed I would be immersed in that green density for a while, so I appreciated every moment of this eagle-eye view.

As I looked out over the immensity, I reflected on returning to the Country of the ancestors of my spiritual path. The ancient ones who for so long had sacrificed and fought to keep alive the Dreaming of their culture, language and knowledge. The Huni Kuin, Yawanawá and many other peoples who have served and kept their culture strong. If it wasn't for them, we wouldn't have the blessings of the music, medicine and wisdom available to us today. They protected the sacred plants and the knowledge of them. They endured the cruelties of colonialism and genocide. Whatever was lost from living memory remained alive in the land. The Dream of Country never dies. The ancestors live on in Spirit, across time and space. They are in the hum of the insects, the songs of the birds, the Dreaming of the Whole Earth. This is the country and source of the teachings of Mestre Irineu, the mission and teachings of Padrinho Sebastião, and the roots of Brazilian Santo Daime, Hoasca and other movements. It was not lost on me that the river where we would be meeting our Huni Kuin hosts was the River Jordan.

The River Jordan, a sacred threshold in the Bible where initiation through water marked the descent of Spirit, mirrors the Amazon's own sacred current — where the force of Ayahuasca flows as the vine of remembrance and the Santo Daime tradition bridges ancient cosmologies with the living gospel of the forest. Country that is the home of the Holy Light of the Queen of the Forest. This is sacred Country: a powerful meeting of the songlines where many tribes also meet, where spiritual doctrine is birthed, where the devotees live in harmony and, with open arms, receive the peoples of the world, to rest in its healing heart.

My Father, I ask that You hear me
So I may ask for forgiveness
I ask not only for myself
But for me and for my brothers and sisters

My Father, when You go to forgive
Forgive in the way that pleases You
I ask that You grant us pardon
As You did in Bethlehem

The boat that sails upon the sea
Sails also within my heart
The one who baptises here
Baptised in the River Jordan

— *Peço Que Vós Me Ouça*, Padrinho Sebastião.

Txaná Ixã met us at the muddy airport when we arrived. He greeted us with a warm, friendly and easy welcome. Ixã Huni Kuin is the *cacique* (chief) and founder of the village called Ni Yuxibu (spirit of the forest) but more commonly known as *Alta Mira* (High Aim). In Huni Kuin tradition, a *txaná* is both a revered ceremonial healer and the sacred teacher bird, the Yellow-rumped *cacique*, known for its wisdom, mimicry and ancestral connection to the forest. To be called 'txaná' is to be recognised as one who carries the song, healing and teachings

With Txana Ixã, João and Huni Kuin friend, Jordão, Acre, Brazil

of nature. Ixã is a strong and jolly man with a seemingly permanent smile who can easily find humour in just about everything. He was wearing a large, colourful necklace of woven beads in the design of a jaguar's face, and I mentioned this was also my totem. We spoke about music and guitars. It was nice to arrive in such a relaxed way. We found somewhere to sit down and chat and talk about the day ahead, as we had much to do to prepare for the boat ride down the river to the village. I noticed that Ixã's way of being reminded me of Australian Indigenous people, especially ones I had spent time with in Central Australia.

We walked a few streets to a house that was empty other than the murals of Huni Kuin art painted all over the walls. There were a few younger Huni Kuin sitting on the floor and some women in the kitchen. Not much was said and I sat down and joined them. Pretty soon we got into the back of a truck with Ixã and some others and went off on a mission around the town to meet with other Huni Kuin and collect supplies to take with us down the river. Jordão is small town where the River Jordão flows into the River Tarauacá. Yawanawá Country was only few days downstream along the Tarauacá, where I had been some years before. The town was neat and orderly with a muddy dirt road and it seemed like the majority of the town was populated mostly by colourful and friendly Huni Kuin, with a few other Indigenous peoples and some non-Indigenous Brazilians running shops and services. Everyone wanted to stop and chat. When I wandered around on my own I was invited to about six different villages. Everyone was so curious, humorous and friendly. The energy seemed light, loving and free of any of the sticky energies or subtle manipulations I had experienced in Peru.

At sunset we took the supplies down to the river, where some other Huni Kuin men were waiting with two canoes. I wondered why they travelled at night, as to me this seemed more dangerous due to the risk of submerged logs that are harder to spot when it's dark. Later I realised it was because during the day was when business could be done in town, and also that it could be torturous spending hours on the river in the full sun. The night journey turned out to be a beautiful blessing.

The chief Ixã and his wife, daughter and youngest son, a 16-year-old named Txanu, were in the first boat and went off ahead of us, with the boat's noisy motor echoing through the forest on its way. João, his girlfriend and I were in the second canoe with some Huni Kuin men and a powerful man captaining at the back. Later I found out that this man was Txaná Kixtin, who is a strong pajé and close ally of Ixã, whom I would go on to have some powerful experiences with. The man was very quiet and humble while working, lifting, carrying and steering the boat, but I could feel his strong, solid and deep presence. His teenage son sat at the front of the boat with a torch, looking out for submerged logs.

We snaked along the winding river, and on the first part of the journey there were a few scattered clearings of farms, but soon we began passing through thick jungle and endless forests. The canoe, with its loud clattering engine, powered us upstream, occasionally bumping into things and passing over swirling rapids. The forest at sunset was sublime, with the beauty of changing colours behind the treelines, and with no people — just forest. After a couple of hours the light had completely gone and everyone in the boat had fallen asleep except me, Kixtin and his son. At some point the son asked if I could hold the torch and look out while he closed his eyes and lay down. As I scanned the waters, we turned another bend in the river and to the left over the trees shone a brilliant full moon, stunningly bright and detailed in the moonlit sky, and perfectly perched over the canopy of the trees. It was so huge, almost surreal. I turned to Kixtin. We were the only ones who saw it; he smiled and nodded.

After about three hours or so we turned a bend and ahead was a long stretch of straight river, as far as I could see. In the distance I could see the other canoe with Ixã and his family and saw them pulling to the side, seemingly having reached the village. As we travelled up this long river-straight, I was struck by how the moon had repositioned to be directly in front of us, perfectly aligned to the centre of the river. It was still huge in the sky, perfectly poised and shining its mysterious silvery light over the waters as we sailed along. Such breathtaking beauty and cosmic alignment was a sign of fate to me, a powerful moment. I remembered the message that had been delivered by the Yolngu and felt that this was some kind of confirmation of a significant Dreaming event.

As we arrived at the landing bank, the other boat was still unloading its cargo. There was a steep hill with a trail up to the village, seemingly perched high to protect it from floods. Ixã walked up onto a rock overlooking the boats being unloaded below; he looked at me and I took that as invitation to join him. I climbed up and stood beside him. We looked at the moon then at each other and both laughed at the wonder of it all, the majesty of creation — another powerful moment. I chose this time to tell him of the message that had been sent from the Yolngu in Australia. He nodded in acknowledgment and gave another laugh. I have been graced with such beauty in this life and the signs were showing me this was a significant and important time to be there with the Huni Kuin for the unfolding of my life's journey.

Some villagers had come down to collect all the cargo, including my bags and guitar. We all walked up the muddy, rocky trail to the top of the hill. As we arrived at the top, a long line of Huni Kuin men each offered a handshake and welcome as we walked past. A beautiful honouring and welcoming to the village. We were ushered towards a large shelter that looked like some kind of church or temple with just a large roof, no walls and a dirt floor. I entered and saw burning in the centre a large fire surrounded by rocks, with two big spears dug into the ground in front of it in a V-shape. This striking scene gave me a sense of tribal strength and power.

As everyone entered, Ixã sat at the head of the space with Kixtin to his right and with senior men beside him, all sitting on chairs. In front of Ixã was a large table full of medicines and medicine tools. The women were all sitting on the ground to the right of Ixã with the children and babies. João and his girlfriend sat to the left of Ixã, followed by me to the left of them, and on my left was Mayá, his eldest son, seemingly in his early twenties, although it is hard to guess the age of most Huni Kuin, as they are all very vibrant, healthy and appear younger than they are. Mayá has a deep and strong, serious presence. All the younger men sat around the edge of the space on the left side. I took it all in: what a beautiful and honouring moment to be invited into Huni Kuin Country and ceremony.

In the light of both the fire and a large candle on the table in front of him, Ixã stood to welcome us to the village, to Huni Kuin Country. He went on to say we were going to drink Nixi Pãe, and we all stood in line to drink their forest tea. When we sat back down Ixã casually commenced singing some traditional songs known as *Huni Meka* with just his voice. It seemed like he was making opening prayers and calls, something I had become accustomed to with the Yawanawá and in the meeting with the Huni Kuin in Rio.

I was surprised when, after he finished his songs, he called me over and offered me the guitar, asking me to sing for everyone. I hadn't really had any expectations or notion of what might happen when we arrived, but here we were going straight into ceremony on the night of an auspicious and aligned full moon, and I was being asked to share my voice and songs for the people. They all sat with their eyes closed, still and listening with intent. Some were tapping their hands or just a finger along with the rhythm. Some of the young boys wandered up and looked right into me, up close. I sang songs for family, for the river, the sweet water (Oxum), and Santo Daime songs for our ancestors.

After those songs, Ixã asked me to pass the guitar to his son Mayá. I passed the guitar to him but he gently pushed it back. I naively said, 'Ixã said to pass you the guitar' and he replied, 'Yes, I know, and I ask you to sing for me because your music is giving me many colours in my visions.' This reminded me of Carioca talking about music as colour, and him teaching me chords, harmonies, arrangements and dynamics to bring colour and beauty into the visions. I was honoured to be seen in such a clear way. I continued to play.

The guitar went on to a couple of the Huni Kuin, one of whom played a Santo Daime-style song, and eventually it went back to Ixã. We felt like we had called the force of the Nixi Pãe and were flowing on its journey. Ixã played for a while then I noticed that the force was starting to fade just slightly. Then Ixã paused in stillness and silence. I heard murmurings amongst the women and eventually they spoke to Ixã, who announced that we would have a break for rapé (snuff) and *xurú* (Amazonian marijuana) before drinking again.

As the force and the visions became quite strong, I drifted deeper into miração with the medicine songs sung by Kixtin. He seemingly knew whenever my mind started to engage and the sounds were doing crazy cosmic dances while apprehending any errant thoughts. Although I was learning from what he was doing, this was also a good challenge and training whilst taking it all in. Some of the Huni Kuin men were lying in the hammocks around the perimeter of the *shubuã* (temple-maloca). I saw many visions that night and the forest spoke to me. I felt like I was being attuned. My experience allowed me to immerse into the miração, guided by the force of the Nixi Pãe and its song.

Nixi Pãe teaches through visions, through songs (Txana), through dreams — and also through silence. — Shakuany Huni Kuin.

At the first hint of morning, Ixã gathered everyone into a large circle and led us through various circular dances accompanied by songs. Some were quite fun and joyous. I was thinking that the spirit of Ciranda had somehow come from the Huni Kuin; I was enjoying the similarities, the depth, the heartfelt sincerity and the joy. Eventually a closing song was played and people dispersed, though some men stayed beside the fire. We shared rapé and xurú and played songs around it. They explained to me the cosmology of the jiboia and their belief that we are awake inside the Dream of the Creator Jiboia, much the same as many Aboriginal cultures believe we are awake inside the Dream of the Rainbow Serpent. The songline trail that had guided me from the rhythms of the Yolngu to the colour and dance of the Huni Kuin unveiled a shared planetary Dreaming. The weaving of my own spirit walk was becoming clearer. The Dreaming of the Whole Earth.

Life with the Huni Kuin got underway very quickly. João, being a very well-disciplined soldier of Santo Daime, was ready for the challenge; I was catching up with myself and a little out of phase. It took me some time to adjust to everything. The Huni Kuin all spoke in the native language *Hãtxa Kuĩ* unless talking to me or João individually, or at times someone would translate when significant things were being spoken, then they would speak in Portuguese. My body was acclimatising: we were on a very minimal diet, and there was a lot to integrate with being immersed in a very different culture, flow and mind space. It took me over a week to fully drop into being there and relaxed in the flow of life with the Huni Kuin and the rainforest.

I set up my hammock on the deck above Ixã's house, and his son Txanu put his hammock next to mine. We got to hang out a lot and he would teach me about the Huni Kuin ways and translate things for me while I would share stories about Australia. He became a guide for me and I noticed that Ixã would instruct him to keep an eye on everything happening around the family and with us as the guests. There was another Huni Kuin man who would sit beside me in circles and at meals and would translate for me. Every night there would be a meal at Ixã's house followed by a circle of sharing and some music. Ixã would lead conversations, speaking very earnestly and strongly. People would also share with passion and conviction. I didn't always understand what was being said but it had a sense of honour and business, of making decisions for the people and the village and sometimes of spiritual conversations.

During the day sometimes I would visit people around the village with João, Txanu and usually a couple of young boys tagging along excitedly. João always had a bottle of the Daime that he had made in Rio. It was beautiful medicine, and he enjoy sharing it with the Huni Kuin, who were very curious and grateful. Every day we would drink in all kinds of settings with Ixã, Kixtin and the others in Ixã's band of warriors. We would visit Mayá's house, drink Daime and have spiritual conversations, talk about our experiences. I asked lots of questions and we would also share music. Sometimes an Elder would join, which I always appreciated due to their wisdom and there being so much to learn from their presence and awareness.

I would ask Mayá, Kixtin and others about the miração and how they had learned their songs, their shamanic skills and knowledge. The answers were always the same: 'From the forest' or 'We learn directly from the forest.' They explained that they learned some things from pajés, fathers and uncles but their training was in the forest. I didn't know at the time because I was just going with the flow and letting them guide me, but collectively they were paying a lot of attention to all the questions I was asking.

I felt that by being there I needed to be of some kind of service; sometimes I felt like an awkward gringo not knowing how to help. I was aware of how dependant on them I was for survival in that forest. I had to make myself useful. It turned out the best way I could do this was to play music for them and at times give guitar lessons or teach songs. All throughout the day people would come and ask me to play a song for them. It was usually the same song that they would ask for, a song called *Família* (Family). Sometimes I felt like a juke box on repeat, but their innocent joy and love for this song and its prayer of connection to Country and family was what they said life was all about for the Huni Kuin. This was such a beautiful sentiment and I was so happy to share. After a few weeks I challenged them a bit to play different songs and teased them about the repetition, which made them laugh.

One night after we came in from the forest there was a big gathering at Ixã's place. I went to the river to swim and wash and came back to a large circle and meal. After we ate a rousing conversation took place and I wondered, 'Wow, what are they talking about?' It seemed to be something really exciting. As I sat there enjoying the vibe, my guide next to me tapped me and said, 'Oi txai (txai means kin or we are one, we are the same), we were talking and decided it would be a good idea if you played *Família*.' Now it made sense and I was very happy to play. As the song finished, more Huni Kuin arrived and the circle of family grew. The village had about 150 people and half of them were there. Another big animated conversation ensued and then again I heard. 'Oi txai, more family have arrived and we were talking and we decided it would be a good idea if you played *Família* again.' I smiled to myself, and soon there I was again rocking the Huni Kuin with my Aussie version of *Família*. They told me that song was so important to them because they see family as sacred and the most important thing in their lives. Beautiful moments like this are life with the Huni Kuin. I reflected a lot on the spirit of Ciranda, the innocence of the inner child and the joy of music.

I will walk in beauty
I will walk in peace

Everything is my family

Everything is sacred
Animals and plants

Everything is sacred
Mountains and the sea

Everything is my family

— *Família*, Alonso del Rio.

A couple of days after we arrived, the Huni Kuin were excited about having another ceremony in the village. The night before I had asked one of the men about *kambô* — the sacred frog medicine. He told me he could find the frog and explained that there were two different types of frogs that have the medicine. As he was talking he paused, tilted his head slightly and said he could hear one. It was so hard, with so many noises coming from the forest's symphony, that I could not tell which sound it was. He ran off and came back 10 minutes later with a big green frog. During the ceremony that night I noticed him running off periodically into the forest. In the morning he explained to me that he had heard seven different kambô frogs during the ceremony and had gone and collected all of them. He had put them all next to where he was sitting in the ceremony. In the morning when he checked he said all had gone except one — and that was the one that we would use for a kambô ceremony later in the morning. Even though kambô can be a strong ordeal to receive, my experience on the frog medicine that day was sublime and it was a great way to enter the rest of the day feeling relaxed and energised, clear-minded and focused.

Village life

Every day Ixã would lead his group of men, with me and João along with them, into the forest for all kinds of missions. They would always be with hunting dogs, a gun and bow and arrow. We would make a few stops during the day where Ixã would announce 'Vamos descançar um pouco, rapézinho, xurú' (Let's rest a while, a little rapê, marijuana). After a few days on our mission through the forest trail, Ixã stopped and called me over to show me a little shrub called *mári taíxski* on the side of the trail. He said it was the plant for singers and took a leaf and told me to put it on my tongue and just leave it there. This became a daily ritual for the next weeks and I started to identify the plant myself and got to know it by holding it on my tongue for hours every day. I didn't notice any effects from this at first, but over time I started to feel the vibrations subtly through my voice, which at this stage I was just observing.

I asked the men what the most efficient tool was for hunting and they told me it was the dogs by far. The dogs would run around in the forest alongside where we were walking and we wouldn't see them but sometimes we would hear them go nuts with a loud and dramatic commotion while the men and everyone would freeze with the gun and arrow ready if the dogs were successful in chasing any animals towards the group. Although these missions were not specifically for hunting, the men were always ready for what they might find. When I was with the Yawanawá I had seen the preparations for hunting missions that would be expeditions lasting many days. These missions were often for collecting different plants, visiting an Elder who lived on top of a hill, visiting what they called their 'sacred space' with medicine gardens and a giant *cumuru* tree where they would do spiritual work and studies with plants, Nixi Pãe and the forest. Sometimes we would be walking and in an instant there would be a commotion with lots of whooping from the men, then before I could hardly blink, two young Huni Kuin would be up in trees shaking them wildly while we were being rained-on by small fruits. Everyone would scramble to eat as much as they could until it was all gone, then we would keep walking. I could really feel the power and force of the forest inside these Huni Kuin warriors, always impressive with their keen, focused awareness and sharp reflexes.

Sometimes Ixã would split us into groups and one day he sent me off with one of the men who was very quiet and hardly spoke a word. He lived mostly in a house near the sacred space where he was the custodian, and occasionally I would see him in the village. As we walked on our mission together he passed me the hunting rifle and asked me to carry it. He was very clear in making sure I knew not to fire it because there was only one bullet. He said he would do the shooting. I smiled to myself, knowing how useless I would be with that gun and that he even felt he needed to tell me. Eventually we found a really tall, thin *açaí* tree. I was excited, as I love açaí so much and here it was growing in the wild. He climbed up with a big machete, almost falling a couple of times as he clung on to the waving tree trying to cut its huge bunches of berries. They eventually all fell to the ground with loud thuds. He came down and we sat there picking all the berries off the bunches. I wondered how we were going to take them back and he went off into the forest and came back with some very large leaves, then tore them in strips and wove them into a basket with a strap. When full with berries, the basket was extremely heavy and I could hardly lift it. He put it on his back, gave me the rifle and we started walking back. That night we feasted on açai prepared by the women.

One day we went up to the old man's house on the hill. We sat around and drank some Nixi Pãe and Ixã sang some songs and then asked me to sing. Later he started speaking in Hãtxa Kuĩ in a formal tone that seemed as though he was making an announcement as he gestured towards João and me. He then repeated what he had said, this time in Portuguese. He told us we were welcome guests and that the people in the village had been happy since we had arrived. He praised our contribution and declared us to be family and offered us both a Huni Kuin name. He gave me the name 'Nawa Ibã', with Nawa meaning 'not Huni Kuin' and Ibã meaning 'the singer who calls the Miração'. I felt very honoured and gratefully accepted the invitation to family and the name he gave me. It was a beautiful moment. I felt happy to receive the name, as it was part of learning about myself but this time through the eyes of the Huni Kuin. Just like Carioca, the Huni Kuin saw me as a singer. Just as my father used to call me. I wondered why it was not so obvious to me at times. The daily ritual of putting the *mári taíxski*, the singers plant's leaf, on my tongue was also making more sense too.

I enjoyed the days where things moved slowly, when I would mostly stay around the village. There was always so much going on in that small village in the forest. At times I would go and lie in the river and just take it all in. I felt like I was immersed in a Huni Kuin universe, often noticing how my thoughts were so deeply embedded in all the learning and culture of the Huni Kuin. Taking time at the river was a great way for me to integrate and get back in touch with myself, to have some time to contemplate my life and make some decisions from a clear and quiet mind space. Some days

Alta Mira, Acre, Brazil

I would be kind-of hiding down at the river and when I sensed the villagers looking for me or psychically calling me back, I would take my time, savouring every moment of my alone time. Like most Indigenous people I know, the concept of being alone or having space to themselves was not something they were happy or comfortable with. Just as their constant communal presence was strange and at times difficult for me, they also seemed curious about me enjoying spending time alone.

One day someone came up to me and João in the village and told us someone was sick, so we went to the house where there were a few people gathered around a middle-aged Huni Kuin man lying on his side in a hammock in the middle of the house. As was typical with Huni Kuin houses, there was no furniture — just a few hammocks and some neatly packed belongings tied to the top of the walls. João took his Daime and offered some to the ill Huni Kuin man in the hammock. People were coming up and trying to help him in all kinds of ways while he moaned and struggled. The air seemed full of fear and great concern. At one point Ixã walked in to the house very casually but holding himself with much grace and strength. I was impressed by his personal power and the manner in which he held himself: it really struck me in that moment. He walked up to the hammock, said a hearty welcome to the sick man, gave the hammock a big shake, then in a very authoritative, impatient way told him to sit up. It seemed he was pushing the man to shift himself. The man sat up and very quickly afterwards had a big purge, vomiting into a bucket, while Ixã walked over to the others and started chatting. After the purging, the man looked completely different. Ixã turned around and gave him a hearty smile and praise, then they both laughed.

That house was the home of an 18-year-old Huni Kuin man who had a very serious demeanour. The others had told me he was intelligent and had been studying Brazilian school books. He showed me the books. They were very carefully packed and neatly wrapped in plastic and cloth. He treated them like treasures, and was extremely careful not to damage them as he opened the pages and showed me different photos, some historical, others geographic or biological. He was much more interested in the historical things and, in particular, a photo of an old Portuguese coin with the image of the emperor on it. I didn't understand the language he used when he spoke about it but I could sense he viewed it with high reverence. At times we would go through the books and I would explain some things to him. I asked him if he studied these books at the school in the village. He said 'no', so I asked him what he learned there. He shared that the teacher at the school was Txaná Kixtin and that the learned about plants and the way of the pajé. He showed me a book which on many of its pages he had numbered every line. The first few pages had the names of plants next to them, with the medicine, use and description written beside. This is what he had been studying at the school. I reflected on how much I respected the way they used the concept of a school to adapt their own traditional knowledge within it. Similarly, the school text books were hidden away as a special treasure for those who were interested. In Australia this level of cultural autonomy has been overrun by governments imposing their stiff curriculums and threatening to take children away if they do not conform — and this is still going on today.

Singing for the plants

> *This knowledge isn't learned from books. It's taught by the beings of the forest in dreams and ceremony.* — Ibã Huni Kuin/ Isaias Sales Kaxinawá.

Txaná Ixã explained to me that in the family the role of the singer who has been given the name Ibã is to call the force and the spirit of all the plants. He was referring to all the medicinal and food plants the Huni Kuin use in their life and practices. He told me he had a nephew called Ibã but the nephew had gone to live on a *fazenda* (farm) further down the river. It was the role, he said, for the carrier of the name Ibã to organise and lead the Katxanawá festival and suggested that would be part of my role now. The Katxanawá is a sacred fertility and harvest ritual of the Huni Kuin people traditionally performed to sing the spirit of the plants, bless the land, ensure abundant crops and harmonise community life with the cycles of nature. It includes days of ritual chants, dance and the symbolic sharing of game and fish, and invokes ancestral presence and reinforces reciprocity between humans, spirits and the Earth. The women make clothing from grasses and other plants that are also worn throughout the event. The ceremony reflects the Huni Kuin's profound relationship with the forest as a living and sentient being. I felt very honoured to be asked to have a role in this, and Ixã suggested I talk to people around the village and ask about the festival and what it required. I wasn't confident I was totally up for this task. It seemed like a daunting undertaking, especially as I felt that I was still so new to their culture and way of life and that I had much to learn. I was aware that most of the gringos I knew who were visiting the Huni Kuin were making them all kinds of promises and offers to make money and do tours to help them get the attention of Westerners. I had gone there making no promises nor asking for anything and had been invited to participate in what Ixã called the most important ceremony of the Huni Kuin.

One of the things I had learned from my time in the villages with the Shipibo, Yawanawá and now the Huni Kuin was that, even as many Westerners go to them with the primary intention of seeking out Ayahuasca, the sacrament does not exist in a vacuum and is intrinsically linked to a vast cosmology of many plants, rites and songs. Ixã explained that for the Huni Kuin it was vital they hold this festival, as it would ensure they would have health, abundance and fertility in all the plants that they depended on for survival in the forest. This was an ancient tradition and similar to other Indigenous practices I had witnessed. He said each plant would have its own dresses, dances and songs which would all be celebrated in succession over multiple days with great feasts and banquets of all the foods. Ixã explained that another Huni Kuin man had agreed with him to develop a farm on some land close by the village, around 15 minutes up the river.

A couple of days later Ixã took me to the farm up the river to meet the man, Maná, who was given the job of caring for and cultivating all of the plants. Ixã explained that I had to stay there for some time to learn from the man. Like everything else the Huni Kuin were offering me, I accepted, even though I didn't feel so secure on this part of the path. It was a bit hard to leave the village, as I had made friends there and felt the warmth of loving care shared amongst the people. When we arrived at the farm, Ixã showed me around and introduced me to Maná and his wife. Ixã's middle son Tuwe was living there with his wife. Ixã went back to Alta Mira and left me there with these new Huni Kuin friends.

Maná took me for a walk during which he explained many things to me. He told me how he had made an agreement with Ixã, whereby Ixã had offered his eldest son Tuwe to marry Maná's daughter in exchange for committing to live and work on this farm in support of the bigger village. I wondered what this must have been like for Tuwe, as I had heard of him but had never seen him in the village in all the weeks I had been there. Maná was a very intense and talkative

Huni Kuin man; I wasn't sure if this was because he felt a bit isolated there and keen to talk a lot or whether that was just his personality. He spent the day showing me many plantations and with Tuwe explained some of the farming techniques they used. It seemed there was a huge amount of work going on there relative to how few of them were living there.

Just before sunset, Maná took me up onto the side of a hill facing west, where I saw rows of terraces carved into the side of the hill, which had been cleared of the rainforest. He said this was a sacred garden that they used to communicate with the plants. He showed me many plants there that they were working with, perhaps ones which they hadn't used previously or which were not traditionally part of Huni Kuin plant lore. We sat down next to one small seedling he said was a new plant that had been gifted from another village. He explained that when new species were introduced to the village part of his role was to germinate the seeds and plant them in this sacred area, and then as they grew he would sit with them to connect spiritually with the plants. He told me that for the Huni Kuin to integrate a new plant into their cosmology they must first understand the plant's spirituality, and that he would drink some Nixi Pãe and sit with a plant and ask to hear its song. Then he would learn that song so that he could then call the spirit of the plant when he wanted to study or work with it. He told me that over time he might learn multiple songs from each plant and he would then know how they would integrate and weave into their existing cosmology — or sometimes he wouldn't know, if they did not harmonise. I was learning about how the Huni Kuin worked spiritually with all their plants and where the songs for the Katxanawá festival came from. We sat and watched the sun set as he sang some songs for the plants.

We then went back to the main house where the women were preparing food — much the same as every meal I had had in the village of small fish, boiled plantains and cassava. I sang some songs for them and then Maná also sang; I noticed his music was just as intense as his personality. Tuwe came back after working all day and I saw that he was very humble and a little shy. I asked if he played guitar and he said that he played a little. So I gave him the guitar and was amazed at how good he was. Most Huni Kuin could string together a few rough chords and a basic strumming pattern, but he had more skill and depth in his guitar playing and I felt a beautiful and refined energy in his voice and songs. He had the same regal grace that I perceived in Ixã's other sons. I also noticed the tone of his playing was not as buoyant and happy as it was in the village. Things seemed more serious here on the fazenda, and when I asked Tuwe about how it was being away from the village I could sense a longing in him for his connection there.

The dance of the jiboia

> *When you're with the people it's made very clear that an icaro is not something you listen to. An icaro is something you look at. You look at it. It is to be seen, even though it is made out of sound, as a composition, as a work of art, it is offered more in the vein of a painting than a song or a poem. What is happening is that in this group state of mind, the intentionality of the singer is beheld as a three-dimensional modality of light and of colour. Well, this is like an ontological transformation of language itself.*
> — Terence McKenna.

When I returned to the village they were already preparing to begin the process of cooking some Nixi Pãe and I was asked to help with harvesting and preparing the plants. João worked closely with them, as they had asked him to teach them some techniques from Santo Daime because they really liked the Daime tea. Firstly we had to walk around the village and ask different Huni Kuin if we could use plants that they were the custodians of, these being the leaves of the chacruna bushes and the vine itself. Once we had permission, I spent some time with others collecting leaves. The next day Kixtin invited me to go with him to harvest the vine. After drinking some Nixi Pãe we walked with some young Huni Kuin to the edge of the village, where there was a vine climbing high up into a tree which had three main trunks winding their way to the top. Kixtin climbed to the top and cut two of the three sections down to the root and left the third one intact so that the vine could keep growing and be used again.

A couple of days later, as the cooking ritual was nearing completion, Kixtin took me and those young men to a little grove where some small plants were growing in a half circle with a bench made out of a large log. He invited me to sit on the log and he applied some sananga, which is a liquid infused with the root of a small shrub, with one drop put in each eye. It was a very painful experience but after the initial ordeal it gave profound mental and sensory clarity. He gave me a strong blow of rapé and asked me to sit while he took a leaf of one of the *mári taíxski* plants I was familiar with. This was the same plant for singers and he told me to put the leaf on my tongue but to leave its stem sticking out of my mouth. He then spoke quietly to the plants, an action I assumed was some kind of prayer of respect and asking of permission. I started to feel the force of the Nixi Pãe and the other plants very strongly as he took another leaf from the singers plant.

Kixtin walked over, stood in front of me and began to sing a song I hadn't heard before. As he sang, he then began to rapidly tap with the leaf he was holding onto the stem of the leaf that was on my tongue. As he did so, I could sense the vibrations of the song and the light tapping sensation, and I entered into the miração. This was a very different kind of experience and it took my mind a while to relax into this. The young Huni Kuin stood around watching. They hadn't explained to me what this was about but I felt it was something significant. After a while I could feel the spiritual enchantment of the plant coming to life; the subtle vibrations became a very powerful wave of spiritual force and took over my attention. While I sat there meditating on this process it seemed that Kixtin had been singing for a long time. His song was very psychedelic and subdued my mind. I began to track the vibrations as they descended throughout my tongue and slowly moved down my throat, vibrating into my vocal chords and further down until I could feel this reach my heart centre. Once this vibrational pathway was fully blessed by the sound and tapping vibrations, he stopped the song and left me sitting there in a meditation for some time.

When we returned to the village there were people waiting and excited for our return. I realised there were some expectations of our

With Txana Kixtin and Huni Kuin children, Alta Mira, Acre, Brazil

arrival in the village and I was offered some gifts and feathers. They told me that we were going to have a ceremony that night. At sunset I made my way to the ceremonial space after I had taken some time to adorn myself with all the gifts that had been given to me that day and during the time in the village. The Huni Kuin usually also adorn themselves with colourful clothing, arts and sacred objects. When I arrived, they were all standing around looking at me and seemed very happy that I had come adorned with all the gifts. Before the ceremony, Ixã told me that my music was appreciated by the people because of the colours that I brought into the miração, and also that my songs made the jiboia dance energetically and with much force. Ixã began the ceremony in the usual way, with prayers and traditional songs, then he made an announcement that I had received the blessings of the singer and he asked me to sing for the jiboia.

As I began to sing, one of the men began the dance of the jiboia and led a line of mostly women and some of the younger men who snaked around doing a little bouncing dance as they wove random patterns around the space, always circling back around the fire. I became aware that as I put more vigour into the music, the line of Huni Kuin dancing the jiboia would gather momentum and energy. A couple of times the leader of the dance led the snake to the opposite end of the ceremonial space and then moved directly toward me in a straight line, turning only as he arrived right in front of me. As this happened, 20 or more Huni Kuin danced up to me and they all gave me a blessing on their way past. I could feel the energy and blessings of the jiboia and the forest very strongly. This force moved through me as I sang — and I felt one with it all. What was most striking was that my voice had a new vibration and a new colour and quality. It felt more stable — something that has stayed with me until this day and that I have studied and developed over time. Everything that had happened to this point was now making sense: from my childhood when I used to sing all the time, then to Carioca training me as a singer, to the daily ritual with the leaf, to being given the name Ibã, the singer who calls the miração, and receiving the blessing and force of the sacred jiboia.

> *Colourful jiboia [boa]*
> *Many dances*
> *Jiboia, colourful arrow*
> *Hands dancing*
> *The force arrives, dancing*
> *Jiboia, colourful borduna [war club]*
> *Strong chest, dancing*
> *Force of the miração*
> *Earrings in the nostrils*
> *Many ears*
> *Sounds dance in the ears*
> *In front of you*
> *Bird with big blue feather*
> *Blue in front of you*
> *In front of you*
> *Arara canindé [blue and yellow macaw] feather*
> *Yellow in front of you*
>
> — Hawẽ Dautibuya Ikirã Ikirã Damibiranai Uikia Tiki (Song of the Colourful Miração), Huni Meka, Romão Sales

Some years later, I met with Ibã Isaias Sales, a famous Elder of the Huni Kuin who is a master of language, arts and music. I told him about my experience and he mentioned that he was the one who taught Ixã and Kixtin these diets and he shared with me the following:

> *There is a plant. You used a sacred plant to remove heaviness, to become lighter. You will never forget how you dreamed. This is the miração, the gift that you received. You are welcome to the forest. The name of the plant is mári taíxski. It is to call the voice closer — the voice, the wisdom — to stay nearer to us. It will not run away anymore. It keeps enchanting you, and you keep enchanting it ... it embraces you, and you stay together with it. You will not forget anymore. Always learning.*

Kingdom of the stars

The day after the ceremony, Ixã's wife set up a loom beside my hammock and began to weave some typical Huni Kuin fabric with *kenê* (designs). The kenê are sacred geometric designs of the Huni Kuin, intricately woven or painted as visual expressions of ancestral knowledge, protection, animal and plant spirits and spiritual alignment. Far more than decoration, each pattern carries symbolic meaning, serving as a living language that connects body, spirit and forest in harmonious resonance. Some examples of kenê can be seen in the chapter titles of this book. I didn't ask why she was doing this beside my hammock, as approaching or talking to the women could make them feel uncomfortable since men's and women's spaces are kept distinctly separate. This culture of gender roles was very similar to that of the Central Australian Indigenous people I had lived with. Some Brazilians I had met over the years complained about it as being discriminatory, but I saw it as traditional culture and not for me to judge.

João had organised with Ixã to visit another village two days by boat up the river Jordão. He had made friends with another, younger

Huni Kuin cacique called Isarawé who lived with his clan in a very remote village called Reino das Estelas (Kingdom of the Stars). Ixã was going to take us to visit the village and told us that Isarawé was his nephew. In Huni Kuin law, once a man has undergone enough training and initiation, he can choose to continue and specialise in the ways of the pajé, or he can diverge and focus on the studies to become a cacique, a village chief. The way of the cacique requires a lot of personal power and responsibility to be able to care for a large family group. It seemed that Isarawé had recently, perhaps a few years earlier, taken some of his family to establish a new village close to the frontier of the protected territory of the uncontacted tribes.

There was much discussion about the agenda and preparations for the journey. As we were getting ready, Ixã's wife painted kenês on my face and arms with jenipapo, which is a plant used for making a black dye/ink which is then used to paint kenê onto the skin. This practice is often used for protection but is also a way to connect to the spirit of the forest and the spirit of the animal or plant that the kenê represents. As the dye penetrates the skin, so the spirit enters the body, and will stay there for five or so days until it naturally fades away. I was painted with a large scorpion kenê on my forehead. Six of us left the village in a canoe and we journeyed downstream on the River Tarauacá towards the junction with the River Yurayá, which has become known as the River Jordão (Jordan). After a supply stop in the town of Jordão, we headed upstream along the river of the same name.

As we began our journey upriver, I contemplated the significance of the name River Jordan. The River Jordan in the Bible marked a crossing from one state of being to another: from the wilderness into the Promised Land, from wandering into fulfilment, from the old self into renewal. Here, in the Upper Amazon lands of the Huni Kuin, where the songlines were waterways of the forest carrying the songs of both the ancient and the new, the sense of a sacred and beautiful Dream-weaving brought powerful feelings of reverence and gratitude to me for the honour of this time and my presence in the forest. As we travelled along the river, I breathed and bathed in the sublime beauty. These were lands where the roots of Santo Daime grew into a beautiful tree, where Christ emerged through the medicine of the

High Aim in the Upper Amazon   493

Receiving kené body paint, Alta Mira, Acre, Brazil

forest, and where the songs of Christ and the chants of Country sang the creation of a new Dreaming. The spirit of the Jordan had found a reflection here, a baptism for the people and for a world in renewal.

> *And Jesus, when he was baptised, went up straightway out of the water: and, lo, the heavens were opened unto him, and he saw the Spirit of God descending like a dove.* — Matthew 3:16.

The first stop along the river was the village of São Joaquin. This is a famous and revered village amongst the Huni Kuin, as it was one of the first places re-occupied when they were granted a reserve of land by the Brazilian Government and were able to return to Country. The village was founded pajé Íka Muru, a major healer, researcher of forest medicines, and cultural leader. Íka Muru 'dreamed' the place and descended the river with his family to found São Joaquim, establishing it as a *Centro de Memória* (Centre for Memory) to preserve Huni Kuin cultural knowledge, plant lore and ritual sciences. Ibã Isaias Sales spoke to me about the movement of the Huni Kuin to recover their culture and spirituality following a long period of genocide: 'I come from the time of greatest knowledge — the one who knows the most about our time, the time of the massacres, the time of captivity. In that time, we could not hold our traditional festivals.'

When we arrived at São Joaquim, Ixã was greeted by family, as he had told us that he was originally from São Joaquin before he founded Alta Mira. A very significant ceremony was underway when we arrived: a multi-day ceremony of baptism that is one of the most important ones for Huni Kuin people. The baptism of Nixpupima is a passage ritual linked to becoming one of the people, stepping into your role in the cycle of life. There was a strong, calm, quiet energy around the village. As I walked around the place many Huni Kuin commented on the kenê design painted on my face, saying it was strong, and praised me with respect. I didn't really know what it meant at that stage. I was soon approached by some young men who were excited to meet a gringo with a guitar. They also commented on the kenê design and invited me to come and try their sananga, which we shared with some rapé and xurú.

There were a group of very old pajés and a group of women who seemed to be leading the baptism ritual. I felt a little uncomfortable being there, as we were not involved in the ritual and I wanted to show respect by keeping my mind and energy out of the field. I won't describe here what I witnessed, as I wasn't part of it, but it was an intense experience being around the ritual all night long and into the morning. Ixã asked the old pajés to do a small ritual for us to drink some Nixi Pãe, and we were blessed to receive it by the fire, where we were served from a traditional clay cup that sat on the raw earth. They sang some chants and said some hearty *haux* (salutation) affirmations. After the pajés went back to the ritual, I grabbed my hammock and found a large shelter with some posts which I tied it to and where I could hide out. The singing and strange sounds coming from the ritual were already calling me into a different state of consciousness, and as I began to feel the force of the Nixi Pãe, I moved into a miração. The miração was pure jungle: I was surrounded by plants and sounds of the forest, and then I saw a vision of a huge scorpion that showed itself to me and stayed for a while. I connected with it telepathically and it told me it had a very strong force, as its lightning-fast sting was very poisonous and deadly. The scorpion hides under rocks and likes to remain unseen. I understood why the scorpion was such a powerful totem ally for protection and I felt gratitude at welcoming its presence and teachings.

We left not long after sunrise and spent the whole day on the river. The usual engine breakdowns and seemingly impossible crossings occurred on our journey. At one point they couldn't get the engine started at all, which was unusual, and I wondered how they would fix it, while we were so far up the river and getting close to the frontier with the uncontacted tribes. The Huni Kuin man who was driving the boat then ran off into the forest and came back a couple of hours later in a boat with a spare engine. The engines were swapped and on we went. Another time there was a giant tree, around two and a half metres wide, crossing the entire river. Sure enough though, we found a way to carry the canoe over the giant trunk and safely into the river on the other side. I was getting into the flow of all the obstacles and was very aware that I would be unable to survive alone in this environment. I was learning to let go of worrying, 'How are we were going to get through *this* one?' All teachings in letting go and trusting in *Yuxibu* (Great Spirit) and the flow of creation and Dreaming.

As we drew closer to the end of the Huni Kuin lands, every time we passed a village people would be waiting on the bank to see if we were going to stop at their village. The loud sound of the boat's motor would echo up and down the river for kilometres, giving the locals notice of our journey. It was some hours after dark when we arrived in Reino das Estelas, and as we approached the village we could see a line of lights descending towards the river bank. As we got off the boats some young men grabbed all our stuff and the rest stood in a long line with each one greeting us. We were all very excited. I had a feeling with the way they received us that somehow they had known we were coming, which struck me as unusual, since João hadn't been able to send them any message. He had just met Isarawé in São Paulo some months before and had been given the invitation to visit.

We walked up the hill towards the village which had a ceremonial space in the centre made up of a doughnut-shaped thatched roof covering a circular ceremonial space. I walked into the hole in the middle, looked up and saw endless stars shining so brightly and was in awe of this beautiful creation that surely was a kingdom of the stars. To one side stood a huge pot of Ayahuasca and a few chairs with Isarawé and another young Huni Kuin man waiting for us. Isarawé explained they had been cooking all day in preparation for a ceremony that night. Our arrival was not just fortuitous but had been divinely orchestrated. Isarawé seemed surprised when I asked him if he had known we were coming, and from his response I realised he had been communicating telepathically and been shown through the miração of our arrival. We drank the Nixi Pãe under the stars and had a beautiful night of chanting, music and sharing stories. Ixã went to sleep in a hammock, while João and I stayed up talking and playing music until the sun came up. By this stage after many weeks in the forest my visions and mirações were filled with teachings from the forest, plus many realisations and deepening cultural understandings. I was processing and integrating the cultural knowledge and experiences, building a constellation of forest wisdom within myself. So much of the transmissions I'd received were through sound, energy and telepathic communication.

In the morning Isarawé talked about his vision to journey and share his culture and medicine. He shared a contemporary Brazilian medicine song, *Caboclo Curador* by Pablo Comesana, about the role of the healer from the forest who travels the world. He played it on guitar and taught it to me — and I still play it to this day:

Arrived! Arrived! The caboclo healer
He circles the whole world
To alleviate our pain

This caboclo is a true caboclo
And aims his arrow way beyond the sea
This caboclo is a caboclo of Jurema
With his feather headdress makes the people balanced

He brings the cures from the forest
And his song of love comes from the heart
Nukum mana ibubu
Mana ibubu butã
Eskwata kai ya uê
Kai ya uê kei kei

As I write about these experiences, I realise that the deeper I have gone into the miração, the harder it becomes to explain what I have seen and the teachings I have received. I understand why Pablo Amaringo ended up painting his visions as his way to convey the cosmology of Ayahuasca and the forest. There is much more to be said about the relationships I have made with spiritual beings, some of whom have become allies and guides for me. Perhaps I will explore in more detail the deeper technology and awareness I have gained in subsequent books, or perhaps this will remain in the realm of oral transmission or communication within the miração.

There were only three more villages along the river before the border with the protected lands. I had previously asked Kixtin about the uncontacted tribes; the Huni Kuin referred to them as the *Indios bravos* (brave Indians) or the *tribos isolados* (isolated tribes). Kixtin told me he had met them at different times when out hunting deeper into the forest. He said they were strong and brave peoples who did not want contact, even with the Huni Kuin. He said there were stories of trading with them, but mostly they were of very different cultures and their languages were full of sounds the Huni Kuin were not familiar with. Kixtin told me that whenever they saw them they were usually hunting in Huni Kuin lands, as they were being pushed out of their protected lands due to encroachments from the Peruvian side, where poachers, bandits and thieves operated. He said they would shout to them: 'This is Brazil! Go back to Peru!' I smiled at hearing they were invoking modern nation boundaries, even though the main reason they didn't want the Huni Kuin on their land was because they were competing for scarce resources, in particular, animals for hunting. Isarawé also had stories of the Indios bravos.

This village had less than 50 people from what I could tell and it seemed most of them were younger than 25 years old. The place was very basic with few dwellings. Isarawé's father was the Elder and he lived on a *terreiro* (sacred ground) on the other side of the river. We spent a couple of days there enjoying the forest, the river and this beautiful, humble, simple and very sweet Huni Kuin family. I felt very honoured to be in their village and to learn about their story of migration and resilience in the forest. Only a few of the older men, who themselves were in their twenties, spoke Portuguese, and even they were a bit rough with the language. Everyone else only spoke their native Hãtxa Kuĩ. The women were very curious and asked the men to ask me if they could look at my necklace and arm band, which were from other Amazonian tribes. I said 'of course' and though they were very shy and scared to come near me they did and marvelled at the designs and colours. We traded some items and I gave what clothes I had with me that I could spare. They gifted me with a *cocar* (feathered headdress) and gave me some *arara* (macaw) feathers which I was very grateful to receive and which I have since used in ceremonies, where my connection to the ancestral bird tribes is one of my main totemic relationships.

We eventually headed off and were a couple of hours away from arriving back at Alta Mira on the River Tarauacá when the boat's engine broke down yet again. After my days of river adventures, at this stage I just smiled and I was offered a spot in another canoe that joined us as we passed through Jordão. We had broken down in a particularly beautiful large bend in the river. I decided to stay with Kixtin, who went off to find some help. I swam in the river as the sun set and watched the colours changing across the forest and the water as the sounds of the animals created a divine soundscape. I just took it all in with much gratitude.

Symphony of the Emerald Forest

I come from the forest
With my song of love
I am an Indian messenger
A messenger of love

I am an Indian messenger
I come from the forest
I will protect you
With my bow and my arrow

I carry peace in my heart
To help you reflect
With the sound of my guitar
This is my tradition

I pray to my Queen Mother
Mother of all beauty
At all times I pray to her
She is my fortress

— *Indio Mensageiro*, Fabricio Ahau.

The day after we settled back into life in Alta Mira, two Brazilian friends of the Huni Kuin arrived from Rio de Janeiro. These people were able to explain a great deal of things to me and fill in some gaps around basic Huni Kuin culture, which was helpful. It was really clear, though, that they had brought with them a kind of 'city energy' that felt a bit stressed and they seemed a little demanding of Ixã and the village people. They came with a lot of expectations which they wanted met in the short time they had available. The contrast with the natural flow, peace and harmony I had experienced until then in Alta Mira was stark. The Brazilians were quick to tell me numerous times how experienced they were with the Huni Kuin and I often felt like they were competing or at least trying to assert some kind of authority over me and João.

Ixã had been planning to take us to the sacred space to continue the spiritual work we had been doing. Suddenly this couple were arguing with him about how and when we would be making this journey. They had a list of demands, some of which Ixã seemed to be questioning, but he didn't seem to want to engage in arguments and — mostly —went along with them. They were a couple and squabbled amongst themselves also. This kind of needy, dominating behaviour was like moving against sandpaper compared to the smooth journey we had been on until they arrived. At one point one of the Huni Kuin men said he thought they were crazy, which made me laugh. I wondered, after all these years they had been coming to the village and helping Ixã and the family there with projects and resources, how they had not learned to respect their ways and the harmony of the forest. Perhaps they didn't get it.

I have come to realise over the years that many people do this. They arrive and start making promises of help and projects and money and Ayahuasca tourism proposals. The native peoples are vulnerable because they need the support and also have a mission to offer their medicines to the world. I felt like these busy people from Rio were missing out on a lot. I had gone there humble and asked for nothing and they had given me so much. This couple were asking a lot and seemingly not comprehending or fully connecting with the spirit of the forest, which the Huni Kuin embody masterfully. I reflected that to be humble and listen, be patient and open, is the way to genuinely access the Dreaming and the spirit of the Huni Kuin. I felt blessed and grateful for my own way and everything that had been given to me. Over the years I have witnessed this kind of attitude increasing, where people go to the villages promising money, fame and support with Ayahuasca tourism. They adopt a performative role in promoting their own connection to the Huni Kuin or other Indigenous peoples and wear it like a badge of honour, even when it lacks substance. Even though the Brazilians' presence was a bit disturbing, it was also a lesson in how not to approach the work in the forest and it also prepared me a little after six weeks there and not having had any contact with the outside world, as it was the end of our journey and we were days away from leaving. It also gave me a new understanding of the peace and harmony of the Huni Kuin and of life in the village.

We journeyed to the sacred space, this time by boat. When we arrived we went straight to the big cumuru tree and all sat around beside one of the big roots. Ixã pulled out some rapé and asked who would like to receive first and I volunteered. When he applied it to me, the blow that he gave was very intense and with a sensation and motion that I had never experienced before. There are many ways to blow the rapé and each may signify or call a different quality of experience; this one felt particularly strong. I immediately knew I was about to have an intense experience and once he had applied the rapé in both nostrils he suggested I go and sit on the root of the cumuru tree and feel its force. I did this and immediately started spinning and feeling dizzy. The force moving through me became far too strong and I thought I was going to fall off the tree, so I crawled over to the side and immediately began vomiting on the ground. This strong force had shifted something deep within that was releasing and anything I may have still been holding onto mentally or emotionally was moving in my physical body. After a while I was able to look around and I noticed everyone else was also on the ground vomiting, while the dogs were running around happily eating the purges.

After a while Ixã calmly walked over and suggested I go to the water and bathe under the waterfall. I was still dizzy and nauseous and did what he said, thinking that perhaps it would help me return to my centre and regain balance. This one was a real struggle. I crawled into the water and made my way to the little waterfall then lay in it but the force of the water also made the rapé effect feel even stronger. The others had all wandered down to the caretaker's house and I eventually gathered my strength and slowly walked down to meet them there, still feeling very nauseous. I sat on the floor of the house with everyone and they began a ritual of xurú. They passed it to me and I tried to smoke but couldn't so I passed it on and just lay on my back on the floor. Then one of the Huni Kuin women came up with a cloth that had sananga in it and she applied two drops, one in each eye. The usual sting came, yet through that ordeal suddenly the nausea was gone and I felt crystal clear and very present. I sat there with my mind blissfully empty and still while some conversations went on amongst the group. As usual, I mostly listened, taking it all in.

After this intense cleansing preparation Ixã then said we would drink some Nixi Pãe. As usual, the friends from Rio started telling him what to do and how we were going to drink it, but this time he ignored them and we sat and he said some prayers as we each drank a large cup of the sacrament. He told us to all lie in the hammocks and we did this in silence, with just the sounds of the jungle as the sun was setting into darkness. Once it was fully dark, Ixã asked me to sing some songs to call the force. I sang a couple of Santo Daime songs and called the force, and then he told me to go back to my hammock. The force duly arrived and I could feel a powerful miração coming. The sounds started to merge into each other and joined with visions into a changing inner landscape that slowly began to form. My thinking mind dissolved into the miração and I found myself feeling buoyant within a stunning beautiful psychedelic forest tinged with emerald colours and golden light. I could see the energy emanating from many plants, some of which looked like they were not of the Earth. I seemed to be floating within this majestic astral forest and I began to perceive a symphony of sounds coming from everything and everywhere within it. I could feel that every plant had a song, and there was music everywhere. I could reach out and grab sound and music with my mind, like picking sonic flowers from this emerald forest.

After all the time in the forest and being immersed in the universe of the Huni Kuin, including the taking of a lot of medicines and finally this big purge, I found myself within the astral dimension of the living forest. After the jarring shock of the mental projections of the friends from Rio and the effect of any remnants of my ego-mind that may have been lingering, the intense purge before this ceremony had apprehended my thoughts, allowing me to fully immerse myself in this divine realm. In that space I knew that I could receive infinite songs and music. It all finally made sense when I asked Ixã's son and others about how they learned some of their craft and, in particular, the songs. As I mentioned earlier, they had always said, 'we learn from the forest' and I now I knew what they meant, having experienced this myself. I was learning to navigate in that space and this was coming to me very naturally and clearly. Then, when one of the Rio friends started talking to Ixã, I dropped right out of the miração and came back to the physical space. Ixã just told them to concentrate. Rather than becoming frustrated and indulging in my own projections, I contemplated the overall experience and was grateful for the teachings. Perhaps these people with their active minds were a reflection of me and what I had brought to Ayahuasca and the forest at some point. This also showed me the importance of taming the mind and being clear and clean in order to reach the elevated and pure astral dimensions. I had some good conversations with Ayahuasca in that space and she explained a lot to me about what was possible and what I was invited to do next. She told me that when I returned this would be the place I would begin to work from at the next level of my studies and training.

This experience was a deeply touching gift from the Huni Kuin and from the forest. They had read me very well through the questions I had been asking. They knew I had a gift of music and singing and had guided me through that process; they had answered my questions by preparing me and guiding me to the answer. I marvelled at this intelligence which reminded me so much of Pablo Amaringo and the way he had taught me and also the way I had learned from so many other clever Indigenous people. The next day we returned to the village and Ixã explained to me that when I returned, the next level of my training would involve a special diet with a songbird, the same as one of Carioca's totems. This would expand my vocal abilities and create an even deeper connection to the forest.

The morning that we left I gave away everything that I had with me, including my hammock and the guitar that I had bought in Rio. I wandered around the village to say goodbye to everyone and made a stop at Ixã's son Mayá's house. We sat out the back chatting, sharing xurú when the old pajé from the house on the hill came by to visit. He sat with us and said, 'You are leaving? But why? You only just got here!' I found myself struggling to answer him, as he was right — I felt that I had only just begun to understand the way of the Huni

Kuin and the gifts and teachings of the forest. I gave him my clumsy explanation and he went on to give me a beautiful blessing for my path forward. He said that since I had arrived, the village was very happy and the children were happy and that my presence and music had brought a lot of joy to their family. He told me I would always be welcome and would never have to bring any money, as my presence was a big gift for them. I had tears in my eyes as he spoke, and I felt so much love and appreciation for this beautiful sharing. That night we had another ceremony and we stayed all night in the temple until it was time to start getting ready for the trip to Jordão.

We drank a cup of Nixi Pãe before getting into the canoe to head back to Jordão to catch the flight to Rio Branco for the journey back to Rio de Janeiro. As I sat in that little plane looking out over the endless forest I felt the loss of leaving the perfect harmony and peace of life in the Amazon forest with the Huni Kuin and I started to cry. I had been deeply touched by their humility and generosity, and I cried all the way to Rio Branco. I knew that I was profoundly changed and life would never be the same again. This is the path of Ayahuasca, the way of the hummingbird.

Silent flight of the mystery of love
I close my eyes to see where I'm going to
Flight to the infinite of that which I am
To reveal and dive in the inner ocean

Hummingbird take me
Hummingbird awaken in me

Take me to the waters of this enchanting river
Golden valley of my beautiful hummingbird
To fly in the blue of the sunset
Soft wind brings me the freshness

Hummingbird take me
Hummingbird awaken in me

Kiss delicately and open all the petals of this flower
Brilliance of the forest that inflames the seeker
Little bird that enchants me, sing the song of love
Take me where you are going

Hummingbird take me
Hummingbird awaken in me

—*Voo da Beija-flor,* Elisa Cristal.

Back in Rio de Janeiro I returned to Ciranda. It was beautiful to be back amongst the family and forest that had been my home for so long, but I found it hard to fully connect and I really struggled. I had become so sensitive after all that time in the forest and amidst a festival and ceremonies at Ciranda with so many people and so many egos I craved silence. I felt alone, like I couldn't connect with anyone. After a few ceremonies I gradually returned and as everyone attuned through the work and through Ayahuasca it also felt like the family there had come to a place where I could connect again. This was good preparation for the journey back to Australia, where there was a big community waiting for my return, knowing that I would have lots to share.

CHAPTER 13

Voices and Perspectives

When I sat down to begin work on this book it was recommended to me to include the voices of other people who have walked alongside me, or have been touched by this journey. As I was chosen by Spirit, my teachers and the community I serve to walk this path and carry this medicine of ceremony, lineage and tradition, I feel that this is a story of many people, and not just me. In this book it is important that we hear from the voices of others and gain insight from their unique perspectives. As you can see from this small sample of voices, everyone who comes to the ceremonies and does this sacred work comes with different life experiences, different intentions and has very unique experiences with Ayahuasca that lead them on their own unique life's journeys.

What I have noticed over the years, with sitting in ceremonies in Australia and Brazil with thousands of people, is that in almost every example, spiritual insight is inevitable. Just as with the ancient stories from the Amazon, where Ayahuasca is the conduit of connection to Country and Spirit, in the modern example people are having the same experience. What a spiritual experience is will differ from person to person but these experiences always seem to bring people into a self-knowing of who they are in relation to creation, ancestors and beliefs. This is a beautiful thing and one of the real treasures our ceremonies and community are able to offer: that no matter who people are, where they come from or what their personal circumstances are, people feel safe and supported to reconnect with themselves. This is where true self-empowerment lies and where we combine with opportunities to sing, dance and celebrate with family. This is where the healing of humanity resides and where we can learn to once again be real humans, guided and taught by our Indigenous Elders, culture, and brothers and sisters, who have never forgotten.

I sent out a call to the community, asking for contributions to this book. People were asked to talk about their experiences with Ayahuasca and ceremony, and I left this open as to how they might like to respond. People were given some guidance on sharing their circumstances coming into their first experiences, how those experiences were for them, what any challenges or benefits they experienced during or after ceremonies were, and they were also invited to share anything they liked to about Ayahuasca use in general. In some cases, people asked to have their names changed for the publication due to social stigma and fear of any persecution that might result from religious and spiritual discrimination in Australia. What I have included is a selection of some of the sharings offered.

So, first up we have the story of Jesse Lethbridge, who is one of my closest brothers, soul mates and allies on the journey of Spirit. It is an honour to share these journeys and experiences with him, and having his voice heard first recognises his dedication and faith in the work with Ayahuasca and in reconnection with Indigenous Earth wisdom. We also hear from Cat, a registered nurse who is one of the most trusted guardians of our temple and our ceremonies, who specialises in deep care and support of the women in our community and is a shining example of healthy integration, self-responsibility and upstanding service to community and society. She also touches on the work she has been involved with in developing psychedelic-assisted therapy. After Cat, we hear from Luís Piazzetta, a master musician with deep roots into Brazilian culture, rhythms and musical styles. From there each voice flows for the reader to gain insight from the kaleidoscope of experiences in our ceremonies. These are just a small snapshot of the hundreds of people touched by these ceremonies and by our community.

Jesse
Male, 49 years, musician/musical instrument craftsman

I was there from the beginning— at the first ceremony Lore facilitated in Australia in 2016. My physical and mental health was in a good space leading up to starting the work with Ayahuasca. I previously had experience with other shamanic practices and meditation teachings and I'd been interested to explore Ayahuasca but was waiting for an environment that I felt safe in. This was it.

I have always had an interest in understanding more of the unseen and the mystery. I think they'd call me 'the seeker'. I have an interest in Indigenous Earth wisdom, which I believe holds great teachings in how to live in harmony with this planet. Let's face it — cutting all the trees and mining all the resources for money and polluting the water and air to the point where we find ourselves today is not healthy or sustainable. I am motivated in seeking better ways to live in harmony with each other and the planet.

So much has happened over the years through supporting and participating in ceremonies. The first years were a steep learning curve, which I took seriously, and still do, in the preparation and cleansing to be ready for Ayahuasca and ceremony. In some ways it's like a university for life, with the arts being one of the main lessons. The art of living is music, singing, dancing, praying together and growing in community. So many people have found their voice through singing in ceremony and many have picked up musical instruments. I've seen Ayahuasca unlock many people's creativity.

Also through the ceremonies many loves and partnerships were healed or formed, babies were born and families created. My personal experience in ceremony included working alongside Lore and others in a supporting/guardianship role at the same time as learning a great deal about myself and about healing. There has been lots of healing — to the point of truly feeling grateful for being alive. I have deep gratitude for the many different experiences along the way. The form and the way the ceremony is conducted maintain a safe space for people to do their own healing and come to a place of self-empowerment. It's a long road to freedom — it's a spiritual journey.

In a way, this is what is lacking in our Western world, and I believe that's why so many people are interested in this path.

My personal growth in this work has been rewarding and life affirming. Not without its challenges, the nature of this work is a kind of training for life. To sit up and meet the challenges in ceremony is training for doing the same in life; transcending physical discomfort, the mental and emotional challenges, to stay clear and focused. Sometimes the integration after ceremonies in trying to relate the new insights I've received has been tough. I walk the path of an artist, so often the integration has been to make art or be inspired to write music. Nature, and my connection to it, have grown stronger. These are the gifts that come with Ayahuasca and I see this a lot with the people who come, that after a retreat they are more connected to nature and with being human. Let's face it, some people never put their bare feet on the earth and ceremony helps them reconnect to the Earth.

I remember when Lore reached out to me when he'd just got back from Brazil and was getting ready to bring his work to Australia and it just felt so right to put my hand up. I remember telling him I'd been journeying deep into the Dreamtime with the yidaki (didgeridoo), and if he needed someone to support, my hand was up. At that stage, I'd already been up to Arnhem Land and visited Djalu Gurruwiwi, a senior Yolngu Elder and master craftsman and player of yidaki.

I'd already been up and connected to that, and then in one of the first Ayahuasca ceremonies with Lore, he asked me to play and I had a really big, deep didge with me. I remember playing that, and it was so strong, like the energy that came through in the temple, in the space, was just so strong with what opened up in the sense of fully being connected. The primal energy that came through that gateway just felt timeless, like the access to the Dreamtime was very easy to slip into, and then later on in that ceremony Lore played the track *Baru* (crocodile) by Gurrumul, and I remember laying down on the temple floor and realising that it was the Yolngu singing.

I started to travel in my vision across the songlines of Australia, up into Arnhem Land, and then standing there to meet me was Djalu. He gave me a transmission, a message that I needed to come and spend time with him, and there were gifts that I needed to bring. I left that ceremony with a really strong conviction to follow through with that. Within about 10 days of the vision, I was up there in the Birritjimi community.

It was 30 hours of travel to get there and when I landed it was so hot. I gave them gifts, and then about half an hour later they said, 'Okay, let's go.' I was thinking, 'Maybe we'll rest tomorrow.' Ten minutes later, they took me out into the forest and we cut these two really big, heavy yidakis, and they sat down with me in the forest, and they just checked me out. They remembered that I'd previously been up there with somebody else, so it was very important for me to go and establish my own connection, from the place where I sit.

Through that experience, I remember Lena, who is one of Djalu's granddaughters, asking me, after a few days of being there, what it was that I wanted. I replied, 'I don't want anything; I've come to give back, to pay my respects, because the instrument has given me so much in my life, for myself and my family and my community. I'm here to give back.' They all sat there quietly for a little moment after that, then she looked at me and said, 'You're different. Everyone who comes here, they come because they want power. They're coming to take old man's power.' I guess when anyone has a position like that, people come and they want something from it. I came purely from that guidance from the ceremony and through the understanding that I needed to deepen my connection. And so, from that point on, they opened a wider door and invited me in.

Over the years since that moment, I've been going up to Arnhem Land every year and taking yidaki students. At one point I became very unwell and a Chinese medicine doctor said it would to be really tough for me in the cold that winter. He recommended that I be somewhere warm, and I immediately saw a vision of Arnhem Land in the winter. Then, right at that time, Djalu passed away. So I went up for about three and a half months during the lead-up to his funeral and did a lot of healing work with the family. They worked a lot with their plant medicines up there, a topical leaf which they used on my body to help with various different healing practices, including their energetic healing. Over the course of those three and a half months, I was nurtured back into strong spirit.

There's an amazing connection there for healing, and one thing that I started to understand through the work in the ceremonies with Lore is that it got me more in touch with a different perception, a different way of looking at things, and a different way of experiencing nature. What I now see in the Yolngu Indigenous culture is that there's no separation between the natural world and their world; that is, to be connected to the elements is just a natural state of being. Through the ceremonial work that Lore holds it opened a deeper connection to that presence in my life, and it is the same for many others, I imagine. My work with the Yolngu helped me to ground and integrate that into my life, so that it wasn't something separate. Quite often through those years that followed, I would be going quite deep in ceremonial work with Ayahuasca and then, soon after, I would be up in Arnhem Land and working with the family and connecting with nature and ceremony up there, which seemed quite complimentary and seamless.

Through that visit — when I went up after those visions — I was given permission to play in Ayahuasca ceremony and I was always encouraged and just asked to always come from the heart, to come with love. It's a very powerful instrument and, like most things, it's got the potential for light and dark. This family, they sit in the light, they pray, they bring the light.

There are some interesting crossovers, where they have a very strong Christian faith, as well as their deep connection to Yolngu *manikay* (clan songs) songlines and *bungul* (ceremonial dance), ceremonies. So that old man Djalu gave me his blessings to play yidaki in ceremony, to share the yidaki and to teach people and to heal with yidaki — so I continue to do that today.

I am soon taking a very special yidaki into a small village in the Amazon to give to the Huni Kuin people. I'm going to share a similar Dreaming they have, where there's jiboia, which has a very similar story to the *Witij*, the Rainbow Serpent. I've been talking with Djalu's family about taking the yidaki to the Huni Kuin and sharing it with them, and his daughter said that's really good to bring, that it'll help them and give them strength to fight for their forest and to help protect their land. She's very connected.

Opening that gateway for others through playing those rhythms in the ceremony, in the surrender, took me deeper into realms of being in that altered state and having the discipline for how I hold myself in that space and going into the Dreamtime. I've had experiences where I deeply understanding how the yidaki is working, how it's clearing, how it's healing, how I've accessed visionary states. On one journey I had a rhythm that I was shown up in Arnhem Land was a dolphin rhythm. I would never seek out and ask to be shown anything up there; if anything was shown, it was always received and appreciated. One day, Djalu came and sat with me, and he started teaching me the rhythm with the tongue and explaining how that was the dolphin swimming then coming up out of the water and blowing — like the blow of air through the blowhole — by pushing the water out and then diving back down. After spending that time and learning that rhythm, I played in this one ceremony with Lore and in my visionary state I suddenly shape-shifted into the eyes of the dolphin swimming underwater. Part of my awareness was still in the circle of the ceremony, and I blended between those two worlds and was swimming.

Through the ceremony this opened my understanding that these rhythms aren't just rhythms. They are gateways and access; they open a gateway into those realms. If someone's playing the big red kangaroo or the dolphin or the Rainbow Serpent or whatever rhythm, it's connecting to those elemental forces, to those beings — or they're strongly connected with bringing the lightning or bringing the rain. So, again this opened my awareness more to the elemental forces. And these things are quite natural for the Indigenous. It's not like a superpower — it's a natural part of life we've been disconnected from through the element of just looking at something but not being able to see it through the journey of playing the didge. Over many years I've had multiple experiences of opening the gateway of seeing — seeing beyond just the looking.

There's been bridging between culture and ceremonies and through teaching a lot of people — that has also been a blessing — to share the yidaki to keep the culture alive. The community aspect of the ceremonies has been very important and we have made countless community events of singing, dancing and togetherness. Lore and I have also recorded music collaborations with Indigenous tribes from the Brazilian Amazon.

Cat
Female, 42 years, registered nurse (mental health/research)

The first time that I drank Ayahuasca with Lore was eight years ago, and [I have done so] many more times since then. Before that, I had drunk twice before. When I met Lore I was very concerned more with other people than I was with myself, more worried about what other people thought, less about what I thought about myself. I was spending more time worrying about what other people were thinking about me.

I'm from England which is very traditional, and where it would be frowned upon to do anything that's considered 'out there'. However, my husband is from Brazil, so from a very different background, and in Brazil they're just more open to different ways of looking at things, and more open to plant medicines, which is something that I never really learned about or heard about before in the UK where I grew up.

The first time that I drank Ayahuasca, I spent a lot of the time worried about what other people were thinking. The key message that I took home was that I've 'got it,' and basically to stop worrying about that and to just focus on myself and the connection to Mother Earth. I feel like it was a big reminder of who I really am, and that in the process of becoming an adult, I'd forgotten that. It just helped me remember the truths about myself that I had chosen to forget.

It reminded me of who I was so I could live with purpose. By the time that I came and sat with Lore and the community, I was already on the path of nursing. So it just connected me to my purpose, the thing that drives me every day, which is to serve my community, and helped me continue my focus on that, while also improving myself as a person. It helped me to be just a regular person in society, to be the person I am, and to do what I believe to be right, true and just.

The Western medicine concept is that the body and the mind are totally separate, and that when you treat the body, you don't need to think about the mind at all. The way that we're supposed to nurse now, or at least 10 years ago when I first started, is to look at things holistically, look at the mental health, and also look at the body and how they're connected. Western medicine, in theory, separates those things. So nursing was saying: look holistically. In my nursing practice, when I was working in surgical and orthopaedic and even in emergency, I was always assessing the mental health. I don't think I ever really thought I would be a mental health nurse until I started to really understand it, and that's how I went on the journey to be a mental health nurse. This was probably partly also due to Ayahuasca helping me to make those connections to the body and the mind and to really see that everything starts in the mind and then manifests in the body.

Ayahuasca helps heal the mind. Well, it helps heal all of you, but it helps you look at the mind and see how you could do things differently, without you being necessarily 'in it'. The way that I see how psychedelics work, is that you take the medicine, you go back to an experience that you've had in the past — good, bad, however you determine it — and then you're removed from it, and you see the situation again. But you're not intrinsically part of it. You're almost looking from the outside, looking in. So you can reconsider how you found the experience and reframe it in your mind to go on more of a healing journey and to learn from the experience, rather than it be a trauma or something that you're holding on to. We don't think about that at all in Western medicine, maybe we do so more in psychiatry, but we just think: 'Oh, this person's broken something. Let's fix that.' We're very good at emergency medicine and those sorts of things, but we're not really good at looking deeply into the mind and the connections.

I think one thing that I got through the ceremonies with Lore, that I wasn't really expecting, was the creativity with the music. I really had it in my mind — a belief, a myth that I made up — that I couldn't sing or play music. I really held to that strongly for a long time. But gradually I was able, with the help of Ayahuasca and ceremony, to break that down and to really tap into my creative side. I realised that not having an outlet for that is something that could definitely make you sick, and in the past, this has definitely made me not feel well. But now I have an outlook for that; I'm able to be a happier and healthier person and contribute to a better society with my work.

I learned it is just so easy to put your problems to one side and go to rescue someone else without really putting yourself first. I grew up in a society where your role as a woman was to do certain things; to put other people before yourself all the time was the message that I was given by society, by my family. So to be able to put myself first and realise that no one else was going to put me first — I had to do it myself. That was a big part of my healing. And I can see how that not only helps me, but also helps the people around me: the people, other women that I work with. And also, like my family, the community, the jiu-jitsu that I do, I can see how the work that I do doesn't just stay with me — it flows through me, which is amazing, and again, something that you don't expect when you're 26 and you go and drink your first cup of Ayahuasca.

In nursing, we have a big problem with martyrdom. It's something that we learned about when we were training to be nurses — don't be the person who never takes a break. There is this culture where if you just work through, keep calm and carry on, that you'll be rewarded, but that's just less and less now. I really don't know if I could have broken out of that pattern, because it was really so ingrained into me and into my sisters, my mother, my grandmother. This was something that I needed Ayahuasca for — knowing to take care of my needs first, and then to go and be able to do the work that I do, because it is very intensive to serve your community. It's incredible to do it and I feel like it's the right thing for me to do. I'm fulfilling my purpose. However, it definitely does take a toll, and if you don't look after yourself first, then you're actually putting yourself at risk. And you're also putting your family and your patients and the people who are looking to you for care at risk, because you haven't cared for yourself first. That is sometimes a very complex thought for people, for women carers — to have to put yourself first. So the medicine helped break that down, and that's why I believe I'm definitely a much better nurse because of it.

We're still fighting to get the psychedelic clinical trials going; it's a work in progress that I have am involved with. However, I do know that there's a lot of research to support psychedelics being used clinically for mental health and possibly in palliative situations. There's lots of research that shows that it would be beneficial. The first psychedelic research in Australia was on palliative patients, to help them come to terms with end of the end of life. And people, although they didn't always necessarily get incredible scores on their mental health questionnaires, they did have a much better understanding of who they were, and the quality of their life improved as it ended. I definitely think there's a place for psychedelics within the mental health system here. In fact, we're in such a crisis now, it seems like it would be so helpful, although we do need to continue with the research. But, like I said, it's a fight to try to get the research going. There's still a lot of stigma around it, but I definitely see a place where we can help a lot of people with psychedelics.

With Ayahuasca — the ceremony of it, the structure and the way everything flows through — it's also really important to then help with the integration by just having a ceremony in your life. And it doesn't even have to be Ayahuasca; it can be drinking tea every morning. It's something that is very beneficial to the human mind and the structure of the ceremonial process: that in surrender it's beautiful, of course, but also that the structure also helps follow through with the integration, which is what you need to bed-down the insights that you've had in ceremony. It's hard to describe how that works, but it's very important for how you're going to make things happen in this reality and such a beautiful process to be part of. Very spiritual. It's difficult to describe it to someone who's never experienced that, but it's very beneficial and very much connecting to the people that you're sharing the space with.

The ceremony is just a drop in a glass of water. Then there's the integration, which is vital. And I think that the structure of the ceremony is important, because you're preparing yourself to go into ceremony. You follow that through, and then you come to the integration and bed-down what you've learned. That's not in the research I've just been reading through. Actually, there's no set way to do an integration. There are lots of ideas, and people have given a lot of different models of how they think people should integrate. But there's no one way that everyone can agree on. What I like to do is always go back to my routine, because that really keeps me grounded in day-to-day life. I try to journal afterwards and then I review that over the following weeks. I don't know if it's because of martial arts, but I like the discipline, as it helps me set things in place.

Those little routines that I have in place now are the foundation of how I get through my week. And those are things that were only dreams back at the beginning, when I started drinking Ayahuasca and thinking I really need to go to the gym. So, over time, when you embed those little rituals, like going to the gym, going to Jiu-Jitsu, you embed them into your life, and every day you just raise the quality of your life. And then when you have the privilege of going and sitting in ceremony, it's a good reminder of how far you've really come in this journey of your healing and putting yourself first.

As a guardian in ceremony I'm definitely more connected to supporting the women, as a woman. I've seen women come into ceremony and go through huge healing processes where they've been battling with their demons. They've also been in love and light. And I've met them in that first ceremony, and then I meet them in the second ceremony, or whenever I see them again, and they look like a different woman. They look like their faces have completely changed. There is a glow to them. They've reconnected with life. When I reflect back on that and I think about the first time I met them, there was definitely a lot of fear there and insecurity and unhappiness. I'm not saying all of that has gone away with one ceremony — it definitely hasn't all disappeared — but they've done integration work, and they come and then look like a different person. It's very similar to my first experience. Drink Ayahuasca and connect with who I really am, and then the light reawakens, you start letting the light back in. To witness that in people is such a blessing. To see them break through and remember who they are — it's just so beautiful to see. For me, when I look at people, I feel like I can really see the good in them most of the time, but for them to see it for themselves is very, very different and very compelling in a different way.

I definitely feel that what we do is very safe. I could see from the perspective of people who don't know, that they may not think that it is safe, but I do feel, as a healthcare practitioner, that what we do is very safe; we keep people safe, and people are our priority. I think that the whole process, the ritual of it, is very beneficial to people's mental health in general. Just that whole commitment to going to ceremony and going to do that is something that people can really connect to and it can help get them through potentially a dark time, or any time. Although I do see that there's a place for psychedelics in our medical system, I see in the public system that what we will struggle with is the set and setting, because we're so sterile and everything has to be like 99.9% germ free. We don't always have that. The therapeutic setting that is very beautiful is something that we're struggling with now. Trying to work with psychedelic research is trying to get that setting into really good place.

I hope that my family would do this, because I feel like it would be of great benefit to them, and I hope one day to share ceremonial space with them. Although I don't think that Ayahuasca is for everyone, there'll be some people who would never want to try it, and I respect that. I feel that people have the ability to choose if they want to partake in something like this and it is safe, and if people within their right mind choose that, then I feel like they should have the right to do that.

Luís
Male, 36 years, musician and music teacher

I'm from Brazil originally and I teach music for a living. I have an online platform through which I teach people about music and their connection with music as a creative expression. I teach the guitar, singing, how to connect with the voice and how to express emotions through that. I've been living in Australia for these past eight years.

I had previous experiences with Ayahuasca before coming to Australia. Those circles in Brazil were intimate, with around

15 participants, and in those circles, throughout the whole night we would be just be listening to recorded music in playlists, diving into the frequency of the medicine through that selection of medicine songs.

After a few years in Australia, I moved to the Byron Bay area and I was looking for a community, a family that would hold me, that would be a space for me to be creative, to connect with music. I landed in a place that was one of the centres of that community, and I ended up teaching music there. I had met Lore previously in Sydney, and he was also visiting the Byron Bay region, and he mentioned that there was a gathering happening in which he would be leading an Ayahuasca ceremony there. I felt the call to attend, which would be the first time with the medicine after many years. Since I'd arrived in Australia, maybe four years before that, I hadn't really been searching for Ayahuasca, but had it in the back of my mind as a possibility, but found nothing that felt right. I felt safe with Lore and the community, and when he invited me to come, I received a full body 'yes' as I was getting ready. It changed my life.

That was my first time in an Ayahuasca ceremony that had live music — different to my experiences in Brazil. I enjoyed the opportunity to be there playing music. The energy that comes when I am in the presence of the medicine, where the movement of my hands and where my voice goes, is a mystery. I found myself amazed by the possibilities that I couldn't have imagined if it wasn't for the experience itself. It's an interesting concept because it's fully trusting that the medicine will support the group, and we can create as a collective, purely in the moment. If I was to think about where that could go, I believe that I wouldn't be able to play any of it because of the physical challenges that come with being with Ayahuasca. At times not knowing what was my hand and what was the arm of the guitar, for example, but as the process is happening, there's a deep trust, and it is as if this presence is using me as an instrument, and I'm just an instrument of Ayahuasca and an instrument of music that's played for us to collectively process emotions, traumas, generational stories, where we can grow as a collective and as individuals as well.

The music has a huge palette of colours and emotions that can be evoked by those experiences. When the music is sounding, the body will synchronise with that frequency and may connect with memories that sometimes hold a level of weight and, possibly, trauma. Through that process, people can connect with their tears, anger, frustration or sadness — those emotions will pop up through the musical experience. This is not something that is specifically related to Ayahuasca, but when you associate this quality of music with the openness of the heart that the medicine brings, it's a very strong teacher and creates a powerful field for healing that people can dive into. I've heard in many of the sharing circles people realise traumas, histories and stories of their life that were hidden, and through that knowing they can be more aware of what they are creating in their lives. They realise they can change and can manifest something better, something lighter, something that can be more loving and supportive for themselves, their loved ones and their environment.

That was the first time I played music in a ceremony of Ayahuasca and I loved it; I felt at home, and it was a good feeling. I realised that there were many people in this circle that held themselves back because they weren't confident enough to play music in front of others. I have been in musical environments since I was young — I was raised in a family of musicians. So I found myself supporting these people, and I now have a group of students. After many people asking me to teach them songs, I was inspired to record some teaching programs, and that was literally the beginning of my project. Nowadays it is my full-time job and my main source of income. It came from experiences of surrender, where I was playing music, and people start to ask me, 'Hey, can you teach me this or that song?' And I found myself supporting them to connect with their creative expression through music. Apart from the songs, there are also many tears and sharing of stories and emotions that come through these lessons. So, I found myself not just as a music teacher, but as a support for the integration of those ceremonies, because the music becomes a familiar language for the people who come to my classes.

As someone that was raised in a musician's family, music was deeply hooked into my identity. The idea that I should be good with music is something that is still present with me today. Ayahuasca can sometimes be strong and it can transform sensations and the capacity to have a fine attunement with the movements of the body that music requires in order to be performed. I had to shift my understanding of music as a performance. Performing for me now is a straight line. I have an objective, I have a place and know how I want to express myself. With Ayahuasca ceremony, when music is happening in that space, it's more like a field, and this field is very alive. If I'm aiming for a straight line, there is a big chance that I'm going to be caught in my identity, and fear will pop up because it's challenging to drive on this slippery road. But then when trust comes, there is a magic that brings an expansion, and I have found myself many times in these ceremonies on the edge, thinking that I couldn't do something, thinking that I couldn't play. There were definitely times where I wasn't able to play, I made a mess, and in the beginning I was very judgmental toward myself, not knowing how to face people that were in the circle, thinking that I was ruining the experience. With time and support from Lore and the community, I could see that we were all doing that together, and whatever was happening was exactly what was needed for me and for people around me as well. I could see the magic unfolding through the sharing circles and through my own integration as well. Nowadays, when I find myself in this situation, where my expectation lies beyond my capacity and I do try, I can just laugh about it. I've come to see it as an opportunity to grow and to surrender to the flow. It has really helped me to connect with music as a vehicle of expression that transmutes emotions and any heaviness I may find in myself.

Over the last three years I have been traveling and learning more about these ceremonial circles. Traveling in the Amazon jungle in Brazil and Peru, and also in Costa Rica, with the intention of having different reference points and to learn from the traditions that have consecrated Ayahuasca for generations, for centuries, maybe millennia. Nowadays, when I'm learning to play songs, most of the time it's connected to these circles or from someone that is involved with a circle somewhere in the world. So, this right now is leading my life — the understanding of these circles, the people that come into these circles. I've found myself with the need to understand and to have better tools in supporting the integration of that. This is now taking me into another phase of my life, in which I might be studying either psychotherapy or psychology, so I can connect with music as a form of therapy as well — not specifically through the field of music therapy, but to connect with music in a therapeutic environment. That way, I can help people to express themselves and their emotions that are held in their truth or in the voice or the idea that they should or should not be doing something in a certain way. I know that there is a lot of healing that can come from that. Because of these circles, I have been involved in this experience, helping people and helping myself to integrate. I'm deeply connected to Ayahuasca nowadays, and it's a big part of my life.

Ayahuasca and the circles where people gather together to sing medicine songs is its own genre of music. You have jazz, you have rock, you have pop, you have punk — and you have medicine music. These medicine songs are in the realm of devotional music which, regardless of the religion they connect to or the spirituality that is expressed through this genre, provides a common ground which is love, reverence to nature, patience, and support of each other, cosmologies that can connect us to the traditions. I believe that if people gather together to sing this collectively, we are going to be anchoring a better way of being and singing together, synchronising through those values. That is a beautiful way for us as a community to grow, to find joy, to connect with ecstasy, to heal traumas, to be held by this transformative flame of music and become better versions of ourselves. I believe that ceremonial Ayahuasca should be legalised; it should be available for people that need to connect with their traumas in a safe, connected and supportive way. There is so much research available nowadays demonstrating the healing properties of Ayahuasca and the healing capacity of the ceremonies themselves, singing circles, dancing circles and drumming circles, where people gather to synchronise and to be together. When you combine these two elements — Ayahuasca and ceremony — it's a great thing, from my perspective, and I'm hoping to see this legalised and respected so the taboos and fear that surround it can be dissolved and we may all grow together.

Dayana
Female, 33 years, yoga teacher

I had consecrated Ayahuasca many times in Brazil from 2016 and it was in 2019 that I first met Lore and the family here in Australia. Being far from family and living in another culture is always very difficult, so finding Lore to consecrate feels like being close to my family again. Additionally, I remember being very disconnected from my spirituality and increasingly drawn towards bodily desires with excesses of sweets, alcohol and other drugs. First of all, my intention when returning to ceremony with Lore was to feel close to my family in Brazil, and then to reconnect with my inner self.

I believe that the first time is always very impactful for many people, and it was no different for me. I remember starting to feel the energy acting, my whole body shaking, my eyes were still closed. Then suddenly I open my eyes and see my caboclo (forest spirit) on the left, on a horse, the *erês* (child spirits) running around the fire, looking at the starry sky, and it was as if I saw Mother Gaia embracing the Earth. And every time I consecrate Ayahuasca I feel the strength of Mother Gaia embracing us, and I always see the same caboclo and various erês. It's divine! Ayahuasca is part of my life and I will always be consecrating. It is also a way for me to connect with my ancestors.

After my first ceremony, it was like a turning point in my life! I began to really see the green of the plants, the blue of the sky, and to embrace other people's problems, seeing the next person. My connection is always active with prayer songs; I never went back to listening to everyday music. I feel more committed to myself, but I also blame myself more. It's as if I'm already on the path of truth and when there's a slip-up, I feel guilty about it.

Bruna
Female, 35 years, human resources

Mother Ayahuasca woke me up for life; I was sleeping in the Matrix before sitting with her. We say 'sitting with her in a ceremony' because one can really feel her presence and guidance. That is why we say 'Mother Ayahuasca', because she is like a mother teaching about past life experiences, present and future, and showing us how everything and everyone is connected in the universe.

I came to Ayahuasca with the intention of spiritual development and she made me connect first with myself; then I was truly able to connect with others, including with my family, friends and Mother Nature. I was reborn on the day that I met her for the first time. Thankfully, she showed me that love is the answer/way. I felt a happiness that I had never felt before afterwards. It is like being in nirvana, feeling a true love for myself, and I understood that the only reason to be living this human experience is to ascend ourselves, to look after each other and Mother *Natureza*. It's something that I would love to continue and I have been continuing to practice, as she makes me a better citizen in the world.

Ayahuasca will be only helping the planet to be that dreamed-of place we all would love to see, as one session of Ayahuasca is the same as 10 years of meditation. Now imagine how the Earth would be different and a much better place with legalisation status [for Ayahuasca]. If we had been modernising our culture to implement meditation in schools for example. This should be the next step of legalisation moving forward.

Majid
Male, 48 years, subspecialist doctor

Drinking Ayahuasca was a hugely positive point in my life. I had heard about it through books and articles and it was my intention to experience it.

I was in good mental, physical and spiritual health when I first did ceremony with Lore and the family in 2019. Since then I have become more humble, more compassionate and considerate of myself and others. I have become aware of my deficiencies and I am trying to resolve them. I have also grown a deep respect for this awesome, mysterious world we live in.

Since drinking Ayahuasca there has been a pronounced improvement in my energy, mood, quality of life and the size of the lens I see the world with. I was also impressed by how good I felt in my body physically, mentally and spiritually weeks and months after drinking.

I had 20 years of IBS (irritable bowel syndrome) type symptoms. After every meal, I had to be sure I was not rushed or I would get very painful spasms and diarrhoea. The third time I drank, I felt an intense pain in my belly. While I looked at the pain, I remembered a painful memory from my childhood when my pet chicken died because I had to rush to school. My mom was late and was screaming at me. The chicken's tongue had gotten trapped in something. So, subconsciously, every time I was rushed, my body was re-experiencing that memory. Upon realising this and forgiving myself and my mum for this, the pain evaporated and never came back.

I have become much kinder to myself and everything around me. A lot more resilient. My base energy has increased substantially. I have come to develop a much broader and healthier view on my life. I just feel better, healthier, kinder and stronger.

The sheer beauty of ceremonies and the music has touched my heart at a level I never imagined, even in dreams. I had read that one Ayahuasca ceremony can change your life and it sure did but I never expected this much beauty, truth and goodness.

I have developed strong friendships through the circle and I have a solid relationship with Lore and some of the guardians. I trust their integrity and goodwill to the extent that I have brought my partner , my sister and multiple friends and colleagues to the ceremonies (several times) with absolutely no reservation or concern regarding trust and integrity.

I have ultimate respect, love and gratitude for Ayahuasca. It has touched my heart so very deeply. I definitely will return to ceremony. I am not drinking at the moment, as I am going through specific spiritual training, but I will.

As a practising medical doctor, I believe with some of the right frameworks, infrastructure and mechanisms there is no reason for Ayahuasca not to become legal. I believe Australia is going through a mental and existential crisis at the moment. Spiritual ceremonies such as Ayahuasca are an invaluable tool to improve the overall mental, physical and spiritual wellbeing of the community. I am astonished how Alcohol is free and openly advertised but Ayahuasca is not. There is room for more understanding from the authorities.

Kane
Male, 30 years, pilot, artist, musician and spiritual healer

My father had been to many of Lore's ceremonies and had asked me if I was interested in coming along. I was physically and mentally healthy, but emotionally quite disconnected. Initially I didn't know a great deal about Ayahuasca, but I was then recommended to read *The Fellowship of the River,* a truly magical book written by psychiatrist Joseph Tafur, a medical doctor who moved to the Amazon to become a shaman. Tafur draws connections between the data of the scientific world and observations of the spiritual realms. This motivated me to experience the healing, metaphysical and visionary powers of Ayahuasca. When I was younger I used to love making music with friends and I was really excited at the prospect of a psychedelic medicine that was activated by the vibration of music.

The ceremonies have taken me on a deep journey through memories and visions of the past, present, love and pain experienced through the interpersonal connections in my life. I have then been able to arrive at an understanding of how I became who I am and why I am walking this path.

The music performed in Lore's ceremonies is truly world class (now that I have travelled to Brazil to experience the original lineages of Lore's ceremony). The lyrics and vibrations are like a magical portal which can take you to a deep place within or to parts of the universe you've never known to exist. Bringing this music into my life has been like a lighthouse of love and self-understanding, illuminating my journey.

Ayahuasca has helped me by awakening my mind to connect back to my heart and, in turn, be able to live intuitively and trust that my heart knows the way. I've been able to empathise with a greater range of people in my day-to-day life, understanding how unique everyone's journey is. This has given me the strength to respond to the world around me rather than react, whether it be the events that are unfolding or daily interactions with people.

My creative development has skyrocketed from my first ceremony. I'm now writing and composing music, painting and creating visionary art, and I have never felt more fulfilled to find these forms of expression in my life which truly make me happy and excited to live in this world.

Ayahuasca has taken me through the astral realms to meet different deities, spirits and ancestors, which continue to teach me the sacred side of the universe. This influenced me to begin Kriya yoga meditation, which has become a regular practice for me. As I've continued to experience Ayahuasca alongside practising meditation in my daily life, this has led me to an understanding of what it is to have faith in God and the Divine Spirit. This connection with God has changed my understanding and enabled me to see that we are all one in this universe.

Lore and the members of DreamingArts community have shown me a beautiful sense of community inclusion which I have never felt before. They all bring years of wisdom and experience of the medicine, while genuinely caring about the social, spiritual and medical progression of our society as a whole — and it shows in their operation.

I now feel I will keep drinking the medicine for self-development. The spirit of Ayahuasca provides insights and guidance not just for the people who come to the ceremony to drink it, but it also has a strong flow-on effect into the greater community, as those who come to experience it bring all the love, insights and positive vibrations into their daily lives and the people around them.

Toni
Female, 52 years, meditation teacher and sound healer

I first drank Ayahuasca with Lore in 2018, shortly after my divorce. Before the ceremony I was depressed from a traumatic divorce from my husband. This is the reason I participated. My intentions were to heal and raise my state of circumstantial depression. I have done large amounts of meditation in the past, so am solid in practice and have used it to break out of depression, which was my mental state at the time.

The ceremonies were beneficial in that they lifted me into the larger picture of my life and helped me get out of the mental rut that I was in, as well as releasing negative states of mind. The Ayahuasca reconnected me consciously to the spirit realms quickly, which I had experienced many times before through meditation but was too depressed to reach through discipline at the time. It was very visionary, insightful and overall uplifting.

The two journeys I took aided me through my healing process after leaving a dysfunctional relationship. This helped me reconnect to myself that is connected to a greater existence. It mostly affected my long-term mental state at the time. I would use it [Ayahuasca] again as a tool if I ever found myself too low to guide myself into deep transcendent states of meditation. It is good for healing chronic, ill states of mind, which for me have been rare, but have happened on the odd circumstantial occasion. I found Ayahuasca to be equivalent in vision to meditation, which has been my long-term practice over most of my life.

Daryl
Male, 50 years, carpenter/men's work facilitator

I was physically tired, as I had gone through a fair amount of adrenal fatigue in the months prior to the first ceremony with Lore. I was quite focused and ready to surrender.

My main intensions were personal development and to work through any traumas that would or could arise during the ceremony. I also was working in a fairly 3D type of job, so I also wanted the connection to Ayahuasca and found it nice to commune with like-minded people who are on a similar path to myself.

For one particular ceremony with Lore, I went in probably the least prepared I had ever been to receive medicine. For me, this was a confirmation that Lore holds space and serves medicine with full integrity, and also that the medicine has its way of moving into the exact part of my psyche that is needed to give the healing which vital in this day and age. Also this was because I was shown, and had let go of such a deep wound from my childhood which had been plaguing me for many years. Aya opens my heart too, which has been a big thing for me throughout my life, due to a traumatic childhood and types of physical and emotional abuse. I find the medicine an essential part of becoming a better person, not just for myself, but for those around me.

I would find that things would almost fall into place after certain realisations experienced during a ceremony, and in waking life it would become apparent as to why you had experienced something particular during a medicine journey. The effects would sometimes be subtle and at other times quite profound. The main thing that happened with having drunk the medicine would be a generally healthier mental state of being. I had improved my relationship with my mother, as during one journey I had forgiven her for things she had done to me as a child. I had also let go of resentment towards my stepfather in a similar way.

My spiritual development also became more heightened and was a massive positive, due to me moving into helping men in my men's group to become better people, due to me being able to guide them to also face their demons so to speak, and to have better relationships with those around them.

Overall for me, I have found that Ayahuasca is a very helpful means of healing traumas and letting go of things that would otherwise take a lot longer using traditional psychotherapy, which I also still do as a method of mental health maintenance. I had done a two- to three-year period where I did Aya often and then have taken a break, as it takes time to integrate the lessons learned from her healings. I will definitely work with Aya again, as required.

I have also been to other gatherings where Lore played music for groups and I found that they are a great way to feel a connection to like-minded people, make new friends and just go home with an overall feeling of joy and happiness after attending.

I believe from my own personal experiences that Ayahuasca can change a person's life for the better. There have been so many stories I have heard of people, including myself, having had a breakthrough type of experience during an Ayahuasca ceremony and even for weeks or months after it. I found it helped me to let go of things that traditional psychotherapy would have taken so much longer to help a person to move through. I believe that Ayahuasca should be made legal and used in shamanic, controlled environments, as it is unquestionably a medicine that helps humans with issues to become a better version of themselves in a relatively short period of time.

People such as Lore are here to help others move through their pain which would otherwise probably never come to light. There are so many damaged people in our society today and they have no idea even why they do the things that they do. In particular, these might be people who have had trouble with the law or are even harming others unintentionally or purposely. I believe that society needs to become more human, and a medicine such as Ayahuasca does exactly that. It can turn a person who has had problems with aggression or even violent tendencies into a peaceful and loving person simply by helping them see into their own hearts and subconscious mind and healing those particular traumas that cause them to act in a way they do not really want to act. Ayahuasca is a medicine and it should be respected. The South American shamans attest to the centuries of these types of healings.

Vivian
Female, 40 years, beauty therapist

When I first met Lore in 2018 I was experiencing disconnection, indecisiveness, victimisation, past issues, ancestral traumas and marijuana addiction. I wanted to try Ayahuasca to improve my emotional and mental health, understand reasons for blockages and traumas, connect with the Divine, discover the truth and learn about medicine.

Ayahuasca brought me many answers, and one of them was the break-up of a toxic marriage. Ayahuasca gave the answer and showed me how it was affecting my life. Ayahuasca gave me the opportunity to encounter "beings" and receive beautiful messages from them.

Afterwards I felt liberation, connection with the cosmos and sky, ancestral understanding, grounding, music, voice, spiritual growth and guidance. I also connected with the community for music circles, one-to-one therapy, birthday parties and made friendships.

Julie
Female, 70 years, family therapist

Before meeting Ayahuasca I was functioning, but understanding the need to continue getting to underlying trauma I had dissociated from with my son's suicide 11 years ago. I was desperate to get down into this stored energy, as I knew part of me was closed off. I asked Ayahuasca for physical healing and cleansing with purging, as handing over to a universal law as meditation was impossible.

My first round absolutely cleansed my system with not only purging but full body release, including vocalising. I am very receptive to imagery, so was shown what I now know was my deep depression as a stone slab down in the depths, with a large anaconda snake slowly moving, sliding through this liminal light. I was shown, in contrast, top side a group of foreign people in a conga line wearing coolie hats and holding lanterns.

The second session was about being shown my avoidant behaviour, the difficulty in being present in groups. I could see how I couldn't open and it was later, under the stars with the dawn coming, that my tears of grief could emerge but needed to be born witness to from Lore — someone who understood the power of medicine and could hold this. Up until then, no conventional method could get close. This was trapped so deeply in my body. The two sessions transformed my dissociation from feeling the loss of my son, and the effects of his suicide lifted. I felt I'd at last let him go and his spirit was now freed. It's hard to explain but I felt he led me to Ayahuasca, as he was trapped, as I was. I have taken up music lessons and feel I am deeper in empathy for others. I am no longer exhausted and now more energised. I'm now interested in going deeper, exploring my ancestry.

I know this has permanently released me where I was completely stuck.

I 'feel' now ... life has a creative flow.

René
Male, 43 years, administration/forklift driver, student (mental health)

I'm very blessed to have come to cross paths with Lore, such a beautiful soul. I came to Ayahuasca wanting to go deeper in my consciousness, my way of behaviour, understand myself better, to see how others perceive me and how to understand others too.

I discovered what I'm seeking in regards to a potential partner. I learned to let things be and not try to control situations — it's okay not to have all the answers about how to parent better. I also understood some disappointments were created by my expectations on people. I learned to forgive and accept love and it brought me closer to God and to appreciate all types of humans. It also showed me how we all suffer and go through pain.

After my first ceremonies I converted to Islam. I have a better relationship with others when I don't expect what I believe I should receive. I'm more peaceful, my OCD (obsessive compulsive disorder) about having to achieve certain things daily is under control, and I'm not disturbed by not achieving things in my mind that had to be done. I decided and commenced to study.

My wellbeing on the surface seems to be okay. I'm clear, focused and I don't get stressed or feel depressed. I'm always busy working, studying and looking after my two boys and my physicality. I don't have any addictions on the surface; I don't smoke nor drink unless there's a reason to. I'm addicted to being active, always on the go, learning and reading books. My mental health is fine and I'm very grateful and like to give to those that are less fortunate.

Fabio
Male, 43 years, artist and art therapist

I was born in Brazil and I've been living in Australia for about eight years. My journey of healing in recent years has fundamentally reshaped my core as a human being, my profession, my role in society, and how I relate to family, friends and partners.

Several years ago during a hypnotherapy session, I discovered two issues that had profoundly impacted my life up until the age of 40: a pervasive sense of abandonment whose origins were unknown to me, and sexual abuse suffered from the ages of five to 10. Despite undergoing conventional therapy for nearly six years, I could never fully explore these two topics (and the consequences they had on practically every aspect of my life). I felt the need to delve deeper to find some answers. Although I was physically healthy, with my wellbeing in a good condition, I was struggling with sex addiction and compulsive behaviours.

After extensive research, I realised that one possible path was to seek support that could help to access my subconscious. That's when I found Lore and the Estrela da Ciranda family. I had the privilege of participating in two workshops, each followed by an Ayahuasca ceremony, with a small group of people (approximately 15 participants). The first focused on honouring the inner child, and the second on ancestral healing. I knew that the karma I carried wasn't solely mine. Other family members had gone through similar situations. That's why I decided to participate in both workshops. Those experiences transformed my entire life.

Having done the groundwork to understand my intention of releasing trauma and recovering my emotional and mental health, the preparation information was crucial in giving me the confidence to participate. I felt welcomed by everyone and was prepared to dive deep into my subconscious. The first workshop began after lunch. We sat in a circle to discuss our intentions, introduce ourselves, clarify any doubts. We did a guided meditation, and an exercise to understand our inner child. During my meditations, I saw a troubled, closed-off, protected boy who didn't feel safe asking for help. I had abandoned him for many years. Today, I share this story with all my art students and people who are in the process of discovering their traumas.

In the ceremony, sometime after taking the medicine, I began to feel physical discomfort. I saw people around me reacting in different ways — some were crying, others smiling, sleeping, purging — but I was there, feeling intense physical discomfort, especially in my abdominal region. Even though I knew that the medicine could induce vomiting as a form of cleansing, I felt that my discomfort was part of what I needed to experience.

Suddenly, I felt the urge to go to the bathroom. As I got up and started walking, I began to experience hallucinations. My body was no longer mine. It was a feminine body, with larger breasts, and I was naked. Although I found it strange, I confess I was curious about that image. I began to touch my body to try to understand why the anatomy was different. That's when I saw a baby in my arms. The baby was calm, quiet. I can't explain why, but when I saw it, I didn't feel well. I felt anger, nervousness. That's when I told the baby: I don't know why you're here, but I don't want you here. The baby disappeared. I went to the bathroom and saw myself with dark skin, as if I were descended from Africa, with a white beard and older skin. I realised that this message would take me to another time or to some mentor who protected me. In Brazil, we call the mix of black and Indigenous peoples 'caboclos'. I saw myself as a caboclo. I felt a very strong ancestral presence and had conversations with departed family members, with great friends, and received many messages of hope and faith. But the physical discomfort remained. It felt like my body was receiving little punches. And I knew that it wasn't because of the medicine. It was trauma stored in my body that needed to be released.

The ceremony lasted almost 12 hours in total. At the end, people were dancing, enjoying the final phase of the ceremony. I was still feeling spasms. It was extremely uncomfortable. That's when Lore came to me and asked if I needed help. I told him that I thought I was going to faint, that I was in a lot of physical pain, and that I was very exhausted. He asked for permission to help me. He put his hands on my back and gave me grounding to let go. My ego didn't want to allow me to go deeper but I felt safe to go. That's when I saw a point of light in front of me opening up, and I felt a sensation of freedom. As if I were everything and nothing at the same time. I was there, present, feeling and hearing everything, but no longer had the sensations of my physical body. With my eyes closed, I was in emptiness. Lore stayed by my side the whole time. Until I gave him permission to leave me there. I had finally reached the end of my process.

Afterwards, we had a group conversation, sharing experiences. I shared everything I had seen and felt. Until the sharing, I hadn't understood the message from the beginning of the ceremony and the physical discomfort that accompanied me throughout the process. When I got home, I ate and rested for about 10 hours. When I woke up, I called my parents in Brazil. As I began to recount the experience to them, my mother's expression completely changed. She seemed worried, uncomfortable. That's when she asked me to repeat what I said to the baby. When I repeated it, she started to cry. She said that my birth was extremely painful for both of us, lasting almost 12 hours, and that both she and I almost died in the process. She was 20 years old at the time, extremely young, and felt very depressed after giving birth. She mentioned that the pain was so intense that she kept pushing with her hands on her belly, not knowing what else to do. She even squatted down to see if the birth would happen. That's when we understood the whole process. I needed to go through all that pain to understand and forgive her for the pain, anger and frustration she felt throughout the process.

That ceremony was the beginning of a healing process for my entire family system. Today, we talk about this issue with respect and curiosity. We are all reassessing our relationship with affection, what we carry from generations of abuse and pain. And we are healing together to change the legacy we will leave for future generations. It was through these two experiences that I made peace with that wounded five-year-old boy, I understood my karma and how I could use it as a tool for my purpose. Today, I understand that I have tools of resilience that can also help many people in similar situations.

These years of investigation brought art as a communication tool. Parallel to a career of almost 20 years in marketing and communication,

I began to express myself through art. In 2023, I held my first solo art exhibition entitled 'Cura', which means healing. I presented 23 pieces that told my entire process of investigating and learning from my traumas, the experiences I lived through, and the tools I gained to move forward.

Today, I have exhibited in galleries in Sydney, London, Spain and across the US, and have been teaching collage-making to students of all ages and skill levels. I'm also studying to work as an art therapist. I run workshops and facilitate experiences that help people reconnect with their bodies, to be present, to value the now, to respect and honour their journeys and, above all, to forgive themselves for their confusion. Today, I see my purpose very clearly: to heal through art.

I have participated in music circles and stayed in contact with the community through different events. I haven't felt the call to repeat the experience. As a Buddhist I'm curious to navigate through my journey moving forward using the breath as medicine. I'm open to experience again if I feel that I need a catalyst again.

Bronwyn
Female, 35 years, environmental community engagement

Before my first of two ceremonies with Lore, my overall wellbeing was a total mess. I had prolonged depression and anxiety, a bunch of grief and unprocessed emotions. I'd entirely lost any appetite and didn't want to eat to the point I had developed a number of nutritional deficiencies. I was suffering from night terrors and insomnia. I was using work as a tool to escape and distract during the day and alcohol to cope at night. Looking back now, I can't believe how terribly I treated myself. I had sought medical help for so many years. I was taking a fistful of prescription pills daily, including anti-depressants, anti-psychotics, and was participating in regular conventional therapy. These were not working.

Whilst recovering my emotional and mental health was the motivation to sit with Ayahuasca, I actually got way more than I was bargaining for. It opened and 'fixed' something deep inside of me. I felt a version of myself that was so connected with the Earth, the universe and other humans.

The first time sitting with Lore and the plants was undoubtedly the most valuable experience I've ever had. I explored my inner world and was taken to the most strange and interesting of places, immersed in a purple forest where I could literally feel the trees pulsating and the heartbeat of the forest. The forest gently plugged me in and merged with me as we shared the same heartbeat. It was as if it became my circulatory system and cleaned out the worry and dread, and absorbed it into the Earth. The experience wasn't all beautiful though. During the journey at some point I was taken to the town where I grew up, and I witnessed an event of horrific child abuse, and quickly realised that the child was me. I suddenly remembered, so vividly, something so dark and traumatic happened to me that I had hidden it from myself for all these years. It was emotional, but I then re-lived the trauma in a way where my child-self was loved and supported, not by anyone else but by my adult self and by mother Ayahuasca. It's really hard to explain. It was healing being able to support, love and forgive myself through the experience. I was able to see how much that suppressed trauma has impacted so many aspects of my experience in this world. That awareness, love, acceptance and support has been so freeing.

While sitting with the medicine for the second time it really hit me how much I had subscribed to being overworked, stressed and had my self-worth tied up in productivity. But Ayahuasca gave me a sense of intrinsic value and such a love for myself and fellow humans. Many of us have been colonised, and that has left a wound on our collective consciousness. That loss of connection is not supposed to be the human experience. The ceremony let me feel the embrace from higher forces and feel the sense of wholeness. It initially made me a little overwhelmed because I connected with so many big feelings throughout the ceremony, but by the afternoon I felt lighter, happier, so tuned in with an authentic sense of gratitude for the moment.

I stopped drinking alcohol. It wasn't even an intentional decision, but my mind and body no longer wanted it anymore.

Soon after, I did feel a sense of anger and resentment that we as humans have been denied so much of this beautiful human experience. I was furious that there exists a beautiful medicine which allows us to remember our connection, but due to political reasons this medicine is not accessible to most people. It feels like it's a breach of basic human rights to deny people access to this medicine. It makes me feel like they don't actually want people to know their own power to heal.

It's now over a year since the two ceremonies and following changes have happened:

- I previously wasn't able to meditate but after Ayahuasca my nervous system and soul are open and able to reach that place of stillness. I do long to do another ceremony but in the meantime, I've been inspired to do breathwork which helps me get into an alternate state of consciousness. I never would have known those states existed if it weren't for Ayahuasca.
- I generally have better awareness of my emotions.
- I studied science and considered myself very analytical. I once believed that what can't be measured must not really exist; that is, I categorised Spirit, God, collective consciousness in the same circle as a fairytale. I can now see how shallow and simple my previous perspective was. I'm so thankful to Ayahuasca for showing worlds beyond the material, for bringing spirituality and gratitude into my life.
- I now prioritise family and loved ones over work and career progression.
- I actually like eating food again and am no longer malnourished.
- I have no night terrors — not a single one.
- I still don't drink alcohol.
- I'm by no means the perfect picture of mental health. I do still go to conventional therapy and occasionally have days of overwhelm. However, I'm able to approach my mental health with compassion and mind-body connection, and I'm not held captive by depression and anxiety.
- I have the deepest of respect for Indigenous cultures.

The ceremonies were run very professionally. They made a safe space throughout the entire process. The application process to join a ceremony was reassuring. I wasn't expecting so many questions but it made me feel safe knowing that they were doing screening before I even arrived, instead of just relying on participants to do their own research and hope for the best. They asked about medical history, our intentions for the ceremony, our experience with plant medicine, etc. They made the medical contraindications clear and invited discussion about any concerns. It was made abundantly clear that the ceremony is a place of healing and growth.

Even going into my first ceremony I could feel such a sense of community that Lore has created. During the ceremony, I really appreciated that they had so many guardians. I don't remember the exact ratio but I felt super safe and that if I needed help it would be accessible. The men and women sit separately, and a female guardian was there to support the women. I loved that they made the ceremony expectations clear with an emphasis on safety.

Their respect and acknowledgement of Indigenous cultures and the origin of the medicine was so authentic and made abundantly clear. Lore encouraged participants to reach out to him or the guides for support if anything came up for us before or after the ceremony. The morning after my second ceremony I had some emotional overwhelm and I reached out to Lore and the guardians for support. Lore and Pedro, without hesitation, sat with me in the ceremony room. We did some breathing, and Lore provided some valuable insights into what I was experiencing. It was probably less than 10 minutes of counselling/support but it was exactly what I needed to re-centre and ground myself. I will forever have gratitude that Lore made plant medicine accessible so close to home. I probably wouldn't have had the courage at the time to go overseas alone as a female, into the forest to seek the medicine.

I will definitely sit with Ayahuasca again.

Renato
Male, 47 years, sales representative

I first drank Ayahuasca back in Brazil in 2003 with some native people in São Paulo, who are from a shamanic lineage. I started drinking because I was taking anxiety medication as a kid, starting when I was eight years old. I took a lot of medication with my parents until I left their place when I was 13. I went to live with my grandma on the condition that I was to stay on the medication, which apparently was because I supposedly had parietal ischemia in the brain. But it wasn't true; it turned out all I had was curiosity and was an inquisitive kid. My mum and my stepfather were in a pretty bad relationship, a very toxic relationship, and I didn't accept that. I always questioned them, and my mother started medicating me. Then, after I went to live with my grandma, I took the medication from 14 until I was around 23 years old. That's when I literally said I had enough. I had been on Prozac, frontal, all sorts of lithium medications that you can imagine, and my mental state was pretty bad, pretty full on.

I was in a family with toxic relationships and fighting and I grew up with this revolt inside me. When I was 23, I decided that if they want to give me medication, I would take it all, and I took around 70 pills in one go. I said, 'Look, if you guys are gonna keep giving me medication, I'm gonna do that all the time.' I ended up in hospital, woke up three days later. Then, six months later, I did it again, because they insisted on the medication, the psychiatrists and psychologists, There were a lot of people insisting that I was the problem. And then I did it again. Went to hospital again.

The family broke down and I went crazy from that time on — and I never came back home. My aunties just said to me that I should try something like a spiritual path to heal my wounds and to never take drugs again. I went to this shamanic temple in São Paulo and I met the people serving Ayahuasca from a very old lineage and tradition. All they said to me was, 'Look, all we want is for you to never take synthetic drugs and Western medicine again; we're going to take you out of that.' I didn't want to commit, because I'm not a religious guy. I normally didn't stick to places. I told them I didn't want the commitment, I didn't want to have the obligations of being there. But they said, 'Don't worry: all we want is to make sure that you don't take these drugs anymore. We're going to heal you, and then you're free to go.' It was then I start drinking Ayahuasca. It was 2003 and I was 26 years old.

I started doing ceremony once every month for around five or six times and by the seventh ceremony I was already convinced that I would never again take a tablet of any type of medication for anxiety, panic attacks, or whatever diagnosis they gave to me, being bi-polar or all that. I opened up my mind and I decided to stay on the path, on this spiritual path and learn more, learn with nature, learn with the natives, learn with the plants.

I stayed there for around 10 years, and that's changed my life. I never took any medicine for anti-depressives ever again. I'm actually very against that, because all these drugs do is just dope you and keep you numb. And, you know, all those years up to age 23 I remember clearly, just acting like a zombie sometimes after taking the medication, because all that it was doing was switching off my brain for some reactions that they didn't want me to have, like questioning who I was and how things work. And as a kid, you were very curious, and I was always very curious about my life and what I wanted to do. So if I'm alive today, it is because of Ayahuasca, it's because that's what I learned, how to deal with my wounds, my fears, and the things that I had to work inside myself to transform all those traumas from childhood and not let that to be something that would affect me for the rest of my life. My mum is still there in her place, dealing with mental health. My sister never left. All those people that were close to me, they are still struggling and my life took a totally different route. I opened up my mind, and I travelled the world. I got married, I built my family and to me, there is nothing more sacred than Ayahuasca.

I've seen literally thousands of people drinking in ceremonies over these 21 years. And it's all good stories to tell. A lot of people healing. I've seen people, like an old lady once — she was an 86-year-old when she did her first ceremony — who said 'I've never seen something more incredible than this in my entire life.' She had the best time of her life. Quite incredible for someone who has lived that long.

In Brazil, as we know, we have the freedom and the rights to practise our spirituality with Ayahuasca. This is amazing, because it's quite a strong community there, healing, transforming a lot of lives. And if there's one thing I can say is that it's the only thing that I've seen in my life that can heal. Like the large amount of people with different types of traumas and addictions and all the negative stuff that you can imagine, they all get better, and they have beautiful journeys. It's hard to describe what Ayahuasca is about, but to me, it's about love. It's about the cosmic love. It's what moved the universe to this expansion and shows us what we are all about.

Ayahuasca pushes us to see our fears and shadows and then we land safely, nicely with a lot of love. We transform our traumas to something better and in total synergy with nature. Because at the end of the day, it's just that. It's a very old tradition. It's two plants which native people figured out thousands of years ago how to combine and use as a medicine for the body, for the soul, for the mind.

In 2016 I was camping with my family and I found someone — another Brazilian guy — who mentioned Lore's work and what I learned in Brazil is it has to be a very serious work. I was pretty wary; I didn't know this person. I don't know what the lineage is and if it is a serious work or not. I actually was very reluctant to have another go, not knowing the work here in Australia. One year later, a friend of mine invited me for New Year's at his place and said that there would be a guy there that lived part of his journey in Brazil with the native people in the Amazon jungle, and I got curious about it. Coincidentally or not, there was Lore, and I could feel in his aura that I should give it a go, especially because I wanted to take my wife with me on the journey. I wouldn't say to my surprise, but it was pretty good to conclude in the end that Lore's work was quite incredible, and serious with a lot of preparation. He really knows what he's doing conducting a ceremony. Now there are a lot of people out there doing ceremonies who don't know what they're doing. Ayahuasca is pretty serious work, in my view, and I come to the conclusion quite quickly that Lore's doing a beautiful type of work with seriousness, respecting the traditions from Brazil, replicating that with his style, and helping hundreds of people to heal.

All that I said before about healing and getting people to live better lives — I was able to experience that quite quickly, and that was incredible, because I then decided to keep going to the ceremonies and seeing Lore. In a sense, somehow this also changed my life again, because I had had a big hiatus of not doing ceremonies for almost seven years. When I restarted the work here in Australia through Lore, I was actually not in a bad place, but I was struggling with the type of work that I was doing, I was working for companies that are not good for the planet. I remember clearly that one of my intentions was to shift from selling food and beverages that were pretty bad for human beings. In a matter of a year, I totally turned the tables and I found a job in a in a company selling only organic stuff, and really healthy products.

Again, coincidentally or not, from that moment on, a lot of great things happened. My professional life took off. I started growing so much as a professional. As a consequence of that, I was able to buy my house, was able to live in a happier environment. I could provide a better education for my kids. I won't say that's because of Ayahuasca, but it's the conjunction of everything. It's professional life and personal life working together. We are human beings at the end of the day, we can succumb to our weaknesses at any time and revisit some patterns and behaviours. If you're firm in the work of Ayahuasca, and you can keep doing the work, I think that's a way of life for me, because it only gets better and better and more clarity and more spiritual firmness that keeps pushing me forward, day by day, to a better position, to a better life, to a better state of mind. It's happiness in the end, and all that comes with love, again. It's been a beautiful journey. I've seen ceremonies of Lore's with so much healing, so many happy people, beautiful music, beautiful traditions, beautiful work. It's amazing.

Because of all the experience that I had in Brazil in terms of groups, like in large groups of people doing ceremonies, from what I saw, Lore's work has always been organised, very safe, well thought out, structured, and with the right instructions to everyone with clarity about what the work is about, what you need to know, all the right recommendations — and the community always responded really well to the dynamics of the work.

Thinking here now and looking back, what I normally say to people who question if they should be doing a ceremony or not (like I did hundreds of times), people wondering, in that week prior, thinking twice *should I do it*? But every time we are in ceremony, you come to think: 'Would I rather be not here, living in community and healing and singing and dancing and praying or should I be in a rock concert? Should I be playing snooker? Should I be in a club? No, this is what I want to be.' I think a lot of the problems in this world now, as we know, are because of the way we live, with all the distractions, social media, politics and dramas, and war and rage and power and all those things that we know that human beings have been doing for centuries. But at least when I put my head on the pillow, I go to bed thinking that I know I'm doing the right thing, just trying to live in the simplicity of life, in synergy with Mother Nature, seeking a spiritual path with the plants, and just being the best human being that I can be.

CHAPTER 14

Rising from the Storm

A point of light: The star of Ciranda

Even better than knowledge is the ability to correct oneself.
— Padrinho Sebastião.

By the time the global COVID crises of lockdowns, medical tyranny and its propaganda arrived, our circles in Australia had grown in popularity and our community was becoming stronger. On one hand I was very happy with what we had created: we had a devoted community of stud=ents and practitioners, some of whom had dedicated to the lineage and to the work of the circles over many years. Many study groups and community events were happening in different regions, where the ceremonies had inspired a new cultural movement.

It was a beautiful thing that through this work and through the strength of our group of ceremonial guardians we were beginning to expand our knowledge of working together, improving safety and care, developing skills on all levels with teamwork, trauma-informed care, intake practices, music production and arrangement and relationship building. This created a powerful environment for a lot of healing to occur. Many people wanted to come to the circles as word got out far and wide, and we were receiving far more applications to come to the circles than we had spaces to accommodate. We were also faced with the challenges of living under a repressive government and in a social environment of prejudice and denial of our freedom of spiritual and religious practice. This oppressive environment never allowed us to feel safe and was a hindrance to doing a lot of the work that was necessary to raise the level across all of our organisation. We had to work in the underground, in fear of persecution.

Despite the challenges, our prayers were gaining a lot of momentum, and a lot of healing was happening. More and more people were coming back to themselves and healing previously chronic wounds, and in many cases people were coming back from the brink of serious addictions, depression and, in some cases, suicidal thoughts. As the community grew, there seemed to be space for everyone to feel welcomed and at home and to feel safe in the embrace of a big, loving community. Many people studied the music, the prayers and the culture of the ceremonies, and many embraced a spiritual path that also embraced them. So much music was flourishing.

Towards the end of 2019 I was getting a lot of requests to host ceremonies in the Northern Rivers of NSW. I had largely avoided the region. Not because I don't love it — it has been a home for me since I was a kid — but because the community is overloaded by new-age spirituality in all its forms, for better or worse. When I arrived and opened the circle in the region there was a lot of buzz and attention and we attracted many people from already existing circles. This brought with it some new skills and some upgrades from people who in turn brought with them experience and knowledge from Brazilian lineages. But it also brought a lot of politics and drama.

The same issues that had kept me away for years were manifesting in my circle. Suddenly we were dealing with power dynamics, manipulation and appropriation that I hadn't seen thus far in my circles in Australia. This was really hard to deal with and affected our group more than I was able to contain at the time. Some of these people were interested in really studying and doing the work, while others were only there for what they could get out of it. At times I felt like I was being used and drained by all the expectations, drama and judgement I was receiving. I found it quite odd that people were coming to us from other circles, attracted to the work we had built and the Ciranda lineage, but were then trying to impose their own agendas and rules from the circles they were leaving. I was learning a lot about boundaries — often the hard way — and I have to admit I was too tolerant and permissive, which led to some good lessons and a strong development curve of strengthening the work and the firmeza amongst the group. But this took time and some chaos ensued. Nevertheless, as in all the regions we had established our ceremonies, a beautiful, loving and joyful spirit emerged that grew into a lot of healing and spiritual development. And as usual, some stayed with the work and when things became tough they faced the shadows and grew in humility and self-awareness, improving their relationships and lives as a result. Others turned to blame and control dramas and stormed away to the next thing when they didn't get what they demanded.

> *Freely we give what we freely receive. The doctrine is going to receive a lot because it gives so freely. We need to navigate with a clean mind, without giving extra work to others. To live while making work for others, in and out of the Daime, to stay stuck in our opinions, to bring sadness and exhaustion to meetings or wherever we may go ... This is not advisable. It is necessary to finish with this attitude quickly ... All of us who take the Daime regularly should clean our minds until these difficulties come to an end. — Padrinho Alfredo.*

I remembered the stories and teachings of both Mestre Irineu and Padrinho Sebastião around the drama and politics amongst the community. Mestre had done the work himself and didn't need anyone to hold his hand while his did his own personal growth and took responsibility for himself. I remembered this amid the complaints from the people who made demands and became angry because they didn't get what they wanted. In all my years of studies and sacrifice, no one had paid my way, no one did the work for me — I just did my work. To this day I feel slightly sad to see that, at times, people are not looking within but rather are looking outside themselves whilst doing the work, looking at others, and they are focused on what they can get rather than what they can do within themselves and what they can give. People choose to go to their identities and their emotional desires and stay in that phenomenal realm. Often these are the very people who speak the loudest about what they know, or think they know, and they have a good performative mask that gets them through. But in their lives outside the ceremonies is where the true test of the integrity of their paths lies. As I had seen most of my adult life, the richly 'spiritual' region of Northern Rivers was also where the most drama, politics and egoic performance existed. A curious phenomenon.

In my prayers and meditations and through ceremonies I asked for guidance on how to bring unity and guide the healing for the community. I was shown that it was time to introduce some stronger practices and processes of initiation as a way to strengthen the work and eliminate the drama through conscious practice and growth. Another thing that kept coming into my visions, often through the miração, was a call from Spirit to found a *ponto de luz* (point of light) that would be akin to founding a 'church-like' organisation. I faced a lot of judgement and resistance to this, yet the guidance and the call was becoming louder. People were encouraging me too, and I came to accept that this wasn't about what I wanted or didn't want; there was a huge community prayer at the altar of this work, and it had taken on a life and a culture of its own. All of those prayers in a sacred alliance with the land were calling for this point of light to be founded, and grounded into physical manifestation.

Then one day a dear brother, who had been in Brazil visiting family, went to Ciranda and did the Cura with Carioca. On his return he gave me a present of six little crystalline stones that came from the waterfall at Ciranda. I was so touched, as I missed that waterfall and Ciranda and it was the place where I had spent so much time in meditation and singing with the spirits of the land in the forest. We sat down and arranged them into a six-pointed star, I fetched a small Santo Daime *cruzeiro* and put it into the centre, and immediately I felt the energy of the point of light. We both felt it. We picked up the guitars and sang at the altar. The point of light that had been coming to me in all those visions was now a grounded reality in the physical dimension through this newly formed altar. That night we both dreamed of it and I was given the name 'Estrela da Ciranda' in my dream while he was given an image of the symbol of the point: a rainbow hummingbird with its wings wrapped around the circle and the altar. Since that manifestation, the work has been much stronger and more grounded but this has also been accompanied by a shifting out of energies that are not in alignment with a stronger grounding of the prayers and the spiritual point of the ceremonial work. Everything changed from then and even led to the writing of this book.

One thing I have learned along the way is that with spiritual gifts and blessings, with Indigenous wisdom and knowledge comes power, and with that power comes responsibility. With the creation of a spiritual ponto de luz as the manifestation of the collective prayers of hundreds of people which were centred in Australia and with our ceremonies but which were also now spreading all around the world, also came the responsibility to honour that ponto and to do the work necessary to hold the light stronger than ever. Sure enough, many storms have come and gone since then that have tested that strength and humbled me and our community to its power.

Lockdowns and meltdowns

As Australia descended into a medical dictatorship in early 2020 through to late 2021 and beyond, our community and I were already caring for many vulnerable people. By its nature, Ayahuasca tends to attract vulnerable and sensitive people who are often spiritually inclined — people who are looking for connection to Country, to Spirit and to community. It also attracts many people seeking healing, especially those who have been unable to find remedy anywhere else in society or within its systems. As shared earlier in this book, the Australian mental health system is particularly poor, and Australian society, with its lack of spirituality, its disconnection, overregulation and materialism, is a hotbed for mental health decline. Ayahuasca ceremonies and their communities have become a safe space for thousands to heal and find that connection their souls are craving.

The period during the authoritarian lockdowns and Orwellian censorship was a frightening time for many of these vulnerable people. It wasn't long before I was receiving many calls and messages from people in crisis and sometimes in critical mental health decline. I spent a lot of time trying to steady people through this critical time whilst at the same time lobbying the government to show some humanity and courage to realise and admit the immensity of the risk and damage that was being created. All of that fell completely on deaf ears, as everyone was asleep and operating in a hypnotised group-think. They were very disturbing times. During this period, whenever there was a break in the oppressive control we were able to gather, and I am very happy to say we had very strong protocols around safety and nobody became sick or infected with the virus they were telling us was so deadly.

By late 2021 we were still living in an era marked by the state-imposed lockdowns and censorship. Police brutality was rampant, along with a sweeping regime of medical coercion driven not by care, but by profit-centred influences that commandeered public policy. These were not benign public health measures but acts of control stripped of freedoms, devoid of compassion and steeped in fear. Across our community, the fallout was profound: we saw a surge in mental breakdowns, anxiety, paranoia, suicidality, addiction relapse, deep spiritual disconnection and widespread job loss. The declining mental health of the people was symptomatic of a total betrayal of trust in the system and a fracturing of society's heart.

During this state of collapse in public trust, our community did its best to respond with humility and responsibility. We had rigorously mitigated any risk of virus spread, having never experienced outbreaks within our circle, and yet we saw lives fraying at the edges. So many people were writing to me asking, pleading, that we gather together and pray again as community. At a time when people were seeking solace, we offered ceremony, healing and reconnection. Instead of supporting us, institutions and media later weaponised what we do. They didn't support the traditions that were holding people together. Instead they attacked, marginalised and silenced us. What many quietly feared has, over time, been revealed as truth: the crisis was not only driven by a virus, but by an abandonment of moral duty. This book bears witness to that betrayal, and hopefully serves as a call back to healing through courage, care and community.

Tragedy

It was during this time of heightened vulnerability that we gathered again, late in 2021. During that retreat, tragedy struck when our brother passed away. He was a dear soul — a valued member of our circle for many years, deeply loved and cared for by all. He carried a strong spiritual fire and a gentle heart. He had a long history of drinking Ayahuasca with various groups and had twice travelled to South America to deepen his path. Though he came from a complicated background and carried many wounds, he walked this road with courage and faith. He identified strongly as an Indigenous man and was well known within the local Aboriginal communities. I had often seen him at Indigenous and Elders gatherings over the years always showing respect, always listening. He was usually the first to book into our retreats and the last to leave, and always available to be of support to others. He learned the hymns by heart and played them with devotion, sharing many beautiful, prayerful moments that touched all of us.

What happened that night was raw, confusing and heartbreaking. We lost a brother, and nothing can soften that truth. Those of us who were present lived through the complexity of it: his refusals of help, our attempts to care for him, the anguish of watching the situation unfold while his Aboriginal Elder was by his side. Everyone deals with grief and shock in different ways. For me it was a very spiritual experience. I had to balance so many things all at once with care for a large group of people who were very vulnerable whilst working with a team of practitioners who were caring for him and then dealing with grief, shock and confusion after he passed. Some people stayed strong and held space for others, some broke down. Others went into fear, blame and panic.

The morning after our brother's passing, before the sun had even risen fully, narratives of blame and condemnation were already swelling across social media. By 6 am, people who had not been present, who had no idea what had truly unfolded, were running public commentaries filled with assumptions, accusations and outrage. While those still in my care were fragile, grieving and needing calming presence, the outside world was already spinning its story. This created a sharp and painful dissonance: inside, the priority was care, grounding and safety; outside, the chorus of judgment was already being amplified by voices which had no responsibility for the people affected.

Holding the centre amidst the storm

My instinct in that moment was to hold space. To focus on those who had lived through the night, many of them shaken and vulnerable, ensuring they had all the support they needed: quiet reassurance, links to community support, external therapists and healers if required, and the stability to process what had just happened without being further destabilised. Many just needed presence. At the same time, I had to navigate the very real fear that police might become aggressive, which, so soon after the abuses of the lockdown era, carried its own risk of panic for some. The reality dawning on many was that we lived in a society where our sacred spiritual practice was criminalised, persecuted and misunderstood. This was a storm of grief, fear and stigma, and in the middle of that I tried to stand, to temper, to balance, to hold the centre.

> *Many I interviewed in Australia were hesitant and often unwilling to talk about their Ayahuasca experiences with non-drinkers due*

to fears of ridicule, discrimination and even persecution. Negative kinds of legal and medical perspectives about "hallucinogens" combined into a uniquely disenchanted view that alienated the practice of drinking Ayahuasca and suspended it beyond civil society. Such alienation further authenticated the intuition that society was existentially toxic and disenchanted and that Ayahuasca and the spirit of nature are powerful antidotes to it. – Alex K Gearin, Global Ayahuasca.

But outside the circle, others did not see what had really happened. Instead, they heard fragments, gossip and media spin. In that vacuum, people in the wider community who had never been there, people who did not know the context, became loud voices on social media, striking the keys of their computers with moral outrage, as though indignation itself were truth. 'Keyboard warriors' amplified themselves, shaping a story that suited their need to be heard, even if it bore little resemblance to the reality. In the noise, the careful voices, the ones who had actually lived it, the ones still grieving, were drowned out. And so the story became less about what truly happened and more about how others chose to posture around it.

What shocked me most was how quickly some people outside our circle, including figures from other medicine communities, leapt onto their soapboxes with campaigns of moral outrage. Some who had never spoken to me directly, some who did not even know me, projected themselves into the tragedy with a kind of righteous certainty. They became loud voices online, feeding into the public narrative of blame. In almost every case, not a single one of them reached out to me with compassion or even curiosity; none asked how people were or asked about what happened that day. They simply took their position in the chorus of accusation. It is quite amazing that a small chorus of people can create so much noise. I was also touched by how much care, love and support was being offered.

Even within traditions that know Ayahuasca well, fear seemed to take over. People in one Brazilian circle, for example, fearing the light might shine on them, sought to divert it by amplifying accusations. This was a reflex of self-preservation, but in doing so they contributed to persecution. Their lack of mindfulness echoed what Alex Polari once described about the sadness of Padrinho Sebastião and Mestre Irineu: that politics and ego too often disrupted the deeper calling of the work. That same ego, cloaked as righteousness, became a force of harm.

The disrespect this showed to our brother was perhaps the deepest wound. He had made a clear spiritual choice that night, refusing medical attention not out of recklessness but because, for him, that was part of his spiritual path, as he was supported by his Aboriginal Elder, who stayed by his side. Yet this truth was hidden from public view, obscured by the narratives pushed strongly even in the coronial inquiry that followed and the ensuing media hysteria. As one respected Aboriginal Elder said to me later, reflecting on the way the community had turned the tragedy into a spectacle: 'They stole death from us as well.' His words pierced through the noise.

And so I found myself in the impossible position of caring for those who were vulnerable, shielding them from panic, while simultaneously enduring a public onslaught of narratives that bore little resemblance to the truth. It was a lesson in how fear, stigma and persecution can ripple through communities, how quickly people can grasp at moral certainty to mask their own anxieties, and how a society that criminalises spiritual practice only fuels misunderstanding. This all revealed less about what actually happened that night than about the way fear moves through people and institutions alike, creating narratives that wound, stigmatise and divide.

Retreat and reckoning

Once the initial storm had passed and I knew that those present were connected with some form of independent support, I had to be very careful not to add to the messy discourse, and so kept to my views to myself. There was still so much we did not understand. Nobody knew, in those first days, how the kambô experience our brother had had that day related to his eventual passing. Fragments of information were coming forward from different people who knew him, but the truth remained unclear.

At the same time, threats were being directed at me, both spoken and relayed through others. I went into retreat for several months. Rather than respond outwardly, I turned inward. I devoted myself to deep spiritual inquiry, going over everything that had happened: the days leading up to the event, the night itself, the reactions in the community. I examined my own behaviour and our protocols, knowing that I am not perfect and that there were definitely things I could have handled better.

The reflections of those who were there that night varied greatly from person to person, and their feelings often evolved over time. Many people expressed gratitude for the way I handled things — for the calm I kept, the reassurance I gave, and the steadiness I held through a very difficult situation. Several told me that, despite the tragedy, they learned a great deal about themselves and about life from that night. Only a very small number, perhaps one or two, came to me with anger or blame. But even then, I was grateful that they had the courage and respect to speak to me directly, unlike those who chose to throw rocks from a distance.

Those months were a time of grief and reckoning. Many times I found myself on my knees, praying, asking for guidance, asking for a sign of where to go and what to do, of what was true in all of this. I bore my soul to the universe and, in return, received solace. I received strong affirmation that my path was a true path; that despite the tragedy and the complex storm of events that day, I did my best. I carried no guilt for the choices that our brother made, even as I mourned his passing. I know we did our best to care for him amidst his choices.

In this process I was guided not only by my own prayers but also by the Aboriginal Elders and Indigenous people around me, whose wisdom and ability to reconcile tragedy with grace became a profound teaching. Their example showed me how to hold loss with dignity and courage. Amidst the media storm I was touched when an Aboriginal Elder drove for one and half hours to show up at my back door simply to tell me that he believed in me and asked me not to give up, that the work was so important for so many people and was supported by Spirit and Country. My spiritual guides and the universe itself also gave me signs — clear and positive affirmations that the story was not over.

From that retreat came change. I sought insight from doctors, nurses, psychiatrists, psychologists — people within our circle and from outside it — so that we could learn from what had happened and identify and mitigate any possible future risks. A lot of work and study was done. Together, we made careful changes to strengthen safety, improve clarity, and ensure that our community continued forward in a way that honoured both the lessons and the spirit of our brother who had passed.

Closed loop of injustice: A modern-day inquisition

Following the subsequent public processes around our brother's passing, I came to see how a coronial narrative, detached from evidence and procedural fairness, could co-opt a genuine investigation and create a presumption of guilt. That narrative was then entangled with other bureaucracies which reinforced it through their administrative powers, producing years of systemic targeting without any factual findings or due process. The media, hungry for sensation, amplified it into a public spectacle of blame.

This closed loop of presumed guilt revealed how easily bureaucratic systems can drift into suppression, how collusion between agencies and media can entrench 'official' truths while evading accountability. What unfolded around me was less a search for justice than a machinery of narrative control.

Spiritually, I experienced this as a kind of cruel mental trap. In vision and prayer, I felt dark forces working through these processes, seeking to dim and destroy the light I am able to bring into the world. Some might dismiss this as 'conspiracy thinking', but many people now see more clearly how our institutions are increasingly subject to authoritarian influence, protecting profit-driven forms of science and medicine that depend on an uninformed and unwell population. The evidence may not always be transparent, but the pattern is undeniable across jurisdictions worldwide.

This entire process has followed a familiar script: establish a narrative, lock it down with media reinforcement, engage government agencies to prop it up administratively, and then obstruct, reinterpret, gaslight or endlessly delay anything that challenges it. This strategy has created immense public harm and forced me, and others, to escalate the matter to the highest oversight and anti-corruption bodies in the state.

Though slow, these processes of oversight are still in motion. My hope remains that somewhere within the system someone will recognise the extreme abuse of procedural fairness, obstruction of natural justice and the dangers of administrative overreach, and act to restore balance, accountability and trust.

As we can see, institutions have built a trap, reinforcing loops of a narrative of guilt without due process, using a public smear campaign to sustain it. I have stayed quiet until now. Writing this book is my way of stepping out of that trap; my way of expressing my truth. There will always be other opinions, other perspectives, other ways of interpreting events — but it is not my role to reconcile those. My role is to speak authentically, to share my truth as I have lived it.

Faith and ancient wisdom

My faith in God, in my Creator, assures me that none of this is accidental. Even Ayahuasca herself has found her way onto the front page of the newspapers. Though the framing has been persecutorial, with the silencing of certain voices, and supported by abuses of process, her presence is undeniable. For those who know and understand her, the distortions will be clear. For those who are curious, they may be inspired to seek further, to research and find their own truth. For others, the fear of the established narrative may prevail. Such divergence of responses is not new; it has always existed.

Throughout history, communities have oscillated between reflexes that lead to growth, evolution, awareness and awakening, and reflexes that fall into denial, avoidance, fear, pride and the ego's defences. This is the nature of societies, particularly those protecting the status quo. Yet this is very different from the Indigenous worldview, which grounds itself in respect, natural law and cultural continuity. My hope is that through telling these stories of my experiences, through the lens of Indigenous wisdom and enduring spiritual practices, a way forward may be found: one based on respect, honouring and mutual understanding.

At the same time, what has unfolded in my case highlights how far our society has degraded into one that can justify, institutionalise and weaponise abuses of process and betrayals of democratic principles. We saw it during lockdowns; we see it again here. The danger is clear: there is a cultural and systemic creep towards legal, political, pharmaceutical and scientific authoritarianism. Even the greatest sceptics can no longer ignore it. This reality is becoming harder and harder to deny, and it calls on us all to seek remedies within our communities and within the jurisdictions in which we live. This pattern of suppression is not new. It echoes throughout history, from the persecution of mystics and healers to the modern-day silencing of spiritual sovereignty.

> *Shamanism has been misunderstood in modern times because it's associated with antiquated ways of thinking and superstition, but the reality is that it was shut down primarily by colonialism and by organised religion. One of the great Catholic mystics of our time, who I talked to, said that the Catholic Church, as an example, had hidden all their mystical practices after Martin Luther and the Reformation because they didn't want people to talk directly to God. They needed people to go through the intermediaries of the priests and the church, and the church was the one that could intermediate between the upper world and the lower world and sell indulgences,*

but nobody else could. And there was something about the colonial and European view that we have the superior way, not just to the Asians or Africans or Latin people and so forth, but even within Europe, in the persecution of the witches and the shamans and the sages. It was really about power and consolidating a kind of vision that was first materialistic and, later on, scientific. The truth is the shamans and shamanism have always existed in cultures. They are the healers, the sages, the ones who live between the two worlds and can open them to you. And it scared people, but now we need them more than ever. — Jack Kornfield, writer and meditation teacher.

Media, medicine and the manipulation of truth

Long before all this went down, in 2018, at a time when the work I was doing was gaining a lot of momentum, when we had a strong, vibrant and growing spiritual community gathering in ceremony, supporting one another, learning the music, practising the dances, reconnecting to country and co-creating a living prayer far beyond the ceremonies themselves, I was approached by two journalists. One was from the Australian Government-funded ABC (Australian Broadcasting Corporation), and the other from Channel 7, a tabloid-style commercial television station renowned for its sensationalist smear campaigns, fearmongering and bottom-feeding brand of journalism.

The ABC journalist had come through mutual friends and initially approached me with a tone of respect. He was working on a piece for *Radio National* about psychedelic medicine, in particular, about the Australian Government's rejection of medical and therapeutic uses of psychedelics. At the time, this felt like a moment when perhaps the broader cultural conversation was shifting, and that maybe there was finally space to speak to something deeper: the spiritual dimensions of this path and the community healing it was fostering.

Before he came to ceremony, the journalist asked to interview me and I told him straight: I didn't want to talk about the same clichés that had been endlessly trotted out in the media. I said to him, 'You've got a choice in how you approach this. You can write yet another tired piece about vomiting in the dark, visions of snakes, strange beliefs and creepy shamans, or you can do something new. You could talk about the spirituality, the lineage, the connection to country, the living prayer that this work represents for so many of us. You could explore how these ceremonies are not just about individual healing but about building culture — real, living culture — for people who've felt alienated or broken by the dominant system. You could speak to how this work is reconnecting people to their roots, to Country, to Spirit, to one another — not in some abstract way, but in real, grounded, community-led practice.'

He nodded and seemed to understand, and he did come to ceremony. But when the final piece aired, it was predictably disappointing. He fell back on the same lazy tropes with anecdotes about someone spending too long on the toilet, the obligatory vomiting stories, the trippy visions, the 'weirdness', of it all. It wasn't exactly a smear piece, but it was certainly a missed opportunity. Another shallow take on something too deep for soundbites. And yet, this didn't surprise me. At least not then.

The second journalist approached me in a similar timeframe. He worked for Channel 7, and while I was naturally sceptical, knowing their reputation for sensationalist tabloid stories masquerading as journalism, I agreed to meet with him. He told me a producer had suggested doing a story on Ayahuasca, and he was curious. We had a good conversation. I approached him the same way I had with the ABC journalist: I spoke about the spiritual context, the deep ceremonial lineage, and the incredible community that was forming around this sacred work. I made it clear that if he wanted a salacious story about vomiting or weirdness in the dark, he could go elsewhere. But if he wanted to understand what was really happening — the reawakening of spirit, the reconnection to country and self, the collective healing — then I was open. I suggested, though, that if he wanted to truly know Ayahuasca and be able to speak about her, then he should put down his journalistic mind and identity and just come and experience. And then decide about a story or not.

To his credit, he was true and he listened. He came to ceremony and was respectful throughout. He didn't act like a journalist poking around for a story. He genuinely consecrated and showed respect in ceremony and in communion with Ayahuasca. He did the work. I thought: fair play, good on him. Later, he contacted me and told me the experience had been life-changing, that Ayahuasca had opened something for him. I appreciated that.

Years later, he reached out again. When we met, he admitted something that truly confirmed my initial suspicion. Back then, he'd been sent to do a 'hit piece'. The story wasn't originally about me; they were targeting Ben Lee, a well-known independent musician from Sydney who had gained mainstream attention and spoken publicly about his transformative Ayahuasca experiences. Channel 7 had wanted to frame it as 'rich eastern suburbs people trading cocaine parties for drug-fuelled jungle ceremonies', spinning it into a narrative of weekend binges disguised as spiritual work.

They had identified that I was hosting ceremonies on the Central Coast of NSW and sent this journalist to covertly film people dancing during ceremony so they could build a case against Ben, and by extension, the entire Ayahuasca movement in Australia. But after being given this assignment, something had shifted for him. He started researching Ayahuasca properly and found it wasn't at all what they were presenting. The more he looked into it, the more genuinely curious he became. He didn't go through with the hit piece. And later, as the story fell apart, the producer behind it apparently faced some internal fallout. Part of me wondered if that was Great Spirit moving through and dismantling the corruption from within once it had been exposed in the light.

I respected him for telling me the truth, even if it came years later. But the irony wasn't lost on me. Not long after, I would find myself at the centre of a sensationalist media storm, with the very same brand of hit-piece journalism turned against me, with all its distortions, cherry-picking and character assassination.

Still, Channel 7 didn't let go of their mission to discredit Ayahuasca. Shortly after, they aired a different hit piece: this one focusing on Australians travelling to Peru for ceremonies. They went so far as to feature a Sydney hospital doctor warning viewers that people were returning from Ayahuasca retreats in the jungle with brain damage. The absurdity of this blatant framing highlighted the lengths they were willing to go to to manipulate public perception and smear sacred ceremonial practices.

It's worth noting that I was also approached by two other journalists, both from publicly funded Australian media: one from the SBS (Special Broadcasting Service), the other from the ABC. These encounters happened in the months leading up to the COVID-19 lockdowns and the wave of authoritarianism that followed. But unlike the earlier journalists who had come with an assignment, these two came through mutual friends, not as reporters but as people: broken, disillusioned and searching for something deeper. They were seeking healing, not stories.

Both had recently left their positions in the mainstream media, shattered by what they'd experienced. Each of them told a version of the same story: editorial pressure, bullying, being forced to push angles they didn't believe in, and the slow erosion of their integrity. They were being asked to bend the truth, twist narratives and ignore facts in favour of political agendas. Eventually, both said no. And for that, they were isolated, marginalised, and ultimately felt they had no choice but to resign.

I felt for them. These were good, intelligent, thoughtful, principled people who had been chewed up and spat out by a system that isn't interested in truth. I could see the toll it had taken on them. The inner fracture of losing faith in the very institution you once served.

These conversations with the former journalists were sobering. But they also affirmed for me that there are still those within the system, and those now outside it, who care about truth, about ethics, about humanity. People who are listening to Spirit in their own way, even as they navigate a crumbling world.

The Australian media also attempted at least two more hit pieces on another well-known practitioner working with psychedelic plant medicines, including Ayahuasca. They ran a smear campaign, a derogatory and manipulative portrayal clearly aimed at turning public sentiment against ceremonial use. It was an obvious effort to delegitimise the spiritual and communal context in which these medicines are traditionally used, while at the very same time they were promoting medicalised psychedelic therapy in hospitals under clinical supervision, using pharmaceutical-branded synthetic compounds.

This wasn't just a coincidence. It was a clear play to shape the narrative: demonise traditional ceremonial spaces whilst elevating state-sanctioned, corporatised models of treatment. Thankfully, that practitioner stood his ground and took legal action. The media outlet was eventually forced to retract the story and issue a public apology. But the damage, and the intent behind it, speaks volumes. It shows just how far the establishment is willing to go to control the narrative and undermine the resurgence of ancient Indigenous spiritual practices that empower individuals and communities, outside of their authority.

The roots of persecution

> *Our society is run by insane people for insane objectives. I think we're being run by maniacs for maniacal ends and I think I'm liable to be put away as insane for expressing that. That's what's insane about it.* — John Lennon.
>
> *LSD is a strange drug that produces fear in people who don't use it.* — Timothy Leary.

The roots of persecution reach deep into the soil of colonialism. Timothy Leary's quote above regarding LSD in the 1960s relates wholly to the way that society has responded to Ayahuasca since the first Jesuit missionaries entered the Amazon basin in the 17th century. They did not come merely as travellers or seekers of knowledge. They came armed with the conviction that they were saving souls from darkness. Their chronicles are filled with images of conquest and purification: the 'cleansing of idolatries', the 'extirpation of the devil's works', where Indigenous cosmologies were seen not as expressions of a divine relationship, but as evidence of spiritual corruption. I have even seen this myself in the Central Australian Indigenous desert communities where young people would approach me on Country and tell me that the priest had told them that their Dreaming and spirituality was the work of the devil, and they were asking me for my opinion about it. This is still going on.

In 1621, the Jesuit Pablo José de Arriaga wrote *La Extirpación de la Idolatría del Perú* (The Extirpation of Idolatry from Peru), a handbook instructing priests how to identify and destroy Indigenous rites. He described healers and ceremonial leaders — *mohanes y hechiceros* — as 'servants of Satan who deceive their people with false visions and enchantments'. That language travelled like a virus. The Jesuits in the Western Amazon such as Cristóbal de Acuña and Pablo Maroni repeated the same imagery, calling Ayahuasca 'the devil's vine' and warning that its visions were demonic illusions. In one report Maroni wrote of 'a vine called vulgarly ayahuasca', through which 'sorcerers trick and deceive the people'. Those words still echo. They established the moral grammar through which the Amazon would be seen. A place of enchantment, yes, but also of danger, witchcraft and sin.

Even as the missionaries learned the languages of the forest, they reshaped them with their demonising intent. The Jesuits compiled vocabularies, catechisms and dictionaries — instruments not of understanding, but of translation into the colonial order. The Huni Kuin call their language Hãtxa Kuĩ, the 'true word'. But this was filtered through the Jesuits who bent it to fit Latin syntax and Christian conceptions. The vocabulary of the forest was recast into moral categories: words for vision, healing or plant intelligence were reinterpreted as temptations, falsehoods or spirits of evil. Even language became a battleground where Indigenous knowledge was domesticated, disciplined and re-spelled into European frames.

The irony is that those same linguistic instruments — the early Jesuit dictionaries, the *Língua Geral* — would later be banned by the Portuguese Crown in the *Diretório dos Índios* (Indian Directorate) of 1757, as the State sought to replace the Jesuit voice with its own. Yet by then the damage had been done. The moral logic of conversion had already colonised perception itself. The 'otherness' of the forest, the sacredness of its medicines, had been encoded as pathology. The contrast with the modern movement of spiritual seekers heading to the Amazon in reverence to the beauty and healing of those native cultures is so vast.

Centuries later, that prejudice continues under new disguises. In our time, it is not the Jesuit's sermon that condemns Ayahuasca, but the bureaucrat's file, the headline, the toxicology report. The same imagination that once saw 'the devil's brew' in the cup of the shaman now calls it a 'hallucinogenic substance' or 'dangerous drugs'. The same fear of Indigenous power that justified the burning of altars now justifies criminal charges, regulatory bans and the presumption of guilt. In the laboratories of science, the legal texts of health authorities and the media's moral theatre, the language has changed, but the story is the same.

During this same period of colonialism, the European witch-hunts of the 15th to 18th centuries were calculated campaigns of repression that accompanied the birth of modern capitalism and the enclosure of the commons. Tens of thousands, mostly women, were tortured and executed under the charge of witchcraft, yet many were midwives, herbalists and keepers of ecological wisdom whose knowledge threatened emerging hierarchies of church, state and commerce. These so-called witches embodied older, Earth-based traditions and communal ways of life that valued interdependence over domination. Their persecution marked the silencing of the feminine principle in both nature and culture, a deliberate severing of humanity's living relationship with the land. As Vandana Shiva and others have observed, the burning of the witches was also the burning of the memory that Nature is sacred and that healing and knowledge were once rooted in our oneness with the Earth.

The witch-hunts were really killing those people who lived and taught the life that we are part of nature. The witches were teachers of oneness with nature. They were the ones who were hunted down and for a century or two centuries nine million people were killed in Europe. It was a killing of the ecological mind. — Vandana Shiva, author and environmentalist.

In Brazil, the long process that led to *CONAD's Resolution No. 1 of 2010* — Brazilian legislation formally recognising the religious legitimacy of Ayahuasca — was a rare moment of reversal, a crack in the old edifice. And in Peru, the 2008 declaration of Ayahuasca as part of the nation's 'Patrimonio Cultural' (cultural heritage) signalled a slow return of dignity to what had been demonised for centuries. Yet these recognitions coexist with ongoing suspicion: the legacy of the Jesuit prejudice. Governments still regulate with a colonial reflex: permission is conditional, belief is tolerated but not trusted, and Indigenous authority remains invisible in the eyes of the law.

To this day, the same hierarchy persists. The Western physician is seen as rational, the Indigenous healer as dangerous; the laboratory as legitimate, the altar as illicit. Beneath the surface of our secular institutions still runs the old theology of domination — the notion that truth belongs to the civilised, and nature is somehow erroneous, the forest a dangerous scourge. The Jesuits may have left their missions long ago, but their dictionaries remain embedded in the structure of our minds, in the language of science and the assumptions of governance. The persecution never ended; it simply changed its dress.

In the early decades of the Santo Daime, from as early as the 1930s both Mestre Irineu and later Padrinho Sebastião lived under relentless attack from police, authorities and religious antagonists. Despite the peace of their spiritual mission, their self-sacrifice in healing many in the community who often came from far and wide, they were treated with suspicion and fear. In the Acre of that era, Ayahuasca was not seen as medicine, but as menace. The Daime's gatherings were forced into secrecy. Even as Mestre Irineu worked tirelessly for the good of his people, he was summoned by police, harassed by officials and accused of practising sorcery. They lived under constant threat of persecution and, in the early days, of even violence. At times the pressure was so intense that Mestre closed one of the early centres of the Daime. His pilgrimage to São Paulo, where he studied esoteric religions, became a quest to find a language that could satisfy the demands of law and society—a way to form alliances and bring legitimacy to the doctrine of the Daime in terms the State might accept.

Padrinho Sebastião would face the same darkness decades later. Police raids, threats and bureaucratic assaults were constant companions. Yet through the persecution he received messages from the astral guides, including hymns that spoke of courage, forgiveness and divine justice. Spiritual guidance told him to keep going amidst the persecution and one hymn came in the midst of that turmoil:

I went on a journey
To see how things are
I found everything obstructed
I almost couldn't go through.

As I was arriving and talking
I was ordered to correct myself
To be sure about
What's going on here.

The Mestre isn't satisfied
With this union
He's seeing everyone as being wicked
Deluded with illusion.

Talking with my Mestre
He said to me
I want to see who is with me
On this very occasion.

The story that's happening
Is null to me
It's like the journey
Of the men who went to the moon.

— Eu Fiz Uma Viagem, Padrinho Sebastião, Hino 126.

Their stories reveal not only faith under fire, but a lineage forged through trial. I relate deeply to those stories. What happened to them continues to happen, only in new guises. I, too, have lived through the machinery of modern institutional suppression, a web of bureaucratic 'investigations' and media distortions aimed at silencing rather than understanding. The New South Wales Health Care Complaints Commission became the formal instrument of this campaign, publishing falsehoods, fabricating evidence, denying every shred of truth and fairness. Millions were spent on prosecuting a ceremonial leader and healing facilitator instead of investigating the truth. Throughout their entire campaign they engaged no experts, did no research and refused to consult with any community, thus erasing all of those voices.

The most alarming aspect was that these public proceedings were led not by impartial oversight but by the state coroner herself, who used her office to mount a covert, parallel public prosecution without due process. What followed was not a fair hearing, but theatre: a modern witch-hunt conducted under the banner of justice. The harm it caused to me, to my community and to those who sought healing, cannot be measured. It revealed how institutions, when blinded by fear and ambition, can lose both compassion and conscience.

How exactly does one quantify consciousness? — Ram Dass, *Being Ram Dass.*

I was just another example in a chain of persecution campaigns against practitioners of psychedelics which included the field of psychology and research. In the 1960s at Harvard University in the US, psychologists Timothy Leary and Richard Alpert (later know as Ram Dass) began studies on psychedelics and their potential for therapy and creativity. In his memoir, Ram Dass later recalled his first experiences of psychedelics:

> *... for the first time, I saw myself from outside, myself who I thought I was; a son, a professor, a psychologist, was not who I actually was. I thought my physical and psychological identity was everything. Psychedelics showed me I was a soul. There were planes of pure being, beyond my achievements, prestige and*

rational understanding. The realisation was cataclysmic. It made me feel, as I would refer to it for many years afterward, that I was finally home, home in my heart, changed by our experiences ... — Being Ram Dass.

Leadership at the University of Harvard went into a fear-based reaction to this groundbreaking work and shut it down, mischaracterising Leary's and Ram Dass' work through the same historical ignorance and stigmas. After the University confiscated their materials, Leary stated: 'What is in question is the freedom or control of consciousness, the limit or expanding of man's [sic] awareness.' The media, predictably, went into a hysterical and exaggerated smear campaign. It was too late for the dominator classes to stop the use of psychedelics, though, as the counter-culture had already been seeded; it was beyond anyone's control or manipulation. This was a remembrance, an awakening within humanity, and an unfolding of our Dreaming as the inevitable return to our true nature.

Sadly, the CIA and other dark agencies which had been doing radical and unethical experiments with psychedelics themselves, conspired to create the 'war on drugs' and prohibition. Leary and Ram Dass were pioneers, serious and careful academics and scientists, but they had also awakened their own consciousness beyond where the limited scope of psychology could have allowed them. Ram Dass went on to reflect: 'What was lost in the media hoopla was our serious effort to develop conceptual models for consciousness itself. Psychology was meant to study the mysteries of the mind but as psychologists, our professional toolbox was too limited to describe these intangible states.'

In these patterns I see a haunting continuity of the same colonial reflex that once branded the forest's medicines as 'the devil's brew', now re-emerging through institutional language and administrative violence. Where the Jesuits once cast the shaman as sorcerer, today's bureaucrats and media cast our ceremonies as threat. The same fear of the sacred that haunted Mestre Irineu's generation still animates the machinery of modern regulation. Yet, as the Daime Elders taught, truth has a longer life than persecution. The vine continues to grow, and so does the light that reveals the darkness for what it is.

> *What we've lost as a culture, at least in the Western world, is a respect for altered states of consciousness. This used to be a very common thing. Every culture throughout history has respected altered states of consciousness. Have had rights and rituals for achieving that, and we swept it all under the rug with a materialistic view of reality.* — William Lyon, PhD.

Toward healing and maturity

Despite the darkness that still hangs over our society with the lingering shadow of old inquisitions now cloaked in bureaucracy, the same ignorance and fear remain. It is astonishing that after centuries, humanity still repeats the same rituals of condemnation, only changing their costume. Yet amid the turmoil and misunderstanding, there is hope.

> *Across the globe, the arrival of "civilization" brought with it the persecution of the seer, the shaman, and the visionary. Why? Perhaps it is because civilization, with its narratives of individual agency and control, its relentless emphasis on forward progress, its commitment to the removal of mystery from daily life, and its encouragement of numbness over feeling, is fundamentally at odds with the seer's sensitivities and alignment to larger forces beyond human control. So modernity pushes the seer to the fringe — and once cast aside, seeing can veer into charlatanry and delusion. The rise of free market spirituality and New Age conspiracy is a result of the unmooring of the seer from traditional context. Yet what this points to isn't something "wrong" with seeing or spirituality. It points to the need for context in a larger culture of disconnect and fragmentation, for slow learning and earned wisdom within a culture that always rushes things outwards. Dichotomized narratives that pit scientific rationalism against the spiritual, shamanic, or oracular ignore the central importance that spiritual*

movements play in culture. Visionary movements drive all aspects of culture, including scientific innovation. And ultimately — as science itself tells us — having a "fringe" that sees things differently than the mainstream is absolutely essential to the growth of culture. So perhaps the modern-day seer must re-learn what it means to find anchor and context and earned wisdom, just as society must remember that the seer is vitally important. In a world of fragmentation and numbness, the seer comes to wake the culture up, to restore its sensitivities, and ultimately to drive culture forward. — Joshua Schrei, The Emerald podcast.

In Brazil, a turning point came in the 1980s with the formation of CONFEN, a national commission that brought government representatives into the Amazon to meet with the Santo Daime and União do Vegetal communities. Those officials, once sceptical, spent days within the forest, consecrating, praying and observing. They emerged with a declaration that these communities were 'healthy, peaceful, and socially beneficial', and that their right to practise should be protected. That recognition became a foundation for Brazil's eventual *CONAD Resolution No. 1/2010*, which formally acknowledged the legitimacy of the religious use of Ayahuasca. This stands as one of the most enlightened acts of governance in modern Latin America — a bridge between the forest and the state.

Across the oceans, in the United States, similar seeds of justice took root. Although Ayahuasca and DMT had been swept into the irrational and unjust so-called war on drugs in the 1970s, the 1990s and early 2000s saw a profound legal reckoning. In *Gonzales v. O Centro Espírita Beneficence União do Vegetal (2006)*, the US Supreme Court delivered a resounding victory for religious freedom, ruling unanimously that the government had failed to demonstrate any compelling reason to prohibit the sacramental use of Ayahuasca. The Court affirmed that the tea, within its ceremonial context, posed no threat to public safety and was protected under the *Religious Freedom Restoration Act*. A few years later, the Church of the Holy Light of the Queen, a Santo Daime congregation in Oregon, won a similar case, gaining the same protection. And most recently, the Church of the

Celestial Heart, founded by a brother of the Ciranda tradition — the same lineage I walk with — became the first syncretic Ayahuasca church blending Daime and Umbanda to receive official recognition in the US.

These are signs of awakening: nations beginning, however slowly, to outgrow the reflex of fear and to recognise the legitimacy of sacred medicine and spiritual healing.

We pray that Australia, too, may grow up into such maturity and that it may find the courage to leave behind its punitive reflexes and follow these examples of wisdom. There is no moral or scientific reason to continue this abuse. Today, thousands of Australians walk the path of Ayahuasca with reverence and respect and are always learning and improving safety and protocols, healing themselves, restoring relationships, deepening their sense of purpose and service. Our holy sacrament keeps people well. It keeps them off destructive drugs. It helps them stay connected to family, to community — to life itself. At a time when the nation's health systems are failing spectacularly, this is not a threat but an opportunity: an opportunity to protect the spiritual rights of those who have found healing, to uphold human rights and Indigenous rights long denied, and to open the doors for genuine collaboration between science and spirituality.

For me, this is not theory. During the darkest years of my persecution, I was banned from all therapeutic work. People who had been stable under my care suffered terribly: some attempted suicide, others relapsed into despair. The Commission ignored every warning, every piece of evidence. This is what the war on drugs looks like when translated into bureaucracy: it destroys lives under the illusion of safety. As Professor David Nutt has shown, tens of millions of lives could have been saved if psychedelic medicines had not been banned in the 1970s. The cost of fear is measurable in human tragedy.

> *The longer the government went on creating policies that conflicted with the scientific evidence, the more harm those policies would do ...* — Professor David Nutt.

It is time for this to end. It is time for Australia to evolve and become a nation that faces its spiritual and historical shadows with maturity and grace; a nation that acknowledges the wisdom of the First Peoples and the sacred medicines of the Earth; a nation that upholds freedom of belief not as a slogan, but as a lived reality. When this country finally honours the ceremonial use of Ayahuasca, it will be healing a great wound whilst protecting sacred rights. And from that healing, perhaps a more truthful and compassionate society can be born.

> *It's important not to lose sight of the bigger picture. Psychedelics may well prove to be an effective new tool in addressing the impacts of trauma on mental health. But it's the war on drugs itself that is fuelling so much trauma. In addition to finding new ways to treat mental health challenges, we should also aspire to address their underlying drivers. Ending the failed war on drugs is one important step in the right direction.* — Richard Branson, entrepreneur.

More so than with government and institutions, the responsibility is on each one of us. We all hold the power to change — no matter how dire the circumstances, how overwhelming the persecution, or how heavy the weight of obstruction. Every hardship can become an invitation. Every challenge, a catalyst. Change is not only possible; it is inevitable when spirit moves. Throughout history, we have endured. We have transformed. We have risen beyond that which seemed insurmountable to create something new. Each of us carries moments of courage, moments where we surrendered, trusted, let go of the known and stepped beyond our limits. And if we can recognise those moments, we can know that faith is not something distant or abstract — it lives within us. Even in the darkest of nights, the light not only persists, it intensifies. And as the world descends deeper into its egoic illusions of domination and control, those aligned with Spirit shine ever brighter. When we choose to return to the light, to walk with the Earth and live in right-relation with all beings, we begin to dissolve the karmas of history. We remember our role as co-creators of a new dream: one of healing, of harmony and of sacred restoration for the whole Earth.

In 2019, I attended the World Ayahuasca Conference in Girona, Spain, a gathering that felt like a living manifestation of this global awakening. More than 1,400 participants came from across 50 countries: scientists, doctors, lawyers, anthropologists, Indigenous Elders, artists, musicians, healers and seekers uniting in dialogue around the cultural, medicinal and spiritual dimensions of Ayahuasca. Over 150 presentations were given by researchers from leading universities, covering neuroscience, psychotherapy, ethnobotany, law and public policy. Yet it was not an academic conference alone. Throughout those days, the voices of Amazonian Elders and shamans spoke eloquently to the people, bringing prayers, songs and ceremony into the heart of Europe. There was a palpable sense of reconciliation between the Indigenous and modern worlds, between science and Spirit. The atmosphere was one of humility and convergence, as if the planet itself were beginning to remember something ancient. Standing there among so many diverse people working for the same vision of healing and understanding, I felt the movement of history turning, felt so many moments of goosebumps and chills along my spine and a glimpse of what a post-prohibition, post-colonial future could truly look like.

A shared path back to truth

If you've made it this far, you've walked with me through a vast and deeply personal journey: of spiritual awakening, revelation, ancestral teaching, initiation and the sacred task of building community. None of it has come easily.

There's been sacrifice. A lot of pain and heartbreak. Many projections and attacks have been directed at me along the way. I've had to stay strong through trials that would've broken others. I've witnessed people take from me, appropriate my teachings, as well as manipulation, betrayal and attempts to gain power within my work, within my circles. It's taken deep vigilance, resilience and a constant return to faith. And through it all, my trust in Spirit has only grown. I'm endlessly grateful to the ancestors and the teachers of my lineages, both living and in Spirit, for their guidance. Without that divine presence, I couldn't do what I do. I'm also humbled by the gratitude I have for the brothers and sisters, Elders and young ones that have stayed true and strong by my side with unconditional love. That sometimes is tough, but we work it out together and how strong in love and unity we are! Haux Haux!

I also want to speak plainly. What I've been subjected to — the persecution, the coordinated targeting by systems and institutions, the media's distortion — is not just about me. This is a much larger cultural struggle. A generational pattern of colonisation that continues to suppress spiritual sovereignty, to silence voices that challenge control.

The lineages I walk with, born of resistance in Brazil and finding deep solidarity with Indigenous peoples here in Australia, have survived centuries of oppression. And what's allowed them to survive is faith. Faith in Spirit. Faith in truth. There were times I wanted to walk away. To take the easier path. But I remembered the responsibility I took on when I accepted the mission Spirit gave me. I didn't ask for it; I was chosen by my teachers, by my community, by Spirit itself.

So if you read this book, you'll see: this isn't just a story. It's a prayer in motion. A living transmission. I've been an instrument of Spirit throughout, and there have been a lot of tough lessons along the way. And though I've endured public prejudice, discrimination and even abuse, I take solace in knowing this isn't just my story. It's humanity's story.

This is about our shared path back to truth. Our reclaiming of spiritual sovereignty. Our remembering that we are children of the Earth, of God, of Spirit. As Uncle BJ once said to me, 'It's hard to believe people can act with such cruelty.' But they do. And still we shine.

To those who haven't yet found the courage to stand in their own light: don't give up. Keep walking. Spirit will keep offering the path of truth. Because there's only one way through this: the way of Spirit. Whether we resist, suffer or rise to be guides for others or shine like a lighthouse in the storm. We are all part of the great Dream of the Earth. And when we walk that path with integrity, we become a force of light. Together, an armada of light.

I'm blessed to walk with the spirit of Ayahuasca in my life. A true voice of nature. A divine gift for these pivotal times. Whether you drink this sacrament or not, I hope this story helps you feel its presence, the Dream of the Earth it carries. Because it belongs to all of us.

Closing reflections: Prayer of remembrance

> *Your life is God's life. The Great Spirit is not just outside you but within you as well. Listen to the Great Spirit. In your innermost thoughts, you will hear teachings superior to any that I or Deganawida will ever share with the words of our mouths.* — Ken Carey, *Return of the Bird Tribes*.

As I bring these words to a close, I am aware that this book has been written during years of turbulence and trial. The ceremonies, stories and yarns I have shared here have been woven not in isolation, but against the backdrop of a society that has, at times, sought to silence and distort them. These pages have been written while carrying the weight of relentless scrutiny, discrimination and persecution, yet also while maintaining faith in Spirit, in Country, in the Elders and ancestors that always guide me.

For me, finishing this book is an act of release. It is a declaration that I will not be defined by the noise of courts, commissions or bureaucracies, but by the truth of lived experience, by the Dreaming that carries me, and by the spiritual currents that no worldly power can contain. The harassment I have endured has been painful and costly, but in the telling of this story I see that this has also been medicine in itself. I have had to protect my field and my work from gossip, drama and community politics. It has deepened my faith, sharpened my voice, and reaffirmed the necessity of walking with integrity, even when shadow forces gather. I have been strengthened by what I have endured. I have been filled with purpose, vision, inspiration and an abundance of support.

This book is not an indictment. It is a prayer. It is not a defence. It is a song. It is not a closing argument. It is an opening to dialogue, to remembrance, to healing. The stories shared here are not only my own; they are threads in a much larger weave, one that belongs to the people who have come to ceremony, to the Elders who have blessed our work, to the ancestors who whisper through the land, and to the Earth herself, who continues to call humanity back into balance.

If there is a final message I leave with you, it is this: Ayahuasca, like Country, like Dreaming, like the great field of Spirit, is not something that can be owned, prohibited or contained. It is a gift. A reminder. A living current of truth that runs through us all. Systems may resist, but truth has a way of rising, of flowering through the cracks of concrete. And as it rises, so too do we.

So let this book be a marker of survival, of resilience, of the possibility of reconciliation between Spirit and society. Let it be a bridge into conversations yet to come and a small light among many in the wider planetary awakening that is already here. My prayer is that these words, however imperfect, may carry some medicine of their own: a spark of remembrance, a nudge towards courage, a reminder that we are not alone, and that another world is not only possible but already breathing among us.

> *We need to understand that we are not outside of nature; we are nature. We are part of the Earth, and it's time for us to become aware of this. We are a part of the river of life, and we need to take care of it.* — Ailton Krenak, Indigenous activist and writer from Brazil.

Shamanism revisited

Now, to return to a question I'm often asked: how did I learn to become a shaman?

Well, I wouldn't call myself a shaman, even if some of the tools I use could be considered shamanic arts. As I've already said, it's not something to be learned in the way society teaches. It's not a certificate to put on the wall. It's a way of walking in the world. It's not a course I did and passed. It's who I am. It's what rests in my soul. It's the knowledge, power, awareness and alliances of natural and spiritual beings that walk with me and move through me. It's my Dreaming.

It's about being in connection with Country. It's about being of service. I believe the way of the shaman is the way of the true self, beyond ambition and mental projections, validation and ego. It's about knowing when and how to stop and sit and listen, to be present, to be guided. To be an empty vessel through which Spirit can flow.

Some weekend workshops or two-week tourist trips to the Amazon might uncover a few things, maybe a skill or two. But this path isn't for show. It's not for Instagram photos. The shamanic path, as I see it, is about walking with Spirit. Being guided. Not having a big list of things I want to do and claim, but uncovering what's already inside, what wisdom lives in my soul, and how that's reflected in community and offered in service. As we walk the true path, we learn that we don't ask or seek to receive gifts of knowledge and power, we embody their teachings in humility and grace, and they are offered to us.

It's about selflessness. It's about putting aside my own agenda. It's about facing the shadows when they arrive. It's not about running or hiding. It's not about bypass and bravado. It's not about the clothes or the language or the theatre of spirituality. I see people appropriating Indigenous culture in performative ways, wearing all the attire and acting out roles they copy from YouTube or from others in social settings. Often they have never even met a Huni Kuin or Yawanawá person, or have only been to one ceremony. We must be mindful of this performative show; when I see this I see a lack of depth and authenticity. Walking a spiritual path is about truth. Aligning ourselves to Spirit's truth. And when we're in that truth, nothing can shake our centre.

I know people who planned to find an Amazonian shaman and tour them around the world like a personal trophy before they had even done any substantial work, either culturally or within themselves. If they had, they wouldn't even be thinking this way. Too many gringos are turning their focus onto Ayahuasca tourism as a business before they have done the deeper work themselves. True shamanism emerges from direct relationship with Country, with ancestors, with the unseen world, and is expressed through quiet integrity, not spectacle. It's not about being seen as powerful; it's about becoming empty enough so that true power can move through us — and it takes deeply committed personal work to get there. This again highlights the shadow side of this path: glamour. Seeking validation and ego gratification on the path is a sign of spiritual immaturity and can be dangerous because if one finds ways to get attention and power from the glamour path then it can develop attachments and become detrimental to the true path — which is finding the power within.

Light and shadow: Beyond separation

The true path of any spiritual development, personal growth, healing or shamanic work demands that we face our shadows. And I mean *really* face them. Not cherry-pick the easy ones. It means sitting with our pain, with the people we may have hurt, with the lives we've shaped and the consequences we've created, and taking full responsibility for all of it. Those running and in avoidance, those putting on masks and performing a role, may be praised by some but to those who have touched the depths, it is obvious where they are at.

In today's world, it's easy to run from shadow. To avoid, to hide, to create stories, to spiritually bypass, and to cloak this all in victimhood, pride and bravado. When one lineage or teacher becomes too confronting, some people monkey-branch to another and tell themselves they've evolved. I've seen so many people in new-age movements flip-flop from one scene to another, hopping and skipping between lineages and practices, never truly attaining depth in any of them, drifting in the realm of phenomenon, the external world. But the answers don't lie out there. The answers come from within and we can only truly touch the depth of that knowing through our faith, where we begin to see the light in the shadows.

> *Curiously, people resist the noble aspects of their shadow more strenuously than they hide the dark sides. To draw the skeleton out of the closet is relatively easy, but to own the gold in the shadows is terrifying.* — Robert A Johnson, *Owning Your Own Shadow*.

Sometimes in new-age movements we become obsessed with the light or we may descend into addictions, where we want only to have good feelings, avoiding the pain or the shadows. But it's not the light alone that does the healing. We must make the darkness conscious. This happens in the place where the light and dark merge in an alchemical union of opposites, where we attain wholeness and find peace. The classic projection of this is when we claim good in ourselves or our tribe through casting blame and calling the other evil or wrong. It is only through traversing darkness that light gains its importance; where fear of life is replaced by the wonders of life.

Everything we manifest is a reflection of who we are inside. Like the hollow reed or the didgeridoo, it's only when we are empty — of ambition, stories, grasping, lack, insecurity — that Spirit can flow through. In that emptiness, our shadows don't disappear. They become illuminated. We learn to embrace them as allies. We begin to see where our wounds are, where our patterns lie. And we walk with them. Not as burdens, but as guides that remind us. When we own our shadows, we take away their power to control us. We invite trust, from ourselves, from others, and from Spirit — and we become transparent to ourselves and to others.

And in that space, we no longer fear being seen. Because what's being seen is truth. And that's what people can meet. Not the persona or the mask, but the whole being. I am so grateful for those on the path who have been able to see through my shadows and guide me to my truth, seeing beyond my illusions and embracing me once I had shed that ego's skin.

This is the training. This is the initiation. I had to weather the storm. Trees with strong roots can withstand a cyclone. Even if they lose a few leaves or branches, the roots endure and grow back stronger. What remained was simple and unbreakable: love and the will to serve. My firmeza stayed rooted like a tree in wind, stripped but unbroken. Those who stood beside me grew strong as well, anchored in love, humility and truth. This was my initiation: to face the shadows of society, to meet the darkness within myself, and to transform both into strength and compassion.

Through the darkest nights I held my firmeza. My faith, loyalty and commitment to this path have been tested and tempered like the steel of Ogum's sword in the fire. The storms stripped away illusion and left only devotion, humility and trust in Spirit.

The lineages I follow and the teachings I've received have all weathered adversity. They come from cultures of resistance, where the Indigenous, the African slaves and the modern Ayahuasca churches had to fight for their survival and stand up as warriors defending the sacred. They have all suffered through history under the march of civilisation. And they still stand. Still reflect. Still mirror society and its leaders. So the question becomes: which side of that mirror are you on?

Now, standing at the edge of 2025, we can see it clearly: a world divided, awash in conflict, corruption, exposure and propaganda. The ego of humanity fights desperately for legitimacy, even as the very structures it relies upon begin to crumble. But beneath the noise, the light of our awakening grows brighter. The swell of change rises from a mighty ocean of truth, and it cannot be stopped.

People say time is speeding up. But time itself hasn't changed, it doesn't go anywhere. What we're experiencing is the compression of greater cycles into shorter spans, lifetimes of humanity's karma, ancestral memory and 6,000 years of civilisational advance resolving itself through increasingly condensed timelines. And if we're still clinging to that history, still identifying with the constructs, identities and entitlements of that civilisational matrix, all of which creates psychic heat, then that internal pressure builds. And for many, this will erupt as collapse, reckoning, suffering and breakdown. We can either choose to let go and face our shadows, to surrender the ego-self, to shed the socially constructed identity and become hollow vessels in connection with Country, or we will be torn apart by the force of what's coming.

As this swell of change arises from the deep ocean of truth, we each face a choice: to ride the wave, or to be taken by it. Those who can empty themselves, who can hear the call of Spirit, will stand upright like surfers balanced on the crest of a mighty tide: alert, awake, strong, clear — and able to see the horizon ahead and ride the force of change with grace. But those still burdened by the weight of the past, those who clutch tightly to the old narratives and false certainties, will find themselves wiped out, tumbling along in the wash, disoriented, gasping for air, dislocated from the truth of what is unfolding. The invitation is not just to survive the wave, but to stand up and surf it. Not just to withstand history, but to rise with what is emerging and become a beacon, one who shows the way for others in alignment with the collective remembrance of the continuum of Indigenous wisdom and the turning of history's tide. When we stand and become channels of the current and force of creation, we become artists of life, of co-creation through vision.

The world is an illusion, a Dream. It only appears to be real to the person who is unaware that it is a Dream. — Alan Watts.

To walk the shamanic path is to awaken within the Dream. It is to see the world not as fixed or final, but as a fluid, living illusion — a Dreaming shaped by stories, symbols, memory and belief. The Dream becomes heavy and imprisoning only when we forget that it is a Dream. But when we wake inside it, we remember that we are co-creators of reality, not just passengers within it. This awareness unlocks deeper levels of perception, presence and power. Not power over, but power with — with Spirit, with Nature, with truth. The systems around us often teach limitation, obedience and fear. But the Dreaming teaches us freedom, sovereignty and deep participation in the mystery of life. When we live from this knowing, we begin to walk *with* the Earth, not on it. And the path of the true shaman is nothing more, and nothing less, than that.

The Dreaming of the Whole Earth is calling. It invites us to listen beyond our personal ambitions and fears, to release the small stories about who we think we are. It's not about humans fixing the world. It's about realising that our disconnection, our ego, our entitlement, our grasping, is the problem.

This Dreaming asks us to surrender the illusion of separation, and to return to the original blueprint encoded in every living being. A blueprint that has never left us, even if we've forgotten how to hear it.

We're all in this together: the truth-seekers and the tyrants, the bureaucrats and the medicine folk, the abusers and the wounded, the light-workers and the dark cabals. There is no picking and choosing. The shamanic way is not about rejecting one side of the mirror. It is about seeing it all. Owning it all. Walking with it all. Living in peace, love and harmony. This is the real work.

> *We are just an unbroken dance of shadows*
> *Formless form*
> *Reflecting the light*
> *Holding to the power of one!*
> *The world will reveal as flawless*
> *One who sees themself in everyone*
> *Is a steady guardian*
> *One who loves themself as everyone*
> *Understands and is a natural teacher*
>
> — Toni Parmer.

Surfing the Zuvuya: The Toltec way and the shamanic gaze

When thinking about shamanism, some of the most important questions we can ask ourselves are: Where is our point of awareness? Where is our attention? Are we anchored in the physical, material world of the *Tonal* — the world of form, order and identity — or are we opening to the unseen, the spiritual dimensions of the *Nagual* — the world of mystery, spirit and formless potential?

In the *Toltec* tradition, the word 'Toltec' means artist — not just in the literal sense, but as a way of being. A Toltec is one who creates art with their life, who consciously shapes reality with awareness, discipline and intent. The shaman, in this sense, is an artist of the invisible, weaving together the seen and unseen worlds. Within this worldview, the mind is the brush and reality is the canvas.

The Tonal is everything we know: our name, our language, our personality, our history, our social roles. And the Nagual is everything else: the ineffable, the spirit, the void, the Dream. Both are essential. But many of us have become overly identified with the Tonal, mistaking it for the whole. We live by the codes of the historical material matrix, getting caught in the dramas of the phenomenal world, forgetting that our deeper guidance and our path beyond history come from the great mystery that lies beyond.

This distinction between the Tonal and the Nagual can often be the dividing line between whether we are truly walking the spiritual path, or merely performing it. Are we accessing the non-world and allowing ourselves to be guided from that place? Or are we reacting to the chaos of the outer world, living from the surface of things, disconnected from source? I have seen many people delve into the world of Ayahuasca and ceremony, come to circle wearing all the feathers and Indigenous Arts, but when they show up their focus is on what others are doing, judgments, dramas and flirtations amongst the group. They are seeking to create identity through the spiritual practice while focused on the phenomenal world. In my experience, it is only deep devotion and faith in the path, in Spirit and in the unfolding of my Dreaming where it all comes together. If I had at any point been focused on material outcomes for all the work and studies I have done, I too would be merely fumbling around in the phenomenal world.

I invite you, the reader, after having been on this journey with me, to reflect on your own point of awareness, your own attention and your own choices. For those of us who already know deep in our bones who we are and what we're here to do, it can still be easy to get pulled off centre by the weight of karma, by emotion, by the noise of the world. But the invitation from Spirit is to return, again and again, to that deep listening, dadirri. To trust the Nagual. To rest in the unformed, in the Dreaming. This is not just abstract philosophy. This is real. This is the path. This is the initiation of our time and the lesson that the Earth is teaching humanity. It is how we evolve. This what Ash talked about in the foreword at the beginning of this book. Holding onto material outcomes of desire — power, control and materialistic gain — only leads to more pain, if that is what you are here to experience. The seeking of identity can dress you in some fancy masks and outfits, whilst the true path strips away the architecture of defence. True liberation of the soul comes through surrendering to the flow of the river of the Dream, listening, emptiness and service to the Divine. Dadirri.

This is the invitation from Spirit: to participate as co-creators in the Dreaming of the Whole Earth. We all have a role to play. What are we dreaming? What are we creating? What is the story we are choosing to live? Are we unconsciously co-authoring a collapse narrative, dreaming up destruction, Armageddon and separation? Or are we dreaming up rebirth? A luminous future of reconnection, balance and harmony with Earth and each other? We need to ask ourselves in all seriousness: if our minds and our attention are what creates our reality — and they are — then what are we investing our creative power in?

We cannot afford to underestimate the strength of the pull of subconscious fears within the social-political matrix our souls have been conditioned by and have participated in for aeons. This is why the training we do in our ceremonies can be rigorous, why we need to be mindful and maintain firmeza, and why the humbling of group practice and lineage is so vital. In Santo Daime traditions, the initiates are considered soldiers in a battalion of love.

The ego is sticky and tricky and we need to work hard, with honesty, vulnerability, devotion and faith, to truly shed the skin of karmic history and rise as the rainbow warriors of the light. So I ask: Where is your attention? What are you feeding with your focus? Are you standing upright on the powerful wave of generational change, riding it with courage, clarity and presence? Or are you caught in the churn, distracted and overwhelmed, paddling in circles, looking down at the waves instead of facing the wide, sacred horizon?

Cactus dust, jagged stones
Wild encounters, alone yet not
Wandering, feeling

Magical places
With deeply mystical sounds
Watching the sun rise

On the horizon — freedom
True green
Green Venus of love

— *Poeira Cactus,* Vasconcelos & Brokow.

At times the density of the Tonal world in our society, in the human constructed field of trauma, becomes unbearably heavy. It is like carrying a heavy burden inside a swamp, and trying to shine light through murk. We feel that weight: everything we carry in our souls, every knot of karma from our lineage, every wound and ancestral burden. It tempts us to give in to our 'safety zones' — what we know and what we are conditioned to be. But it is all illusion, temporary satisfaction and avoidance. Yet Spirit calls us to lighten ourselves. To stand firm. To refuse to be dominated by unconscious fear, grief, betrayal and trauma.

Sometimes standing upright demands that last ember of faith. Don't give up. Don't surrender to the heaviness. Instead, resist the pull of mindless scrolling, of distraction, of hiding in the noise, and replace it with a meditative walk in nature, with art, with music, with reconnection to the Nagual. Strengthen that inner channel. The more of us who do this, the more who individually turn toward the unseen, the more the *Zuvuya* (cosmic wave) awakens in our lives. Then the wave of change becomes something that does not happen to us, but something we ride, something we co-create.

This moment in time is a swell of spiritual potential. And as José Argüelles writes in his book *Surfers of the Zuvuya*: 'The Zuvuya is the wave, and to surf this wave is to be at the dynamic crest that interfaces our 3rd-dimensional physical reality with the reality of the 4th-dimension.' The Zuvuya is a two-way flow circuit: the in-and-out breath of the galaxy, the pulse of creation and return. It is the current that reminds us of our true nature as inter-dimensional travellers returning to conscious awareness. When we go beyond even needing that concept, and we fully let go into faith and trust, then we become that flow. This is our evolution from moments of consciousness, in meditation or ceremony, to continuing consciousness and beyond.

To surf this wave, we must overcome the gravity of ego, the static blocks of the false self. Argüelles speaks of the ego as 'the secretary of defence, the CIA mastermind of all denial mechanisms' — the one who resists surrender. But when we lighten our emotional, mental and energetic load, we rise. We become awake in the Dream. We become capable of riding the great wave of change with strength, confidence and grace.

You are not just a character in the Dream; you are also the Dreamer. You are not just watching the wave; you are the one who surfs. It is the same with Ayahuasca. We are not just patients who lie back and wait for her to 'fix' us; we are co-creators in an artful relationship with a divine being. In the ancient Toltec way, let your life become a work of art, shaped by intention, inspired by Spirit and grounded in truth.

Ayahuasca and ceremony: The Holy Sacrament and the chalice

Ayahuasca, as a holy sacrament of light and dark, offers us a bridge and a path into balance. For those who hear the call, for those who choose the path, this is an ancient, ancient remembering. And as many Elders, researchers and seers have said: it is through the medicines, through these sacred sacraments, that human consciousness first arose. This is our birthright. No government, no prosecution, no campaign of fear can take that from us. Spirit always rises. Spirit never dies.

When we align ourselves with the Dreaming of the Whole Earth, we begin to shift our perception. We begin to see the Earth not as a backdrop to human experience, but as a single, vast, living being — a being in which all realms of consciousness, all creatures and forces, have an equal part to play. In this Dreaming, we are not separate. We are being dreamed as much as we are dreaming. And in our humility, we are co-creators within the Dreaming.

> *Just as you do not see the leaves on any healthy tree in the forest contending among themselves or fighting with one another, so neither is there any need for people to contend or fight or in anything but friendliness compete. When the Great Spirit is known within, in communities where truth and honesty are honoured, people live in harmony with one another. They experience their own life and the life of the Creator as one. They know that our people are like the leaves and our tribes like the branches of a wondrous tree. They know that the life of the two-footed and four-footed and winged ones, the life of the plants, the rivers and seas, the life of the very sun, moon and stars grows also from that tree. All come from one single trunk of being — the eternal Being that we know as God. In this way, the Great Spirit lives within all things, within every plant and animal, every tree, every one of us here present.* — Ken Carey, Return of the Bird Tribes.

In this deeper awareness, we start to see how even the light and the dark, the manipulators and the surrendered, the oppressors and the awakened — all of these things — are playing a role and nothing is excluded. As we step into these prophetic times, the ancient vision of the eagle and the condor reminds us of a sacred reunion: the marriage of the rational, technological mind with the intuitive, healing heart. This is where Ayahuasca plays a significant role.

This is not just a union of cultures or hemispheres. It is the union of the fragmented human psyche with the Earth herself, with the Dreaming, with Spirit.

True healing at the end of time is not about domination, or one force winning over another. Not light vanquishing dark. That's the old paradigm. That's the dream that's dying. The new Dreaming is a shared Dream: a weaving of the divine will with the human will in a sacred alliance. This new narrative is not based on control, but on co-creation. And as the world races toward digital illusion, with artificial intelligence, synthetic realities and separation from the natural, we see the impact on our collective soul. Mental, emotional and spiritual health is crumbling under the weight of disconnection. And that, in turn, shows up as planetary destruction.

Ayahuasca offers a remedy for this condition of humanity, as alongside its visionary power it has a powerful ability to reconnect us to the Earth, to Great Spirit and to our own inner truth. Millions have experienced its healing as real, embodied and transformative. Ayahuasca reveals what must be healed and then gives us a roadmap. But we must be brave in stillness and listen to truly receive it. Ayahuasca brings ceremony back into our lives. And it does so not through dogma, but through direct experience, through truth.

When held in sacred, respectful ways, Ayahuasca ceremony becomes a cultural anchor. It reminds us that we are not lost, that we are not alone. All ceremony, whether it's a collective ceremony or a quiet personal ritual, calls us back to the sacred. It gives us a lens, a point of light, an axis around which our humanity can revolve. But with this gift comes responsibility.

We must not outsource our spiritual sovereignty. Ceremony is not about projecting our power onto a shaman, onto Ayahuasca itself, or turning facilitators into messianic figures who act as father-surrogates for our cultural wounds. The medicine is not about personality or about charisma or control. The ceremonial leader holds a role, yes, but we must not forget our own. Each of us is responsible for what we think, feel, create and contribute. If we're still blaming others, still chasing external saviours, we haven't understood the teaching. I encourage people to come to me with solutions, not with the problem, and if we see something that needs attention or repair, then we step forward and do what needs to be done, we embody self-responsibility within the whole. If we are unsure, or we meet our limitations, we can ask for guidance or support, a reflection or a reminder on the path.

We remember the teachings of Jesus Christ and *Quetzalcoatl* (Toltec shaman-prophet), both of whom walked a path of humility and service. When the eyes of the world were upon them, when they were being followed, adored, accused or persecuted, they didn't cling to that power or try to control the narrative. They chose sacrifice. They stepped back, surrendered themselves and, in doing so, planted the seeds for generations to learn the deeper teaching: that the journey is ultimately about taking responsibility for ourselves.

Their example reminds us that the path is not about elevating any one individual as the sole bearer of truth. It's not about projecting our need for certainty, direction, salvation, blame or fear onto another. Rather, it's about turning inward, listening deeply, and walking our own path with courage and discernment. This is where the wisdom of Indigenous cultures shines. They do not centralise power in messiahs or external saviours. Their ceremonies, councils and spiritual traditions have long reflected a more egalitarian, Earth-connected way of being, where each person holds a role and no one is above the Dreaming.

From the perspective of the Santo Daime, the awakening to Christ is a journey of self-awareness and self-responsibility. The heart of Christ resides within us all. These are not times for mobilising ourselves around a single person, guru, dogma or organisation, even if that prayer is a beautiful path. We are called to mobilise in love. Love for the sacred, for the Earth, for one another, which we find in ourselves and then share with the world. Together, we stand in harmony as our sovereign selves.

Through thousands of years of unbroken practice and evolution, Ayahuasca shows us that healing is possible. It reveals the pattern and also provides the way out. When we engage with it humbly and with respect for its cultural roots and traditional knowledge, it becomes a vehicle that can endure through this time of transition. Despite resistance, judgment and attempts to discredit or destroy it, the sacrament will not go away. Too many have already received its blessings. Too many have been healed — and this is in the Dreaming of the planet.

For the sceptics, I invite you to reconcile your scepticism with the lived experiences of those who have found their way back through this path. Ayahuasca is a path amongst many and it is time to end the religious wars that claim superiority over spiritual belief and practice. This is not a passing trend. This is an ancient remembering and a living gift for humanity in a time of great forgetting. It is time to embrace it, celebrate it, and walk with it — in reverence and in truth.

> *And people who might be sceptical about shamanism, they're giving up without even trying it. This is a way to multiply your opportunities of solving problems, of asking for healing for the planet, getting in touch with all the beings of the planet. This goes beyond compassion. People often speak of compassion. That's a wonderful path. But in shamanism, it's not just being compassionate for other beings, other animals, plants, the planet. So it's becoming one with it. So you feel compassion toward and yourself at the same time. We are working in consent with the agenda of the compassionate ones. It's much bigger than just us.*
> — Michael Harner, anthropologist & author.

Ceremony itself is a cornerstone of our humanity. Across all cultures, throughout time, human beings have gathered in honour of the sacred. This practice is embedded in our ancestral memory, our spiritual DNA. It is our legacy and our birthright. Ceremony offers a central axis for our spiritual work, a place where the threads of community, culture, reverence and remembrance are united. It is where we come home to ourselves, to each other, to Country and to Spirit.

If Ayahuasca is the Holy Sacrament, then ceremony itself is the sacred chalice that holds it — a vessel of divine unity, coherence and intention through which the medicine can truly do its work. Ceremony embodies the culture of the medicine, of the music and the sacrament that work in a sacred unity. In true ceremony, we gather as equals. We sit in a sacred circle that mirrors the wheel of life, the directions, ancestors and the elements. We bring our stories, our songs, our silence and our presence. We are seen, and we see each other. In these spaces, we remember who we really are. We come as co-creators in a sacred Dreaming that is bigger than any one of us.

> *Today we make a covenant with the peoples of our five nations. We make an agreement to honour the ways of love, the ways of justice, the ways of peace. We are not in truth a separate people. Each one of us here in this multitude is a single leaf on the Great Spirit tree. When we go within ourselves to touch the river of life that runs at the heart of our innermost being, each one of us touches the same life that flows within our sisters and brothers, even as the same sap flows through all the leaves of the tree.* — Ken Carey, Return of the Bird Tribes.

Living the prayer: Ceremony as a way of life

The evolution of ceremonial work, particularly through the graceful and joyful work of Carioca and the global Ciranda community, is a shining example of how this sacred container can reflect the changing needs of our people. The ceremonies of Carioca are not only profoundly beautiful, held in harmony, in rhythm and in deep reverence, they also invite a kind of spiritual authenticity where participants can drop their masks and discover their own unique expression within the greater song of life. In Ciranda, we see the dance of Spirit and culture, form and freedom, devotion and creativity — ceremony as a truly living entity.

But the power of ceremony goes even further. When held in the right way — with real listening, real devotion and the presence of spirit — it has the capacity to awaken something deep within us. It teaches us reverence in action. It prepares us to live our lives as ceremony, so that the grace and awareness cultivated in the circle extend into our relationships, our work and our life's choices. Ceremony, in its highest expression, trains us not just to pray, but to become the prayer and to walk the sacred way in everything we do.

Perhaps this is one of the greatest teachings gifted to us through the ceremonial use of Ayahuasca: that healing — true healing — is not about fixing what is broken, but about remembering what is whole. Through the alchemy of Spirit and sacrament, we can release the mental confusion of this age, set down the armour of defensiveness, and open ourselves, naked, vulnerable and present, to the Divine. And in doing so, we become instruments of the great spiritual work of creation.

Through devotion, through courage, through the fires of initiation, we embody the regeneration of the garden of divine beauty that lives not only in the Earth, but within each of us. This, I believe, is the evolutionary calling of our times. The lineages that carry these medicines, many of which are born in the vibrant forests and deep soul of Brazil, offer us blueprints for how to return — not as dominators, but as custodians in service and co-creation with nature. When we go beyond performance, we truly arrive as embodied humans.

This is the sacred role of ceremony as a living container for the remembrance of who we are, and who we are becoming, together. This isn't theatre or performance when we are connected to Spirit. When we are free of the burdens and shackles of history and our wounded souls, then we can really return to the work of caring for this Earth and enjoying all the fruits of her being.

But this is not always easy. The integration of Ayahuasca experience and healing can be the hardest part of the journey as we face all of those accumulated soul remembrances, mental habits and emotional reactions. But this is part of the work and cannot be avoided. If you choose this path, don't complain. It is a big and, at times, arduous path. Without concerted effort towards effective and healthy integration, the work is lost in meaning and authenticity. This is why there is a growing movement towards creating cultures of integration not just around Ayahuasca communities, but with all plant medicines.

Most importantly, our spiritual evolution as humanity represents a return to honouring the spirit of Country, respect for Indigenous wisdom and holding deep reverence for the majesty and wonder of all of creation and for the Earth that nourishes us and supports us in all ways. At this time, the Earth is offering us gifts of knowledge and healing. Will we receive and honour them with grace? And do we return these gifts in kind with the wholeness of our beings in love and humility?

If this book serves any purpose, I hope that it is to give the reader a glimpse of that depth. Though my words may be imperfect, though language may falter in trying to express the immensity of this path, I trust that the openness of these yarns might open something in you. I hope they stir a presence in your own life, and remind you of what it means to walk the sacred way — with heart, with listening, with courage, and with Country.

May these yarns find you well, and may they remind you of your own Dreaming and be a welcome home to the Dreaming of the whole Earth.

I'll go following this path
To always be grateful
Each step a lesson
For all to see

Come from the forest, come from the sea
From the waterfall to your eyes
This infinite love

My sweet, sweet hummingbird
When I feel you singing
My heart starts opening
Lotus flower in the astral

I receive the light with joy
My heart the guiding star
I feel the divine power

— *Eu Vou Seguindo,* Unknown composer.

And in the end

And in the end, there are always beginnings. Every closing brings the seed of new birth. As this book finds its way into the world, more stories are already forming. There are more songs to be sung, more pages waiting to be written. The creativity flows through me like a river and, to me, that's the greatest gift life offers. I feel blessed to share this work, and it continues. The music still plays. The prayers grow stronger. The light in our hearts shines ever brighter, and the songlines of this new Dreaming of the Whole Earth are still being woven.

This book holds a collection of yarns: moments, memories and messages carried through years of walking this Earth with Spirit guiding me. As it goes to print, I find myself at a point of convergence: personal healing, cultural reconciliation, and a growing collective dialogue around Ayahuasca and plant medicine in Australia. I reflect on my journey — from a wounded, silent child to a painfully shy teenager, and through decades of deep healing and self-discovery. No one carried me through it. No one handed me a path. I had to carve it alone, guided by Spirit, held by Country, with ancestors by my side.

And still I carry the scars. I feel the echoes of abandonment, the grief of betrayal, the weight of the Earth's suffering, and the pain of those silenced or unseen. At times, those wounds stir again. But I've learned how to stay balanced, how to return to centre without drowning in them. The real work has been to find peace — not from escaping pain, but from learning to sit with it, learning to forgive, and to keep walking with humility and faith.

I've made mistakes. I've been misunderstood. But I've also grown, softened and deepened. And I remain endlessly grateful for the ancient wisdom still accessible to us — for the spirits, the Elders, the teachers, and the unseen forces that walk with us when we choose to listen.

There is so much potential for humanity's healing through Ayahuasca and traditional ceremony. It's not for everyone; but for many, it has brought deep relief, reconnection, and a sense of belonging. Around the world, a living culture is rising — rooted in community, in reverence, in care. It wasn't manufactured. It wasn't sold. It grew organically, quietly, through love.

And no matter what narratives try to erase us — we're not going anywhere. The old systems of control and domination are cracking. And in those cracks, the seeds of a brighter future are already sprouting.

May the Earth Dream awaken again through us, and may we move beyond healing into the creation and live as true humans in a time of renewal held by the pillars of love, peace and harmony. Beyond healing we are still humans, and we will still ride the waves of joy, pain, tears, ecstasy, fear and stillness. May we stay firm on that journey, in all its forms.

May we rise in salutation of the magnificence of Divinity and the mysteries of creation, as we sing out the calls to Spirit from each of the lines that weave this Dreaming:

Haux! – Huni Kuin.

Axé! – Umbanda / Candomblé.

Viva! – Santo Daime.

Yoeway! – Bunjalung.

Afterword

A fireside yarn with Uncle BJ, Galibal-Bunjalung Elder

Author's note:

During the writing of this book, I sat by the fire with Uncle BJ, a Galibal-Bunjalung Elder and cultural guide, and we yarned for about eight hours, talking about life, culture, Dreaming, Spirit, family and our community. These yarns are always big learning for me. At times, I found myself apologising for my clumsy use of language or the way I framed my questions. I'm still learning, still reaching for a deeper understanding. I was deeply moved by Uncle's patience, his intelligence and his generosity of Spirit.

After hours of conversation, I asked to record a short segment — about an hour and a half — for inclusion in this book. He agreed, and I feel honoured to include that here. As I've said throughout these pages, it's important to me that this work reflects not just my own perspective, but the voices of others. Especially those who carry the ancestral wisdom of this land.

Many times Uncle was at our ceremonies, lighting the sacred fire, welcoming us to Country, guiding, supporting and moving with the spirit of Country. For me, the support and love I've received from Uncle has got me through some really difficult times and, more than that, has expanded my knowledge and skills in navigating ceremony and sacred spaces. He has been like a father-figure and mentor for me, and I'm honoured to give him the final voice of this book, to acknowledge that this really is about so much more than me. It is a transmission on behalf of the Earth and the Dreaming.

I was born here in Australia, and I feel very privileged to have been guided, seen and supported by Indigenous Australians over the years. I can't imagine who I would be without that. My hope is that this book both begins and ends on a note of cultural respect: honouring Country, tradition, Elders and the spirit of place. On my own journey, I continue to learn, to listen and to deepen into humility and reverence. This afterword is part of that.

Uncle BJ's voice here is not only a grounding conclusion, but also a rare and significant contribution. It is uncommon for Aboriginal Elders to engage publicly with other ceremonial traditions like those of Amazonian and Brazilian Ayahuasca. His reflections and blessing represent a sacred bridge, a weaving between worlds. May it inspire a deeper dialogue in this emerging global culture of plant medicines, and carry forward the sacred alliance as depicted by the prophecy of the eagle and the condor.

As a cultural note: in many Aboriginal communities along the east coast of Australia, Elders are respectfully addressed as 'Uncle' or 'Auntie', regardless of direct kinship, thereby acknowledging and honouring their role as wisdom-keepers and cultural guardians.

Uncle's fireside yarn

Yarning about my life's journey is like a novel in itself. It is a natural process, we go through things, go through early parts of life. We formulate different things about where we get different impressions about this and that. One theme that you really notice, even your perception of events, so to speak, changes all the time. Being an Elder or having the honour to be able to reach this point of life, it's really all the same: you just got a different perspective on it.

But in terms of things that people like to consume as their intellectual diet, I do actually remember Aboriginal people living in the wild and swagmen and people just out in the bush, not going anywhere, just living in the bush. To me, that's actually a really awesome memory, even though back then they probably weren't really having a good time. They were probably being affected by the domination of white colonialism, but they were still out there in the bush. So, I've seen that kind of beginning, that essence of the way people lived on the land, or with the land, or as part of the land, which is truly what we mean by spiritual in those terms. And to this modern context now of someone doing a welcome to Country in Parliament House or whatever, or actually having some kind of recognition of the fact, or genuine inquiry of Aboriginal culture, especially Aboriginal land management inquiries, wanting to understand how we manage the land and what relevance that actually has to do with the so-called 'modern' times — it's extremely relevant. I'd say I wouldn't have had a normal life, but whoever does, you know? It's been a different kind of life, but it has really been important for me to formulate and understand some of these things that I'm doing now. I don't think it's very likely to change. There's three mysteries. A mystery that we really don't know, that everyone has theories about and like, where did we come from? When you're born, you're born, you're here. I'm not saying that our culture, or any other culture, has all the answers — but in some ways, the mystery remains. We know we're born, and we grow up in this world.

People tell us of that time we're going to leave this world, that no one lives forever. There hasn't been anyone who hasn't died who has preceded us. Then there's that mystery of what happens when we die? Where are we going? And then the other mystery, which we never even think very often about is: we're dreaming our own Dream. We are technical. We are creating our own life. By dreaming our own Dream, we can't necessarily totally relate to other people, even though we try hard, and I think it's good to do that. But there's something about our experience that's very much our own Dream. And I think we need to understand that — we're dreaming our own Dream. I think it's very important.

But also, of course, there is the big Dream, the collective Dream of the tribe or the society or the world or the universe or whatever, for sure. But I think if we really contemplate this and look into it, we can see that we really are dreaming our own Dream, and this so-called 'waking experience' is kind of like a dream, and it's been used by many traditions. We're (Aboriginal Australians) very famous for the Dreamtime and all this story. But there really is something in that word being chosen. You know, sometimes dream is used as 'dream-like,' or means that someone's kind of vague, or they're not somehow practical. But really, when you're dealing with this kind of mystery that I've spoken of, practicalities aren't really the thing that's going to unpack it. It becomes the area, like spiritual or philosophy, these kind of things. I've had a strange life, but at the same time, I've always really wanted to learn about other cultures as well, like all the cultures of the world. I see a lot of my people aren't necessarily doing that. They don't even know about their own culture. They're not what they may learn on TV, incidentally, and that ends up being the whole of what they know. That's not necessarily a racial thing. I think that's probably the same for everyone.

I always felt a bit like an alien or something, or there's quite often that feeling of not fitting in. I grew up largely in a white kind of scenario. I didn't grow up on a mission or connected to a huge Aboriginal community at the time. In fact, the place where I live, basically there were very few Aboriginal people there. You don't even think racially when you're young, people are just people. I remember they used to call us 'coons'. That was one of the words they used back in those days. I didn't really understand that at the time; it was the name of a famous generic brand of cheese, when there were hardly any choices in your delicatessen. Anyone just came home and said, 'Oh, Mum, why are they calling us cheese?' She didn't answer. I didn't really understand a lot of what all that was at the time. I just bunkered down; I suppose that's where I was. There's just so many mysteries of life, so many unanswered questions. That was only just one of them when I'm trying to understand society or whatever.

So then with that, I'm sort of feeling like an alien, metaphorically, feeling different, so that I couldn't have conversed like this with my fellow man. I really wanted to, and I started to try a bit, but then realised that it wasn't going to be, it wasn't the thing to do, and they just really had no idea what I was talking about. Well, they didn't seem to anyway, and whether that was or wasn't necessarily the case, maybe they were just caught up in other trivialities of growing up and wanting things, wanting this and that.

I really don't think I understood it that well at the time. This is just a reflection, looking back at it — I think it was kept away from not only me, but from people, on purpose. That somehow we'd be better if we threw off those things, became modern and more savvy in the ways of the world. Honestly, I just couldn't do it. I had this 'mother nature's son' running within me, and I used to just walk off into the bush and do fire stuff, even when I was young, without anyone telling me or teaching me anything.

Somehow my parents didn't care. Maybe they were trying to get rid of me; I was pretty annoying, perhaps. I had a brother and sister and they never would have let them do that. They had them wrapped up in cotton wool. I was allowed to wander in the bush. I felt very at home in the bush. In some ways, I never wanted to leave it. I always had this kind of fantasy of just living in a cave and things like that.

Those things didn't seem alien to me and when I think about it now, in this context, where did that even come from? It's like an instinct or your spirit — kind of like an instant 'guiding spirit'. I was giving a talk the other day about cultural fire, and I always say the main reason we do cultural burning or look after Country is for spiritual reasons. But someone completely misinterpreted that. I think they thought I was speaking in some kind of Byron Bay spiritual lingo. I just find it funny — to use those ordinary new-age words when really, that was the furthest thing from what I meant.

It's made me feel like you always got to be on guard too, even if you don't say these things. In some ways, it doesn't make any difference to really explain something in more detail. People just take what they want to hear. They take home with them what they want to take home. And I think we're all kind of guilty of that actually, to be honest.

They felt that to some degree in the bush illusion, but at least it's your memory and your experience, and then you took yourself into the bush, and were bathing in the peace of nature, at home. I didn't feel scared of snakes and things like that. People were worried about being unsupervised in the bush, or that the bush was out to get them. I've never felt like that. You see that with modern people today. It's almost like a bellyful of hysterical laughter, they're frightened of themselves — a disconnection from nature. Part of our spiritual nature is not being too scared of yourself and everything going around in culture. Everybody has different approaches, but that's a goal.

In terms of initiation for men, I can speak about that, of how the young men were sent out into the bush, to hunt and collect food, prepare food for people and then not eat any, go through fasting of 10 days. It's toughening people up. Or you could see that by putting a modern lens on it — that it's really making people strong and content with having basically nothing and also content with helping others.

First and foremost, they're helping others. The rest of the tribe is as it always was and always will be — more important than you, the individual. So you're just part of that network. It's really about the whole; it's a totally holistic kind of thing. The individual being in the background is almost non-existing, whereas in the modern sense, it's all about the individual. You know, the ads on TV we get the most — you get the right house and you've got the right kitchen and you can get extra money on credit, on your phone or whatever, so you can just be you, and you can prove to the world, get those artificial dreadlocks at your hairdresser. You can show the world that you're you and you're perfect and you will create this perfect world. But where is it? I see people getting older, getting more miserable, more bitter, worrying about their possessions, endlessly trying to protect them.

The face of Indigenous people, First Nations people all over the world is basically having very few personal possessions. In our case, basically we had none. Everything was shared, and there was just that reality, or that baseline — and there is nothing that you can have on your own. And to me, that just seems like an incredible wisdom as a remedy, or an antidote actually, for the people. They lose all their money, so they go and jump off a cliff. That kind of thing.

You mentioned the philosophy of sharing and caring. I think it actually goes beyond being a philosophy; it's a way of being in those terms. You describe it like that, for sure. Honestly, it is a way of being.

It's just like any way of being that you're taught from day one, then that just becomes the fabric of your life. Now we're talking about how we're being taught the cult of the individual, and how with tribal people it's creating this great schism, or it's kind of like war — an internal war — maintaining the cultural perspectives that are innate, bringing them more to the surface. It's with Indigenous people, but it's in all people, obviously, is what I'm saying. It's just been conditioned out of them, where we're fresh on the block of modern consumerism.

I always laugh at them, and people like mining companies that somehow have given some Elders a Land Rover or whatever, and they run out of petrol and just fucking walk away, leave it there. I've seen that. Ran out of petrol, gotta walk — and I guess you've also experienced that, and you probably see it in a lot of other young Aboriginal people. So, how are they reconciling that within our society, and how's the society dealing with it? What's the effect of that? What's the carnage? What happens there? I think it's generally a pretty bad effect too.

What I've seen within the 'mob' [Aboriginal people] is that culture of sharing is still very, very strong, even with people that have no cultural knowledge, when all the cultural knowledge is not there for whatever reason. So, they have very little, not just because they don't want to talk about it; they just haven't got it. And still that sharing is there and it's what makes the mobs who they are. A lot of times I see with some individuals that that extends to anybody. They want to make sure everybody's happy, or have got whatever's there, a big packet of chips or whatever, that everyone gets a share of it. Somehow, the only way that so-called individual can truly be happy is if everyone else is happy. What a revolutionary thing to say. And yet, to me, it's just common sense. All this disconnection we see is amazingly artificial. It has to be held up by propaganda and, at times, even literally by fascist-like behaviours just so that it seems like it makes sense.

Encountering Tibetan Buddhism

It's a funny kind of thing, because with the Himalayan people, which always was Tibet, they came here to Galibal Country and I actually felt very much on the same page with them, even though their outside looked vastly different, with all the ceremonial, ritual paraphernalia involved with Tibetan Buddhism. It's massive. It must be one so-called religion. They wouldn't necessarily call it religion just because it has so much ritual, has so much paraphernalia in regards to ceremony, the bells, the drums, the oboe trumpets, the Tibetan orchestras. Oh, it's just ... it's phenomenally huge. But at the same time, the feeling of these people — I just felt the same. I felt much greater affinity with them than with the non-Indigenous people of this land, honestly, which was a bit of a shock at first, but it was also a bit of a hook as well. I've always been interested in religions; not to necessarily join them. Like when I was presented with the Bible when I was young, I thought: 'It's a book, people are quoting out of this book. You know, John, Chapter three, verse two, consonant one, and the Lord went ...' Ah, but I thought, 'No, it's a book, I'll read it.' So I started at the beginning and I read the whole book. I think very few people have done that. And I've read others, like the Koran, Bible sort of things I suppose. I'd always been fascinated with those. My criticisms of Buddhism were, 'God, they're all just talking about death and suffering all the time. Can't they ... ? Just, like, get a life, you know?'

Anyway, I discovered in some small way the teachings of the Lord Buddha, who we say is our main guru, our main teacher or whatever. The founder of all schools of Buddhism and the tantric or the Vajrayana Buddhism, which basically means enlightenment in one lifetime, came and got protected in the land called Tibet and a few of the other Himalayan countries there, which actually all through time, were Tibet. Tibet was this huge country. And I was fascinated by the fact that there were these incredibly fierce warriors who the vast majority of them got converted to Buddhism, into prayer, wheel spinning — a kind of peace. Spinning the prayer wheel, sending out the feelings of compassion and love and blessing to all beings, not just humans. It seemed fascinating that actually could happen. And I think in our original states of mind we're very similar. So I found that kind of connection, which helped me become more open to the Buddhist teachings.

Ayahuasca and psychedelics

Growing up in the 1960s, I'd heard the word LSD, but I didn't even know what it was. The first time I smoked *yandhi* [cannabis] was in a scripture period during school. I was 15 or 16 or something, and all the ministers — there was like five or six different ones, like Church of England, Baptist, Methodist, whatever — they all came to the school. They all stated that they didn't want to teach our year. Maybe we were real revolutionist troublemakers who spoke our mind, I don't know. But anyway, so we got a free period, when we could actually do what we liked. We sat out on the lawn and this little girl said, 'Oh, friend, smoke some marijuana.' Then I discovered LSD. I had a deep connection with Indian culture, as in India from Central Asia, but also Indians from the Americas as well, and also got really fascinated, especially with Timothy Leary and the *[Tibetan] Book of the Dead*, which was one of those treasure teachings I was talking about early on that came to me at the right time, speaking of the journey of death. It's really erroneously called the *Book of the Dead*, of course, but that's what it's famously known as.

Those people who took the psychedelics and had big sessions out of it and then read or had some kind of teachings on the *Book of the Dead* — there was a huge similarity. This is a huge subject that I really can't talk about at the moment because it's a book in itself. But from this point of view it's much more like states of mind, how Indigenous people were much more original or much less conditioned, in terms of the universe, everything, and also the mind itself, which again, is a huge area to talk about. I suppose we could just use that word 'awareness'. For example, you are holding a recording instrument at the moment. You're aware that you're doing that. You're aware that you're asking me questions. You're aware that you're talking to me. So it's nothing more than that. It's just that kind of awareness without any analysis, without trying to fathom it. Just pure awareness.

So when I say mind, I'm talking like that, because I think when average people are talking mind, they really mean all their thoughts, without the awareness. They wouldn't really be having the thoughts, because then there wouldn't be anyone to be aware of the thought, if you follow my kind of logic.

The moral of the story here is that with LSD I instantly had this feeling it was connecting me back into those original states, like a child sees the world in wonder, and isn't really unpacking it, isn't really trying to understand it particularly; they're just doing it. Then, with the help of our parents, God love them. It's not like they really tried to condition us into this artificial, virtual world, but they had the same thing done to them. They feel it was their duty as a parent to do it to you, and if they weren't doing it well, then they had their peers to be on their case, and right down to the fact that they would come and take your children away from you if you didn't send them to school, if you didn't teach them to wear clothes and uniform and all these kind of things.

But one of my influential teachers — let's just call him uncle C — he told me this story once of when he was a child and he was living at the house in the bush, near Tabulum, and the officials came around to his mum and said, 'Look, you've got to send your kid to school. That's it.' They made all sorts of threats and stuff too, as you can imagine at the time, whatever they were. When she broached it with the young Uncle C, she said, 'Oh, look, you've got to go to school, you got to go to the white man school.' Whatever he knew that as, every day. But he said, 'Mum, I go to school every day. Uncle comes around in the morning, and he takes me for walks in the bush, and he teaches me things about animals, about plants, about everything. So I go to school every day.' And she just said, 'Oh no, no. Well this is it; you gotta do it.'

I soon had enough of LSD and then discovered psilocybin mushrooms. They became my main teacher in connection with psychedelic things. It was probably all over the place, without proper ceremony. They do actually say that psilocybin is probably one of the safest so-called 'drug' experiences. I would never call these things 'drugs'. It introduces you to heightened states, which a lot of the time you don't really remember much of when you come back into your so-called normal state, which really is just a virtual world of conditioning and has no connection with reality whatsoever. We tend to think of that as reality or normal, but the psychedelic experiences teach you otherwise, and they really teach you succinctly. They teach you like a headmaster that really does get the message through to you.

So when I came across Ayahuasca, it honestly happened kind of randomly. I did have a deep reverence for it — not from direct experience, but from reading books about psychedelic plants. Those books came into my life through the powerful effects and insights I'd had with other plant medicines. They opened me up to new ways of thinking, different channels of thought, and broader worldviews, I suppose. But anyway, I never thought I would encounter it, because it's there in South America — the vine of death, the vine of the soul. And it was just something that was interesting to read about, and obviously had parallels with other psychedelic pharmacopeia.

When I met you, Lore, and your group, I really appreciated the actual ceremony of it, the way that it was conducted, how authentically it was conducted, even though, albeit, it was a mixture of Western people and people from Brazil, who were perhaps a bit more culturally connected to it, or had red Indian in their family, or they grew up around those kind of people. Somehow it was more available to them. So, I really liked the ceremony, and I think that helps big-time, and also the fact the people who run the ceremony have vast experience with Ayahuasca, otherwise they couldn't be a helper or an aide or, literally, a nursemaid at times for people, especially if they haven't had previous psychedelic experiences.

Anyway, I found a very powerful, very strong one, and I wouldn't say it was entirely different from other psychedelic substances, which is strange talking about them like that — plant energies, deities that you connect with through the Ayahuasca. That's why I really don't like describing them as drugs at all. They're portals into other worlds, other experiences, other perceptions. I think to round us off as human beings that we need to have a completely open world viewpoint. And I think especially people of the Western world, but maybe all people really to different extents, depending on the so-called individual in this modern context, need these kind of things to open them up into the world viewpoint that they weren't brought up with, or awareness of the virtual-world viewpoint that they were brought up in — to know that it isn't the whole thing of the universe. In fact, it's absolutely nothing at all. It's complete fabrication. I'm not totally against having a society that has rules to say, 'this is good, this is bad' sort of thing. I think that's important for humans to relate to each other in groups, but not being the sole guide or the sole reality, or 'this is exactly how it is'.

So pathways. We talked about Tibetan Buddhism before, or Buddhism. We talk about meditation, we say that meditation is completely important, and that a scholarly intellect is also important as kind of guideline. But really this pathway through meditation, this insight that we gain through meditation, is just the same as the insight we gain through experiences with so-called psychedelic plants and ceremonies. To me, it's exactly the same thing. It's just this journey into who we really are, which at the end of the day we possibly could never put into words. Initiation, in the case of the people of this world, is to open us up to all these different kinds of possibilities, so that we have this view. We have this vision that we can't even really talk about, honestly.

That is who we are. We know who we are. So these lineages, like Buddhist or the Ayahuasca lineages, I think that's really what it's all about: to learn who we truly are, and to work with that space all our lives til we pass on to whatever's coming next. As I said, it is a kind of a mystery. Some people think oh yeah, they're going to heaven, where it's all really great, or they know they're really bad, so they probably think they might be going to hell, that kind of thing. The whole thing is just stupid to be like that. I mean, it just shows unawareness, really, just lacks insight of who we actually really are. So when we get on that journey of who we really are, then we don't bother with these kind of conjectures, around the coffee table or getting drunk at a party with discussions: 'I don't believe in God', 'I really believe in God', or whatever. All these things with scientists, with their belief in logic and science and analysis — I think all these things are kind of good, but when they just become a totalitarian thing, then no, it's like authoritarianism and I think that's where meditation and the psychedelic journeys really help with that. I'm not saying that because that was just my own experience. I've seen it with other people too.

And even though we can't totally share, like I said, the Dreaming, our Dream, we can get some kinds of ideas, we can get a feeling that other people are sharing similar experiences which have similar kinds of themes to what I'm alluding to or talking to here. Even though I'm talking about this lack of individual in reality, it's the contrary. I'm saying it's a personal experience that leads us to the non-personal. So, take what you will out of that.

There is a lot of contradictions. Meditation and psychedelic journeys can really help us with those contradictions, to come to terms with those and actually work with them to have a greater deal of happiness and contentment. This is one of the reasons why people with whatever kind of upbringings they have get attracted to drugs — the kind we really do call drugs — like heroin, methamphetamine, cocaine, MDMA, ecstasy. There's a whole range of these designer drugs. People are somehow looking for something. They're perhaps looking for something spiritual, even though they may not use that word, or use words that are tricky such as an 'altered state'. At the end of the day, the completely irony of it is that it's actually arriving in an unaltered state of who we actually, truly are — the baseline. Somehow we need to bring a purpose and a contentment in our life, even if we just have some glimpse of that. Some people might describe it as the 'enlightened state'. Some people might describe it as who they really are, or some people may choose not to describe it in any way, shape or form. Just try to get on with living it, being it, doing it, and then sharing, or trying to share, some of the outcomes of these so-called spiritual journeys. This is actually a true compassion for other beings and their journeys and their sufferings, and relating to that and saying; 'Well, I don't think I can really feel good when other people are really suffering. I want to help these other people. I want to see them suffer less, and then perhaps as a result of that, then maybe I might not suffer as much, but it's just that I don't know.' I've met people like that who've come through the various journeys, whatever the lineage is, meditation, Ayahuasca — let's call them shamanic, pathways. There's some other famous ones like peyote or San Pedro.

I think in the Western world, we don't really know that many shamanic pathways. Yet of course, here in this land you call Australia, there's the tradition of the wattle plants, which contain a high amount of DMT. All plants contain DMT, this genetic key, this fascinating thing. That's not something I really want to talk about, of course. There's various usages. One usage that I can talk about in terms of wattle or DMT is how it was used as a smoke. I can't speak for all nations, all Aboriginal people, all over Australia, but it's quite common in a lot of tribes, a lot of nations, where they use the smoke of certain wattle leaves, certain branches, or parts of the wattle plant to, what we'd call these days, immunise babies. When a baby's born in the Western world, we take them off and we give them all these injections or whatever to immunise them. The way the mob saw that was, as soon as they got the baby, they also rubbed oils and things into them, ash and various things like that. This main key thing was to keep away the bad spirits, to deal with spiritual things. But really, at the end of the day, when you look practically at it, it's just actually the health of the baby. So they use the smoke of the wattle to immunise, and really honestly, that's the best word. I don't care if people argue. That word 'immunise' these days is a bit taboo, isn't it? It's probably why I love it, but just in its actual sense.

The importance and role of ceremony

Ayahuasca ceremony — it's a real leveller, isn't it? I would say the Ayahuasca is an incredible leveller. Whether someone was an accountant or a flash lawyer, or whether they were just someone wanting to wander around in the bush from Nimbin, or be an influencer from Byron Bay, I think it really levelled them all into the same space. These things are highly important.

In the Ayahuasca ceremony I just seemed to be in the flow of it at the time. It's interesting because there's different kinds of logics in that heightened awareness. I don't really want to call it an 'altered state', but from the so-called point of view of people who watch the news or whatever and go to work at nine and come home at five, I guess it certainly is like an altered state. It's not anything in their normal perceptions of things. I think it creates an incredible equality, where it's not making anyone better or anyone lesser. And I think as human beings, that's probably the biggest medicine that we need. We see the world leaders at the moment, and it's been a theme, obviously, for the time of humanity, that they're kind of drunk with this power of being able to manipulate people. Sometimes it's hard to believe that people even want to do that. A lot of the time they actually start off wanting to do good, but once they drink the water of power, they lose all that. They lose all that humanitarianism and things that maybe they wanted in the first place to become.

From there we can go into the role of ceremony. Because ceremony is something that is endured across all cultures, all around the world. We talked about singing and dancing — and you've been to plenty of ceremonies, so you've seen how that's affecting the people. So then what is the benefit of ceremony, not just in the healing and the experience of the ceremony itself, but everything that comes from it? Well, there's a hardline thing. I think it's totally essential. And I think as human beings, we know that we recognise that we're doing it all the time. We have rituals. We have ceremonies. It's like we can't stop doing them. I think it's important to know that the ceremony, or whatever, is kind of like a spark point. It's not the actual thing itself. It's like it's facilitating something; it's not the ceremony itself. I see so many people that get caught up in the ceremony. Like in Vajrayana, or whatever, you have these offering ceremonies where you fill up bowls full of water, and people are going: 'Oh, you got the right amount,'

'There's too much.' 'Oh, there's not enough water,' or 'Oh, we have held it with our left hand; we should have been facing Mecca.' You can get anal retentive, or whatever. There's so much of that in ceremony that we can lose the point of ceremonial thinking. Yours was good ceremony; it's like another program happening. It's almost impossible to do that in your ceremony because you're being literally carried away by the energy, the plant energy. It's all in your mind. It's not anywhere else. It's not taking you to another planet. It's only just taking you somewhere in your own mind, some realm that was previously undiscovered, and even modern psychology lacks the ability to say what I'm just saying.

But when, in the 1960s they discovered so-called psychedelic substances or started to use them and study them in psychology and psychiatry, they instantly saw that there was something there, there was some kind of value. Then the political and some kind of criminal thing or corruption came in to upturn that. Now, in the case of psilocybin, it's been reversed. And now they just talk about the beneficial things in terms of people with addiction problems, with relationship problems, and they're saying that there's clearly therapy involved, even with little ceremony involved. That's not really what we would call traditional ceremony. Maybe because I'm a traditional person, I've got that in there. I could always just keep coming back to that. I think it's so important to have the good facilitation of the ceremony, and people are being equal, as well, within the ceremony. Even though there might be people like helpers or aides that are looking after less experienced people. I never get the feeling from those people at all that they try to lord it over anyone. They've had the experience, you know, and it's like they brought a map and they followed it, and are able to guide others with that map, helping them if they get off track.

Through meditation or through psychedelic experiences we can unlock, or shine a light on, the untapped vast, expansive awareness. Some people may struggle with these things, but I think it goes hand-in-hand that we need to jump into that unknown, jump into the mystery, become the mystery — not get caught in the need for analysis.

Connection to Country

You asked me about plant ceremonies from South America being held on Country. From an Aboriginal worldview, there are no other countries. There is no other world. This is all just one world. We're all human beings. It's really that all these things like countries are fabrications. All these things are used for all the wrong purposes. We're human beings. We have a similar Dream. Speaking Dreaming, we have a human Dream. So with our human Dream, we can relate whether we come from Alice Springs or whether we come from the upper reaches of the Amazon. We have that in common. We have a human Dream. We all take a shit, we all need water; it's a real basic thing. Everybody's complicating the whole thing with all this other stuff. Honestly, I don't really care what people think about this. 'Oh, you're making it too simple.' Or 'Oh, I don't like that approach.' But I do. It's that one Dream that we share as humanity that permeates through all of it.

There's also right-relationship to Country. We can also see that other animals had their dream, like the porcupine or the echidna. There was no word for that. That's why we call them porcupines, because when the West, when the Europeans first came to Australia, there was no such class of animals that had echidna in it. So they called it a porcupine. We can't necessarily perceive it, but the echidnas, they have their Dream, they have their Dreaming. And if they come along and they meet another Echidna, or take them up to be their wife and raise up little echidnas together, it's exactly the same, and we can relate to that. Or really we should relate to that — it's actually the echidna Dreaming. It's no different or no better, or no worse, or no less or no greater than human Dreaming. We should also appreciate that the human Dream is where we are — that's where we're at. And then through that, also related to all those animals. We actually have an important responsibility to look after Country for all the other animals, all the other beings. Even the ones you can't see, like life in the soil, for example, are also beings. The life of the soil is like a base level when talking about Country, even when Country is so much greater and vaster than that. Without that life in the soil, there's going to be no life on the top of the soil. Maybe people see things in different ways. They understand what I'm saying in different ways, but I think it's hard to argue with.

This law was taught to us, passed on through generation to generation. It wasn't kept in books; it was an oral story that was spoken as an oral lineage. One of the key marks of an oral lineage is that when a knowledge keeper — and they don't have to be an Elder — is passing on knowledge that they really know, they understand it. The key mark of that is when you're passing on that knowledge, then you know, quite subtly, you might be asking the knowledge holder questions or whatever, but through those questions or even just looks on their face or their body language, you're seeing whether they're actually understanding what they're being taught, and you would never let that person go in an oral tradition, til you really felt like they actually understood, so you knew that they were going to pass on that knowledge correctly, and they weren't going to just take on their own bent of it. That is seemingly something that's really lacking in the world when it comes to books. I'm not against books particularly, but so many people can go away from a meeting with a different understanding, and a book is just so much like that. We have the meeting I'm alluding to. I see lots of them, whether they're a tribal meeting, a company meeting or whatever, where people leave that meeting or that conference table with so many different understandings of things. So, an oral age is just so different, and people can interpret books in so many different ways, even if they got some hardline person, like an old-time hell and brimstone teacher, really drilling them on how they've got to understand that book. Even with all that, still a book is just so much open to interpretation. Even just one fucking word is just so open to interpretation or whatever. Through the correct maintenance of an oral tradition, that's really cut down in the middle. There's something really beautiful about that, because it's always this human connection, and we also believe that's what your echidnas are doing, or what the bush turkey is doing.

Something I love — and this actually relates to your question about looking after Country, or the ability to look after Country — is the bush turkey is a fantastic example for us blokes or those identifying with being a male. The male bush turkey builds the nest. He builds a nest, and he makes it real fucking greedy, and he attracts the female, because he's gotta have a big proud nest. It looks real good, looks a little deadly [good] there. So he gets the female, she lays the eggs in there, and then because the nest is kind of like a compost thing, he controls the temperature of the compost with his tribal knowledge, because he's the bush turkey tribe, that's his Dreaming. He's actually the Dreaming of the turkey. He knows what the eggs are going to be like, male and female, and if he sees there's maybe going to be two males, or too many males, or, on the other hand, too many females, he actually controls that temperature of the composting nest. It's something like about half a degree that science has discovered between the male and the female. Maybe the female eggs are somewhere else, so he's on the male place there. So they do it all and it's like this scientific knowledge, right down to the knowledge of composting for the temperature. How random is that? It's unbelievable. But even the best part of this story, the only reason I'm telling you the story, is that when the little bush turkeys leave the nest, they're ready to go. They don't have to go to turkey school. They know how to carry out their Dreaming. It's within them, and they don't even have any doubt. Maybe they make little mistakes here and there and get guided by the social structure of the turkeys that are still there with all their family and all the mobs still around them. Old man turkey isn't going to go, 'Oh, you're going to come. You know, I'll teach you how to be a turkey.' They just do it. They go off into the world with their genetic memory or their Dreaming or whatever is instilled within. But of course, people would argue with that. But even if they studied scientifically, they'd see the evidence of what we're saying, because it's not just me saying it. All I'm saying to the best of my ability or protocol responsibilities is cultural stories about one animal.

You told me the story about the Amazon people learning alone, directly from the forest. I've got absolutely no problem with that. It aligns with what I'm saying. It's like I'm coming on a different road to Sydney but know that if we follow that map, we'll get to Sydney. So that's good. I like it, that's awesome. And so those kind of stories work together in a way, and ultimately that would be my answer too. I just see that the wisdom of — I don't want to talk about myself as some kind of traditional healer or shaman or whatever the word is — but maybe there's some kind of enlightenment there in those terms. And really also my main reason for that is because I believe that every human being is capable of this, just the same as every little turkey in those little eggs is capable of doing what they do. It sounds really awesome, but then the bigger picture of reality is it's just how it is.

Somehow we've got to do all this analysis and all this unpacking and all this everything, and basically, like yourself, be persecuted, or whatever, for having the audacity to try and present this knowledge to the Western world. That's one of the reasons why I'm happy to tell these little stories or tell the group and give this yarn. So we call it yarn. Technically, yarn really is that no one, no one's knowing what they say is more important than anyone else's, and they're all just perspectives. They're all just yarns. And also, it literally could mean everybody talks at once. This actually happened — people take it in. Modern people, they can't do that. They can only listen to one talker.

Makes me want to talk about shamanic skills of having multiple points of perception in the same conscious moment. I often had experiences of that during the Ayahuasca, where I felt like I was in 50 different places at once, and I was also very cognisant of people's thoughts or where they were at. Maybe not their thoughts exactly, but where they're at, even if only just in that moment, just coming from a point of kindness or helpfulness, like a mother. They call her 'Mother Ayahuasca', I believe, and it's what a mother does. They would swim a river, they would risk their own life, they would die in the river to get their baby onto the other shore. They're really coming from that practical compassion, the direct compassion. Especially in the Western world, you walk down the street and you see someone starving, and they tell you that they're starving, or whatever. Can you give them some money so they can eat? Maybe they just want to get some more heroin, or get more alcohol. But anyway, just on the face value, you give them some money, you feel good, or generosity, or whatever. But that's not compassion, see, because all you've done is feed them for that hour or for that day or whatever. And if you come back along that street and give them money, and then to continually keep doing that, you give them an impression, then they get thinking, well, actually, I don't need to go and look for food. I've got someone who's going to come along and give it to me every day. So that's why that compassion would be completely wrong, because it's uncompassionate. You're taking away that person's livelihood; you're taking away their ability to be a balanced human being. So all that thing of kindness — it's not being kind at all. You're actually being unkind, because we can always cross over into enabling behaviours too. I'm sure you've already got that on board.

At the end of the day as a parent — and I've got many kids — I want them to be self-reliant. That was always my mission: that when I'm not here, or when I'm still here, that they wouldn't be a burden on the world. They wouldn't be like a parasite on the world. They could actually go out, get their food or get whatever they think makes them happy. Not just have everything, but work for it. They got to do things, collect things, preserve them, look after them, whatever it is. Little kids, you give them stuff, and as a dad, like mums too, you become everything that your kids are looking for in a parent. Because you see things from the bigger picture. You're thinking ahead, wanting to guide them, protect them, and prepare them for life. You don't want them to be a parasite on the world, like any sane parent would really think. Or my child, my prodigy. Because if I'm an accountant, I don't necessarily want them to be an accountant. I want them to be a contributor in the world, someone that is not a burden. Sometimes we do need help from others, but I'm just talking specifically on that modus operandi — that if they know how to fish, they go and get fish, and what they've got left, they give to other people. Really, that's it.

In my opinion, considering how the world is, it's a projection of how we are as a group. Individually too, I suppose, but really more as a group. If we think the world is completely fucked up, then our natural feeling would be to try and make it better. If we're ravaged with war — I'm not completely discounting war — but I'm just saying if we feel like that, then we'd be doing everything to bring peace to alleviate that situation, especially alleviate people cause it's seemingly unjust.

Ceremony and the rightness of a ceremony, the tangible outcomes of ceremony — it may be closer to us Indigenous people. In the Western world they're still just the same with their marriage ceremonies, for example, for all the stuff around when babies are born, or even before the baby's born, the baby showers. They're all ceremonies. So we've really had that in us. I just think that there's a better intent. I think it's really to do with intent. And the mind is all about intent, or the awareness is it's all about intent. Even in worldly terms, if people just set their mind on something, they can do it. Ceremony helps with that. It's like a greaser or it oils the wheels of intent. With our tribal kind of thing, it's in that DNA. Ceremony is important, as long as we don't believe that ceremony is the only thing. It's a facilitator. Especially in the group situation, we all recognise how we can become a slightly different person in a group, or things can become more enjoyable, or we can learn better. There are so many examples of why a group works better, and honestly as human beings, that's what we are really. We are like ants and bees and stuff. We need that community. We're not loners; we really are community. Whenever people stray away from those community situations for whatever reason, which is something that we always safeguard in the tribal situation, they can become quite twisted and bizarre people — that is well documented. Serial killers and murderers all have this story of where they're disconnected from the group, isolated. They often use that as a justification of why. And believe it or not, I think about all these things all the time.

It comes back to this ceremony. We could just talk about ceremony for about five volumes, and we still wouldn't be covering it, because the ceremony transcends. It's like a living entity evolving, and such a beautiful thing really. As human beings, we all like beautiful things. We know the world's full of shit things. A lot is just our perception, but at the same time, essentially as a human being, we're kind of like an artist, and life is a canvas. I think most of us generally sane human beings, one way or another, whether we're striving for it or we just found ourselves like that, want to do that. It changes too, as our lives evolve. Some people might say 'grow old', but I would just say, 'evolve'. There's too much emphasis on young and old. I'm just eternally young, the whole time growing up. But when I do it, when I do grow up, I do want to be a fireman — living that dream a little bit.

People are going to be reading this book for all different kinds of reasons. Ayahuasca is a bit of a topic. Shamanism is a bit of a topic that people are interested in these days, and you already talked about why people are attracted to it. And sometimes people are also reading, reading, reading, because they want the answer: what is Ayahuasca? How am I going to do it? Is it safe? What's going to happen? What did that person do? What did this person do? Is it real? Does it work? All these kinds of questions, and you may have conflicts. Writing a book, from my perspective, is a way of trying to share my stories and my perspective, and asking you, what's your perspective? So that people can just share those different perspectives. And to show that there's a diversity of perspectives too, and is there anything that you want to share with the audience about any of that?

Honestly, I think these things are important to the human race, and you gotta get a bit brave. Like I said, you don't know when you're going to die. So, what are your real priorities in life? If I said you had 24 hours to live, what would you do with that? At the end of the day, our culture is 100,000 years old, maybe the culture, or the Ayahuasca is 100,000 years old too. I don't know or even care that much, but these things aren't something that happened last week. They're not something like a drug that was invented in 1990. Or in the case of the COVID drugs, or inventing the vaccinations, obviously it was experimental. These practices, I'd like to say that they were tried and true, but I don't think we necessarily need to say that. Basically they have been happening for thousands of years. They're not new practices, and that should at least in some part of our mind trigger something that gives a sense of viability, that these truths have been tested over a long period of time on many generations of human beings. To me, it makes more sense, even though I might be biased in some ways, with a tradition that goes back to the beginning of time, while people are not feeling so confident with the Western world. You might say Western practices are a new tradition, but it's still based on a lot of old traditions.

Western ways shouldn't just be totally discarded. And at the same time, I don't think we shouldn't totally embrace them either, because the facts are that it is polluting the world. It is taking away a lot of species of animals and plants, beings that we don't even know exist, things challenging their world. This is something that we should really think about at the same time. It needs an element of bravery if you are feeling that all the answers, all the teachings that were given to you as you were growing up — whether by your parents, by your school teachers, by scientists, by books or whatever — are not really completely fulfilling your expectations. Never stop seeking, never stop trying to understand the fabric of reality and just get off at the station. Like, yeah, I've got it now, it's alright, or, the scientists are working on it now, or philosophers. Don't give up. Keep on searching, keep on thinking, go with your intuitive mind, rather than a logical mind, or a balance between the two.

We're specifically talking about plant medicines and plant technologies. I think they're more relevant to the world than ever, and they need to be. They need to be facilitated by good leaders who are not driven by their own ego, so to speak. Leaders that have been levelled out by some kind of tradition, one way or another, and they must see some kind of benefit towards humanity, and they just want to be helpful. Ones that are not claiming to have all the answers at all. Who does? Nobody should make that claim, yet everyone knows that that thinking is at the base of modern sciences.

I believe these things are very important to the world today. Honestly, I do, and actually could be crucial to the survival of mankind. I don't know how humans can just assume that their longevity is based on the fact that they're humans. The whole thing is preposterous. They're overtaken by a great inflated importance of themselves, human beings. They think that humans on Earth are the only important beings in the whole universe — and how preposterous is that? They think they're the boss of the universe, because they're human beings. The whole thing is ridiculous. We need to humble ourselves. We need to just see ourselves as part of the jigsaw of infinite life, infinite worlds, infinite understandings, which in some ways we can never understand completely. Then to be able to function in some way that makes a better world, if it's only just for our children, some kind of legacy, for their grandchildren and great grandchildren. That's what First Nations people normally say: we're doing this for our grandchildren in terms of caring for Country, looking after Country, understanding Country.

These things we talk about are very deep. It's not referring to the land we're standing on top of the soil. It's referring to everything in connection with everything, and a vast majority don't understand. I always emphasise that I don't think every human being needs these specific ceremonies, specific plant medicines, but they need something. They need some kind of journey, some kind of inner journey to understand that the Dream is a Dream that they're having, and it's their own Dream. And they have responsibility to be accountable for that, and also be accountable for the group Dream. If we're humans then we need to be accountable to the group Dream, the group experience, and not just say, 'Oh, it's them, it's not me.' It's all of us; we're all in this together and we can't divorce ourselves. You will divorce yourselves at your own peril, and this is the most important thing I can say. The value of our so-called ancient cultures. Don't even want to use the word 'ancient' really, because it means that it's some kind of relic, or some kind of myth, something that is not relevant anymore. Indigenous culture is very relevant, and it's enduring. And for every human being, in fact every being, it is also their heritage. Just because you were born in Russia or born in Greece or born on the 25th floor of a building in New York, doesn't divorce you at all from any of these things.

Yoeway.

Glossary

Author's note on spiritual language

The terms defined in this glossary come from rich and diverse spiritual traditions—many rooted in ancestral and Indigenous knowledge systems. Defining them in modern language is inherently limited. Even with familiar concepts like 'God,' countless perspectives exist. Spiritual terminology must always be understood within its cultural, historical, and ancestral context.

As shared by Ibã Sales, a Huni Kuin Elder, pajé, cacique and visionary artist, many sacred chants and words are not meant to be translated literally into Portuguese—or English. Their origins lie in spiritual dimensions, carried by ancestral beings and received through dreams, visions, and ceremonial states. He explains that these sacred songs (called *txirin* or *ishkavo*) often resist simple verbal interpretation. Instead, the Huni Kuin convey their meanings through painting, body art, kenê (sacred geometric design), and the layered symbols of visionary art.

> *Because our sacred songs are like a language of the forest... it's not possible to translate directly into Portuguese or English and have the same power. But when we paint them, the song is still alive.* — Ibã Huni Kuin / Isaias Sales Kaxinawá

Rather than fixed definitions, this glossary offers signposts—a guide to further inquiry and respectful learning. These terms cannot be fully grasped outside the land, people, and ceremonial life that gave rise to them. To truly understand many of these concepts, one must sit with the songs, witness the designs, and enter into relationship with the cultural and spiritual worlds they reflect.

Use this glossary not as an endpoint, but as a doorway—an invitation to listen, to feel, and to deepen your connection with the living traditions from which these words emerge.

Aboriginal: Refers to the First Peoples of the Australian continent, whose lineages, languages, and Dreamings have sustained an unbroken relationship with Country for tens of thousands of years. The term encompasses hundreds of distinct Nations and cultural identities, each with its own law, kinship, and cosmology. *Note: Some Indigenous Australians prefer the term* Original *or their specific Nation name rather than* Aboriginal.

Amazon: The vast living forest and river basin spanning much of South America — a breathing, interwoven ecosystem of immense biodiversity and spiritual intelligence. It is both a physical region and a sacred organism, the heart-lung of the Earth, where forest, river, human, and spirit exist as one continuous field of life.

Avalon: The mystical island of the Celtic and Arthurian traditions — a realm of mist and enchantment said to lie beyond the mortal world, where heroes journey for healing and initiation. Known as the 'Isle of Apples,' it symbolizes renewal, immortality, and the eternal feminine. In myth, Avalon is where King Arthur is taken to recover from his wounds and where priestesses, often associated with Morgan le Fay, guard the secrets of balance and transformation. Spiritually, Avalon represents the threshold between worlds — a sanctuary of divine mystery, the heart of the old ways where the Earth's magic and the soul's wisdom meet

Axé: Creative power. Sacred vitality. The current of divine authority that turns intention into reality. The vital force that animates all existence — the current of divine potency that flows through nature, ancestors, orixás, humans, and sacred ritual. In Candomblé, Axé is a metaphysical substance as real as breath or blood: it can be cultivated, transmitted, strengthened, or diminished. It is the power that allows a work to manifest, a prayer to take root, a healing to hold. Axé is carried in gestures, songs, offerings, herbs, consecrated objects, and the disciplined presence of the initiated. It is generated through alignment with one's ori (crown), with the orixás, and with the ethical harmony of community.

Ayahuasca: A sacred Amazonian sacrament born from the union of two plants — the *Banisteriopsis caapi* vine and *Psychotria viridis* leaves — Ayahuasca, the 'vine of the soul,' opens gateways into expanded states of consciousness. It is revered across Indigenous Amazonian cultures as a living, intelligent spirit and divine teacher that bridges the physical and spiritual worlds, guiding humanity toward healing, humility, and remembrance of our unity with nature. More than a brew, Ayahuasca is a being — a mirror of creation's mystery that reveals the heart of the forest and the Dreaming of the Earth.

Bailado: In Brazilian spiritual traditions, particularly within *Santo Daime*, the *bailado* refers to the sacred dance performed during ritual works. It is a rhythmic, meditative movement in concentric lines, embodying harmony, discipline, and devotion. Each step follows the compass of the hymns (*hinos*), expressing the integration of body, spirit, and cosmos. Through the *bailado*, participants align with the current of the Divine — a choreography of prayer where every motion becomes an offering of light, balance, and unity.

Caboclo: A term with layered meaning in Brazilian culture and spirituality. Culturally, it refers to people of mixed Indigenous and African ancestry — the forest people, strong, humble, and deeply connected to the land. In the spiritual traditions of **Umbanda** and **Candomblé**, *Caboclos* are powerful ancestral spirits of Indigenous origin who work through mediums in ceremony, bringing healing, protection, and wisdom. They are the guardians of nature and courage, embodying the strength of the forest and the clarity of truth. When a Caboclo speaks through a medium, it is said that the voice of the forest itself is speaking — firm, direct, and full of heart.

Cacique: A term commonly used in Brazilian Portuguese to refer to an Indigenous chief, leader, or Elder responsible for guiding a community. The word originates from the Taíno language of the Caribbean and was adopted by Portuguese and Spanish colonisers to describe tribal leaders across the Americas. In contemporary Brazil, *cacique* carries both cultural and political weight, often representing a traditional authority who embodies the wisdom, responsibility, and leadership within Indigenous villages. While the role and recognition of a *cacique* may vary between Indigenous nations, it is typically rooted in communal respect, responsibility, ancestral lineage, and a deep commitment to cultural preservation and protection of the land.

Callanish (Calanais): A large stone circle, rising from the moors of the Isle of Lewis in Scotland's Outer Hebrides, is a neolithic temple aligned with the movements of the Sun, Moon, and stars. Erected over 5,000 years ago, these standing stones mark a place where sky and earth converse — a site of ancient ritual, astronomical observation, and spiritual communion. Callanish stands as a sentinel of the old ways — a timeless circle of stone and silence bridging human consciousness with the cosmos.

Candomblé: An Afro-Brazilian religion rooted in West African Yoruba, Bantu, and Fon traditions, brought to Brazil by enslaved Africans and preserved through centuries of resistance and adaptation. Centred around devotion to the *Orixás* — divine forces of nature — Candomblé honours the cycles of life through drumming, dance, song, and sacred offerings. Each ritual celebrates the unity of Earth and spirit, where the human body becomes an instrument through which the forces express their power, beauty, and wisdom

Ciranda: In Brazilian culture refers to a traditional circle dance of the Northeast region of Pernambuco — a communal rhythm of joy, unity, and movement where people join hands and step together to the beat of drums and song. It celebrates equality and belonging, dissolving barriers between dancer and dance, individual and community. For **Carioca Freitas**, *Ciranda* became the name of his spiritual house and centre — a living temple of music, prayer, and ceremony where the circle is both literal and symbolic. It's a weaving of Santo Daime, Afro-Brazilian, Indigenous, and universal traditions into a ceremonial culture of joy and happiness — the great dance of life where all paths meet in song, healing, and beauty.

Clever-man: A traditional Aboriginal healer, lawman, and spiritual intermediary — one who has undergone deep initiation and training to work with the powers of the unseen. Guided by ancestral spirits and the lore of Country, the Clever Man heals, protects, and restores balance within community and land. His knowledge is not learned from books but through direct transmission from the Elders and the spirit world — a sacred responsibility carried with discipline, humility, and respect.

Country: Country is not just land — it is a living presence that holds spirit, ancestry, language, and law. For Aboriginal peoples of Australia, Country is family and consciousness itself; it breathes through songlines, animals, plants, waters, rocks, and sky. To care for Country is to be in right relationship with the Earth and all beings — a reciprocal bond of belonging, responsibility, and reverence that connects past, present, and future as one unbroken Dreaming.

Cultural appropriation: The act of adopting elements of a culture—such as its symbols, language, dress, ceremonies, or spiritual practices—without permission, deep understanding, or respectful relationship with the people who carry it. In this book's context, it particularly refers to those who mimic or commercialise Indigenous or traditional identities (such as Amazonian or Aboriginal practices) without having done the relational, initiatory, or respectful work required. It often involves taking without giving back, misrepresenting sacred knowledge, and can cause harm to both the integrity of the culture and the individuals who carry it.

Cura: Meaning 'healing,' is one of the principal Santo Daime works and the root of Carioca's Ciranda tradition— a ceremony dedicated to physical, emotional, and spiritual restoration. Conducted through song, prayer, and the sacramental use of Daime, it aligns participants with Divine harmony and invokes the healing presence of the forest and the celestial realms. In contemporary expressions, such as those developed by students of Mestre Irineu, Padrinho Sebastião and other spiritual leaders such as Carioca, the Cura has evolved into multi-day ceremonies that unite practices of discipline and firmeza, joy, and freedom — healing through the vibration of sound and love.

Curandeiro: A *curandeiro* (*curandeira* for women) is a traditional healer — one who works with sacred plants, songs, and spirits to restore harmony between body, mind, and soul. Within Ayahuasca traditions, the curandeiro/a serves as an intermediary between worlds, guided by the living intelligence of the plants and the spiritual forces of the forest. Their art is not only in curing illness, but in realigning the soul with its natural rhythm and reawakening connection to the Divine — a practice of deep listening, prayer, and communion with the unseen.

Dadirri: A Ngangikurungkurr word from the Daly River region in northern Australia, means 'deep listening' — an inner stillness and receptive awareness of the world around and within. It is a contemplative way of being that listens not only with the ears, but with the whole being: to Country, to spirit, to others, and to the silence between words. Practising dadirri awakens communion with the land and the unseen, fostering respect, patience, and relational balance — a spiritual discipline of attunement to the living intelligence of creation.

Daime: The Holy sacrament used within the Santo Daime spiritual doctrine of Brazil, which blends Indigenous Amazonian plant medicine with Christian, African, and esoteric mysticism. While the brew itself is the same concoction as Ayahuasca, *Daime* is understood as the 'Holy giving' — a communion with the Divine Light of Christ through the forest's spirit. Its ceremonies are disciplined, musical, and devotional, embodying a theology of love, harmony, and service. In Daime, the sacrament carries doctrine and traditions and is seen as a living bridge between the human heart, the forest, and the celestial realms.

Didgeridoo / Yidaki: An ancient wind instrument originating from the Yolngu people of Arnhem Land in Northern Australia. Carved from termite-hollowed eucalyptus trees, it produces a deep, resonant drone used in ceremony, healing, and storytelling. Beyond music, the Yidaki is a sacred voice of Country — a bridge between human breath and the spirit of the land, echoing the sounds of creation. Its song carries law, lineage, and the vibration of ancestral presence.

Dreaming: Also called *Dreamtime* or *Tjukurpa* in some Aboriginal cultures refers to the spiritual, ancestral, and cosmological order of existence — the great Storying that shapes all life. It encompasses creation, law, ceremony, and the ongoing presence of ancestral beings who continue to animate the land. Dreaming is not a past event but a continuous field of consciousness; every person, mountain, river, and being carries its Dreaming, a thread that flows as the eternal song of creation.

Dreamspell: A modern interpretation, living prophecy and continuation of the ancient Mayan calendar, developed by José Argüelles as a spiritual framework for re-synchronising human consciousness with natural time. Based on the 13-Moon, 28-day cycle and the Tzolkin harmonic matrix, it encodes a cosmology of harmony, galactic resonance, and evolutionary awakening. The Dreamspell invites participants to live in rhythm with the "law of time" — *time as art* — and to awaken to the multidimensional unity of self, planet, and cosmos.

Druid: A spiritual practitioner and wisdom-keeper from the ancient Celtic world, revered as a mediator between nature, humanity, and the unseen. In both historical and modern contexts, Druids embody the sacred sciences of the Earth — blending philosophy, poetry, astronomy, and ritual to honour the cycles of life. They serve as guardians of natural law and memory, keepers of ceremony who listen to the voice of the land and uphold the harmony between all realms.

Ego: In psycho-spiritual understanding, the ego is the constructed identity — the story of 'I' — that filters experience and seeks control or validation. It is neither enemy nor essence, but a temporary structure that allows consciousness to navigate human life. Through inner work and expanded awareness, the ego can be integrated rather than dissolved — transformed from an architecture of defence into a transparent vessel through which higher awareness, compassion, and authenticity may flow.

Estrela da Ciranda: The living prayer and spiritual point of light established in Australia by Lore Solaris and the community around his work. With roots in Amazonian Indigenous practices and a deep connection with Country in Australia, the culture of this point of light follows the tradition of Carioca Freitas and his global Ciranda community. The practices have roots in Santo Daime, from the lineage of Padrinho Sebastião and Mestre Ireneu and the Afro-Brazilian traditions of Umbanda and Candomblé.

Firmeza: Literally means firmness, yet in the Santo Daime and other Brazilian Ayahuasca traditions it signifies an inner spiritual alignment — the capacity to remain centred, steady, and clear within the current of the ceremony and life itself. It is the discipline of presence: holding faith, posture, and prayer even amid challenge or visionary turbulence. To have firmeza is to stand rooted in the Light, anchored in truth, service and devotion, allowing the Divine force to work through one's being with grace and strength and without the interference of ego.

Gira: In the Brazilian Umbanda tradition, a gira is a ritual ceremony or spiritual gathering in which spirits or entities (such as *Orixás, caboclos, pretosvelhos, Exus, Pombagiras*) are invoked and may manifest through mediumship/incorporation.

Great Spirit: The animating force that breathes life into all beings — the eternal consciousness that connects Earth, sky, and every living thing. In both North and South American Indigenous traditions, the Great Spirit is not separate from nature but embodied within it: the wind, the water, the fire, and the heartbeat of the land. It is the unifying mystery behind creation, honoured through prayer, ceremony, and right relationship — a reminder that Spirit moves through all things and that life itself is sacred.

God: In the Santo Daime doctrine, *God* is experienced not as a distant figure but as the living presence of divine love and consciousness within all creation. The teachings reveal that the essence of Christ — the spirit of universal truth — resides in every heart, and that the forest itself is an expression of this divine intelligence. Through the sacrament of Daime, practitioners seek direct communion with God as light, love, and wisdom — the source from which all life flows and to which all returns.

Hãtxa Kuĩ: Translates as 'true language,' or 'true word,' is the ancestral tongue of the Huni Kuin people, belonging to the Pano linguistic family of the western Amazon. More than a means of communication, it is a vessel of ceremony, cosmology, and ecological knowledge — each word carrying layers of mythic, spiritual, and environmental meaning. Through *Hãtxa Kuĩ*, songs (*huni meka*), prayers, and teachings transmit the living consciousness of the forest, preserving the tribe's sacred connection to the spirits of nature and the universe.

Haux: A sacred ceremonial word from the Huni Kuin people of the Brazilian Amazon. In ritual contexts, *haux* of *haux haux* is used by ritual leaders (pajés/txanã) at the start or end of prayer, song or healing, signifying a deep spiritual invocation or commitment. Symbolically, it invokes the first sound of creation, the first sound uttered by the creator serpent, the Jiboia, and carries the force of acknowledgement, agreement, and alignment with the spirit world. In contemporary practice it may also be used more broadly as a greeting, affirmation or expression of thanks—but always retains ancestral resonance, and is not treated lightly in ceremonial settings. Huni Kuin leader and pajé *Ibã Isaias Sales* explained: '*The meaning of Haux is peace, love and harmony. This language is from the Enchanted Jiboia — not from the Huni Kuin. Through these sounds, this language, we can travel in the miração.*'

Hinário: A sacred collection of hymns or spiritual songs received through vision, prayer, or divine inspiration during Ayahuasca work. In the Santo Daime and related lineages, it forms the living scripture of the doctrine — each hymn a calling, a teaching, a healing, and a transmission of spiritual force. Sung collectively in ceremony, a hinário is both a map and a medicine, guiding participants through cycles of learning, purification, and revelation. In the broader Ayahuasca movement, the hinário is a song book that represents the evolving voice of the forest — the continual unfolding of sacred song as a pathway of remembrance, harmony, and awakening.

Huni Kuin: The Huni Kuin (Huni Kuĩ), whose name means 'true people,' are an Indigenous nation of the western Amazon, living primarily along the rivers of Acre, Brazil, and eastern Peru. They are also known by the anthropological term 'Kaxinawá.' Their culture is rooted in a profound reciprocity with the forest — expressed through art, song, ceremony, and the sacred medicine *Nixi Pãe* (Ayahuasca). The Huni Kuin see life as an interwoven field of beings and forces, where humans, animals, plants, and spirits coexist in mutual respect. Their traditions embody beauty, discipline, and harmony — a living cosmology in which every act, from painting *kenê* designs to singing to the fire, reaffirms humanity's place within the Dreaming heart of the forest.

Huni Meka: means 'songs of the true people' for the Huni Kuin people. These are the sacred healing songs sung during *Nixi Pae* (Ayahuasca) ceremonies, carrying the voice and wisdom of the forest. Each *meka* is a living prayer — a bridge between human and spirit, guiding the visions, invoking the plant teachers, and harmonising the energies of the participants. Through the *Huni Meka*, the Huni Kuin connect with their ancestors, the forces of nature, and the great spirit *Yuxibu*, maintaining balance and remembrance of their place in the web of life. The true meaning of the songs cannot be translated cleanly into English or Portuguese, their translation is through art. *"The healing work — the work with our relatives, with the receiving, with the visitor who comes to be healed in the forest... all of this speech, everything I'm saying here, this is healing. This healing plant of Nixi Pãe, from the pedagogy of the Huni Kuin, is the spirit, it is the language of the Jiboia. This song he is singing — this is the language of the Jiboia."* - Ibã Huni Kuin / Isaias Sales Kaxinawá

Icaro: A sacred medicine song — a vibrational technology sung by shamans, curanderos, and plant healers during ceremony to summon, guide, and harmonise spiritual forces. In native Amazonian cultures, icaros are not simply melodies but living entities, each carrying the consciousness of the plant spirits and the forest from which it was learned. They weave sound into healing, vision, and transformation — sonic maps through which the unseen realms are navigated. Across cultures and lineages, icaros express the voice of the forest itself, a bridge between human breath and the vast intelligence of nature.

Incorporation: In Brazilian Portuguese, *Incorporação* refers to the process by which a spiritual entity temporarily enters and animates the body of a medium. In Afro-Brazilian traditions, it is considered a sacred act of service — a moment where divine or ancestral forces work through the practitioner to offer healing, protection, or teaching. It is approached with discipline and humility, cultivated through years of spiritual training and devotion

Indigenous: refers to both the First Peoples of specific lands, and to the deeper ancestral consciousness within all humans that remember how to live in harmony with Earth and Spirit. It honours those cultures that have preserved this wisdom through ceremony, song, and reciprocity / connection to Country — the living custodians of planetary balance. To be Indigenous, in this sense, is to belong to the Earth as kin: to walk with reverence, responsibility, and awareness of the invisible threads that unite all beings in the Dreaming of the Whole Earth.

Jiboia: The boa-constrictor, is one of the most revered spiritual beings within Brazilian Indigenous Ayahuasca traditions, especially among the Huni Kuin and Yawanawá peoples. Seen as an ancient ancestor and master of transformation, the Jiboia is the keeper of the mysteries of *Nixi Pae* (Ayahuasca) and a bridge between the worlds of water, earth, and Spirit. Its shedding of skin embodies renewal and healing, teaching humans to release what no longer serves and to awaken their vision. In ceremony, the Jiboia's spirit is invoked through song and vision as a guardian, healer, and cosmic teacher — the great serpent of the forest that dreams the world into being.

Juramidam: The sacred name for the spiritual current or Christic consciousness at the heart of Santo Daime — the universal spirit of love, light, and truth that flows through all creation. Followers often describe Juramidam as both the collective brotherhood [sic] of all beings working in this light and the divine force that unites them in harmony with God, nature, and humanity.

Kambô: a traditional Amazonian medicine derived from the secretion of the *Phyllomedusa bicolor* tree frog, used by Indigenous peoples such as the Huni Kuin and Yawanawá for purification, strength, and spiritual cleansing. Applied through small burns on the skin, it is believed to clear toxins and dense energies from the body and energetic field. Within Ayahuasca lineages, Kambô is seen as a complementary ally — a warrior medicine that fortifies the body, heightens awareness, and restores equilibrium between the physical and spiritual realms.

Katxanawa: Within the culture of the Huni Kuin of the western, upper Amazon, the Katxanawa is a ceremonial celebration of harvest, fertility, and the renewing life-force of the forest. It brings together songs, dance, sacred plants and community in a deep ritual of communion with the ancestral, vegetal and animal realms.

Kené: A sacred term among the Huni Kuin and other peoples of the BrazilianPeruvian Amazon, often translated as the 'true design' or 'true drawing.' It refers to the complex geometric patterns used in textile weaving, body and face painting, basketry and other art forms. The Huni Kuin have 62 different types of kené. These designs are also a spiritual language and carry cosmological meaning, serve as identity markers and link craft, ritual, and ancestral knowledge. Because the practice is both aesthetic and symbolic, the word is best understood as a cultural concept rather than a simple 'pattern.'

Loch: the Scottish Gaelic word for 'lake' or 'sea inlet,' yet in Celtic tradition it carries deeper resonance — a place where the veil between worlds grows thin. Lochs are often associated with mystery, guardianship, and ancient feminine energies of water and transformation. Across Scotland and Ireland, sacred lochs mark liminal thresholds between the material and the mystical, where myth, landscape, and spirit flow together in the living memory of the land.

Madrinha: Meaning "godmother" in Portuguese, *Madrinha* refers to a female spiritual guide or elder in Brazilian traditions such as Santo Daime and occasionally Umbanda. A *Madrinha* holds a similar role to a *Padrinho* (male counterpart), embodying wisdom, nurturing, and ceremonial leadership. Often revered for her intuition, compassion, and depth of experience, the *Madrinha* plays a vital role in transmitting spiritual teachings, holding space in ceremony, and supporting the wellbeing and development of the community.

Mãe de Santo: In Candomblé and Umbanda, an initiated high priestess and spiritual leader who serves as guardian of the *terreiro*, guiding rituals, initiations, and the relationship between the community and the *Orixás*. She embodies wisdom, discipline, and devotion — the maternal channel through which the divine forces of nature are honoured and balanced.

Mayan Calendar: an ancient Mesoamerican system of timekeeping developed by the Mayan civilisation, designed not merely to mark days but to reflect the sacred rhythm of cosmic and earthly cycles. It interweaves the *Tzolk'in* (a 260-day harmonic module) with the **Haab'** (a 365-day solar cycle), creating the *Calendar Round*, and extends into vast epochs through a long count, which tracks the unfolding of world ages. For the Maya, time is alive — a spiralling continuum of artful creation where each moment carries its own spiritual essence and purpose. The calendar is a tool of prophecy, ceremony, and alignment, guiding human consciousness to live in harmony with cosmic order and the evolving Dream of the Earth.

Mediumship: The spiritual practice of communicating with or embodying spirits for healing and guidance. In Umbanda and Candomblé, mediums (*médiuns*) act as channels for ancestral and elemental entities — such as *caboclos*, *pretos velhos*, and *exús* — during sacred ceremonies known as *giras*. In Santo Daime, mediumistic sensitivity is integrated more subtly into the collective ritual, expressed through song, prayer, and intuitive communion with divine beings

Miração: From the Portuguese *mirar* — 'to see' or 'to gaze' — and refers to the visionary experience within Ayahuasca ceremonies. In Brazilian Indigenous and Santo Daime contexts, it is understood not as hallucination, but as *revelation*: a spiritual visionary state through which the drinker perceives deeper dimensions of reality. The miração is both a teaching and a healing — an encounter with the intelligence of the forest, the Divine, or one's own soul. Guided by sacred songs and disciplined intention, it becomes a bridge between worlds where insight, purification, and communion with Spirit unfold through light, sound, and inner vision.

Nagual: In Toltec cosmology, the *Nagual* is the unseen realm of energy and spirit — the infinite mystery that exists beyond the boundaries of the rational mind. It is also the term for the spiritual guide or master who can navigate both the ordinary world (*Tonal*) and the unseen (*Nagual*) with awareness. The Nagual is the field of pure potential, the source from which all forms arise, teaching that true freedom comes from awakening to what exists beyond personal identity and illusion.

Nixi Pãe: Translates as 'vine of vision' or 'enchanted vine' — is the Huni Kuin name for Ayahuasca. Within their cosmology it is a sacred, conscious being and teacher, guiding practitioners to heal, learn, and remember their interconnectedness with the forest and all life. Nixi Pãe ceremony is a dialogue between human and plant spirit, conducted through songs (*huni meka*), prayer, and disciplined presence.

Noosphere: The emerging field of planetary consciousness — the living mind of the Earth awakening through humanity. As envisioned by José Argüelles, it is an emergent layer of planetary consciousness, where human thought, art, and spirit unify with the biosphere in a field of collective awareness. In Argüelles's vision, the noosphere is the next evolutionary stage of Earth — a telepathic web of harmony between humanity and nature, guided by the rhythms of the natural time (Mayan Calendar). In the *Dreaming of the Whole Earth*, the noosphere is the planet's own Dream of unity — the moment when human awareness and the Earth's intelligence remember themselves as one.

Orixá: A divine force of nature — a living expression of the sacred that bridges the human and cosmic realms. Originating in the Yoruba traditions of West Africa and carried to Brazil through Candomblé and Umbanda, each Orixá embodies an element of creation: the rivers, the ocean, the thunder, the wind, the forest, the fire. They are deities and energies, ancestors and archetypes, guiding human life through rhythm, song, and ritual. To honour an Orixá is to honour the natural world itself — the luminous intelligence flowing through all existence, reminding us that the Divine moves through every breath, heartbeat, and wave. More details of specific Orixás can be found in Chapter 4: *The Way of the Hummingbird*.

Neo-Shamanism: A modern, often Western interpretation and adaptation of Indigenous shamanic practices. It typically draws from various global traditions—Amazonian, Native North American, Siberian, Celtic, and others—blending them into new spiritual frameworks that often lack direct transmission or cultural grounding. While some neo-shamanic paths are approached with sincere respect and careful study, many risk appropriation, commodification, or distortion of sacred traditions. This term is not inherently negative, but it does raise critical questions about authenticity, responsibility, and the importance of context. In today's rapidly evolving spiritual landscape, neo-shamanism can be a doorway for healing and connection, but it must be approached with humility, discernment, and deep respect for the Indigenous cultures from which its practices are inspired.

Padrinho: A Portuguese term meaning 'godfather,' used within Brazilian spiritual traditions such as Santo Daime and sometimes in Umbanda. A *Padrinho* is a respected male spiritual guide, elder, or ceremonial leader—often someone who has undergone deep initiatory processes and holds responsibility for guiding others on the spiritual path. The role is relational rather than hierarchical, grounded in trust, humility, and service to the community. It signifies a mentor or guardian within the lineage of sacred teachings. The female equivalent is *Madrinha*.

Pai de Santo: The male counterpart of *Mãe de Santo* — the initiated priest or father of the terreiro — who leads ceremonies and mediates between the *Orixás*, the spirits, and the people.

Pajé: A traditional Indigenous healer and spiritual leader in Brazil — one who bridges the worlds of human and spirit through prayer, plant medicine, and song. The Pajé carries deep ancestral knowledge of nature's forces and works to restore harmony between body, community, and the unseen realms. Outside of Brazilian culture they may be referred to as 'shaman.'

Peyote: A small cactus (*Lophophora williamsii*) native to the deserts of Mexico and the southwestern United States, revered by many Indigenous peoples of North America as a sacred teacher and medicine. Containing the psychoactive alkaloid mescaline, Peyote is used ceremonially within the Native American Church and other traditional contexts to promote healing, vision, and communion with the Great Spirit. Its use is guided by prayer, song, and deep respect, serving as a path of purification and truth. For many nations, Peyote is not a drug but a living sacrament — a doorway to divine understanding and right relationship with creation.

Queen of the Forest: In the Santo Daime tradition, the *Queen of the Forest* is the divine feminine spirit of the Daime — the celestial presence who revealed the doctrine to Mestre Irineu in the Amazon. She embodies the living consciousness of the forest, the maternal face of God manifest through nature, and serves as teacher, healer, and guide for humanity. Through her visions and hymns, she instructed Irineu in the ways of love, discipline, and self-transformation, giving rise to a global spiritual movement that unites Christianity, Indigenous wisdom, and the mystical intelligence of the Earth.

Quetzalcoatl: An important deity in ancient Mesoamerican spirituality, particularly among the Aztec, Toltec, and Maya civilizations. The name *Quetzalcoatl* means "Feathered Serpent" in Nahuatl—symbolizing a fusion of sky (quetzal bird) and earth (serpent). Revered as a god of wind, learning, creation, and cultural evolution, Quetzalcoatl is also seen as a civilizing figure who brought knowledge, language, and sacred rituals to humanity. In modern spiritual circles, Quetzalcoatl is often invoked as a symbol of awakened consciousness, spiritual sovereignty, and the balance of dual forces—such as heaven and earth, masculine and feminine. Some Amazonian and pan-Indigenous movements include references to Quetzalcoatl in visions, dreams, or ceremonies as part of a shared ancestral cosmology.

Rapé: pronounced 'ha-peh' is a sacred Amazonian snuff made from finely ground medicinal plants, ashes, and seeds. Blown into the nostrils through a pipe called a *tepi* or *kuripe*, it is used to cleanse, ground, and align the mind and spirit. Indigenous peoples regard rapé as a medicine of cleansing, focus and protection — a prayer carried on the breath that clears stagnant energy and reconnects the individual with the spirit of the forest.

Sananga: A traditional medicine prepared from the roots and bark of the *Tabernaemontana* shrub, used by Indigenous healers to purify physical and spiritual vision. When applied as eye drops, it produces a sharp, brief pain followed by clarity and energetic cleansing. Sananga is believed to balance inner sight, dispel negative energies, and open perception — a luminous medicine that awakens the light of truth within the eyes and soul.

Santo Daime: A Brazilian spiritual doctrine founded in the early 20th century by Mestre Irineu in Acre, blending Amazonian shamanism with Christian, Afro-Brazilian, and esoteric influences. The word *Daime* means 'give me,' reflecting a prayerful request for Divine guidance — *give me strength, give me faith, give me love*. The religion centres on the sacramental use of *Daime* [Ayahuasca], in ceremonial 'works' of prayer, song, and discipline, designed to align the soul with divine light and service.

Saravá: A ritual greeting and blessing meaning 'salutations,' 'may it be blessed,' or 'hail the sacred force.' Saravá is both a word and an energetic gesture — an invocation of harmony, respect, and the living presence of the spiritual lines that support the work. Spoken to honor the orixás, to greet the spirits, to acknowledge another practitioner, or to sanctify a moment within ritual. 'Saravá' carries the vibration of opening a path, aligning intentions, clearing interference, and affirming that the *Axé* is flowing. A blessing that affirms connection. A recognition of the sacred current moving between people, spirits, and the *terreiro* itself.

Shamanism: A term used to describe a wide range of ancestral spiritual practices found across Indigenous cultures worldwide, shamanism is a way of connecting with the spirit world through altered states of consciousness, ritual, prayer, and communion with nature. In many cultures, the shaman is a healer, guide, and bridge between the physical and spiritual realms, often called upon for insight, medicine, or ceremonial leadership. The word 'shaman' originates from the Tungusic

Evenki people of Siberia, but the practices it points to are far older and more widespread. The term 'shamanism' is a broad label placed by outsiders, and many cultures have their own unique names, cosmologies, and protocols that differ greatly. True shamanic practice is rooted in lineage, land, and lived initiatory experience, and cannot be detached from its cultural context without losing its integrity.

Songlines: Sacred pathways that map both land and spirit — routes of ancestral journeys remembered and evoked in song, story, dance, and art. They are living networks of electromagnetic vibration that transmit knowledge connecting places, peoples, and cosmologies across the continent and the world. To follow a songline is to walk in the footsteps of the ancestors, reactivating creation through memory, rhythm, and respect. These songs are both geography and theology — the landscape sung into being and sustained through ceremony.

Spirit: The animating essence that moves through all things — the invisible current of life, consciousness, and creation. It is both immanent and transcendent: the breath within every being and the vast intelligence beyond form. Across traditions, Spirit is known by many names — *Yuxibu, Orixá, Great Spirit, Divine Light* — yet always points to the same truth: that all existence is alive, interconnected, and sacred. To live in communion with Spirit is to remember our origin and our purpose — to walk with awareness that every thought, song, and breath participates in the dreaming of the whole.

Syncretism: The sacred blending of spiritual lineages — the meeting of Indigenous, African, and Christian cosmologies into a unified current of faith and devotion. In Brazil's sacred traditions such as Santo Daime, Umbanda, and Candomblé, syncretism is seen as evolution; a living dialogue between ancestral wisdoms, each contributing its own melody to the same divine song. Through this merging, Spirit expresses itself in new forms of ceremony, song, and symbolism, revealing that the essence of truth is universal and can wear many faces while flowing from the same source of Divine light.

Terreiro: The sacred ground or temple where ceremonies of Candomblé, Umbanda, and other Afro-Brazilian traditions are held. It is both a physical and energetic space — an altar of Earth, song, and Spirit where humans commune with the *Orixás*, ancestral forces, spirits of the land and ancestral beings. Every terreiro is considered a living being, consecrated to specific deities, where the rhythms of drumming, prayer, dance and herbalism awaken the harmony between the human community and the powers of nature

Toltec: A culture and tradition originating from the ancient wisdom of Central Mexico, later carried forward through lineages of seers and teachers such as those described by Don Miguel Ruiz and Carlos Castaneda. In its deeper sense, 'Toltec' means *artist of the spirit* — one who shapes reality consciously through awareness, impeccability, and intent. The Toltec path is not a religion but a way of mastery: transforming the Dream of life from fear into love, and awakening the creative power to dream the world awake.

Tonal: For the Toltecs is the realm of the known — the structured, visible world of names, roles, and perception that forms our everyday reality. It encompasses language, personality, and the order we impose upon existence. In Toltec teaching, balance between *Tonal* and *Nagual* is essential: the Tonal grounds and gives form to life, while the Nagual dissolves boundaries and reconnects us to the vastness of Spirit. Mastery lies in walking with awareness in both worlds — shaping the dream consciously while remembering the mystery from which it arises.

Totem: A spiritual ally or ancestral being that embodies the deep kinship between humans, animals, and the natural world. In many Indigenous traditions, a totem represents both lineage and guidance — a living symbol of one's spiritual family in nature. It may appear as an animal, plant, or elemental force that reflects the qualities and teachings of the person or community it protects. To walk with a totem is to recognise the mirror of spirit in all forms of life — to honour the web of relationship that unites the human soul with the greater consciousness of the Earth.

Txai: Traditionally a specifically masculine kinship term of respect amongst the Huni Kuin, meaning 'brother,' 'ally,' or 'companion on the path.' It expresses reciprocity and kinship — the recognition that all beings are relatives in the great web of life. To call someone *Txai* is to acknowledge shared spirit and equality, affirming the sacred bond of friendship and harmony that unites human and non-human worlds.

Txana: Both the name of a sacred bird and an honorific title among the Huni Kuin people of the western Amazon. As a title, it denotes a spiritual singer or leader who channels the healing force of the *huni meka* — the sacred songs of the forest. The Txana carries the voice of the plants, animals, and spirits, weaving songlines that guide ceremony and sustain the community's connection to the living cosmos. The bird known as txana has the ability to imitate the sounds of other birds in the forest.

Umbanda: a syncretic Brazilian spiritual tradition blending African, Indigenous, and Catholic elements with Spiritism. It honours the *Orixás* as divine embodiments of nature's forces and works with spiritual entities such as *caboclos, pretos velhos, exús* and others through mediumship, music, prayers, offerings and healing practices including with natural plants, flowers and herbs. Umbanda's ceremonies, called *giras*, are celebrations of healing, charity, and balance — a living dialogue between the material and spiritual worlds where love and service are the highest offerings.

Uní: The Yawanawá people's name for Ayahuasca, revered as a divine sacrament that opens vision, purifies the heart, and strengthens one's relationship with the spiritual world. For the Yawanawá, Uní is both medicine and spirit — a path to knowledge, courage, and truth guided by ancestral song and sacred tradition.

União do Vegetal (UDV): Meaning 'Union of the Plants' — is a Brazilian spiritual doctrine founded in 1961 by Mestre José Gabriel da Costa. The tradition centres on the ceremonial use of *Hoasca* (Ayahuasca) as a sacrament for spiritual study and moral development. Rooted in Christian ethics yet deeply influenced by Indigenous and esoteric teachings, the UDV emphasises discipline, fraternity, and direct experience of the Divine through clarity of mind rather than vision. Its ceremonies are structured, guided by dialogue and reflection, aiming to unite science and spirit, reason and faith, the human being and the living intelligence of nature.

Wachuma: Also known as *San Pedro* — is a sacred cactus (*Echinopsis pachanoi*) native to the Andes, used for thousands of years in Peruvian and other South American Indigenous traditions. Containing mescaline, it is revered as a plant teacher that opens the heart, expands perception, and connects the practitioner to the living consciousness of nature. In Andean cosmology, Wachuma is associated with the great serpent and the Christic light — a bridge between heaven and earth. Ceremonies with Wachuma are guided by prayer, music, and silence, inviting deep healing, compassion, and the remembrance that all life is woven in a single field of spirit.

Xurú: Within the cosmology of the Huni Kuin people, *Xurú* carries layered meaning that interweaves plant, song, and spirit. In the context of the Katxanawa, a traditional fertility and renewal ceremony, *Xurú* is invoked both as a sacred plant — the name given to marijuana within Huni Kuin culture — and as an energetic ally sung into the ritual through prayer and *huni meka* (sacred songs). Rather than being used recreationally, *Xurú* is woven into the ceremonial field as part of the living cosmology of the forest, representing growth, sensuality, and the creative life force.

Yarn: a conversational practice of storytelling and truth-sharing grounded in deep listening, equality, and relational respect. In Aboriginal culture, yarning is how knowledge is passed — not through debate or hierarchy, but through story, presence, and shared understanding. Each person's voice is honoured as part of the collective narrative. To yarn is to weave truth, to listen with heart, and to build connection — a sacred conversation where wisdom moves through the circle, not from the top down

Yawanawá: The 'people of the wild boar,' are an Indigenous nation of the upper Amazon in Acre, Brazil. Their culture is rooted in harmony with the forest, expressed through intricate body art, vibrant music, and devotion to sacred ceremonies with Uní (Ayahuasca). The Yawanawá language, part of the Pano linguistic family, carries their cosmology, myths, and spiritual teachings — a living voice of the forest that embodies their resilience, beauty, and ancestral wisdom.

Yolngu: *(pronounced yolngoo)* A collective term used by Aboriginal people of northeastern Arnhem Land, Australia to describe themselves. In Yolngu Matha (their language), it simply means 'people,' similar to the term 'Anangu,' used by Indigenous peoples of Central Australia. Yolngu refers not to a single tribe but to a network of interrelated clans united by kinship systems, ceremonial law, and shared ancestral songlines. Yolngu culture is among the oldest continuously practiced cultural systems on Earth, rich in art, music, governance, and sacred law (*Madayin*). Their knowledge systems include oral histories, *manikay* (clan songs), and *buŋgul* (ceremonial dance), and are deeply embedded in land, language, and the Dreaming.

Yuxibu: The supreme creative spirit in Huni Kuin cosmology — the great consciousness from which all life emerges. Often described as the source of the forest's intelligence, Yuxibu is both creator and sustainer, present in every being, song, and element of nature. Yuxiu is the origin of the sacred medicines, the dreamer of the world, and the guiding spirit who teaches humans to live in harmony with the web of existence.

Zuvuya: A term from José Argüelles's interpretation of Mayan cosmology, meaning the great interdimensional memory circuit that connects all things across time and space — the return path to source. It represents the ever-flowing current of synchronicity through which the universe remembers itself. To follow the Zuvuya is to awaken to the holographic nature of reality, where past and future, self and cosmos, are reflections of one living pattern. It is the wave of remembrance — the spiral of energy linking individual consciousness with the collective dream of the whole Earth.

Bibliography

Amaringo, Pablo. *Ayahuasca Visions: The Religious Iconography of a Peruvian Shaman* (1991)

Amaringo, Pablo, Howard G. Charing, and Peter Cloudsley. *The Ayahuasca Visions of Pablo Amaringo* (2011)

Arguelles, Jose. *Manifesto for the Noosphere: The Next Stage in the Evolution of Human Consciousness* (2011)

Arguelles, Jose. *Surfers of the Zuvuya: Tales of Interdimensional Travel* (1988)

Arguelles, Jose. *Time and the Technosphere: The Law of Time in Human Affairs* (2002)

Atkinson, Judy. *Trauma Trails, Recreating Song Lines: The Transgenerational Effects of Trauma in Indigenous Australia* (2002)

Barnard, G. William. *Liquid Light: Ayahuasca Spirituality and the Santo Daime Tradition* (2022)

Barnard, G. William. *The Life and Work of Mestre Irineu* (2022)

Berendt, Joachim-Ernst. *The World Is Sound: Nada Brahma — Music and the Landscape of Consciousness* (1987)

Campos, Don Jose. *The Shaman and Ayahuasca: Journeys to Sacred Realms* (2011)

Carey, Ken. *The Return of the Bird Tribes* (1991)

Charing, Howard G. *The Amazonian Angel Oracle: Working with Angels, Devas, and Plant Spirits* (2022)

Dass, Ram. *Being Ram Dass* (2021)

Dobkin de Rios, Marlene, and Alberto Groisman. *Ayahuasca, Religion and the U.S. Supreme Court: Cultural Context and Implications of a Legal Dispute* (2007)

Elkin, A. P. *Aboriginal Men of High Degree* (1945; later edition 1993)

Gearin, Alex K. *Global Ayahuasca: Wondrous Visions and Modern Worlds* (2024)

Geraci, Massimiliano. *The Divine Birth of Ayahuasca: Myths on the Visionary Vine* (2024)

Gordon, Charles, and Roger Walsh. *Higher Wisdom: Eminent Elders Explore the Continuing Impact of Psychedelics* (2005)

Hamel, Peter Michael. *Through Music to the Self: How to Appreciate and Experience Music Anew* (1979)

Harris, Rachel. *Listening to Ayahuasca: New Hope for Depression, Addiction, PTSD, and Anxiety* (2017)

Huni Kuin Artists Movement. *Mahku: Visions* (2023)

Huni Kuĩ, Ibã / Sales Kaxinawá, Isaías. *Nixi Pãe: Espírito da Floresta* (2024)

Johnson, Robert A. *Owning Your Own Shadow: Understanding the Dark Side of the Psyche* (1991)

Lawler, Robert. *Voices of the First Day: Awakening in the Aboriginal Dreamtime* (1991)

Leary, Timonthy et. al. *The Psychedelic Experience* (1964)

Leonard, George. *The Silent Pulse: A Search for the Perfect Rhythm That Exists in Each of Us* (1978)

Luz, Cristina Rego Monteiro da. *Master Gabriel, the Messenger of God* (2011)

Matus, Lujan. *The Art of Stalking Parallel Perception: Revised 10th Anniversary Edition – The Living Tapestry of Lujan Matus* (2015)

McAdam, Charlotte. "The River of Dreams." *Mind Medicine Australia*, (2020).

Multiple Indigenous Nations. *Declaration of the 3rd Brazilian Indigenous Conference on Ayahuasca* (2023)

Neale, Margo, and Lynne Kelly. *Songlines: The Power and Promise* (2020)

Nutt, David. *Psychedelics: The Revolutionary Drugs That Could Change Your Life – A Guide from the Expert* (2023)

Pinchbeck, Daniel, and Sophia Rokhlin. *When Plants Dream: Ayahuasca, Amazonian Shamanism and the Global Psychedelic Renaissance* (2019)

Polari de Alverga, Alex. *The Religion of Ayahuasca: The Teachings of the Church of Santo Daime* (2010)

Rinpoche, Sogyal. *The Tibetan Book of Living and Dying* (1992)

Roth, Gabrielle. *Maps to Ecstasy: A Healing Journey for the Untamed Spirit* (1998)

Ruiz, Don Miguel Jr. *The Mastery of Self: A Toltec Guide to Personal Freedom* (2016)

Ruiz, Don Miguel Jr. *The Mastery of Life: A Toltec Guide to Personal Freedom* (2021)

Santo Daime Community. *Baixinha: Como nos ensina o Caboclo Tupinambá* (n.d.)

Sheldrake, Rupert. *A New Science of Life: The Hypothesis of Morphic Resonance* (1981)

Soriano Yawanawá, Luna Rosa. *Yawanawá: The People of Queixada* (n.d.)

Strassman, Rick. *DMT: The Spirit Molecule – A Doctor's Revolutionary Research into the Biology of Near-Death and Mystical Experiences* (2001)

Tafur, Joseph. *The Fellowship of the River: A Medical Doctor's Exploration into Traditional Amazonian Plant Medicine* (2017)

Yunkaporta, Tyson. *Sand Talk: How Indigenous Thinking Can Save the World* (2020)

Albums by Lore Solaris

Irradia (2022)

We are – Estrela da Ciranda Live in Ceremony (2025)

Listen and download

www.ingramcontent.com/pod-product-compliance
Lightning Source LLC
Chambersburg PA
CBHW071327080526
44587CB00017B/2749